American Indian Economic Development

World Anthropology

General Editor

SOL TAX

Patrons

CLAUDE LÉVI-STRAUSS
MARGARET MEAD
LAILA SHUKRY EL HAMAMSY
M. N. SRINIVAS

MOUTON PUBLISHERS · THE HAGUE · PARIS

DISTRIBUTED IN THE USA AND CANADA BY ALDINE, CHICAGO

American Indian Economic Development

Editor

SAM STANLEY

MOUTON PUBLISHERS · THE HAGUE · PARIS

DISTRIBUTED IN THE USA AND CANADA BY ALDINE, CHICAGO

General Editor's Preface

Among the indigenous peoples of the world who resist absorption into the industrializing juggernaut are hundreds of American Indian communities dotting the whole of North America. Without the resources which once enabled them as communities to adapt to changes in their own ways, individual families now have no alternative but to make their own reluctant way — usually by migrating to cities — in the cash economy. They often do not disappear into the general population, so that whatever problems there were are complicated rather than solved. Hence there are continuing efforts toward "development" in the locations of the communities themselves. Remarkably, this book is the first careful study of a sample of seven of these efforts. It provides basic and very striking lessons applicable wherever people with distinctive identities and cultures are pressured to join another people's "mainstream" — even the best of intentions simply do not succeed. Whether or not governments heed the lessons, they are consonant with what anthropology has learned and a remarkably worldwide congress provided a forum for their presentation.

Like most contemporary sciences, anthropology is a product of the European tradition. Some argue that it is a product of colonialism, with one small and self-interested part of the species dominating the study of the whole. If we are to understand the species, our science needs substantial input from scholars who represent a variety of the world's cultures. It was a deliberate purpose of the IXth International Congress of Anthropological and Ethnological Sciences to provide impetus in this direction. The *World Anthropology* volumes, therefore, offer a first glimpse of a human science in which members from all societies have played an active role. Each of the books is designed to be self-contained; each is an attempt to update its particular sector of scientific knowledge and is written by specialists from all parts of the world. Each volume should be read and reviewed individually as a separate volume on its own given subject. The set as a whole will indicate what changes are in store for anthropology as scholars from the developing countries join in studying the species of which we are all a part.

The IXth Congress was planned from the beginning not only to include as many of the scholars from every part of the world as possible, but also with a view toward the eventual publication of the papers in high-quality volumes. At previous Congresses scholars were invited to bring papers which were then read out loud. They were necessarily limited in length; many were only summarized; there was little time for discussion; and the sparse discussion could only be in one language. The IXth Congress was an experiment aimed at changing this. Papers were written with the intention of exchanging them before the Congress, particularly in extensive pre-Congress sessions; they were not intended to be read aloud at the Congress, that time being devoted to discussions — discussions which were simultaneously and professionally translated into five languages. The method for eliciting the papers was structured to make as representative a sample as was allowable when scholarly creativity — hence self-selection — was critically important. Scholars were asked both to propose papers of their own and to suggest topics for sessions of the Congress which they might edit into volumes. All were then informed of the suggestions and encouraged to re-think their own papers and the topics. The process, therefore, was a continuous one of feedback and exchange and it has continued to be so even after the Congress. The some two thousand papers comprising *World Anthropology* certainly then offer a substantial sample of world anthropology. It has been said that anthropology is at a turning point; if this is so, these volumes will be the historical direction-markers.

As might have been foreseen in the first post-colonial generation, the large majority of the Congress papers (82 percent) are the work of scholars identified with the industrialized world which fathered our traditional discipline and the institution of the Congress itself: Eastern Europe (15 percent); Western Europe (16 percent); North America (47 percent); Japan, South Africa, Australia, and New Zealand (4 percent). Only 18 percent of the papers are from developing areas: Africa (4 percent); Asia-Oceania (9 percent); Latin America (5 percent). Aside from the substantial representation from the U.S.S.R. and the nations of Eastern Europe, a significant difference between this corpus of written material and that of other Congresses is the addition of the large proportion of contributions from Africa, Asia, and Latin America. "Only 18 percent" is two to four times as great a proportion as that of other Congresses; moreover, 18 percent of 2,000 papers is 360 papers, 10 times the number of "Third World" papers presented at previous Congresses. In fact, these 360 papers are more than the total of ALL papers published after the last International Congress of Anthropological and Ethnological Sciences which was held in the United States (Philadelphia, 1956).

The significance of the increase is not simply quantitative. The input of scholars from areas which have until recently been no more than subject matter for anthropology represents both feedback and also long-awaited theoretical contributions from the perspectives of very different cultural, social, and historical traditions. Many who attended the IXth Congress were convinced that anthropology would not be the same in the future. The fact that the next Congress (India, 1978) will be our first in the "Third World" may be symbolic of the change. Meanwhile, sober consideration of the present set of books will show how much, and just where and how, our discipline is being revolutionized.

Other books in this series which will interest readers deal with migration, development, ethnicity, urbanization and other such topics as well as with relevant social and cultural theory and with different geographic areas of the world in which situations similar to those of American Indians are numerous.

Chicago, Illinois   SOL TAX
January 19, 1978

Table of Contents

Introduction

SAM STANLEY

This volume is the result of efforts on the part of Indians and anthropologists to gain a better understanding of what is involved in the process of economic development as it affects American Indian communities. The aim of the study was to try to develop an Indian point of view on the concept of "economic development" and on efforts to improve conditions in Indian reservations and communities. The study also proposed to pinpoint factors contributing to or detracting from the success of such efforts.

Former Secretary of the Interior Rogers B. Morton noted in a speech that economic development is " . . . a slow and arduous task. The investment of capital is only a small part of it. Great magazines, for example, are not just printing presses and pulp forests. They are an organized group of dedicated, skilled people. The same is true for a successful Indian enterprise, but it doesn't come about over night" (Morton 1973).

Economic development does indeed take an organized group of dedicated, skilled people, and Indian tribes have shown themselves to

This study was supported with a grant from the Office of Economic Research of the Economic Development Administration, U.S. Department of Commerce, under grant #99-7-13229.

I should like to thank the authors who wrote the individual reports, and all those who assisted them. They provided me with valuable suggestions and criticisms in preparing the introduction and conclusion, though I alone am responsible for the results. I also wish to thank Ms. Lee Massey for copy editing the original manuscripts. Thanks are due to the Economic Development Administration personnel who offered suggestions and criticisms on the project. In particular Ms. Charlotte Breckenridge, as project liason, was helpful from the beginning to the end. Ms. Jo Ann Moore did the very fine maps and illustrations. Finally, I would like to thank Ms. Valerie Ashenfelter, Ms. Lydia Ratliff, Ms. Priscilla Weatherly, Ms. Judith Wojcik, and Mr. William Douglass for the typing, proofreading, and other important tasks.

be this for thousands of years. Yet, if measured by the criteria for twentieth century economic development, most Indian tribes fall far short of the mark. How is it that a self-reliant, completely competent group of tribal people cannot get above the generally acknowledged poverty level of the United States? And is it true, as Vine Deloria Jr, has asserted, that those tribes which hewed most closely to traditional forms of governing themselves have been much more successful in achieving some modicum of economic development?

These are not new questions but they are implicit in the recent publication of a body of materials by the Joint Committee on Economics of the U.S. Congress (U.S. Congress Joint Economic Committee 1969). The articles compiled in those two volumes, edited by Frazier Kellogg, focused specifically on problems broadly related to Indian economic development, and they attracted the attention of many who were concerned about the government's role with respect to this problem.

The Economic Development Administration Office of Economic Research saw that the Joint Committee Report raised a series of interesting research problems which could only be solved empirically. They knew an on-the-ground, factual fieldwork approach was required. As a result talks began between representatives of EDA-OER and the editor of this report. Because the funds available were quite modest, it was agreed that only a minimum amount of fieldwork could be accomplished. At the same time everyone expressed a firm desire to involve Indians as fully as possible in all phases of the work. It fell upon the principal investigator/editor to enlist the services of as many Indians as possible in the research. Originally six tribes were selected —Lummi, Morongo, Navajo, Papago, Cherokee, and Passamaquoddy. Later, it was possible to add the Pine Ridge Sioux. The selection of the tribes was governed by a number of considerations. First, it was desirable to get a geographic spread. Second, we wanted a spread in terms of population size and land area. Third, we wanted tribes with very different histories of white contact. Fourth, we wanted tribes with various experiences of economic development, including at least one successful group as well as at least one very doubtful case. Finally, we had to choose tribes that had been recently studied by people who would be willing to prepare monographs.

On the whole it would seem that Indians benefited both directly and indirectly from this research. The Lummi work was done by Vine Deloria, a Sioux, with the assistance of some Lummi students at Western Washington State University at Bellingham. Morongo reservation was done by Dr. Lowell Bean and Madeline Ball (a Cahuilla) with assistance from many of the Morongo people. The Navajo work began under the direction of Milton Bluehouse, a Navajo, who unfortunately had to withdraw because of a number of overwhelming commitments. He was succeeded by Dr. Lorraine Ruffing, an economist, who lived for a few months at Shonto, and was able, with the assistance of the Navajo people, to get a good basic grasp of the Navajo economic situation. The Papago study combined the efforts of Dr. Bernard Fontana and two Papagos, Juliann Ramon and Henry Manuel. The Eastern Oklahoma Cherokee research was conducted by Albert Wahrhaftig with the assistance of a number of native Cherokee people. The Passamaquoddy study was carried out by Susan Stevens, wife of former Governor of the Passamaquoddy and presently Commissioner of Indian Affairs for the State of Maine, John Stevens. The Pine Ridge study, carried out by Dr. Ray DeMallie, was commissioned well after the other studies and required somewhat more fieldwork, and a portion of the funds for it went to Indians who assisted him in the field.

After the initial researchers were selected, the group met in Tucson, Arizona, to discuss the strategy of research and the procedures to be followed. Most of those who met there were familiar with other anthropological examinations of Indian economic behavior. In particular, they knew of the volume entitled, *Human problems in technological change*, edited by Edward Spicer and published by Russell Sage Foundation in 1952. Many of the lessons of that volume would be repeated in this study, but everyone realized there would be important differences. The Spicer volume consisted of a whole series of case studies, many of which emphasized the futility of trying to impose outside programs upon Indian tribes. The present study concurs with it on this point, as well as many others. However, the basic approach of this study differs primarily in that it looks at economic behavior within an even wider context. Our strategy and procedure were quite different from that of the Spicer study, with the possible exception of the Papago monograph with its emphasis on a case study approach. To begin with we agreed to try to adhere to a suggested check list of factors that seem to be somewhat closely related to economic development.[1] No one was expected to modify his or her material to conform to the list, but everyone was asked to use it in carrying out their research. The categories of the list seem to come from the "dismal science" — economics — and as such are foreign to most anthropologists and to almost all Indians. This is not to disparage the efforts of economists, but rather to point up the fact that when man is viewed holistically, i.e. anthropologically, it requires some effort to understand the narrower focus of the economist. Similarly, while anthropologists do not "think" like Indians, they tend, at their best, to

[1]   Appendix, page 590

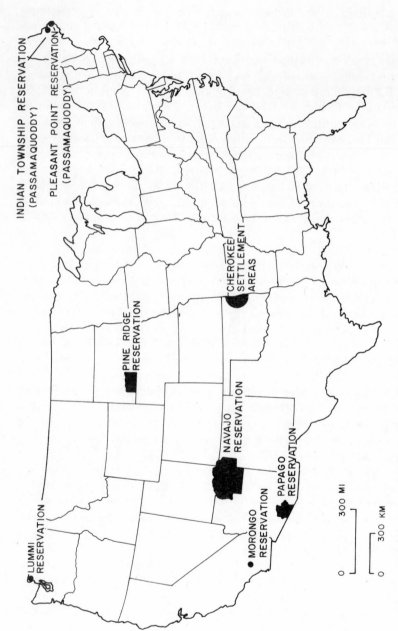

INDIAN TOWNSHIP RESERVATION
(PASSAMAQUODDY)

PLEASANT POINT RESERVATION
(PASSAMAQUODDY)

CHEROKEE
SETTLEMENT
AREAS

PINE RIDGE
RESERVATION

NAVAJO
RESERVATION

PAPAGO
RESERVATION

MORONGO
RESERVATION

LUMMI
RESERVATION

300 MI

300 KM

Map 1.   Location of seven Indian tribes described in this volume

have a world view with many similarities. In other words, when anthropologists are attempting to understand and interpret Indian behavior, their accounts will come close to those which the Indians themselves express, albeit somewhat removed from a pure economic interpretation.

Following the Tucson meeting, each researcher commenced serious work on his/her respective group. Then, from July 5 through July 9, 1972, everyone met again in Seattle, Washington, for three days. At this meeting progress reports were given and all had an opportunity to go to the Lummi reservation and observe the aquaculture project. We are indebted to Lummi tribal officials and Dr. Wally Heath for their gracious hospitality and careful description of the project. Our visit provided us with an unusual view of what can be accomplished when Indians are permitted to go at their own pace on tasks which they wish to accomplish.

Our next meeting took place in San Francisco from February 15 to February 17, 1973. By that time most of the manuscripts had been finished, and our major purpose was to try to test generalizations about American Indian economic development as described in each of the reports. Considerable discussion took place and a kind of consensus emerged. In effect everyone agreed that the key to economic development for American Indians lies in the extent to which they feel involved at the grass-roots level. The kinds of problems which this conclusion produces varies for each of the communities discussed and undoubtably for every one of the Indian tribes not included in this particular study. The nature of the variation will be apparent to the reader and it is spelled out conceptually later in this introduction. On April 19, 1973, most of those involved in the project participated in the presentation of our tentative results at the Southwestern Anthropological Association Meeting in San Francisco. Dr. Sol Tax served as a discussant at this meeting, and much valuable criticism resulted. Our final review and airing of the project took place in Oshkosh, Wisconsin (August 27–31, 1973) followed by a formal presentation at the IXth International Congress of Anthropological and Ethnological Sciences in Chicago (September 1–8, 1973).

In writing these accounts each of the authors was asked to imagine that his work was being read by Indians, bureaucrats, legislators, and anthropologists, economists, etc. in that order. This is a pretty heavy order, but because there was heavy Indian involvement it was not impossible. Moreover, Indians will have no difficulty in recognizing the processes described by each of the authors. They know that for a long period of time they have been subjected to the power of the federal government with respect to the conduct of their own affairs. The nature of this subjection is well spelled out in the administrative

structures of the Bureau of Indian Affairs (BIA). The BIA in turn
simply refers to the Acts of Congress which grant them the authority to
do whatever it is that they do. All kinds of legal questions can be
raised concerning the relationship of Indians and the federal government, but these are not the subject of our report. This, of course, does
not mean that we can or will ignore the nature of the relationship, but
we shall try to keep it in proper perspective.

The reader of this volume will doubtless be struck by the seemingly
heavy historical input in each of the accounts. There are reasons for
this. In the first place Indians have a perspective toward modern life
which involves their own past deeply. The treaties, which most non-
Indians regard trivially, are a sacred part of their life. They are part
and parcel of their identity as Indians and nonfulfillment of the treaty
obligations is tantamount to stripping Indians of their special status
vis-à-vis the rest of the American citizenry. Each treaty has its special
history usually more in the breaking than the keeping. Second, modern
Indians know that they are the descendants of the original occupants of
this land. They had their roots here thousands of years before Europeans arrived. They are acutely aware of the specific ways in which
they lost possession of over 98 percent of the land to non-Indians. All
of this involves history, and it is living history to Indians — handed
down orally in every tribe, a part of their collective bitter experience.

Finally, there is another important reason for all of this history.
Economic development generally implies capital accumulation and the
ability to increase production of goods and services as well as their
distribution. Prior to European presence, Indians were as developed
economically as they needed to be (Tax and Stanley 1969). Even after
Europeans began to gain control of the continent, Indians experienced
an economic florescence based on the fur trade, the horse, metal, and
adaptation of some European sociopolitical institutions. Despite their
initial successes in continuing their own economic development, they
subsequently came less and less to share in the nation's progress
economically. It is this historical fact which constitutes the present
Indian economic development problem. Any understanding of the
Indian's present plight must include a grasp of the processes by which
it has come to be as it is.

This report, then, is derived from the anthropological perspective
rather than the economic. Above all, this means that every action has a
context and makes no real sense outside of it. Specifically, this means
that Indians are suspicious of development projects which ignore the
existing system of social relationships and ideas about land use. The
failure of so many development projects on the Papago reservation
and at Pine Ridge are good examples of this dictum. With the

exception of the Lummi aquaculture project, it holds true for every development project discussed in this report.

With this and other points in mind it seems appropriate to briefly review each study so that a cursory reader might get a quick grasp of the thrust of each report.

Beginning in the east, the first point of European contact, we can look at the Passamaquoddy Indians in the state of Maine. The report by Ms. Susan Stevens is remarkable. To begin with, it is the first clear account of how the Passamaquoddy came to be in their present plight. From an historical point of view it is the first history of the Passamaquoddy which corresponds to their own view of themselves. Second, it brings to our attention the present condition of a tribe which has been ignored by the Federal Government since the founding of the American Republic. They are an Eastern United States Indian group which has been swept under the table for almost 200 years. A third significant fact, which incidentally characterizes all of the reports, is the strong emphasis on their persistence as an identifiable American Indian social group. Despite enormous pressures to "disappear," the Passamaquoddy are very much with us today and have every intention of remaining highly visible. Ms. Stevens's account deserves especially close perusal because as indicated above, she writes from the vantage point of being married to the long time Governor of the Passamaquoddy who is presently Commissioner of the Maine Bureau of Indian Affairs.

To understand more clearly what contributes to Passamaquoddy persistence as a people, one must read Stevens's section on values, entitled "The Implementation of Federal Social Programs." It spells out the ways in which cultural differences have contributed to the failure of many development programs. At the same time she shows positively how an understanding of basic Passamaquoddy values could make the difference between success and failure in economic development. Her recommendation is that programs must be shaped to fit the culture before they will succeed. It is clear that most prior efforts have been based on the premise that the culture must be changed to fit the program. Her most devastating example was the tribe's refusal of a $100,000 OEO program until it could be shaped to fit their own existing institutions.

Ms. Stevens makes the point that whatever contributes to and supports traditional Passamaquoddy values has a positive effect on development. The Dana Point School is an example of this principle. Another important area of development is in leadership. This is a somewhat intangible area, yet her case is explicit and certainly the Passamaquoddy would not have been able to do as well without. She correctly credits the influx of federal funds for new programs as the catalyst for the new leadership.

In concluding her monograph, Ms. Stevens makes a number of positive suggestions for bringing improvements to the Passamaquoddy economic development scene. They are highly specific and should be read in context. Suffice to say she "covers the waterfront", including building on existing activities as well as suggesting new logical extensions of the potential of the Passamaquoddy land and people.

Dr. DeMallie's monograph on the Pine Ridge Sioux is carefully written. It follows the course of Oglala history from a time when they were the mounted masters of the Plains until the present day. He spends some time discussing the traditional subsistence pattern and the sociopolitical organization. Next he does a very succinct and important analysis of Lakota world view. An understanding of this is crucial if one wishes to communicate meaningfully with Sioux people. After this, he establishes the initial economic independence of the Sioux, which is then followed by an increasing dependence upon the goods of the white trader. Historically he recognizes three distinct economic periods following the establishment of the reservation. From 1869–1915, the reservation is developed. The years 1915–1934 are a period of economic crisis and from 1935 to the present there is a New Order.

The modern period really consists of a synthesis of data that spans the decade from 1962–1972. Two-thirds of DeMallie's work is focused on this period. He presents the basic statistics on land, resources, population, and income. The land base is a little over 50 percent owned, there are few resources, the population is increasing steadily, and income is far below the national average.

Dr. DeMallie next examines the modern economy of Pine Ridge. The picture is one of almost grinding dependency. During 1966–1967, 91 percent of all funds expended or generated directly on Pine Ridge Reservation originated in off-reservation public and private social service agencies. When he examines other sources of income, the picture is depressing. In agriculture there are the familiar problems of fractured landholdings, low quality grazing land, and an absence of viable groups to carry out successful exploitation of the land. Only a White run moccasin factory seems able to function profitably on the reservation. It makes few concessions to Lakota culture, and, while many Sioux work in it, they are unable to fit it to their values.

In summing up his monograph, Dr. DeMallie outlines a number of themes related to economic concerns which he considers within the total historical and cultural context of Pine Ridge reservation. They include dependency, lack of tribal unity, management problems, leadership, overlapping and conflicting planning agencies, lack of continuity, and absence of a profit incentive. He does not attempt to judge whether these themes are good or bad, but rather he uses the theme concept to show some of the important concepts which add up to the present Pine Ridge situation.

Professor Wahrhaftig's description and analysis of the traditional Oklahoma Cherokee is a most original contribution. He states clearly in his introduction that there is a strong dividing line between the descendants of the traditional Cherokee, numbering about 10,000 in 1907, and the persons who identify as being of Cherokee descent (legal Cherokee) totaling about 40,000 when the roll was compiled. One may seriously question his polemic division of Cherokees into traditionals and nontraditionals, but he points out that this is the view of the traditionalists, and as a good anthropologist he is faithfully following their analysis. The issue is difficult to resolve, but what comes out most clearly is the plight of the traditional Cherokee. Wahrhaftig establishes that they are at the bottom of the heap in terms of modern American values of economic, social, and political status. The insidious part of their plight is that they are the true carriers of the Cherokee tradition on cultural, linguistic, and literate (in Cherokee) grounds. They are locked into a system from which they are unable to escape.

In addition to establishing that there is a viable group of traditional Cherokee who struggle daily to maintain themselves, he is able to detail the mechanisms by which they survive. Not surprisingly to students of Cherokee life, we learn the importance of kinship, neighborhood, and religious organization in supporting life. These institutions go far beyond survival — they give meaning to life and therein lies their power.

But survival imposes harsh conditions on many Cherokee families. It involves long connecting trips to uncertain employment. It means going far from one's own community in order to make money. It also involves working for the very lowest wages paid in this region. Cherokee want and need jobs, but they also need to insure the continued existence of their communities and themselves as a people. The traditional Cherokee have no desire to join Eastern Oklahoma's mainstream as white people.

Yet as Wahrhaftig points out in his long final chapter on "The Cherokee Establishment", it is an assumption of those who control the tribal government that traditional Cherokee are moving in that direction. For the Cherokee Establishment, the Cherokee are a resource in two senses. First, they are a cheap supply of labor. Second, they are the means by which the government and tourist dollars can be attracted to northeastern Oklahoma.

Wahrhaftig is not sanguine about the economic future of the traditional Cherokee. Their communities cannot develop without threatening the present system of exploitation. Any independent move toward development would doubtless be opposed by the present tribal leadership. Yet clearly, the Cherokee settlements will continue to resist all efforts to "develop" them as long as they emanate from "outsiders." The total situation has all the ingredients of a Greek tragedy.

The Papago monograph is a joint project of an anthropologist (Fontana) and two Papagos (Juliann Ramon and Henry Manuel). They utilized a case study approach to economic development on the Papago reservation over the past 16 years. The record is a dismal one — 13 cases and 12 failures — measured by any criteria! In making their point the authors review the history of the Papago tribe from Western contact to modern times. They graphically detail the manner in which a large amorphous group of people, occupying a contiguous land mass in southern Arizona and northern Mexico, were first separated by a political boundary and then told (on this side of the line) to organize themselves as a political entity. This has been a common experience for tribal peoples, but few nontribals realize what extraordinary demands and hardships it imposes. One can almost predict the factionalism and bewilderment which follow attempts to organize a people along lines and principles both unknown and reprehensible to them.

The record of the 12 failures is, on the one hand, a testimonial to the tenaciousness of non-Indians in pushing their view of the world, while, on the other hand, it documents the deep resistance which Papagos have to those views. Again, it is not a question of resistance to change—it is resistance to performing acts that are contrary to their own views of correct behavior. They cannot act in un-Papago ways.

There is a pattern which characterizes the way in which economic development makes its appearance on the reservation. A development project is proposed either by or to the Bureau of Indian Affairs. The Bureau may then take an active role in persuading the Tribal Council to act or it may (as in leasing) go to individual allottees and gather the requisite signatures. Eventually the project reaches a point where some Papago begin to question it. Those who press for answers do not receive explanations, but are told to either accept the money or lose it. *Alternatives and clarification of the issues and their implications are not offered.* The usual result is that people take the money without ever understanding or feeling involved with the project. Papago remain in the dark about complex legal and economic matters because no one will undertake to explain them. As long as this is the case, there is very little chance that they will be able to participate meaningfully in the development of their own resources.

The authors of the Papago monograph point out that Papagos have been burnt so often by schemes of outsiders that they inevitably react negatively to each new proposal. They have come to fear the unexpected changes which follow the introduction of new projects. It would appear that any development on the Papago Reservation must proceed slowly and must be very well understood by the Papago people.

The Navajo article is the only account by an economist— Lorraine Ruffing. Her work grew out of her belief that Indian culture may contain institutions which could perform economic tasks carried out by different institutions in Western society. If free enterprise was anathema to Navajo, then what about a cooperative economic system? To learn more about Navajo economy, Dr. Ruffing went to live for a few months at Shonto. She interviewed numerous Navajo and had an opportunity to observe and note their economic activities. She was also able to compare her work with another study of Shonto done in 1955, by Richard Adams, an anthropologist, who worked at the trading post. The results are instructive.

Dr. Ruffing finds that the basic production unit of the Navajo is the extended local kin group that occupies a particular territory. In this area they graze their sheep and other livestock. The sheep provide wool, cash, hides, and meat for the extended kin group. This has been a successful adaptation since the days of Spanish contact, and it is complemented by agriculture, especially the growing of corn.

Together with the traditional subsistance activities there is federal assistance, under a number of guises, plus some industrial employment and income from leases. To some, the newer sources of income represent the future, yet Ruffing questions the extent to which they maximize Navajo economic development opportunities. Her statistical tables suggest that leasing of mineral rights is not necessarily the most economically advantageous policy for the tribe to follow.

Dr. Ruffing had hoped to test alternative models for economic development on the Navajo reservation. She argues that Navajo culture is antithetical to Western capitalistic entrepreneurship. In this respect she is almost surely correct. Capitalism involves assumptions about the relationship of man to man, man to nature, and man to the processes of production, and these assumptions are foreign to the Navajo.

In searching for an alternative development model, Dr. Ruffing seems to settle for expanding the traditional economic activities of the Navajo. Any other model would seem too abstract. The advantages of her suggestion is that it would use the most abundant resources: land and labor. It would cushion the fluctuations of temporary wage labor by providing an important supplement — stock raising — and it would take advantage of the existing investments and knowledge while involving a majority of the population. Such a development would also involve existing production units with a long tradition of doing the job.

She also suggests that a cooperative livestock marketing program could be established and run by the tribe.

In summarizing her report, Dr. Ruffing emphasizes the continuity of Navajo social institutions over time and their close interconnections with traditional economic activities. Their interdependence is such that changes in one will have serious repercussions in the other. Her conclusion is that the investment in an infrastructure must be accompanied by an intelligent focus upon increasing productive capacity. If these two are not coordinated there will be more grief in the future for the Navajo people.

In his monograph on the southern California Morongo reservation, Dr. Lowell Bean chooses to emphasize those processes which have permitted the Morongo people *to survive as a people* for the past century. Within the context of this overall theme, he is able to analyze the past and present behavior of Morongo people. One of the principal strengths of his report is the deep involvement of Morongo people in the research, and they are responsible for much of the evidence which supports his general theme.

He begins with a description of his methodology and procedure. This is followed by a history of the Morongo people. In approaching the modern day he distinguishes between a Mission period, a Rancho period, and an early American period. He follows this by describing the kinds of associations which carry the "load" of Morongo culture in facing up to the pressures of the dominant society.

Bean then proceeds to describe the basis for ethnic identity at Morongo. This turns out to be a concatenation of history, tribalism, and a sense of being different from outsiders. The key element here is their reluctance to get into economic planning unless it matches their own notions of what is proper for Morongo people to do. The rule tends to be that if members of the tribe can organize to carry out some entrepreneural activity then this is perfectly all right as long as it does not jeopardize the integrity of the reservation. This, of course, is a powerful rule since it simultaneously encourages all to be entrepreneurs while making clear that their activities can never be at the expense of community integrity. One gets the clear impression that community values reign paramount over any individual's personal aspirations.

To outsiders, Morongo appears fractionated and hopelessly divided. Any casual observation would confirm this picture, but Bean is able to demonstrate that this apparent "anarchy" is precisely what insures the continued existence of the Morongo people. The apparent paralysis of the tribe in making decisions about programs "aimed at their own benefit" is really a mechanism by which they closely examine what they do not thoroughly understand.

The Morongo people are highly suspicious of any economic development schemes. They even turned down a planning development grant. Clearly they are only interested in development projects which they thoroughly understand. The challenge is to come up with some realistic programs which fit the needs of the Morongo people and which will not violate their own sense of being a people.

The Morongo paper has an appendix which responds specifically to the list of questions and categories (pages 214–235) suggested by the EDA research branch. This response addresses itself to each of the variables which economists consider crucial in measuring economic development. Bean does the best job in responding to these economic categories, and his report is the richer for this. At the same time, because he is an anthropologist, he insists on seeing it all in context. The real value of the questions raised by the EDA is that they turn the attention of noneconomists to areas of human behavior not previously considered. The great value of Bean's report turns on three important points: first, an account of Morongo, historical and contemporary, which reflects considerable Morongo input; second, a detailed description of the essentials of Morongo survival as a people; and third, a detailed response to the EDA list which insists on bringing it into the context of a living people.

The Lummi Indians, a small tribe of the northwest coast in western Washington, are described by Vine Deloria, a Standing Rock Sioux from South Dakota. Mr. Deloria became acquainted with the Lummis while on the faculty of Western Washington State University at Bellingham. In compiling his monograph, Deloria worked closely with Lummi tribal officials and enlisted the services of Lummi students enrolled in studies at his university.

Deloria establishes the independence of the Lummi people prior to White encroachment. He details the treaties which led to the establishment of the reservation together with the problem of implementing all of their provisions. In this respect he cites three of the more important treaty rights' cases which the Lummi engaged in after their signing. The cases describe a continual struggle between the Lummi and the State of Washington over the limits of Lummi fishing rights. According to Deloria, the Bureau of Indian Affairs remained silent throughout all these controversies, though they were bound to protect the Indian rights. In spite of harrassment by the state, Lummis were able to survive comfortably until about 1890. For the ensuing 74 years, the Lummis found themselves on the defensive. The surrounding white communities clamored to have the reservation open up to white settlement. There was also pressure on the Lummi to become farmers and turn away from the sea. Eventually whites were able to buy Lummi land and a considerable amount has been alienated.

Throughout the period from 1890 to 1964, the Lummi economic situation deteriorated. The fishing industry fell off as the salmon decreased in number each year. It also became prohibitively competitive as sophisticated technology began to dominate the boats and fishing gear. Logging without re-forestation left the Lummi without commercial stands of timber. Migratory labor and seasonal cannery work were major sources of income to the people.

In the early 1960's the Bureau of Indian Affairs started cottage industries on the reservation. The industry groups were called Lummi Knitters, Lummi Weavers, and Lummi Arts and Crafts. None of these programs, conceived by outsiders, was able to provide income for the workers, and each quietly faded away.

The central theme of Deloria's account is the development of aquaculture. He describes how, in 1967, the tribe chose to develop the tidelands of Lummi Bay for the commercial production of seafood, instead of building a magnesium oxide plant. They made this choice, he believes, because it permitted them to continue to be fishermen and because there would be community control of the whole project.

Deloria points out that it is not possible to discuss the development of aquaculture without discussing the development of the community. They have grown together and are closely intertwined. Economic development *is* community development in this particular case, and it follows a concept which has been internalized by the Indians. Above all, the Lummi understand themselves and what they are doing on this project. They are comfortable and secure in the knowledge that they are continuous with and faithful to their past tribal experience. They are into a fascinating development and they control it. The Lummi aquaculture scheme is a superior model for other Indian tribes to scrutinize.

REFERENCES

MORTON, ROGERS B.
   1973   Speech on economic development at Menlo Park, California. Office of Communications, U.S. Department of Interior, Washington, D.C.
TAX, SOL, SAM STANLEY
   1969   "Indian identity and economic development." 75–96 Joint Economic Committee, Congress of the United States, Washington, D.C.: Government Printing Office.
U.S. CONGRESS JOINT ECONOMIC COMMITTEE
   1969   Toward economic development for native American communities, Volume one/two. Washington, D.C.: Government Printing Office.

Navajo Economic Development: A Dual Perspective

LORRAINE TURNER RUFFING

This study is another attempt to analyze the many diverse aspects of Navajo underdevelopment with the hope of isolating the most important stumbling blocks. It is an exercise undertaken primarily to aid the planners charged with promoting Navajo development.

It contains a brief history of Navajo development, an examination of the obstacles to development, an analysis of federal attempts to promote development, and an evaluation of the present development strategy. Much of the report is written from the perspective of the Navajo tribal government, since it is the entity charged with promoting development and responsible to the Navajo people. Implicitly, the Navajo government is treated as if it perfectly reflected the desires of the Navajo people. This assumption does violence to reality, because there is often a divergence of opinion on methods and rates of development between the Navajo executive branch and the Navajo people. If this report treated the development dilemma at only the tribal level it would contribute little new to the existing state of knowledge. Therefore, the section "Development and the Traditional Community" contains an examination of development at the grass-roots or community level.

HISTORY OF NAVAJO DEVELOPMENT: FROM A SELF-SUFFICIENT TO A DEPENDENT ECONOMY

The surrender of the Navajos in 1863–1864 marked the beginning of their government wardship. Eight thousand five hundred Navajos and four hundred fifty Mescalero Apaches were confined to 40 square miles of poor land known as "Bosque Redondo." Here government agents attempted to transform Navajos into peaceful, village-dwelling, Christian farmers. The projects failed for a number of reasons. Drought, hail, and worms attacked the crops; Comanches raided the sheep; Navajos quarreled with Mescaleros; and Congress objected to the cost: $1,114,981 for the first 20 months of the experiment and $750,000 annually for rations (Kelly 1968: 7).

In 1868, after four dismal years of captivity, twelve Navajo leaders signed a treaty with General W. T. Sherman. The United States Government agreed to establish a reservation and to erect an agency building, a warehouse, a carpenter/blacksmith shop, a schoolhouse, and a chapel. Each Navajo family head who wished to farm would be allowed to select a 160-acre plot (80 acres for single adults) to be retained as long as he chose to cultivate the acreage. The government issued 15,000 sheep and goats, nearly two animals for every man, woman, and child. In 1872, 10,000 more sheep were issued (Shepardson 1963: 12). In return, the Navajos promised to give up raiding and pillaging as a way of life.

The treaty makers of 1868 assumed that the Navajo would be assimilated into the American mainstream if he were made a property owner, an entrepreneur farmer, and economically independent of the United States government. The allotment of land to family heads or individuals ignored several facts: Navajos believe that individuals do not "own" land, they merely enjoy "use" rights; Navajos did not have the capital or technical knowledge necessary to develop the land; the Navajos belonged to extended families in which economic support was mutual.

From 1863 to 1913 the lot of the Navajos was seemingly profitable and peaceable. Their numbers had increased from 8,000 to 30,000 by 1912. Animals increased from 15,000 sheep to their preconquest number. The federal government, recognizing that the original four-million-acre grant was too small to support a pastoral economy, enlarged it by 1911 to 12 million acres. Navajos engaged in a number of activities, principally subsistence agriculture, herding, and weaving. They were economically self-sufficient. However, it was an illusory type of self-sufficiency. The fixing of boundaries insured that it would only be a matter of time before the increasing population would overburden the fragile resources.

Until the 1920's, the Navajos lived in relative isolation. Because they did not occupy prime land, they were bypassed by White settlers. The only pressure for their land came from prospectors who suspected its mineral wealth, which remained unexploited until the 1920's.

The most significant change in Navajo land resulted from erosion caused by overgrazing. In 1930 there were nearly 1,300,000 sheep and goats on the Navajo reservation and approximately 40,000 Navajos, or 32.4 animals per capita (Young 1961: 150). The estimated carrying capacity of the range was 513,000 sheep units. (One sheep or goat = 1 sheep unit; one burro = 3 sheep units; one cow = 4 sheep units; one horse = 5 sheep units. There is presently no legal penalty for exceeding the "permitted" number of sheep units.) Overgrazing lowered the productivity efficiency of the land by denuding it of a protective cover of vegetation, which increased the rapidity of run-off. The most conspicuous evidence of overgrazing was the increase in the size of gullies that gashed the reservation. In 1897, Orabi Wash was no more than twenty feet across and twelve feet deep; in 1937 it measured 150 to 300 feet wide and 30 to 35 feet deep (Hoover 1937: 289).

A federal livestock-reduction program was instituted, and between 1934 and 1940 reservation stock was reduced by one-half. Stock reduction, combined with population increase, lowered the livestock per capita ratio from 32 to 8; Navajos could no longer depend solely on their own resources for support. As a result of the reduction program, the Navajos suffered a severe economic shock — and psychological shock as well. When it proved impossible or too costly to move animals to packing plants, these indicators of Navajo wealth were shot and left to rot or were set on fire. During a Senate hearing in 1936, a Navajo from Tuba City asked how the Senators would feel if he asked them for a $5 bill and then burned it in front of them. "That," he said, "was what the Navajos felt when their valuable livestock was destroyed" (Aberle 1966: 61–62).

The Navajos, embittered by the reduction program, became suspicious of all programs to improve their range. Tall John, when confronted by government reduction agents said, "If you take my sheep, you kill me. So kill me now. Let's fight right here and decide this thing" (Downs 1964: 20). The program was a failure politically, economically, and ecologically.

The fault can be laid to federal planners who failed to see that sheep were a way of life for the Navajos. Reduction of sheep meant abandoning old ways and values; it meant a cultural transformation as well as an economic one. Because the federal government did not offer viable economic activities, one could hardly expect the Navajo to scuttle both the traditional economy and their culture.

Although the program did not restore the Navajo range, it did end the self-sufficient nature of the traditional economy. Before the imposition of reservation boundaries, the Navajos could expand their use areas as population and livestock increased. After 1911 it was impossible to maintain a pastoral economy which used the land extensively. The fact that the Navajo population expanded from 8,000 to 40,000 and their livestock from 15,000 to 1,300,000 testifies to the capacity of the land. However, the population would eventually overtax this capacity. Thus, the Navajo nation with or without stock reduction would have eventually faced the problem of supporting an expanding population on a limited resource base.

There are a number of alternatives open to such an economy. First, excess population can migrate, allowing those who remain to live on the fixed resources. An induced migration, euphemistically referred to as "relocation", was attempted by the Bureau of Indian Affairs (BIA) in the 1950's and was unsuccessful. Second, the Navajos could export products in which they have a comparative advantage and import those they do not produce. This has been occurring since 1921 when Navajos began to lease their mineral wealth. However, the minerals are exported in their crude state and the Navajos receive very little of their final value. Mineral and timber resources should be processed before they are exported in order to capture as much as possible of the "value-added" and to generate additional jobs.

Federal interference was not limited to stock reduction. In 1934 Congress passed the Indian Reorganization Act (IRA) which among other things provided for democratically elected tribal governments. The Navajos, smarting from the recent economic hardships visited upon them by the reduction program, voted down the opportunity to organize under the IRA. The current tribal council functions under special bylaws issued by the Secretary of Interior in 1938 (Goldberg 1976: 3). Even though the Navajo rejected the IRA government, they have not been able to avoid the hiatus between the values of traditional Navajo people and the actions of tribal government officials.

To supplement the decline in stock income which resulted from reduction, the government planned a series of public works projects, but federal budgets were subject to political whims. When funds were decreased, the government was unable to compensate the Navajo people for their investment loss or even maintain their annual income at former levels. The Navajo were forced to seek wage work off the reservation. World War II catapulted 3,600 Navajos into the armed forces and 15,000 Navajo men and women into off-reservation work in war plants and agriculture. The end of World War II precipitated an economic crisis, as the Navajo labor force reluctantly returned to a substandard level of living on the reservation (Shepardson 1963: 16–17).

Under the Navajo-Hopi Long-Range Rehabilitation Act of 1950, the federal government began its first program to promote economic development. The act was intended to assist Navajos in re-creating a self-supporting economy and, ultimately, in attaining standards of living enjoyed by other citizens. The act financed school construction, soil conservation, and relocation. Of the appropriated $89,946,240, 78 percent was allocated to roads, education, health, housing, and com-

Table 1. Allocation of development funds (1950–1961)

Activity	Dollar amount	Percent of total funds
Roads	$38,237,680	0.425
School construction	24,997,295	0.277
Health	4,750,000	0.052
Service facilities	495,100	0.005
Housing	26,300	0.0002
Water	1,356,670	0.015
Irrigation	6,616,775	0.073
Conservation	7,097,175	0.078
Colorado Irrigation Project	3,449,750	0.038
Survey of timber, coal, minerals	436,895	0.004
Placement and relocation	194,600	0.002
Revolving loan	1,800,000	0.020
Business development	238,000	0.002
Telephone and communications	250,000	0.002
Total	$89,946,240	

munications; 20 percent was invested in improving the productivity of subsistence agriculture and sheep raising; and a mere 2 percent was appropriated for starting new enterprises (see Table 1). Although investment in infrastructure was necessary for development, it was not sufficient. Roads and an educated, healthy labor force do not in themselves generate productive enterprises. Simultaneously with the Rehabilitation Act, income acquired from the exploitation of mineral leases increased. By 1975 tribal mineral revenues from oil, gas, coal, and uranium amounted to $305,914,831 (see Table 2). Of this large total, $34,418,112 (11 percent) was invested in job generating enterprises (Navajo Tribe 1975, Financial Statement). The remainder was used for tribal administration, services, maintenance of productive resources or was invested in securities.

Table 2. Tribal mineral production and revenues (1922–1975)

Mineral	Amount produced	Revenue received
Oil	333,259,441 barrels	$272,716,931
Gas	Not available	7,836,661
Coal	Not available	10,490,233*
Uranium	Not available	14,871,006*
Total		$305,914,831

Source: *Annual report of mineral leasing activities, June 30, 1975.* (U.S. Department of Interior 1975).
* This figure includes income only from 1967–1975.

The Rehabilitation Act was followed by a host of antipoverty programs. It would be interesting to compute what each federal agency spent on the Navajo reservation from the initiation of the War on Poverty. However, there is no on-going information system which automatically collects, compiles, and analyzes information on programs operated for the benefit of the tribe by federal, state, and private agencies, though such an analysis was undertaken for one year (Fiscal Year 1972) by the accounting firm of Ernst and Ernst (Table 3). In

Table 3. Federal programs (FY 1972)

Agency	Amount
U.S. Department of Agriculture	$ 375,000
U.S. Department of Commerce	3,711,000
U.S. Department of Health, Education, Welfare	47,858,000
U.S. Department of Housing & Urban Develop.	25,000,000
U.S. Department of Justice	50,000
U.S. Department of Labor	6,853,000
U.S. Department of Interior	170,478,000
U.S. Office of Economic Opportunity	10,042,000
Total United States government	$264,367,000

Source: Ernst and Ernst 1973.

addition to direct federal funding, the Navajo economy benefited from indirect federal assistance ($73 million), state agency contributions ($9.7 million), Four Corners Regional Commission contributions ($4.8 million), private, religious, charitable contributions ($7.4 million) and Navajo tribal funds ($45.9 million). These contributions to the Navajo economy totaled $406.9 million in FY 1972 or $3,124 per Navajo. When one learns that Navajo income per capita from all sources, including welfare was $900 and compares this figure with health and education statistics, one wonders who benefited from such public expenditures. Ernst and Ernst analyzed how $331 million of the $406.9 million was spent (Table 4). As can be seen from Table 4, 59.9 percent of all public sector funds were spent on health, education, housing, and welfare. Little was available for job creation.

The results of this pattern of spending have been described by David Aberle:

At the end of 100 years of administration we find an undereducated, unhealthy, overcrowded population with a primitive livestock and farming pattern, with [an inadequate] technological substratum for development, and with almost no development save for exploitation of mineral resources by outside private capital (Aberle 1969: 243).

Such underdevelopment is confirmed by the socioeconomic statistics on income, employment, education, health, housing, and transportation.

Table 4. Federal, state, tribal, and private spending (FY 1972)

Category	Amount	Percent of total
Health and medical care	$ 34,034,000	10.28
Education	97,720,000	29.51
Public assistance	41,491,000	12.53
Construction	36,015,000	10.87
Agriculture and land management	3,521,000	1.06
Economic development*	12,909,000	3.90
Housing	25,178,000	7.60
Administration, planning, miscellaneous, assistance	57,833,000	17.46
Earned tribal income	22,488,000	6.79
Total	$331,189,000	100.00

Source: Ernst and Ernst 1973.
* Economic development included SBA loans, EDA loans and grants, OEO loans and grants, and BIA industrial development funds.

Income and Employment

When income (cash and kind) from subsistence activities, wage work, and welfare are taken into account, average Navajo income per capita in 1970 was a mere $900, compared to $3,921 for the U.S. The 1971 average per capita income for the Navajo living in an isolated community was even lower, $725, compared to the national poverty level of $1,727 for unrelated rural individuals. Sources of Navajo community income are contained in Table 5.

Table 5. Source of Navajo community income, 1971

Source	Percent
Livestock	10.1
Agriculture	1.1
Weaving and singing	2.3
Local wage work	44.4
Nonlocal wage work	15.1
Welfare (cash & kind)	26.6

Sources: Ruffing 1973: 162.

A Navajo living in an isolated community derives 71 percent of his income from welfare and public sector employments. Low income can be partially explained by unemployment, low educational levels, and poor health. The rate of unemployment and underemployment was a staggering 54 percent in 1971 (see Appendix I, Note A).

Education

The average educational level in 1970 for all Navajos was five years, as compared to the national average of twelve years.

More important, a large segment of the Navajo population has not attained functional literacy in English; 17 percent of the adults over 25 years were not literate, and 12 percent did not speak English. The preferred language of communication for adults is Navajo. If any English is known, it is used with reluctance.

Although the educational level is abnormally low for Navajo adults, the situation is changing for Navajo children. At Shonto individuals between 16 and 25 years of age showed an astonishing average of 10.25 years completed schooling. In 1971 all but 9 percent of the 56,797 children between 5 and 18 years of age were in school — 40 percent being educated by the BIA, 46 percent by public schools, and 5 percent by private schools. Of the 32,982 Navajos 25 years and older by 1970, 4,576 had completed high school (14 percent) and 325 had completed college (1 percent) (U.S. Bureau of Census 1970: 146). A recent demographic survey verified these small gains when it found that female household heads (average age, 42.6 years) had 8.6 years of schooling, while male household heads (average age 45.1 years) had 8.5 years (Wistisen 1975, vol. 1, p. 28).

The BIA spent approximately $2,505 per Navajo child in 1971. For all children, including Indians, the state and local authorities of Arizona spent $637 per child, New Mexico spent $547 per child, Utah spent $560 per child, and the United States average was $761 per child. BIA expenses are greater because 49 of the 60 BIA schools are boarding schools. Approximately 19,600 Navajo children (35 percent) must leave home to attend BIA and public schools, and private schools have been severely criticized for lack of community control and lack of acceptance of bilingual education. These failings, no doubt, contribute to the slow progress made in Indian education, but we cannot examine them in depth here.

Tribal and BIA scholarships, combined with the efforts of the Navajo Community College and of private individuals or groups, annually send between 1,000 and 1,500 Navajo students to colleges and universities. Little is known about how Navajo students fare, what they study, or where they go after college. It appears that few return to the reservation, because most teachers are non-Navajo (93 percent), even though educating Navajo teachers has been a BIA priority since the late 1930's (U.S. Commission on Civil Rights 1975: 72). The tribal scholarship fund has been depleted from $10,121,724 in 1967 to $8,600,235 in 1971, because expenditures have exceeded revenues from the fund. In 1971 tribal scholarship grants amounted to $526,157, while scholarship revenues totaled $378,302. To ease the strain on the educational fund and to benefit from its investment in education, the tribe could consider requiring repayment either in cash or in service to the reservation school system. The brain drain will have to cease if the Navajo nation is going to acquire the management skills necessary for development.

Health

The Navajo people are served by 6 hospitals and 24 health clinics. In 1971 there were 230 Navajos for every hospital bed and one doctor for every 1,195 Navajos, compared to one doctor for every 613 United States citizens. The Indian Health Service spent $30,941,000 during 1972 for health care on the reservation, or approximately $237 per Navajo. Even though the average United States citizen spent only $177 for health care in 1968, he was considerably healthier (Table 6). The fact that the average United States citizen spends less on health care and is healthier results from the fact that he has better health-care facilities and living conditions. Ninety percent of Navajo families lived in houses without indoor plumbing, which accounted for the high rates of gastritis and enteritis. Most Navajo families slept on earthen floors, which contributed to the high incidence of tuberculosis.

Table 6. Comparative health statistics

	Navajo[a]		United States[b]	
	Incidence	Mortality	Incidence	Mortality
Tuberculosis (per 100,000)	176.7	15.7	—	2.6
Gastritis, enteritis (per 100,000)	11,914.2	18.9	—	1.4
Infant mortality (per 1,000)	—	35.5	—	20.7
	American Indian[c]		United States	
Average age at death in 1964	43.8		63.6	
Life expectancy	64.0		70.5	

Source: [a] Navajo figures: Indian Health Service files, [b] United States figures, U.S. Bureau of Census, *Statistical Abstract of U.S.*, 1971, [c] American Indian and United States figures: U.S. Department of Health, Education and Welfare 1966: 16–17.

Housing

In a 1971 Chinle Agency study, it was found that 90 percent of Navajo families lived in substandard housing. The Navajo Housing Authority was formed in 1963 to implement federal housing programs. Since then 4,000 new homes have been built. However, in examining the FY 1975 housing inventory, only 4,753 houses or 20 percent of the total

Table 7.   Navajo housing inventory FY 1975

Total number of houses		23,315
standard condition	4,753	
substandard	18,562	
needing rennovation	8,325	
needing replacement	10,237	
families needing housing	2,662	
houses needing replacement	10,237	
Total housing deficit		12,899

Source: Housing inventory FY 1975 (U.S. Department of Interior 1975).

housing stock were rated in standard condition. Thus, 80 percent of Navajo homes are still substandard. The total housing deficit is almost 13,000 units (see Table 7).

There have been numerous studies and congressional investigations of Indian housing. There are not only problems with the actual delivery of housing to Indian people, but there is also a more serious problem with the type of housing delivered. Federal housing is based on standard designs which have not been successfully adapted to differences in income levels, climate, cultural life-styles, or settlement patterns. As a result, low income Indian families have not been able to properly maintain their surburban ranch style homes or even heat them properly. Federal units built in 1963 already are substandard because of rapid deterioration. The Navajo hogan, while lacking electricity and plumbing, is notably cooler in summer without air-conditioning and warmer in winter without the use of expensive fuels. Federal designs do not accommodate extended families, thus old people must go to nursing homes. While there is little individual land ownership on the reservation, families usually have claim to traditional use areas where they graze their livestock. Their summer and winter hogans are located within this use area. With federal cluster housing, it is no longer possible to live within one's use area. Thus, federal housing will have an impact on Navajo culture, particularly on family structure, on land-use practices, and ultimately on traditional economic activities such as sheep herding and weaving. Such changes will increase Navajo economic dependency, since there will be a greater need for welfare aid to pay utilities and repairs. There will be less opportunity to engage in traditional economic activities, because place of residence is removed from the use area. Nevertheless, the Navajo people are very receptive to federal housing because it has improved health conditions.

In 1976, the Navajo housing effort began to flounder badly due to financial mismanagement. The Navajo Housing Authority invested $13 million in federal funds in the American Funding Corporation, which was unable to produce the money needed by the authority to defray construction costs. This has stalled the completion of 480 units.

Transportation

Throughout the Southwest, there are generally 154 miles of surfaced road for every 1,000 square miles of area. On the Navajo reservation, there are only 60 miles of surfaced roads for every 1,000 square miles. Two east/west and north/south highways cross the reservation, but only 1,500 miles of road are paved. Although state highway programs are supplemented by federal funds, and Navajos pay state gasoline taxes, the states do little to build reservation roads, which have primarily been built by the federal government (Aberle 1969: 237). The isolation of the reservation is extreme. If Navajos living in Shonto wish to shop at a nontrader grocery store, they must travel 54 miles to Tuba City; shopping at a major shopping center requires a trip to Flagstaff, 132 miles away.

Lack of adequate transportation facilities adds to the major Navajo problems: boarding school education, independent medical care, high prices, and the lack of industrial and commercial development. To bring the present road system up to surrounding state standards will require an estimated $600 million. (MacDonald 1972: 21).

RESOURCES FOR DEVELOPMENT

While one is perplexed by the coexistence of high public spending and low socioeconomic indicators, Navajo underdevelopment is even more puzzling when one considers the fact that Navajos are wealthy in natural resources.

LAND. The Navajo reservation occupies a tract of land about the size of West Virginia (See Map 1). Its 14,124,069 acres include contiguous areas in Arizona, New Mexico, and Utah and noncontiguous areas such as Alamo, Canocito, and Ramah. (Hopi reservation is omitted from the total.) The Navajo reservation, one of the most scenic areas in the world, has three distinct climates: the cold, humid climate of the mountain heights; the steppe climate of the mesas and the high plains; the comparatively warm climate of the desert. The topography varies from the 11,000-foot Chuska Mountains, which traverse the reservation from north to south along the Arizona-New Mexico border, to desert lands at 4,500 feet. Annual rainfall averages from 27 inches, reached only at the highest elevations, to 7 inches (Aberle 1969: 229).

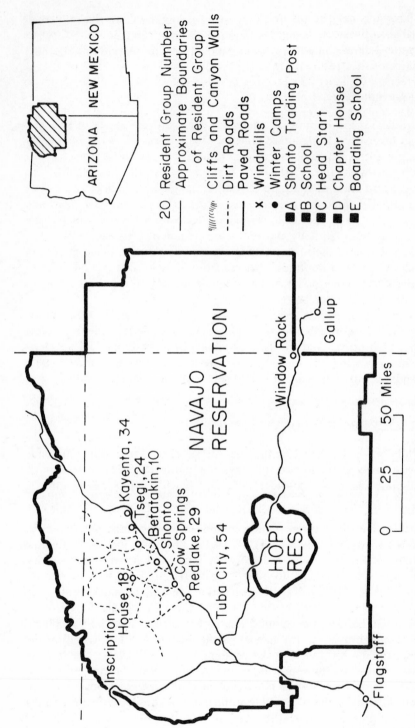

Map. 1.   Navajo Reservation with Shonto and surrounding area indicated.

The soils may be divided into five classes, based on the criteria of available livestock forage, soil permeability, water retention, slope, erosion, alkali content, drainage, and vegetation. According to these characteristics reservation soils fall into the following categories: 11 percent, excellent; 22 percent, good but more susceptible to erosion; 29 percent, fair; 23 percent, poor; 15 percent, unproductive.

The soils of the humid area are highly productive and are suitable for dry farm agriculture. Such crops as grains, alfalfa, sweet clover, hay, corn, potatoes, turnips, carrots, and cabbage grow readily. The steppe climate is of medium productivity, but, because of the greater acreage involved, this area exceeds the remainder of the reservation in total yield from dry farming and irrigated crops. The rest of the reservation is unsuitable for the growing of crops (Shepardson 1963: 18–19). The BIA land-use inventory for 1971 classified reservation land according to usage (Table 8).

Table 8.   Reservation land

Use	Number of acres	Percent of total acres
Dry farming	9,039	0.0006
Grazing	9,069,077	0.6480
Irrigated farming	36,830	0.0026
Timber	3,502,533	0.2500
(commercial timber)	(439,402)	(0.0314)
Unproductive	1,359,063	0.0970

WATER. This is a land of little rain; large areas are unproductive, others are capable only of low productivity. In assessing land values, access to water is more important than amount of acreage. Usable water can be found on only about 39 percent of the reservation, 32 percent of the area has brackish water, and 29 percent has almost no water potential. About 45,000 acres can be cultivated, and, if the maximum expansion possible under the Navajo Irrigation Project is attained, an estimated 156,500 acres could be farmed. The tribe has historic water rights to the Colorado River (50,000 acre feet) and the San Juan River (508,000 acre feet).

However, it signed over 68 percent of its rights to the Colorado to the Navajo Generating Station in the hope of creating employment for local Navajos. It has been unable to secure its full entitlement to the San Juan because that river is already overcommitted to the surrounding non-Indian community.

The Navajo tribe has not developed any overall water plan, although it has been estimated that the use of water in rural areas on the reservation, which was 6,000 acre feet in 1966, will increase to 30,000 acre feet or more by the end of this century. The Navajo population has been outpacing the development of reservation water resources. During the past twenty years the reservation has suffered repeatedly from droughts, and indiscriminate use of water by non-Navajo enterprises makes the situation even more difficult. For example, Peabody Coal chose a slurry operation to transport coal to Nevada in preference to other means. Clearly, it is the least costly method for Peabody, but the cost to the tribe has not yet been estimated. To supply water for the operation at least four wells 2,500 feet in depth were dug, each of which will have pumping capacity of 2,000 gallons per minute. There is a possibility that the water table will be permanently lowered, eliminating the Navajo livelihoods of livestock raising and occasional farming in that area.

LIVESTOCK.   Sheep raising has been an integral part of Navajo culture since the sixteenth century. Prior to the livestock-reduction program, sheep yielded a sizeable portion of Navajo income, but today yield only 10 percent. Nevertheless, the unemployed labor force spends the bulk of its time in stock-raising activities.

The total carrying capacity of the range in 1974 was 1,587,763 animal units. Actually, the reservation supported nearly 2,512,007 animal units: 526,864 sheep and goats, 49,201 cattle, and 29,353 horses (Figures from U.S. Department of Interior 1974 *Annual range management report*). The reservation was 63 percent overgrazed, with some areas more seriously depleted than others. The situation could be eased by a more equal distribution of animals over the range, but the unequal distribution of water makes this impossible. The failure to develop adequate resources for watering stock limits the number of animals that Navajos can graze.

TIMBER.   As early as 1888, a sawmill was built to exploit the reservation's timber resources, which now include some 430,302 acres of commercial forest. The Navajo Forest Products Industry annually harvests stumpage valued at $1–3 million. The resulting lumber sales earn $7–11 million. NFPI employs 564 Navajos (1975) and in 1976 installed a particle board plant which employs 80 additional Navajos.

OIL, GAS, COAL, AND URANIUM.   The reservation is rich in subsurface minerals, with vast reserves amounting to 100 million barrels of oil, 23 billion cubic feet of natural gas, 5 billion tons of easily accessible coal, and 80 million pounds of uranium (Table 9). Other materials that could be exploited are helium, copper, bleaching clay, puzzolan, and "frac" sand.

Table 9. Known physical resources (1975)

Resource	Amount
Sheep and goats	526,864
Cattle	49,201
Commercial timber	1,524,537 M ft. BM
Oil	100,000,000 barrels
Gas	23,000,000,000 cubic feet
Coal	5,000,000,000 tons
Uranium	80,000,000 pounds

Source: Livestock: *Annual range management report* (U.S. Department of Interior 1974); Timber: *Forestry report* (U.S. Department of Interior 1975); Oil, gas, coal, uranium: *Business Week* (May 3, 1976).

HUMAN RESOURCES. There is a sharp contrast between the wealth of Navajo mineral resources and the dire poverty of human resources. In 1975 there were 147,210 Navajos. Annual population growth exceeds 2.5 percent compared with 1.1 percent for the total United States population, and the tribe will have doubled in 28 years (1999). A slowing of this rate is not expected; on the contrary, with 59 percent of the population below 24 years of age, growth will probably accelerate. Median Navajo age is 17, compared with 29 for the United States (MacDonald 1972: 10); average family size is 6.5 compared to 3.6. Unless the external economy improves and racial discrimination diminishes, 80 to 90 percent of the reservation population will wish to remain on the reservation. Planning must be based on a maximum estimate of population and population growth (Aberle 1969: 252).

LABOR FORCE. More than 1,000 Navajos enter the labor force each year, and job development must stay ahead of this increase. The 1975 Navajo labor force was estimated to be 41,075, with 50 percent permanently employed, 32 percent temporarily employed, and 18 percent completely unemployed. Thus, 50 percent of the labor force was either unemployed or underemployed (see Appendix, Note B).

The permanently employed are active in the modern sector of the economy while the unemployed and underemployed participate in the traditional sector.

A 1974 labor survey reviewed the sources of modern sector employment (Table 10). Of the existing 20,140 permanent jobs, 14,280 jobs were held by Navajos. As can be seen, the Navajos have had great difficulty in obtaining employment in the construction industry. Sixty-six percent of all permanently employed Navajos were in the public sector. Even if Navajos were to take over the 5,860 positions held by non-Navajos, unemployment and underemployment would remain

Table 10.   Source of employment

Industry	Total number	Navajos	Percent
Mining	794	518	65.2
Agriculture and forestry	890	840	94.3
Tourism	240	217	90.4
Manufacturing and processing	1,383*	1,281	92.6
Commercial trades and services	1,156	892	77.1
Transportation communication, and utilities	348	333	95.6
Construction	2,716	741	27.3
Public services	12,613	9,458	74.9
Total	20,140	14,280	70.9

Source: 'Overall Economic Development Program (OEDP) (Navajo Tribe 1974: 23).
* This total includes Fairchild Semi-Conductor which accounted for 950 employees. The plant closed down in 1974.

high. In 1975 a total of 20,576 Navajos needed full-time jobs; only subsistence activities, the Navajo system of extended family sharing, welfare, and government education and health care have made this amount of unemployment tolerable.

OBSTACLES TO DEVELOPMENT

Economic development can be analyzed from many perspectives. Examining public expenditures and taking an inventory of natural resources does little to explain the dismal socioeconomic statistics of the Navajo nation. Furthermore, it is not the purpose of this report to imply that public funds are being misspent. The expenditures for health, education, and welfare are necessary and are required by treaty. However, these expenditures merely maintain the people. Their living standard will not improve appreciably unless they are able to obtain jobs. Such jobs can be generated by the development of Navajo resources. However, there are numerous obstacles which prevent the beneficial development of these resources.

LACK OF CONTROL.   The first obstacle to Navajo development is the fact that Navajos do not control their own resources. The Commissioner of Indian Affairs, acting for the Secretary of Interior, manages all Indian affairs, even though the United States Constitution only empowers the federal government to "regulate Commerce ... with Indian tribes".

The commissioner in effect has been transformed from a trade commissioner to a colonial governor. In commenting on how federal-Indian relations could be improved, the general counsel for the Navajo tribe, George Vlassis, suggested that "Section 2 of U.S. Code

Title 25 (pertaining to the Commissioner's duties) should be eradicated from the books tomorrow" (American Indian Policy Review Commission, Task Force #9 correspondence from George Vlassis March 24, 1976). Not only does the BIA control Navajo resources, but they control the actions of the Navajo government. Virtually every act of the tribal council must receive the approval of the BIA before it can become law or be acted upon by the tribe.

In a hearing for the U.S. Commission on Civil Rights, the Navajo chairman, Peter MacDonald testified that many of the tribe's plans and proposals for development "have sat in the hands of the bureaucrats for 2 to 3 years — a frustrating and backbreaking situation" (U.S. Commission on Civil Rights: 1975: 89).

Having ultimate control, the BIA has consistently favored one method of exploitation of Indian resources, and that is, to lease them to non-Indians. The BIA had chosen this option because they felt that Indians lacked the skill and capital to properly develop their resources. In the case of the Navajo, the BIA formed the first tribal council in order to sign oil leases. Mineral leasing under the technical guidance of the BIA has resulted in suboptimal rates of return for these resources.

The royalty rates negotiated by the BIA were fixed in dollars per unit of the mineral produced rather than being made a percentage of the value of production. In four out of five coal leases negotiated between 1957 and 1968, the royalty was fixed between $0.15–0.375 a ton. Since then the value per ton has more than doubled. There is no way to adjust these inequitable royalties because the leases are for ten years or "as long thereafter as minerals are produced in paying quantities". The royalty is thus fixed for the life of the deposit or until the mining company develops a social conscience. To make low royalties even worse the BIA does not verify the companies' production records or insure that the royalty is paid on time. One year (1974) the auditor general of the Navajo nation investigated the United States Geological Service in Roswell and found that various companies were in arrears. In addition to these defects, the leases contain provisions for environmental protection and preferences for Indian hiring which are wholly inadequate. These provisions have been so vaguely worded that the lessee cannot be successfully prosecuted in court for noncompliance.

In a conference on Indian Land Development, Peter MacDonald told the audience that mineral contracts would have to be renegotiated to meet five minimum demands: (1) a fair return, a royalty based on market value; (2) an option for the tribe to participate in the venture as a partner; (3) Indian employment throughout the company, not just in unskilled positions; (4) use of the best technology to protect the environment; and (5) compliance with tribal laws and courts.

However, to date the Navajos have been able to renegotiate only the El Paso Natural Gas coal lease and obtain slightly more favorable terms. They have also set up the Office of Navajo Labor Relations to enforce preferential hiring provisions. The Navajos might realize a greater return for their minerals by direct exploitation or by forming joint ventures with mining companies. Thus far, it has been difficult if not impossible to form joint ventures due to the reluctance of both the mining companies and the BIA.

In the U.S. Commission hearing Carl Todacheene, chairman of the tribal council resources committee, recalled that in the mid-1950's the tribe approached the Delhi-Taylor Corporation with a 50–50 partnership proposal for the development of oil and gas resources. He blamed the proposal's eventual defeat on intensive lobbying at the Department of Interior by industry competitors (U.S. Commission on Civil Rights 1975: 29). Mineral producers themselves have made it difficult for the Navajo to become partners by demanding that the tribe contribute an equal share of equity and working capital, a difficult requirement in view of the scarcity of capital. The lack of capital could be remedied by permitting the tribe to mortgage its royalties in exchange for equity. This supposes of course that royalties are fairly calculated. However, is it fair that the mining company receive $83\frac{1}{3}$ percent of the market value just for delivering it to the market, with royalties accounting for only $16\frac{2}{3}$ percent? Royalties should more accurately reflect the value of the resource which can be calculated as that portion of total sales revenue which remains after the company has deducted all the cost of delivering it to the market: wages, depreciation on equipment, material costs, interest on capital. At present royalties are almost always less than this remainder, most of which accrues to the company as excess profit. If the value of the resource were always computed in this manner, then both the company and the Indian owner would know what value could be attached to the Indian equity share.

Even when the tribe has been able to work out a joint venture agreement, it has not been able to secure prompt BIA approval. For example, in January 1973 the Navajo nation sent out 25 invitations for bids for uranium exploration. By January 1974, they had determined that Exxon had made the best offer, and entered into a joint venture agreement. After a deposit is found, the Navajos can choose whether they want to receive a negotiated royalty or up to a 49 percent working interest with Navajos contributing up to 49 percent of the remaining future capital requirements and receiving 49 percent of the future profits. The Navajo nation requested BIA approval of the agreement. On April 2, 1974 the Commissioner of Indian Affairs requested the Navajo area director to undertake an environmental impact statement. This was not initiated until January 1976. The Navajo Minerals Department felt that the BIA Area Office delayed because they had been left out of the original negotiations. Since the Area Office does not have a mining engineer or a geologist and has a record of approving inequitable leases, what could it have contributed? By March 10, 1975, an assistant interior secretary for energy and minerals made the following assessment of the Exxon agreement:

The enclosed analyses indicate there is no reason for the Secretary (of Interior) to disapprove the proposed contract because it contains financial terms which are inequitable to the Navajo nation. On the contrary the financial terms are attractive. Given the lapse of time that has already taken place (14 months), I recommend that the Department of Interior expeditiously complete the Environmental Impact Statement.

The lease was approved in late January 1977. The three year delay cost the Navajos $1,500 a day in unpaid interest on the $6 million bid price to be paid by Exxon but held in escrow until the lease was approved.

Navajo mineral revenues are reduced not only by poorly negotiated leases but by some types of state taxation of non-Indian mineral producers. A tax on mineral production falls in the long run upon the owner of the resource rather than on the developer because the developer will pass on the tax in the form of lower royalties. Since state taxes increase the cost of mineral production to the developers, Navajos will encounter increasing reluctance on the part of the developers to renegotiate old leases with low royalties or negotiate new leases with higher royalty rates. Therefore, a state tax upon mineral developers can be regarded as a tax upon Indians no matter who, in fact, pays the tax. Peter MacDonald has called this the "legal theft" of Navajo resources. Presently, Navajos are writing a tax code, but it remains to be seen if they can displace state taxes. Mineral developers place little credence in the tribal power to tax which originates from its sovereignty and prefer instead to continue to pay state taxes.

The magnitude of lost revenue or the burden imposed on the Navajo by state taxation is staggering. The states of Arizona and New Mexico will collect more in taxes after 1976 from energy producing companies on the Navajo reservation than the Navajo nation will receive from the sum total of coal royalties, rentals, bonuses, and wages. After 1976 approximately 500 Navajos will be employed in coal mining enterprises, energy producing plants, and energy-related pipelines and railroads and will earn $5.5 million in wages. The tribe will receive $4.5 million in rents and royalties, $402,000 in rights of way and water charges. Total energy revenues will be approximately $10.5 million. In 1974 Peabody Coal Company paid $1.6 million in Arizona sales and property taxes. Black Mesa Pipeline paid $1.5 million in property taxes. The Navajo Generating Station will pay $10.5 million after 1976

(Robbins 1975: 12). The state of New Mexico expects to collect $12.6 million per annum in sales taxes alone from coal gasification on Navajo lands (Aberle 1976: 18). State taxes will exceed Navajo revenues 2.5 times. Thus, while the Navajo nation is rich in resources, the benefits from these resources accrue to mineral developers and the states.

Lack of Capital

One reason that the Navajo nation has not been able to mine and process its mineral wealth itself or even enter joint ventures is because it lacks the capital. Ironically, its main source of revenue is mineral royalties. However, in three out of the last six years, tribal government expenditures have exceeded these revenues, and it has been forced to dip into its accumulated capital reserves (see Table 11). Tribal capital

Table 11.   Tribal revenues and expenditures in thousands of dollars

Year	1970	1971	1972	1973	1974	1975
Revenues	17,989	26,448	19,561	26,316	20,583	27,549
Percent derived from minerals	45	51	41	28	49	70
Expenditures	18,537	21,381	25,928	29,928	20,209	27,057
Excess (deficit)	(547)	5,067	(6,366)	(3,260)	374	491
Accumulated capital	47,597	54,131	47,443	47,420	49,725	45,112

Source: Financial statements (Navajo tribe 1971–1975).

available for investment during 1970–1975 fluctuated around $45 million. A joint venture in uranium would cost the tribe $25 million, in coal, $50 million, and for a solely owned venture, double — (estimates based on Department of Interior calculations and Navajo Minerals Department). Obviously, if Navajos are going to enter joint or solely owned ventures, they are going to need federal loans, or advance mineral sales, or bond issues. Since their status as a local government equal to any municipality or state has not been recognized by financial markets, they cannot issue bonds.

A Navajo resource development authority should be created. Tribal exploitation of the resource would eliminate state taxation. The authority's equity and working capital would come from federal loans, tribal bonds, advance mineral sales. It could hire a mining company to do the actual exploitation just as in the Blackfoot-Damson agreement.

Working within the current capital constraints, the Navajo tribal government should increase its rate of investment in job-generating enterprises. Its rate of investment in tribal enterprises has not been

Table 12.   Rate of investment in thousands of dollars

Year	1970	1971	1972	1973	1974	1975
Revenue	17,989	26,448	19,561	26,316	20,583	27,549
Cost of tribal enterprises	27,005	27,024	27,593	30,831	32,040	34,418
Change in cost of Tribal enterprises		18	569	3,237	1,209	2,377
Rate of investment*		0.0007	0.0291	0.1230	0.0587	0.0863

Source: Financial statements (Navajo tribe 1970–1975).

$$\text{* Rate of investment} = \frac{\text{Changes in cost of tribal enterprises}}{\text{Revenue}_t}(t)-(t-1)$$

very stable nor adequate for development (Table 12). Most developing countries are urged to invest at least 20 percent of current income. Current tribal budgets reveal that the bulk of current revenue is spent on administration (31 percent) and social services (57 percent) (Table 13).

Table 13.   Actual net expenditures, 1975

Budget category		Amount	Percent	Type of expenditure
Legislative		$2,054,889		Administration
Judiciary		395,490		Administration
Executive		2,331,204		Administration
Administration		1,998,591		Administration
Controller		455,541		Administration
Business management		499,628		Administration
Services		835,287		Administration
Subtotal		8,570,630	31	Administration
Division of law		3,204,013		Service
Operations		4,005,318		Resources maintenance
Education		2,059,802		Service
Social Service		1,566,077		Service
Contributions–charity		126,608		Service
–NAPI		1,876,000		Job creation
Continuing net expenditures		3,205,825		Emergency programs
Revolving net expenditures		143,341		Service
No year expenditures		1,518,493		Service
	NIP	1,583,478		Infrastructures
Subtotal	Service	15,830,478	57	
	Other	3,352,809	12	
Total		$27,753,917	100	

Source: Financial statement FY 1975 (Navajo tribe 1975)

Uses of Capital

Even though the tribe has not been able to invest at a rapid rate, it is helpful to examine the types of investments they have made and their contribution toward increasing employment and capturing an increased share of the value added (Table 14).

Table 14.   Navajo tribal enterprises

Enterprise		Amount invested at cost	Number of employees in 1974
Navajo Tribal Utility Authority		$ 17,299,296	89
	(in notes)	3,974,926†	
Navajo Forest Product Industries (NFPI)		6,486,127	644*
Navajo Housing & Development Enterprise		1,337,303	N.A.
	(in notes)	1,200,000†	
	(performance bond)	10,000,000†	
Navajo Agricultural Products Industries		4,323,375	209
Navajo Engineering & Construction Authority		772,234	218
	(in notes)	500,000†	
Navajo Arts & Crafts		724,580	56
Shiprock Motel		316,274	N.A.
Navajo Aviation Authority		716,200	N.A.
Revolving Credit		2,397,723	N.A.
Wool Plant‡		65,084	N.A.
Window Rock Motor Inn‡		136,000	38

Source: Financial statement FY 1975 (Navajo tribe 1975); annual report (Navajo Forest Products Industries 1975); Overall economic development plan (Navajo tribe 1974).
*   Figure is for 1976.
†   Notes are actually held by the tribe or the tribe is a cosigner.
‡   The wool plant is merely a sorting operation and is not a bonafide enterprise. The Motor Inn did not appear in the 1975 statement and so was either omitted or sold.

The Navajo Tribal Utility Authority provides the Navajo with electricity, gas, and water. By 1973 nearly 40 percent of households had electrical service, but only 20 percent had water and sewer services. The OEDP (Navajo Tribe 1974) suggested that it is impossible to provide small outlying communities with electricity. This suggestion is ridiculous when one realizes that Navajo resources (namely coal and water) supply the Page, Mohave, and Fruitland generating stations which provide power for Phoenix and Los Angeles.

The ironies of NTUA operation have been described in detail by David Aberle. The NTUA buys power from an Arizona Public Service Company power plant near Fruitland, which burns coal supplied by Utah Construction and Mining Company from Navajo mineral leases. Thus, the Navajo buy back their coal in the form of electric current, which they sell at a profit locally (Aberle 1969: 255).

This is the ultimate economic absurdity: to export a resource in its crude form, and then import it in its processed form allowing non-Navajos to reap the value-added. We have explored the costs of mineral extraction ($100 million for coal) but not for the generation of electricity. The Navajos could supply their own power with the assistance of federal subsidies.

One of the oldest (1958) and most successful enterprises is the Navajo Forest Products Industries (NFPI). It now includes a sawmill, a bark-processing plant, a millwork and cut-stock plant, and a particle board plant. NFPI annually increases the return from the tribe's timber resource by allowing it to be sold as finished lumber instead of stumpage. The difference between stumpage receipts and lumber sales is $6–8 million. This is the value-added from processing. Net profits average $3 million a year. NFPI employs 644 Navajos and generates $3 million in wages. The recent addition of a particle board plant allows it to make use of its waste material. At the dedication ceremonies Chairman MacDonald praised the new plant as a means to "employ more of our people and provide the economic self-sufficiency we all are looking for. It is incumbent on us . . . to extract the most benefit from our resources as possible — resources such as uranium, coal, oil, and timber" (*Navajo Times,* September 23, 1976). NFPI is the only tribal enterprise which annually repays part of the original tribal investment.

The continued growth of NFPI necessitated the development of the new town of Navajo: the Economic Development Administration (EDA) assisted by providing a business loan to NFPI of $550,000, a public works grant of $130,000 for town-site preparation, $270,000 for a business loan for a commercial center, and $160,000 for the town water supply. In this unique case, a viable industry sparked the development of infrastructure. A considerable body of economic literature is devoted to the question of whether infrastructure or productive enterprises should come first. It seems that the past 20 years of investment in infrastructure has generated little complementary investment in productive enterprises. Rather than waiting for spontaneous investment in productive activities, the tribe could initiate productive enterprises based on their natural resources.

The most ambitious development project undertaken by the tribe is the Navajo Irrigation Project on the San Juan River, which will increase irrigable land by 110,630 acres. The project was proposed more than a century ago and field surveys, preliminary reports, and feasibility studies were prepared between 1945 and 1955. In the interim, a proposal was made for the diversion of water from the San Juan to the Chama River to serve the growing city of Albuquerque. Laws were passed authorizing the necessary construction. The Navajo dam and reservoir were completed at a cost of $22,822,624. The reservoir is the principal source of water to serve the irrigation project. In 1960 Senator Anderson introduced a bill to authorize construction of the irrigation project. Secretary of Interior Udall stated, "that authorization of an irrigation development such as the proposed Navajo Indian irrigation project would implement the recognition given in 1956 of the nation's responsibility to help alleviate the severe economic distress among the Navajo people by providing them an opportunity to earn a respectable standard of living." The bill became law in 1962. But the Navajo will be lucky to see the completion of their project by the year 2000 due to federal impoundments of funds.

The first 10,000 acres of land on the project received water and were farmed in 1976. Ten thousand acres are to be added each year, but it is questionable if the Navajo tribe will be able to secure all 508,000 acre feet of water per annum assigned to them. The water in the San Juan-Chama system has been overcommitted and overestimated. The Bureau of Reclamation would like to cut the assignment and is claiming that the Navajos will not be able to "reasonably" use all 508,000 acre feet and insists that the water be used only for irrigation. The real problem is that if the Navajo take their full entitlement there will not be enough water for proposed coal gasification plants.

To control and develop the productive capacity of the 110,630 acres, the Navajo have established a tribally owned enterprise, the Navajo Agricultural Projects Industries (NAPI). The project is being developed as a tribal farm, but it is unlikely that one tribal agribusiness could efficiently manage 110,630 acres. Most economics of scale are obtained by the time a farm reaches 750 acres (Carter and Dean 1936: 264–277). Thus, 150 efficient-sized farms could be set up.

The actual organizational structure of the project should not be viewed as a strict "either-or" choice. There is room for a sizeable tribal farm as well as for a number of family farms of efficient size. Tribal farms and family farms could cooperate on a number of levels such as joint buying and selling, use of specialized farm machinery, and sharing of technology.

Either approach will generate 2,500 jobs during the peak growing season. Total development costs for irrigation, roads, and the farming enterprise will exceed $400 million (personal communication from Bahe Billy, director, NAPI, April 30, 1976). The federal government is funding the irrigation project as required by law, but the tribal government must finance the farming enterprise.

In addition to planting the first 10,000 acres, NAPI has successfully run a small lamb feedlot since 1973.

Normally, Navajos sell their lambs a few at a time to various traders — when they need the cash, where the price is the highest, and sometimes where they have a debt to cancel.

Lambs produced on the Navajo range and in the Western states in general are sold as feeder lambs. In 1968 the average Utah feedlot bought a lamb for $19.43 and sold it for $28.81, for an average net return per pound gained of 8 cents. The tribe has the opportunity to put low cost gains on light lambs by establishing a feedlot. A tribal feedlot could take advantage of the annual price cycle for lambs (see Table 15). Generally, prices are at their peak in spring and

Table 15. Slaughter lamb prices: average per 100 pounds

Jan.	Feb.	Mar.	Apr.	May	June	July	Aug.	Sept.	Oct.	Nov.	Dec.
24.00	25.12	26.88	30.25	31.12	31.12	28.88	27.75	27.50	25.88	24.75	25.75

Source: U.S. Department of Agriculture 1972: 118

are lowest in late fall, when supply is greatest. If individual Navajos could sell to the feedlot in fall, the tribe could fatten the lambs and sell them the following spring at higher prices. The gain would accrue to the tribe instead of to a commercial feeder. Whether actual production is tribal, individual, or both, there are certain complementary activities that should be undertaken. Some have already been mentioned, such as joint buying, marketing, transportation of products, water delivery, provision of utilities, buildings, and maintenance. Other secondary activities could be developed, such as food processing and canning, which would create employment and increase the value-added of agricultural products. Canning and processing will require water, and so it is essential that the Navajo receive their full 508,000 acre feet. Primary and secondary agricultural activities and service-related activities are expected to employ 6,000 Navajos by the year 2000.

In 1971 the Navajo tribe was forced to undertake a tribal wool marketing program because of the collapse of the wool market. Shorn wool prices dropped from a high of 41.8¢ a pound in 1969 to 19.4¢ a pound in 1971. Traders were unable to even market Navajo wool, since domestic manufacturers could buy better quality wool at low prices. The Navajo tribe paid individual Navajo growers a fair selling price, plus an advance on incentive payments, minus handling costs. The program has been successful in finding buyers, in large measure because of the uniform product presented. The program offers advantages which traders cannot offer such as standardized grading and processing, and collective marketing to obtain the best prices. Reservation sheep produce about 3 million pounds annually, or 2 percent of national production. The program markets about 2.2 million pounds all over the world. There are tentative plans for the wool program to expand into fleece-scouring operations. Wool processing is not a novel suggestion. In 1876 John W. Young started a mill in Tuba City that was to use local Navajo wool, but it failed because Mormon women could make better cloth at home (Haskett 1936: 22–23). In 1949 the

Agriculture Industry Service, Inc., recommended a wool processing plant, on the premise that 1.5 million pounds of wool could profitably be bought, sorted, and sold to Eastern markets. This possibility has been demonstrated by the present wool program.

A wool spinning operation to process all Navajo raw wool could be set up for less than $1 million. During scouring 3,036,522 pounds of raw wool (1971 wool clip) is subject to 65 percent shrinkage. Thus, 1,062,782 pounds of scoured wool would be yielded; 631,578 pounds of scoured wool produce 600,000 pounds of spinning yarn for Navajo weavers; the rest could be sold as clean wool to national or international buyers. The tribe has a good local market for semi-processed weaving wool, which many Navajo weavers prefer to buy from traders instead of processing themselves. The wholesale price of this yarn is $2.25 a pound (1971), but it often retails at the trading post for $3.80 a pound. By supplying semiprocessed woolen yarn at lower retail prices, the tribe could cut the price of woolen yarn to the weaver and also receive for itself a higher per pound price than from selling raw wool. In 1971 a pound of carpet yarn sold for $1.17, compared with 19.4 cents for a pound of raw wool. Table 16 shows the relative returns from selling raw wool as the marketing program presently does, versus processing and selling it.

Table 16. Alternative investments

Investment	Price × pounds	= Revenue	− Costs	= Profit
Raw wool sale	$0.126 × 3,036,522 =	$364,382	− $62,000	$302,382
Wool processing				
Scoured wool sale	0.66 × 431,204 =	284,594		
Spinning yarn	1.17 × 600,000 =	702,000		
		986,594	− 748,319 =	238,275
Wages				209,900
Social return (wages + profits)				448,175
Weavers' savings ($3.80–$1.17)(600,000)				1,578,000
Total social gain (wages + profits + weavers' savings)				$2,026,175

Source: Ruffing 1973: 226.

The processing operation would yield a social return of $448,175 (profits plus wages). This is $145,793 more than is yielded by merely selling raw wool. If weavers' savings are included, total gain is a phenomenal $2,026,175.

As a complementary activity to wool marketing and wool processing, an effective marketing service should be created for Navajo rugs. Most unmarketed Navajo wool, 800,000 pounds (1975), is used for making rugs. At present these rugs are marketed through the traders and the Navajo Arts and Crafts Enterprise. Neither has been able to form an energetic marketing chain. The sale of Navajo rugs is dependent on tourists and intermittent sales to large department stores even though there is a growing market for craft articles.

Rug marketing must be on a tribal level and not on a chapter level, because the production of Navajo rugs is sporadic. In previous years there was a seasonal cycle; women produced more rugs during the long daylight hours of summer. Women now weave whenever they need the cash, so production is greater when other economic activities decline or when the chapter provides funds for weaving projects. Small chapter cooperatives have done poorly in the past, because they could not advance payment before they sold the rug. Because the weaver is usually in need of cash and can readily obtain credit from a trader with the rug, there is no incentive to use a marketing service unless it pays on delivery. If the tribe processed the wool, cut weavers' costs, and increased the price per rug by tapping urban markets, production would probably increase, because the weavers — women between 25 and 65 years — have the lowest opportunity cost on the reservation.

The tribal motels like most ventures in Indian tourism have consistently produced a deficit. A consultant on Indian tourism, Harry Clement stated, "It is difficult to make profits on tourism anywhere, much less on Indian reservations which are often located in remote areas" (American Indian Policy Review Commission 1976: 123, *Report*). Faltering tourism projects impose burdens on the tribe that they can ill afford since they are liable for the bad debts. But even if the projects were favorable they provide little employment relative to investment. The jobs are also seasonal and pay minimum wages. It is not surprising the tribes have overhired in an effort to provide more employment. In examining the balance sheets for the Window Rock Motor Inn and the Shiprock Motel, salaries either exceeded total revenues or were 70 percent of them. The tribe should defer investment in tourism since other projects will generate more employment. The Navajo can eventually capture tourist dollars if managers are trained, tourist facilities are placed in the scenic areas, and complementary infrastructure such as stores and restaurants are developed.

More recent ventures are the Navajo Housing and Development Enterprise, the Navajo Engineering and Construction Authority, and the Navajo Aviation Authority. These provide opportunities for Navajos to contract with the federal government for business that has been going to private, non-Navajo firms. Even though 4,000 housing units have been built on the reservation, this activity has had little impact on employment due to the lack of Indian contractors. The formation of the Navajo Engineering and Construction Authority is an attempt to increase the impact of federal spending by having Navajos participate directly in utility construction. The Navajo Housing and Development

Enterprise (NHDE) is supposed to develop middle-class housing. The tribe has directly invested $2,109,537 in these companies, has accepted notes or cosigned notes for another $1,700,000, and has guaranteed a $10,000,000 performance bond for the enterprise. However, NHDE is suffering from the repercussions of the misdirected investment of $13 million in HUD construction funds by the Navajo Housing Authority. NHDE's financial management has been less than adequate, and with the temporary interruption in funding they are on the verge of bankruptcy. Given that the Navajo housing deficit is so great and the rate of deterioration of federal housing so rapid, it is likely that with proper management a new tribal or private company could achieve the objective of making greater use of federal funds by generating employment as well as providing housing.

Another activity of the Navajo tribe is the operation of a revolving loan fund for the benefit of tribal enterprises and individual Navajo businesses. The fund $2,397,723 (FY 1975) was hopelessly inadequate for the task. This lack of capital is the chief obstacle to the increase of Navajo retail establishments.

Since 1965 the tribe has been cooperating with a federal effort to attract non-Navajo manufacturing firms to the reservation. The tribe provides the facilities and sometimes the equipment. The government subsidizes the wage bill. The companies provide the management and working capital. Thus far, four plants, Fairchild Semi-Conductor, General Dynamics, Utah Navajo Industries, and Navajo Trailers have located on the reservation.

In 1967 the tribe spent $600,000 in plant and $220,000 in equipment to attract General Dynamics (see Table 17). With defense cutbacks, employment dropped from the original 250 to 75 (1974).

Table 17.   General Dynamics set-up costs in 1971

Investment	Investor	Amount	Type of funding	Interest
Fort Defiance	EDA	$101,000	Grant	—
Industrial Park	Tribe	25,000	EDA loan	$611,611
	Tribe	17,000	Own funds	11,360
General Dynamics Building	Tribe	600,000	Own funds	48,000
General Dynamics Equipment	Tribe	220,000	Own funds	17,600

Source: Statistics supplied by the EDA 1971

The initial cost of job creation was $3,852, which is very low compared to the industry average of $30,000. In 1971 rentals from General Dynamics exceeded tribal interest payments and foregone interest on capital invested. Salaries generated amounted to $480,000 annually.

Facilities were also provided for Fairchild Semi-Conductor at the cost of $3,301,267 (see Table 18). Fairchild, at its height, employed 1,200 workers. Job creation therefore cost $2,751 per employee. Tribal interest payments to EDA and foregone interest exceeded the rental paid by Fairchild. Nevertheless, salaries contributed between $4.5–5.6 million to the local economy. Thus, while the plant functioned, it was a very successful investment.

Table 18. Fairchild Semi-conductor set-up costs in 1971

Investment	Investor	Amount	Type of Funds	Interest
Shiprock Ind. Park	EDA	$ 122,400	Grant	—
	Tribe	30,600	EDA loan	$ 705
Shiprock Water	EDA	1,000,000	Grant	—
	Tribe	650,000	EDA loan	24,375
Facility	Tribe	462,800	EDA loan	19,665
	Tribe	678,467	EDA loan	28,834
	Tribe	366,000	Own funds	29,280

Source: EDA 1971.

In 1970 Fairchild Camera, the parent company lost $19 million, in 1971, $7.8 million. The company was adversely affected by the slow-down in defense activities and by the 1974 recession. In 1975 they radically reduced their labor force and American Indian Movement demonstrators occupied the plant in protest. This provided the company with the perfect pretext for closing down the operation.

Unfortunately, the Navajo will not be able to depend on branch plants for the industrialization of their reservation. Companies set up such plants during good times, and, since they have little invested in the facilities, close them down just as easily during bad times. The chief disadvantage of this operation is that the Navajos have no control over the decision to close down and have their scarce funds tied up in idle buildings. As Aberle has said, "This episode supplies further evidence that these industries were exotic growths . . . unrelated to the assets of the region, with minimal stakes in Navajoland" (Aberle 1976: 19).

Nevertheless, the tribe has not been deterred from its campaign of industrial promotion. Given an unemployment rate of 50 percent, the tribe is under great pressure to pursue any scheme that might generate employment. It hopes to lure other non-Indian companies onto the reservation with the promise of low cost facilities, access to Western markets, abundance of raw materials, and, most importantly, its inexpensive and readily available labor force. The only success it has had recently is the establishment of a glove manufacturing plant in a remote Utah area of the reservation. Forty people are employed. The remaining non-Navajo industry is Navajo Trailers, Inc. which employs

43 Navajos. Unlike Fairchild and General Dynamics it is not a branch plant, but a self-contained enterprise. Foot-loose industries account for 158 jobs, a disappointing record.

Lack of Managerial Skills

In the preceding section we considered the effect of lack of development capital. However, in a few instances where the tribe invested its scarce capital the results were disappointing. Lack of managerial skill limited the amount of development capital that could be productively used. By now the tribe has learned that capital alone will not increase income or produce jobs.

Experience with the Navajo Housing Authority, the Navajo Housing and Development Enterprise, and two tribal motels reveals a lack of basic business skills and effective tribal control. Other ventures such as Navajo Forest Products and Navajo Agricultural Products demonstrate that well-trained key personnel can put scarce capital to effective use.

As was mentioned earlier, between 100 and 1,500 Navajo students go to college each year. Every effort should be made to ensure that they acquire the technical skills the tribe needs. Furthermore, once they have been trained there should be a mechanism to ensure that they return to the reservation. In examining a 1975 tribal government organizational chart (Figure 1) it appears that the tribal bureaucracy consumes much of the managerial talent of the Navajo nation. If some of the 19 separate offices were combined, competent administrators could be freed to manage new tribal enterprises or could become private entrepreneurs.

Lack of Commercial Infrastructure

Federal, state, county, and tribal expenditures have little effect on the income of the Navajo nation because of leakages to the outside economy. Federal dollars which are used to buy nonreservation products never even reach Navajo hands. Those dollars which accrue to Navajos in the form of wages are usually spent off the reservation.

The multiplier allows us to calculate for a given expenditure what will be the impact on gross reservation product or income. If the government spends $1,000 and the multiplier is 1.5, the gross reservation product will be $1,500. A multiplier of 1.5 is very low and indicates an extremely underdeveloped retail and commercial sector. A metropolitan area such as New York–New Jersey–Connecticut has a multiplier of 3.36. The more isolated and the smaller the community, the smaller will be the multiplier because smaller communities depend much more heavily on imports from outside. Much of the increased government expenditures in a small community "leaks out" through payments for imported goods and services.

While an income multiplier has not been calculated for the Navajo nation, a recent study on income and expenditures revealed some interesting facts (Wistisen 1975, vol. 2). Forty-nine percent of all household expenditures are made off the reservation. When the informants were asked why they left the reservation, the two major reasons given were to sell rugs and jewelry and to seek a job. The response is indicative of the poor marketing record of the Navajo Arts and Crafts Enterprise and the high rate of unemployment. The purchase of groceries and clothing ranked fourth among the reasons for leaving. In 1970 there were 196 commercial establishments on the reservation: 171 retail stores, 1 wholesale store, and 24 service establishments. As a result there was a very large number of potential customers per business (see Table 19).

Table 19. Customers per business

Location	Retail	Wholesale	Services
Navajo reservation	616	105,291	4387
New Mexico	110	721	278
Arizona	115	726	160
United States	112	635	167

Source: Gilbreath 1975: 10.

The difference is so great between the number of Navajo customers per business and the number of United States customers per business that there appears to be room for more Navajo commercial establishments. Navajo entrepreneurship has been impeded for a number of reasons, but largely due to the lack of capital. The Navajo Revolving Loan Fund is inadequate ($2,397,723), and commercial credit is not available due to lack of collateral. The Navajo Small Business Development Corporation (NSBDC) was established to assist entrepreneurs to obtain capital. Between 1972–1975 NSBDC received only $319,610 from the Small Business Development Administration. Under the 1973 Indian Finance Act, $30 million was allocated for all Indians for small business grants of $50,000. By 1976, the funds that had been appropriated were completely committed.

The survey also determined the leakages for other sectors of the economy. Retail establishments spent 77.3 percent of their revenues off the reservation. Most of these off-reservation expenditures were for

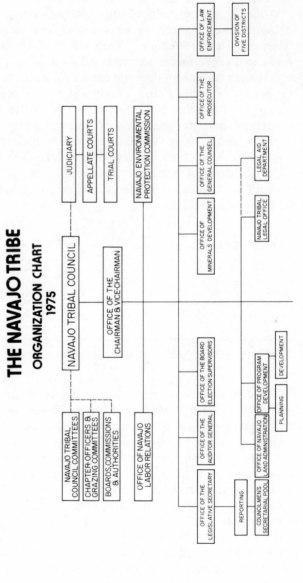

THE NAVAJO TRIBE
ORGANIZATION CHART
1975

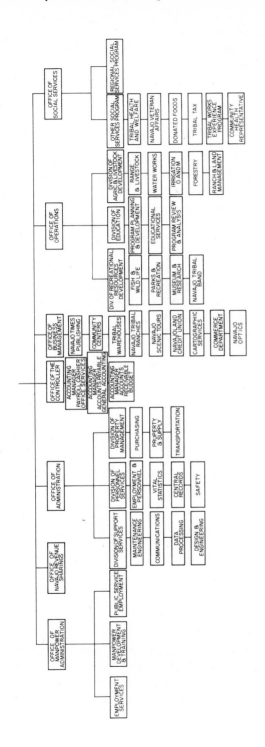

general merchandise. Industries and manufacturers spent 62.6 percent of their funds off the reservation. Thirty-two percent of institutional expenditures were made off the reservation. Institutions had the smallest leakage because 61 percent of their funds accrued directly to reservation labor. Table 20 illustrates what items accounted for the 32 percent leakage. It is surprising that some of these expenditures are made off the reservation when the item could have easily been purchased on the reservation as in the case of lumber and laundry. In fact a group of Navajos from Tuba City wanted to start a commercial laundry facility but could not get an SBA loan because the BIA refused to guarantee them a 3 year contract. Instead the laundry was sent to a firm in Cortez, Colorado, 200 miles away (U.S. Commission on Civil Rights 1975: 36).

The income and expenditure study traced the effect of an additional dollar of household spending on the reservation economy. The household would spend $0.59 on and $0.49 off the reservation. The retail stores received $0.57 and respent $0.13 on and $0.44 off the reservation. Firms received $02 and respent $0.0075 on and $0.0125 off the reservation. For every dollar spent, about 12 cents of indirect income is generated on the reservation — a very low expenditure multiplier (Wistisen 1975, vol. 2, p. 141).

Table 20.   Institutional expenditure leakage in thousands of dollars

Item	Total	On	Off	Leakage percent
Auto and farm parts	$2,164	$66	$2,098	97.0
Furniture	1,763	44	1,719	97.5
Lumber	5,320	677	4,652	87.3
Minerals	131	—	131	100.0
Hardware	3,776	27	3,749	99.3
Machinery and equipment	2,435	82	2,353	96.6
Office supplies	2,310	80	2,230	96.6
Food	4,938	327	4,611	93.4
Laundry	1,003	0	1,003	100.0

Source: Wistisen 1975, vol. 2, pp. 126–127.

Conflicting Philosophies

The last obstacle to development is the neglect by modern Navajo bureaucracy of the traditional sector. Until recently they have ignored the desires of traditional Navajos, and they have not invested in traditional economic activities. Such neglect is no longer possible for political and economic reasons.

The Navajo tribe has a tripartite government with legislative, executive, and judicial branches. The tribal council (legislative branch) is composed of 74 members elected by Navajos from 102 chapters on the reservation. It has standing committees and an advisory council that exercises the tribal council's powers when it is not in session. The executive branch consists of the chairman, vice-chairman, and numerous administrative departments. The chairman usually prepares the agendas for the tribal council for review and debate. The councilmen are at an immediate disadvantage in that they have no offices and no staff to provide information about the issues the chairman has presented (Robbins 1976: 18).

Furthermore, most councilmen spend a large share of their time attending to local matters on the chapter level, rather than having time to study issues of tribal-wide importance. If the councilmen cannot obtain information to make intelligent decisions, they will not be able to adequately inform their chapters of the issues. Often the councilmen have been asked to ratify *de facto* decisions or negotiations made by the administration. This resulted in serious economic consequences for the tribe. In the case of the Exxon agreement, the council was asked for its approval after the contract conditions had been decided. As a result, a former councilman filed suit in December 1976 to block the Department of Interior approval of the lease by alleging that the environmental impact statement is inadequate. This new delay might result in additional foregone interest from the bonus which is in escrow.

Exclusion from the initial decision-making process has been the source of great bitterness between the council and the chairman. It is lamentable because there is probably a great deal of consensus on development. Traditional councilmen and modern administrators feel that the resources should be used for the benefit of the Navajo people. Peaceful coexistence with plenty of aid and no strings attached is what all Navajos would like to enjoy. They want the reservation "developed" so they and their children can stay near home, and they want to avoid relocation, off-reservation work, and boarding schools. They need jobs, houses, schools, and hospitals.

Given this basic consensus it is unfortunate that a dichotomy has occurred between the "modern elite" administrators and the people at the grass roots. The executive branch relies heavily on its own personnel for the initiation and development of projects for the Navajo nation. The chapters are not involved in any real development planning. They merely participate in programs once they are initiated. Local communities are less interested than the executive branch in "national" development. They want roads, schools, wells, bridges, hospitals, sheep, and jobs — and if not jobs, then welfare checks. Indeed, with the exception of the wool program, the tribal projects reviewed did not affect the local community. If he is to benefit the traditional Navajo must go where the project is located.

Before 1974 when an intensive range restoration and range management education program was announced, almost all Navajo development planning by-passed the traditional livestock economy. Yet the Navajo tribe estimates that 35,000 Navajos (5,000 families) engage primarily in traditional agriculture, and the majority of the population obtains at least supplemental income from livestock activities.

In the FY 1975 tribal budget most of the funds were committed to administration and maintenance of resources and to emergency programs necessary to prevent severe economic hardship in the traditional economy. No expenditures appear for range restoration (Table 21). Eight percent was for water (both human and livestock) and sewer development in local communities.

Table 21.   Tribal expenditures on traditional activities (FY 1975)

Account	Amount	Purpose	Percent of total budget
Division of Agriculture and Livestock	$24,510	Administration	0.0009
Range and Livestock Department	457,049	Administration and Maintenance	0.0165
Range and Land Management	76,332	Maintenance	0.0027
Livestock Marketing	28,360	Marketing	0.0010
Water Works Department	2,307,368	Community Water Development	0.0831
Irrigation O & N Department	347,104	Maintenance	0.0125
Emergency Haylift	14,891	Emergency	0.0005
Emergency Feed Grain	259,216	Emergency	0.0093
Emergency Water	129,563	Emergency	0.0046
Total	$3,644,393		0.1300

Although the tribe is aware of the need to upgrade productivity in the traditional sector, it has not enacted any program capable of so doing. It undertook the wool marketing only because the wool market collapsed, leaving Navajo growers without an outlet. Fortunately, the utility of the program has become obvious to Navajo administrators and in FY 1975 the tribe invested $65,084 in a wool processing (sorting) plant. The neglect of the livestock economy is the result of the belief that stock raising cannot yield an adequate living for the entire Navajo population. But no one activity will solve the economic problems of the Navajo, and continued neglect of the livestock economy ensures that eventually it will be unable to provide even supplemental income, further increasing Navajo dependency on welfare.

Because most Navajo still receive supplemental income from their small herds, investment in the livestock economy would benefit a large part of the population. Investment in industrialization will reach only young, educated Navajos in the immediate vicinity of the industry, but investment in livestock will reach a majority of Navajo families, regardless of education, age, or location.

The neglect of the traditional economy is probably just another manifestation of the gulf between grass-roots councilmen and Window Rock administrators.

The Navajo executive branch might also be accused of a schizophrenic attitude toward development. The Overall Economic Development Program states "... it is not the policy of the tribe to preempt Navajo entrepreneurs who are capable. Rather, it is tribal policy to pursue tribal development possibilities in a manner that will foster Navajo entrepreneurship and encourage the development of the private sector in related activities" (Navajo Tribe 1974: 72). If one interprets this literally, it is the Navajo businessman, driven by profit-maximizing motivations, who should create jobs for other Navajos. Accordingly, the only valid role for the tribal government is to create those conditions whereby these entrepreneurs can prosper. Since there is no developed Navajo private sector, the tribal government has been forced to assume a major role in promoting development. However, the tribal government views its involvement as short run. It is crucial to distinguish which sectors are appropriate for tribal action and which can safely be left to Navajo entrepreneurs. Obviously, the development of Navajo tribal resources should be a tribal activity. The benefits from oil, gas, timber, land, and water should accrue to all Navajos, since they are the collective owners of these resources.

Fortunately, the tribe has developed some of these resources through tribal enterprises, so that theoretically all Navajos have an opportunity to benefit. The most appropriate spheres for individual Navajo entrepreneurship are the retail, service, and construction activities. Here, whatever profit an entrepreneur makes will have originated from his own efforts and not from the use of tribal resources. Entrepreneurs might also engage in manufacturing provided they pay fair market value for whatever tribal raw material they use.

Thus, there is room for both tribal and entrepreneurial initiative in development. Tribal leaders should reconsider what is the proper scope for tribal and entrepreneurial action not from the point of view of how the dominant society functions, but from the point of view of the values of Navajo society.

FEDERAL EFFORTS TO PROMOTE ECONOMIC DEVELOPMENT

As every federal official knows, the federal effort to promote Indian economic development is underfunded, uncoordinated, and based on legislation which does not realize the unique position of American Indians. The only agencies with programs to promote economic development in terms of job creation or job training are the Bureau of Indian Affairs (BIA), the Economic Development Administration (EDA), the Small Business Administration (SBA), and the Department of Labor Manpower Administration. These four agencies' appropriations for development accounted for approximately 15 percent of the total federal FY 1976 Indian Budget (Table 22). It is questionable how representative these figures are of the magnitude of annual appropriations or if they really represent expenditures on job creation and training. For example, transportation expenditures are also included in the budget of the Office of Resource Development. The additions to the Revolving Loan Fund and Loan Guarantee are special appropriations which end in 1976.

Table 22. Agency spending on Indian economic development, FY 1976 in millions of dollars

Agency	Amount	Purpose
BIA Office of Tribal Resource Development	$86.5	Enterprise development, manpower training, transportation
BIA Revolving Loan Fund and Loan Guarantee	32.0	Capital formation
EDA Indian Desk	32.5	Public works, business loans planning
DOL Manpower Administration, Indian Desk	67.9	Manpower training
SBA	8.5	Business loans
Total	$227.4	

Source: Napoli report (American Indian Policy Review Commission 1976).

One of the difficulties of the current federal method of promoting Indian development is that the funds are dispersed among a number of agencies which are unable or unwilling to coordinate their activities. For example, more than one agency is responsible for supplying some essential factor necessary for development projects: DOL supplies manpower training; EDA supplies public works, business loans, technical assistance, planning; SBA supplies business loans; BIA supplies business loans and grants, manpower training, and technical assistance. However, each program operates in a vacuum, manpower training is provided for nonexistent jobs; non-Indian enterprises are attracted to reservations which lack trained manpower; Indian enterprises are started but often lack trained manpower, management, and working capital. Such difficulties have been adequately elaborated in two 1975 General Accounting Office reports: *Improving small business opportunities on reservations* and *Better overall planning needed to improve the standard of living of White Mountain Apaches of Arizona* (Comptroller General of U.S. 1975).

The recommendations of both reports were identical: that the Office of Management & Budget set up an interagency coordinating committee. Two full years later (1977) the federal agencies involved are unable and unwilling to set up or participate in such a committee.

Federal efforts are also hampered because the enabling legislation authorizing programs ignores the unique status of American Indians or is interpreted in such a way that American Indians are ineligible. For example, under Title I of the Comprehensive Training and Employment Act, funds are provided to local governments. However, DOL does not consider Indian tribes as local governments.

The Public Works and Economic Development Act of 1965 allows EDA to provide 100 percent financing for a public works project. However, for a tribally owned business, EDA can only contribute part (50–80 percent). Since Indian tribes do not have access to commercial credit to raise the remaining capital required, they have opted to apply for public works projects instead of starting tribal businesses.

SBA has three types of loan programs: direct loans, indirect loans, and guaranteed loans. Actually, Indians receive only direct loans and guaranteed loans, because SBA has not been able to put pressure on banks to make indirect loans. The following excerpt from a Small Business Administration letter of April 30, 1975 points up the problems of Indians seeking to do business with SBA:

... corporations chartered by Indian tribes to carry out business projects are not eligible for SBA assistance unless such businesses are incorporated under state law. If the private profit subsidiary will operate within the private enterprise system, i.e. operate for a profit, pay corporate taxes, and produce distributable income for its stockholders, it would be eligible ... it is our opinion that, unless a business entity is formed subject to the laws of a particular state subject to the taxes and regulations of like enterprises, that business entity is not operating within the competitive free enterprise system which is contemplated by the Small Business Act (Napoli 1976).

Thus a tribally owned business would not qualify for an SBA loan because it is outside the system as defined by the federal bureaucrats.

The Navajo Area Office of the BIA spends very little on reservation development. Seventy percent of the FY 1972 budget went for education and welfare, 12.8 percent for infrastructure, and 1.8 percent for resource maintenance. The BIA allocated $154,900 out of $108.8 million to promoting industrial development (Table 23).

The BIA suffers not only from lack of development funds, but also from clear-cut development plans. Aberle explains the deficiencies of the BIA: "The BIA is what local and national popular pressures and Congress have made it; an understaffed, underbudgeted operation with no control over many salient factors that would make a difference" (Aberle 1969: 243).

Table 23. BIA Navajo area budget: funds obligated in 1972

Categories	Amount	Subtotals	Percent of total budget
Resources:			
Irrigation construction	$148,800		
Forestry	234,100		
Range management	321,400		
Extension	298,500		
Soil and moisture	849,400		
Indian water rights	65,000		
Credit operations	135,400		
		$2,052,600	1.8
Education and Welfare:			
Educational assistance	51,921,900		
Adult education	402,200		
Welfare	19,676,700		
Title One	4,546,700		
		$76,547,500	70.2
Infrastructure:			
Road construction	10,751,500		
Housing improvement	1,265,400		
Law and Order	299,700		
Housing development	170,000		
Road maintenance	1,275,500		
Real property management	203,800		
Real estate management	16,700		
		$13,982,600	12.8
Administration and Repairs:			
MA & I	611,400		
Administrative support	2,155,500		
General trustee	88,900		
R & M, B & U	6,078,300		
Plant operations	5,419,400		
		$14,353,500	13.1
Miscellaneous:			
Reservation programs	131,100		
Tribal operations	21,300		
Industrial development	154,900		
Employment assistance	702,100		
AVT Area	32,500		
AVT Agency	918,500		
		$1,960,400	1.7
Total		$108,896,600	

Bureau officials are constrained in many ways: they wish to be primarily concerned for Navajos, but also have assigned roles as trustees for Indian property; they must not upset local interests, which could put pressure on Congress, which can in turn put pressure on the Bureau. BIA structure impedes progressive leadership by making every idea, every hypothesis, every adaptive change run the gauntlet of area branch personnel, area director, Washington division personnel, and assistant commissioner — whose tight budgets and spending constraints make new ideas less attractive than nonpostponable functions.

Economic Development Administration assistance to the Navajo tribe, which has been substantial, includes $1.8 million in business loans, $3.9 million for industrial parks, $190,114 in technical assistance studies, $12.4 million in water and sewer systems, $586,082 in planning funds, and $7.5 million for enterprise development and $67,783 for tourism (U.S. Department of Commerce 1975: 16–19). A program of attracting industry to the reservation begun by the BIA in 1955 is presently supported by EDA. Under this program the tribes provided the facility and sometimes the equipment while the BIA provided on-the-job training subsidies. The firms did not have to agree to stay for a minimum period, nor try to retain their Indian workers. When the BIA ceased collecting information on the program in 1968, 110 firms were in operation in Indian country and provided 8,487 jobs of which 48 percent were held by Indians.

EDA invested almost $4 million in three Navajo industrial parks with the intention of attracting footloose industry to the reservation. Presently, the parks have two occupants which employ 118 Navajos. The instability of footloose industries became apparent with the abrupt departure of the Fairchild Semi-Conductor plant. Fortunately, federal officials at EDA do analyze the results of their projects. They have found that those enterprises which are most likely to succeed on reservations are those which are tribally owned and are based on local resources. EDA has invested both in NFPI and NAPI.

The Small Business Administration's loan programs are ill suited to serve the Navajo nation or southwest Indian communities in general. The SBA Arizona director himself found that SBA regulations and policies were not adapted to serving Indian applicants. For example, when the minority enterprise program was conceived, no special consideration was made for the Indian because the Washington administrators were not acquainted with the habits and cultural background of the Indian. The program they devised excluded aid to Indians per se. Only 35 loans, totaling $460,800, were made by SBA to Indians on the Navajo reservation during the three fiscal years ending June 30, 1973 (U.S. Commission on Civil Rights 1975: 34).

DEVELOPMENT AND THE TRADITIONAL COMMUNITY[1]

The situation of the Navajo people, as described in the *Overall economic development program*, is that of a traditional society being forced for economic reasons to adapt to the technologically advanced

---

[1] The section is based on an article, "Shonto revisited: measures of social and economic change in a Navajo community 1955–1971" by William Y. Adams and Lorraine R. Ruffing. It appeared in the February 1977 issue of the *American Anthropologist.*

society which surrounds it (Navajo tribe 1974: 68). The OEDP assumes that the Navajo must surrender their traditional life-styles in order to improve their living standard.

Navajo society is a traditional society whose social structure and values are communal rather than individualistic. Its outstanding characteristic is a remarkable flexibility in adapting to changing economic conditions. Together with this flexibility is a tenacious hold on the core values that define Navajoness. This section examines the extent to which Navajos are willing to trade life-styles for materially improved living standards, if at all.

Until recently, development experts felt that traditional society was itself a barrier to development. The sooner traditional social structures and values could be transformed, the sooner development would occur. Of the American Indian, a noted land economist asserted, "that Indian culture can somehow be preserved in fact, along with the achievement of economic success is largely a delusion" (Dorner 1959: 57). Although deliberate attempts at cultural transformation are slow, costly, and unpredictable, development planners have given little serious thought to ways of utilizing the existing social structures and values. One can argue that a development strategy which minimizes social costs is a far more successful strategy than one which requires cultural change as a precondition for economic development.

Social Structure of Navajo Society

Most of the Navajo people have chosen to live on the reservation. Although their material culture is in many ways indistinguishable from that of non-Navajo society, their family and kin institutions are unique. Southwestern tribal representatives recently completed a list of traits that they felt were still dominant in their societies and in conflict with non-Indian society: a preference for the group versus the individual, and emphasis on the present versus the future, a respect for age versus youth, a preference for cooperation versus competition, a choice of nonmaterial versus material goals, a desire to share versus a desire to accumulate wealth.

The social organization of the Navajo people is complex. It appears that each anthropologist has analyzed the existing social structures and has devised a different system of classification, yet all anthropologists agree that the residence group is the social unit that controls the livestock economy and makes most economic decisions.

The social structure is formed of a series of basic functional and non-functional units (Figure 2). For example, the tribal council and the chapter are functional on a political level, the clan on a social level; the

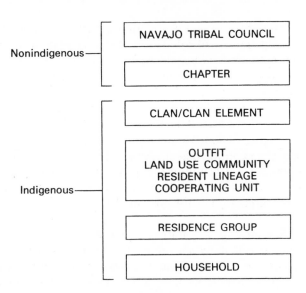

Figure 2. Navajo social structure

outfit is functional as a unit of infrequent cooperation; the residence group is functional as unit of production; the household is functional as a unit of consumption.

TRIBAL COUNCIL. Both the tribal council and the chapter are new to Navajo society, being artificial constructs of the federal government created expressly for the administration of Navajo affairs. Historically, the Navajo people were not a corporate group and never had a centrally organized unit. After the acquisition of livestock from the Spaniards, the Navajos began an existence of pastoral migration. They moved about the Southwest in small bands, seeking pastures for their livestock. The term "tribe" could be applied to them only as it signified a community of language and culture (Shepardson 1963: 37). Yet in 1923, sixty years after the subjugation of the Navajo by the United States Army, a tribal government was formed by twelve Navajo representatives who had been handpicked by federal authorities. The function of this government was to sign leases for non-Indian use of Indian mineral resources.

The reservation is divided into 102 districts called chapters which are represented by 74 council delegates. The tribal council is accepted and integrated into the present-day Navajo social system as the focus of an emerging tribe-centered culture. Most Navajos feel that the tribal council is capable of meeting important needs of the tribe; increasingly, they accept its authority, regard its rules as binding, and view as legitimate its right to use force within the limits permitted by the federal government. Broad tribal authority is legitimized by the United States Supreme Court, is upheld by the federal government and the BIA, and is recognized, with some reluctance, by the states of Arizona, New Mexico, and Utah.

The BIA has gradually relinquished control over some aspects of Navajo life to the tribal council, which is in charge of developing natural resources, human resources, agriculture and livestock, local industries, and law enforcement. Although the Navajo tribal council functions without a constitution, it is the *de facto* government of the tribe and has preempted the authority accorded to the Navajo people as a treaty sovereign (Shepardson 1963: 3).

CHAPTER. The local representatives of the Navajo Tribal Council, the chapters, are certified by the council, which requires them to file regular reports of meetings and pays *per diem* salaries to chapter officers. Chapters handle welfare applications, conduct primary elections, plan and administer public works programs, and are the principal means of communication between the council and the communities. Tribal programs and policies reach the community through the chapter. Although these local organizations are nearly as old as the tribal council, not until 1955 did they become an integral part of Navajo government.

The division of the reservation into 102 chapter areas not only created political units but also imposed geographical limits on grazing rights (Lingenfelter 1966: 7). Permits to graze animals are issued only to the inhabitants of chapter areas, and trespassing of animals owned by members from another chapter is fiercely resented. Thus, the movement of animals, and consequently of people, across chapter boundaries is restricted.

The chapter house is the focal point for the community. The chapter is represented in the tribal council by a delegate and is administered by three elected officials: president, vice-president, and secretary. Another important elected figure is the chairman of the grazing committee, an office created in 1952 to put into effect the joint BIA-tribal range management program. The chairman conducts official livestock inventories and organizes branding, spraying, and vaccinating of community livestock. Chapter officers normally oversee elections and the administration of tribal projects such as the 10-day work projects, Office of Navajo Economic Opportunity, Neighborhood Youth Corps, Tribal Work Experience Program, and food and grain distribution. The bimonthly chapter meeting is a sounding board where tribal officers present new programs and ideas, where community problems are resolved, where participants in tribal work programs are chosen. Tribal news is discussed, and the meeting is also an important social event for the community. Formly, chapter houses were known as centers for gossip and agitation. Chapters became centers of resistence to the stock reduction program, and the government withdrew its aid from them. But chapters endured, because they were fulfilling a local need for liaison between the tribal council and the people. The chapter movement is truly a grass-roots movement in Navajo political life; it is the means by which the traditional society, with its traditional problems, is channeled into the modern tribal government system.

HOUSEHOLD AND RESIDENCE GROUPS.   The fundamental social unit of Navajo society is the household or nuclear family. Adams has defined the household as "a group that regularly eats together and shares food resources in common, forming a minimum subsistence unit" (Adams 1963: 54). The most important social unit of Navajo society, the residence group, is an extended family composed of several households that live in close proximity, share certain basic resources in common, and are usually organized around a matrifocal head (Witherspoon n.d.: 5).

Anthropologists have devoted considerable research to classifying Navajo families according to residence patterns: in a matrilocal household, a married daughter lives with her parents (or, if her parents are dead, with the people with whom she grew up). In a patrilocal household, a married son lives with his parents; a neolocal household is a solitary household or where one lives in a residence group of which neither party is a native member. Analyzing communities according to the percentage of households in each category is a static analysis that fails to capture the dynamics of Navajo society. Almost all of the above patterns and more can be observed with regularity in Navajo communities, for young married daughters and sons apparently move back and forth between the two parental residence groups as occasion necessitates.

Navajo residence rules are a function of normal mother-child and husband-wife relationships. According to Witherspoon:

A Navajo may live wherever his mother has the right to live. His mother has the right to live wherever her mother lived. A Navajo may live wherever his or her spouse has the right to live. Upon the death of the spouse or divorce, the partner may be forced to return to his or her mother's residence group. As long as one's mother is alive, one may go anywhere, do anything and still return to one's mother's unit to live, eat, and help care for sheep (Witherspoon 1970: 202).

On the mother's death, residence rights must be asserted or they are lost. The head mother is the person around whom the unit is organized. All residence rights can be traced to her, and her wishes most often predominate.

The residence group, using a common grazing area to which the head mother inherited use rights from her mother, operates a cooperative enterprise, the sheep herd. Residence group members share the task of caring for the herd, although the sheep are individually owned. Cooperation rests on generalized reciprocity or the injunction that one should help other people (Lamphere 1967: 134). Noncooperation is cause for public disapproval, which is expressed in ridicule, gossip, and accusations of witchcraft.

At the residence group level, social groups correspond to those that hold sheep in common. The residence group controls the livestock economy (goats and cattle as well as sheep) and makes the relevant decisions in other productive activities, such as field agriculture and wage work. In each residence group there is likely to be a male who is considered to be most competent in the management of resources, to whom the head mother delegates much of her role and prestige. Usually he is her husband, but if her husband is deceased or incompetent, the oldest son or the husband of the oldest daughter will be the resource controller or "headman" (Witherspoon 1970). With the consent of the adults, and respectful of their individual autonomy, he organizes the movement of the herd, breeding, lambing, shearing, spraying, plowing, planting, and harvesting (Reynolds et al. 1967: 191). Even though inheritance is matrilineal, political and social control have been abdicated to the men.

OUTFIT.   The definition of the social unit as a unit larger than the residence group but smaller than a clan is subject to considerable dispute. Kluckhohn and Leighton (1962: 109–110) used the term "outfit" to designate a group of relatives, larger than the extended family, which regularly cooperate for certain purposes. Sometimes the members of an outfit live on lands that are geographically contiguous. In this case the outfit constitutes a "land-use community," a term first used by Kimball and Provinse (1942: 13). The basic principle integrating land-use communities is occasional participation, under a single leader, in common enterprises such as range use, water development, or development of farmland. Kimball and Provinse suggested that it is the logical unit to use in dividing the reservation into land-management districts, because land-use communities already control the use of resources, have adequate management personnel, and are sufficiently large in size and population for efficient management planning (1942: 18).

William Adams (1963: 59, 100–104) divided the community of Shonto into twelve resident lineages, which are land-use communities composed of related residence groups. These related residence or sibling groups inherit use rights to the specific and contiguous area that they occupy. However, these use rights are adjusted among residence groups according to need. The residence lineage is, therefore, the highest level of economic organization, but it is not a unit of production or consumption. There is a high degree of interaction within resident lineage because of consanguinity and geographical proximity; but the interaction between them is just as likely to be hostile as cooperative.

CLAN. The largest original social unit on the reservation is the clan. A Navajo clan is a consanguineous kin group whose members acknowledge a traditional common descent in the maternal line but are unable to trace actual relationships. Clan affiliation regulates marriage and stipulates the proper behavior between members. Clans own no property, are responsible for no rituals, and have never functioned as units (Shepardson and Hammond 1970: 48). Aberle (1963) uses the term "local clan element" to designate members of a clan who reside in a given locale; several local clan elements comprise a community. The local clan element functions to demand damages from another local clan element, to cooperate in ceremonies, and to spread news.

SOCIAL STRUCTURE AND THE ECONOMY IN A TRADITIONAL NAVAJO COMMUNITY

The community of Shonto provides an excellent opportunity to study how these traditional residence groups respond to economic changes. Income and resource data have been collected for two separate years, 1955 and 1971. This fifteen year span enables us to evaluate how traditional structures and values influence economic decisions. Shonto is a sparsely settled rural district of upland mesas and canyons which encompass 147,000 acres in the northwest section of the Navajo reservation.

The most conspicuous social development at Shonto since 1955 is the sheer numerical increase of the population from 568 to 762 persons. The population of 568 individuals enumerated in 1955 comprised 100 households which were further clustered in 38 residence groups, that is, groups of cooperating households which lived close together and shared in common basic productive resources such as livestock, fields, and water supplies. In 1971 the number of households had increased to 128 and the number of residence groups to 60. The increase resulted in every case from the orderly and predictable fissioning of already existing groups. A new household was formed whenever a young couple married; initially in every case it was established by building a new home within the encampment in which the wife or (somewhat less commonly) the husband had grown up. Later on, after the birth of a substantial number of children or the acquisition of large livestock holdings, the household might move a short distance away from its original locus, to form the nucleus of a new residence group which would in its turn expand as children of the original couple married and set up households of their own. In no case, however, did a newly married couple set up their initial residence anywhere except within the already established group in which one or other of the partners had grown up.

Economic Changes 1955-1971

In 1955 Shonto's annual per capita income from all sources (cash and kind) was $301. Sixteen years later it had risen to $724. Deflating the second figure to 1955 values yields a real income of $510. Real income thus increased at a rate of 3.3 percent annually, which is a respectable growth rate by the standards of developed countries. However, if one compares Shonto's per capita income of $724 with the "acceptable" United States minimum of $1,727, it is clear that the Navajo community lags far behind the rest of the nation, and there is no prospect that the gap will be closed within this century even if the rest of the United States should experience a zero growth rate.

Income per capita is of course a measure of a country's level of economic development and/or its standard of living. It is not a good measure of actual welfare because it indicates only what each person's income would be if all income were equally distributed. In actuality, at Shonto as in the rest of the world, there are substantial discrepancies between the wealthiest and the poorest families.

Family income was the direct result of the productivity of various economic activities in which Shonto Navajos engaged, and this in turn was determined by the quality and quantity of available productive resources, and their allocation among different activities. In order to understand Shonto's low general income level, it is necessary to understand the community's traditional resource base and its allocation.

The traditional resources of the Navajo residence group are labor, land, and livestock. They are traditional in the sense the Navajos have derived their livelihood from land and labor since their first entry into the southwest several centuries ago, and from livestock for well over a hundred years.

Labor resources comprise the able-bodied adults in the community between the ages of about 16 and 65. There were 259 such individuals

(45 percent of the total population) in 1955 and 530 (58 percent of the population) in 1971. From the standpoint of employability the educational level of Shonto adults had improved only very slightly, from an average of less than one year to about three years' schooling, and most were still functionally illiterate in 1971.

The land resources of Shonto comprised 147,000 acres or an average of 3,873 acres per residence group in 1955, which had diminished to 2,453 acres per residence group in 1971. The increasingly overcrowded range conditions are indicated by a comparison of Maps 2 and 3. Ninety-nine percent of the land at Shonto was and still is devoted to grazing.

The problem of a diminishing land base per family was compounded by a deterioration in the quality of the range due to overgrazing. In 1955 Shonto's livestock holdings amounted collectively to 6,563 sheep units, or considerably in excess of the permitted capacity of 5,225. By 1971 permitted capacity had been increased to 5,845 units, but actual livestock holdings stood at 12,517 units. Overgrazing, in other words, had increased from 25 percent to 113 percent in a period of sixteen years. Large areas had been denuded of grass and sagebrush, and deep gullies gashed the terrain.

The 38 residence groups extant in 1955 possessed a total of 3,525 sheep, 1,158 goats, and 120 cattle; by 1971 the respective figures were 4,995 sheep, 2,899 goats, and 735 cattle. Dividing these figures by the respective populations for the two baseline years provides a measure of personal wealth in livestock, and the income-generating capacity thereof. Additional data from a United States Government survey in 1935 make it possible to trace livestock holdings and income at Shonto over a 36-year period, as shown in Table 24. These figures make it obvious that the stock of animal wealth has declined, as has its capacity to provide food for home consumption and cash income from sales. In the years since 1935, livestock raising alone has never provided a sufficient basis of livelihood for the Navajos.

Table 24. Animal wealth, consumption, and income in 1935, 1955, and 1971

	1935	1955	1971
Sheep per capita	16.4	6.2	6.3
Goats and cattle per capita	6.9	2.2	4.5
Sheep sold per capita	1.3*	1.1*	1.3†
Sheep consumed per capita	3.6	2.3	2.0
Sheep income per capita	$64.35	$49.23	$28.11§
Income per sheep	$3.96	$7.93‡	$4.45§

*   Includes sheep and lambs.
†   Includes sheep, lambs and goats.
‡   Excludes wool subsidy payments.
§   Figures adjusted to 1955 levels.

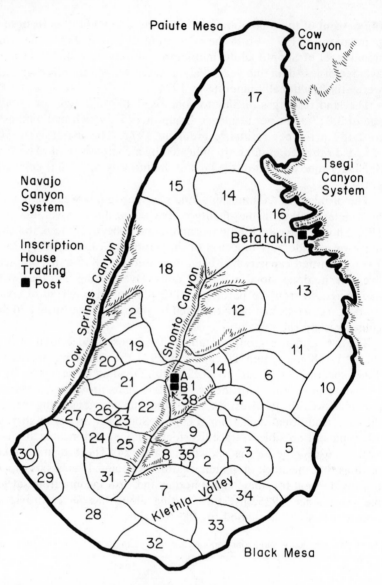

Map 2. Shonto divided among 38 residence groups, 1955

Since the 1930's the Navajos have supported themselves by a mixture of sheep and cattle raising, field agriculture, weaving, welfare, and occasional wage work. These diverse economic bases were integrated into an annual round of activity as shown in Figure 3. Although the traditional pursuits of agriculture and stock rearing have not, in the last generation, provided the main bulk of Navajo income, they still

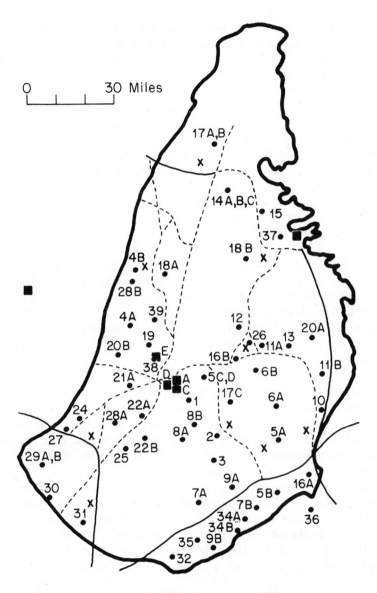

Map 3.   Shonto divided among 60 residence groups 1971

dominated the annual work cycle and were accorded most importance by Navajos themselves.

There has always been a lively debate among scholars as to whether the very loose and pragmatic nature of Navajo social structure (cf. Aberle 1963) is the result of their distinctive livestock rearing practices, or vice versa. Whatever the answer may be, it remained as true in

1971 as in 1955 that sheep raising dominated the Navajo way of life at Shonto. As already noted, the community's holdings in sheep increased by 41 percent, from 3,525 to 4,995, between 1955 and 1971. Yet they did not keep pace with the even more rapid growth of the human population, with the result that average herd size at Shonto (sheep only) diminished from 93 to 83 sheep per residence group. Sheep-raising practices and tasks remained much the same, and included herding, lambing, shearing, wool and lamb sales, spraying and breeding. Herding duties were usually rotated among member families in the residence group, while lambing and shearing required the simultaneous cooperation of most group members.

Navajos have been criticized in the past for their poor animal husbandry practices (Adams: 1963: 111–120), and these have not changed significantly since 1955. Sheep are herded during only part of the day, and are corraled in the camp at night. As a result they travel the same daily route between corral, forage, and water sources. causing excessive overgrazing along these routes while other parts of the range are underutilized. If herds were allowed to follow more varied routes, and to bed down in different places at night, grazing areas could support many more animals. Overgrazing is also caused by an excessive number of commercially unproductive animals, such as goats and horses.

Most Shonto livestock owners did not and do not breed their sheep at one time or selectively. Lambs born during the winter often freeze. Navajos usually sold their best animals, retaining the less desirable for breeding stock, which resulted in a gradual decline in herd quality. Owners did not dip or inoculate their sheep regularly. Poor management was not entirely the result of cultural traditions; there was very limited technical assistance and no agricultural education. The long-range effects of poor livestock practice were nevertheless reflected in a decline in average income per sheep at Shonto, as shown in Table 25.

Income per sheep is a function in part of physical productivity in wool and lambs and in part of market prices. Physical productivity includes the size of the lamb chop, the average weight per lamb sold, and the average weight per fleece sold. These variables are of course

Table 25.   Sheep income and productivity, 1955 and 1971

	1955	1971
Income per sheep	$8.77	$5.68
Lamb crop	51%	57%
Lamb weight	67 lbs.	48 lbs.
Fleece weight	5 lbs.	7.2 lbs.

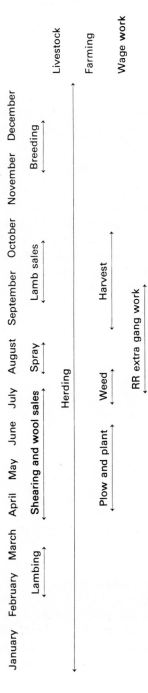

Figure 3. The annual round of productive activity at Shonto, 1955

related to climatic conditions, i.e. temperature, moisture (which influences the amount of available feed), breeding practices, and the type of sheep. The abnormally low lamb crop and weight in 1971 were due to a combination of poor animal husbandry techniques, principally progressive and continued overgrazing, and a record drought. Fleece weight, on the other hand, improved through the interbreeding of a good wool producing species of sheep, the Rambouillet. Improvement in fleece weight was, however, offset by a precipitous decline in wool prices, from $0.42 a pound in 1955 to a record low of $0.19 in 1971.

Surprisingly, herd size also affected income per sheep. Measuring income per sheep against the size of the herd shows that the highest incomes were obtained from medium sized herds comprising between 50 and 150 sheep, as indicated in Table 26. The explanation for these figures lies in the fact that small herds comprising fewer than 25 animals have little commercial value and are allowed to roam under scant supervision. While large herds (151 head or more) can be managed during most of the year by one herder, there are certain critical periods such as lambing and bad weather when the labor demand increased rapidly. Residence groups with large herds generally did not meet the peak labor demand as effectively as did groups with medium sized herds.

Table 26.   Herd size and sheep income, 1955 and 1971

Herd size	1955		1971	
	Income per sheep	Sheep* per laborer	Income per sheep	Ewes per laborer
1– 24	$8.56	3.8	$4.57	11.8
25– 37	8.56	3.8	5.44	11.8
38– 50	8.56	3.8	5.85	14.0
51–100	9.33	9.3	5.79	28.0
101–150	9.72	13.8	5.76	37.0
151–200	8.33	23.0	5.63	60.0
201+	7.63	27.0	5.61	60.0
Average	$8.77	15.3	$5.68	30.1

*   Includes rams and ewes.

By far the most significant change in Shonto's livestock rearing activities since 1955 is reflected in the increase in cattle owernership by members of the community. Cattle holdings actually increased six-fold, from 120 to 735 head, in the interval of 16 years between the first and second studies. In 1955 only half the residence groups in the community (17) owned cattle, and the average herd size was seven. By 1971 40 of 59 residence groups had cattle, averaging no fewer than 18 head per group. As a result of this increase cattle sales accounted for about 19 percent of livestock income in 1971, as against virtually nothing in 1955. The increasing popularity of cattle is due to the fact that calves bring a higher price per pound than do lambs; cattle are also easier on the range since they do not crop as close as do sheep and goats. Probably the biggest factor contributing to their popularity, however, is the fact that cattle require very little attention, since a full-time herder is unnecessary. Thus, Shonto men could participate in wage work and at the same time take responsibility for their cattle herds.

Farming continues to be economically unimportant but nevertheless engages some of the activity of nearly every Shonto family. The Shonto region has never been climatically suited for more than 100 days of dry farming annually. Average annual rainfall is only slightly over twelve inches, though there are considerable variations within the community area, depending chiefly on altitude. Total arable land was estimated at between 200 and 400 acres, most of which is located in the two canyons which have permanent surface streams. Some adult males in each residence group annually prepared and plowed the fields, while the labor of planting, weeding, and harvesting was normally shared among whole families. Nearly every Shonto residence group engaged in some farming activity, but not every family in each group participated. Abnormal drought conditions contributed to the diminished area actually planted and the diminished yield per acre in 1971 as compared to 1955 (Table 27).

Table 27. Agricultural productivity, 1955 and 1971

	1955	1971
Number of cornfields reported	42	63
Average field size	5.0 acres	6.6 acres
Area actually planted	105 acres	73 acres
Yield per acre	12.6 bushels	8–10 bushels

In 1955 agricultural foodstuffs consumed at home made a small but significant contribution to the Navajo diet; their total value was estimated as comprising 5 percent of the community's income. Agricultural activity also affected Navajo settlement patterns in that summer residences were located primarily with reference to cornfields rather than to good grazing land. This picture has hardly altered in the years since 1955; dietary preferences as well as ceremonial necessity assure the continued cultivation of corn, and to a lesser extent of squash, pumpkins, and melon. Reliance on home-grown foodstuffs as a significant component of the diet has been diminished as a result of the federal food subsidy program which donated some $24,608 worth of food to Shonto families in 1971.

In 1955 all but six of Shonto's married women wove, though they were noted more for the quantity than for the quality of their work. They usually produced saddle blankets of a plain weave and simple banded design. Single saddle blankets (30″×30″) sold for $4.00, and double blankets (30″×60″) for $8.00 at the trading post. The average weaver produced about one saddle blanket a month. Only six women in the community regularly wove larger rugs of good quality, valued at $50.00 and up, and the highest price ever paid for any one rug was $95.00. Total income from weaving was $2,685 equal to about 1.6 percent of the community's aggregate income from all sources (Adams 1963: 137). Weaving was nevertheless a source both of recreation and of prestige for Shonto women, and these factors probably contributed more to its continuation than did its economic rewards (Adams 1963: 83–84).

In 1971, 89 women (32 percent of the adult female population and 76 percent of the married female population) reported that they did some weaving during the year. Weaving has been encouraged in recent years by the artifically high prices paid by Navajo tribal weaving projects. Under such a project in 1971, 31 Shonto weavers were employed for 10 days each, mostly to weave double saddle blankets. They were reimbursed $102 each regardless of the quality of their products. As a result, the tribe was frequently unable to sell the Shonto rugs for the same price which had been paid for them. Two women continued to weave rugs of high quality, sometimes measuring as large as 9′×12′ and selling from prices between $1,000 and $2,000. Total income from weaving was $11,286, or $128.25 per weaver; an increase of 420 percent since 1955. This increase was due wholly to the dramatic rise in the demand for Navajo rugs in recent years, rather than to any improvement in the quality of the community's woven products.

Although traditional economic pursuits continued to absorb a great deal of Navajo time and effort between 1955 and 1971, by far the most renumerative outlet for labor was not in these activities but in wage work. It is principally here that a significant change can be observed in the Shonto economy in the recent past. Over time the rate of unemployment in wage work has declined considerably, while opportunities for employment have increased both in number and in variety (Table 28).

In 1955 there were very few temporary or permanent local jobs. Men seeking wage work were largely forced to look outside the community, and the Santa Fe Railroad was by far the single most important source of temporary employment. The combination of

Table 28.   Status of the Shonto labor force, 1955 and 1972[2]

	1955		1971	
	Number	Percent	Number	Percent
Permanently employed	79	43.0	36	17.4
Temporarily employed			84	40.7
Unemployed	103	57.0	86	41.7
Total	182	100.0	206	100.0

wages and unemployment compensation from this one source in fact accounted for more than half of Shonto's total aggregate income in 1955 (Adams 1963: 137). In 1971, on the other hand, temporary local jobs had displaced the railroad as the most frequent source of employment. Local employment opportunities multiplied with the construction of the large Shonto boarding school and the increase in community work projects funded by the Navajo tribe (Table 29).

Table 29.   Changes in employment patterns, 1955 to 1971

	1955		1971	
	Number	Percent	Number	Percent
Local permanent jobs	8	8.8	38	22.2
Local temporary tribal jobs	2	2.2	63	37.3
Local temporary jobs, nontribal	14	15.5	33	19.5
Railroad jobs	63	70.0	30	17.7
Other nonlocal temporary jobs	3	3.3	5	2.9
Total	90	100.0	169	100.0

The type of job most preferred by Shonto Navajos was and is a permanent local job. It not only yielded the highest income (Table 30) but did not impose the social cost of having to leave the community. The number of such jobs was however far too limited (8 in 1955; 38 in 1971) to provide a viable alternative for the bulk of the labor force. Shonto Navajos were therefore obliged either to combine traditional subsistence activities with temporary wage work or to leave the reservation in search of employment.

The largest potential source of local employment in 1976 was Peabody Coal Company which does strip mining on Black Mesa.

[2]   Labor force is here defined as those persons 16 to 65 years old residing within the community and either working or actually looking for work. Students, absentees, and women without child-care facilities are automatically excluded by this definition. Thus, the size of the labor force is substantially less than the community's total labor resources, as discussed in earlier pages.

Table 30.   Average income per worker in different activities, 1955 and 1971

	1955	1971	1971 adjusted*
Subsistence			
Livestock	$ 96	$ 139	$ 98
Agriculture	26	18	13
Combined livestock and agriculture	122	157	111
Wage Work			
Local permanent jobs	2,090	4,875	3,436
Local temporary tribal jobs	254	737	519
Local temporary jobs, nontribal		1,171	824
Railroad jobs	1,460	3,349	2,158
Other nonlocal temporary jobs	933	710	500

*   Deflated to 1955 prices paid to farmers.

Peabody is being paid $750 million to supply coal to two power plants, one at Page, Arizona, and the other (Mohava) at Bullhead City, Nevada, during the next 35 years. The Mohava plant consumes 15,000 tons per day to produce 1,580,000 kilowatts of power, 76 percent of which will be used by residents of southern California. The Page plant consumes 23,000 tons per day and produces 2,310,000 kilowatts. Thus, the coal reserves on Black Mesa will be exhausted after 35 years. A 273-mile pipeline slurries a mixture of 50 percent pulverized coal powder and 50 percent water to the Mohava plant. In one 60-second period, it uses 2,000 gallons of water (Clemmer 1970: 3–5).

To transport coal to Page, Morrison-Knudsen Company constructed an 80-mile railroad, which bisects the entire width of Shonto at its southern end and intrudes upon numerous grazing areas. This will have a direct impact on traditional activities. Already one family's entire herd has been wiped out. The impact of the mining and power-plant complex on the level of the water table, on local drainage areas and lakes, and on atmospheric conditions unfortunately cannot be evaluated here although clearly the moisture and atmospheric conditions will have considerable influence on the productivity of livestock and crops.

Peabody Coal Company, located within 45 minutes of Shonto, employs over 200 men. The Black Mesa Pipeline Company employs approximately 38 men. The Page plant, which is within weekend commuting distance of Shonto, will employ 175 men. At least 425 jobs are available to Shonto Navajos. These companies can employ unskilled laborers and gradually train them, because they will be in operation for 35 years or more. However, Morrison-Knudsen did not employ a single Shonto Navajo in 1971; the company said that it could not employ unskilled labor and meet its deadline and also that hiring was under tight union control. The Navajo tribe was reluctant to impose the extra cost of generating local employment on the company. However, Shonto Navajos were not very successful in securing employment with Peabody and Black Mesa Pipeline, which prefer local labor. In 1971 two Shonto Navajos worked at Peabody, one worked at Black Mesa Pipeline, two worked on the construction of the Page plant. Hopefully, as these companies expand operations, Shonto Navajos will be aware of such openings.

Table 30 discloses that, if a Shonto man managed to find a temporary construction job on the reservation in 1971 and if at the same time he continued to participate in traditional subsistence activities, his average combined income from the two sources would have been $1,328, as compared to an average $3,349 that he could have earned by working on the railroad during the same period. Thus, the "opportunity cost" of remaining in the community instead of going abroad to work was $2,021 per individual. (This figure might be considered too high if Navajos had to incur extra transportation or living costs when working on the railroad. In fact, however, transportation was regularly provided by the traders, while housing and food were furnished by the railroad itself, so that there were almost no incidental expenses connected with this particular form of off-reservation employment.) This $2,000 could be considered a measure of the amount of material living standard a traditional Navajo is willing to forego to maintain a preferred life-style.

Notwithstanding the high "opportunity cost" of remaining at home, it was a cost which the great majority of Shonto men were willing to pay. Preference was nearly always given to temporary reservation jobs rather than to railroad jobs when there was a choice between the two, and a good many Shonto men preferred to remain entirely unemployed rather than leave the reservation in search of work. The demand for railroad labor in fact considerably exceeded the number of individuals willing to engage in it in 1971. During that year the railroad recruiting office sent job orders for 125 men to Shonto, but received only 96 responses, despite the fact that there were at least 30 completely unemployed men who were qualified for these jobs. (Qualification for railroad work is purely a matter of age and physical fitness, since the work is unskilled and is carried out by all-Navajo gangs, in which even a knowledge of English is not required.) In 1971, no less than in 1955, remaining within the Navajo community and participating in traditional subsistence and social activities were more important than maximizing cash income to the average Shonto man.

The men who did participate in railroad work in 1971 comprised a very well-defined group. They were members of a long-established work gang and were not only accustomed to working together but had accumulated sizable retirement benefits (drawn partly in the form of unemployment compensation during winter months) for which temporary wage work did not provide an adequate substitute. Seventeen of the men had been working for the railroad since 1955, and the new entrants were their relatives or members of the same residence group. In a way, these men were carrying on an older subsistence pattern; one which was almost "traditional" in 1955, but which seems to have lost much of its appeal for the better educated Navajos who have come to maturity since that time.

Of all the sources of livelihood upon which Shonto Navajos depend, none shows a more dramatic increase between 1955 and 1971 than the unearned income derived from welfare payments. In 1955 the community received $13,598, or approximately 7.9 percent of its total income, from this source (Adams 1963: 137). By 1971 welfare payments in cash had increased by over 900 percent to $124,881. Altogether, income from these two sources accounted for more than one quarter of the community's income.

In addition to welfare payments in the form of cash, Shonto in 1971 was the recipient of food commodities which were valued at $24,608. It is believed that this program contributed in part to a declining interest in local agriculture, as already mentioned. Shonto also participated in a drought-relief program which contributed $4,120 worth of grain supplies to the community. The overall effect of welfare income has been to bolster the traditional subsistence economy and the traditional social structure with which it is integrated. Able-bodied men can remain within the community, participate in traditional activities supplemented by temporary wage work, and fall back on assistance payments when these resources prove inadequate.

The economic results of the various activities discussed in these pages, and their changing importance over time, are summarized in Table 31. Two changes are particularly apparent: the displacement of railroad work by local wage work as the single most important source of income, and the dramatic increase in welfare income. At the same time the monetary importance of "traditional" Navajo economic activities (livestock rearing, agriculture, singing, and weaving), which even in 1955 contributed only a quarter of Shonto's total income, has declined still further. It should be noted nevertheless that actual income in each of the traditional categories has increased since 1955; the rate of increase, on the other hand, has not kept pace with the much more rapid increase in wage and welfare income.

It seems apparent that there continues to be little relationship between economic return and the allocation of time and personnel among different productive activities (cf. Adams 1963: 148). In 1971 no less than in 1955, the preferential ordering of activities was a

Table 31. Total Shonto community income, 1955 and 1971

	1955		1971		
Source	Amount	Percent	Amount	Amount adj.*	Percent
Livestock	$ 31,405	18.3	$ 57,967	$ 40,858	10.0
Agriculture	8,600	5.0	6,310	4,450	1.1
Singing, weaving	6,360	3.2	13,566	9,154	2.3
Local wage work	22,624	13.2	248,141	171,748	44.4
Railroad wages and compensation	85,779	50.1	83,735	58,968	14.5
Other nonlocal	2,800	1.6	3,552	2,501	0.6
Welfare, cash	13,598	7.9	124,881	87,944	21.7
Welfare, kind			28,728	20,230	4.9
Total	$171,166	99.8	$566,880	$395,853	99.9

* Deflated to 1955 prices paid to farmers.

function not so much of their economic return as of their consistency with Navajo tradition and with the fulfillment of traditional social and ritual obligations. Those activities like livestock rearing, agriculture, weaving, and to a lesser extent local wage work, which were most conducive to the maintenance of familiar lifeways, were consistently preferred to those which, while financially more rewarding, required a disruption of family and community life.

Implications of the Economic Changes

Although economic change is somewhat more conspicuous at Shonto than is social change, even in this area the transformations that have taken place since 1955 are far less pronounced than might have been expected in view of the advent of paved roads and tourist travel, the railroad, the Black Mesa mining operation, and other material advances. Four main aspects of economic change have been noted: a substantial increase in cattle holdings; a decline in off-reservation wage work; and particularly in railroad work, a corresponding increase in local wage work; and a dramatic increase in unearned income from various forms of welfare. A common theme runs through all of these developments: they are changes which do not threaten, but which rather tend to reinforce the traditional fabric of Navajo society. Cattle ownership as practiced at Shonto does not involve any significant investment of labor; the decline of off-reservation labor and its replacement by temporary local jobs mean that households and residence groups are kept more nearly intact for more of the year than was true a generation ago; welfare payments lessen altogether the necessity for off-reservation wage work, releasing more time for traditional economic, social and ritual activities. Once again, as so often in the past, economic change has been limited to what was possible within the context of an unyielding social and cultural value system. As our figures show, the cost in terms of potential income lost has been considerable.

A generation ago, off-reservation wage work was widely regarded as the best solution to the economic dilemma of an exploding population and diminishing native resources (cf. Young 1957: 87–98). Such employment was already, at that time, furnishing over 50 percent of all income not only at Shonto but for the whole Navajo population (Adams 1963: 146), and a continuing increase was anticipated. New off-reservation job opportunities for Navajos were continually sought by the BIA Placement Service and the Arizona State Employment Service, even though it was recognized that dependence on off-reservation employment would ultimately modify or disrupt the traditional fabric of Navajo society.

It is clear from a number of studies (e.g. Sasaki 1960: 52–69, 126–134; McCracken n.d.; Graves 1970) that the anticipated migration and concomitant social disruption have in part taken place, yet their scope has been far more limited than might have been expected in 1955. Admittedly, few planners at that time adequately foresaw the rapid modernization of the Navajo reservation and the consequent growth of local employment opportunities as an alternative to off-reservation work, yet this development alone does not fully account for the declining interest in off-reservation labor. As our figures show, the majority of Shonto men could still have earned far more money on the railroad than they were able to do at home in 1971, yet many declined to avail themselves of it,

A more fundamental source of misperception lies in the fact that economic planners have always taken it for granted that Navajos, once educated in Anglo-ways and in Anglo-schools, would learn to set economic values above social values and would seek to maximize income and property, in the approved American tradition. Clearly this ideological change has yet to come about. The somewhat paradoxical result is that, at Shonto and elsewhere, the Navajos' involvement in some of the most remunerative fields of employment have decreased significantly (cf. Johnston 1966: 44, 50).

An unyielding adherence to traditional values, even when neighboring peoples seemed to offer other and more "rational" ones, is precisely what has enabled the Navajos to retain their social and cultural integrity through four centuries of environmental and political transformations, and apparently it is still doing so today. In an age when Americans are becoming increasingly disillusioned both with material incentives and with the "melting-pot" ideal, and are coming to value ethnic and cultural diversity for their own sakes, perhaps we are moving more toward the Navajo point of view than vice versa.

DEVELOPMENT STRATEGY PRESENT AND FUTURE

Navajo development is limited by many factors, the most important of which is the fact that the Navajo nation does not control its own government or economy. As any other colonial possession, its resources serve outside interests. In addition to this the Navajo nation is pursuing a development strategy which is open to serious question.

The economic plan for the Navajo nation asserts the impossibility of preserving traditional society and attaining an improved standard of living:

The rapid population growth of the Navajos coupled with the current rate at which their land is deteriorating make it *no longer possible* for the majority of Navajos to choose the traditional style of living, livestock herding and, at the same time have their demands for an increased standard of living met without extensive subsidization from both within and outside the Navajo tribe. (Navajo Tribe 1974: 68)

Complete dependence on traditional activities has not been possible since 1935, yet the Navajos, with their usual flexibility, have maintained themselves by participating in a number of activities while at the same time retaining their life-style and values. Therefore, it is not likely that traditional society will meet an early or easy demise.

The assumption that Navajos want a traditional life-style and an adequate standard of living is probably true. However, if they are faced with a choice as they were in 1955 and 1971 and are today, they will choose those economic pursuits which do not disrupt traditional life-styles even though it means a lower material standard of living.

The development plan requires that Navajos leave their traditional use-areas and migrate to the so-called "growth centers" of the Navajo nation in order to obtain employment in the modern sector. But there is little chance that the Navajo nation will be able to create enough jobs for all those who are currently unemployed or underemployed, or who have stopped looking for work. Since 1958 the tribe has only been able to create 1,400 jobs. This would not even employ the annual increase in the labor force. The importance of job creation has been pointed out by the British economist, E. F. Schumacher, author of *Small is beautiful.* "The central concern of a development policy must be the creation of work opportunities; for those who are unemployed are consuming without contributing anything to the (economy) . . . The output of an idle man is nil, whereas the output of even a poorly equipped man can be a positive contribution" (Schumacher 1973: 183).

The tribe should promote employment wherever it can whether it be in the modern or traditional sector, or in a growth center or a remote community. Schumacher recommends the following steps to generate jobs:

1.   Create workplaces where people are living, thus ending the rural-urban migration which intensifies congestion without alleviating poverty.
2.   Workplaces should utilize as little capital as possible; they can do this by employing the "appropriate technology".
3.   Methods employed must be relatively simple; equipment should be easy to operate, maintain, and repair; men should be easily trained and supervised.
4.   Production should be based on local materials and for local use.

Schumacher's suggested solution for Third World countries has some applicability to the development problems of Navajos. The dilemma facing the Navajo tribal government is how to create jobs given their limited financial and managerial resources. But then according to Schumacher, money alone cannot solve the problem nor should a lack of it prevent a solution. "If the policy is wrong, money will not make it right; if the policy is right, money may not, in fact, present an unduly difficult problem" (Schumacher 1973: 196). The task then is to find the right policy. Given the fact that the Navajo nation is not able to employ all traditional Navajos in the modern sector, it should not encourage premature migration to its so-called growth centers. Better to have the population at home even at a relatively low wage than unemployed and completely dependent on welfare in Window Rock. It might be better to invest in strategic areas dispersed throughout the Navajo nation such as Tuba City, Kayenta, Leupp, Chinle, and Crownpoint as well as Shiprock and Window Rock so that people could obtain local employment and still live in their local communities.

Following Schumacher's advice, new tribal enterprises should, as far as possible, use local resources and simple but modern techniques. This does not mean substandard techniques or substandard wages. Ideally, tribal enterprises should increase the value-added of Navajo resources (land, timber, minerals, labor, capital) and traditional activities. Among the possible enterprises and activities which fulfill some of these requisites are furniture making, feedlots (lamb and cattle), slaughter houses, meat-packing, tanneries, leather goods, wool spinning, food processing and canning. If the appropriate technology for a given task is chosen, it need not be terribly expensive nor require an exorbitant amount of capital. It might be more desirable to set up a modest operation which is labor-intensive and will do well in the local market rather than doing nothing because one cannot afford a more capital-intensive operation. Reservation enterprises with the appropriate technology should have a cost advantage over remote city plants because they use local materials and labor and have lower transport costs. The reservation might engage in reverse exploitation by selling to local towns and cities instead of being bled dry by them.

In addition to starting tribal resource-based enterprises, some effort should be made to increase the productivity of the livestock economy. Traditional activities utilize two of the most abundant Navajo resources: land and labor. They cushion the income against fluctuations in temporary wage work; the reservation cannot presently provide steady jobs for the entire labor force, and stock raising provides an important supplement to welfare for those who are not able to secure permanent wage employment.

Livestock activities take advantage of existing investment and knowledge, and reach most of the population as well. The tribe should pursue a more vigorous program of range restoration and education in range and livestock management in order to increase productivity in the livestock economy. Unfortunately, a few of these suggestions are contained in the present tribal development strategy.

The success and beneficial results of the tribal wool program have already been discussed. Obviously, this activity should be continued and expanded to include wool scouring in order to further increase the wool income of Navajo families. National marketing of Navajo rugs should be undertaken. Tribal feedlots and marketing of sheep and cattle should be undertaken by NAPI.

The development goal of the Navajo nation as expressed in its 1974 OEDP is "the efficient development of a viable Navajo economy, which will afford the Navajo people the maximum opportunity for choice of both style and standard of living" (Navajo Tribe 1974: 72). This goal is to be achieved by encouraging private entrepreneurship and by choosing the most efficient mode of organization for an economic enterprise. The incongruity of Navajo values and those of entrepreneurs has already been explored. Creating entrepreneurs will be difficult, but there is room in the Navajo economy for their ventures, especially in the commercial sector. Still, a development strategy should not depend on them, even in the long run.

The tribal plan defines "most efficient" as that method of combining productive factors which produces maximum income. Maximizing income, apparently means maximizing profit or the return on invested capital. Thus, income or profit maximizing projects are preferred to job maximizing ones because ... "the resulting increases in

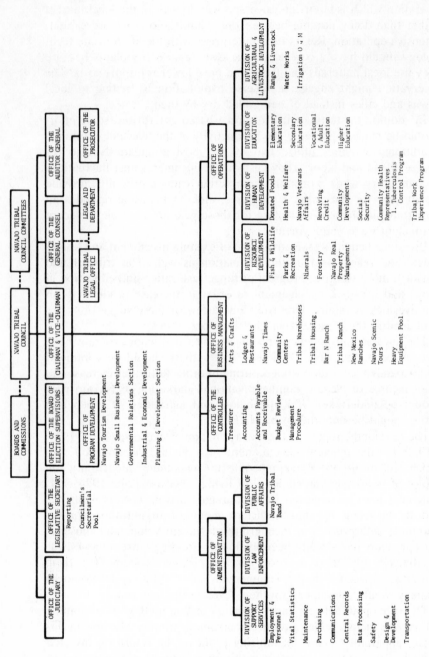

Figure 4.   Organization chart of the Navajo tribe, 1972

income . . . can provide funds for further investment . . . and also enable the tribe to finance its growing social service programs and the labor-intensive employment it creates through the extension of government services" (Navajo Tribe 1974: 73).

If investment projects are chosen solely on the basis of their return to capital, capital-intensive projects will be favored over labor-intensive ones. This criterion is characteristic of the capital-intensive investment approach to development. The capital-intensive strategy depends on the creation of growth centers, where capital may be concentrated and benefit from close markets, infrastructure, trained labor, and ancillary services. Capital-intensive projects will make possible a more rapid rate of investment (so the argument runs), because it will not be necessary to distribute so much income to labor as under a labor-intensive approach. This argument assumes that the profits from capital-intensive projects will be reinvested. From the above quote it appears that the tribal government does not intend to reinvest all the profits but spend a portion for social services. Thus, they will violate the rationale for choosing capital-intensive projects over labor-intensive projects. Worse yet, they will be substituting social services for jobs in productive enterprises.

Given that the rate of unemployment is at least 50 percent it would seem that job maximizing projects should be preferred to those which employ fewer people but have a higher return to capital. When evaluating projects the tribe should compare the cost of the project with the return or the total value added to all reservation resources including labor. The fact that wages are included in the calculation of value-added will increase the probability that labor-intensive projects will be chosen *vis-à-vis* capital-intensive ones. Of course any new project or enterprise should cover all costs of operation such as wages, depreciation, and raw materials.

Investment in enterprises which use local resources and are based on traditional activities would probably result in maximum job creation and allow maintenance of cultural values. To date, few of the programs for economic development deal directly with increasing the productive capacity of the livestock economy. The present strategy favors the modern sector over the traditional economy. It has also resulted in choosing a capital-intensive investment criterion which may not lead to the greatest economic and social good for the Navajo nation.

APPENDIX

A. The Overall Economic Development Program itself (Bureau of Indian Affairs 1971) states that "demographic statistics are woefully inadequate". For example the number of Navajos on the reservation in 1970 according to the BIA was 126,265 while the U.S. Census enumerated only 64,675. However, BIA statistics have their own particular problems. The statistics are compiled on an annual basis by the area office. However, it does not take any sample survey to establish these figures but merely adjusts the previous year's figures to reflect any changes it thinks occurred. The Bureau's justification for lack of accurate statistics is twofold. One, it claims lack of personnel. Two, its response through its representative is sufficient, "What good are accurate statistics?" There are also definitional problems with the labor force statistics reported by the BIA. The U.S. Census defines an unemployed person as one who had been seeking work within the four week period previous to the interview. The BIA is aware that it defines unemployment differently but it justifies the difference by saying that the nature of job search is different on the reservation and so the U.S. Census definition has little relevance. On the reservation there is almost perfect job information. Everyone knows where there is a job opening and therefore does not have to search continuously. Therefore, if a Census taken asked a Navajo "Have you looked for a job in the past few weeks?" he might reply no because there had been no job openings and being rational he didn't seek what didn't exist. If the BIA is correct then the U.S. Census figures for Navajo unemployment are under-estimates, the BIA figures overestimates. The truth is somewhere in-between. There should be someway to determine what portion of those not seeking work have withdrawn from the labor force.

The rates of unemployment and underemployment are based on the following adjustments to BIA data for 1971.

	Original BIA figure		Adjusted figure	
Population	130,231		130,231	
Labor Force	40,346	100%	38,570	100%
Employed	26,000	64.4	26,000	67.4
permanently	17,532	43.4	17,532	45.5
temporarily	8,468	20.9	8,468	21.9
Unemployed	14,346	35.5	12,570	32.5
seeking work	12,570	31.2	12,570	32.5

The original BIA figures overestimate unemployment (35.5%), as computed by the U.S. Census because it included 1,776 persons who were not looking for work. If 1,776 persons are subtracted from the labor force the unemployment rate is 32.5%.

B. In 1975, the BIA reported a labor force of 61,182 persons, 27,633 of whom were unemployed, and only 7,259 of these were looking for work. This means that 20,107 were not looking for work. The BIA rate of unemployment was 44.7 percent. Using U.S. Census definitions it would have been 17.6 percent. As stated in Note 1 the truth is somewhere in between.

	Original BIA figure		Adjusted figure	
Population	147,210		147,210	
Labor Force	61,182		41,075	
employed	33,816		33,816	
permanently	20,505		20,505	
temporarily	13,311		13,311	
Unemployed	27,366	44.7%	7,259	17.6%
seeking work	7,259			

REFERENCES

ABERLE, DAVID
1963 *Peyote religion and the Navajo.* Viking Fund Publication in Anthropology. No. 421.
1966 "Navajo matrilineal kinship," in *Matrilineal kinship.* Edited by D. M. Schneider and K. Gough. Berkeley and Los Angeles: University of California Press.
1969 "A plan for Navajo economic development," in *Toward economic development for native American communities,* volume one. United States Congress Joint Economic Committee. Washington, D.C.: United States Government Printing Office.
1976 "The emergent Navajo nation: economic development." Unpublished manuscript.

ADAMS, WILLIAM Y.
1963 *Shonto: a study of the role of the trader in a modern Navajo community.* Washington, D.C.: Bureau of Ethnology. No. 186.

AMERICAN INDIAN POLICY REVIEW COMMISSION
1976 *Report on reservation and resource development and protection,* Washington, D.C.: United States Government Printing Office.
1976 Task Force #9, Correspondence with George Vlassis. March 24, 1976

BUREAU OF INDIAN AFFAIRS
1971 *Labor force report.*

Business Week
1976 "Indians want a bigger share of their wealth." *Business Week.* May 3, 1976.

CAHN, EDGAR, *editor*
1969 *Our brother's keeper.* New York: World Publishing Company.

CARTER, H., G. DEAN
1936 Cost-size relationships for cash crop farms in a highly commercialized agriculture. *Journal of Farm Economics* 17(2).

CLEMMER, R.
1970 "Economic development versus aboriginal land use: an attempt to predict culture change on an Indian reservation in Arizona." Unpublished manuscript.

COMPTROLLER GENERAL OF U.S.
1975 *Better overall planning needed to improve the standard of living of White Mountain Apaches of Azirona.* Washington, D.C.: General Accounting Office.
1975 *Improving small business opportunities on reservations.* Washington, D.C.: General Accounting Office.

DELORIA, VINE, JR.
1969 *Custer died for your sins.* New York: Macmillan.

DORNER, PETER
1959 "The economic position of the American Indians:" "Their Resources and Potential for Development." Unpublished Ph.D. dissertation, Harvard University.

DOWNS, JOHN
1964 *Animal husbandry in Navajo society and culture.* Berkeley and Los Angeles: University of California Press.

ERNST AND ERNST
   1973   "Phase one survey-sources of revenues, goods & services received by
          the Navajo tribe fiscal year ended June 30, 1972."
GILBREATH, KENT
   1972   Business development on the Navajo reservation. *New Mexico
          Business* 25 (March).
GOLDBERG, CAROLE E.
   1976   The Prospects of Navajo taxation of non-Indians. *Lake Powell Re-
          search Bulletin* No. 19.
GORMAN, W., R. LANSFORD
   1972   "Alternative farm organizational structures for Navajo Indian irriga-
          tion projects." New Mexico State University. Agricultural Experi-
          ment Station Special Report No. 17.
GRAVES, THEODORE
   1970   The personal adjustment of Navajo Indian migrants to Denver,
          Colorado. *American Anthropologist* 72: 35–54.
HASKETT, B.
   1936   Sheep industry in Arizona. *Arizona Historical Review* 7(3).
HOOVER, J. H.
   1937   Navajo land problems. *Economic Geography* 7.
JOHNSTON, DENIS F.
   1966   *An analysis of sources of information on the population of the Navaho.*
          Washington: Bureau of American Ethnology Bulletin. No. 197.
KELLY, LAWRENCE
   1968   *The Navajo Indians and federal Indian policy.* Tucson: University of
          Arizona Press.
KIMBALL, S., J. PROVINSE
   1942   Navajo social organization in land use planning. *Applied Anthropol-
          ogy* 4.
KLUCKHOHN, C., D. LEIGHTON
   1962   *The Navaho.* New York: American Museum of Natural History.
KUNKEL, J.
   1965   Values and behavior in economic development. *Economic Develop-
          ment and Cultural Change* 13 (April).
LAMPHERE, LOUISE
   1967   "Social organization in a Navajo community." Unpublished Ph.D.
          dissertation, Harvard University.
LEVITAN, SAR, B. HETRICK
   1971   *Big Brother's Indian programs with reservations.* New York: McGraw-
          Hill.
LINGENFELTER, SHERMAN
   1966   "The Navajo Cow Springs area." Unpublished manuscript. Tri-
          Institute Field Program in Cultural Anthropology.
LUNDGREN, H.
   1964   "Hope for wool through research," in *The future of sheep.* Edited by
          C. Terril et al. Center for Agriculture and Economic Development.
          Ames: Iowa State University of Science and Technology. No. 21.
MAC DONALD, PETER
   1972   *The Navajo ten year plan.* Window Rock, Arizona: The Navajo
          Nation.
MACGREGOR, GORDON
   n.d.   *The Navajo study.* Navajo Indian Irrigation Project.

MC CRACKEN, ROBERT
n.d.   "Urban migration and the changing structure of Navajo social relations." Unpublished Ph.D. dissertation, Department of Anthropology, University of Colorado.

MADDEN, J. P.
1967   *Economics in size of farming.* United States Department of Agriculture Economic Report No. 107, Washington, D.C.

NAPOLI, JOSEPH
1976   "The Indian budget." Unpublished report. American Indian Policy
Review Commission, Washington, D.C.

NAVAJO FOREST PRODUCT INDUSTRIES
1975   *Annual report.* Window Rock, Arizona.

Navajo Times
1976   "Particleboard plant dedicated." *Navajo Times* 17(39) (September
23).

NAVAJO TRIBE
1971–1975   Financial statements, Window Rock, Arizona.
1974   *Overall economic development program.* Window Rock, Arizona:
Office of Program Development, Navajo Tribe.

NEILS, ELAINE
1971   *Reservation to city: Indian migration and federal relocation.* University of Chicago Research Paper No. 131. Chicago: University of
Chicago.

RENO, PHILIP
1970   Manpower planning for Navajo employment: training for jobs in a
surplus-labor area. *New Mexico Business* 23: 8–16 (November–
December).

RENO, P., BAHE BILLY
1973   Navajo Indian economic planning: the Navajo Indian Irrigation Project. *New Mexico Business* 26(11): 3–12 (*November*).

REYNOLDS, TERRY *et al.*
1967   Time, resources and authority in a Navajo community. *American
Anthropologist* 69.

ROBBINS, L.
1975   The impact of power development on the Navajo nation. *Lake
Powell Research Project Bulletin* (7).
1976   Navajo energy politics. *Lake Powell Research Project Bulletin.*

RUFFING, L.
1973   "An alternative approach to economic development in a traditional
Navajo community." Unpublished Ph.D. Dissertation, Columbia
University.
1976   Navajo Economic Development Subject to Cultural Constraints.
Economic Development and Cultural Change 24(3).

SASAKI, TOM
1960   *Fruitland, New Mexico: a Navajo community in transition.* Ithaca:
Cornell University Press.

SCHUMACHER, E. F.
1973   *Small is beautiful.* New York: Harper and Row.

SHEPARDSON, MARY
1963   *Navajo ways in government.* American Anthropological Association.
64(3). Part 2 Memoirs 96.

SHEPARDSON, MARY, B. HAMMOND
    1970   *The Navajo mountain community.* Berkeley and Los Angeles: University of California Press.
SORKIN, ALAN
    1971   *American Indians and federal aid.* Washington, D.C.: Brookings Institution.
TWEETEN, L.
    1970   *Foundations of farm policy.* Lincoln: University of Nebraska Press.
U.S. BUREAU OF CENSUS
    1970   Census of Population 1970, Subject Reports, Final Report PC(2)–1F "American Indians," Washington, D.C.
    1971   *Statistical abstract of U.S.* Washington, D.C.
U.S. COMMISSION ON CIVIL RIGHTS
    1975   *The Navajo nation, an American colony.* Washington, D.C.
U.S. DEPARTMENT OF AGRICULTURE
    1972   Livestock and meat statistics. Supplement for 1971 to Statistical Bulletin 333: 118.
U.S. DEPARTMENT OF COMMERCE
    1975   "Results of a partnership between the American Indian and the economic development administration." Washington, D.C.
U.S. DEPARTMENT OF HEALTH, EDUCATION AND WELFARE
    1966   "Indian health highlights." Public Health Service, Washington, D.C.
U.S. DEPARTMENT OF INTERIOR
    1974   *Annual range management report.* Navajo Area Office. Bureau of Indian Affairs.
    1975   *Annual report of mineral leasing activities, June 30, 1975.* Washington, D.C.: Bureau of Indian Affairs.
            Forestry report. Navajo Area Office. Bureau of Indian Affairs.
            Housing inventory FY 1975. Navajo Area Office. Bureau of Indian Affairs.
WITHERSPOON, GARY
    n.d.   "Cultural meaning and social function of the Navajo sheep herd," Unpublished paper.
    1970   "Social and cultural analysis of Navajo kinship and social organization." Unpublished Ph.D. dissertation, University of Chicago.
WISTISEN, MARTIN, *et al.*
    1975   *A study to identify potential feasible small businesses for the Navajo nation. Phase 1-an evaluation of income and expenditure patterns,* volumes one, two, and three. Provo, Utah: Center for Business and Economic Research, Survey Research Center, Brigham Young University.
YOUNG, ROBERT
    1957   *The Navajo yearbook, FY 1957.* Window Rock, Arizona: Navajo Agency.
    1961   *The Navajo yearbook.* Window Rock, Arizona: Navajo Agency.

The Lummi Indian Community: The Fishermen of the Pacific Northwest

VINE DELORIA, JR.

INTRODUCTION

The vast majority of Indian tribes lived in nonindustrial and nonagricultural settings until the closing decades of the last century. At that time, government policy dictated that tribal land estates be divided among individual tribal members and that hunting and fishing economies, which had sustained the tribes for centuries, be exchanged for sedentary agricultural patterns of economic subsistence.

Where Indian tribes had already made the transition from hunting to farming, the translation of economic factors did not radically disorient the community. In some instances, however, tribal members made adjustments — only to find that their loyal pursuit of the American economic system was fruitless, for it was changing faster than they were able to adjust. The allotment ideology dictated that rural farming would continue to dominate those areas in which it was already entrenched and that it would conquer the regions in which it had not yet taken root. Yet the very decade in which most allotments were made, the 1890's, brought the official end of the American frontier and the prelude to the end of rural economy as the mainstay of American society.

The allotment method of holding lands was introduced by the government as a panacea for the cultural gaps between Indian communal existence and the highly individualistic conception of society as a conglomerate of property owners, which was then held by the American people and their political policymakers. Regardless of the quality or the nature of the lands on the reservations that had been set aside for Indian tribes in the treaties, federal policy demanded that the tribe divide its lands and that it stake its communal existence on the ability of its members to conform to the disintegrating economic and social world view of Western civilization.

The pronounced cultural and religious differences between red men and white men were seen as differences in their ideas of what elements constituted wealth and prosperity for a particular community. Adjustments of property and property rights were seen by government officials as motivating factors in changing Indians from a savage and unhappy state to an economic status that exemplified, in the philosophy of white American society, the progressive refinement of civilization. Having subscribed to a particular theory of history, white America viewed Indian reservations and communities as laboratories where white economic beliefs could be validated through humane, although dictatorial, guidance.

The Lummi Indians of western Washington state were merely one group of American Indians who suffered from the continually changing political adjustments of the last century. Considered as a community in forced transition, the Lummi did not go through an experience radically different from that of many other tribes. They signed a treaty, were given allotments, and were threatened by whites' constant demands for more land. And they survived continual efforts by the federal government to extinguish their political independence.

Today the Lummi tribe stands on the threshhold of success. It has developed an aquaculture project on Lummi Bay, a small portion of its reservation. In four short years, the tribe has climbed steadily into a position of major influence in the field of sea farming, and it has achieved a national reputation among American Indian tribes as a leading proponent of self-determination through creative programming and community development of resources.

As originally conceived, this study of the Lummi Indians was to seek out the peculiar factors that enabled this particular Indian tribe to achieve so much in so short a time with such limited resources. Finding the hidden key to Lummi progress, it was supposed, might unlock the energies of many other tribes in developing their resources through reliance on the particular strengths of tribal culture which do not exist in non-Indian communities.

The Lummi story is at once more complicated and much simpler than originally conceived. It is a fortunate and, at times, rather sophisticated intertwining of a number of factors, some of which are directly dependent on Lummi culture, some of which are dependent on the attitudes of the Lummis. Over and above the peculiarities of tribal existence, however, are factors that cannot be found in the present situations of many Indian tribes. These factors are the product of historical accident. That they have been exploited by the Lummi Indians to their distinct advantage is a testimony to the astuteness of the Lummi people. It is also a verification of the arbitrary nature of history and the irrationality of man's life experience.

Three significant factors appear to emerge from the history and present success of the Lummi Indians — factors over which they had no apparent control. Early in the 1900's the tribe was singularly fortunate in winning a series of law suits that preserved a 5,000-acre tract of tidal lands in tribal hands. It is upon these tidelands that the present successful aquaculture is built.

The government did not, at any time, have the energy and resources to provide constant supervision over the Lummis. Government control, as arbitrarily exercized over Indian tribes much larger than the Lummi, never existed with respect to them. Benign neglect, then, may be a valid concept in the social development of communities. The neglect of the Lummi Indians by the federal government was, however, never benign. They were simply too isolated from the administrative offices of the Bureau of Indian Affairs to be considered for pilot projects.

The third influential factor over which the Lummis had no control was the inability of the people who had political and administrative power over their lives and property to understand them. Administrative arrogance can be useful, when it allows a people to maintain themselves as an intact community because they are regarded as powerless. When the opportunity to charge forward comes, the community rises as one and moves, catching the experts totally off guard and carrying the day.

The changes of recent years, in which the Lummi people suddenly created a totally new concept of community development, were not as radical as they would appear. Throughout Lummi history the community had shown itself devoted to the integrity of its ancient fishing culture. Almost every force that attempted to change the Lummi people failed to comprehend the nature of Lummi existence: to be a Lummi meant to be involved with the sea, the water, the fish, the shellfish, and the traditional lands of the tribe.

From their very beginning the Lummi people had been fishermen. After a century and a quarter of continual contact with whites, after a series of disastrous experiments by the federal government, the Lummi people were still fishermen. But in the interim they had created a new meaning for the word. The Lummi story begins, takes place, and will continue on the lands where the people originated.

If the success of the Lummis is to have any relevance to the other tribes of the continent, certain interpretations must be drawn from it. The tribe must have sufficient leeway to define its own conceptions of community needs. The policy of "self-determination" is now standard rhetoric among government agencies that deal with Indian tribes. But it is not understood by them. Success did not come to the Lummis because the Bureau of Indian Affairs advocated a policy of self-determination for a period of years; the BIA simply neglected the tribe in almost every respect, thus giving it sufficient freedom to work out its problems.

The Lummi people have persisted in maintaining a close relationship with their ancient way of life. Whenever and wherever they had the opportunity to fish, they did so. Perhaps other tribes that persist in valuing the old ways should consider means of translating traditional life-styles into contemporary enterprises. Former buffalo hunters might well consider tribal herds of buffalo instead of cattle. Tribes that depended on trade with neighboring tribes might well look into marketing programs. Agricultural tribes might well develop specialty farming for selected markets.

Probably the most important lesson to be learned from the Lummi experience is that the traditional reverence for the land and an intimate knowledge of its spiritual and life-giving powers is an extremely valuable asset in confronting the contemporary problems of Indian communities. Lands appear to be destined for certain uses. Proper appreciation of the lands on which the people live may be the most necessary component of modern economic development of Indian tribes.

After the United States government had finished with the Lummi Indian tribe, all that the Lummi had left was the land that lay exposed between low tide and high tide. A mud flat. Yet, clinging to this mere fragment of aboriginal existence, the tribe conceived one of the most advanced programs any community has ever created. Other Indian tribes, too, should learn to view their land as peculiarly adapted for certain activities. Instead of setting land aside for programs, programs should be tailored around the land.

The Lummi story opens with the land and sea. Before the coming of the white man, the Lummi Indians ranged over a large area that centered at "the island called Chah-choo-sen, situated in the Lummi River at a point of separation of the mouths emptying respectively into Bellingham Bay and the Gulf of Georgia" (Point Elliott Treaty, signed January 22, 1855). From this homeland base on the northwest coast of what has since become Washington state, the Lummi people traveled east to the Cascades to trade with the Nooksacks, mountain people who lived in the foothills of the range that divides the present state. Further to the east, the Lummis traded salmon to the Kootenais of the Columbia Plateau (*Bellingham Herald*, May 11, 1893).

Throughout the year, the Lummi people followed the natural cycle of fish life. They spent the summer season fishing in the San Juan Islands. As fall came they moved to the mainland site of their present reservation and continued fishing. Winter and spring were also spent on the mainland. The seasonal runs of salmon, the availability of shellfish, and the abundance of berries and camas roots determined where the people would go and when they would move on (Suttles 1954: 31; Stern 1969: 49). The Lummis lived *with* the lands and seasons, not against them.

Lummi territory then extended over an island-dotted inland waterway off the end of Vancouver Island, now San Juan County, and the shoreline that is now the western part of Whatcom County. The territorial area was bounded by the Strait of Georgia in the northwest and the flood plain of the Fraser River in the north, and it included most of the San Juan Islands, which lie across Hale passage from Lummi Island. Lummi territory also extended eastward along the shores of Bellingham Bay. (The territory is elaborately discussed in *Lummi Tribe of Indians* v. *United States of America* in Spier [1936]).

The area where the Lummis lived was particularly well suited for settlement. The land was heavily forested with stands of gigantic Douglas fir (Taylor 1969: 11). Rainfall averaged some 33 inches a year, with December having about 5 inches of rain. Various species of salmon traveled the Nooksack River, which divides south of present-day Ferndale: the main channel of the Nooksack — later to become the eastern boundary of the reservation — empties into Bellingham Bay; the Lummi (or Red) River veers westward after its separation from the Nooksack and empties into Lummi Bay, near the present site of the aquaculture project.

Inland, a rugged terrain and dense rainforest vegetation made travel difficult. Further to the east, on the opposite side of the Cascades, was a high, desert plateau; although there were fish and game animals, resources were not as abundant as they were along the coasts.

The coastal tribes were of one basic cultural stock, with a variety of differences. The Lummis, Swinomish, Tulalip, Duwamish, Clallams, and other tribes occupied a series of fishing villages that extended from the present international boundary to the region now encompassed by the Seattle-Tacoma-Olympia-Bremerton complex. The most common political unit of the coastal tribes was the extended family group, whose members shared a cedar longhouse. A rather strict definition of family groupings, coupled with intermarriage according to certain customs, enabled the tribes to extend political and cultural alliances among other villages for a considerable distance along the coast. The Lummis at one time had apparently divided into three groups of families, according to where they lived (Commissioner of Indian Affairs 1857, No. 135, 327).

Perhaps more significant than formal village organization was the division of people into classes, which were based partly on religious considerations and more largely on accumulated wealth, as defined primarily in terms of fishing locations, tools, household goods, and other personal property. Fishing-site ownerships, in particular, defined political status in the tribe. Slaves from the wars between the coastal villages and the marauding tribes that lived further north along the coast of what is now British Columbia provided the lowest class, albeit temporary in terms of individual people, in the political organization of the Lummi tribal structure.

Religious differences among the coastal tribes were slight. Sharing a common group of creation myths, orienting interpretations of life around their relationship with the salmon and the traditional practices of fishing, the coastal peoples — including the Lummi people — held to a basic conception of life as it had been revealed to them in olden days. Most influential in community religious life were the religious power songs and spirit dances in which people expressed their deepest feelings. The Lummis were, on the whole, a highly religious people with a profound ability to comprehend the spiritual powers of their land (Suttles 1957: 352–397). This genius continues today.

ABORIGINAL ECONOMY AND STATUS

In aboriginal days there was apparently a great deal of strife among the various villages, as groups shifted about between the islands of the inland waters and the mainland. The presence of slaves in the Lummi social structure would seem to indicate intertribal warfare at an early date (Suttles 1954: 46). However, here as elsewhere, it is virtually impossible to distinguish the general shifting of Indians from the dislocations created by the pressure of white settlement along the coast and by the fur trade in the interior (Suttles 1954: 42).

One cannot conclude, therefore, that aboriginal days were necessarily more disrupted than were the years immediately preceding the arrival of whites in the Lummi lands. The Indians in what is now British Columbia, primarily the Yukulta, received guns in the fur trade and escalated their raids against the Lummi. The repeated loss of women and children to these pirates resulted in great disruption of Lummi family life. Perhaps the move from the islands to the mainland and the subsequent construction of large stockades was a direct effect of such raids (Suttles 1954: 42).

The stabilization of village groups and the creation of classes within the communal Lummi structure were probably as much a response to the antagonistic forces without as to the cultural developments within. The most notable aspect of the Lummi political structure appears to have been the absence of authoritarianism. Family heads came to direct the fortunes of Lummi bands by example and personal influence, rather than solely by formal acknowledgment of authority (Suttles 1963: 513).

The social and political life of the tribe revolved about its fishing activities. Fish were caught by reef netting, a unique method developed by the Indians of the area, in midsummer and early fall, in the waters around Lummi Island and Point Francis (Spier 1936: 5530). Reef nets were made of logs and twisted bark ropes, and the stationary fishing sites were owned by family heads as individual enterprises (Taylor 1969: 19–21). Family heads gathered men in their immediate family group into crews that worked for each fishing season, dividing the catch according to previously agreed formulas.

At the end of the reef-netting season the Indians usually moved onto the mainland near what is now Lummi Bay, where the Lummi River originally drained into the waters of the Gulf of Georgia (at the end of the similarly named strait). A large weir was maintained there while the salmon were running upstream to spawn. Weir fishing was apparently a communal rather than an individual venture. The salmon were caught and dried in the sun, thus preserving them for winter (Suttles 1954: 53–54; Taylor 1969: 16–18).

Spring was devoted to digging camas roots on the islands, trolling for salmon, digging clams, and hunting deer. Most of this activity centered in the northern San Juan Islands. With the exception of salmon traded to other tribes, there was little commercial exchange among the coastal villages. The various species of salmon provided people with everything they needed economically.

The weir at the mouth of the Lummi River apparently established a sense of communal ownership of economic functions. When private property was introduced through allotments, the Lummi continued to recognize a communally centered function in fishing, relying on their memories of village existence and the annual salmon runs (Taylor 1969: 21–22).

THE PERIOD OF WHITE SETTLEMENT

The first evidence the Lummi had of white intruders was the devastating smallpox epidemic that ravaged coastal villages during the 1870's (Suttles 1954: 37ff.). Helpless because they had no immunity to the disease, the coastal peoples were nearly wiped out. At about the same time, fur traders with horses had apparently come to the northwest coast — the first Indians encountered by Spanish expeditions of the 1790's told of trading with mounted men who had come from the Fraser River.

According to European accounts, the first recorded contact with any of the coastal peoples was that of the Spanish explorer Quimper, who in 1790 explored both sides of the Strait of Juan de Fuca, in addition to visiting the Makah. (The Makah traditionally tell of repelling the Spaniards at Neah Bay). The next year, the Eliza expedition explored inland waters, including Bellingham and Padilla bays, and sailed at least to Point Roberts. Because the migratory pattern of the Lummis involved movement between the northern San Juans and Bellingham Bay, it is probable that Spaniards made some contact with Lummi villagers during this expedition.

The English entered the area the following year, when Vancouver's expedition sailed into the lower Strait of Georgia. A fiercely competitive trade in furs had begun, and the tribes of the inland waterways found themselves caught between the coastal sea-otter traders and the interior beaver traders. Although invaded, coastal tribes were the subject of pressure on both their eastern and western borders.

Increasing rivalry between John Jacob Astor's fur company and British fur traders brought the first Americans to the area. In 1824 McMillan and Work, Astorians, came into the straits country from the lower Columbia River, where they had been in competition with the Hudson's Bay people. Three years later, McMillan returned to the lower Fraser region, where he established Fort Langley as an American trading post. The Americans were eventually overwhelmed by the growth of Victoria, the settlement on Vancouver's island that served as a trade and administrative center for British interests in the northwest.

In 1837 two Roman Catholic missionaries, Fathers Blanchet and Demers, came from the Columbia River to establish a mission settlement on the Cowlitz River. For the next five years they preached at coastal villages, visiting the Nisquallies and the people of Whidbey Island, and made occasional trips to Fort Langley and Victoria. No systematic mission activity was established among the Lummis until Father Casmir Chirouse came to the Tulalip region in 1857, following the treaty of Point Elliott (Suttles 1954: 57).

The fur trade rather profoundly affected the coastal villages. Competition started as a three-way struggle between the Hudson's Bay Company, the Northwest Company (a rival British concern), and the American Fur Company of Astoria. The major struggles were fought on the Fraser and Columbia rivers. Emphasis was on beaver pelts; thus, the inland tribes received the attention of the fur traders, while the coastal villages developed a trade in supplying the expeditions into the interior.

The coastal villages began supplying salmon, vegetables, and other foodstuffs to the trading posts, in exchange for metal implements, blankets, and other manufactured articles. Indians began to cultivate small plots of potatoes and to establish an ongoing relationship with the whites at Fort Langley and, later, Victoria. Firearms acquired in trade enabled the coastal people to more easily repel the raids of their northern enemies (Commissioner of Indian Affairs 1857: 326).

The Lummi people may at this time have become established in the role of commercial food producers. The important influence of the fur trade on subsistence patterns was that the Lummi people themselves developed the idea of raising vegetables for sale to the whites. Concluding that food production was a sensible way to expand their trading relationships, the people undertook to develop this entrée into the economic system. They did not, however, believe that expansion into agricultural production would make total cultural change inevitable. The government's later determination to convert the Lummis from fishermen to grain farmers was totally without precedent or rational basis.

Although a number of Americans passed through Lummi territory, no settlement was made until a few years prior to the treaty of Point Elliott in 1855. Two white men set up a sawmill in 1852, at the falls just above the entry of Whatcom Creek into Bellingham Bay. (Over the years, this industry has evolved into the gigantic Georgia-Pacific wood processing complex of Bellingham.) Later, coal was discovered nearby (Suttles 1954: 54). For some time Lummi men were employed in the mines, but they sought such employment only as a means of supplementing their ordinary fishing activities (Commissioner of Indian Affairs 1870: 43–44, 1871: 121).

The northern tribes continued to launch attacks on the Indian villages on the American side of the inland coast, and in 1857 Fort Bellingham was established, to discourage American Indians from joining in the fighting (Commissioner of Indian Affairs 1870: 54). The fort also served notice on Canada that the United States was affirming its claim to the northern territory. The following year gold was discovered in Canada on the Fraser and Thompson rivers. Thousands of gold-crazed whites stormed north in search of instant riches. Bellingham was directly in the path of the rabid migration, and the Lummis took full advantage of the gold rush. Although the fishing season was due shortly, they sold their canoes at very high prices to the migrating gold seekers, thus making a temporary profit but hampering their fishing for several seasons to come.

Treaties and Agreements in the Northwest Territory

Great Britain and the United States had quarreled for years over the boundary of the Oregon country, which then extended over a large part of the Pacific Northwest. The British seemed to have the edge initially, with Victoria established as a major trading center in the area. The Americans, under John Jacob Astor, proved themselves to be a match for the English, however, and, while the Hudson's Bay Company edged ahead in the fur trade, the Astorians cleverly publicized the riches of the country, encouraging settlers to travel the Oregon Trail to the promised land. In this way, settlement of the territory became a *de facto* American enterprise.

The boundary dispute reached serious propositions in 1844, when James K. Polk ran for president on a platform of "54–40 or fight," a slogan that belied traditional interpretation of peaceful American settlement of continental lands (Josephy 1965: 673). A treaty with Great Britain was signed June 15, 1846, settling the white ownership of the northwest coast.

The boundary, set at 49 degrees latitude and rigidly followed, severed a peninsula, thereby leaving a tiny piece of American land — Point Roberts — detached from the United States mainland. No sooner had the line been drawn than Congress created Oregon Territory and began to make plans to populate it. The Oregon Trail had only been open for three years at this time.

On September 27, 1850, Congress passed the Oregon Donation Act, which allowed each settler who made the long journey west a tract of 320 acres. The act was designed to settle the Willamette Valley in north-central Oregon, but its provisions began to be used by whites coming into the Nisqually Delta and the lower parts of Puget Sound. By clever manipulation of the law, a man and wife could double their land, each taking an allotment (American Friends Service Committee 1970: 16). Complications arose in administering such a liberal land law, and three years later Congress separated the northern half of the territory at the Columbia River, creating the territory of Washington.

Isaac Ingalls Stevens was appointed governor of the new territory and superintendent of Indian affairs, with supervisory responsibility over the new policy of freeing large areas of land for white settlers by restricting Indians to small reservations (Act of March 2, 1853). Stevens, who took his responsibilities very seriously, immediately set out to get as much land as possible away from the tribes of the region.

In a series of five treaties signed over a two-year period — Medicine Creek (December 26, 1854); Point Elliott (January 22, 1855); Point No Point (January 26, 1855); Neah Bay (January 31, 1855); and Quinault (May 8, 1859) — Stevens managed to trick the Indians west of the Cascades out of some 64 million acres, or 100,000 square miles. The lands were heavily forested with virgin Douglas fir and western cedar. The rivers were full of salmon and trout. The bays and inlets teemed with shellfish. And the area had some notable mineral deposits. Original payment for the lands was grossly inadequate, and subsequent litigation for true value by the tribes of the area has also returned insignificant amounts of money. (See *Duwamish et al. Tribes of Indians* v. *United States* 1934; *The Lummi Tribe of Indians* v. *United States* 1957. In the latter, some $57,000 was awarded to the Indians for the San Juan Islands and most of Whatcom County.) The treaties may be classified either as sophisticated forms of theft, or as some of the best real estate deals ever made.

Stevens had visions of being the first senator from the new state of Washington. His object was to clear the land of Indians as quickly as possible and to get the necessary population into the new territory, so that it would be eligible for statehood. With his eye fixed firmly on the nation's capital, Stevens did not try to clarify the provisions of any of the treaties; instead, he made them deliberately vague, so that there would be no outcry from the Indians before he could achieve higher political status (Josephy 1965: 293–294).

The Indians never understood the provisions of the treaties they were told to sign. They did not conceive of the western Cascade lands in terms of measurable distances, but as a series of river valleys and tributaries where their fishing villages were located. They could not understand why anyone would want inland tracts for agriculture, when everyone knew that the action was on the rivers. They did not ask very much for the lands they were ceding, because they did not use them in the manner in which the whites intended to use them.

The Lummis — whose annual migrations took them from the northern San Juan Islands to Lummi and Bellingham bays, along the Nooksack and Lummi rivers, and back to the San Juans—visualized this region not as an area with clearly defined boundaries, but as a series of sites to be occupied at certain times of the year. The Lummi concern was that traditional fishing stations and grounds should be guaranteed to them in perpetuity. Almost every treaty of the Northwest region specifically guaranteed to the tribes concerned the right to continue to make their living by fishing.

The difficulty in reviewing the treaties has been that Stevens deliberately used trickery in explaining the provisions of the various articles. He insisted on having the interpreter use the Chinook jargon, a conglomerate of sign language and code words that combined several Indian languages with French and English (American Friends Service Committee 1970: 16; Suttles 1954: 46–47). Chinook had been used by Indians and traders during the decade immediately preceding treaty negotiations; it was more of pidgin commercial shorthand than a language.

Thus, the Indians were given one understanding of the treaty provisions, while Stevens was busy writing up, in English, another version of what the documents contained. When asked if they would remove to the reservations that were to be established under the treaty, the Indians agreed; they could visualize only moving their fishing villages from one part of the region to another. Stern has listed seven widely scattered places where Lummis traditionally fished: Sxoletc (a point on Lopez Island opposite Lopez); Tceltenum (Point Roberts); Xoxalos (on Orcas Island, south of Freeman Island); Tlqwoloqs (Point Doughty, on Orcas Island); Xwitcosang (in Upright Channel, south of Shaw Island); Xwitcosang (Bee Station, north of Sandy Point on Lopez Island); and Village Point, on Lummi Island (Stern 1969: 126) (see Map 1).

The Lummis insisted that traditional fishing sites, grounds, and stations apart from the reservation be confirmed to them, so that they could continue to fish and bring their catches back to the villages, as before. They also insisted on continuing their traditional rights to pasture horses on the small meadows that dotted the forests and to dig camas and other roots in these grassy places. They wanted places to gather berries, to establish curing houses, and to gather shellfish. Stevens agreed to all the provisions and ignored how intimately the people were tied to the land and waters, and to the life that these supported.

By emphasizing the fact that "bad" men would come and kill the Indians if they did not remove to the reservations, Stevens got a reluctant gathering of Indians to touch the pen, indicating their acceptance of the treaty terms. It was said that "haste, high pressure, and no little chicanery on the part of the whites was predominant throughout the meetings from start to finish" (American Friends Service Committee 1970: 20).

The pertinent parts of the Point Elliott treaty, to which the Lummi were signatories, are important for understanding the historical problems of the tribe. Article V provided that:

· · · the right of taking fish at usual and accustomed grounds and stations is further secured to said Indians in common with all citizens of the Territory, and of erecting temporary houses for the purpose of curing, together with the privilege of hunting and gathering roots and berries on open and unclaimed lands. Provided, however, that they shall not take shellfish from any beds staked or cultivated by citizens (7 Stat.).

The distinction between fishing "grounds" and fishing "stations" may yet prove to be critical to contemporary economic development of the Lummi people. Fishing grounds, it would appear, refer primarily to river fishing, which at the time of the treaties involved weir fishing but is today done with gill nets. Fishing stations, however, seem to refer to reef netting, which is practiced in deeper waters with the apparatus previously described. The treaty apparently has preserved both kinds

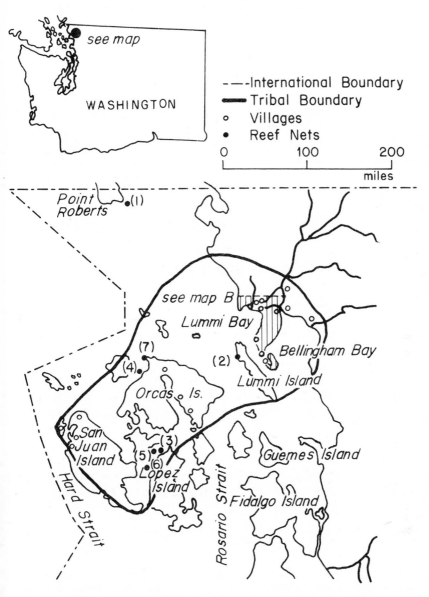

Map 1. Historic Lummi village and reef net sites; (1) Point Roberts, (2) Village Point, (3) Bee Station, (4) Orcas Island, (5) Upright Channel, (6) Lopez Island, (7) Point Doughty

of fishing for the tribe, as a superior and prior right over anyone else who may wish to use the natural resources of the area.

In Article II of the treaty, four reservations were established for the Point Elliott tribes, to be established in two sections each at four different points. The Lummis received the land between the main channel of the Nooksack River and its tributary, the Lummi River, which emptied into Lummi Bay near the site of the present aquaculture.

Article VII considered the creation of a large reservation some time in the future, for all of the Indians of the treaty area. So it provided that the president could remove the Indians from the reservations delineated in Article II if, in his opinion, the interests of the territory and the welfare of the Indians made such a move necessary. During the period of allotment it became necessary to add to the original area of the Lummi reservation in order that every individual tribal member have an allotment (Executive Order November 22, 1873). Article VII then came into effect, giving the president the executive power to extend the limits of the reservation from some 9,570 acres to more than 12,560 acres during allotment (*Duwamish et al. Tribes of Indians v. United States* 1934: 530, 549).

The final important provision of the treaty gave the future state of Washington the right to incorporate the reservation into the political system whenever it received Congressional approval to do so. White settlers did not make the Indians feel welcome in the county, however, so there was never any sustained move to give the Lummi equal political rights with other state citizens. The only effort of whites to accommodate the Lummis was the continual agitation in Bellingham newspapers, over a thirty year period, to give the Indians their lands in fee simple. This, of course, was a desire to get the Indian's lands, not a desire to vest them with full political rights. The *Bellingham Herald* (January 23, 1910; June 11, 1911) looked forward to the tidelines being used as factory sites by the whites of Bellingham, now that they believed they had forced the reservation lands open to themselves.

EARLY RESERVATION DAYS (1855–1890)

A general survey of the conditions of the Lummi people during the first three decades of reservation life provides a necessary background for discussing the sharpening conflict that the early decades of the twentieth century were to bring. The general data available on this period is the *Annual report of the Commissioner of Indian Affairs* series, which gives the reports of the various agents assigned to federal Indian reservations. These reports outline the expectations of the federal government and Christian churches rather than those of the Indian people.

Several themes consistently run through these reports. One theme concerns the continuing problem of the missionary: how to make the Indians conform to Christian ideas of religious and moral behavior, while the neighboring whites were busy breaking every commandment in the book. The frustration is compounded when the "falling away" of the Indians from missionary teachings is held to be the reason for their "inability" to become successful farmers.

Actually, the Lummis apparently fit into the neighboring economy as well as they were able or desired to — but their chief preoccupation was the preservation of their fishing. Reports on the Lummi are scattered and vary considerably, but close examination reveals the range of activities that Indian agents felt demonstrated the Lummi acculturation to white social and economic forms. (This attitude, evidenced again in the 1950's and 1960's, caused the Bureau of Indian Affairs to neglect the Lummi business council, which gave it the chance to plan the aquaculture project.)

E. C. Fitzhugh, the first agent to record anything of note with respect to the Lummi, wrote in the annual report that:

As a general thing their women are very industrious, and do most of the work, and procure the principal part of their sustenance; they cultivate potatoes, and generally have a superabundance, so that they dispose of a great many to the whites, by which means they procure the greater part of their clothing. They have an abundance of fish; salmon is the principal stand-by, also shell fish of all kinds; *in fact, I think I never saw a country so well adapted for the Indians to live in as this* (Commissioner of Indian Affairs 1857: 326; emphasis added).

Fitzhugh had come to the Lummi reservation just two years after the treaty of Point Elliott; thus, he had not yet been prejudiced by the formal federal policies toward acculturating the Indians. Within two years, however, a sterile pattern of analysis is apparent in the attitudes and outlook of the Indian agents. B. F. Shaw began the long series of reports emphasizing the agricultural program for the Lummis. He reported:

The Lummis are at home on the reservation, and are well pleased with the location, and are very anxious to get a team and plows, so that they can go to work on a large scale. There is under cultivation on this reservation (mostly in potatoes) thirty-five or forty acres of land, about six or seven acres of which are attached to the agency, and the remainder on the two branches of the Lummi (Commissioner of Indian Affairs 1859:767).

But whites were already making trouble for the Lummis; Shaw recounted that he had "also been informed that some whites have taken claims (since the treaties were confirmed) on the reservation, for the purpose of bringing claims against the government." He recommended that the reservation be surveyed as quickly as possible to avoid a confrontation (1859: 768).

Farming continued to be emphasized by the Indian agents, who frequently had to bend to the obvious facts of life. The reservation was heavily forested with Douglas fir, and farming required clearing the land. A sawmill was built, and the wood that was cleared was used to build houses. Thus, in 1865 C. C. Finkbonner was able to state enthusiastically in his annual report (1865: 74) that "we built seven good substantial houses with shingle roofs, chimneys, etc., cleared off about thirty acres of new land, and planted about one hundred and fifty acres in potatoes and vegetables" (Commissioner of Indian Affairs 1865: 74). Clearly the bureau was concerned with full agricultural development of the reservation.

But Finkbonner was to discover that the old cultural habits died hard. He advocated good housing as "more conducive" to the acculturation of the Indians than any other thing the government could provide, yet he noted that, even with good housing, "most Indians naturally yield their lands and old homes very reluctantly to move and live on the reservations." A small band, probably the Mount Baker Nooksacks, "persistently refuse to come and live on the reservation. They tell me other Indians on the sound are permitted to live, build, and roam at will, and they think the same privilege ought to be extended to them, which is in a measure true" (Commissioner of Indian Affairs 1867: 58–59).

The life of an Indian agent must have been very bitter. To the south the Upper Skagits continued to live in the Cascades, refusing to take allotments or to come into the reservations. Upriver from the Lummis, the Nooksacks continued to hunt and fish; whites defended the Indian right to remain in high country, even though some people occasionally sided with the agent and demanded that all Indians go to the reservations. (The *Bellingham Bay Mail* on March 14, 1874, demanded that all Indians go to the reservation; on February 20, 1875, it demanded that they be left alone off the reservation.) And Indians from British Columbia continued to visit the American tribes, stirring up trouble and refusing to acknowledge the authority of Indian agents (*Bellingham Bay Mail*, July 12, 1873).

Finkbonner's report of 1867 contained the first exhaustive statement of life on the Lummi reservation (1867: 58–59). The agent apparently did not see that the Lummi people were gradually adapting to a modified fishing economy, for he still enthusiastically endorsed farming as the future for the Lummi:

These Indians cultivate their land in severalty, i.e. each head of family clears off and cultivates from one to four acres, the principal crop being potatoes. There is planted in all this spring about 150 acres in potatoes and other vegetables, and five acres in wheat. These Indians raise all the potatoes and vegetables they can eat, and sell all they can find a market for, which enables them to buy their necessities, such as flour, clothing, groceries, etc., etc.

It is very difficult for me to approximate at anything near the amount of principal labor performed on a reservation. I will, however, give some of the principal labor performed: First, in clearing off the land and planting their crops in the spring, and hoeing during the summer; second, in gathering berries, which grow in great abundance and variety. Those which prove the most profitable are the cranberry.

From June to October salmon commence running, during which time all the Indians are engaged taking, curing, and salting for winter use. During the winter months they are engaged in various occupations; some are employed by the whites; some are engaged in the chase and hunt, and others are at work on the reservation, making canoes, and improvements around home.

The Indians also make all the shingles used on the reservation, cut roads, make repairs and other improvements for their comfort, etc., etc.

Finkbonner obviously regarded fishing as a part-time occupation for the Lummis.

The federal government was determined to transform the Indian fisherman into farmers, and agents could do no more than try to be optimistic about the whole program (Suttles 1954: 64). Thus, Finkbonner compiled a list of the livestock owned by the Lummi (1867: 59); he included 15 head of cattle, 50 swine, 500 chickens, 150 ducks and geese, and 5 horses as evidence of his success as their reservation farmer. In 1870 his report listed the occupations and sources of income for the Lummis. Of a total of $12,939.52, more than half came from incidental jobs and products not directly related to farming (1870:43–44).

Finkbonner's successors continued the practice of issuing very optimistic reports on Lummi agriculture. Patrick Buckley in the annual report of 1885 commented on their fine farming practices (1885: 169). W. H. Talbot, Buckley's successor, made long lists of the crops that had been raised by the Lummi, as if he were personally responsible for planting and harvesting them (Commissioner of Indian Affairs 1888: 217, 1889: 229).

Throughout this period, no agent seemed to understand that farming was at best a marginal operation, that it could not support an expanding population, nor that it required an increasingly complicated investment in machines and techniques, which were far beyond the financial and educational means of the Indians who had been limited to allotments of 40 acres by the Coke Act. Lummi farming success had crested by 1891 or 1893 (Suttles 1954: 76; Taylor 1969: 65). Reports became less optimistic and it became increasingly obvious that the Lummi people were indeed fishermen, not farmers.

By 1895 Indian agents were forced to admit that the program had not succeeded in stamping out the Lummi culture and turning the people into sedate farmers. The annual report of that year chronicles the admission by the federal government that the Lummi had survived the agricultural phase of government programs intact (1895: 319):

The Indians, as a rule, are not systematic farmers. Farming is with them the incident and not the business of everyday life. Some of them, the more thrifty and industrious, have well-cultivated farms and comfortable houses, and are anxious to have their children educated. They generally live like white people. *Those, however, are the exception. A large majority spend most of their time in their canoes, fishing, especially during the salmon season.* In the summer they are absent most of the time picking berries. In early fall, with few exceptions, all, little and big, young and old, go to the hop fields, where they meet old friends from all over the sound and east of the mountains. Here they drink, gamble, and, as they say, have a good time generally. This annual pilgrimage to the hop fields is very demoralizing and positively injurious; but as it has been their custom for many years, and always permitted by former agents, I did not feel justified in interfering with what they seemed to regard as one of their vested rights (Commissioner of Indian Affairs 1895: 319, emphasis added).

Farming activities continued to expand until just before World War I, when nearly half the reservation was given to cultivated crops, berries, or orchards (Taylor 1969: 64). But agriculture did not produce sufficient cash income to allow the Lummis to live as well as they had before the arrival of whites in their land. They had to find wage jobs to supplement farming, and they regarded farming as supplemental to fishing.

A variety of other occupations beckoned to them. Shortly after the fishing season in 1871, Felix Brunot visited the Lummi reservation on a good will tour for President Grant and was disturbed to find that it had not yet been surveyed and confirmed to them (Commissioner of Indian Affairs 1871, Appendix A, d. No. 4). Brunot got the reservation established two years later; another result of his visit seems to have been a sawmill, which was erected in 1872 to clear reservation lands and provide lumber for houses.

The reservation sawmill enabled Lummi men to learn skills in the lumbering industry, which was booming in Whatcom County, and many Lummi people began to regard lumber camps as a source of income to supplement that received from fishing. In the 1904 annual report, agents acknowledged that lumbering and fishing-related activities provided the main sources of Lummi income (Commissioner of Indian Affairs 1904: 336). In 1900 there were said to be "sixty-eight mills in Whatcom County employing 1200 men" (Taylor 1969: 67). Lummi men undoubtedly provided a percentage of these workers.

Fishing remained the favorite occupation of the Lummi people. In their early contacts with whites, they provided fish oil for use as a lubricant in lumbering, and they continued to fish for this purpose

(Suttles 1954: 61). Large companies began to establish fish canneries along the west coast of upper Washington in the 1880's; the Lummis sold their fish to the companies and also worked in the canneries. In 1893 the canneries at Semiahmoo and Point Roberts employed 140 Indians (Taylor 1969: 67).

The Struggle to Preserve Treaty Rights

The precipitous decline in the Lummi standard of living during the 1880's and into the 1960's can best be understood in terms of the ongoing struggle of the tribe to preserve its treaty right to fish in usual and accustomed places. The legal history of the tribe is unique, indicating a protection of the tidelands that seems almost predestined for creation of the aquaculture project.

Generally, treaty fishing rights of Indians were protected during the period of territorial government. At first, whites were satisfied to buy fish from the Indians, and it was not until the 1880's that they began aggressive commercial fishing. In 1880 the Alaska Packers Association set up a fish trap at Point Roberts, just outside the area that had been reserved for the Lummi as a traditional fishing ground (Taylor 1969: 40). The Lummis, enticed to the site by liquor, had apparently helped to build the fish trap and were thus implicated in the machinations of the company.

From earliest times, the Lummi had trekked annually to Point Roberts, where they had extensive reef nets for catching the salmon that swam upstream to spawn in summer and early fall. The sockeye run usually appeared early in July and lasted for a period of about twenty days. Other species returned to the nearby river later, so the site continued to be profitable.

In 1893 the state of Washington passed a law regulating the construction of fish traps and authorizing the issuance of licenses for the construction, maintenance, and operation of fish traps and appliances for catching salmon. The licensing meant that reef nets and other gear used by Indians could not be used near the fish traps. In effect, it precluded Indian fishing (Laws of Washington 1893: 15).

The annual report of 1898 includes this wistful statement:

The Alaska Packing Company and other cannery companies have practically appropriated all the best fishing grounds at Point Roberts and Village Point, where the Lummi Indians have been in the habit of fishing from time immemorial. The State legislature, at its last session, passed an act imposing a tax upon all persons fishing with nets within its waters, and at the same time prohibiting persons using nets from fishing within 240 feet of any fish trap (Commissioner of Indian Affairs 1898: 297).

Point Roberts had been government land, but an American named Kate Waller had leased part of her homestead to the Alaska Packers Association, a large corporate group that dominated the fish-canning industry in the northern part of the state. The company constructed a massive series of traps, which took almost all the fish that were legally available under Washington law.

The United States sued Mrs. Waller and the Alaska Packers Association on behalf of the Lummi, contending that the treaty gave tribal members the right to fish at the site, it being a "usual, traditional, and accustomed fishing ground" (*United States et al.* v. *Alaska Packers Association* 1897: 152, 153). The judge disregarded the provisions of the fifth article of the Treaty of 1855, indicating that although the evidence did seem to give a favored position to the Indians he felt that fishing only in the traditional and accustomed manner of white citizens had been intended.

The court found that the tribe had no easement on the lands because of the treaty and that the lands, having passed to private ownership under the state, were subject to state law. The evidence presented to the court tended to cloud the issue of fishing rights. The Lummis usually sold their catch to the canning company and usually had access to other species of salmon on the same grounds at different times of the year. Judge Hanford implied that a decision favorable to the Lummis would prejudice their profitable relationships with the canning company. He remarked that such a decision might possibly put the company out of business, which would result in Lummis losing their cannery jobs and suffering an economic loss. The court did not feel that losing the primary resource, the sockeye salmon, was an economic loss to the Indians.

In making his decision, the judge remarked that in interpreting the Point Elliott treaty provisions he had used the same rationale in deciding two other Indian treaty cases, *United States* v. *Winans* 1896, involving the Yakimas, and *The James G. Swan Case* 1892, involving the Makah treaty. The Winans case, like the Lummi suit against the Alaska Packers, contested the interpretation of fishing rights in accustomed fishing stations and grounds, and the Swan case dealt with the rights of the Makah Indians to hunt seals in the northern waters.

The Alaska Packers case was appealed to the Supreme Court after the United States Attorney requested permission, remarking that "testimony in the case is very voluminous and that an appeal would be expensive, but that the Government ought not to hesitate on the ground of expense to carry out its obligation to the Indians" (Commissioner of Indian Affairs 1897: 93–94). The case was dismissed on stipulation of the same attorney who was supposed to defend the Lummi treaty rights. The appeal on the Winans case straggled through the federal court system and was not heard by the Supreme Court until 1905, nearly nine years later. In the meantime the court had changed and now viewed the treaty provisions entirely differently. The Supreme Court reversed the decision of Judge Hanford, commenting adversely on his interpretation of the article and following the original interpretation advocated by the Lummi tribe.

Meanwhile, the state did not hesitate to harass the Lummi people as they pursued their legally established right to fish. In 1906, Francis Celestin, a Lummi, was arrested for fishing without a state license at a point directly offshore from the reservation (*Bellingham Herald*, October 5 and 6, 1906). The Indians testified that they were fishing for salmon to dry and salt for winter use and that they had been fishing well within reservation boundaries. One aspect of the case was the determination of the reservation boundary, which was to create immense problems in later years. The Lummi won the case.

Less than seven years later the issue was in court again. A story in the *Bellingham Herald* related that:

In order to bring about a final and peaceful settlement of the differences existing between the state fish commissioner and the Lummi Indians, and in order to establish definitely the redskins' rights under the Treaty of 1868, the prearranged arrest of Harry Price, a Lummi Indian, will be effected by the commissioner in order that the case may be taken direct either into the state supreme court or the district federal court. Attorney R. W. Greene, who has represented the Indians in recent similar cases, had announced that the arrest will be made for the express purpose of having the higher courts determine whether or not the Indians can fish outside their reservation lands without licenses (*Bellingham Herald*, November 7, 1913).

The Indians won this case, too, and it was officially decreed that they could fish outside the reservation without state licenses. But the state commissioner, who had cooperated in setting up the test case, refused to be bound by the court decision. His arbitrary actions against Indians led to a massive protest by the tribes of the upper Puget Sound region less than two years later. Federal officials ignored the issue, leaving the local Indians and their attorneys to carry on the fight.

The Lummi fishermen asked for a permanent injunction to restrain the state fish commissioner from interfering with their fishing. The *Bellingham Herald* related:

··· at least it will force Commissioner Darwin to come into court and file informations to which demurrers can be taken, something which, the petition recites, he has heretofore refused to do. Instead in each instance where he has had Indians arrested for alleged unlawful fishing off the shore of Lummi Island he has refused to file any information of facts or showing that the fishermen were Indians or claimed any treaty rights, or at the time of their arrest they were fishing at any 'usual and accustomed ground or station' as provided by treaty (*Bellingham Herald*, January 15, 1916).

The Indian strategy would have worked with anyone who felt impelled to follow the laws of the land or to abide by the laws of the state. However, the article outlined Darwin's attitude thus:

As for the court's decision, Commissioner Darwin has said that he would not be bound by it, the petition says, but would continue not only to arrest the petitioners, but would file informations of the same character as those already filed. In brief, it seems, according to the petition, that Mr. Darwin has determined to make it as troublesome and expensive as possible for Lummi tribesmen in an effort to make them live up to his interpretation of the law, and at the same time afford them no opportunity to demur (*Bellingham Herald*, January 15, 1916).

One of the Indians involved in the suit against Commissioner Darwin was Dan Ross, the Indian who had already been cleared two years earlier in the test case.

Darwin bided his time and, a year later, involved the Lummis in a serious confrontation. An Austrian-owned commercial fishing boat came into the Lummi fishing grounds to fish for halibut. The Lummi refused to allow them to fish, and Darwin, with the county sheriff, filed a series of charges against them. State officials backed the Austrians, even though they were not United States citizens, and claimed that the Lummi reservation did not extend seaward from the high-tide line. The United States Attorney sided with the state officials.

Then, the Lummis arrested the Austrians and held them at the reservation home of August Lane. With foreign citizens being held on the reservation, the Bureau of Indian Affairs began to consider the situation serious; Dr. Buchanan, the agent at Tulalip, came to Bellingham and talked with the Lummis, who informed him of Darwin's persistent attitude toward their fishing. Buchanan backed the Lummi fishermen against the state and the Department of Justice in Seattle. Then it became known that Darwin had deliberately told the Austrians to fish in Hale Passage, which was definitely within the reservation waters. The Austrians, who had debarked on the reservation beach to unload their purse seine and had been arrested by Indian police, were finally released. Darwin continued to make false charges against the Indians, however.

The Lummis had won cases in 1913, 1915, and 1916, and by now it should have been obvious to the people of Bellingham and surrounding areas that the law supported the Lummi right to fish in waters near the reservation. But the state continued its harassment. In September of 1918 three Lummis were arrested for fishing without a license (*Bellingham Herald*, September 10, 1918). They were made to plead guilty and then let off, foreclosing any appeal of the arrest.

Four years later, a Lummi, John Finkbonner, and the Lummi Bay Packing Company were both fined — Finkbonner for fishing out of season and the company for buying the fish he had caught (*Bellingham Herald*, October 19 and November 16, 1922). This pattern of persecution and arbitrary action has continued. The Indians have rarely lost a fishing rights case — yet state and county officials seem determined to reject the decisions of state and federal court systems, which have upheld the Indian rights to fish.

The moral case for Indian rights was presented several times by the agent who supervised the Tulalip and Lummi reservations. He noted that the government had been notoriously lax in defending Indian fishing rights and that it appeared to the Indians as if laws existed primarily to assist the white man in depriving the Indians of their ancient means of subsistence (see Appendix).

In 1948, the Lummi Tribal Council was browbeaten by local whites into closing their river to Indian fishing during the fall salmon run, as an "effort to rebuild the Nooksack salmon stock." A year later, under severe political pressure from the Bellingham Sportsmen's Club, Lummi tribal officials were again forced to close the river for a period of ten days, as a conservation measure. Lummi tribal officials had to come to Bellingham and meet state fisheries director Alvin Anderson and, in the presence of Bruce Lintz, president of the sportsmen's club, sign the formal agreement; local whites were not content with merely breaking the law — they insisted on humiliating the Lummis, in addition (*Bellingham Herald*, September 20, 1948; November 22, 1949).

By 1959 the state fisheries department had so coerced the Indians of Washington that it was able to publicize a list of the most "cooperative tribes" — those that had practically given up fishing (*Bellingham Herald*, November 5, 1959). The Lummi fought back. After propaganda was put out by the State Sportsmen's Council accusing the Indians of destroying the salmon in the state, tribal chairman Forrest Kinley pointed out that in a recent "fishing derby" sportsmen had taken 7,000 salmon in one weekend — more than the Lummi fishermen had caught in all of 1959 (*Bellingham Herald*, November 3, 1961).

The local sportsmen's group continued its persecution of the Lummi fishermen, however. Once again, in 1964, a meeting was called to force the Lummi into accepting new regulations on their fishing. This meeting was sponsored by the Bellingham Chamber of Commerce and was marked, as usual, by the absence of officials from the Bureau of Indian Affairs or other federal agencies who might well be expected to defend the Lummis' court-established rights to fish. At no time was it ever suggested that the sportsmen consider regulating themselves, although they fish for recreation, while the Indians fish to provide food for their families and to derive a small income from the sale of fish (*Bellingham Herald*, March 10, 1964).

The struggle of the Lummi people against the unfair, immoral, and arbitrary rejection of state laws has been spectacular and not without its dramatic confrontations. The issue of traditional fishing grounds and stations has not yet been resolved. It is not the fault of the Lummis, who have been upheld in every case involving their reservation fishing, except the first one in 1897. Rather, the solution of the problem lies in getting officials who will uphold and enforce the laws and court decisions.

The clashes over fishing rights have partially obscured the fight that the Lummi tribe has also waged against the efforts of the state to take their tidal lands. In this struggle, too, court decisions have upheld the tribe on every point that the state has raised. The story began with the continuing refusal of the federal government to survey the Lummi reservation. When President Grant's representative Felix Brunot visited the Lummis in 1871, he held a council with the tribe's elders and noted their frustration at not being able to have their lands surveyed (Commissioner of Indian Affairs 1871: Appendix A. d. No. 4).

The president set aside the Lummi reservation by executive order in 1871. The order gave the Lummi tribe a little more land than had originally been set aside, because in the interim between the signings of the treaty and the surveying of the lands the Nooksack River had shifted (*Lummi Tribe of Indians* v. *United States* 1957). The key phrase in the order, however, was that the reservation was to extend to the low-tide mark. This inexplicit language was not common in treaties; the Treaty of Medicine Creek, for example, mentioned fishing grounds but did not describe the reservation boundaries to include waters to which the Indians had exclusive rights.

The Romaine Case (1919)

The Romaine case was triggered by the sale of tidelands to Romaine and other whites by the state of Washington (*United States* v. *Romaine et al.* 1919). The group was made up primarily of prominent citizens of Bellingham who based their case on the interpretation of the nature of grants by the federal government regarding streams and waters of public lands. They contended that the authority of the president to "move the reservations, if necessary," (included in Article 7 of the Point Elliott treaty of 1855) was fulfilled in a surveyor's report that appeared to shorten the boundaries of the reservation to the farthest western channel of the Nooksack River.

Previous case law indicated that grants by the government of public lands bounded on streams or other waters without reservation or restriction were to be construed in accordance with the laws of the state if the land lay within the state, or in accordance with the common law if it lay within a territory. Romaine contended that "a reservation to Indians of land on tidewater in Washington Territory is presumed to extend to high-water marks only." (Romaine's point appeared to be substantiated by *Pollard* v. *Hagan* 1845, and *Shively* v. *Bowlby* 1893.)

Such an interpretation would have effectively cut off the Lummis from the water, thus negating the obvious intent of the treaty. However, the Quilleute reservation had been denied rights to tidelands earlier so the case was not without either precedent or peril to the Lummi tribe. The tribe lost the case in the federal district court for the northern district of Washington, but it was reversed on appeal to the Ninth Circuit Court in San Francisco. (The *Bellingham Herald* on January 10, 1919, deplored the court's ruling for "interested Indians" against "disinterested whites.")

The case was not appealed to the United States Supreme Court, and the tidelands were confirmed as Lummi tribal land. Perhaps the most important effect of the decision was the reaffirmation by the circuit court of the traditional doctrine of land titles as confirmed to Indian tribes in treaties. Citing the decision of *Gaines* v. *Nicholson* 1850, a landmark decision on Choctaw lands made half a century earlier, the court stated that the Lummi title, which was derived from the Treaty of 1855, and the subsequent executive order, which established the reservation, were confirmation of the aboriginal title of the Lummi; not a grant by the federal government of lands to them. This decision refuted the state's contention that the tidelands became state property upon its admission to the Union.

The Stotts Case (1930)

Eleven years after the Romaine case had settled the tidelands issue, the Stotts case attempted relitigation of the same issue under slightly different conditions. Allotments had been made to individual Indians in 1884 under the Coke bill, and some of the shoreline allotments had been sold. When Stotts and his friends purchased shore allotments, the state of Washington then attempted to give them title to the tidelands immediately adjoining their tracts of land.

The legal question involved definition of allotment boundaries. Did they extend into the water to include the beach and tidelands? If so, were the tidelands included in any sale by individual Indian allottees? Two cases appeared to dominate this legal question. In *Taylor et al.* v. *United States* 1930, the court had denied the Quilleute tribe's ownership of tidelands, and *United States* v. *Holt* 1931 in Minnesota had denied title to the Red Lake Chippewa of lands uncovered by the draining of a lake on their reservation.

The circuit court ruled that, although the highlands of the reservation had been allotted, not all of the tribe had received allotments. The tidelands had been common property and, therefore, were considered exempt from allotment. It would have been grossly unfair to tribal members who held inland tracts to have included tidelands in the shoreland allotments.

It is significant that the court took official notice of the fact that the Lummi Indians, at the time of the treaty, had subsisted on hunting and fishing and that they had been promised the right to continue this type of existence by Article V of the Point Elliott agreement. The tidelands were not merely preserved — they were preserved specifically for tribal hunting and fishing activities.

The Lummis had turned back two efforts to take their tidelands away from them. The Romaine decision generally upheld their rights as federally recognized Indians against the state of Washington; the Stotts decision defined the distinction between tribally owned lands and individual allotments. The next year, another case was to finally confirm, beyond doubt, the tribal ownership of tidelands for tribally defined uses.

The Boynton Case (1931)

When John Snow surveyed the Lummi reservation in 1873, he had to indicate the general meanders of the shoreline for allotments bordering the water. When allotments were mapped, the beach side was indicated by a general line describing the high-water mark in 1873.

Lot 1, a triangular plot on a headland, was assigned to Tsumilano, a tribal member. Tsumilano died in 1929, and his heirs sold the land to Boynton and others. Had the shoreline remained the same during the interval between 1873 and 1928, the situation would have been covered by the Stotts case. But it had not. Instead, the sea had deposited land in some places and had eroded it in others, changing the shoreline.

The question before the court involved the determination of the nature of the lines drawn in 1873. If they were held to be rigid, then the deposition and erosion had given some tidelands to the groups represented by Boynton and his friends — thus effectively breaking the tribal stranglehold on tide flats. However, if the lines describing the shoreline were only meander lines indicating high water in 1873, the shifting of the shoreline would change the shape of the allotment. Then, the actual area of the tract would follow the shore and not the description lines: when the tract was eroded, land would be lost; when the water deposited land, the tract would grow larger.

Relying on the testimony of an Indian who had been Snow's surveying chain man, the Ninth District Court of Appeals interpreted the lines of the survey as meander lines, thus denying tidelands to Boynton. (Judge Jeremiah Neterer, who had decided against the Lummis in both the Romaine and Boynton cases in federal district court, was overruled on appeals of the cases to the higher court in San Francisco.)

The three cases, taken together as a series, effectively established total ownership of the tidelands for the Lummi people. The state of Washington was precluded from claiming a right to pass title to whites. The tribe was singularly fortunate in that these legal decisions were made at a time when no one realized that the Lummis would someday find a way to make the tide flats commercially valuable. The courts in Washington have been notoriously predatory in their seizure of Indian lands, and it is doubtful that the Lummis could receive a fair hearing today on this question.

Both state and federal courts have failed to approach Lummi treaty rights in a consistent manner. Rights to fish within reservation waters and at traditional fishing grounds and stations, guaranteed by treaty, have been buffeted about. Yet in the tidelands case, hunting and fishing rights were the basis of court interpretation that the tidelands were specifically reserved for Lummi tribal activity. The legal distinction between the two conflicting doctrines is puzzling, at best.

THE YEARS OF POVERTY (1890–1964)

The fishing rights struggle dominated Lummi relations with the formal world of political structures, from 1890 until the mid-1960's. The whites of Whatcom County maintained a consistent anti-Indian attitude during these years, and newspaper reports indicate that their primary desire was to take over the Lummi lands and turn Bellingham Bay into a seaport and industrial center rivaling Seattle. Witness the special story in the *Bellingham Herald*:

Few people realize that at last the great fight for the opening of the Lummi Indian Reservation has been virtually won, and that from now on it is only a matter of time until a huge area of tidelands flats will be available for Bellingham Bay factory sites and from 12,000 and 13,000 acres of the finest agricultural land in the Northwest opened for development. It is more than probable that at least fairly big cities will be established in the course of time at Lummi Bay and Birch Bay, which is already fairly well settled, and that direct access will be given to the people of the Mountain View section into the City of Bellingham. In addition to all this a quick route will probably be established to Lummi Island and the whole fertile section opened up by railroad transportation.

The tidelands at Marietta comprise from 15 to 20 square miles and are of such a nature that they may be easily reclaimed. These being added to Bellingham's resources, will give this city factory and industrial possibilities such as are to be found in or near no other town on the whole entire Pacific coast (*Bellingham Herald*, June 11, 1911).

As early as 1891, the local press had advocated that Lummi lands be sold to local whites and that the money be invested in securities. "This plan," the *Bellingham Bay Express* noted, "if adopted, would wrong no one, but would assist the Indians now living and add very materially to the wealth of our county by getting under cultivation some of the splendid land which is now primeval forest and doing nobody any good" (June 9, 1891). The writer had not been out to Lummi very often if he considered it still to be a "primeval forest." The annual report for 1889 had reported the following agricultural products for that year: "6,000 bushels of oats, 10,000 bushels of potatoes, 2,000 bushels of turnips, 3,000 bushels of other vegetables, 600 pounds of butter and 300 tons of hay." (Commissioner of Indian Affairs 1889: 229). By 1893 agriculture had begun to decline, as previously noted, but the reservation was hardly a forest. That year the Lummis produced "50 bushels of wheat, 500 bushels of oats, 1,000 bushels of potatoes, 1,180 bushels of other vegetables, 214 tons of hay, 1,000 pounds of butter, 50 cords of wood." The Lummis had 192 horses, 500 cattle (presumably dairy cattle), 400 swine, 700 sheep and 1,200 domesticated fowl (Commissioner of Indian Affairs 1893: 505).

Agitation for Lummi lands continued to increase throughout the 1890's and by 1904 was getting results. Local pressure had crystallized in a petition to bridge the Nooksack at Marietta and build a road through the reservation that would link Bellingham with the farms of whites at Birch Bay (*Bellingham Herald*, May 18, June 8, and June 29, 1904). Such a road would obviously increase the value of the Lummi lands when they were finally obtained by non-Indians.

By 1909 the white businessmen of Whatcom County were united in their determination to get the reservation lands. Ed Brown, Whatcom County's state senator, asked the state legislature to memorialize Congress to open the Lummi reservation for white settlement (*Bellingham Herald*, February 8, 1909). The lands had already been allotted in 1884, so it is obvious that sale of the lands was intended. C. T. Canfield, on behalf of the Bellingham Chamber of Commerce, began a new plat of the Lummi reservation. According to a story in the *Bellingham Herald*:

The new plat will cover the entire area of the land, showing the portions best adapted for different lines of development in farming, stock raising and fruit growing. Statistics and all general data showing how much land is under cultivation now and the amount of good which will accrue to the county at large by having the tract open to white settlers will be gathered also, and according to the general opinion of the members of the committee the probabilities for changing the status of the land are very good (*Bellingham Herald*, October 1, 1909).

By early February the Bellingham Chamber of Commerce was holding weekly open meetings in an apparent attempt to stimulate citizen interest in getting reservation lands taken away from the Lummis and opened to non-Indians. The pressure was not sufficient to convince everyone, however; Congressman W. E. Humphrey warned that "the mere fact that the City of Bellingham sees in the reservation a commercial advantage would make the national legislature suspicious" (*Bellingham Herald*, September 4, 1909). Humphrey advised that the best he could do would be to get legislation allowing part of the allotments to be sold, with the remainder retained in federal trust as home sites.

The president of the chamber of commerce, W. R. Moultray, appealed to Secretary of the Interior Richard Ballinger for special permission to have the legal status of Lummi allottees "clarified"; that is to say, to find a way to force their allotments out of federal trust (*Bellingham Herald*, October 1, 1909). But Ballinger had a survey conducted on the reservation and determined that only nine out of sixty Lummis wanted to sell their lands. He promised to support Humphrey's original suggestion that the Lummis be allowed to sell parts of their allotments. By 1910 land sales had begun on the reservation. The lands that were sold belonged, strangely enough, to "non-competent Indians ... because many of the Indians owning choice farming lots are unable to make their living." (These reputed "incompetents," of course, were the very people that Ballinger, as secretary of the interior, was legally responsible to protect).

By 1911 the whites at Bellingham had won the struggle. A general act of Congress the previous year had allowed the Secretary of the Interior to issue patents to any Indian allottee at his request (U.S. *Statutes at Large* 1911, vol. 36, p. 855). It then became a simple matter to get the Indian drunk or in a financial crisis and take his land. The *Bellingham Herald* rejoiced at the prospect:

... the announcement that seven patents will be issued will undoubtedly be received with great joy by local residents. The granting of the patents will be the opening wedge for the opening of the entire reservation, comprising about 12,000 acres. Some of the finest agricultural land in the entire Northwest is within the confines of the Indian reserve and is lying idle when it might be yielding rich crops (*Bellingham Herald*, January 7, 1911).

But the Lummis did not exactly rush to sell their land. Many wanted to keep their allotments and live on the reservation, combining the income obtained from fishing, farming, and leasing their farm lands. The state of Washington, which had steadfastly maintained that Lummi lands were within state jurisdiction, now suddenly decided that Indian lands were federal property. The reason for this defection became clear in 1915. A destitute Lummi woman applied for a mother's pension and was disqualified from receiving it because her husband still owned 20 acres of land. So the court and the Indian agent decided that selling her husband's land might qualify her for the pension (*Bellingham Herald*, January 27, 1915).

Once the Lummis began to sell their lands, county officials began to agitate for the building of a road to Gooseberry Point, the southernmost tip of the reservation peninsula — and prime recreation land. For a period of nearly two years, pressure to build the road continued. At one point, two Lummis refused to sign a simple waiver of the right of way, which all the other allottees had accepted at the request of the Indian agent. They demanded a payment of $450 for the use of their lands. The whites of Bellingham immediately started a drive to raise the money. After several years of controversy during which, at one time, the county offered to invest $6,000, the road was finally built — by a special federal appropriation to "help the Lummis" (45 Stat. 902).

The agitation over the road was reported in the *Bellingham Herald* (March 18, September 30, and October 3, 1921). It was partially built, according to federal reports, by Whatcom County, when it was discovered that if it appeared to be an Indian project federal funds could be made available. A special appropriation of $20,000 was made in 1928 to help regravel (45 Stat. 366).

No sooner had the road been approved than the people of Bellingham were at it again. They proposed that a large diking project be started to reclaim some of the tide flats where the Lummi River had emptied into Lummi Bay. Two dikes were proposed, one to cost $50,000 and the other $1.1 million. Some 3,400 acres of tribally owned Lummi tidelands were involved in the project (*Bellingham Herald*, May 26, 1923). It was to be federally funded, with the lands recovered to be leased to white farmers and the income from the leases to be repaid to the federal treasury. All things considered, it was a most sophisticated swindle of the Lummi tribe.

The federal government approved the appropriations in the Act of March 16, 1926 (44 Stat. 211–212), and a sum of $65,000 was initially approved to begin the project. Assessments were to be levied against the Indian allottees at an interest rate of 5 percent annually. The appropriations continued sporadically for years (44 Stat. 841; 45 Stat. 200; 47 Stat. 1602; 49 Stat. 176, 1597, 1757; 52 Stat. 291). Not until the mid-1960's were the costs of the project finally canceled by the government (Public Law 89–190).

Throughout the years of this century, the Bureau of Indian Affairs has evidenced a steady determination to cooperate with the whites of Bellingham in opening Lummi lands to non-Indian settlement. The people of Bellingham lived with a fantasy: should they ever get control of the Lummi lands, their city would soon surpass Seattle as the industrial center of the northwest. The *Bellingham Herald* of June 11, 1911, includes an extensive article on this scheme. In the 1950's, when the policy of Congress was to "terminate" Indian tribes, the superintendent of the agency at Tulalip deliberately began to push shoreline allotments out of Lummi hands by virtually forcing sales. The tribe lost some 5,000 acres of individual allotments (see Map 2 for distribution of lands lost); more than 40 percent of the Lummi lands passed into non-Indian ownership during the 1950's (Lummi Indian Tribal OEDP 1968: 9).

The Lummi people should be compensated for the blatant breach of federal responsibilility that occurred during this century. In the mid-1950's, for example, shoreline allotments were sold at $100 an acre. Today they are worth between $10,000 and $20,000 an acre. Quite obviously there has been wrongdoing by the Bureau of Indian Affairs officials who sold these lands, when such a disparity of value develops in less than two decades.

The economic condition of the Lummi people continued to deteriorate. The lumber industry continued to clear the Douglas fir without making any provisions for reforestation. Lummi lands were logged fairly early and, as farming was gradually abandoned, they reverted to scattered patches of alder, vine maple, birch, and western cedar — none of commercial value (Taylor 1969: 11). By the late 1960's lumbering was not available to most Lummis because it required transportation to distant places of work (Taylor 1969: 76).

Hop picking remained a favorite migratory job. Hop picking was considered as work fit for Indians until the depression years of the 1890's. A letter from a "workingman" to the editor of the *Bellingham Bay Express* expresses the sentiment that during the economic crisis only whites should be hired to pick hops, as the "government provides a reservation for the Indians and gives them plenty, why have them compete with us?" (*Bellingham Bay Express*, August 23, 1893).

Initially the Lummis went to British Columbia only to pick hops, but gradually expanded their activity to include work in the fish canneries, making long and extensive trips around the Strait of Georgia region (*Bellingham Herald*, September 29, 1913). The circuit would start in the hop fields at Chilliwack, British Columbia, and after finishing this work the Lummis sought employment at the canneries located at Lummi Bay and Carlisle.

After fish traps were outlawed in 1935, more fish came up the

Nooksack River for the Lummis, but they were generally denied the right to go back to Point Roberts, their traditional reef-netting grounds. At the onset of World War II the Lummi began extensive purse-seine fishing. The wartime shortage of fishermen increased the individual catch and considerably raised the price received for fish. But whites were using the same fishing techniques and had much better access to funds for purchasing boats and equipment, so it was not until after the war that the Lummi were able to make any significant progress in this field.

During the late 1940's and early 1950's the fishing industry developed incredibly in the State of Washington (Taylor 1969: 41–45). Salmon runs were greater than any since the late 1920's, and the only requirement for commercial fishing was a state license. By the early 1950's the Lummis had 25 to 30 purse-seine boats operating regularly (Suttles 1954: 88). These boats required a crew of seven men and provided employment for most of the men on the reservation.

Financing the boats was a hazardous venture for the Lummi fishermen. A great many of the Lummi took out what came to be known as "first marine mortgages" (Taylor 1969: 50–52). Salmon-canning companies would lend the Indians money for purchase of the boats and gear, with the provision that the fish caught would be sold to the company. If the season were good, the Indian could redeem his boat at its end. If it were bad, he lost everything. One Lummi became rather prosperous and at one time owned three purse-seining boats.

The fishing industry, like other technical occupations, soon began improving its equipment, and this increased the cost of operating a boat far beyond the limited financial resources of the average Lummi. An indication of how quickly the costs escalated in this industry is seen in the cost of building the boats:

One Seattle builder, who wished to remain anonymous, claimed that the construction cost of a 57-foot steel seine boat, completely equipped, rose from $49,000 in 1955 to $133,000 in 1968. A second builder located in Blaine, suggested that for a 58-foot 'Alaska limit' boat, the price rose from $50,000 in 1945 to $110,000 in 1968 (Taylor 1969: 52).

It was obvious that the Lummis could not afford to compete with whites who had access to capital for the purchase of boats and equipment. Left to the mercy of the canning companies, most of the Lummi went broke and lost their boats. Some continued to fish — not as boat owners, but as hired men for corporate boats.

"The elimination of the purse seine fleet from the Lummi fishing economy was nothing short of catastrophic" according to one observer (Taylor 1969: 56). The men were forced back to gill-net fishing in the Nooksack River (Taylor 1969: 31; Suttles 1954: 88). Gill netting involves much smaller boats and depends primarily on the run of fish coming up river rather than on trips out into open water. By the late 1960's between 70 and 80 gill-netting skiffs were operated by the Lummi people on the Nooksack River and the tidal flats owned by the tribe. But gill netting provided less than a living wage. Sportsmen accused the Lummi of having destroyed the fish runs on the Nooksack, and the state fisheries department refused to stock the river until the Indians quit fishing it.

The accusation that the Indian had destroyed the Nooksack River fishery was ironic, indeed. Local writer Lottie Roth, perhaps not realizing that she was providing a dissident voice to the accusation, had written that:

As late as 1890 many farmers of Whatcom County pitchforked the lordly salmon out of the streams during the spring and summer spawning season, and used them by the wagonloads as fertilizer for the soil, or as feed for hogs. The latter soon became unprofitable, because the ration imparted a certain fishy or salmony flavor to the pork (Roth 1926: 66).

Ever since they had arrived in the region, whites had acted as if the salmon resources were virtually inexhaustible, and for a long period of time salmon were plentiful. But eventually the supply became exhausted because of overexploitation. The attitude of the local whites can be seen in an article from the *Daily Reveille:*

Pike, Goodfellow and other fishermen exported the following fish to British Columbia this year from Point Roberts: 174,861 fish weighing 1,041,655 pounds for which they received the sum of $25,442.28. The steamer Angeles also cleared for British Columbia with the following: 12,235 fish weighing 85,575 pounds, worth $1,078.75, making a grand total of 187,096 fish weighing 1,127,230 pounds worth $26,521.03. *It does not look as if any one had a monopoly, when a couple of fishermen without capital, and with one trap apiece can in a short season in the off year of the sockeye run, sell over* $26,000 *worth of fish, or nearly* 200,000 *salmon* (*Daily Reveille*, October 23, 1895; emphasis added).

The Lummis faced a real crisis economically during the 1930's when they had to sell their lands in order to remain solvent. The banning of fish traps alleviated the situation somewhat, and the purse-seining days of the 1950's provided a temporary source of income. On the whole, however, the tribe was greatly depressed economically. During the late 1950's and early 1960's the Bureau of Indian Affairs could well have applied its bureaucratic genius to the problem of Lummi economic development.

The bureau had spent the 1950's selling off the Lummi shorelands for a song. Its record over the previous decades had been just as sterling. It had gained increasing control over the lives and property of the Lummis in the first decade of the twentieth century, when it was given the task of administering the allotments for individual Indians and determining heirs of Indian estates.

In 1910 the Indian agent had stood by while a white man, M. J. Clarke, had taken Lummi water by running a pipe across the Indian lands (*Bellingham Herald*, September 22, 23, 1910). The bureau had stood by during the crisis with the Austrian fishermen — but not until several Lummis were arrested by the county sheriff. In 1921 Superintendent W. F. Dickens of the Tulalip Agency had casually allowed that he thought the Lummis were taxable by the county for their personal goods and for the poll tax. It has usually been the custom of civilized countries to pass laws prior to taxation and to refrain from taxing without any authority. The Lummi, following the advice of the BIA, paid their taxes, although if they had taken their case to court they would undoubtedly have won (*Bellingham Herald*, August 11, 1921).

The same fall that the Indians had been made taxable, their agent, Captain J. Shanners, took some of their money, went on a "drunk," and fled to British Columbia. Shanners had been highly recommended by the American Legion Post and was a Harvard graduate (either of which may have explained his behavior). The bureau quickly appointed another agent for the "incompetent" Lummis; their string of agents apparently were considered competent to conduct Lummi affairs, but no mention is made of the money ever being restored by the government (*Bellingham Herald*, November 3, 1921).

With this record, subsequent proposals for solving the economic problems of the Lummi that were developed by the BIA make a certain amount of sense. The bureau, convinced that the Lummi Indians, like the other tribes, were natural artisans, based its plans for their economic development on three arts and crafts projects. They visualized a number of cottage industries, combining to provide the Lummi people with sufficient income to survive.

LUMMI KNITTERS.   The first project was the Lummi knitters, a basic home industry in which women worked at home, knitting wool sweaters, wool socks, gloves, and caps. The program, established in 1964, depended primarily on the bureau's ability to invoke sympathy for the Indians and to conjure up purchases for the products of the Lummi women who remained home knitting, but it never developed a significant source of income. In 1967, this industry employed some 65 women, more than half of whom were Lummis and the remainder from other tribes. The total income of all 65 women for that year was $17,823, or an average of some $274.42 each. The program did not, needless to say, cut deeply into the poverty of the tribe (Taylor 1969: 73).

LUMMI WEAVERS.   Undeterred, the bureau established another industry that projected more optimistic returns. Lummi weavers, the pride and joy of the Portland Area Office of the BIA, was created by a loan from the bureau in 1963 of $30,000. It employed, at its height (if such a term can be used), about a dozen people who wove cloth and made finished garments for special order customers. The women also made dresses, place mats, and drapes. The program lasted until 1968 and paid an average $15,000 in wages annually. This industry thus returned something close to $1,000 to each of its employees every year.

One can conclude that the program was somewhat less than successful. When it went bankrupt in 1969, with a debt of some $24,000, it was apparent that the project could only have functioned with no loan to repay and a large subsidy for its workers (Taylor 1969: 74). This program was the "high-water mark" of BIA ideas for assisting the Lummis. Confident that the Lummi were incapable of being helped, the bureau thereafter left them alone, giving them sufficient flexibility to create aquaculture. In fact, this project was being discussed during the very weeks when the famous Lummi weavers went under; but the bureau failed to notice that anything was happening on the reservation.

LUMMI ARTS AND CRAFTS. The third major project of the Bureau of Indian Affairs was the Lummi arts and crafts program. In this program, Lummi men were encouraged to carve totem poles, women to make Christmas cards, and all to make other carvings and baskets. The project depended primarily on part-time workers. The total income for the Lummis in 1967 from this industry was $5,000 for nearly 30 Lummis. This meant an average of some $172.41 a year per person (Taylor 1969: 74).

It is difficult to be serious when evaluating the programs of the BIA in assisting the Lummi Indians to enter the economic mainstream of American life. The proposals made by the bureau were so incredibly bizarre, so ineptly planned, and so incapable of being sustained that one questions whether or not the bureau itself was serious. One note may be added to indicate the general progress of the BIA over the three-quarters of a century in which it had virtual control of the Lummi people. In 1911 the *Bellingham Herald* (June 11) indicated that the Lummis could anticipate an annual rental of $20 an acre for the lease of their lands. In 1967 the lease income "from 1,551 acres of farmland was $24,243 averaging $9.18 per acre" (Taylor 1969: 65). In 56 years the BIA had managed to reduce the value of the Lummi lands by half!

POLITICAL DEVELOPMENT

Originally, Lummi political structure was based on the strength of major families in the villages. The heads of these families owned the fishing sites, and tribal members with less status gathered around these families to join the fishing crews and general households of the leaders. The advent of reservation days meant that the United States government began to recognize the influence of family heads, considering them as "chiefs" in the sense that the plains and eastern woodlands leaders had been considered chiefs (Suttles 1963: 513, 514).

Catholic missionaries seemed to consider their leading converts to be the leaders of the community, and during the merging of spirit dancing and Christian services several Lummis apparently held the reins of leadership in both camps (Suttles 1957: 359). During the first decades of the present century, the Lummi men who resisted the constant intrusion on their fishing grounds can be said to have led the community, and economic leadership undoubtedly passed to the owners of purse-seine boats in the 1950's.

The organization of formal political structures appears to have been triggered by the Indian Reorganization Act of 1934. BIA representatives visited most of the tribes in the upper reaches of the state and explained the provisions of the law in a perfunctory manner. When this task had been accomplished — and few Indians in the state understood what the whole thing was about — elections were called on the various reservations to determine whether or not the tribes would accept the act. The Lummis turned down the Indian Reorganization Act but recognized the value of having a formal government through which they could deal with the federal government.

In 1937 the Lummi tribe gathered as a general council, somewhat in the tradition of their village meetings of the distant past, and adopted a constitution and bylaws. Under this new constitution the highest political body of the tribe was the general council, which was formed from all the enrolled members of the tribe. The general council had annual elections to choose members of the Lummi Indian Business Council, a smaller committee-type structure that could conduct business for the tribe between meetings of the general council (Lummi Overall Development Plan 1969: 10).

Terms of the members of the Lummi Indian Business Council were for three years with a certain number of positions filled each year. (Candidates run "at large," so each election serves as a sort of referendum on current tribal programs.) Eleven members of the council were elected, and the hereditary chief of the village was made the twelfth member. This hereditary position was dropped by a constitutional amendment in 1969. After the annual election of the council, the chairman, vice-chairman, secretary, and treasurer are elected by the newly formed council for terms of one year.

For many years, the main task of the tribal government was simply to attempt to protect the dwindling Lummi treaty rights and land base and to try and get some assistance from the federal government (Lummi Overall Development Plan 1969: 10). From 1937 to 1966 the Lummi council had no significant income. In 1953, for example, the income to the tribe derived primarily from leasing the tidelands as boom grounds for timber, as oyster beds, and as resort beaches. "Additional income derived from the sale to non-Indians of permits to hunt on the reservation, and from the sale to members of the tribe of permits to fish in the tribally owned waters of Bellingham Bay and the mouth of the Nooksack River" (Suttles 1954: 84). Tribal income was used to keep up the tribal cemetery and to pay the tribal policeman's salary at community functions where he was needed.

Operating the tribal government was extremely difficult for nearly a generation. The tribe had no funds for travel and was, therefore, unaware of the programs it might have been able to get. It was all council members could do to attend meetings. The people knew pretty much what they wanted to do, but there were no chances to do anything without funds for development.

An article in the *Bellingham Herald* (March 4, 1961) outlined the attitude of the tribe." 'We need direction and purpose, both within and from outside the tribe,' one of the Indians said. 'We need decent jobs and the opportunity to compete, both legally and morally,' says another. 'We need land reclamation and improvements if it means loss of the few rights we still have,' another added."

The Lummis knew what they wanted. They didn't know how to get it. In April of 1961, they asked for a loan from the government to develop an industrial site. The Employment Club, a group of Lummis that had organized to try to get jobs brought to the reservation, sent a petition to John O. Crow, then acting commissioner of the Bureau of Indian Affairs. The club proposed to get enough money to purchase 80 acres of reservation land and the heavy equipment necessary to develop an industrial park by themselves. Already they were figuring the chances of having an integrated development scheme for the reservation (*Bellingham Herald*, April 11, 1961).

In addition to the industrial park, the Lummis wanted housing programs. They urged that a "point four" program be initiated for the reservation (forgetting that foreign countries have priority over Indian reservations). The situation appeared hopeless. In 1957 there had been a chance to get a Navy ammunition depot established on the reservation, but the Navy had finally decided to expand its existing facilities in California. The Navy claimed as the reason why it could not relocate at

Lummi that an oil refinery was being considered for the reservation, thus precluding the depot (*Bellingham Herald*, May 13, 1959). (Needless to say, the oil company did nothing.)

In the winter of 1962 Forrest Kinley, then tribal chairman, got the tribe to support the development of Century 21, a tourist facility for arts and crafts. The community pulled together and fixed up old buildings through volunteer labor. The gymnasium was repaired so that it could be used by the people, and a large barbecue pit was made for salmon feasts. People even began to talk about having a Lummi museum in the newly repaired buildings. A sense of community unity began to pervade the Lummi reservation once again (*Bellingham Herald*, February 25, 1962).

During the first years of the Kennedy administration, Indian tribes began to receive the benefits of the social programs that were being created in Washington, D.C. The Area Redevelopment Administration, later renamed the Economic Development Administration (EDA), made Indian tribes eligible for grants for economic development. The Lummis were able to gain some benefit from this law in 1963, when United States Senator Henry Jackson assisted in getting a grant of $91,000 for work in the improvement of soil productivity (January 16, 1963). No one, at this point in time, seemed to be able to figure out exactly what projects should be undertaken to improve the economic stability of the reservation. But everyone wanted to do something definite.

The grant was used to hire Lummi men in alternating two-week jobs, so that everyone on the reservation could receive some wages from the project. The Lummis cleared the dike on the east side of the reservation near the Nooksack River. The most important development of this project was the establishment of the precedent that every Lummi would share the benefits of whatever federal projects the tribe received.

The following month the Lummis received another federal grant for work on the reservation; $50,000 was authorized by the Department of Health, Education and Welfare for installation of water systems and sanitation. Again, Senator Jackson's office had helped the tribe get final approval for the program. The funds were to be used to provide septic tanks for about 70 percent of the homes on the reservation, most of which had previously been without running water. This grant was the first investment of federal money ever made on the Lummi reservation. Prior to this time the federal government had never thought to build any of the ordinary municipal service structures that almost every other American community had had since its inception (*Bellingham Herald*, February 8 and March 17, 1963).

The Economic Opportunity Act of 1964 was a major event for the

Lummis. During the early 1960's, they had been able to get federal grants on a temporary basis, such as those listed above, but no funds were available for a survey or for development of total community needs. The tribe had no funds that could be used for speculative analysis of tribal needs. There were no full-time workers for the Lummi tribe itself during the early 1960's — there were merely temporary supervisors of temporary federal projects.

The War on Poverty, as it came to be called, had specific provisions for community action projects. The Lummis received a grant of $40,000 in 1966, two years after the Office of Economic Opportunity was established (*Bellingham Herald*, May 10, 1968). This grant provided the first full-time salaried job in the history of the tribe for a Lummi on the reservation. The Lummi Indian Business Council finally had a staff to carry out its ideas on reservation development.

The first major program that the people undertook was a housing project. Working nearly three years in the maze of federal agencies, with their conflicting guidelines and qualifications, the Lummi Community Action Program (CAP) was able to combine funding — from the Office of Economic Opportunity, the Department of Housing and Urban Development, the Department of Health, Education and Welfare, and the Bureau of Indian Affairs — to get a housing program to build twenty new houses on the reservation (Lummi Overall Development Plan 1969: 11). This program began in 1969 and was completed in 1971.

But the problem of establishing a solid economic base for the reservation people still plagued the Lummi tribe. New houses are useful only when there is a continuing economic base to allow for their upkeep and for continuing expansion of community development opportunities. In late 1967, the Lummis were approached by a corporation that wanted to build a magnesium oxide reduction plant at Lummi Bay. The company had already approached the Port of Bellingham, the Whatcom County Development Council, the Whatcom County Commission, and the Whatcom County Planner; all had turned down the project as being too detrimental to the fishing industries to be considered.

The company's plan was to ship ore from the Twin Sisters Mountains and process it in Lummi Bay, on land that certain families owned. A mountain of green olivine ore would be processed at the plant, leaving tailings of silica deposited in Lummi Bay. Economic development of the tidelands would include a dredged seaport facility, large sea traffic (complete with oil spills), and other pollution that would have made the destruction of the bay irreversible.

The Lummis were greatly concerned at the thought of the final destruction of their tidal lands. For more than a century they had preserved this area for tribal use. They dug for oysters and clams in the tidelands. It supported the migratory birds that traveled from Canada to the south and back again each year. The traditional fishing grounds in Hale Passage and western Bellingham Bay, which they had fought so hard to protect, would be ruined by the presence of an industry with such extensive polluting potential.

Some of the Lummi people began to search for another means of using the bay, hoping that they could find an alternative to the magnesium oxide reduction plant. Word got around Bellingham that the heavy industry might be approved by the tribe, if it could find no other opportunity for development. At that point, fate appeared to intervene in the affairs of men. On the faculty of Western Washington State College at that time was Dr. Wallace Heath, who had studied desert ecology at the University of Arizona as a graduate student and who was well versed in natural-life systems. He was also a consultant to the Oceanic Foundation of California, which at the time was studying the mariculture of the ancient Hawaiians.

Heath discovered that the Lummis were searching for an alternative to the magnesium plant, because he had volunteered to work with an ecological group in planning a county-wide program for Whatcom County's lands and waters. Part of his work was to survey the remaining natural features of the county and to seek ways of preserving them ecologically. Heath paid a visit to the Lummi reservation to determine the status of the magnesium oxide plant and found that the Lummis were just as anxious as he was that an alternative use be found for the bay.

As part of his inspection of the Lummi reservation, Heath visited the tidelands. He asked the older Lummis how the tribe had traditionally used the tidelands and discovered that the people had always considered the bay as the most important part of their land, because of its ability to support a great variety of sea life. As he walked the sandy beaches, Heath began to visualize the creation of an aquaculture, comparable to those he had studied in Hawaii. Finally he asked the Lummis if they had ever considered using the bay for the commercial production of seafood. They had not considered such a use, but, after hearing Heath's description of the Hawaiian aquacultures, they decided that they wanted to try the idea.

The next tribal meeting was crucial. It was basically a contest between the two conceptions — white and Indian — of the Lummi world. Advocates of the magnesium oxide plant visualized not only the creation of industrial jobs for the tribe, but the transformation of a fishing community to a wage-earning community that would no longer be dependent on the sea and its produce. Advocates of aquaculture visualized the whole community participating in the transformation of fishing techniques into sea farming of the most sophisticated nature. The Lummis could continue to be fishermen, aquaculture proponents argued, and everyone could participate in all the decisions; with the magnesium oxide plant, however, the Lummis would once again be laborers for some outside group.

The final factor in the tribe's decision to undertake the aquaculture project was probably the feature of community control, combined with the deep desire to maintain the reservation as a source of community life rather than as an adjunct of corporate exploitation. The recent past years of sharing projects on a total community basis undoubtedly influenced the decision.

In March of 1968, the final arguments between aquaculture and magnesium oxide sharpened, and by April the subject finally arose in tribal council meeting (*Bellingham Herald*, March 30, 1968). The Lummis voted to embark on the aquaculture project and agreed to spend the following summer exploring the bay to see if the project were feasible. An initial grant of $1,000 from the State Oceanographic Commission enabled Heath and four Lummi teenagers to do basic surveys of the aquatic life in the bay during the summer of 1968. A milestone in tribal life had been reached.

THE LUMMI AQUACULTURE PROJECT

The Aquaculture Project is so complex and so intimately intertwined with other development projects of the community — and it holds so much promise for the future, not simply for the tribe but for other tribes and for the Pacific Northwest—that it is extremely difficult to place the proper emphasis on each part of it. The concepts of developing the aquaculture and developing the community have continually gone hand in hand in tribal planning.

Unique Factors

Possibly the most basic and unique feature of the aquaculture project is the land itself (Map 2). Lummi tidelands extend a considerable distance at low tide, exposing an extensive mud flat. This land was preserved for the tribe through a series of unusual law suits that upheld the boundaries set by the Treaty of Point Elliott and the Executive Order of 1873, which gave boundaries in detail. The loss of these tidal flats would, of course, have precluded any development of the area whatsoever, at least by the Lummi tribe as a concerned community.

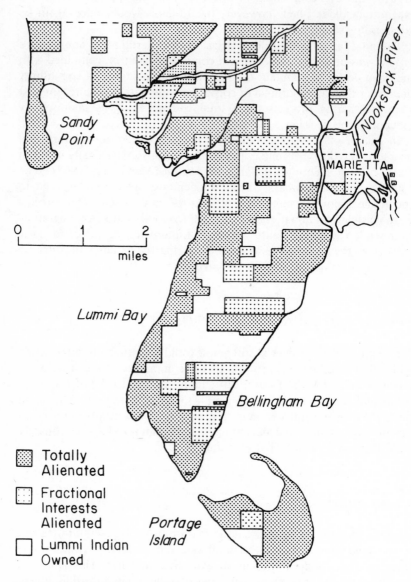

Map 2.   Land alienation on the Lummi reservation

In July of 1967, the regional solicitor of the Bureau of Indian Affairs, at the request of Congresswoman Julia Butler Hansen of Washington, issued a general opinion on the rights of Indian tribes to control the waters and lands of their reservations. The memorandum was originally issued in reference to the Quinault reservation on Washington's Olympic Peninsula, but its principles applied to most of the tribes in the state whose treaty and executive order boundary provisions coincided (Memorandum 1967). This memorandum had already widely circulated throughout the BIA and was well known to the tribes and their lawyers, so the BIA could not negate the right of the Lummi Tribal Council to determine how it would use its lands, particularly its tidelands.

Had this particular memorandum not been issued and publicly known prior to the creation of the aquaculture project, the BIA personnel in the Everett, Washington agency and Portland Area office would almost certainly have found some way to stop the Lummis from developing their plans. (The pattern of BIA interference with tribally planned programs, and its near-direct sabotage of Indian projects, can be documented in almost every reservation in the country on a variety of projects.)

The unique feature of the aquaculture project with respect to the lands was, first, that the tidelands had been preserved in tribal title through a series of law suits, all of which reaffirmed and clearly set forth tribal ownership, thus preempting any question concerning ownership of tidelands and beaches by any individual, white or Indian, or by any state, federal, or local governmental units.

The second unique feature of the land use was that the BIA was barred from interfering with the development at any point, because it had just issued an extensive memorandum on the rights of tribes to control and zone tribal property. With the BIA precluded from raising extraneous questions and hampering the project at every step, the Lummis had a clear path to development of the aquaculture project.

Another distinguishing factor of the Lummi project was the early development of a powerful and responsible political team as key figures. Sam Cagey and Vernon Lane assumed political control of the Lummi Indian Business Council in 1968 and worked in tandem to push the development. The two complemented each other to an amazing degree, were singularly devoted to the total development of the tribe, spent every waking hour working out the details of the project, and, if any dissension existed between them, kept personal matters out of sight. They inspired everyone to continue to support aquaculture and also formed a devastating political front that was united against all critics, white and Indian.

Lane is a quiet and unassuming man, handsome and dignified; his calm demeanor hides a razor-sharp mind that instantly cuts through rhetoric to the issues. Lane handled the major public relations tasks, absorbed the indignities of ignorant and uninformed critics, and generally acted as the Lummis' "velvet glove" in transactions with outside groups, agencies, and individuals.

Sam Cagey, although not a tall man, is a giant. He is one of the sharpest political minds in Indian country and was the "Hammer of Thor" for the tribe. Anyone who would not deal reasonably with Vernon Lane soon discovered that he had taken on the wrong opponents when the Lummis unloosed Sam Cagey. Cagey, as the saying goes, could make offers that people could not refuse.

The astute negotiating of the Lummis for project funds, for consideration by government agencies, and for shifting emphasis to accomplish the community goals — in spite of the red tape requirements of government bureaucrats — was possible only through the magnificent teamwork of the Lummi business committee led by Cagey and Lane.

Any project, particularly one with the scope of the aquaculture project, is ultimately dependent on the political skills of tribal leaders. They must keep tribal members concerned about the total development in community terms, and they must not yield to what appear to be impossible odds held by outside forces that desire the community to fulfill their wishes. The Lummis were extremely fortunate in having, at the right time, two capable and devoted leaders.

The fourth factor was the presence of Wallace Heath, whose flexible and inquiring mind was not subject to doctrinal stubbornness. Instead of adhering to establishment ideas, Heath was always ready to adapt to the actual situation. He had served on the National Indian Service Committee in Phoenix, Arizona, from 1953 to 1959, had helped organize the American Indian Club at the University of Arizona while a graduate student there, and had worked with the Papago Indians for a period of six years during the 1950's. Heath understood Indians fairly well; even more, he felt that he had something to learn from working with Indian people—(A rare quality for a white man with an education.)

Heath also had good relationships with the foremost people in marine science. When he and the tribe began to talk about aquaculture, he was already involved with the Makapuu Oceanic Institute as assistant director. It was through Heath that Victor Loosanoof, professor of marine biology at the University of the Pacific, and one of the world's top shellfish experts, visited the Lummi reservation and offered constructive comments. Charles A. Black, San Francisco mariculturist and businessman, who helped develop a firm that produces millions of oysters at Pescadero Bay in California, also assisted the project. Heath was able to call on Tim Joyner and Anthony Novotny, fisheries biologists of the Bureau of Commercial Fisheries; James Ellis of the Oceanic Institute and Taylor A. Pryor, its president; and Richard Poole, who had designed the shellfish hatchery at Monterey Bay for the State of California. Thus, the Lummis not only found a devoted scientist to help them but also received the benefit of his extensive and knowledgeable colleagues from all over the world.

The Lummi business council designed and directed the project and used non-Indian experts to provide the needed technical skills. Its goal, however, was to train Lummi people for every job that the project would produce. Thus, the technical experts employed by the tribe were directed from the beginning to train Lummis to replace them. Lummis have used the technical skills of non-Indians and the non-Indians — who have had the sense to recognize the strong tribal desire to conduct its own business — have remained in the background as advisers.

Another important factor in the development of the project has been the willingness of government agencies to support the project without imposing unnecessary restrictions on the tribe. The Economic Development Administration, in particular, has responded to the funding requests of the tribe with careful and thoughtful granting of funds for specific portions of the overall development. Perhaps realizing that aquaculture was a unique undertaking, EDA in general gave excellent support (in contrast to the negative attitude taken by the Department of the Interior and other agencies, which have perhaps viewed tribal development as threatening to their authority).

The final significant factor in the development of Lummi aquaculture has been the response of the Lummi community to the project. As a group, the Lummis have not allowed themselves to be led astray by unfounded accusations against the project, they have not allowed personal or family preferences to sway them from completing the task of building the project, and they have insisted on allowing all members of the community to participate in the work. Visitors to the project are as likely to see the tribal chairman wielding a shovel as anyone else. The whole tribe, from grandmothers to children, has had a hand in building the dikes, harvesting the fish, and determining the priority of grant proposals to be submitted to foundations and government agencies.

The combination of all these factors has produced the Lummi aquaculture project, which will soon be producing oysters, salmon, sea trout, clams, and other seafood products. It is extremely doubtful if this same combination could ever be duplicated with another group of people. Altering any one of these factors would certainly result in a less satisfactory outcome.

Construction Activities

To determine if Lummi Bay could be used as a site for aquaculture, the physical aspects of the bay had to be evaluated. Dr. Heath and four young Lummis spent the summer of 1968 plotting the geography of Lummi Bay; they laid out a grid and charted the total acreage available for use at each level of tide. Water levels were crucial to the planning; for example, ponds for oysters must be deep enough to prevent the oysters from being frozen by winter cold or burned by summer sun.

The project seemed feasible, so the tribe decided to apply to the EDA for technical assistance grants to build a 4.4-acre research pond for testing the development of oysters and trout in salt water. In February of 1969 the EDA granted the tribe $143,220 to begin research and training; in June the Indian Desk of the OEO granted $300,000 to begin construction of the pond.

The Lummis decided that they would build the pond themselves, although none of them had ever built anything of the kind before. When work on the test pond dike began, the construction engineers estimated that the Indians could complete, at most, 50 feet a day. Lummi enthusiasm was so great that these untrained builders were soon putting in more than 100 feet a day. Tribal members handled everything — manual labor, heavy equipment operations, and supervision of construction. In short order the Lummis had a research pond, which was dedicated with a host of dignitaries present. It was to be the first of a series of astounding achievements by the Lummi people.

Research in the pond rapidly confirmed the feasibility of the project that had been proposed by the planners. Original projections had been cautious — to expand the pond in another year, if all went well, to an area between 220 and 400 acres. But the results of research in the small pond were so spectacular that the tribe decided to go ahead with a 750-acre pond, which would give them a greater chance at success much sooner than originally anticipated.

The 750-acre pond brought certain technical problems. It was one thing to close off several acres for testing and another to develop a pond with an area of more than a square mile. Tides are not severe in Lummi Bay, but projecting the arms of a large dike out into the bay would create additional water action, which would tend to erode construction. Final work on the dike would mean filling in a considerable distance in a single day, to prevent tidal action from washing everything out in a final movement through the reduced opening.

Everyone appeared to be a little skeptical about the larger pond project, except the Lummis. No one had ever built a dike of this type before in the United States, and only one other existed in the world —

in Holland, land of master dike builders. Thus the major pond project was experimental in every sense. No one really knew what would happen.

In July of 1970 the EDA, through its public works fund, made a major grant of $1.5 million for the large pond and work began. The Jansen Construction Company was hired to build the dike, with the major work force to be composed of Lummi men. Construction of the steel intake and outlet gates required substantial skills, and Jansen was responsible for making sure that this job was handled by its technicians. The remainder of the work, including most of the welding on the gates, was done by the Lummis.

The EDA agreed that the tribe could function as prime contractor on the project. (EDA probably made Indian history, in that this was the first time that a government agency had given an Indian tribe a contract for major construction. It is especially significant because this particular kind of structure had never been built in North America previously. Because of delays in funding caused by opponents of the program, pond construction began in bad weather, thus increasing the actual final cost to $1.9 million.) The Lummis purchased a tract of 140 acres on the reservation (which had gone out of Indian hands long before) as a source of sand and gravel. Some nineteen gravel trucks, owned or leased by Lummi men, were used in building the dike. In almost every way possible, the people scrimped, saved, adapted, modified, and conserved resources and funding.

Closing the dike — which extended for about three miles, from Sandy Point around the major part of Lummi Bay to the site where the research pond had been built — was the most severe technical test that the project had yet entailed. As the arms of the dike were extended forward to their meeting point, the action of the tides became more severe.

By late fall the Lummis were averaging better than 200 feet of dike per day, hauling tons of rock for a base, hundreds of tons of sand and gravel for filler, and a great deal of dirt for the top of the dike. Problems increased as the dike's two sides edged closer to one another. Even the rains — expectable in western Washington — seemed to increase as spring began to turn to summer. As the day approached to push for closing the dike, the tribe called on a Dutch expert, who advised building a $300,00 complex to regulate tidal pressure while the gap was being closed. It looked as if the dike would be much more expensive than any of the planners had foreseen.

But Dave Hudson, Jansen's chief engineer, came up with a novel idea that solved the closure problems. He had Lummi aqualung divers pin nine acres of polyvinyl filter cloth to the bottom of the opening of the dike; this caused the tide to depress the sand at the entrance instead of scooping it away. June 4th, the day with the lowest tide of the year, was picked as the day to close.

During previous weeks the Lummis had piled massive mounds of sand and gravel on the ends of the dike arms, so that on the final day they could bring in heavy equipment to push materials into the 800-foot expanse that remained open. Nearly everyone in the tribe turned out for the final push. Working for a period of thirty hours without rest, the Lummis closed the dike without incident — seven hours short of the time predicted — the great pond was complete.

Twenty-seven dump trucks, ten earth movers, and a number of bulldozers had pushed 15,000 cubic feet of dirt into the opening in little more than a day. The Lummis had exceeded even their own wildest and most optimistic hopes. While most of the tribe spent the day celebrating, a hardy crew remained to complete the top of the dike to specifications: 90 feet of width and 16 feet of crown. Then the whole community celebrated with a fish barbecue and oyster bake. The tribe had completed the task so quickly that television crews who arrived to film the scheduled closure found a completed dike and the Lummis off at Birch Bay feasting.

To enable the Lummis to qualify for additional government funding, the EDA had invested an additional $350,000 in the large pond, and the Oceanic Foundation had given $100,000 in cash for matching funds. The grant from Oceanic was particularly significant during the construction period, providing the tribe with the funds that enabled them to qualify for an EDA grant.

The large pond was only the first construction required for the aquaculture project, however; smaller ponds were also needed. In July of 1970, the OEO had granted the tribe $500,000 for construction of breeding ponds for oysters and fish. But in their extensive testing of the Nooksack, the Lummis had discovered that the water that reached the river's delta was highly polluted because of upstream industries. So the tribe constructed a trout breeding pond farther up the river in the foothills of the Cascades, where fish could be raised to fingerlings in clear mountain water, and later transported to the larger shoreline pool in tank trucks.

In June of 1971, shortly after the completion of the large pond, another EDA grant of $408,000 was made to the Lummis, for a complete oyster hatchery on the shore of the larger pond. The hatchery, finished in August of 1972, was built in the style of a Lummi longhouse. It has the most modern conveniences available and is capable of producing 100 million seed oysters a year — which is the highest production for the money invested of any oyster hatchery in existence.

The fish hatchery was built through combination of a number of grants: $290,000 from OEO, Economic Development Division; $100,000 from OEO, Indian Division; and a special $118,000 supplement that was added to the Indian Appropriations Bill. When completed and fully operative the fish hatchery will produce between 5 and 10 million fingerlings a year, comparable to hatcheries costing double the amount.

The initial construction phase of the aquaculture project is now finished. Should the Lummis decide to expand the operation to several thousand acres in a few years they can do so. For the present, however, they are concentrating on making all phases of the project commercially profitable.

Table 1 gives the total cost of construction of the aquaculture project, to date. Had the large pond been built without the enthusiastic

Table 1. Total cost of construction of aquaculture project

Granted by:	Date	Amount in dollars
OEO experimental pond	June 1969	300,000
EDA sea pond	July 1970	1,500,000
Oceanic matching cash	July 1970	100,000
OEO-EDD fish and oyster hatcheries	July 1970	500,000
EDA sea pond	June 1971	350,000
EDA oyster hatchery	June 1971	408,000
Total		3,158,000

and creative work of the Lummis, the cost would probably have been double the actual expenditures. Not figured into the cost are the countless hours volunteered by the people, the expenses taken out of individual pockets, the sleepless nights given to make the project a success. The total administrative overhead on the project construction was $38,000. The Economic Development Division of the OEO added another grant of $1.7 million to assist in the budgeting of operating costs through 1973.

Training Programs

The programs developed by the Lummi people involved a total concept of community development. The various features of that program have been treated separately here, to allow analysis of the whole community development movement of the Lummis, but all of these operations were in progress simultaneously, involving nearly all of the people living on the reservation. The various aspects of the program were never conceived by the Lummi people as distinctive in nature or as separate from the entire needs of the community.

Most development projects on Indian reservations are imposed from the top down. Construction is begun and programs are started without any thought as to the eventual impact on the people. Countless reservation industries are operated without a single Indian in a management or technically skilled position; the employment provided for Indian people is usually custodial or service-oriented, with top management and professional jobs going to non-Indians.

The Lummi project is distinctive, in that Lummis matched every construction project with a training program that prepared people to assume leadership at the highest levels. The preliminary survey of the bay, carried out by Dr. Heath and four young Lummi surveyors, included two young people who had hopelessly dropped out of the American educational system. In view of their subsequent success, it seems obvious that the vaunted American educational system had failed to meet their needs — possibly because it was too rigid and boring for these bright young Indian people.

Of the four young Lummis employed the first summer, one returned to Skagit Valley College and a second went back to high school; both were fired with the idea of becoming marine biologists by their summer's experience. A third enlisted four of his friends, and all are studying fisheries technology at Peninsula College. The fourth and a friend got jobs with the Bureau of Commercial Fisheries where they have been gaining valuable experience in fish biology. The idea of the project so excited the young Lummis who had heard of it that another six enrolled to study business at Bellingham Technical School. In one summer the whole concept of education had changed for the young people of the tribe — and so had their perception of their roles in life.

From the very beginning, the Lummis wanted the training that would enable them to operate the aquaculture project themselves when construction was finished. In 1969 a special aquaculture training program was designed by the Lummi Education Committee and Dr. Heath, in the hope of providing knowledge that would compensate for the educational deficiencies of the public education system. The Manpower Development Training Administration (MDTA) provided a training grant of $150,000 for eighteen Lummis. Of this number, eight went on to college for advanced work in fisheries, eight became instructors in the next year's program, and two immediately became technicians at the research pond.

The training program was successful beyond anyone's expectations. In September of 1970, a new program was begun, with sixty-four trainees. Fifty-eight people finished the one-year course, which by this time had become scientifically rigorous. Eight people from this training class went on to college, and most of the remainder demanded further training in marine biology. Much of the success of the training course must be credited to the instructors, Roy Nakamura and Judy Trout, who view their academic training as applicable to the real problems of practical marine biology and who work very closely with the Lummi trainees, proceeding as fast as the students are able to master the subject. It is probably because of their shared love of both the project and each other that the Lummis and the two instructors, Roy and Judy, have created a wholly unique training program, which has demonstrated the value of a practical and concentrated approach to education.

The demand for advanced training presented a novel difficulty for the tribe. Most training programs funded for poverty-level people are not concerned with a field so complex as aquaculture. The fact that the Lummi trainees had absorbed several years of advanced marine biology and science in a relatively brief time failed to register on the people for training program grants. The tribe could not make it clear to people who had never seen the reservation development that they were not simply retraining their people in the same subject matter but were offering a program that in some respects was equatable in difficulty with a college program.

The Lummis were finally able to prove the worth of the advanced training program, and in July of 1971 they received a grant of $306,000 from the MDTA to give forty of the previous class an advanced program in aquaculture. The problem at that point, of course, was success itself. Few people other than the Lummis knew anything about aquaculture and its potential. The advanced training program will enable the trainees not only to handle all phases of aquaculture but also to qualify as instructors for future classes.

Ironically, the final training grant received to date was from an agency that for years had avoided its legally established responsibility for the Lummis, whose officials had grumblingly predicted the failure of the aquaculture program. The Bureau of Indian Affairs, having finally decided that the project was going to succeed, in July of 1971 gave the tribe a grant of $193,000 for management training. It was a tacit acknowledgement that the Lummis had become a power to be reckoned with.

After the takeover and destruction of the BIA's Washington, D.C. headquarters in November of 1972, a great many BIA programs were cut back. The Lummi program was one of those that came under the scalpel. As this study was being finished, a promised grant of some $100,000 for additional training was being cut back to less than half that amount. Whether or not the grant will be restored will probably depend on the extent to which the White House allows cuts in the Indian budget to remain in effect.

The Lummi project was being carefully watched by other tribes across the country. Lummi tribal members and Dr. Heath made a trip to Nevada in 1972 to discuss the aquaculture program with Indians of the Pyramid Lake Paiute reservation. Other tribes began to ask for a training program comparable to that of the Lummis, so in the fall of 1972 the tribe began planning for a massive training program, which would involve some eighty Indian people from about forty tribes that have substantial aquatic resources. The Lummis are busy developing a nine-month course that will give the basic principles of aquaculture. After taking this course, Indian trainees will be able either to go on to college for advanced theoretical work or to return to their home reservations for work on tribal development projects.

The training project in aquaculture is tentatively set to be funded by a combination of six agencies. An interagency committee, which includes representatives from HEW, EDA, and the Department of Labor, has approved the project as a basic program to be supervised by the department. Its initial budget will be some $700,000, which will hopefully include $300,000 from the Bureau of Indian Affairs. Again, the immediate problem the tribe faced, as 1973 began, was the series of drastic cuts envisioned by the Nixon administration as part of its general curtailment of federal expenditures. Everyone connected with the program — particularly the tribes that had asked the Lummis to develop it — hoped that this training project would be spared by the federal budget cutters.

It is strange that no large private foundations have come forward with support for the Lummi project. The Ford Foundation, for example, has poured millions of dollars into Indian projects involving both education and economic development — with little to show for its philanthropic efforts. This foundation presently appears to be gearing up for a major effort in the field of Indian economic development, but it has not made an effort to closely examine the Lummi project. Yet, of the projects developed in Indian country during the whole decade of the frantic 1960's, the most outstanding and promising to date — and certainly the most innovative — has been Lummi aquaculture.

Public Relations and Marketing

From the very beginning of the project, the Lummis have been keenly aware of the forces that were opposing them. Opponents of the project, Indian and non-Indian, maintained sniping fire from the safety of ignorance. The project almost immediately attracted every type of critic imaginable, and the critics spared no ammunition in trying to stop aquaculture. Foremost in the fight were the dissident Lummis, who had wanted the magnesium oxide plant, and the Lummi Bay Beach Owners Association, which was composed of non-Indian property owners who had purchased land during the 1950's when the BIA was gaily selling Lummi beach property at pennies on the dollar.

The Indian critics, who hoped to reap personal benefit from shoreline family lands that would be leased to the magnesium-producing industry, staged a running fight against the incumbent tribal council. They continued to fire at the chairman and vice-chairman, Vernon Lane and Sam Cagey, insisting that the actions taken to approve the aquaculture project were made illegally and in secret and that few members of the tribe understood what was happening (*Bellingham Herald*, November 21, 24, 1969).

This campaign backfired somewhat, because the supporters of aquaculture had held open meetings at each step of development. The attacks of the Indian critics served only to unite the tribe in defensive protection of aquaculture. In the minds of most of the tribe, the project became a personal venture involving their whole future. Instead of fostering tribal disunity, the critics' attacks fostered an incredible tribal strength.

The crisis came in December of 1969, when the dissident group demanded a change of the constitution and bylaws that would have made recall of tribal officials possible. They apparently figured that this device would stir up discontent against individual council members, who could be removed from office in gradual succession.

The BIA, which appears ever eager to foster tribal dissension, insisted that the tribal rolls be brought up to date before a vote on the constitution could be taken. Off-reservation people had generally been negative towards previous development plans, and BIA people apparently believed that most of these members would approve the new articles of the constitution, thus virtually gutting aquaculture before it could be put to a test.

The supporters of aquaculture, however, had a much better understanding of tribal attitudes than did their opponents and the BIA; they knew that many off-reservation people were hoping that aquaculture would succeed, providing them with jobs. A great many Lummis wanted to return home to the reservation, but they did not want to leave their current jobs unless there were prospects of work on the reservation. When the vote was taken, the amendments were defeated by substantial margins. But BIA intervention had accomplished two things: tribal rolls had been updated and aquaculture had been publicized (*Bellingham Herald*, November 20, 1969; *Seattle Post-Intelligencer*, February 15, 1970).

The non-Indian Lummi Bay Beach Owners Association was a much more dangerous group of critics than was the group of Indian dissenters. The people of Bellingham were inclined to believe what white landowners said about aquaculture in preference to the facts that tribal officials were releasing about the project. Throughout the three years of aquaculture development, the local newspaper consistently under-played Lummi successes and overemphasized tribal disunity and the temporary setbacks suffered. The letters of white critics were usually published in the paper at length, while Lummi replies were often not printed at all, or relevant points were deleted.

The first major attack against the project was launched prior to a hearing to determine whether or not the United States Army Corps of Engineers would issue a license to the tribe to build the research pond. It is still questionable that the tribe really had to get a license from the corps — but in covering all possible bets, it applied for one. Im-mediately prior to the hearing, a whispering campaign of incredible distortions was carried on by opponents of the project.

Four petitions were sent to the army, listing various reasons why the project should not be undertaken. On the four petitions, 59 people had contributed 139 signatures — for an average of 3.27 signatures per person. On one single petition five people had signed three times. Apparently it had been concluded that the army would not investigate who the opponents actually were. (See Lummi Indian Business Council 1969).

All of the petitions objected to the proposed 2,000-acre pond, rather than to the 4.4-acre research pond for which the permit was requested. It was stated that the creation of the pond on a tidal flat of 4,500 acres would cause great pollution, affect boating and wildlife, and greatly devaluate property. No one seemed to recognize that the alternative, a magnesium oxide reduction plant, was not about to skyrocket their property values by any startling percentage.

The petitions were discredited (one person in Texas even wrote in to object), but a letter-writing campaign was initiated in the effort to stop approval of the license. When the Corps of Engineers turned the letters over to the Lummi council to get their answers to the objec-tions, it was as if a slow fat pitch were drifting over the plate with Babe Ruth at bat.

Ninety percent of the people who wrote letters about the extensive property damage they would suffer from aquaculture did not live within sight of the project; many did not even own property near the reservation. Most of the letters reflected an astounding ignorance of the project. They charged that the Lummis intended to extend dikes for miles in every direction, thus cutting off swimming, boating, and fishing around the islands near the reservation.

The opponents probably lost their case when they waxed poetic about the evil intentions of the Lummis. Some had the tribe deliber-ately putting oysters on the beaches to cut the feet of recreationists, others claimed that roving bands of Indians would attack the people using the beaches. Some claimed it was a plot to cut off the wind, others maintained that all wildlife would be removed and the smell from the fish would pollute the whole county. The most astounding objection, however, was that Indians, unlike many of the protestors, paid no taxes. The Lummis, however, pay everything but real estate taxes — but what paying taxes had to do with creating a research pond for aquaculture was puzzling, even to the Corps of Engineers.

When the hearing was finally held, the room was swamped with Lummis, who were so well informed on the various parts of the proposal that it was obvious that the project had been designed and created by the people themselves and not by Dr. Heath or any of the scientists employed by the tribe. The permit was approved.

A student at a nearby college was the most violent opponent of the project, and he continued as its major critic during the three years of its development. He wrote to President Nixon — with copies to senators, congressmen, government agencies, and the Bureau of the Budget — demanding that all funds for the project be cut off immediately. He charged that all the fish had died, that the pond emitted powerful odors, that all the migratory birds would be driven away, that fish would pollute the waters for twenty miles around, and that outside interests would soon take over the project. He saw a general conspiracy of frightening proportions evolving at Lummi, with the Indians as helpless victims. Facts did not support any of the man's contentions. (Ironically, after the Lummis had received funding for a large training program, he walked into the tribal office and asked for a job as a counselor.)

Faced with ongoing flank attacks of this type, the tribal business committee decided early that it would carefully inform as many people as possible about the project. Open meetings were held on the proposal in March of 1969 with over 250 people attending; more than 300 people attended a similar meeting in July. The Lummi Indian Business Council sought full disclosure in newspaper stories throughout the period of project development. There was practically no feature of aquaculture that was not repeatedly put before the tribe and the general public, while each step was proposed, debated, and approved by the tribal members.

Aquaculture itself attracted a significant number of visitors. Senator Henry Jackson and Congressman Lloyd Meeds both attended the opening of the research pond, and Shirley Temple Black brought a delegation from the United Nations to visit the project while it was being built. Officially, the Lummis took care to inform the government agencies that were funding construction and training as to successes and failures, so that no federal officials were ever unaware of what was happening.

Time magazine mentioned the aquaculture project favorably (August 31, 1970), and Lummis appeared on television, showing the hosts of the "Today" Show what they were doing. The favorable publicity continued to snowball — the project was, all things considered, the most spectacular development that had ever occurred in Indian country.

The result of the publicity was astounding. Some thirty Indian tribes around the nation have talked with the Lummis about aquaculture; a delegation of Florida Seminoles visited with the Lummis to confer about assisting them in developing similar projects. Film crews began to make regular visits to Lummi when out filming stories on Indian progress.

Early in 1972, Lummis were invited to the National Press Club in Washington, D.C., for dinner. Sam Cagey put a poster-sized display featuring aquaculture in the lobby, because it was too large to be placed in the dining room. The Lummis had barely begun to eat when they were paged by Christopher Blake, a playwright and noted gourmet cook. Blake heard their story and became so fascinated that he promised to create some specialty dishes, using food produced by aquaculture.

Blake returned to New Orleans, where he was then living, and the Lummis sent him trout, oysters, clams, and salmonettes. Jim Thomas, head of an Indian public relations firm in the nation's capitol, helped to coordinate the effort. The result was the creation of several gourmet recipes featuring Lummi aquacultural products. The tribe had an initial dinner in Bellingham, where its perennial critics ate their words and also feasted on the Lummi delicacies. Dinners followed in San Francisco, and, finally, a special seafood demonstration was given at the National Press Club. Lummi foods were a smashing success. (The *Bellingham Herald*, May 19, 1972.)

Aquaculture will not, however, depend on specialty markets for commercial success. During the period of development the tribe had been keenly aware of the necessity for finding an outlet for its products. Early in August of 1970, Dr. Heath visited Japan to determine the extent of their seafood needs. Increasing industrialization in Japan has produced so much pollution that the Japanese now depend on imported seafood to a greater degree than at any time in their history (Lummi Overall Development Plan 1969: 48).

Discussions with Japanese businessmen indicated that the Lummis could find a ready market for smoked salmon, for sea urchin roe, and for edible seaweeds. All signs appear to indicate that the tribe can build up a strong market position with Japanese fish dealers, who are already importing large amounts of salmon from Alaska every year.

In January of 1971 a delegation of Lummis explored the New York fish market (Lummi Indian Tribal OEDP 1969: 50). A number of dealers were contacted about the variety of food available through aquaculture, and some indicated an interest in both fish and oysters. With the speciality market being oriented toward recipes specifically devised for Lummi products, the New York market is looking increasingly stronger.

The Lummi have considered processing plants for handling both fresh and frozen seafood and have made contacts in Bellingham and Seattle. At present it appears as if satisfactory arrangements can be made in either city. Eventual plans call for the creation of a special Lummi label and possibly, in the distant future, a processing plant on the reservation (Lummi Indian Tribal OEDP 1969: 54).

The commercial exploitation of aquacultural products has scarcely been touched. The possible use of any and every form of sea life is now being evaluated. Red algae, used as emulsifier in foods, is already being harvested from rocks in depths of twenty or more feet and will provide a significant income as the harvest is stabilized. The long-term future of aquaculture appears to be quite bright.

Political Changes

The development at the Lummi reservation is certainly without parallel on any other Indian reservation in the nation. Some tribes have come into sudden wealth, others have embarked on expansive developments. But few tribes have built a project of this magnitude with practically no income whatsoever. The Lummis have had a desperate time maintaining their administrative balance during this period of development. Tribal income has remained at a very low level, because the project has not been in operation for a sufficient time to produce an income of any significance.

Over the past several years, therefore, Lummi councilmen have had to double as administrators of some of the major projects, in order to provide matching services "in kind" to qualify the tribe for grants. Some tribal members have literally been working eighteen to twenty hours a day for several years. The strain is beginning to tell at this point; the necessity of writing and rewriting proposals, of filing reports and evaluating progress, and of keeping everyone informed as to events and developments is simply wearing the people out.

During a period of three years the Lummis have administered more than $5 million in program costs, with overall administrative costs of 3.2 percent, or $163,000 (Lummi Indian Tribal OEDP 1969: 57). There is now a desperate need for administrative funds that will

provide trained managers, administrative assistants, researchers, proposal writers, and other necessary service-support personnel to
stabilize the projects now being operated.

Some fifty Lummis are now in college, being trained for all phases of
aquaculture and business administration. During the next five years the
massive structure of community development must be coordinated,
and people must be placed where they can be the most useful. Such
training and placement necessarily involves being able to expand the
administration functions of the total program to take advantage of
every possibility that can be developed as supportive of both aquaculture and community programs.

A great many communities would have attempted to struggle along,
using outmoded political forms to manage an increasingly complicated
situation. The Lummis recognized fairly early how complicated things
were becoming, however, and ingeniously began to create separate
organizations to handle functions that could effectively be made into
separate programs.

The regular political body of the tribe, the general council, includes
all adult members of the tribe. This council elects a business council of
eleven people to handle the ongoing political needs of the tribe
between general council meetings. In order to keep aquaculture
separate from the political struggles of the tribe, a new organization —
a new vehicle for economic and community development — was
created in 1969 to handle the expanded business functions of the tribe
(Lummi Indian Tribal OEDP 1969: 12 ff.).

The Lummi Indian Tribal Enterprise (LITE) is seen by the Lummis
as an innovative type of community development corporation. The
initial board of LITE consisted of five members appointed by the
Lummi Indian Business Council to serve for a term of three years. To
ensure that the two bodies worked together, the vice-chairman of the
tribal business council was appointed to the LITE board. The LITE
board has usually elected the vice-chairman to the position of chairman of its board. In 1972, the LITE board was expanded to seven
members, thereby including two non-Lummi business experts who are
expected to give professional advice on decisions involving substantial
technical problems.

The LITE board has recently undertaken an extensive training
program to prepare itself for a role as supervisor of total community
development efforts. In conjunction with a number of departments at
Western Washington State College, members of the LITE board are
being educated in such fields as sensitivity training, corporate management, social theory, the dominant culture and its economic, social and
political values, and selected individual courses designed to quickly

upgrade existing knowledge and skills of board members in their areas of interest and specialization.

LITE is presently dividing its time between general supervision of the aquaculture development and creation of a reservation-wide housing program that involves the building of some 150 new houses (*Ferndale Record*, August 4, 1971). It has at present only the administrative staff allowed under the various existing programs; thus, it is handicapped in terms of ongoing development by not having sufficient staff to systematically exploit existing opportunities for the tribal community.

In addition to the requirements of funding LITE, the Lummis discovered that funds were needed to give them flexibility in educational development. Some Lummis wanted special training, others needed assistance with college expenses. Research into conservation measures was another need. In most instances government funds could not be used for these special purposes. Consequently, in 1971 the Lummi Indian Foundation Trust was formed as a nonprofit tax-exempt development arm for tribal educational and research purposes. The trust is just now beginning to attract donors. The initial contributors were people generally involved with aquaculture, who saw the desperate need for funds to further educational needs in specific areas. The tribe is presently hoping to attract larger foundation grants to support this trust.

THE LUMMI CONCEPT

One of the most unique aspects of the overall development at the Lummi reservation is the manner in which the various needs of the people have been considered. The emphasis has not been placed totally on development of aquaculture. Training programs have tended to look into the future and balance community needs in other areas with the specific needs of aquaculture and related activities.

One of the training programs has been the development of skilled carpenters through a grant from the Manpower Development Training Administration. The people who chose to enter this course have found employment on the reservation in the housing programs that the tribe has sponsored. Besides building houses, Lummi trainees have also salvaged and remodeled condemned buildings for use as offices, have built three laboratories for the training sessions in aquaculture, and have converted a large room into a lecture hall.

Another training program was designed to help Lummi people gain experience in office and clerical skills. Almost all of the people going into this program have worked for aquaculture and other tribal enterprises after finishing the course; they have become valuable members of the management team at the reservation.

Present plans call for the creation of a Lummi construction company to subcontract for the building of the 150 new houses that have been authorized for the reservation. The proposed Chief Kwina Community Development will be located on 125 acres of land near St. Joachim's Catholic Church, near the present tribal headquarters (*Ferndale Record*, August 4, 1971). By making use of the construction skills of tribal members, it is hoped that a permanent, tribally owned construction company can eventually be created to handle tribal projects and to work on individual and regional jobs as a general contractor.

LITE is continually developing projects such as these, in order to provide backup service occupations, which will allow those tribal members who would prefer work in fields other than aquaculture to have good jobs on the reservation. Although aquaculture remains a major project at Lummi, the trend is presently to search out subsidiary occupations that will support total community development and will, in addition, provide services that previously have been unavailable to tribal members.

LITE has planned, and is now working to get funded, a number of programs that will alleviate some of the detrimental conditions that have always existed on the reservation. Reservation people have never had basic community commercial services. Except for sporadically operated "trading posts" and small stores, they have never had access to a shopping district near their homes. The nearest supermarket closed about a year ago, making the trip for groceries about six miles each way.

LITE plans to use some of its income as a recycling loan fund to support the development of small businesses on the reservation where the Lummi people live. In addition, board members visualize smaller water-oriented enterprises deriving from the investment mix of aquaculture income and LITE loans to individual members. Suggested enterprises include a marina, a motel, commercial fishing boat moorage, a seafood processing plant, tourist boat rentals, ship building and repair yards, a shopping center with a variety of service and speciality stores, and recreational facilities.

The importance of the emphasis now being placed on subsidiary activities is that the LITE board recognizes that a stable community cannot afford to remain economically based on a single industry. They feel that the task at present is to build in as many supporting economic ventures as possible, to avoid depending totally on aquaculture to provide the jobs that will be needed by the Lummis in the future.

In the field of social services and activities, the LITE board has already determined a number of high-priority items. The tribe presently has two full-time counselors in its alcoholism program, as well as the beginnings of a "half-way house." It needs two more counselors, a secretary, and a live-in caretaker. The approximate cost is $20,000 a year. The tribe hopes to get this program funded in the coming year, in order to help with the adjustment problems of Lummis who are now attempting to work in reservation programs instead of seeking the only solace previously available to them: alcohol.

A youth program with an estimated cost of $15,000 a year is also being planned. Adequate facilities for young people have never been available at the small town of Marietta. Day-care and health-care centers of some size are being requested through the Department of Health, Education and Welfare, and a program for elderly Indians will be needed for several years, until the majority of the tribe has a steady income from the various developments now underway.

Immediate Problems

One of the major failures of government agencies and private foundations has been that each has rather nebulously supported "pilot projects," with the assumption that the other will somehow pick up ongoing administrative costs once the feasibility of a program has been determined. The construction phase of aquaculture is now basically finished. It now needs continued support through its first half-decade, to ensure that it can face every conceivable fiscal pressure with cash flow adequate for survival.

The major — and immediate — danger facing the Lummi people and the aquaculture project is that federal agencies will not recognize their responsibility to continue funding the project at reasonable support levels so that the project can survive. Some agencies have a habit of planting a little seed money and then running for cover when it looks as if the project has a chance of succeeding. The result is that the project promptly collapses and the seed money is wasted.

In view of both the past history of the Lummi people and the current survival struggles of their aquaculture and housing programs, there is no doubt that the Lummis must continue to receive high-level support for their project for a minimum period of five years. The aquaculture project has the potential to change the economic climate of the Pacific Coast. It is a program of highest national priority. As such, it should not be subjected to undue restriction of funds; its program of funding should be expanded to allow exploration of all phases of mariculture.

The second, and almost as pressing, need of the Lummi people is the clarification of their legal rights. Industries in Whatcom County are presently polluting the Nooksack River at unreasonable levels. An aluminum reduction plant upriver is polluting the Nooksack, because state agencies do not yet regulate water pollution. But the state of Washington is presently contemplating the taxation of cigarettes on reservations, even though federal law prohibits such action. Questions have also been raised with respect to the authority of the state to zone lands within Indian reservations, and it appears that the state may attempt to illegally seize power in this area. (See *Bellingham Herald*, June 7, 1970, October 26, 1971, December 1, 1971, to understand the complexity of this particular problem.)

Probably most crucial is the announcement by the Washington State Department of Fisheries that it plans to establish regulations governing commercial aquaculture of salmon. Historically, the fisheries department's specific persecution of the Lummi tribe has been documented. This last invidious move by the notoriously anti-Indian state of Washington bodes ill for the Lummi people.

The records of the Bureau of Indian Affairs, the Department of the Interior, and the Department of Justice with respect to the fishing rights of Washington Indians — particularly the Lummis — are records of treachery, betrayal, ineptitude, and incompetence so gross that their legal role as trustees for the Lummis can only be considered as some ludicrous and tragic joke.

The ultimate success of the whole aquaculture project, therefore, depends on the ability of the Lummi people to defend their legal rights against the state of Washington and against the behind-the-scenes collusion of the federal agencies that have been directed to defend the interests of the Lummi people. In order that the United States may adequately fulfill its treaty responsibility to the Lummi people, it is the conclusion of this study that a special grant of $100,000 a year for a minimum period of five years should be granted to the Lummi tribe for use in the litigation necessary to uphold its rights.

THE LUMMI EXPERIENCE AND OTHER INDIAN TRIBES

The present development of the Lummi Reservation is a total community effort. Its outstanding feature is the aquaculture project, a new and innovative economic program that symbolizes the blossoming of a new concept of tribal life and culture. The question of how the experience and understanding gained by the Lummi people may be transferred to other tribes involves a number of factors that can be considered only tentatively at this time. This study should be regarded as a preliminary sketch of the ongoing development of the Lummi community. A specific study by the Lummi people of the difficulties encountered in the various phases of community development is imperative, if the projected analysis of this paper is to have more than passing relevance. Community development and community identity can be realized only within a community and not by an outside observer, no matter how vigorously he strives for understanding.

The following factors, therefore, are probably unique at Lummi and may not be realized with respect to other tribes in other situations.

Human Resources

The Lummi community is more solidly a community than the vast majority of non-Indian communities. Originally a series of closely related fishing villages, the community merged into one general group with the establishment of the reservation in 1873. During the past century the Lummi people have engaged in lumbering, hop picking, fishing — and presently aquaculture — as a community.

Almost every cultural tradition of the Lummis relates back to the early period when people acted in concert to follow the sea-life cycle of their territory. Members of other tribes who came to live on the reservation had lived much the same type of life as had the Lummis, and they made the transition on the same terms as did the Lummi people.

The programs that have been proposed by the federal government — designed to turn the Lummis into farmers, to make wage earners out of them, to relocate them in the cities, even to make craftsmen out of them — were all activities that did not speak to the Lummi community in terms of its deepest striving: to be itself. The aquaculture project related directly to Lummi traditions. It involved work at which the Lummi people were expert. It reaffirmed their dignity, by once again allowing them to become master fishermen of the Northwest.

The use of human resources of other tribes, if anything is to be learned from the Lummi experience, must be closely related to the cultural and historical conception that the tribe has of itself. It must correspond to what people remember as being the best in their community life, at that point at which memories are most vivid. Without this factor, it is doubtful that any lasting success can be made with proposed developments to assist the tribe.

Capital Resources

The only property that the Lummi tribe owned communally was some 5,000 acres of tidal flatland. Before the development of aquaculture, the tidal flats were regarded as community property for clamming, fishing, and recreation. A substantial amount of federal funding was received, enabling the Lummi people to develop the tidelands for aquaculture. However, the concept of community development, as directly opposed to individual development, played a very important part in the willingness of the Lummi people to attempt the development of aquaculture.

Almost every tribe has some communally owned land. The possibility of developing an economic base for every tribe theoretically exists. The important aspect of the Lummi development has been that it is creating jobs for individuals, through the total concept of a community that has almost exclusively dominated the outlook of the Lummi people.

It would be singularly tragic for other tribes to take community lands or property and attempt to use them to create a certain number of jobs for a certain group of individuals. Tribes could better concentrate, instead, on building a total community with a discernable future. The jobs, individual betterment, and subsidiary programs will fit themselves into a community that looks to the future as a psychic unity, as has the Lummi community. Without this orientation it is doubtful that any significant programs can be sustained. For confirmation of this analysis, a reading of the Commissioner of Indian Affairs regional conferences in the fall of 1966, with respect to tribal investments of judgment funds, should be sufficient.

Management

With the exception of several non-Lummi people who have provided the technical scientific knowledge needed to develop aquaculture and the employment of business managers for setting up projects during the first years, the Lummi development has been a community effort. Had the Lummi people possessed the technical skills, which most certainly must include experience, they would have been able to do almost everything that has previously been or is now done by non-Lummis.

Personnel has shifted continually throughout the development of the project. However, in comparison with other Indian tribes and with a substantial number of non-Indian communities, this shifting has been notably free of personality conflict, petty jealousies, and favoritism. The political and economic structures that the Lummi people have set up — the Lummi Indian Business Council, the Lummi Indian Tribal Enterprises, and the Lummi Indian Foundation Trust — have generally chosen their personnel according to the ability of the person to perform.

Management, as practiced by the Lummis, has entailed properly identifying what the community is, rather than merely training people to fulfill certain functions. Lummi people who were considered failures in the non-Indian educational system, who had been losers in the economic competition of non-Indian society, have assumed very complicated responsibilities in the aquaculture project and have handled them with amazing expertise.

Natural Resources

The Lummi attitude toward natural resources has been consistent throughout the recorded history of the tribe. Religious and cultural values revolved around the salmon, the plants and animals of the immediate environment, and the particular lands on which the people have traditionally lived. Even during the darkest days when fishing was restricted to gill netting in the Nooksack River, the tribe had rules for regulating tribal fishing so that there would be a sufficient return of salmon to the river.

The stripping of the reservation's original stand of Douglas fir and the failure to replant the forest was not a Lummi failure. Rather, it was government policy to turn a magnificent forest into farmlands. The Lummi preservation of tidelands is certainly the most significant indication of the Lummi attitude toward conservation of natural resources.

The development of aquaculture, as previously noted, was not originally an effort to exploit the tidelands. It was an attempt to find an activity that could be conducted there without damaging the environment. In Lummi aquaculture the tides, not pumps, circulate water through the ponds; every natural force that can be applied is favored over mechanical devices.

Can other tribes make the same adjustments to their lands? In many cases Indian tribes have been greatly misled as to the consequences of long-term leasing, industrial development, and exploitation of mineral resources. This factor is probably not as relevant for consideration in dealing with the development of other tribes as others that have been presented. The Lummi attitude of disturbing the land and water as little as possible is hardly an uncommon attitude among Indian tribes.

Markets

The next task of the aquaculturalists, according to the Lummi people who have responsibility for the marketing phase of the project, is to determine where and how the seafood products will be sold. As previously noted, reef netting was regarded as an individual right, and weir netting was regarded as a community enterprise. Both traditions are present in the Lummi community. For that reason a further study of the Lummi development by the Lummis themselves is recommended. This particular question can be resolved by such a study.

Profits

It is very difficult to determine exactly how the profit motive is operating in the Lummi community. All families want a decent living and recognize the need for income above the subsistance level at which Lummis have lived ever since the reservation was established. Aquaculture is designed to produce an annual gross income of $4 million a year by 1975, with a profit of $1 million (Lummi Indian Tribal OEDP 1969: 21 ff.). Projections of income are revised very frequently according to the actual production schedule of aquaculture, so it is virtually impossible to determine exactly what the income and profit for the project will be until the project is in full operation.

Profit, however, is hardly a term that can be used with respect to this particular development. The Lummi people have projected a need for 600 additional jobs within the next twenty years. What the ordinary corporation would call income and profit cannot be said to be either income or profit in terms of the Lummi development. The LITE board has already projected the expenditure of what could be called "surplus funds" into a revolving loan fund, to ensure that sufficient jobs will be available for all Lummis who want to live and work on the reservation.

Instead of categorizing Lummi aquaculture as a profit-making venture, one could more adequately characterize it as a generating source of development and social service funds. At no forseeable time in the future will the excess produced by aquaculture be available for investment or distribution to tribal members. Rather, it will continue to provide funds for community and individual development. Aquaculture must provide surplus funds to make the entire Lummi development plan come to fruition. However, the profit motive as traditionally known is not a significant factor in the Lummi community.

Some Indian tribes presently have sufficient income from oil and gas royalties or timber stumpage to distribute their funds on a per capita basis. This type of tribal income distribution is probably the closest comparison to traditionally conceived ventures that can be found in Indian country. The Lummi conception of community-generated and supporting funds should certainly be considered by other tribes seeking long-term community development.

Income Distribution

Current development plans in the Lummi community appear to be moving toward creation of a reasonable income for all tribal members. Employment on tribal projects, specialization and resulting financial rewards, and eventual creation of economic classes within the tribal community appear to be problems that the community must face as aquaculture and other tribal projects get under way. For that reason a further study by the Lummi people themselves as to the ultimate meaning of their community development has been recommended.

Methods of Dealing with Crises

The Lummi people have responded to natural crises with a unified effort. Closing the retaining wall appeared to be the crucial event of the construction of the aquaculture facility. Almost the whole tribe turned out to work at whatever jobs were required, for a period of some thirty hours, in order to close the dike.

On one occasion, several thousand trout froze because of a sudden dip in temperature. Lummis gathered at the pond and promptly harvested all the fish, thereby saving a considerable amount of food that otherwise would have spoiled. Markets in the local region were found and the loss was held to a minimum.

The constant attacks by the Lummi Bay Beach Owners Association have served to unify the community as no other force could have done. At every point at which it appeared that the aquaculture project was threatened, the Lummi community — with the exception of the few magnesium-oxide dissidents — rallied behind the tribal program.

The concept of unexpected natural or unnatural crises is a difficult one to chart for any Indian community. Probably the best parallel that could be drawn would be to compare the Lummi response to crises with the reaction of Indian people to termination of specific reservations. The Klamaths, for example, grew so tired of controversy that they simply refused to do anything, a response that guaranteed the termination of their tribe. The Lummis, on the other hand, do not usually back away from controversy.

Tribal Wealth

In comparison with other tribes in the nation, the Lummi people have very little material wealth. They have lost a substantial amount of their land base, including most of the shoreline allotments (They received a magnificent settlement of $57,000 from the Indian Claims Commission for their aboriginally held lands.). The Nooksack River, their traditional fishing site and the river on which they have primary water rights, has been all but destroyed for fishing by industrial pollution.

Projecting the possible success of tribal economic ventures by evaluating natural resources or treasury accounts is, at best, hazardous. The Lummi tribe, for example, possessed practically nothing. Tribal income was sufficient only to pay the wages of the tribal policeman when he served at celebrations. For years the tribal chairman and council members have worked with no per diem compensation. Lummi tribal officials could not afford to travel until the tribe received a grant from the Office of Economic Opportunity.

The absolutely unique factor of the creation of Lummi wealth, which is as yet a future event, is the ownership of Lummi Bay tidelands. The particular use to which this area has been put probably cannot be duplicated in more than two or three places in Indian country. Other tribes should consider the unique features of particular lands that they own and develop specific programs revolving around the unique uses of these lands. Other than projecting that possible insight, the Lummi experience is so totally unique that no conclusions can be drawn from it.

VALUES AND GOALS OF THE RESERVATION

Perhaps the most significant lesson that can be learned from the developments of the Lummi community is that economic development should not be conceived as economic development, but as community development. The orientation of the Lummi people has been to accomplish something on a community basis, because the community has been looking for a means of asserting itself. Lummi community life has traditionally revolved around the ecological values of the immediate area. From precontact times until the present, the Lummi people have been a community in the process of discovering itself.

Indian communities have always found themselves torn between two abstract conceptions of what they are, as defined by outsiders. One interpretation, favored in the academic community, is that Indian culture, religion, and political development reached its highest and most pristine point at precisely that time when it was first observed by a scholar. From that point on, the Indian community is graded negatively as it varies from the behavior patterns originally observed.

The other interpretation, favored by government agencies and policy makers, places a positive value on any community development that appears to indicate that the Indian community is beginning to behave as the government agent or politician himself believes that men should act. The series of optimistic reports of Indian agents during the 1860 to 1890 period, stating that the Lummis were becoming successful farmers, is an indication that expectations often cloud bureaucratic reality.

The fundamental meaning of the current development of aquaculture by the Lummi Indian people is contained in their understanding of themselves at every point at which we have knowledge of them. Their singleness of purpose is notable. In the 1890's they fought to preserve their reef-netting sites at Point Roberts and lost. In the 1915–1917 years they fought against the state and fishermen from Austria to protect their fishing grounds. They lost. In the 1930's they managed to stay alive in a severe depression because they were fishermen. After World War II they developed a purse-seine fleet so that they could continue to fish. They were forced out of the market. Finally, they have become world-famous aquaculturists.

The Lummi people have evolved over a period of time, and they have maintained themselves as what they have wanted to be from the very beginning. The Lummi people are fishermen, perhaps at one time the most primitive, perhaps today the most sophisticated. If they continue to receive adequate support until they complete the planned development of their community, the world will have learned something from them. If they are thwarted, they will simply retreat and retrench — until they find another way to be fishermen. For it appears that fishermen and Lummi are identical terms for a very tough and flexible community of people.

REFERENCES

AMERICAN FRIENDS SERVICE COMMITTEE
  1970   *Uncommon controversy.* Seattle: University of Washington Press.
Bellingham Bay Express
  1891   Article in *Bellingham Bay Express*, June 9. Bellingham, Washington.
  1893   Article in *Bellingham Bay Express*, August 23. Bellingham, Washington.

Bellingham Bay Mail
  1873–1875   Articles in *Bellingham Bay Mail.* Bellingham, Washington.

Bellingham Herald
  1893   Article in *Bellingham Herald*, May 11. Bellingham, Washington.
  1904   Articles in *Bellingham Herald*, May 18, June 8, and June 29. Bellingham, Washington.
  1906   Articles in *Bellingham Herald*, October 5 and October 6. Bellingham, Washington.
  1909   Articles in *Bellingham Herald*, February 8, September 4, and October 1. Bellingham, Washington.

1910   Articles in *Bellingham Herald*, January 23, September 22, 23. Bellingham Washington.

1911   Articles in *Bellingham Herald*, January 7 and June 11. Bellingham, Washington.

1913   Articles in *Bellingham Herald*, September 29 and November 7. Bellingham, Washington.

1915   Article in *Bellingham Herald*, January 27. Bellingham, Washington.

1916   Article in *Bellingham Herald*, January 15. Bellingham, Washington.

1918   Article in *Bellingham Herald*, September 10. Bellingham, Washington.

1919   Article in *Bellingham Herald*, January 10. Bellingham, Washington.

1921   Articles in *Bellingham Herald*, March 18, August 11, September 30, and November 3. Bellingham, Washington.

1922   Articles in *Bellingham Herald*, October 19 and November 16. Bellingham, Washington.

1923   Article in *Bellingham Herald*, May 26. Bellingham, Washington.

1948   Article in *Bellingham Herald*, September 20. Bellingham, Washington.

1949   Article in *Bellingham Herald*, November 22. Bellingham, Washington.

1959   Articles in *Bellingham Herald*, May 13 and November 5. Bellingham, Washington.

1961   Articles in *Bellingham Herald*, March 4, April 11, and November 3. Bellingham, Washington.

1962   Article in *Bellingham Herald*, February 25. Bellingham, Washington.

1963   Articles in *Bellingham Herald*, February 8 and March 17. Bellingham, Washington.

1964   Article in *Bellingham Herald*, March 10. Bellingham, Washington.

1968   Articles in *Bellingham Herald*, March 30 and May 10. Bellingham, Washington.

1969   Article in *Bellingham Herald*, November 20, 21, and 24. Bellingham, Washington.

1970   "County zoning on Indian land allowed in special cases." *Bellingham Herald*, June 7. Bellingham, Washington.

1971   "Non-Indian land owners on reservation plan meetings." *Bellingham Herald*, October 26. Bellingham, Washington.
        "Reservation water rights get court test by Lummis." *Bellingham Herald*, December 1. Bellingham, Washington.

1972   Section on featured recipes, *Bellingham Herald*, May 19. Bellingham, Washington.

Board of Indian Commissioners
1884   *Sixteenth annual report.*

COMMISSIONER OF INDIAN AFFAIRS

1857   *Annual report of the Commissioner of Indian Affairs.* Washington, D.C.: Government Printing Office.

1859   *Annual report of the Commissioner of Indian Affairs.* Washington, D.C.: Government Printing Office.

1865   *Annual report of the Commissioner of Indian Affairs.* Washington, D.C.: Government Printing Office.

1867   *Annual report of the Commissioner of Indian Affairs.* Washington, D.C.: Government Printing Office.

1870   *Annual report of the Commissioner of Indian Affairs.* Washington, D.C.: Government Printing Office.

1871 *Annual report of the Commissioner of Indian Affairs.* Washington, D.C.: Government Printing Office.

1872 *Annual report of the Commissioner of Indian Affairs.* Washington, D.C.: Government Printing Office.

1885 *Annual report of the Commissioner of Indian Affairs.* Washington, D.C.: Government Printing Office.

1888 *Annual report of the Commissioner of Indian Affairs.* Washington, D.C.: Government Printing Office.

1889 *Annual report of the Commissioner of Indian Affairs.* Washington, D.C.: Government Printing Office.

1893 *Annual report of the Commissioner of Indian Affairs.* Washington, D.C.: Government Printing Office.

1895 *Annual report of the Commissioner of Indian Affairs.* Washington, D.C.: Government Printing Office.

1897 *Annual report of the Commissioner of Indian Affairs.* Washington, D.C.: Government Printing Office.

1898 *Annual report of the Commissioner of Indian Affairs.* Washington, D.C.: Government Printing Office.

1904 *Annual report of the Commissioner of Indian Affairs.* Washington, D.C.: Government Printing Office.

Daily Reveille
1895 Article in *Daily Reveille*, October 23.

Duwamish et al. tribes of Indians v. United States
1934 79 C. Cls. 530 (1934) cert. den. 295 U.S. 755.

Executive Order
1873 1 Kapp. 917.

Ferndale Record
1971 Article in *Ferndale Record*, August 4. Ferndale, Washington.

JAMES G. SWAN CASE
1972 50 Fed. 108 (D.C. Wash. 1892).

JOSEPHY, ALVIN
1965 *The Nez Perce Indians and the opening of the Northwest.* New Haven: Yale University Press.

LOWMAN, BEATRICE AUNETTE
1939 Reef nets come back in Puget Sound salmon fishery. *Pacific Fisherman* (June): 45–48.

LUMMI INDIAN BUSINESS COUNCIL
1969 "Rebuttal to letters from opponents of the Lummi Aquaculture Development Research Ponds in Lummi Bay," in *Memorandum of 15 August*, 1969.

Lummi Tribe of Indians v. United States
1957 5 Indian Claims Commission 525 Findings of Fact.

Memorandum
1967 "Comments on Quinault Ordance No. 1." Office of the Regional Solicitor. Portland Area Office, Bureau of Indian Affairs, July 26, 1967.

Pollard v. Hagan
1845 3 How. 212–235.

ROTH, LOTTIE
1926 *A history of Whatcom County*, volume one. Chicago: Pioneer Historical Publishing Company.

Seattle Post-Intelligencer
1970 Article in *Seattle Post-Intelligencer*, February 15.

Shively v. Bowlby
   1893   152 U.S. 1, 14 S. Ct. 548 (1893).
SPIER, LESLIE
   1936   Indian Claims Commission Hearings. Findings of Fact, *The Lummi Tribe of Indians v. United States of America*, Docket no. 110. "Tribal distribution in Washington."
STERN, B. J.
   1969   *The Lummi Indians of Northwest Washington*. Columbia University Contributions to Antropology Series, volume seventeen. New York: A.M.S, Press. (Reprint of the 1934 edition.)
SUTTLES, WAYNE
   1954   Post-contact culture change among the Lummi Indians. *British Columbia Historical Quarterly* 18(1,2).
   1957   The Plateau Prophet Dance among the coastal Salish. *Southwestern Journal of Anthropology* 13(4).
   1963   The persistence of intervillage ties among the coastal Salish. *Ethnology* 2(4).
TAYLOR, DON NEWMAN
   1969   "Changes in the economy of the Lummi Indians of northwest Washington." Unpublished M.A. thesis, Western Washington State College, Bellingham, Washington.
Taylor et al. v. United States
   1930   44 F. 2d. 53 (C.C.A. 9, 1930).
Time
   1914   Article in *Time*, August 31.
Tulalip Reservation
   1914–1927   *Annual report.*
United States et al. v. Alaska Packers' Association
   1897   79 Fed. 152 (C.C. Wash. 1897), app. dism. 19 Sup. Ct. 881 (1899).
United States v. Holt
   1923   270 U.S. 49,46 S. Ct. 197(1923).
United States v. Romaine
   1919   255 Fed. 253 (C.C.A. 9, 1919).
United States v. Winans
   1896   198 U.S. 371 (1905), rev'g 73 Fed. 72 (C.C. Wash. 1896).

Morongo Indian Reservation:
A Century of Adaptive Strategies

LOWELL JOHN BEAN

The failures of American Indians to fully exploit the economic resources of their lands is sometimes blamed on social pathologies and disorganization. Lack of management training, education, capital, and access to markets are other reasons that have been given for Indian "backwardness." Another point of view suggests that the organization and management that have been imposed on Indians by the dominant white culture may be the main cause of Indian problems.

But these theories do not explain Indian problems, because they are based on the premise that failure exists. The reputed "failures" may actually be successful adaptive strategies — strategies that have enabled a subordinate population to maintain its local power, autonomy, ethnic boundaries, and traditional value system, while surrounded by threatening and conflicting views.

Since 1890, leaders of the Morongo Indian reservation have been allied closely with federal agencies and their representatives — while they have simultaneously battled vigorously with these same agencies about how their mutual relationships were to be conducted. Consequently, for more than ninety years, Morongo reservation has been reported by Bureau of Indian Affairs officials as a model and progressive reservation—and as southern California's most contentious and difficult reservation. Morongo obviously provides a dynamic example of what may happen when two contrasting and interacting cultural systems meet in a long-range relationship that is fixed, yet alterable.

Traditional Indian approaches to the production, distribution, and management of resources usually differ significantly from those of the white community. The free enterprise economy of the United States includes "private property, market-determined prices, decentralized

decision making, consumer sovereignty, competition, entrepreneurship, etc. It also establishes certain goals, such as maximization of
economic returns, including profit and other economic returns to
individuals, accumulation of wealth and physical possessions, and so
forth" (Stanley 1971).

Indian societies may emphasize, instead, communal property and
communal objectives. Interaction with white society has affected traditional Indian economic strategies and values, but at least one native
American scholar maintains that "tribes that can handle their reservation conflicts in traditional Indian fashion generally make more progress and have better programs than do tribes that continually make
adaptations to the white value system" (Deloria 1970: 28).

Our preliminary study, which has been appended, deals with a
number of specific variables which provide documentation for those
who wish to compare reservations in terms of: (1) ownership of
production factors; (2) management of those resources (Indian and
non-Indian); (3) planning and goals; (4) social organization that affects
labor force participation, scheduling and work hours, and personal and
economic growth; (5) methods of dealing with crises (e.g., drought,
floods, etc.); (6) land tenure, community vs. individual ownership of
land; and (7) profit motive.

This report will provide additional data and background for native
Americans involved in economic development, as well as non-Indians
dealing with reservation problems so they can become more aware of
the historical, cultural, and economic variables which affect their
interactions with reservation communities. There are very few studies
of recent developments on California Indian reservations, and this
study and Bee's study (Bee 1967) of the Quechen reservation are
unique, since they direct attention to economic development and social
organization. The processes of culture change and adaptation in
California, especially in relationship to the reservation milieu, can now
be compared on a broader range, since this study complements others
which have dealt with variables of culture change (Theodoratus 1970)
on the Point Arena reservation, Robert Bee's study (1967) of the
Quechen, Imre Sutton's study (1964) of land tenure on southern
California reservations, Richard Thomas' study (1964) of leadership in
context of culture change, and Kennedy's study (1955) of culture
change at Kashia Indian reservation.

This study will also provide data useful to researchers interested in
the political adaptations which reservation populations have made to
changing policies, opportunities and withdrawals, and new forms of
welfare capitalization. The politically dynamic reactions to these factors are major considerations in this study, and they demonstrate ways
in which reservation people have utilized non-Indian resources.

METHODOLOGY

While it was not intended that significant new data would be needed for this study, the present state of readily available materials was deemed inadequate, and a large body of archival resources was collected to provide a supportive base for our generalizations. Morongo residents and non-Indians who have had extensive experience with economic affairs on the reservation were interviewed concerning the historical aspects of the reservation economic and social history.

Whenever it was possible, respondents were asked to describe the reservation's economic background, and economic development plans that are now being presented to the tribe.

Our study carries a historic dimension indicating the adaptive strategies of Morongo people to changes in their circumstances, so that we can see if traditional ways persist through time, and what new strategies were developed with each generation of change in economic and political life. While continuity with the distant past becomes less and less clear at a casual level, it is dramatically persistent when seen over several generations.

The social groupings at Morongo are primarily based on kinship, tribal affiliation, religion, economic orientation, and, to some extent, class. Each of the components enters into our discussions. The kinds of jobs people have had access to and the overall organization of the community have been discussed in our preliminary report, but enter into this one as well.

We have found that Morongo cannot be isolated from its surrounding community. At whatever level of organization one looks at — federal, state, county, city, Indian Service, or the subculture of southern California reservations themselves — Morongo is but a part of a complicated ecosystem, more influenced by than influential to it. As reservations function in the local area, Morongo has been an unusually innovative and adaptable part of the whole.

We are including maps and charts which indicate Morongo's place within the California and southern California Bureau of Indian Affairs, the nature of landholding and use, population patterns, and organizational charts which indicate the complex milieu of which they are a part (see Maps 1–4 and Figure 1-3).

PROCEDURE

This study was begun in December of 1971, when the author met with four members of the Morongo Indian reservation: James Martin, tribal chairman, Jane Penn, curator, Malki Museum and former tribal councilwoman, Madeline Ball, tribal councilwoman and an O.E.O. neighborhood worker for the Banning area, Thomas Lyons, councilman of the Morongo reservation, Michael Black, architect and planner who was working with an economic development committee on the reservation.

The goals of the research project were discussed and all agreed to act as a committee to assist and evaluate various stages of the research.

Mrs. Ball and Katherine Siva Saubel, president of Malki Museum, subsequently visited the State University at Hayward and discussed reservation conditions and procedure and research objectives with the author and oriented a group of students who were preparing to go to Morongo to assist in this project. Initially the author surveyed bibliographic sources and outlined the goals of the project. Ten students from the Department of Anthropology of California State University at Hayward prepared research schedules for reservation residents and aided the author's and the reservation committee's search of archival resources at the Federal Records Center, Bell, California, and at the Riverside office of the Bureau of Indian Affairs. Madeline Ball and Jane Penn, as well as the other committee members, assisted in archival searches and introduced students to reservation members, set up meetings with Morongo reservation high school students who acted as research assistants, and arranged meetings with various individuals and groups. Most of these meetings were held in the tribal hall, but formal and informal interviews with individuals were conducted in private homes or where convenience dictated.

Formal seminars were held with older residents — Margaret Cline, Marianno Saubel, and with William Gianelli, a Bureau of Indian Affairs officer. Various residents of the reservation sat in on these sessions.

Upon returning from the field, students wrote reports on the particular subjects covered in their research, such as the history of agriculture, education, leadership patterns, health, stock raising, and allotments.

Ten weeks later a second group of students was brought into the project; their orientation was similar to the previous group — Mrs. Ball prepared special lectures for them and some students who had worked on the previous trip went along to introduce the new students to the community. They proceded to interview and work on archival materials.

Upon completion of the first phase, a preliminary report was submitted by the senior investigator to the reservation advisory committee. This committee met privately, exchanged views, and relayed criticism back to the author.

In effect, most of the residents of the reservation participated in our study. Some were especially active and served as formal consultants: Mr. and Mrs. Orlin Hough, Miss Margaret Cline, Mr. Walter Linton, Mrs. Victoria Lomas, Mr. and Mrs. Sam and Dorothy Lugo, Mrs. Sarah Martin, Mr. Clifford Matthews, Mr. and Mrs. Henry Matthews, Miss Viola Matthews, Miss Rose Meserve, Mrs. Adelaide Presley, Mr. and Mrs. E. Miguel, Miss Irene Miguel, Mr. Marianno Saubel, Mrs. Ray Valenzuela, and Mr. and Mrs. Leonard Siva.

The Reservation Advisory Committee arranged for a group of high school students to assist in a work/study capacity in local arrangements and research. They were James Lugo, Luanne Martin, Roy Matthews, Joletta Miguel, Pauline Miguel, and Phillip Siva.

Twenty students from the Department of Anthropology at California State University, Hayward, participated in data collection and analysis for this report. Four graduate students, Thomas Kirkland, Jaynel Hatlen, and John Mahon continued with the project to its completion. Jack Young assisted throughout in data retrieval and manuscript preparation.

Several non-Indian residents of Banning, California, were also consulted: George Barker, Francis Johnston, and Bert Jost.

TRIBAL BACKGROUND

In aboriginal times, the region where the Morongo Indians now reside was part of the homeland of Cahuilla-speaking peoples who lived in and exploited the general area of San Gorgonio Pass (Bean 1969): 111–113). The Wanikik clan of this region included twelve confederated lineages which recognized descent from a common ancestral lineage. Each lineage owned a village location in one of the area's canyons, and each had its own ceremonial house, a *net* [political and ceremonial leader] and *paha* [*net*'s assistant], shamans, and other officials who fulfilled ritual, philosophical, economic, and political roles. One *net* was recognized as titular head of the clan that numbered perhaps 1,200 people.

The general boundaries of Wanikik territories were the higher parts of the San Bernardino Mountains and the San Jacintos on the north of San Gorgonio Pass (Map 1A, 1B). Within this general area—which included canyons, valley floor, foothills, and mountains—each lineage owned specific food-collecting and hunting areas, as well as resource areas for other valuable products.

Villages were occupied year round, although people left temporarily for activities such as the collecting of acorns in the fall. The concept of private ownership was intense; all resources within the tribal area were

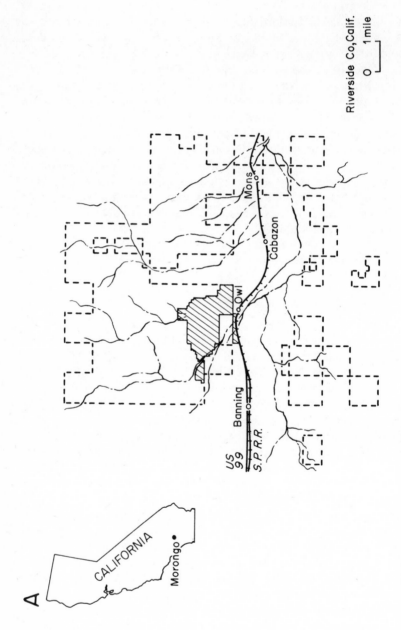

Map 1A.   Morongo Indian reservation

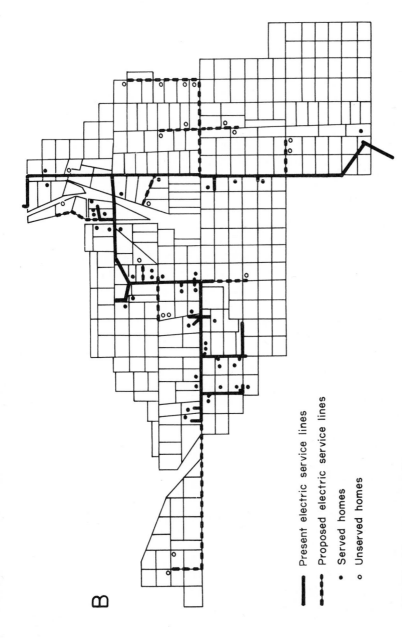

B

Present electric service lines

Proposed electric service lines

• Served homes

○ Unserved homes

Map 1B. Morongo community

attached to social units, ranging in level from the individual to the collective Wanikik group. Ownership and the exclusive use of produce and capital equipment were jealously guarded.

Economic exchange involved an elaborate system of exchange rules, associated with kinship and marriage regulations and controlled by ritual obligations. As a result, Wanikik groups always had relatives in several Cahuilla, Serrano, or other neighboring groups, and economic and political alliances extend in broad networks for many miles. These exchange relationships were supported by elaborate ritual mechanisms and philosophical assumptions (Bean 1972).

Labor within a lineage village was divided principally by age and sex. Men did most of the hunting, food collecting that required heavy work or long-distance travel, manufacturing of some goods, trading, and supervision of ritual activities. Women collected plant foods, raised the children, and manufactured materials associated with cooking, food storage, and clothing.

Cahuilla philosophical concepts defined a complex cosmology, which was described in epic poems that were memorized by specialists and accompanied by music. In the poetic texts, Cahuilla values were clearly stated.

In historic times, peoples from variant tribal backgrounds came to the Morongo reservation — other Cahuillas, Serranos, Cupeños, Diegueños, and some Luiseños. All have cultural backgrounds in which social and economic arrangements are similar to those described for the Wanikiktum, and differences are not significant to this report. Most of them (excluding the Diegueños) shared a Shoshonean language and a philosophical system. They participated in very broad ritual congregations of peoples who had shared and exchanged ideas, wives, and economic goods for several centuries prior to the arrival of white people.

Mission Period

News of the arrival of the Anza expedition in Cahuilla territory, via Los Coyotes Canyon, must have spread quickly to nearby San Gorgonio Pass. There is no recorded contact with non-Indians, however, until 1809, when Wanikik Cahuillas living at San Gorgonio Pass were baptized at Mission San Gabriel.

Within a decade, missionaries had explored as far as the present city of Redlands and had established the *assistencia* of San Bernardino (reportedly by request of the Indians at Guachama). Serrano and Wanikik Cahuilla Indians who came to the mission acquired not only instruction in the Catholic faith but also agricultural knowledge (including that of stock raising) and various European crafts which they incorporated with their own traditions. The people of San Gorgonio Pass seem to have been only slightly involved with the Spaniards, although Cahuillas, as far east as the present Indio, dealt on friendly terms with the Romero Expeditions that traveled through the area in 1819 and 1823, apparently without interpreters. Mission cattle were then being grazed as far south and east as Palm Springs.

There is no evidence that significant changes occurred in Indian settlement patterns, social structure, or economic development during the mission period, although it is probable that European diseases spread throughout many Indian communities, killing many people. Historic and oral records of the Cahuillas indicate that some Gabrielinos had come into the Wanikik–Serrano area during the mission period, and the establishment of the San Bernardino *assistencia* brought Cahuillas together with Serranos in a new manner, for they united to attack the mission settlement in 1834.

The missions brought new leadership roles such as majordomos, *regidores*, and others to Cahuillas and Serranos. These roles were sometimes taken by traditional chiefs, although opportunities were provided for new leaders to emerge and for chiefs to extend their authority to new peoples.

Economic changes were brought about by new agricultural knowledge. Cattle from Mission San Gabriel were occasionally hunted by Indians.

Rancho Period

During the "rancho" period in California history, several socioeconomic patterns developed among native populations. Indians had already learned the rudiments of Spanish living patterns, so when ranches supplanted missions as the dominant institution, Indians continued to provide the primary labor force. They often lived at ranches or migrated to them seasonally, in groups or as individuals, to find work and wages. In the small settlements of Los Angeles and San Diego, Indians found work, liquor, and more diseases; they brought back wages to their people — along with new goods and new illnesses. During this period the system of wage labor was established, allowing the Cahuillas to acquire goods and money from outsiders while maintaining the integrity of their own cultural system.

Several ranches near San Gorgonio Pass provided employment and wage-earning opportunities for native peoples. The ranchers needed laborers for vineyards, orchards, irrigation, sheep herding, and sheep shearing. These occupations were integrated with the widely diversified

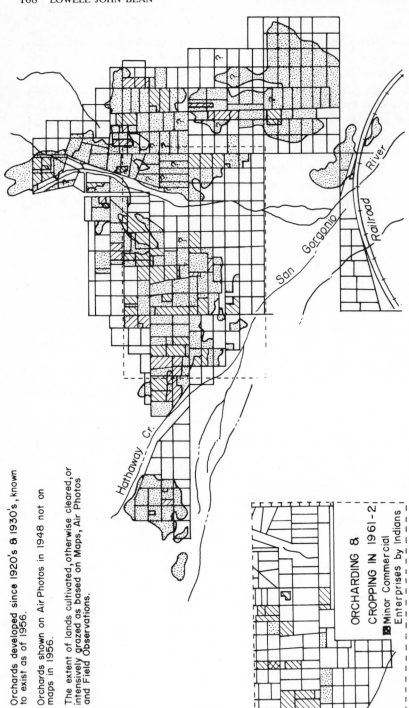

Orchards developed since 1920's & 1930's, known
to exist as of 1956.

Orchards shown on Air Photos in 1948 not on
maps in 1956.

The extent of lands cultivated, otherwise cleared, or
intensively grazed as based on Maps, Air Photos
and Field Observations.

ORCHARDING &
CROPPING IN 1961-2
Minor Commercial
Enterprises by Indians

Map 2.   Composite land use (allotted areas to 1956)

hunting-and-gathering economy of traditional settlements, and new village locations became centers of living from which members went out periodically to "collect" the new products of the Europeans. By 1840, Indians from the Cahuilla and Serrano areas worked at Jurupa (now Colton) in the upper end of San Gorgonio Pass, at the ranch of Duff Weaver.

This ranch at the head of San Gorgonio Pass, which was still the eastern frontier of Mexican California, was freely controlled by Cahuillas. One famous leader, Juan Antonio, headquartered at a very large village near the pass. The ancestors of Morongo people were even further isolated and were relatively undisturbed, except by migrants from other tribes and by the few white people who had previously established ranches.

EARLY AMERICAN PERIOD

The ancestors of the Morongo people were represented at the signing of the treaties between southern California Indians and the United States government in 1851. The original inhabitants who remained lived in small settlements throughout the San Gorgonio Pass; many of them clustered at Ajenios village, near Banning. Although they continued many of their native traditions, they also migrated to work for white settlers in the area.

Troubles with whites increased rapidly, and a reservation system was suggested by a local authority, B. D. Wilson, who was quoted in the *Los Angeles Star* on February 26, 1853:

They are the only places where the different nations could be colonized and established in large numbers, with sufficient land for cultivation. San Gorgonio and San Jacinto each has more than 2,000 acres capable of raising barley and wheat, without irrigation; and sufficient water, husbanded as the Missions taught Indians to manage this matter, to supply in abundance beans, pumpkins, and the other crops Indians are familiar with, or can soon be made so . . . . The Cahuillas can raise 100,000 bushels of wheat or barley annually, at San Jacinto or San Gorgonio. Temecula and Agua Caliente would yield $300,000 worth . . . .
San Gorgonio, for example, would not support a hundred small farmers, seeking to satisfy the wants of civilization; while, under a common cultivation, and a systematic and economical appropriation of the water for irrigation, it will amply support three thousand souls and more . . . .
Frequent rumors reach our city from San Gorgonio, that the Indians are deprived of the use of the water, by Mr. Weaver, and that in consequence they are unable to sow their grain. We hope the rumors may not prove true; for the acts complained of are outrages which may provoke retaliation. The law expressly provides that the Indians shall retain uninterrupted possession of

lands they may have occupied for a series of years. Moreover, these Indians are Juan Antonio's Cahuillas, with whom Gen. Bean formed a treaty, pledging the faith of the State that they should not be molested so long as they observed its terms. Thus, to deprive them of any of their privileges would be a violation of both the law and the treaty, and may lead to serious difficulties. We hope Mr. Weaver appreciates the importance of maintaining inviolate the pledged faith of the State with these Indians, and the dangers he may incur by provoking them to hostilities (Caughey 1952: 37, 55–56, 90).

The treaty of 1851 had not been ratified, and Indians of the pass had no legal claim to the lands they had owned for centuries. Many more whites came to the area and made claim to these lands, and conflict between Indians and settlers became acute. Finally, the federal government restricted the settlements of Indians; Morongo reservation was established in 1877, in a checkerboard pattern of alternate sections of white-owned and Indian-owned lands.

Conflicts over land continued, and a government commission was set up to establish new reservation boundaries. Several white families were removed and the checkerboard holdings of the Indians were consolidated into a single parcel. They were now more isolated from, but not independent of white settlements.

During these early years, the reservation was managed only minimally by the Bureau of Indian Affairs, with the agent located at either Colton or Soboba. Home rule and traditional leadership patterns were still in operation. In the 1880's a day school was established, and the new teacher took an interest in reservation life. She encouraged the entrance of a Protestant missionary in 1899, and a new era of reservation affairs was initiated.

LEADERSHIP DEVELOPS NEW STRATEGIES

One of the first major conflicts between traditional Morongo leadership patterns and outside authority began shortly before 1900. H. N. Rust, Indian agent for southern California, attempting to place Indian leadership under the control of the Bureau of Indian Affairs, opposed the traditional captaincy system in which the Indian people selected their own leaders. He insisted on final approval of captains selected in his jurisdiction, repeatedly blocked those of whom he disapproved (often on personal grounds) from taking office, and consistently interfered with decisions made by the Indian people. Rust directly opposed the captaincy of a young Indian leader named Cabeson. Cabeson commanded great respect among the Cahuilla — he was the son of a *net* and himself a *net* of a Cahuilla clan from the Colorado Desert.

Rust went to the desert and influenced the Indians to hold an election, in which an opponent of Cabeson was elected leader by a considerable majority. H. N. Rust leased Morongo reservation grazing and agricultural lands, which had been developed by Indians, to whites —privately maintaining the rent payments (about $3,000; $1,500 in cash and the rest in grain). (Later, he alleged that he was saving it for the development of an irrigation system on the reservation.)

Rust's authority was challenged by William Pablo, a young Wanikik leader who was a friend, relative, and political ally of Cabeson. Pablo collected petitions from Indians of several reservations, sought the aid of a lawyer, talked to a reporter from the *San Francisco Chronicle*, and in general organized the Indian people in an attempt to unseat Rust from his position. Rust requested that Pablo be put in jail, and he appointed John Morongo, an interpreter, as captain of the Morongo reservation. Morongo was a Serrano whose people had been accepted at Morongo by the Cahuilla some years before because of marriage alliances, with the condition that the authority of the traditional leaders would be recognized by the Serranos.

Thus, the self-determination of the people at Morongo to elect leaders by the traditional process was seriously challenged for the first time.

Religious alliances also emerged about this time. Rust, John Morongo, and Protestant school teacher Sarah Morriss had encouraged William H. Weinland, a Moravian missionary, to conduct missionary work at Morongo reservation. Weinland was successful in bringing members of all reservation tribes and many families into his church, but soon members of the Pablo family and other Cahuillas left the Moravian church to return to Indian and Catholic rituals. (William Pablo was both a respected shaman and a Catholic.)

The Catholic priests of southern California, who had previously blocked the acceptance of Weinland at both the Cahuilla and Soboba reservations, also opposed him at Poterero and were joined by Catholic reservation residents. Pablo encouraged parents to send their children to a Catholic school where he had once been employed, at Banning, and as a result the Protestant day school was closed for a time.

After this dissension, leadership at Morongo was never again to be stable. A two-party system developed, and each leader allied with an agent — one in favor, one out. Solidarity was rarely achieved, but a fluid power structure was developed; a system that was learned and applied with consummate skill by the Indians who practiced it. The traditions that each group had brought to Poterero from the past became a system that was dimly recalled by older people, desired by many, but never again freely achieved.

Power(less) Elite

The power(less) elite of Morongo represent many groups, in which membership is variously fixed and is formed through negative integrating devices — the forming of factions, the splitting-up of previous relationships, and other nonpositive means. The majority of the power(less) elite of Morongo have major access to economic production, money, political decisions, control of associations and groups. The status and power of most of the elite comes from a combination of ownership of cattle and/or land, membership in the Moravian church, Serrano–Cupeño ancestry, and the ability to articulate to outside agencies for reservation members. The tribal council is dominated by leaders who have these indicators of status.

Most of the members of the power(less) elite seem to form closer relationships with whites in the city of Banning, where they are characterized as "better Indians," "progressive Indians," "white Indians," or other terms indicating that they are more closely identified with and accepted by the members of the white community than are other residents of Morongo. These Morongans frequently belong to voluntary associations in Banning, and they receive visits from whites and in turn visit in Banning. In the past, their children have been more vigorously encouraged to seek an education and other achievements in Banning. There is a subtle, but clear self-concept of subethnicity among reservation members of this group, which is reflected in folk vocabulary. Members often refer to other reservation residents as "the Indians," in contrast to themselves.

The power elite is not composed exclusively of this group however. Other members represent less dominant groups. Some reservation people belong to all groups in part, to none entirely. Others are associated with the "Indianness" of minority factions — "Cahuillaness," Catholicism, tradition, and farming. These people, too, have extensive off-reservation contacts. But unlike the majority elitists, who tend to associate and identify with the city of Banning and its conservative interests and attitudes, they usually associate with more distant and politically liberal outsiders (such as lawyers, anthropologists, and others who are oriented toward social welfare) who are interested in the Indian and his problems.

There are significant contrasts in the behavioral patterns of these two types of elite. The majority elite accepts local values, while the minority may be opposed to — or even openly hostile and critical of — the "town's" values and its relationships to the reservation. Members of the minority elite are rarely deferential to non-Indians and even openly hostile or defensive, although they may seek out whites for service roles.

In recent years, as federal funding programs have become more accessible and Indian protest groups have developed, new power elite groups have been formed. Their members cut across older factions, integrating skilfully with local and distinct organizations as well as with reservation members. A significant new type of leader, who acts as a catalyst of change, has appeared. He brings together older factions, canceling or smoothing out ancient "feud type" behavior and competitive behavior. Factional leaders appear to be joining together and supporting a younger group of leaders. But such leaders lack the large support bases that older faction leaders could draw upon; only a small group of kin can now be counted on to provide predictable support for a leader. Thus, these younger elitists must have a more flexible approach to the community than was necessary in the past, with issues, not personal loyalties, as a central influence.

The new leaders are more innovative in their approach to reservation affairs. Most of them are associated with specific programs that are beneficial to the reservation but are "managed" by an elite person rather than a broad-based group or faction.

A complete picture of the power elite operating at Morongo must include local and state personnel of the Bureau of Indian Affairs. The role of the BIA has diminished since the passage of Public Law 280, but it is still influential in matters concerned with inheritance, probate, leases, expenditure of tribal funds, research and development grants, and educational grants. The BIA remains a distant authority, but one that is necessarily encountered frequently, because of legal technicalities as well as the dependence that reservation people have on those who have been mandated to serve their interests. BIA personnel are often called upon to provide advisory or informational assistance to Indians, referring them to agencies or persons who can assist them in matters beyond the BIA's authority. The bureau also functions in the role of archivist, by maintaining tribal records and censuses, enrolment data, probate, control funds, correspondence, and historical records.

These roles of the bureau have a permanency, although the actual personnel is ephemeral. The resulting power elite has little predictive value to the people it serves, because policy is interpreted differently by the carriers of the role.

Personnel of other federal agencies — as well as local, state, and federal politicians — may also be considered as members of a power elite, because their activities appreciably affect the quality of life on the reservation, although they are essentially beyond the control of the reservation population. The personal, idiosyncratic, and unpredictable behaviors of this bureaucratic elite cause anxieties and tensions which pervade all relationships on the reservation.

In recent times, Morongans have reasserted self-determination and learned new ways of acquiring power. An example is the present role of Moravian missionaries on the reservation. Missionaries of this religion once wielded significant power with Indians and Indian agents, influencing almost every phase of reservation life — economic, religious, and political. Today the role of the missionary is clearly defined, compartmentalized as that of a religious administrator, and he is expected to restrict his activities to church business. In the past, groups frequently asked missionaries and other non-Indians to attend tribal meetings, to write letters and petitions, and to set guidelines. Such requests are still occasionally made today, but the role of advisor is more controlled than formerly.

Information Control: A Basic Function of Leaders

The demands of normal day-to-day behavior at Morongo requires large amounts of information. During our brief visits, there have been several crises involving land annexations, elections, economic development, arson, water pollution, and adult educational opportunities. These crises were of an intensity that would be considered highly stressful in any community.

The amount of data coming into the Morongo reservation is overwhelming, and the communication networks may react efficiently, inefficiently, aggressively or passively when information is faulty. As in the past, a principal function of today's leader is to control information. People route both problems and outsiders to the leaders, and they are responsible for receiving and evaluating information about problems or outsiders. A new person or a new idea is inevitably routed to one or several people who assume the functions of finding out if anything of merit is being offered to the community, or consulting with others, of sending people's ideas further along the routes of information, and — ultimately — of rejecting or accepting them. Such leaders carry a great trust in the community, plus the responsibility of protecting and informing its people of possible exploitative or useful roles which strangers might play.

Today's leader, often criticized for not giving out enough information, is still subject to yesterday's traditions. In ancient times, the traditional flow of information was vertical. It was received by the elite, who reviewed it, synthesized it, and then told the people about it. This tradition is still a feature of the reservation, for residents say they need more information in the form of newsletters. Leaders are constantly accused of having secrets or of hiding facts from the people, and there they are in a double bind: expected to be discreet and careful about information, but expected to act on it wisely, fairly, and freely. Leaders are not provided with the facilities for adequate communication, but they have the responsibilities of management. There is little power or privilege attached to the role.

Leadership Selection

Morongo residents feel that the children of leaders grow up with a sense of responsibility toward the community. Although individuals may not define themselves as potential leaders, they are subtly trained for such roles. Some develop a sense of responsibility because they are treated by the community as potential leaders, and they are encouraged to assume leadership in either formal or informal roles.

Another group of leaders, who are called "influencers" by some Morongans, are often those who will not seek public office, but who are influential within the community because of their wisdom, good sense, and *independence.* People consult them about decisions. They are often active in forming committees, associations, and clubs. As often as not, they have leadership backgrounds. They usually deny interest in formal leadership because of the inconveniences that accompany it but may serve actively for the duration of a crisis, after which they withdraw to an informal role.

Younger people are now given more opportunity to assume tribal responsibility, and more praise should they accept such responsibility. Although leadership positions are still held most often by older persons, the age norm has dropped perhaps a decade during the past few years. The teenage population is becoming more aware of reservation politics and more vocal about their future on the reservation. They articulate a firm desire to leave the reservation for an education, but to return and maintain it as it is now. They do not, however, take public roles in reservation affairs; their concerns are expressed primarily within their own peer group and to their immediate families.

More dramatic changes have occurred since aboriginal times in the political roles of women. In the early part of this century, when diminishing ceremonial activity drastically decreased the power and economic advantages formerly associated with ritual leadership, Morongo men reduced their participation in ritual and spent more time seeking employment in positions within the BIA, seeking jobs in a wage market, or creating new economic institutions outside the BIA. As a result, women became more actively responsible in managing the complex rituals associated with funerals and wakes. Although the older

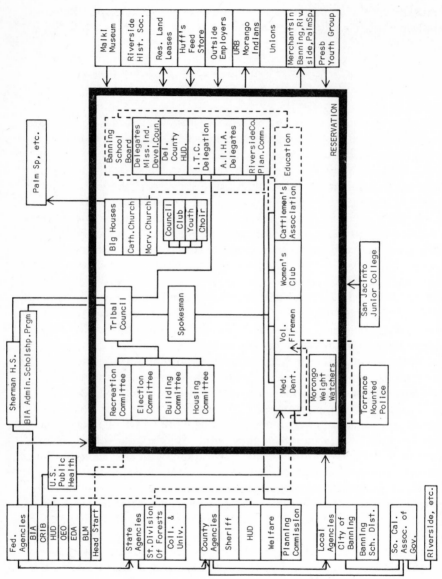

Figure 1. Social organization of the Morongo reservation, 1972

men and some politically active men maintained ritual positions in performance, much of the administrative, social, and economic aspects were left to the women.

Associated with the formation of the militant Mission Indian Federation (whose first president was a Morongo resident), women for the first time were elected to council office in southern California. Significantly, the wife of one of the leaders of the federation was the first chairwoman of the reservation council some years later. Women's roles were also expanded, when they gained the right to vote in reservation elections, to receive allotments, to own property, and to receive an education (Bean 1964: 2–10). An important factor here too was that since 1890 Morongan women had been actively encouraged by the Moravian missionary to engage in administrative affairs.

Throughout the 1930's, money became more accessible to them — older women and those with dependent children were able to receive small welfare incomes. These incomes, when combined with the right of private ownership of land, meant that women were more independent of men; they became more concerned with their futures, which were now directly tied to decisions made by the tribe as a whole (particularly when land tenure was involved). This concern, and the fact that political alliances were formed primarily by kin ties, and decisions made by majority vote led women to become formally involved in all tribal affairs. They have subsequently made a very significant — at times a seemingly dominant — contribution to activities of the tribe. Reservation members attribute progress in housing and planning to women's interest and to their willingness to work for extra incomes that will increase standards of living.

Being a reservation leader involves many problems. Publicly, leaders receive very little positive reinforcement; they are more usually damned, criticized, and suspected than praised. (Some of the Morongans have stated that they value the *lack* of public praise.) Little or no remuneration accompanies responsibility, except in the jobs (usually temporary) that are funded by the BIA, Office of Economic Opportunity (OEO), and similar organizations. As a consequence, leadership roles are necessarily secondary to subsistence or career goals. At best, leadership responsibilities bring perhaps an honorarium or travel pay.

The constant criticism aimed at leaders causes them to be wary when making decisions. Investigators working among a small group of reservation leaders in San Diego County made an observation that also seems relevant to the Morongans. They pointed out that "the pace of problem solving seems to be dictated in part by the attitudes that one should not make a social move unless it can be made perfectly and that imperfect social problems are hindered at times by a tendency to undermine the personal responsibility for a problem before correcting it." (Benedict and Shipek 1972)

These investigators found that the time necessary to attend meetings and solve problems reduced the time devoted to constructive action, because the number of people who were able to serve on committees was small, and those few were especially pressed. The situation at Morongo is similar. Accountability to the tribe remains a principal value, which is enforced by community attitude. However, willingness to recognize that tribal offices border on professional positions, and that they demand much of the people who hold them, is increasing. In recent years, funds have been voted to pay partial expenses incurred by the tribal chairman ($100 per month), by the committee (for travel), and by the tribal secretary (honorariums).

Professional Leadership

The time when the Morongo tribe will have funds to finance positions of managerial sophistication is near. The willingness to pay, which has evolved during the present generation, has been brought about in part by the federal funds that have supported professional positions at Morongo — a health officer, nurses, paramedical aides, community development officers, and neighborhood youth workers. Although invidious distinctions are sometimes made about salaries and the attendant advantages of these jobs, it is also realized that leadership and professional positions must be salaried. This realization is not new — BIA and other personnel have always been paid, and traditional leaders, curers, craftsmen and other specialists always anticipated some form of payment for the services they rendered. The difference today is that the tribe sees itself instead of some distant agency as the corporate unit that pays. It also sees payments as being direct, rather than through some subtle system of economic reciprocity, such as those of the traditional ritual systems which were sanctioned by cosmological criteria. Now the source of payment is clearly attached to the reservation and to group-owned resources.

This seemingly dysfunctional relationship between leaders and people may actually be a strategy for maintaining equality in social and economic relationships. At the very least, dysfunction allows the myth of equality and of popular control over public affairs. When an individual succeeds in one activity, the group criticizes that activity or some other area of his conduct. ("Yes, he is good with outsiders and in dealing with whites, but he doesn't understand the Morongo people.")

Thus ambivalence functions in part to control the actions of leaders, who are always made conscious of public opinion. It allows the community to draw on a greater proportion of its personnel resources, without overidealistic criteria that would remove a potentially successful person from community action.

As leaders develop prestige and crystallize their power bases, particularly in nonelective positions, they are isolated and prevented from expanding their power. Once they are well established in a capacity that the community does not control, they may not be elected to a public office. It is as if the group recognizes the necessity for moving new people into elected positions of leadership — where they can have an opportunity to serve and to become successful. Thus the group simultaneously prevents individuals from acquiring too much power and maximizes the use of its "people resources."

Nevertheless, leadership recruitment and removal is guided by the powerful persons themselves. Somewhat young, or less experienced and less securely based, persons may be elected to committees or to the tribal council, while former elected leaders are placed on committees and continue to serve as informal opinion makers. As young people move up in the reservation heirarchy, they are both learning and being tested for future leadership roles. The committee system is used by the people to try new leaders on for size, and younger people are consciously recruited with this in mind.

SEVEN VIABLE EXPRESSIVE-INSTRUMENTAL ASSOCIATIONS

Seven successful adaptations to reservation needs have evolved in historic and recent times: the Big Houses, the Moravian churches, the Malki Fruit Association, the Cattlemen's Association, the Malki Museum, the health clinic, and the Morongo Fire Department.

The Big House

For more than a century, the traditional ceremonial units of southern California — Big Houses — have adapted to social pressures and economic change. These ritual congregations maintain a continuity with the past and a ritual reciprocity with similar units on other reservations, such as Palm Springs and Soboba.

The principal functions of ceremonial units were the perfomance of rituals for the dead and rituals that focused on lineage, clan, or ethnic identity. Participation in these rituals identified those who were most committed to Indian ways, and were especially useful for distinguishing those who considered themselves "Indians" from those who considered themselves "non-Indians." Rituals also helped to establish political and economic alliances.

In the early 1900's, there were several active ceremonial Big Houses at Morongo, each owned by a lineage. But maintaining Big House ceremonies was expensive and time-consuming, and it required a great commitment and highly specialized knowledge. As the ritualists who knew the esoteric knowledge of each Big House tradition died, and as the older people who were deeply committed to its functioning died, participation and economic support decreased. Transportation problems, loss of ritual accuracy, and antisocial behavior that came to be associated with the rituals also diminished the quality of Big House ceremonies. As a result of all these factors, attendances decreased.

As lineages gradually ceased to operate as discrete units and the Big Houses were phased out, groups became smaller, and membership became more flexible. As individual decision making became more independent, members of the remaining ceremonial units extended their services and membership criteria in order to survive.

The last Big House was formally reorganized in 1960, when the Pablo family met together after the death of ceremonial leader Victoria Wierick to decide whether or not the house and the rituals performed in it should be continued. The family decided to offer the Big House for use in funeral ceremonies to all of the Cahuilla people, rather than for the Wanikik lineage alone. A meeting of the older people from various reservations was held, and the group decided that the house should be retained and that Jane Penn should be responsible for its management. Ownership, ethnic boundaries, use, and responsibility were extended to the Cahuillas as a whole.

A significant feature to the understanding of Morongan life-style is that Big House activity demonstrates how outside resources and people may be used for the community good, while keeping the "in group" separate. The rituals brought people and goods into the community — but always as invited guests, not as community members. This basic strategy is still applied, but now in an on-reservation and off-reservation sense.

The Big House also demonstrates how community values may become more predominant when the survival of an important institution is threatened: the remaining small units combine into larger groups, for the basic purpose of saving the institution. Ideologically, the people of Morongo recognize the larger identity boundaries in times of crisis, when they have no difficulty in enveloping otherwise discrete and competitive groups.

A third principle demonstrated by the Big House is that the selection of leaders is explicitly democratic, although implicitly controlled by a few influential people. When a new leader was selected in 1960, all who were concerned with the decision — young, old, male, female — were informed, discussions were held, a decision was reached, and all returned to their communities to relate the new status of the Big House.

Other traditional values were also exhibited in the selection of the new leader. Age, lineal closeness, and specific ritual knowledge were significant criteria in the decision. The fact that a woman was selected indicates the firm power base that women held aboriginally, which explains in part their ready election to leadership positions in later years.

The Moravian Church

The acceptance of the Moravian church, like the acceptance of the Catholic church and other non-Indian organizations, exemplifies the readiness of the Morongo people to use non-Indian devices in meeting their own needs.

Protestant-Catholic rivalries were intense toward the end of the nineteenth century, and the Indian agent, reservation schoolteacher, and Banning citizens were interested in bringing a Protestant orientation to the Indians. In aiding their cause, reservation resident John Morongo established very powerful outside allies and advocates who could aid him in his quest for leadership and power.

With the eclecticism typical of southern California groups, Morongo was able to adopt a new religious structure while maintaining basic Serrano customs (as his rivals the Pablos had adopted Catholic institutions while maintaining those of the Cahuillas). The Moravian church thus became the focal point for one political faction. In view of the missionary's ability to serve as a liaison to outsiders, and the general hostility of middle-class whites and bureaucratic institutions toward Catholics, John Morongo's alliance was politically astute since he was able to acquire advantages for himself and other Morongoans. William H. Weinland, the Moravian missionary, was an experienced and fierce advocate for his parishioners; he guided them into Anglo-American ways, encouraged interaction with whites and attendance at government boarding schools, placed his Indian converts in administrative posts. He entered into every aspect of Morongo life and actively campaigned against all who disagreed with his programs.

The Moravian church has maintained a viable congregation at Morongo since 1889. It developed the first of many welfare programs on the reservation and operated the first health clinic and an organization for alcoholics, as well as other social activities. Church members extended their activities to other communities and reservations and developed and still maintain close working relations with residents in Banning. Moravian children, especially girls, were encouraged to enter government schools, to organize church associations and clubs, to take responsibility for fund-raising programs, and to seek careers such as teaching in the reservation schools and nursing. The Moravian church became an intensely integrated, highly organized group in which praise, prestige positions, and economic reinforcement quickly accrued to the faithful.

The church today serves as the basic organization for articulating reservation affairs. Out of thirty-one tribal officers who have been elected since 1948, twenty-three were members of the Moravian Church. Four out of five large-scale cattle owners are also members of this church. Membership is correlated with power, wealth, and acceptance of and by non-Indians.

The multiple functions of the church continue, although less overtly than thirty years ago. The church performs social and welfare services for both young and old and also functions as a base for reaching outsiders, through activities that bring contact with other Protestant groups.

Today, leaders of the church are Indians who refuse to accept significant input from whites. The non-Indian pastor is clearly "kept in his place" by an independent congregation. Members of the Moravian church readily accept non-Indian strategies and apply them for the welfare of the congregation, and they also demonstrate a basic commitment to the reservation as a whole. Despite being the focus of a faction, the church group has tried to maintain a mixed membership. Church officials and church business are kept formally separated from non-church affairs, and decision making within the church is kept in the hands of the Indian congregation.

The Malki Fruit Association

Before the establishment of a reservation, Indian residents of the Morongo area were successful farmers, who marketed the produce of vineyards and orchards. Beans, melons, and barley were later grown extensively in reservation fields in the 1890's. Reservation entrepreneurs bought — or acquired by loan or work in kind — the equipment necessary to participate in the agricultural industry of southern California.

Marketing of farm products involved wholesaling, processing, shipping, and packaging — all of which were carried out with Indian managements. Many farm laborers were employed during the harvest season, including local residents as well as Indians from other reservations and migrant Mexican farm workers. Camping accommodations and, sometimes, subsistence were provided. Field workers were paid in cash and in kind, or both. Customarily, several boxcars were rented for rail transport of produce to market. These agricultural operations were financed by private capital. The industry suffered when the tribe accepted individual allotments in 1919, after almost a decade of argument.

When it was first proposed to divide tribal land into individual allotments, BIA agents and the Moravians approved the proposal. It was argued that the allotment program would protect individuals, minors, widows, and others and that it would introduce the concept of private ownership to the reservation. After much argument, individual allotments were accepted by a narrow voting margin. The new allotments of five or six acres were impractical for commercial farming. Geographer Imre Sutton, who has examined the nature of land tenure in southern California (1964: 134), has commented that the government "was quite slow to realize that the changing realities of commercial agriculture in the drylands would vary quickly making these subsistence units inadequate . . . it is hard to believe that any Indian family could support itself by means of working a single allotment," a point that the dissenting minority had realized itself in the arguments made prior to the allotment procedure.

Morongans, who wanted to continue in commercial agriculture, necessarily developed a new strategy. Families merged several allotments into 30-to-40-acre land parcels; thus, relatives could continue their commercial activities by farming their own and their children's allotments. Other Morongans became discouraged and reduced their efforts to subsistence gardening and relied on other sources of income.

The most successful adaptation, however, was achieved by the Malki Fruit Association. This group was formed by Segundo Chino and Bartisal Rice, who had also been founders of the Mission Indian Federation (an early protest association). The Malki Fruit Association hired seasonal laborers, bought hauling equipment, and built drying sheds, work platforms, and processing facilities; it also arranged for financing and shipping. Through the cooperative association, small landowners could pool their resources and maximize their assets, thus overcoming the disadvantages of the small allotments. Under the management of Chino and Rice, both traditionalists who objected to BIA interference in reservation affairs, the Malki Fruit Association operated for nearly twenty years — until the age of its leaders and an increasingly difficult marketing situation forced discontinuance of the enterprise.

The limitation of commercial agriculture at Morongo was not caused by internal stress. Off-reservation commercial orchardists had phased out of agriculture even before the people of Morongo, because old

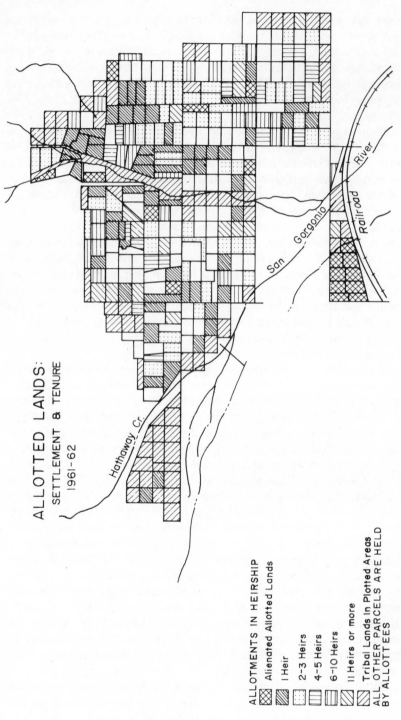

Map 3.   Allotted lands: settlement and tenure (1961–1962)

trees had ceased to be profitably productive and the planting of new orchards would require major capitalization. As orchard agriculture declined, Morongo men were forced to take jobs that took them farther away from the reservation for longer periods of time. The situation was complicated by the fractionating of land as a result of inheritance laws.

The history of commercial agriculture at Morongo demonstrates that management and marketing potential has always been available and that economic success has been vigorous under Indian management, when there was an opportunity to exploit a reservation resource profitably. Cooperation and innovative strategy were clearly manifest in the agricultural arena.

The Cattlemen's Association

Stock raising, like the raising of fruit, is not new to Morongo people. By 1819, Mission San Gabriel was running cattle through San Gorgonio Pass. Cahuilla, Serrano, and Cupeño men were experienced cattlemen long before the reservation was established, and Morongans worked as professional cowboys for white ranchers during the early years of the reservation.

The cattle industry flourished during the early 1900's. No formal organization is recalled; families worked together as necessary. Work activities were organized by the heads of families who owned cattle, meeting informally. (Later, range leaders were hired.)

The first major recorded conflict involving reservation cattle occurred when an Indian agent actively interfered with the round-up. In later years, when the BIA officially became interested in the management and "progress" of the cattle industry, conflict increased as owners and bureau experts disagreed. Occasional crises also occurred when cattle of individual owners roamed into agricultural and residential areas owned by others to graze. When conflicts escalated during the 1930's, the Cattlemen's Association was formed to help solve problems. The association hired a full-time ranger, who supervised fence repair. It also worked actively with the BIA, the tribal committee, and other groups in developing policies for range management and marketing. Since its beginning, the Cattlemen's Association has been either an organization or a clique that acts formally when there is a need and disbands when there are no problems.

The Cattlemen's Association is a special interest group that is always well represented in tribal politics; there is usually a cattleman on the elected tribal committee. Association members are watchful of tribal plans or resolutions that may effect grazing lands, and they act informally as an action group both on and off the reservation.

According to government officials and economic planners, Morongo people have misused their grazing lands for several generations. Experts have tried to encourage rigorous management procedures that would maximize the productivity of herds and also maintain the productivity of the land. Yet, although each succeeding generation recognized the obvious signs of poor management, the lands remain overgrazed.

Why, then, do experienced cattlemen continue to overgraze and undermanage their land resources? Several answers seem to make sense, in view of the overall Morongo economic system. Despite overgrazing and undermanagement, cattle raising is obviously one of the more successful Morongo enterprises. This industry requires little investment, it may be combined successfully with other income-producing activities, and it may provide considerable profit. Although it is possible that the ideal stock-raising procedures suggested by experts would yield an adequate return in terms of time and capital investment, this conclusion has yet to be adequately demonstrated.

The present *laissez-faire* attitude toward range management also allows the possibility of options. When grazing is good, the cattleman can expand his operations; during a drought, he can cull his herds. In addition, he has the traditional strategem of hidden assets and floating stock, with opportunities for profiting from exceptional — even extra-legal — arrangements.

The sentiment that the presence of herds engenders also provides a considerable argument against the leasing of Morongo lands for non-Indian development. The grazing of cattle is considered as a proper and traditional use of the land, and it does not bring intruders to the reservation. The undeveloped range lands also provide game.

The history of the cattle industry demonstrates several strategies used at Morongo. Cattlemen organize flexibly and democratically, taking active interest in tribal politics through their special interest as businessmen and maintaining a philosophy that allows them to keep their options open while protecting the land base for the tribe as a whole. Cattlemen have adopted new ideas that seem to be effective and have ignored those that are not visibly productive; they continue to maintain a concept of diversified economics by also farming or working for wages.

Malki Museum

Malki Museum, the result of a desire to enhance ethnicity, was founded in 1964 by people who had worked together for a number of years in various political, scientific, and social projects. The museum began with administrative talent of a high order, which was brought together by Jane Penn, the politically active daughter of a former tribal leader William Pablo. Indian and non-Indian talents have combined to develop exhibits, an ethnobotanical garden, scholarship and publications programs, and to reinstitute a defunct "fiesta" celebration. The museum complex has served as a model and a catalyst for other reservations throughout the state of California.

During its first years, Malki Museum was viewed by some Morongans as a factionally based institution, and, in spite of public statements of its intention to serve all the peoples on the reservation, many Morongans avoided its activities. In time, the institution began to receive support from all reservation factions, through its publication of material about the reservation's major ethnic groups and its providing of scholarships for children without regard to reservation politics.

Malki Museum provides an example of a contemporary adaptation to new conditions. The basic strategy of involving off-reservation experts to integrate internal reservation groups about a single activity — with a goal of bringing services and funds to the reservation — is as old as Cahuilla society itself. The museum brought together outsiders, who were encouraged to extend their services to other reservation activities as their involvement with the museum was recognized. As each member of Malki increased his activity, reservation people became reciprocally involved in museum activities — although to the community at large, it is explicitly not a reservation association.

The museum has provided a more positive relationship with the community of Banning, where its activities are recognized and praised in the local press; the power elite of Banning have begun to consider the reservation with new respect, and interaction between Indians and Banning residents has improved. Morongans have also become involved in educational activities and local festivals (especially Pioneer Days) of the town. The Indian component of local history now had a resource base, and Indian members of the museum became involved in local historical, archaeological, and conservation groups. This process indicates that Indian members of the museum recognized the need to extend their influence to outsiders in order to control outsiders' activities in relation to the reservation.

The museum's success in attaining goals indicates that Morongo people have the skills necessary for establishing and managing large-scale business enterprises. The bookkeeper/manager is Indian, the majority of board members are Indian, and white influence in decision making has decreased with each year of operation.

The fiesta, the museum's largest activity, was initially managed by committees, most of whom were non-Indian. Although the fiesta itself was a great public success, committee planning operations were chaotic, wasteful, and stress-inducing for many years. The museum association turned over management of the fiesta to Marianno Saubel, an Indian member of the board of trustees. Although the planning group seemed to be disorganized, the infighting and bickering characteristic of earlier years diminished, work schedules were completed ahead of time, and a small profit began to come in.

Since that first Indian-directed fiesta, most committees of the museum have been managed by Indians, with superior organizational success. After three years of successful operation, manager Saubel has decided to turn his responsibilities over to another Indian, Matthew Pablo, who has been involved only slightly in the past. This deliberate training component of Morongo social structure of assigning responsibility seems to be characteristic of certain leaders, who are willing to do necessary work during developmental stages of an activity because it is necessary, but who do not wish to participate beyond this period.

The Health Clinic

Health services and health education have been areas of community concern for several generations. Until a few years ago, shamans continued to practice their traditional roles as curers and healers. During the 1920's, the Moravian church established a clinic that provided health care to the reservation. Under the Bureau of Indian Affairs, the people of Morongo have been provided with contract doctors and nursing services and an Indian hospital, which was located at the nearby Soboba reservation. These services varied in efficiency but, in retrospect, are considered to have been more valuable than the services received after the passing of Public Law 280 which placed Indian medical care in the same status as that of other California citizens.

The inadequacies of community health care had become increasingly serious by 1960 — medical care was expensive and distant, and many Morongans needed accessible clinic and referral services.

In 1965–1966, a private and nonprofit institution, the Harridge Foundation, began to provide medical services without cost to Morongans, largely through the efforts of the American Indian Service Committee and the active interest of individual Morongans. Critical need helped to generate the idea that a medical alternative was possible for the people of the reservation; doctors and hospital personnel in the area (at Loma Linda, for example) occasionally provided help in an inadequate building provided by the tribe.

A survey made in 1967 pointed out that medical needs were critical at Morongo and that a local system of providing health care would be enthusiastically accepted (Bean and Wood 1969: 29–31). Simultaneously, the state of California's public health office, working with a statewide Indian organization, California Rural Indian Health Service (CRIHS), acquired partial funding for a program of paramedical training. Action for improving health care was taken by Clifford Matthews, the tribal council, and other reservation members, and a serious effort was made to acquire funds for a building and equipment. Various non-Indians helped in acquiring funds from federal, state, and private resources, and fund-raising activities were sponsored by the reservation Firemen's Association. Finally, a medical facility was built on tribal land.

This sizeable health center received 6,400 patient visits from Indians during its first years of operation, and it has served as a model for the entire state. An annex is presently being planned.

The example of the health clinic demonstrates several recurrent themes in Morongo life. Traditional modes were utilized simultaneously with Anglo medical procedures during the early part of the century. Reservation people used the health care later provided by the Moravian church and the BIA, while still seeking private medical attention. The crisis created by the change to Medi-Cal facilities was solved by another strategy.

Morongans have sought help from outside private agencies when public agencies were slow to meet their needs, have simultaneously used public health facilities, and have also used the services of local doctors whenever they could afford private treatment. This constant adaptation emphasizes still another strategy — that of maximizing the potentials of the environment by keeping options to the outside open, while simultaneously developing local solutions to problems. Such a strategy is selective, in that it accepts outside services but controls them.

Firemen's Association

The most recently developed formal association on the reservation is the Morongo Volunteer Fire Department, which was organized in 1969 because community service did not offer adequate protection against brushfires that threatened homes and lives. Elected to association offices were first aid chaplain, traffic control officer, dispatcher, master-at-arms, and an election committee; bylaws outlined goals, rules of membership, and procedures. Non-Indians and Indians who are not Morongans may become members; thus, the association allies all residents of the reservation. The organization functions to conserve resources and to train local men in fire-fighting techniques and first aid. It is prepared to act in time of any general emergency, and it also functions as a social club. Firemen have taken dominant roles in establishing the health clinic, organizing the Malki Museum fiesta, and campaigning for candidates to tribal office.

The association also appears to perform several informal policing functions. Firemen have argued for the development of a police force to maintain internal peace and order and to keep trespassers off reservation land. Their arguments reflect a general concern for a situation where the legal implications of Public Law 280 are still not absolutely clear. Generally, the organization induces cooperative action on the reservation by linking other organizations, groups, and interests and by integrating opposition perhaps more effectively than any other association in Morongo history.

Ephemeral Organizations

Morongans, throughout their history, have evidenced a tendency to organize rapidly but ephemerally when needs arise. These organizational responses have varied from reactions to termination (in general a critical event for California Indians), to local and family crisis (such as assisting a family whose home has burned). The most dramatic of these ephemeral organizations was the Mission Indian Federation, which was organized by Johnathan Tibbets, a white advocate for Indian affairs.

Tibbets, a master organizer, developed a multiethnic organization, one part of which was the Mission Indian Federation. The federation attracted conservative Indians and served as a major force in protesting BIA policies during the 1920's. Tibbets was tried for sedition, on a charge of alienating Indians from the federal government; the government as well as Indians who had been officials in his organization accused him of misusing funds collected to aid Indian causes and of using threats, coercion, and violence. Nevertheless, the federation continued as an organization long after Tibbets' death, under the guidance of another white advocate, Purl Willis.

The founding leaders of the MIF were Morongo residents, some of whom later were associated with the very successful Malki Fruit Association. Shortly after World War I, MIF vigorously protested against the management of reservation affairs. Its members wanted home rule, and they wanted to block non-Indian participation in reservation policies.

At Morongo, most of the long-lasting organizations have begun as ad hoc committees. Fixed membership groups apparently know how to expand and contract social relationships in correlation with need, and, although decision making is constantly criticized as being slow and backward, it is the slowness and backwardness of a carefully articulated network system that combines the democratic process with balancing power mechanisms. There are indications that Morongans are suspicious of any emergence of an authoritarian or power elite control. This is not to say that they do not trust leaders, but it does suggest that they do not trust leadership. Traditionally their philosophy expressed the adage that power corrupts, and more power corrupts more (Bean 1972).

MORONGO AND THE MISSION INDIAN SUBCULTURE

Southern California is a subcultural domain today, as it was in aboriginal times. Within its boundaries lie the lands that have been known bureaucratically as the Mission Indian jurisdiction. (Excepted is the Santa Ynez group, which is effectively outside the interacting system. Indians at Parker and Yuma, although outside the area, have more contact with Mission Indians than with other reservations.)

The Mission Indian subculture has been formally organized in various ways. The Mission Indian Federation is the most outstanding example, but organizations of tribal chairmen and other groups have been formed as common causes have been recognized. The subculture is in effect a macrocosm of reservation social structure. Members group situationally and participate selectively in organizational activities — usually becoming united only when the group as a whole is threatened by a common crisis, such as termination, claims case participation, etc.

Links with Other Reservations

Morongo social structure cannot be understood without considering this group within the context of this total reservation system in southern California. Morongans have always been leaders in establishing relations with white institutions. Members of other reservations have sought residence at Morongo or nearby Banning, because these locations are situated within the fruit-raising zone of southern California, where there is access to jobs (at least seasonally).

The Morongo reservation has also become a "local" center for BIA activities — perhaps because it is a "progressive reservation" that learned early the sophisticated machinations of Indian-affairs bureaucracy.

It is no accident that Morongo is a center of political organization.

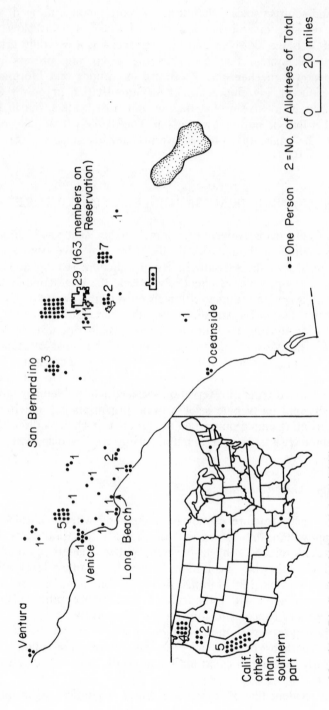

Map 4A.   Distribution of Morongo band (1962)

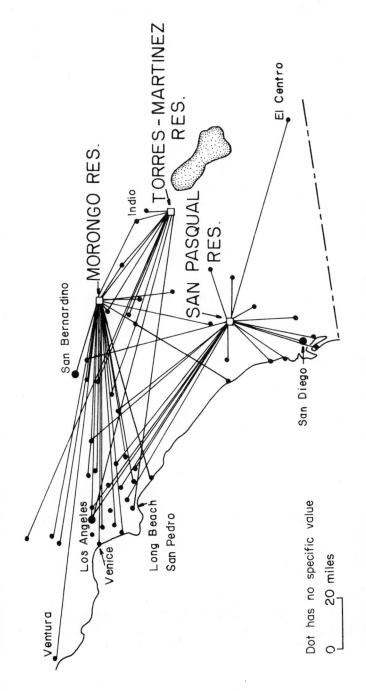

Map 4B. Comparative distribution of selective band membership in southern California (1960–1961)

The first reservation population, drawn from several heterogeneous tribes and many clans, was in effect related everywhere in southern California. All of the southern California tribes were represented at Morongo. From the first Indian protest movements, during the 1860's, BIA personnel noted that leaders at Morongo had very wide networks of political support, which cut across various reservations and tribes. Tribal members formed alliances by marriage, were consciously active politically, and were continuously involved in the fiesta system and rituals that were the principal interactive institutions in southern California until the 1920's. There were remnants at Morongo of ritual units that had originally been located in other areas, including some five ritual houses representing Cahuilla and Serrano lineages. Throughout the winter months, ritual activity and the resultant social and economic exchange brought other Indians to Morongo, as it took Morongans to other areas.

After tribal lands were divided into allotments, Morongans inherited land throughout southern California. Some tribal members owned land on several reservations and were thus linked with the economic interests of other areas. Such links have become more frequent as the population increases and intermarriage continues among members of various reservations.

Morongo continues to be a pacesetter. Its institutions, such as its health clinic and museum, serve as models to other reservations, and the BIA has actively sought to replicate innovative activities originated at Morongo on other reservations. (Although Morongo residents take some pride in this compliment, they have also criticized BIA people for passing along Morongo ideas without properly crediting the source.)

The personnel policies of the BIA have also helped to create a Mission Indian subculture, by placing Indians hired to work in bureau-funded jobs on reservations other than their own. Educational and medical institutions have had the same effect; Indians from many reservations have worked at medical institutions such as Soboba Hospital, and reservation children have gone to boarding schools (St. Boniface in Banning, or Sherman Institute in Riverside). Southern California Indians established friendships and sometimes met their future spouses while attending these schools. By the early 1900's more than thirty reservations and several cultural nationalities were interfaced in a broader manner than the traditional ritual congregations had allowed. Intercultural and interpolitical mechanisms, although not new, had been expanded considerably by processes generated off the reservation.

These processes of integration continue with increased intensity now, as federal funding encourages reservations to ally in their planning for education, housing, and economic development. In organizations such as the Mission Indian Development council and the All-Mission Housing Authority, the Mission Indian sense of identity and interreservation communication is reinforced.

ETHNIC IDENTITY AT MORONGO

The people of Morongo form a community apart from any other, with a fixed membership that is based on a tribal roll and is reinforced by similar sociocultural background and a common history. The reservation has become an identity focus — and a positive one. As a Morongan has put it, "When a person is a member of the reservation, he has something. He is not lost. He is not like people in an urban ghetto — where the only identity you have is your job. We are not just shiftless people. We are Morongo Indians." Fixed membership, tradition, kinship, and a basic economic security combine to create an ethnic identity that, although not clearly defined, is very real.

Within the reservation, people classify themselves and each other according to tribal background, as well as by degree of Indian ancestry, participation in Indian activities, and acknowledgement of "Indianness." In general, models are Indian versus non-Indian, traditional versus progressive. One group, the Serrano–Cupeño alliance, apparently considers itself distinct from other groups on the reservation by its maintaining a sentimental attachment to traditional language and culture. Some of this group's members express fierce pride in speaking their Indian language, deriding those who cannot, who "do not know who they are" in traditional terms.

Pride versus Stigma

Pride in Indianness now stimulates individuals to achieve skills that will allow them to exploit off-reservation opportunities. When Indian problems are discussed today, outsiders are less welcome than in times past; there is explicit acknowledgment that Indians should think out and determine their own direction. This attitude is not new at Morongo, but it is more directly stated than formerly, and outsiders are now more quickly put in "their places" when they overstep the bounds that are recognized as "their positions."

A few years ago, some stigma-associated personality traits were commonly evidenced at Morongo by statements such as "We are just poor dumb Indians.... Indians are poor — that's why we are poor.... Our young people are just drunkards ... we are ugly, fat, and don't eat good food." Such things were said in both a joking and a serious manner.

The stigmatic self-image often fulfilled its own prophesy. Some parents encouraged children to leave the reservation and not return, because "it's a loser's life on the reservation." Other parents discouraged children from studies by saying, "It's just a waste of time — whites won't hire you anyway," or, "Whites will only tell you lies." In some activities, this type of negativism often defeated action before it began. Within the Morongo community, distinctions were based on race and acculturation. Indians distinguished themselves in hierarchically arranged sets, depending on the prestige of their political or family units. At the same time, Indians from less progressive reservations were compared unfavorably to Morongo people.

A poverty image at Morongo is associated primarily with lack of opportunity rather than with cultural differences or Indianness versus non-Indianness. As opportunities have expanded and incomes have increased, Indians who seemed very conservative have acquired new houses, automobiles, and other material possessions that have improved the general quality of reservation life. Twelve years ago there was one telephone on the Morongo reservation; now the telephone has become a basic communication device. With new federal rulings on housing — many families have built new homes — the association of old homes with Indianness applies less aptly than before.

Negative self-evaluations are still occasionally expressed, especially among older people. But the decrease of stigma-related behavior during the past dozen years is reflected in a lessening of factional disputes and negative gossip, as Indianness becomes more acceptable and as the demands for Indian rights are more forcefully expressed throughout the nation. The values openly expressed by politicians and the communications media have significantly improved the reservation's view of itself. Only a few years ago, the media commented on local Indian affairs with sarcasm or a "tongue-in-cheek" style; its recent change to a more positive and advocative approach has affected the Indian self-image, as has the success of the Malki Museum.

The Malki Museum has received assistance and widespread publicity from prestigious non-Indian institutions, from non-Indian individuals, and from militant Indians as well. Several thousand people attended its first public fiesta. The community of Banning, which had previously been rather prejudiced against local Indians, shortly afterward began to cooperate with the reservation by inviting reservation people to participate in socially significant activities, such as speaking before businessmen's associations and women's clubs. Morongans were invited to join county organizations and citizens' advisory groups, such as the Riverside Historical Commission. The museum reinforced its position through its educational relationship with children; local school districts for miles around bring busloads of children to the museum. Local Indian children now take special pride in the fact that their culture is a focus of attention, and they enthusiastically point out aspects of the exhibits that may pertain to their own families.

Children's reactions feed back to adults on the reservation, and the museum consciously attempts to represent all groups and all families in its activities. These activities have helped to break down many previous barriers to positive communication among reservation members.

As the chronic defeatism of the past is gradually being replaced by a more positive and hopeful attitude, older people are beginning to accept younger persons in leadership capacities. The present feeling toward young people who seek leadership roles is not one of, "They can't be trusted until they are over forty," but rather, "Let's give them a chance — maybe they can solve problems that we haven't been able to solve." Still, the testing remains cautious.

The "Outsiders"

Some residents of Morongo reservation are not members of the tribe. These people include spouses of tribal members, people who have purchased land allotments and live on them, heirs to allotted land, and renters. Most residents are Indian, but some are not. All are distinctly classed as outsiders.

The degree to which outsiders are brought into community affairs apparently varies according to behavior, length of residence, and Indianness. Outsiders are self-interested advocates, because decisions regarding reservation assets or behavior affect them directly. But the fixed membership tribal group is very jealous of its prerogatives, and opinionated outsiders are often reminded that they do not have decision-making rights. ("Who are you? You do not belong here. You have no rights to speak.") For this reason, outsiders usually abstain from comment on reservation affairs, saying, "I don't know about that, this is my wife's [husband's] reservation." Mothers who are not residents may join the Mother's Club, however, and men may belong to the Firemen's Association; the Malki Museum and the health clinic provide other roles. Outsiders sometimes influence relatives and friends who are tribal members, and in general they have contributed significantly to political and economic affairs, although, occasionally, they have been the instigators of rather severe conflict.

The Morongo community holds its outsiders in second-class status. They are exploited by the group when their services are needed, but barred from participation when formal decisions are made. The degree

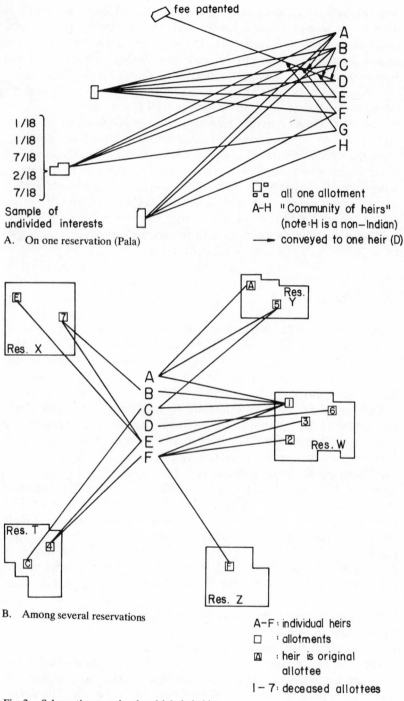

fee patented

A
B
C
D
E
F
G
H

1/18
1/18
7/18
2/18
7/18

Sample of
undivided interests

⊓⸳⊔ all one allotment
A-H "Community of heirs"
     (note:H is a non−Indian)
━▶ conveyed to one heir (D)

A. On one reservation (Pala)

Res. X

Res. Y

Res. W

Res. T

Res. Z

A
B
C
D
E
F

B. Among several reservations

A−F: individual heirs
□   : allotments
▣   : heir is original
      allottee
1−7: deceased allottees

Fig. 2. Schematic example of multiple heirship

to which they are eventually allowed to serve and to become active members of the community appears to depend on their relationships with tribal members and their attention to the subtle rules long established for nonmembers' role behavior.

Ethnicity and Economic Planning

One of the basic stratagems in maintaining economic and political autonomy at Morongo has been to develop sources of wage earning or off-reservation income, while keeping the reservation intact for subsistence and social use. The exclusion of non-Indians from ritual and other cultural-related activities has emphasized in-group identity and has controlled the influence of outsiders. Ethnic independence is reflected futher in reservation land use. There is a reluctance to will land to outside heirs; and the peripheral boundaries of the reservation are kept in a nonuse category, providing a buffer zone between the reservation and the world outside.

The Wanikik group has thwarted serious threats to its basic way of life for more than a century, by continuing the process of extracting income from the outside while maintaining its ethnic boundaries. As new outside elements threaten the reservation's self-maintained independence, new techniques for preserving exclusiveness will be developed. The Morongans' desire for ethnic independence explains in part their basic reluctance to enter into any significant long-range economic planning, as well as their negative attitudes toward seemingly valuable projects, such as county roads and the concept of Malki Museum. As a consequence, the proposals of economic planners often conflict directly with the basic and traditional patterns of Morongan survival.

ADVOCATES: THEIR ROLE IN ECONOMIC DEVELOPMENT AND POLITICAL AFFAIRS

"We know what's good for them."

Before Morongo Reservation was established, Indian leader Juan Antonio and his non-Indian supporter Judge Benjamin Hayes sought non-Indian advocates to aid in protesting against BIA policies. After the establishment of the reservation, William Pablo hired attorney John Brown in San Bernardino and talked to newsman J. H. Gilmour, whose stories about Morongo protests were carried in newspapers across the country; as a result H. N. Rust was exposed for marginal business procedures with Indian property and leases and was accused of confiscating artifacts which he later sold. Later, Pablo received aid for economic development projects from southern California Catholic leaders and businessmen. John Morongo's advocates were H. N. Rust and other BIA personnel, and Moravian missionary William Weinland. Historically, Morongo leaders have aggressively sought the assistance of agencies and individuals for services not readily available within their own population — or the Indian Service — such as those of missionaries, lawyers, politician, educators, and businessmen.

The role of these advocates in economic development and social change cannot be underestimated. They have been intimately associated with the introduction of factors that have greatly influenced reservation life and day-to-day behavior. The Moravian church, for example, developed and articulated political aspirations. From 1889 to 1930 the church was intimately involved by invitation, design, or propinquity in every major affair having to do with economic, political, social, and religious matters. Non-Indian William Weinland wielded power on the reservation for forty years; BIA personnel changed frequently during that time — often because of Weinland — and tribal leadership changed, but his involvement remained constant.

As BIA bureaucracy developed, agents, farmers, and other personnel became the principal advocates at Morongo. This new service created a need for more advocates, because BIA bureaucracy entered into every phase of Morongo existence — health, welfare, education, law, economy, politics and even "moral" behavior. Nonbureau advocates were needed to provide a balance.

As the bureau phased out its services in the 1950's, new services and advocates were again needed. A need for acquiring and utilizing advocates was increased, very often by people who had returned from off-reservation residence because of the jobs available during the war years. Non-Indian spouses and friends helped recruit advocates, and many attempts to stimulate new economic developments were made. New federal agencies, such as "farmers' administration" for training programs in agriculture, were sought out. New ideas and skills such as chicken-ranching were taught. Leadership was often challenged, and conflicts needed to be resolved.

Transitions to New Advocates

The withdrawal of federal personnel and the formal rules, regulations, and direct institutions of federal and state government made it difficult for Morongans to proceed in problem solving. A period of administrative chaos followed: state agencies were unable to define their responsibilities, and local law agencies were unwilling to accept new responsibilities. Indians consequently had to learn an entirely new bureaucratic system, as the bureaucrats had to learn about a set of clients whose problems and ways of dealing with bureaucrats were different from those of non-Indians.

The change brought conflict, because Indians felt they had a right to seek and accept the services of advocates, without guilt or gratuitous responses; welfare and social agencies were not accustomed to such an attitude. The Indian often approached these agencies in a more aggressive and anticipatory manner than others and thus received a new kind of rebuff. He frequently received offhand treatment, and many agencies formally refused services until forced to do so by legal actions.

The Indians' "you owe us this" attitude was new to many welfare-oriented people, who tended to see themselves as dispensing gratuities rather than fulfilling legal and moral obligations. *Noblesse oblige* did not work with Indians, who in some instances reacted aggressively or innovatively with their own resources (for example, in developing a health clinic). Other Indians retreated from the new bureaucracy, which did not meet them with the attitudes they had come to expect from federal or Indian service bureaucracies (BIA officials had known the game of "Indian bureau interaction").

Tribal relationships with new agencies and new kinds of advocates led to an awareness of realities that in the past had been padded or obscured by the traditional paternalism of the Bureau of Indian Affairs. Morongans began to seek professional help from advocates who dealt with them as clients, hiring people to provide services for them rather than depending on bureaucratic personnel.

They also met a new kind of bureaucrat, one who could provide benefits and services but imposed new criteria, such as a demonstration of self-help and proof of motivation, which were deemed essential for acquiring funds. Economic Development Administration personnel, for example, approached the reservation in "hard terms." As the EDA liaison agent explained, "We have what they want — money for development. I tell them I will not put up with any nonsense. You organize effectively so your leaders can make rapid decisions or we don't fund you." The leaders were told to be more assertive. This was a different approach, because most advocates come to the Indian community with a program to sell — the "candied apple" approach, or, "If you will stop bothering us, we will help out a little." As the advocates' strategies change, becoming oriented toward long-range programs developed by the community rather than piecemeal crisis-solving strategies, a futuristic attitude is becoming evident. Programs that insist on long-range planning, with built-in responsibilities, have had a very direct effect on Morongo thinking and planning, but assertive leadership is very suspect.

Advocates Among Themselves

Competitiveness sometimes develops among advocates, with results that are not beneficial to their mutually "shared" clients. To some degree this is because clients fail to communicate the same sort of information to their advocates. Advocates working on other reservations have complained that they are told different versions of a particular incident or given only parts of data; thus, they cannot make full use of their talents. Shipek has described such a situation in a southern California reservation leadership management program (Benedict and Shipek 1972). Advocates may jealously guard their "important" and unique statuses as an expert or friend. The roles they are assigned by their clients may be only partially integrated into reservation problems, so that fractionalism among the advocates reflects fractionalism on the reservation, or vice versa.

Problems of the Advocate

Advocates may also be caught between opposing values — their own and those of their clients. Their private and professional values and goals may also conflict. A case in point is the social scientist who observes phenomenon of great interest and value to his discipline but is constrained from presenting the reality as he sees it because it may threaten the community or the observer's relationship with the community.

Advocates frequently write reports or present views to outsiders which bridge a number of realities, which have no definite outcome — in fact skewed positively or quite frankly ignoring or obscuring negative factors which may be critical in understanding the dynamics of Indian affairs in order to maintain or protect the advocate-client relationship, or the advocate's relationship to funding institutions. This phenomenon occurs at the bureaucratic level, too. It is a constant factor of Indian/non-Indian affairs. It is talked about, complained about, and may, in fact, lead to continued dependency relationships.

Ultimately, relationships are structured by the client who is the purchaser of services in an independent marketplace. If the advocate does not fulfill his expected role, he is almost guaranteed of rapid removal from the system — by Indians as well as by other clients and advocates. His functions are completely dependent, unless he is protected by a bureaucratic powerbase, such as the BIA and EDA. The advocate walks the finest line sociologically and psychologically — perhaps equalled in Indian affairs only by the Indian leader with whom he is usually associated.

Contractual relations between the Indians and advocate preclude dependence, to some degree. When the advocate is employed by the tribe on a contract basis, more honest relationships are sometimes elicited — the advocate can quit or the tribe can fire him. The possibility for frankness on both sides is facilitated by the monied relationship, which frees both advocate and client from the benevolence syndrome and "fuzzy-informal" role that some advocates maintain. Advocates who fulfill personal needs through advocative roles often establish highly inter-personal relationships; because they are more subject to rejection and threats of broken relationships, they appear to have the greatest difficulty in performing objective services, perhaps becoming neutralized to the point of ineffectiveness.

Control

The contribution of advocates is difficult to evaluate. Many officials and Indians cite individual advocates as being detrimental to the smooth running of reservation affairs, accusing them of causing trouble among groups within the reservation, and between the reservation and the established bureaucracy. Often the advocates appear to be fighting among themselves for the privilege of being "the advocate," and they are accused by some of inserting conflicting data into a community in order to further their own personal needs for power and influence.

Observations at Morongo indicate that, while these conditions have operated, in general the people are quite aware of the multifaceted role of the people they select to be of service to them. Morongans are apparently able to assess conflicting opinions, while maintaining good relationships with (and among) various outsiders. There are many nonresident advocates. Each is associated with leaders — rarely more than two or three — who articulate his activities, regulate his role, and screen the information that comes to him.

Although individual advocates usually have a sponsor among the reservation leaders, each leader draws on a more-or-less exclusive set of advocative relationships. These relationships tend to be jealously protected. Therefore, the various facets of an advocate's role are correlated with particular leaders. Conflicts may occur when exclusive control of the relationships is threatened. Sometimes an advocate may become acceptable to other elites. The present tribal attorney, for example, is an engaging and personable man who has assiduously developed relationships that cut across individual or subgroup affiliations.

Non-BIA advocates have been particularly important for minority leaders, while majority leaders have looked toward the bureau as their principal source of support.

DISORGANIZATION IS IN THE EYE OF THE BEHOLDER

Almost axiomatically, it is said that American Indian reservations are dysfunctionally organized. This image of reservation social disorganization may exist primarily in the eye of the beholder. The seeming lack of structure at Morongo is an elaborate and subtle self-protective mechanism developed to maintain self-determination in reservation affairs. The most common complaint voiced by outsiders is that they can't "get" the people at Morongo to make a decision, that the machinery of leadership is unwieldily slow, or that leadership is powerless and unwilling to assume an assertive role. Although no one has clear access to power, this "powerlessness" results in latent power to the people, who have the power to veto by demanding consensus, to prevent leaders from taking unfair advantage of them, and to stop the federal bureaucracy from continuing to give persons in power advantages that the people do not want them to have.

It has been said that Indians use up leaders and then throw them away when they are tired and no longer useful. At Morongo, leaders are used and later recycled. They remain in power for a time, are then harassed out of office, but return again in later years to the former or another position. This pattern is a century old. When leaders finally retire permanently, new persons take up the positions — the same complaints are made, they suffer the same inequities and have the same privilege power. (For some prestige and advantages do accrue to leaders, unclear as these may seem at any given time.)

When one considers all the organizational devices of the reservation, it is clear that, when Morongo residents want things done, action is successful and rapid. When Morongans wish to organize, they do; when they do not want action, decision making is slowed down. Strategies such as accusation of cupidity, purported failure to understand details, or refusal to attend meetings are used.

Factionalism

Factions are usually named the villains in explaining why reservations do not "progress." This convenient scapegoat theory is presented by economic development specialists whose plans have been inoperable, insufficiently funded, or unacceptable to the people at Morongo. At Morongo, factions have served the people very well. Although generally considered impediments to progress and community action, it is clear that, during the past century, factions have been developed to replace the institutions that formerly served as integrative mechanisms for the community. At the very least, they have created a balance of power.

As early as 1891, factions were observed and complained about, but utilized by BIA personnel at Morongo. The author and Brickman studied the phenomenon at Morongo in the early 1960's; this research was reported in 1964 by Brickman, in association with an analysis of the changing political role of women among the Cahuilla (Bean 1964).

Factions at that time seemed to have crystallized about two major groups. Since that time — and apparently before it — factions were highly flexible: persons on the reservation changed affiliations and loyalties as political and economic needs and goals changed and as leaders came and went. Generally, however, alliances have remained stable, with a core of one family predominating in each faction. Conflict led to complete cessation of reservation activities in the 1960's. In order to resolve the stalemate, new leaders who could cut across the disruptive lines were encouraged; persons were selected who had recently returned to the reservation, who were not clearly identified with either of the two historic factions and who had prospective ties to both. These new leaders were in office when federal funding opportunities increased during the 1960's. A social structure characterized by a process of atomization began to supplant factionalism as an adaptive device.

Atomism

An atomistic social structure developed from the structural background at Morongo and the proliferation of resource potentials in recent years. The complexity of Morongo life provided more opportunity for leaders to emerge. As the factional structure became unwieldy, the nuclear family became the major social unit. As this was accompanied by a more complex social system outside the reservation, normative disaffection increased. The intense interest in one another that is characteristic of normative disaffection is a binding element in the community; it balances power and keeps channels of information and options open. On a psychological-interpersonal level it appears that, by directing antipathy toward the same persons or institutions on the reservation, the closeness of relationships among otherwise fragmented social units is increased. The same processes and functions operate in the reservation's relations with outside institutions.

Unfortunately some observers have sometimes viewed cooperation as a universal ethic or have attributed problems of today to the failure of reservation society to cooperate. Both kinship and nonkinship groups do cooperate, but the cooperative groups have become smaller

as the kin groups have declined and no longer extend to five generations of people and hundreds of individuals. As the kin-term relationships are reduced, so are the rules, expectations, and ethical proscription for reciprocal behavior. This result of conquest is complicated
even more by the placement on one reservation of remnants of
previously independent and autonomous corporate kin groups, who
cooperated with one another only in reciprocal ritual contexts and
when marriage contracts anticipated reciprocal behavior.

The continuity of the traditional pattern is demonstrated at Morongo
in the fact that the organizing mechanisms — factions, cliques, and
families — are still based primarily on kinship, although on a more
atomistic level. Traditional kin groups have been reduced and relationships attenuated because people have moved away from the reservation; they marry within wider perimeters, they receive an education
and find jobs further from their home base. Consequently, the ethical
proscription attached to kin relations, formerly drilled into each family
member, is difficult to maintain. Degree of adherence to traditional
kinship obligations depends on the individual training experience of
the person. Those raised by or with grandparents in an extended family
context tend to amalgamate and act cooperatively on a family basis.
Most of the successful economic efforts of the reservation indicate this
pattern. Close relatives form the basic core of the Moravian church
and, to some degree, the Malki Museum and the health clinic.

Some argue that this pattern generates nepotism, but it is also the
most familiar mechanism for cooperating groups. It continues to be a
viable method, despite the many minor problems it engenders (such as
people being reluctant to go to the health clinic because the family
members associated with it might learn too much about their business).
Further, the appearance of nepotism is inevitable in a population as
small as Morongo.

The cooperative groups of the historic past are fondly praised today,
but the situation has changed since the old days. Many kinds of
activities that required mutual aid in the past are no longer important
to the individual's basic welfare. Stock raising and commercial agriculture, which required coordinated efforts, have been replaced by wage
labor as the principal economic mode. Health and medical services and
aid to the indigent take care of other responsibilities once assumed by
extended families.

Cooperative behavior does exist, but the cooperative groups are now
different. Today's cooperative groups may be small kin groups, voluntary associations that are often reacting to crises, or the reservation as
a whole (when the issue is significant to all). Thus, it can be argued that
Morongo has raised its level of sociocultural integration to incorporate
groups that were previously disparate.

FUTURISM OR REALISM IN ECONOMIC DEVELOPMENT

In the marginal economy of the Morongo people, development is seen in very practical and immediate terms that often conflict with the views of economic developers, whether they be BIA personnel, advocates, or other Morongans who have a futuristic orientation. Generally, aid programs, from both within or without the community, are evaluated in terms of whether or not they provide immediate income or training possibilities the reservation members see as productive. Although "pie in the sky" philosophy motivates some thinking and action, it does not seem to apply to final decision making in programs.

The September 1972 rejection of the reservation's economic planning committee's suggestions may have occurred because the direct benefits and implications of the program were not highly visible. In addition, there was an immediate cost because of changes in land use and monies, and the fear of losing control of individual allotted lands to a board of directors. Present techniques for handling decision-making situations are familiar to Morongans — they can anticipate how to control or block an action. They do not know how to handle a corporation board and are reluctant to give powers to that type of organization.

Lack of futuristic orientation clearly stems from a cautiousness traditional to these people, whose philosophies emphasized the negative possibilities of an erratic universe. Traditional views have been even more strongly reinforced by the past 100 years of experience with whites, as each generation of promises appears to be unfulfilled and the privileges of wardship have been threatened over and over again.

Morongo reactions are realistic, when assessed in terms of the erratic distribution of the "favors" that have been granted them. The government gives in one administration and takes away in the next; thus, every new program is received with an "I'll wait and see, prove it to me" attitude. A negative prediction is probably correct more often than not, as the reservation has been the experimental playground of various advocates and Indian leaders, and more ideas have failed than succeeded. Waiting and seeing before joining a program is characteristic of the recent successful programs at Morongo. The "talking stages" of the health clinic lasted some ten years, with several starts and stops; when it finally received sufficient popular support, it succeeded. Malki Museum required five years of steady and continual growth through a fiesta program, a publications program, and — perhaps most significantly — a vigorous public relations program emphasizing non-political scholarship programs for Indian youngsters, before it received widespread community support — albeit still somewhat hesitant.

The carefully worked out economic development study, although rejected, was influential. A committee worked very hard, large amounts of time and money were invested in the study, information was widely distributed to the tribe, numerous mass and committee meetings were held, and finally every family was contacted for discussion and explanation. The denial of the program does not indicate a negation of futurism but a rejection of a specific plan in which the immediate advantages and the means of implementation were not clear. A similar situation regarding economic development programs was noted at Yuma by Bee (1967), who noted that most programs which would have benefited the people were rejected not for the programs per se, but because of disagreement about the details.

INNOVATION

Innovation and experimentation have been constant themes throughout the history of Morongo.

Morongans — often without help from the BIA — have experimented with new crops, such as potatoes, with mining and chicken farming, seemingly with every feasible economic activity. For several generations agriculture and stock raising were successful, and new ideas were tried. Morongo is also recognized as a reservation where social innovations have been devised.

From an economic point of view, the principal impediments to general economic development are:

1. Faulty and inadequate water systems and supplies.
2. Small labor force caused by large numbers of people leaving the reservation due to a lack of economic potential, the poor quality of life available (in the recent past) on the reservation and in the surrounding area.
3. Market conditions in the area not having been practical for the land use processes available to the group for which they have been trained (e.g. orchards).
4. Lack of a proper and practical educational system. The people were trained in, and for, a system that was already unfeasible at the time they were being trained (i.e. agriculture was phasing out of their area while they were still being trained for it). Allotments were set up in undesirable, small parcels.
5. Fractionated lands, due to heirship rules, which complicate land use to the point where some people must sell or lease land in order to acquire an income. Then the income isn't very significant, due to the small amount of capital which could accrue to any one person or heir.

Furthermore, alienation or use of reservation lands by nonmembers is generally repugnant to community life.

6. Lack of capitalization over long periods of time and improper training of reservation personnel toward productive economic goals. Although many programs have been set up on the reservation, it does not appear that reservation personnel have ever been routed towards active management or other programs requiring skills necessary to manage 30,000 acres of resources. Managerial positions and final decision-making powers have always been in the hands of outsiders. This was complicated in the 1950's when termination proceedings were attempted throughout California.

7. Shifting policies and high turnover of advocative personnel which have led to conflicting information being placed in the community about what is good or proper or what can be attained. At no time in their history has there been a carry-through on advice or funding. Blame for the failure of programs has invariably been placed upon the tribe itself as programs have not been immediately successful on the reservation, whatever the evaluation.

Morongo has not utilized all of its resources in an efficient and profitable manner, so it cannot be argued that the community is successful economically. Yet, it is questionable if Morongans are any less competent in meeting the ideals of the larger society than are many non-Indian communities. When the complications of land tenure are taken into consideration, they may in fact demonstrate a rather remarkable level of economic and political integration.

Viewed as an independent body of people holding land through perpetuity, who have developed their own value system and goals, the Morongo reservation has been a success for 100 years. In comparison with other reservations sharing similar environmental and administrative circumstances, it ranks among the highest in terms of exploiting potentials and coping with limitations. Morongans have demonstrated that they can adjust and change, can revise criteria for selecting leaders, can maintain sophisticated political tactics for solving and allaying crises. In terms of maintaining community viability in an environment that has been erratic, unstable, and varyingly discouraging, they have developed strategic mechanisms of a high order. They have not at any time in their history accepted unquestioningly the decisions of the larger society that governs them; they have not expediently abandoned their community life and land base as have other groups in their area.

Instead, the Morongans have adapted to their life circumstances. Actively but cautiously oriented toward the future, they have insisted on maintaining their community as an income-producing area, as an identity base — and as a homeland.

SUMMARY AND CONCLUSIONS

It is almost axiomatic to students of American Indian affairs that reservation political structures are dysfunctionally organized. The general image of reservations is one of faction-ridden or atomistically structured groups that compete with one another to the point where positive economic or political actions are invariably destroyed before they can even approach successful completion.

A second assumption of many students is that traditional Indian systems are so divergent from those of the dominant culture, with which they necessarily interact, that mutually exclusive organizational principles come into conflict. Because the dominant culture holds the ultimate sources of power and decision making, the result is that Indians who insist on maintaining traditional institutions are necessarily barred from successful economic ventures or from being able to satisfactorily maintain effective internal social structures.

Neither of these assumptions seems to explain the situation at Morongo. We examined seven expressive-instrumental, voluntary associations that have a continuous history of successful operation and Indian management: Big House or ceremonial units, churches, Cattlemen's Association, Malki Fruit Cooperative, Malki Museum, health clinic, and Morongo Fire Department.

The first assumption, that disorganization is so pervasive that continuous positive actions are impossible because of internal stress, proved to be invalid. In fact, the conditions that non-Indians have assumed are empirical indicators of social disorganization (factionalism or internal feuding, rapid turnover of leaders, and slowness or apathy in decision making) are institutional strategies that the people of Morongo use deliberately, to protect themselves from massive exploitation by a dominant culture.

Consequently, we have seen that the refusal of the Morongo people to allow elected leaders a broad range of discretionary powers serves as a fail-safe mechanism, which the people overtly acknowledge will impede leaders from being unduly or precipitously influenced by outside interests that have designs on reservation activities or resources. It matters not whether the innovations come from exploiters, benevolent advocates, or whatever. It is not feasible to anticipate that truly useful, badly needed programs could be scuttled, because it may be important that the people, in order to maintain fail-safe mechanisms, are themselves more significant to long-range survival than is any single program or idea.

The second assumption, that traditional systems are dysfunctional or incompatible in a contemporary context, is also invalid at Morongo. In this assumption, such indications as the fear of kinship-based decision making and consequent nepotism, religious rules that impede a people's potential to get things done, and concepts of time (colloquially referred to as "Indian time") that might interfere with progressive institutions also did not stand up to the test of the Morongo case.

At Morongo, we see that traditional values such as these and others actually integrate rather well in both reservation and off-reservation affairs.

In almost every situation examined, extended kinship relations have contributed to the successful organization of political protest organizations, with factional and atomistic units providing an assumed political or economic pose for innovative leaders. Furthermore, the traditional strategies of expanding or contracting fictively and utilizing extended networks of kin to five generations have, in some cases, allowed leaders to draw upon a large reservoir of talents for whatever actions they deem significant to the well-being of the group.

In traditional religious affairs, we found that ritual requirements served to enforce group identity and social cohesion, and their performances have adjusted in several ways so that severe competition with economic conditions is not felt. As the society was able to introduce flexible standards to changing ecologic conditions in prewhite times, so it has today.

Divergent concepts of time are present, but they are used practically, as occasion demands. Local employers have not expressed dissatisfaction with employees in this regard. In fact, attention to detail and a sense of commitment in reciprocal relations continue, as in the past, to place the people at Morongo in an excellent employment situation.

Factions are the villains usually named in explaining why reservations do not "progress." This is a convenient scapegoat theory for economic development specialists whose plans have been inoperable, insufficiently funded, or unacceptable to the people at Morongo. At Morongo, factions have served the people very well. Although factions are generally characterized as impediments to progress and community action, it is clear that during the past century the development of factional parties has led to goal attainment and sociopsychological adaptive functions in the absence of institutions that more naturally served in the past as integrative mechanisms for the community. At the very least, factions have served to allow a balance of power structure to develop. As the older, larger factional structure became unwieldy, a social structure formed in which the nuclear family became the major social unit, the major social unit upon which an individual could rely. As this was accompanied by a more complex social system outside the reservation, normative disaffection increased, but contributed to the maintenance of a system the people wanted. The personal hardships of this are mitigated by tribal membership, being clearly defined and irrevocable. In fact, the intense interest in one another that is so often reflected in disaffection is a binding element in the community; it balances power and keeps channels of information and options open in a powerless but completely structured society. On a psychological-interpersonal level, it appears that by directing antithetical feelings toward the same persons or institutions on the reservation, closeness of relationships among other fragmented and potentially unorganized social units is increased. The same processes and functions operate with regard to the reservation and outside institutions.

When the community is seen as an independent body of people, holding land through perpetuity and developing its own value system and goals (present and future), the reservation has been a success for 100 years. In comparison with other reservations sharing similar environmental and administrative circumstances, it ranks among the highest in terms of coping with the potentials and limitations it is offered.

The Morongo people have demonstrated that they can adjust and change, that they can revise leadership criteria and selection processes, and that they can maintain sophisticated political tactics for solving and allaying crises with an eye towards the community as a whole and toward the survival of a fixed membership group. In terms of maintaining community viability, despite erratic and unstable environment and the vacillating administrative policies of the larger society, they have developed strategic mechanisms of a high order and have shown an inclination to adaptive and creative change.

They have not at any time in their history sat back and unquestioningly accepted the decisions of the larger society that governs them. They have found abandonment of the community life and land base less expedient than continuing to struggle. Instead, they have adapted their life circumstances toward an active but cautious future orientation about their community, insisting on maintaining their land and using it as an income-producing resource, a homeland, and an identity base.

When one looks at all of the organizational devices of the reservation, it is clear that when Morongo residents want things done, action is successfully and rapidly accomplished. When they wish to organize, they do; when they don't want action, a system of checks and balances is brought about to slow down decisions. Accusations of cupidity, failure to understand the details, and refusal to attend meetings are examples of strategies used.

The characterization of Morongo as a reservation that is factioned to the point where members can't reach decisions, who are so suspicious of one another that they won't trust their own leaders with the

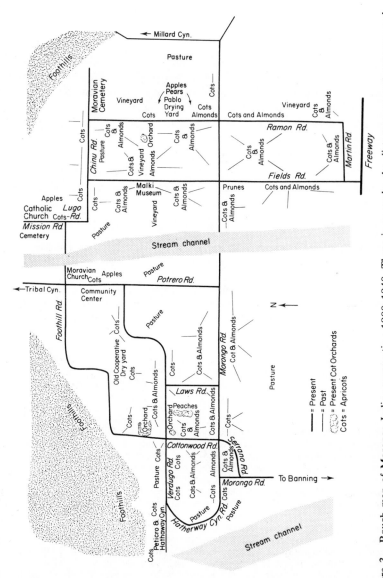

Figure 3. Rough map of Morongo Indian reservation 1900–1940. There is no scale, the distances are not accurate and descriptions are tentative. The map is intended mainly as a starting point for any subsequent work in this area

responsibility for the group future, is highly exaggerated. These seem to be, at least in part, rationalizations by outsiders whose ideas have not been successful. The seeming lack of economic development is caused by influences outside the control of Morongo. Individual entrepreneurship and small associational successes are seen, but only as they are able to operate separately from the built-in restrictions associated with trust statuses of the land, or the conflicting land-tenure concepts of the reservation members and the larger society.

In conclusion, the Morongo case demonstrates a century of successful and profitable organizational skills, despite impediments from the larger society, and these successes directly occur when Indian leadership and participation are in firm control of the decision-making processes of the organization itself.

A principal point demonstrated in this case is that profit as well as control must remain in the community for acceptance by the community, and that the people want to maintain the reservation as an exclusive Morongo Indian domain.

APPENDIX: A CENTURY OF ADAPTIVE STRATEGIES ON THE MORONGO INDIAN RESERVATION

This preliminary report is designed to answer specific questions posed by the Economic Development Agency; consequently, it deviates considerably from the project outline as previously submitted. The final report includes more details on historical and cultural factors and expanded notes on the points covered in report.[1]

[1]   Mr. William Gianelli of the Bureau of Indian Affairs in Riverside, California, was consulted and generously provided his time and insight. Mr. Michael Black of Economic Development Collaborative has been of special help in talking to us and generously provided reports concerning Morongo Indian reservation prepared for him by the Economic Development Collaborative and other consultants. Several archival resources and extensive library resources provided materials for this report: the Bureau of Indian Affairs, Riverside Office; the Federal Records Center at Bell, California; the Huntington Library in San Marino. The services of the Huntington Library manuscript section were valuable in providing access to the William Weinland papers. Mr. Dorme, Mr. Jordan, and their staff at the Federal Records Center were especially helpful.

The members of the research committee of the Morongo Indian reservation who participated in this project were: James Martin, tribal spokesman; Thomas Lyons, member, tribal council; Madeline Ball, member, tribal council and trustee, Malki Museum; Jane Penn, former member, tribal council and trustee, Malki Museum. The following persons at Morongo reservation participated significantly in data collection and analysis: Mr. and Mrs. Orlin Hough, Margaret Cline, Walter Linton, Victoria Lomas, Sam and Dorothy Lugo, Sarah Martin, Clifford Matthews, Mr. and Mrs. Henry Matthews, Viola Matthews, Rose Meserve, Adelaide Presley, Marianno and Katherine Saubel, Ray Valenzuela, and Leonard, Anna Siva, Mr. and Mrs. E. Miguel and Miss Irene Miguel. In addition, the following high school students from the reservation aided in data collection: James Lugo, Luanne Martin, Roy Matthews, Joletta Miguel, Pauline Miguel, and Phillip Siva.

George Barker, Francis Johnston, and Bert Jost, non-Indian residents of Banning, California, were also consulted.

Members of the research committee at Morongo reservation were consulted on all aspects of this report, and numberous members of the reservation served as consultants. All age and social groups have been represented.

Tribal Wealth

The principal capital resource of Morongo Indian reservation is 32,300.58 acres of land. This includes tribally owned land (30,873.75 acres or 95.6 percent), allotted land (1,327.27 acres or 4.1 percent), and fee lands (99.56 acres or 0.3 percent). Of the allotted land, 30 acres or 2.4 percent is used for housing; 1,068 acres or 80.2 percent is used for nonirrigated agriculture; and 155 acres or 11.7 percent is used for irrigated agriculture. Community buildings occupy 4 acres or 5.4 percent of the allotted lands, and roads take up 70 acres or 5.4 percent of the reservation's land.

Each allotment has an area of five acres and contains a house or trailer. Some allotments are still used for agriculture. Fruit trees occupy about 8 percent of the irrigated lands. Community buildings include a hall, a health clinic, Malki Museum, a Catholic church, a Pentecostal church, and a Moravian church. There is also a privately owned feed store.

The use of lands as a capital resource is complicated by the several kinds of ownership. Tribal lands are owned by the tribe and held in trust by the Department of the Interior. These lands are used for various community facilities and activities — a community house, health clinic, recreational groups, grazing cattle, and leasing to utility companies and businesses. These activities provide services and modest, but regular, income to the tribe. The income from these sources and the specific use to which tribal lands are put are controlled by the voting members of the band (people over 21 years of age who are recognized as members of the reservation). These voting members, assisted by an elected tribal council, decide how the lands belonging to the group are to be handled. They vote on all matters concerning use of the land, and the band maintains final authority over all tribally owned lands.

The allotted lands can be divided into two types — those owned by single individuals who have full rights over the use of that land, and lands that have been fractionated because of inheritance. The former lands are potentially exploitable for income by owners and their families. These lands are sometimes rented or leased for income (Malki Museum leases five acres), used for private business (the feed store), agriculture (orchards), and as feed lots for stock and chickens. Generally they are used for home sites and gardens, with some commercial orchards. The 5-acre allotments are too small for successful commercial farming, however, so the fractionated lands are used as living sites or are leased. In some cases the mutual interest of heirs has been arranged so one heir or several have the permission of other owners to use the lands for a business purpose or as a home site, with the co-owners subordinating their interests for the time being. One allotment owned commonly by several people provides a homesite for a family that has many children as well as land for stock raising and gardening, which add income for that family without any cost to the family for rental to the other co-owners.

Some of the land owned by individuals is no longer in federal trust: allotments sold to nontribal members or inherited by Indians who are not members of the Morongo band. Some of these lands have been put up for sale, and the tribe has purchased several to keep the land in federal trust and under control of the Morongo band.

The tribe owns no buildings that produce income, although pumps that provide water for domestic agriculture are owned by the tribe. A fire truck is owned by the firemen's association, and the medical clinic owns equipment but uses its building without cost.

In the canyon a corral used for cattle is owned by the tribe. Breeding bulls have been purchased periodically by the tribe and are available to all cattle owners.

A major capital asset of the band is grazing land, which cattle owners use without cost. Individuals own capital equipment for farming and cattle raising, including horses, riding equipment, branding instruments, and trucks.

Leases are another capital resource. Tribal lands are leased for highway signs and businesses. It is anticipated by the economic development committee of the reservation that leases could be used in the future as collateral for borrowing funds for building facilities, which then could be leased to businesses such as restaurants, mobile home parks, and produce centers.

The intangibles of tribal wealth revolve around the general potential of both the land and the people. Located strategically as a link in the traditional "tourist belt" through the Southwest and into southern California, Morongo reservation itself has potential for tourism. Both climate and natural resources are conducive to success in this particular type of economic activity, and the population has demonstrated its ability to handle such ventures. Extremes of temperature and general scarcity of water are not nearly as bad as in nearby areas already developed successfully, and the people have themselves developed tourist attractions known throughout the region. Malki Museum, the annual Malki fiesta, and other affairs demonstrate that the Morongo people are capable of exploiting the outsider's widespread fascinations for things that are "Indian."

The basis for the Morongo community's talent for handling this and many other types of enterprise stems mostly from a basic set of values necessary in such pursuits. Great patience in the completion of a task is a recognized trait of the people, as is their sense of responsibility in maintaining steady work habits. In general they show a high work drive, value those who work diligently and exert an extra effort. Many households include both a working husband and a working wife, and most adolescents work when able.

The human potential aspect of tribal wealth is apparent, when one takes into account the large number of people who have acquired considerable social and intellectual skills without the benefit of a formal education. Training in leadership and organizational skills in association with the maintenance of various traditional social institutions through the years has been keenly developed. Today these same skills have been utilized to successfully promote community members in ventures outside the reservation. Morongo women were active for organizing employment service industries in nearby Banning, and two served as union presidents in local factories. Others have displayed unusual skill in working cross-culturally in the Office of Economic Opportunity and in educational programs as community organizers.

The possession of various technical skills adds to the reservation's intangible wealth. Many adults have been trained in skilled occupations as a result of vocational training opportunities, and their expertise in livestock and in agriculture is well known. Morongans work in maintenance and construction trades and hold jobs in nurseries and forestry. Community members have a local reputation for excellent physical coordination and manipulative skills; and many are employed in light industries such as electronic assembly and handicraft manufacturing.

Human Resources

There are no formal organizational means by which the Morongo community directly affects participation in the labor force, nor is there any organizational framework that attempts to influence the scheduling of work hours, the development or seeking of new jobs, or preparation or technical training for careers.

The social factors affecting who takes part in the labor force and where and when jobs are taken include restrictions imposed by family ties, time demands imposed on individuals by ceremonial and tribal affairs, and individuals' value orientations. Other factors exist but are too individualistic to be described here.

Familial ties are important, and Morongans are reluctant to take jobs away from the reservation. There is a deep commitment to the reservation as a residence base and to the family as a primary referent-support group. Participation of women and children in the labor market is usually limited to jobs on or near the reservation. The exigencies of family emergencies and child-care needs often impede the job-holding ability of women. Relatives are often called upon to care for younger children so mothers can work. However, a problem still exists for many families, as evidenced by a recent proposal that the tribal committee established a child-care center.

Although factions have been considered by many observers and members of Morongo reservation to be a pervasive problem, factions do not seem to impede reservation public works projects, although participation and cooperation often fall along factional or familial lines. Numerous organizations on the reservation tend to alleviate and cut across alliances, intermeshing personnel in cooperative activities that encourage the formation of groups oriented toward specific goals. Examples of such groups are the Firemen's Association, health clinic, museum, churches, recreational and political associations, and youth group.

SCHEDULING OF WORK HOURS. Scheduling of work hours is not seriously affected by traditional customs. For several generations, traditional ceremonies have been well coordinated with local work schedules. This is not always possible for all people, because rituals — like candlelighting, flower decoration day, funerals, wakes—may conflict with the ordinary work schedules of participants who serve as singers and cooks. Usually participants make arrangements with employers in advance so others may substitute on the job. No serious conflicts between employers and reservation members seem to have developed. Nevertheless, traditional funerals and memorial wakes are decreasing in importance to community members. It is generally expected that friends and relatives will attend these affairs despite personal inconveniences that may arise, but they are not expected to remain for the entire 36-hour ritual. In recent years, fewer and fewer people have been honored by traditional funeral rituals. When they do occur, a local administrative office may be closed for the occasion. But because most funerals today take place in the Cahuilla ceremonial house, Catholic, or Moravian churches, whose leaders recognize local work schedules, a simple one-day leave of absence from a job is all that is usually required of individuals.

Tribal meetings are usually held on Saturday or Sunday evenings, so that only a few of the members have conflicts with work schedules. The most serious problem for members participating in reservation affairs is the need to live off the reservation to maintain steady employment. Members of the

Morongo tribe who live at great distances from the reservation must participate in reservation affairs through letters, personal contacts, and newsletters from the business committee when they cannot attend meetings. They can vote in tribal decisions by mail. Their questions about election matters are often answered by mail. Members of the tribal council, Bureau of Indian Affairs officials in the Riverside office, and kinsmen or friends may correspond privately.

Certain value orientations affect the allocation of human resources on the Morongo reservation. Because Morongans see themselves as members of a fixed membership group, they are sometimes unwilling to accept jobs that are located far away. On the family organizational level, individuals sometimes approach the question of job allocation with the view of maximizing the participation of family members to the exclusion of others. Individual self-interest, too, plays a part, because jobs are approached in terms of achieving greater participation in the general consumer market. This is evidenced in an increasing desire for higher cash incomes and more costly personal possessions, such as a new house, television sets, and cars, and in an increasing concern for clothing styles.

Ancillary factors affecting the participation of community members in the labor market include attitudes of local businessmen and alcoholism. Local businessmen have developed an increasing interest in career preparation and technical training of younger Indians, and their participation in the local job market has increased recently. Government agencies have assisted in developing manpower training programs and in opening labor possibilities not previously available to Indians.

Although alcoholism has been at times a factor in the loss to the labor market potential, it has never been an acute problem at Morongo and has decreased significantly in the past decade. A local chapter of Alcoholics Anonymous has been effective in this regard.

Awareness of opportunities available to Indians for advancement through education has also increased. Several Morongans have entered adult educational programs, and a larger number of young people are now encouraged by adults to finish high school and consider college educations. High school students are performing better than in past years, according to teachers in the Banning school district, and Indian students have organized a Native American Club with the backing of reservation adults, Malki Museum, and local school officials. This club has raised funds for student activities, developed curriculum suggestions, and investigated post-high-school job and educational programs. Several young people are enrolled in colleges: San Jacinto Junior College, Humboldt State College, and the University of California at Riverside. Their education goals include two-year trade degrees, teaching credentials, and postgraduate degrees. Dr. Marigold Linton, a scholar from Morongo, has received a doctoral degree in psychology and is now active in teaching and research at California State University at San Diego, while participating in reservation affairs and other Indian affairs.

The women of Morongo are directly promoting their own personal growth and development. Several have entered adult training programs for nursing and leadership training and now work in local hospitals and service organizations. The job potential for women was investigated by several reservation women a dozen years ago; several became active in union activities, two served as president of their union local. They encouraged others on the reservation to seek jobs in local industries. Women also are employed in secretarial, clerical, paramedical and social service work. Desire for personal growth was also evidenced in the development of a mother's club which was a catalyst to the development of various women's associations which have stimulated useful programs among reservation women. Two specific examples of this were: a class in nutrition and a successful diet-and-health club. On a more extensive level, women's organizations have participated significantly in local and national community development programs. Reservation women take part in the Banning City Headstart program, sit on the steering committee of the Riverside County Board of Education, and have successfully set up Morongo as a recipient of Title I educational support funds (1965–1966). The organizing efforts of Morongo women have also promoted interaction with non-Indians, by establishing the community hall as an official voting station and starting an arts and crafts program that has attracted many people from off the reservation.

Throughout the reservation a growing concern for personal growth and an increased standard of living is seen in escalating individual goals. Many have increased their incomes by actively pursuing better-paying jobs; this has been coupled with a rise in expenditures for personal (durable and nondurable) goods and services. The general level of wages is a matter of concern to everyone in the community, and their expectations are at pace with the standard of pay in the area as a whole. Morongans have been able to acquire high-cost consumer goods, such as household appliances and furniture, carpets, television sets, and new kitchen equipment. More money is being spent on new cars, and there is greater interest in subscribing to local and national mass publications and in keeping up with the dress styles of large metropolitan areas.

The desire of Morongo residents for personal growth is also evidenced in the greater awareness of the need to pursue education opportunities. Many people in the community are adopting an acquisitive attitude toward education, e.g. a summer tutorial program for reservation children. Intense interest is shown in maintaining the quality of education in the local schools, through direct action and confrontation with the local school boards and school officials.

A desire for personal growth is also reflected by recent changes in outward material appearance at Morongo. Housing began to improve in 1952, when federal surplus houses became available to southern California Indians. But it was necessary for reservation members to initiate a long, drawn-out struggle with county officials over restrictive zoning ordinances to build them. The vigor and success of this contest indicates the strong desire for better housing on the part of the community. Some new homes were erected as a result of this opportunity, but the frustration of inadequate housing on the reservation continued. In 1967, funding for more new houses was arranged through the Federal Housing Authority. More improvements in housing have been recommended by the economic planning committee of the reservation, and many people are building new houses on their own initiative. Several residents have built their own homes, thereby cutting down initial capital investment, while others have arranged for architectural planning. These changes in the housing situation at Morongo have been caused not only by increased personal incomes and greater access to financing, but also by the fact that younger people now see the reservation as a place where they can raise their families. While many people wait for financial aid, others have found temporary solutions to the housing goals by acquiring mobile homes.

Management

The role of managers at the Morongo Indian reservation is marked by a long continuity from the aboriginal past down to the present. Traditionally, lineage leaders (*net, kika*) carried out managerial tasks in economic activities. Leadership succession today is often held by the children of past leaders. This tendency is clearly seen when one examines the family backgrounds of tribal council members and those who are identified as decision makers or "influencers." One person in the community suggested this came about because children of leader families grow up with a sense of responsibility toward the community. While such individuals may not define themselves as potential leaders, they have been taught leadership role behavior and a sense of responsibility or "mission" toward the community. Respect for a family's past capacity for leadership continues to place them in, or influence them toward, formal and informal leadership roles.

In addition to official managerial roles, there are unofficial leaders who do not actively seek public office but exercise substantial influence and power within the community. These influencers are consulted frequently by officials before making important decisions. They are generative figures in the formation of committees, associations, and clubs. More often than not, they are also descended from families of past leaders.

Thus, continuity with the past is demonstrated in managerial selection and conduct. Traditional checks and balances remain, e.g. gossip. The principal means of selection is election, since members of the tribal council are elected and hold office for two years. They do not control the resources of the community. Permission by the majority of reservation adults is required before contracts of leases can be signed. Distribution or disbursement of tribal funds requires a majority vote. This is accomplished by presenting a formal reslou- tion to the tribe, which votes by secret ballot. Elected tribal council members must be enrolled, adult members of the fixed membership group; thus, all management decisions are ultimately decisions made by the tribe at large.

The major role of the tribal council is to formulate committees and investi- gate problems generated by the council or reservation members. The council and selected committees place recommendations before the tribe in the form of resolutions. These are discussed privately in council, committee meetings, and, finally, public open meetings (of which all members are notified by mail) before voting. Members who cannot attend the meetings mail in their ballots.

This limited managerial responsibility is related to and reflected in the feeling held by community members that concentrated executive power in the hands of a few could be detrimental to the tribe as a whole. There is presently (1973) considerable discussion about incorporating the tribe, so that a manager can be selected and a board of directors appointed with the power to make binding decisions without majority consent in a rapid decision-making process. Some argue that this move would attract business interests who wish to lease lands from the tribe. The Bureau of Indian Affairs, other agencies, and a private attorney have been asked to advise the tribe in this matter. The proposed change is presently a hotly contested and unresolved issue. It is clear that most Morongans are reluctant to allow any tribal member to assume a position of significant managerial strength or of permitting any elected commit- tee to make binding decisions without tribal consent. Some have stated that a nonmember (even a non-Indian) would be the most acceptable manager, because inequities in management, favoritism, and nepotism would not become major problems. There has been a long history of controversy over the manner in which assets have been managed. This was publicly acknowledged when a resolution was passed ten years ago which requires that all decisions concern- ing the use of tribal assets receive a majority vote from tribal members before binding decisions can be made.

While some have suggested that non-Indian management would be prefer-
able, others would prefer an Indian from another area. Others suggest that the
manager should be selected from the reservation, after completing a management training program designed for reservation needs. The decision about
future management roles has been postponed, because the tribe has not yet
decided if it will incorporate — although the economic development committee
of the reservation has recommended that it should do so and the tribal
attorney has worked out a plan for incorporation (this plan was rejected in
1973).

The disadvantages of a central management with limited responsibility may
be more apparent than real. Morongans have a definite preference for doing
things without a boss or overseer. Fund-raising affairs and large communal
gatherings like the annual fiesta and barbecue are quite successfully handled
without a rigid sociostructural format.

Natural Resources

Tribally owned natural resources of the reservation are valued as assets to be
preserved, maintained, and kept in Indian ownership for exclusive Indian use
and occupancy. These lands, owned in common, are a permanent land base
closely associated with ethnicity, Indianness, and group identity. Morongans
are acutely conscious of their natural resources and share the view that these
resources are more than just real estate or deposits of natural wealth. Reservation land is more than a source of cash income, a place of refuge, or a "nest
egg" to fall back on in time of need. The land has not been overexploited, and
reservation residents are concerned about conservation.

Reservation lands, however, are exploited for recreational, economic, or
community help projects. A large part of the tribally owned lands are used for
cattle grazing, as sources of individual leases (for example, signboard space)
and small amounts of money paid into the tribal fund, and as rights-of-way to
outside agencies serving reservation members. Land bordering Highway 10
and lands distant from the residential area are exploited for profit to outside
tourist-recreational and other commercial ventures, with the condition that
they remain in tribal ownership and those who use them do not interfere with
the quality of community life.

Some assets have been sold to outsiders. In these instances, reservation
members were employed by businessmen who leased assets from the tribe, e.g.
peat moss. Considerable interest has been expressed over the years in potential
mineral resources that could be exploited. While there is a willingness to earn
income from tribal lands, this motive has never outweighed that of protecting
the reservation from exploitation from non-Indians and maintaining it as an
exclusively Indian community. Occasionally myths have been circulated, hint-
ing at vast and undiscovered deposits of mineral wealth underlying reservation
land. These myths of hidden resources have served to protect the loss of
natural resources — both real and fictional — to the group as a whole, by
impeding other land-use suggestions.

Tribal policies for managing tribal resources are not clearly defined (perhaps
deliberately), except that exploitation of any community asset is presumably
impossible without a majority ruling by the tribe's voting members. Thus,
management decisions regarding resources are, in effect, made by a majority of
the adult population and accomplished only after complex decision-making
processes. The basic point of this arrangement is an assumption that any
benefits accruing from exploitation of tribal resources must be distributed on a

comprehensive basis throughout the fixed-member group and not in a piecemeal manner among either a minority of the community or a few individuals. This means that proposals for economic exploitation of natural resources are more likely to be implemented if they involve projects explicitly beneficial to the population as a whole rather than projects having only indirect benefit to the community and possible wealth for a few. Thus, matters such as the request for utility right-of-way leases, which serve to bring conveniences to most reservation members, stand a better chance of being adopted than do such recent proposals as the establishment of a casino or mobile park utilities, which would serve outside business interests more than they would the reservation.

The fear that outside business will profit from reservation resources is reinforced by a fear that outsiders will be brought into the reservation. This has been made explicit by a rule the tribal council passed to guarantee close privacy for reservation people, such as the "no-trespassing" law. It is assumed that ecological damage as well as increased litter, smog, and overcrowding would result from any influx of strangers. Less explicit, but nevertheless real, is a fear that outside resource exploitation projects will end up in the hands of non-Indians for the sole benefit of non-Indians. Such fear may be the reason that a feedlot proposal was turned down by the tribe, although it would have provided jobs for Indians. In the recent past local resistance against plans to exploit peat moss deposits and a gravel pit on reservation may have been similarly motivated.

Long-range policies are being developed by the economic development committee of the reservation, the Economic Development Collaborative (a private planning firm), and the tribal attorney, who are preparing recommendations for the tribe. This has come about because of a clear recognition that long-range planning is necessary for the group to protect itself from the increasing economic and political pressures of private, city, county, state, and federal actions, which affect the reservation. Some leaders fear that, if the reservation makes decisions only as crises emerge, control of land, freedom to choose traditional life-styles, and economic advantages will be lost to the group by a slow attrition of rights and privileges.

The idea that the resources should be saved until they are maximally beneficial to the band as a whole and to its decendants underlies some decisions. Meanwhile, the reservation can be used as an economic refuge — a place for people with modest incomes to retire. It is the Morongans' savings account, their "ace in the hole" — a combination of assets whose potential uses they keep as flexible as possible. Reservation members agree that resources must be protected from internal forces as well. This explains the restrictions on executive power, and controls against personal aggrandizement and favoritism. For example, contacts with outside business interests and cash expenditures are closely watched. The tribe will cautiously advance funds for maintenance of the clubhouse but not for development beyond its present state. It will vote funds to hire outside legal help but will restrict reimbursement of business committee travel expenses. Expenditures for other than bare support of administrative work are considered cosmetic expenditures, while outside legal help costs are necessary for impartial legal advice.

Various resolutions have been passed by the tribal council to control unauthorized use of tribal assets. For example, nonmembers are prohibited from collecting firewood and hunting on tribal lands. There is considerable concern when reservation lands are used to raise secondary crops such as hay or fertilizer materials, or when cattlemen do not control grazing in unauthorized areas. These matters have been difficult to deal with on an official level, because the conflicts involve tribal members rather than outsiders.

Two other critical issues are: (1) the various uses of allotted lands and (2) the distribution of income from tribal land. The issuance of a per capita payment of cash income several years ago received a mixed reaction in the community. Some members see that tribal resources can be directly beneficial to individuals; others feel that tribal income should be used for the common good of members. Problems have arisen because some landowners have put their land up for sale. The tribe has purchased some of these lands with tribal funds. Funds are limited, however, and, as individuals sell, the tribe uses its cash resources in a holding action to keep Indian land in trust and non-Indians out of the reservation. Most people want the future generations to be guaranteed a piece of land of their own, but the suggestion that young persons presently without allotments be given allotments further complicates the picture. If all unalloted members are given allotments according to the specification of economic planners, the most valuable lands that the tribe has for future economic development will go into private ownership and perhaps will be sold at a later time to nonmembers.

Two new major problems affecting the attitude of reservation members toward their land developed in 1973. A federal court ruled that the city of Palm Springs could make zoning restrictions on federal trust land within that city's boundaries, and the city of Banning received a favorable ruling in a bid to annex a small but lucrative strip of land from the Morongo Indian reservation.

These two cases are significant to Morongo, because Morongans feel that the Palm Springs ruling may apply to Riverside County, which has already stated that the Morongo reservation area should be zoned for recreational use. A fear that the city of Banning may, through a series of rulings, gradually incorporate reservation lands or diminish the land value of the reservation is strong, since zoning authority would limit possibilities for economic development. The psychological impact of this new indicator of powerlessness could be profound. The tribe has invested thousands of man hours and a great deal of money in economic development plans. Already working relationships between reservation members and city officials, which have gradually developed over a period of years, are at a low point, because Banning officials bypassed Indian representation in this matter. Bureau of Indian Affairs officials assured the band that they need not worry, because the land in question was in federal trust. This error has somewhat undermined the faith and good working relationship that had developed over the past few years between the bureau and the reservation leaders. The reservation has placed the matter in the hands of a private attorney.

Many recognize that planning for the future should begin now. Others feel that a holding action should be maintained until they can judge the direction in which to change; in this way land can be most useful to them. A very small minority see the lands as immediately productive of income, but the forces of farsightedness and tradition seem to outnumber them.

Markets

Markets for cattle, agricultural produce, and crafts are accessible to Morongo band members, although not so conveniently as they were when produce buyers came to the reservation to contract and pay advances for agricultural products.

Today, agricultural production is minimal and unfeasible as a major economic activity for individual entrepreneurs on the reservation. Those who have produce to sell market it in local outlets. The situational nature of demand on the market places them in a considerable risk situation, and in years when abundant crops are available in the area they may either receive very little for their produce or be forced to sell it themselves.

Marketing of produce, e.g. fruit, has become difficult as access to large-scale buyers has been more and more restricted. Local canneries purchase infrequently, because they prefer to deal with large growers' and producers' cooperatives, in which membership requires greater agricultural output than is possible for reservation members. Now people grow only enough to distribute among their neighbors and through small roadside stands.

Cattle are marketed in nearby communities, although some distant buyers still visit the reservation. Each individual brings his cattle to market as he deems necessary. There is no longer a routinized cooperative activity; consequently there is little preparation of cattle for market. Most cows are brood cows, the calves being the primary marketable product. Agricultural products and cattle are sometimes used within the community. The cattle are a significant component of the household economy of cattle owners, who regularly butcher meat and keep it in freezers for home consumption. Occasionally cattle are sold to band members, usually at bargain prices. Sometimes band members donate cattle to community activities, such as barbecues, and to raise funds for band activities.

The cooperative aspects of cattle raising have weakened recently. In the past many corrals were used, as were winter and summer pasturage areas, but these features have disappeared from the community's cattle-raising practices. Cooperative fence-mending operations have also been less successful than in the past. The only significant cooperative efforts among cattlemen now are the common purchase of calves and political cooperation to protect their prerogative of using tribal land for private gain.

There is no real pattern of community sharing of goods produced on the reservation, although familial ties induce a great deal of reciprocal exchange in economic goods and services. The creation and sale of craft goods represents a minor economic activity. Several people supplement their incomes making jewelry and artifacts, and by tanning hides. These are sold by the individuals or left on consignment at small retail outlets in the pass area such as Malki Museum, which is on the reservation. Some items are sold at an annual fiesta, sponsored by Malki Museum, that attracts several thousand visitors each Memorial Day.

Prices to outsiders are determined by market conditions but are modified by community attitudes when selling to family members or band members. There is usually, but not necessarily, a feeling that Indian buyers should be given a lower price. (This sometimes applies also to non-Indian friends or relatives.) This notion extends to goods manufactured outside and then sold within the reservation community. The local feedstore, which is privately owned and run by a member of the community, is sometimes criticized because it does not regularly provide a discount for local people.

Cash marketing is obviously not an extensive activity of the reservation community as a whole. On a per capita basis, income-producing efforts are rather minor in terms of agriculture, consisting mostly of subsistence production of beef, poultry, and garden crops for home consumption. The same is true in manufacturing; anything approaching the establishment of a reservation cottage industry is again concerned with home consumption and probably as much is produced for barter, gift exchange, or community fund-raising efforts as is produced for off-reservation marketing.

Cooperative efforts have been frequent in the past. There have been successful cooperatives such as the Malki Fruit Association, and the Cattlemen's Association which acts as a cooperative attending to problems concerning them as a group. Yet, as mentioned earlier, the cattlemen act independently when selling products, so the cooperative aspects are limited to production and to acting as a group to protect cattle owner's prerogatives rather than as a production and distribution group. This cooperation appears to be breaking down except when a crisis occurs in the cattlemen's affairs. Although the Cattlemen's Association exists as a formal organization, it is relatively inactive.

Profit Motive

The degree to which the concept of a profit motive operates among the people of Morongo was difficult to determine, but several general principles emerged as this study progressed. Community members strive to use their private resources as advantageously as possible, given their circumstances and their need for income. A profit orientation is especially evident in dealings with persons outside the community, but when dealing concerns private resources within the fixed membership group, profit and a drive for maximization of profit do not seem to apply.

In many small-scale transactions, the concept "one price for the Indians, another price for the outsider or white man" is expressed especially if this can be done inconspicuously. A fair or nonexploiting transaction is expected between reservation members. For example, joint owners of land frequently allow a co-owner to live on and to exploit land without reimbursement to co-owners. This sort of arrangement would be severely criticized if it were granted to non-Indians. A buyer from outside is likely to be dealt with harshly and in a demanding fashion, and the price may be as high as the circumstances will bear. He may be expected to pay more because of a "bad deal" the Indian has had in dealing with non-Indians in the past. In this circumstance, a hard sell and a profit motive are associated with a desire for reparation, and an expression of residual power against the outsider. This strategy is justified by recalling that many businessmen have overcharged Indians or when purchasing lands offer a lower price to Indians than non-Indians. Transactions with outsiders may also be accompanied by rituals of denigration that have economic, psychological, and political functions. These serve to lower the sales resistance of the prospect, satisfy personal needs for aggressive behavior, give prospective notice that Indians are no longer to be cheated, and provide leaders with an opportunity to publicly express concern for the communal good. These rituals may begin by placing "ridiculous, or exorbitant prices on things," in the manner of, "It's Indian land, so it's worth a million dollars an acre." They may end in an adamant and vigorous refusal to negotiate at all if the buyer does not indicate an acceptance of the positive values of Indian ethnicity or a public recognition of the maltreatment of Indians by whites. This type of negotiation ritual intensifies group identity by calling attention to the common history and concerns of the group today.

The same dualistic system is at work in the use of tribal lands. Outsiders are expected to pay a good price for the land they acquire, unless the transaction is especially useful to the community as a whole, for example, if it includes services to the reservation. When the tribe buys allotted lands from an Indian, however, sharp bargaining is not expected.

When ancillary benefits to the tribe are clearly involved in a transaction with an outsider, the Morongo people show a decided ability to effectively weigh advantages and disadvantages in maintaining the dualistic price-setting pattern. The residents of the reservation are aware of the valuable geographic position of their lands and the expansionist desires of surrounding non-Indian communities. Right-of-way applications are granted if their completion across reservation land will provide access to public utilities and services for the Morongo community at large but not if they are meant solely to facilitate the operation of some neighboring non-Indian-owned enterprise.

The individual operates with a profit motive in his pursuit of various economic enterprises, in agriculture, and in the manufacturing of small items for the express purpose of sale. Cattle raising, for example, is today the most obvious and extensive usage to which land is put for generating cash income through profit-seeking activities. Although fruit raising for cash is no longer a major enterprise on the reservation, commercial cattle raising is, and cattlemen continue to show their concern for greater profits by seeking lucrative markets more distant than those normally used in the past. Fruit growers are not as numerous as they once were, but those who remain reflect a profit motive in their attempts to devise ways of reducing costs, such as adopting local means of preparing the produce they manage to sell to canneries or other markets.

Profit motive is also reflected by them in the manufacture of tourist items sold at fiestas and fairs. Fund-raising events to support reservation institutions like the churches, the volunteer fire department, and the museum are clearly motivated by a profit incentive.

While the profit motive is not always apparent in interpersonal economic relationships, people at Morongo anticipate value for value received. Morongans are aware that the reservation offers an opportunity for a diversified economy, a factor many people consider when deciding whether or not to move off the reservation. In spite of the fact they are likely to receive more cash income in absolute terms off the reservation than on, the costs of living on the reservation are less, and an individual can make extra money by grazing cattle, or supplement income by having a garden or orchard.

The profit motive is also at work in the thinking of those who live off the reservation. One member of Morongo who did not need her allotment of land considered selling it. It was obvious in her dealings with potential buyers that she was aware of the future value of an unbroken block acreage, so she refused attractive offers for smaller parcels. She recognized that there was no cost for holding it, but a potential profit was likely. This sort of sophistication is not uncommon, as evidenced by the remark of one community leader that no one at Morongo will do anything unless there is profit potential. Another member of the community interviewed about the fruit-growing situation reflected similar consideration by placing the blame for the disappearance of the cash-crop industry at Morongo on the fact that "it doesn't pay anything." Profit motives operate in acquiring personal material items, and the extent and frequency of gift giving and reciprocal aid among the people at Morongo obscure but do not negate it. The profit motive may sometimes operate on rather subtle levels; it is not uncommon for a member of the group to give another a high-cost durable consumer item simply because a new one has been purchased. Yet there is no obvious overt requisite that this must be done and surplus goods are sometimes sold.

Community members are keen to get their money's worth when buying personal items. They will travel long distances or use mail-order catalogs to buy items that are available locally at a higher price; discount stores in distant metropolitan areas are used frequently when buying high-cost durable goods. In addition, the advantages of convenience are weighed against the disadvantages of high maintenance cost when purchases are made. For example, one woman decided to purchase an old-fashioned washing machine with a wringer instead of a modern type, when it became clear she might be unable to repair the latter herself in case of breakdown.

Morongans save cash and other resources for future use and exploitation. They tend to make the most out of manufactured items as they age or wear. They conserve raw materials such as lumber and yard-goods for later use. Yardage is carefully used and odd pieces are saved for making quilts. Older people seem particularly conscious of this form of efficient resource utilization.

There are indications that a true profit motive is not a principle value nor is the conspicuous display of personal wealth for the purposes of prestige or individual advancement in the community a desired or rewarded mode of behavior. On the other hand, the absence of conspicuous consumption may reflect a traditional secrecy motif regarding expenditures and may be related to the need today for a shrewd handling of private resources for personal gain and profit in order to make do with the few resources available on or near the reservation.

Nevertheless, there are some instances of persons pursuing economic activity without obvious or immediate return on investments. Cattle raising provides an example. Some of the herds were established on a reimbursable basis. That is, the Indians return an equal number of cattle from the first generation on calves given to them by the Indian Service. It was expected that Morongo cattle raising would expand rapidly as soon as the government was reimbursed, but in fact this has not happened to any great extent. Indeed, one of the cattlemen has been quite neglectful of a cash-profit potential from his herd. He continues to build his herd despite poor grazing conditions. But he is an exception to the rule, and, because economic transactions are very private affairs, it is not known whether or not his cattle-raising efforts are profitable.

In general, the profit motive is present in the community, despite the few real opportunities for it to be conspicuously successful on the reservation.

Income Distribution

Tribal income is derived primarily from the lease of tribal lands for right-of-way, utility lines, and highway signs. The income derived from the leases is held in a trust account for the tribe by the Department of the Interior, and it draws a modest interest for the band. Funds may be withdrawn on request of the band and used for community projects. On one occasion a per capita payment was made to the tribal members; each member received $200. In retrospect the general feeling among the people is that this was not the best way to use tribal funds. Funds have also been used for building and maintaining a community house, honorariums for elected tribal officers, hiring consultants for economic planning, surveys of reservation assets and potentials, legal fees, repair of the domestic water system, and the support of various recreational activities. When per capita payments were made, the money was used for home improvements, building materials, paying debts, purchasing household goods and clothing, and savings. Several families used these funds for their children's educational expenses. No appreciable change occurred in the community, although members have suggested that once per capita payment occurred it tended to change the attitudes of some members, especially those living off the reservation, about tribal assets. Some members have been concerned that others would now see tribal income as desirable on a per capita basis, although in the past they only voted funding for tribal community interest. The reality of this fear remains to be proved.

Generally, the community feels that funds coming from tribal resources should be used for the benefit of all and not for special groups or persons. In this regard there is a history of controversy, because tribal funds are sometimes used for the special interests of cattlemen, a strong and vigorous special-interest group within the reservation.

The continued use of tribal resources and grazing land by cattle owners unquestionably provides a considerable but immeasurable economic advantage to those who take advantage of it. All tribal members have the privilege of using these lands, but actually only twenty-nine people were listed as users in 1973. Because a reimbursable cattle program is no longer available, young people who are without capital find it difficult to get started as cattlemen.

Tribal funds, for the most part, are used for legal council for the group and for maintenance of the community hall, which provides a meeting place for various social and instrumental groups who bring aid and advice to the community. Consequently, tribal resources, although not dramatic, are significant in maintaining a quality of life the people want and in reinforcing a sense of group and corporate identity.

Methods of Dealing with Crisis

There have been numerous crises, both natural and man-made, at Morongo in recent years. Floods, water pollution, fires, and drought have occurred, but man-made crises have been more frequent; these have involved legal problems arising from the passing of Public Law 280, claims cases, urban sprawl, economic development, allotment programs, and law and order.

Natural crisis are dealt with in ways consistent with the flexible and democratic style of social order at Morongo. Individuals apply political pressure and acquire services by contacting elected tribal officials as well as federal, county, and city agencies — sometimes simultaneously. Almost invariably the Bureau of Indian Affairs is called in for advice, whether the crisis concerns it or not. Local newspapers are used to call public attention to a problem and alert reservation members of particular problems. A telephone committee has been organized on the reservation so individuals can be contacted rapidly. Some individuals take it upon themselves to drive to each home to inform people of crises; elected committee persons usually see this as part of their role as councilmen. Natural (informal) leaders generally express themselves in these situations, and persons not ordinarily involved in band political affairs regularly step forward and assume responsibilities during crises. Several members were so named.

Crisis management has been more acute since the 1950's because of the partial withdrawal of the Bureau of Indian Affairs from responsibilities in California. This major crisis remains one that is still apparent on all California reservations, because the bureau and the new agencies that Indians now deal with are only beginning to adjust to the changes that occurred seventeen years ago. The relationship of reservation members and the BIA has remained fluid, confused, and erratic as new rulings and policies meet new demands and problems.

Because of these conditions, several organizations have been formed to anticipate and meet crises. The Firemen's Association was formed two years ago, because of an unusual problem with small fires (there were fifty on the reservation in one year). An individual called a number of volunteer speakers from state and county agencies to come to the reservation and speak on fire-control methods. Shortly thereafter, because meetings at private homes are somewhat suspect, the volunteer group met in the community house, where any reservation member would feel free to take part. They formed a firemen's association, a group of volunteers, mostly reservation members; the association was soon recognized and approved by the tribal council and the band. They established procedures for the prevention and fighting of fires, and raised funds through various activities, (grossing $1,000 on one breakfast) to purchase or otherwise acquire equipment, e.g. government surplus. A very significant outgrowth of their work was the placement of fire plugs on the reservation.

Firemen have become involved in other crisis-solving situations. They were instrumental in acquiring permission from the tribe to use tribal land, construct the building, and acquire equipment for the public health center that now serves several reservations. Firemen's Association members are active in political problems and express support for particular candidates in tribal elections.

Floods in recent years have caused dangerous situations on the reservation, blocking roads and isolating people in their homes for several days. During the last flood there was a keen sense of cooperation and closeness. Everyone looked out for others. After the flood, the community pressed county officials to take preventive action against future flood problems. The business committee wrote letters to county supervisors and representatives who came out to see reservation conditions. Consequently, roads were repaired and reinforced.

More recently there was concern that domestic drinking water might be polluted. Several illnesses were thought to have been so caused. Various agencies were contacted immediately by individuals. Health clinic personnel contacted medical and public health authorities at county and state levels. Individuals were called and warned about the possible effects of drinking the water, and information was rapidly disseminated to band members as progress was made toward solving the crisis.

Southern California has suffered from drought for a number of years, limiting agriculture, gardening, and cattle grazing in gardens, destroying fruit trees, and, in general, constituting a public nuisance in people's attempt to acquire food. This crisis led to new resolutions providing financing from tribal funds for fences, and regulations regarding free-ranging cattle. The problem continues and procedures are presently being discussed that would provide further solutions.

Despite the seemingly high degree of internal conflict and arduous decision-making processes that characterize this community, it is obvious to the outside observer that rapid, efficient, and responsible action can be anticipated when crises develop. In personal crises such as death or the destruction of property by fire, local aid from individuals and groups is immediate and is related to the specifics of the situation. Legal problems that have arisen because of the "fuzzy" relationship established between the reservation and local law enforcement agencies have recently been taken more clearly in hand. Members of the reservation are more willing to bring in outside authority as legal problems become acute, and more willing to vote on tribal resolutions restricting individual action and to carry through legal action controlling reservation members who act against the best interests of the group.

Transportation problems that sometimes interfere with getting jobs and getting to work are often solved by car pools.

The major crises that continue and are now becoming critical because of Public Law 280 are the recent legal decisions threatening zoning restrictions on federal trust land and annexation procedures undertaken by the city of Banning against Indian lands. After an initial shock, tribal council members and individuals sought advice from various agencies and their tribal attorney, who is now investigating the legal implication of these rulings for them. At this time the crisis has yet to be solved.

Value and Goals Related to Economic Development

Several clearly defined goals emerge from reports of reservation committees, tribal resolutions, and conversations with band members. These goals often overlap. The major goals and values most explicitly examined are presented below.

JOBS. Morongo members want to increase the number of employment opportunities and heighten their efficiency in gaining access to employment and services by developing service industries near or perhaps on the reservation. It is firmly believed that more job opportunities should be made available to tribal members near the reservation, in order to eliminate the need for long-distance driving or settling off the reservation for long periods of time. This is fully in accord with conditions of the recent past, when government and local economic institutions provided a large number of jobs on or near the reservation on a fairly regular and equitable basis. This, combined with a diversified use of reservation resources, resulted in an economic pattern that provided the possibility of combining the production of reservation and off-reservation income.

HOUSING. A principle concern of the community appears to be improved housing despite discouraging problems with lending agencies, contractors, and contracting agencies. There have been conflicts with contractors and house owners because of poor construction standards and litigation has been instigated. Little has occurred on a higher organizational level, because the tribal council itself has adopted no specific overall program for new housing construction. The economic planning committee, however, has recommended that the tribe take part in federally financed housing programs.

COMMUNITY FACILITIES. The community of Morongo as a fixed membership group usually establishes goals which serve large segments or all of the group. The tribal hall is an example of how the members acquire and maintain community facilities. Tribal funds were approved for its building and maintenance. It is used for expressive and instrumental needs that are both political and social — study groups, women's societies meetings, and recreation. It is "neutral ground" — a center that everyone has the right to use. Members feel free to attend functions held there, in contrast to those held in private homes or in other facilities associated with individuals or groups. Recreational facilities for children and adults is another area of concern, and ground has been set aside for other community facilities such as a health clinic, a fire station, a graveyard, and churches (although it should be noted that the churches are primarily the concern of their congregations). The water system is a community facility supported by the membership.

All tribal land is considered a community asset. Land is valued in and of itself, and many would have it remain as it is. Public sentiment is divided regarding immediate versus deferred exploitation of community land. There is an expressed desire to produce income from the land while ensuring that the natural resources and future values will be available for future use.

MAINTENANCE OF PRIVACY AND A RURAL ENVIRONMENT. Voting trends on tribal resolutions indicate that members value their privacy as a fixed membership group. They will not voluntarily include outsiders within their domain. They resent changes that occur because of marriages to outsiders and the occasional sale of allotted lands to outsiders. This is reflected in the purchase by the tribe of allotments that have come up for sale (despite the great cost to tribal resources), the passing of trespassing ordinances, and the rejection of certain business offers that would bring more whites onto the reservation. It has been suggested that reservation lands distant from the Morongo residential area, such as One Horse Springs, could be used for industrial or recreational purposes. Some members of the tribe feel this would be a solution to conflicts arising between economic goals and the desire to maintain a rural and exclusive living area.

Privacy is highly valued and is reflected in a dispersed settlement pattern. Housing is scattered, and people interviewed — from children to adults — expressed concern that this pattern continue.

Reservation members are offended because outsiders apparently drive through the reservation just to "see Indians." People stop in front of houses, take pictures and ask questions that are often personally offensive. These incidents are recognized as gross invasions of privacy. Members of the local white communities also use the reservation roads (county-maintained and therefore accessible) for activities such as drinking, and they dump garbage and trash on reservation lands.

Intimately connected to feelings for privacy is a desire to maintain a rural environment and the natural beauty of the area. The economic development committee of the reservation has stated in its report to the people that:

Conservation of the land, streams, and plant growth is important to the continued full use and enjoyment of the land by the band. The land, water, and air resources must be continually protected. Efforts are necessary to control flooding and waste of water resources. Care should be taken in allotment of lands and in the use of allotted land so that the maximum benefit to the band members, present and future, can be achieved.... The appearance of the reservation should be protected and improved. The natural landscape should be conserved. Landscaping and good architectural design should be considered in all new development. Disposal of trash and waste materials should be improved.

Yet it should be noted that the Morongo community is caught in a basic conflict of values regarding economic allocation of resources and the desire for independence, privacy, and preservation of the environment. On one hand people recognize that, in dealing with outsiders, their land is a basic commodity that can provide cash income. On the other hand, Morongo residents are very eager to avoid intimate, prolonged contact with outsiders and are deeply concerned that land exploitation will substantially alter the rural environment of the reservation. There is also some conflict concerning the distribution of cash income on an individual basis. Long-term community projects would not be possible if income were distributed to individuals.

EDUCATION. While education has always been highly valued at Morongo, opportunities were limited. Recently adult educational programs in high schools are popular, and the establishment of the Malki Museum scholarship committee for the funding of college students has been vigorously supported. Education goals have broadened. In the past, the focus was on skills directly applicable to the local labor market, e.g. carpentry, masonry, and agricultural activities. Limited goals were related to community relations between Morongo and the city of Banning which were so negative that some parents didn't want their children to attend the school of Banning. In the cultural milieu of that time, public school education was often seen as a waste of time by teachers and Indian parents alike.

In recent years educational opportunities have improved, and the relationships between the reservation, the school district, and the community of Banning have improved. This is related to the general public awareness of Indian problems, but it is more directly based on the active interest of band members aggressively seeking information, funds, and tutorial help from various agencies. Clubs and associations on the reservation have organized toward this end, and now educational achievement is a principal goal. In meetings with children and parents it is clear that educational achievement from preschool through college is keenly sought. Adult educational programs have been carried on, and tutorial programs and Headstart programs for younger children have been established. Several young adults are successfully pursuing higher degrees in local colleges and universities.

The concern of reservation residents for the future of their children is seen in the considerable effort to get a Headstart program for preschool-age children. The effort failed, however, because the community's income was too high according to federal regulations. Another move in this direction can be seen in the desire of many for the establishment of a reservation day-care center. Many preschoolers are already cared for by their grandmothers, but some parents want formal preschool education rather than supervision.

Adults have taken advantage of training opportunities (in nursing, for example) making successful career changes as a consequence. Local officials speak of the remarkable success ratio of reservation members. One family in particular consistently performs at the very highest academic levels in the local schools.

At the same time the social value of maintaining native educational mechanisms has been decidedly weakened in the recent past at Morongo. The pedagogical function held by old people in the past has largely been supplemented by outside sources of knowledge. Old people no longer serve as repositories of group records and knowledge through the memorizing of oral tradition, nor do they actively pass on these materials to the young. Instead, Morongo people now rely on agencies such as the public school systems, the BIA, and Malki Museum for the storage and retrieval of knowledge.

The educational needs of the group are clearly seen. They want training for jobs and careers that will not be disruptive to family and reservation ties. The young want to retain their reservation life style after college. At the same time, they seek a broadening of the range of skills required for future successful management of reservation resources.

FREEDOM OF CHOICE AND LOCAL POWER. Powerlessness and subordination under a federal bureaucracy, limited decision-making powers, economic disadvantages, and cultural downgrading by the dominant culture have led to very special adaptations on Morongo for the expression of cultural integrity and self-help.

Throughout the history of Morongo, traditional values and customs have persistently been maintained in religious institutions, decision-making situations, language, pride in knowledge of the environment and its efficient use, and "Indianness." Community self-government has been an expressed goal since the beginning of federal management over Indian affairs, and it is still an area of conflict. One protest after another has been mounted on the reservation because of agents and officials who attempted to impose federal regulations or policies that are offensive to the group.

In recent years — after the activation of Public Law 280 — the tribe has begun to work out problems of management with less reliance on federal agencies. It has developed a series of resolutions guaranteeing each individual member of the tribe a decision-making role. One resolution requires all decisions affecting tribal resources or affairs be voted on and passed by a majority before they can become legal. Voting and attendance at tribal meetings tend to be high, indicating a broad community interest in this process. In fact, members of the band complain vociferously when they feel they have not been properly informed on public issues.

The tribe is reluctant to grant authority to any outside agency, or allow major decision-making powers to its own elected council. There is vigorous public debate, as well as private debate, on all issues on the reservation. Much time is spent communicating information among members. It is clearly stated to any outside interest — whether it be BIA, a consulting agency, or whatever — that its role is advisory at best. Outsiders are welcome in tribal meetings only when they serve the interest of the tribe. Numerous "fail-safe" mechanisms have developed in order to limit the length of time individuals may acquire power. This concern for minimizing local power is expressed in a variety of subtle and complex strategies for blocking suggestions that are not clearly agreed upon; at the same time, when there is consensus, decisions can be made rapidly and clearly.

HEALTH AND SAFETY. Other values relevant to economic development concern health and safety. The economic development committee recommended to the band that improvements were necessary in the water system and that provisions for industrial, agricultural, livestock, and commercial uses be established or improved. Significant improvements in the water system have been made in the past several years, yet a general concern still exists for this aspect of reservation life.

The health clinic on the reservation was organized as a response to community frustrations. A volunteer group (mainly members of the fire department) acted as catalyst, donated labor, and raised funds so the health clinic could be established. The band voted to provide some aid and outside funding was acquired from the Intertribal Council of California, the Harridge Foundation, and others.

In addition to an active health clinic, which cares for the general medical and dental problems of the community, a weight-losing club has started and instruction on nutritional concepts has developed. Recreational facilities and improved waste disposal systems are recognized as related to general health and welfare problems of the community.

Although protection from environmental hazards is rarely needed, the anticipation of such hazards causes anxiety. Numerous fires occur, some caused by accident and some by arson. The fact that the reservation borders a hazardous fire area in the national forest adds to the concern. Earthquakes, high winds, and severe flooding caused by heavy rains also occur. In recent times these crises have been met by direct individual and community actions.

TRIBAL CULTURE AND IDENTITY. One goal outlined in the report of Morongo's economic development committee is an "increased identity as Indians, as band members and as individuals." Certainly, a sense of community membership is felt at Morongo, a sense of Indian versus non-Indian, member versus nonmember, reservation versus town resident. In addition, gradations of "Indianness" exist on the reservation as reflected in a folk taxonomy used by the people at Morongo in various situations.

The desirability of maintaining a separate and viable group identity as Indians is a principle value at Morongo. On an individual level this value is implicit in the continued use of the native Cahuilla, Serrano, and Cupeño languages within the community, and in the survival of a number of various traditional ceremonies. The value placed on traditional culture can also be seen in the struggles waged against the incursions of church groups and the oft-mentioned concern for the loss of ethnic integration through marriages with those outside the reservation. The currency of this value has increased in recent years. Some, who in the past disclaimed or downgraded their Indian identity, are now proudly claiming their heritage.

The social context in which these values have operated has brought about the evolution of informal social mechanisms to maintain the consciousness of separate identity. The Protestant church groups on the reservation give those who associate with them an identity as both an Indian and as a member of their particular denomination, which is apart from other Indians who remained unconverted. Those who marry with outsiders receive dual identity, too, as both an Indian and as an out-marrying Indian. The public school system, as a whole, is a social mechanism for the maintenance of a separate identity as an Indian on the part of the Morongo children. Many have said they did not identify themselves as really separate from other peoples until they entered public schools and came face-to-face with racist discrimination and prejudice that instilled in them a source of separateness.

A more formal mechanism for maintaining ethnicity is the museum complex that has emerged on the reservation. It is not a tribal venture, nor is it supported by all members of the tribe; although its accomplishments are respected, complaints about its presence and its operation are still heard. The influence of Malki Museum has been subtle, but effective, in restoring certain institutions and in increasing interest in historical, educational, and community development programs. It has provided a channel for outside and inside people to operate together effectively. It has aided in bringing the several cultures of the reservation closer together and has also brought Indians from other reservations to Morongo for various activities.

Although Indianness — or "Morongoness" — is not clearly defined, it is clearly felt, especially by the young people, who vividly express their pride in Indianness and their desire to maintain the Indianness of the reservation. The popularity of classes in native American culture among school children from Morongo is an example of this. The young say they need to learn more about their traditional cultures than they are taught in school.

The goal of increasing Indian identity is also reflected in a developing interest in tribal history as well as in plans to save certain historic buildings on the reservation and to place commemorative plaques honoring persons and events of the past. Many families maintain historical records, save photographs, and keep artifacts (especially baskets) as cultural treasures; they pridefully talk of these things and pass them on to their heirs.

At Morongo, social values surrounding the maintenance of "Indianness" were given a good deal of support and a chance for expression when funding programs became available through the federal Office of Economic Opportunity. The programs provided a thrust to the movement for a better Indian image and also made it possible to profit from the guilt felt by many Anglos for past mistreatment of Indians by whites.

But Indianness does not stretch to "Pan-Indianism," for Morongo attitudes concerning other reservations are in line with their general desire for isolation and privacy. They do not seem to be especially concerned about the affairs of other Indian groups in the area, although they do maintain membership in many Indian associations and organizations, such as Intertribal Council of California, Mission Indian Development Council, and the California Indian Education Association.

INDUSTRIAL AND COMMERCIAL DEVELOPMENT. The inevitability of increasing numbers of people in and around the reservation is discomforting to the Morongans, but the economic advantages that would occur are generally sought. The economic planning committee of the reservation has recommended that lands most distant from the present residential area be developed industrially and commercially, in consideration of the clearly expressed desires of the people concerning the use of reservation land by outside interests.

It should be pointed out that, although privacy is almost a universal value at Morongo, it does not seem to have been an impediment to the development of future economic planning. Industrially developed lands are available at a considerable distance from the reservation where they will be visually distant from the residential community.

REFERENCES

BEAN, LOWELL JOHN
    1964   "Cultural changes in Cahuilla religious and political leadership patterns," in *Culture change and stability, essays in memory of Olive Ruth Barker and George C. Barker.* Edited by R. L. Beals, 1–10. Los Angeles: University of California Press.
    1969   The Wanikik Cahuilla. *The Masterkey* 34(3): 111–119.
    1972   *Mukat's people: the Cahuilla Indians of southern California.* Berkeley and Los Angeles: University of California Press.
BEAN, LOWELL JOHN, CORRINE WOOD
    1969   The crisis in Indian health. *The Indian Historian* 2(3): 29–33.
BEE, ROBERT L.
    1967   "Sociological change and persistence in the Yuma Indian Reservation." Ann Arbor, Michigan: University Microfilms.
BENEDICT, JULIE, FLORENCE SHIPEK
    1972   "A report of an adult education program on San Diego County reservations." Manuscript, University of San Diego. (Manuscript in possession of authors.)
CAUGHEY, JOHN WALTON, *editor*
    1952   *The Indians of southern California in 1852.* The B. D. Wilson report and a selection of contemporary comment. Huntington Library, San Marino.
DELORIA, VINE
    1970   *Custer died for your sins: an Indian manifesto.* New York: Macmillan.

KENNEDY, MARY JEAN
   1955   "Culture contact and acculturation of the South-western Pomo."
          Ph.D. dissertation, University of California.
STANLEY, SAM
   1971   E.D.A. Research Proposal.
SUTTON, IMRE
   1964   "Land tenure and changing occupations on Indian reservations in
          southern California." Ph.D. dissertation in geography on file at the
          University of California, Los Angeles.
THEODORATUS, DOROTHY J.
   1970   "Identity crisis: changes in life style of the Manchester Band of
          Pomo Indians." Ph.D. dissertation, Syracuse University.
THOMAS, RICHARD
   1964   "The Mission Indians: a study of leadership and cultural change."
          Ph.D. dissertation on file at the University of California at Los
          Angeles.

APPENDIX: A MORAL CASE FOR GAME LAWS AND INDIAN TREATY RIGHTS (1914)*

Several cases have occurred during the year that seemed for a time to threaten or jeopardize the Indians' right to secure his natural food supplies in his ancient and accustomed ways. These are sufficiently serious and sufficiently important to seem to warrent a consideration at some length.

The first case threatened the Indians' fishing rights, more particularly at Lummi. Under date of February 11th, 1914 your Office called for a report upon the application of a Mr. Mattson of Bellingham, Washington, for a right to construct a fish trap adjacent to Point Francis of Lummi Reservation on Hale's Pass. At this point Lummi Island (which is not a portion of the Lummi Reservation) is separated from Lummi Reservation by a narrow channel or passage variously termed "Hale Passage" or "Hale's Pass". From time immemorial this place (long before the advent of the white man) has been a valuable fisheries location for the Lummi Indians and upon it some of the self-supporting Lummi Indians have been dependent from ancient times. These locations (here and elsewhere) have been causes of controversy between Indians and whites for years. They have been the cause of endless disputes which the agency had been able to handle itself prior to this case — in this case the appeal was made by appelant to your Office. The matter has several very important phases.

The economic side of the matter may be stated thus: Naturally, inevitably, the aborigines inhabiting the littoral are in large measure, like other such people, dependent upon the bounty of the sea for support and maintenance — it is for this reason of environment that they are a fisher folk, from circumstances rather than from choice. For this reason the United States Government found these people a self-supporting people, and for the same reason they have since so remained. The shell fish and fishery locations adjacent to the mouths of the great rivers of Puget Sound have been the ancient natural larders of these Indians ever since they can remember. These resources have hitherto been sufficient to subsist and maintain these Indians dependent upon same. With the advent of the white man these resources have

---

* This case was presented by an agent who supervised the Tulalip and Lummi reservations.

naturally lessened. More recently, the use of labor-saving appliances, mechanical assistance, numerous great fish traps, canaries, etc. and other activities of the industries allied to the fisheries, have greatly lessened and depleted the Indians' natural sources of feed supply. In addition to this economic burden an even heavier one has been laid upon him by the harsh, stringent, and technical application to Indians of the State game and fish laws. It is becoming increasingly precarious, unnaturally precarious for him to procure his natural foods in his natural way. All of this, or most of it, at least, has been done under color of law — in most cases it cannot be denied that the letter of the law may have been observed *so far as the State laws are concerned.* An empty larder and an empty stomach however are arguments from which there is an appeal and can be no appeal — regardless of the legality or lack of legality of the means by which the larders were emptied or the stomachs remained empty. The pinch of poverty and hunger are none the less severe because the man who has taken your means of subsistence has been careful to observe State law in so doing. The Indian is aware of no defect, default or transgression upon his part — he has always secured his natural food supplies from his natural larders in his accustomed ways, and, until recently, there has been no question raised of his rights in doing so. *Ergo, post hoc propter hoc,* he argues, it must be the white man who is the transgressor as well as aggressor. One by one his remote fishery locations (his from ancient times and customs) have been stripped from him while the law held him helpless and resourceless — but not so the white man. Driven back to his reservation (in spite of the treaty right of taking fish "at usual and accustomed grounds"), under cover of the operation of State laws in State territory (the State game laws apprehend an Indian seeking a duck for dinner for his family if it be in the "closed" season), he is compelled to utilize the fishery locations immediately adjacent to his reservation. The aggressors are even now endeavoring to oust him from these last; they are seeking to drive him from these — still under cover of "law", perhaps, but none the less rigorously and certainly. The fishery rights adjacent to the Lummi littoral have been held in common by the Lummis from ancient times — it is these, for this reason, that the whites are now seeking.

To this the Indian objects for several reasons (aside from the fact that it is practically his last stand) as follows: (1) it seeks to deprive the Indian of a natural right further guaranteed to him by a treaty, (2) it seeks to deprive him of his natural food supplies taken in his accustomed way and at his accustomed and usual grounds, and (3) even the aboriginal fisherman must fish in the water and not on the land. The Lummi Indians, therefore, as a body protested vehemently against the encroachments of the whites upon these ancient fisheries of theirs (the Indians') immediately adjacent to their reservation, regardless of such rights as the white man may give *himself* in the premises. If the white man takes from the Indian the latter's natural means of support, the white man is then also in honor bound and in equity bound to supply the Indians with other, adequate and immediate means of support. It is neither a full nor a direct answer to this question to state that it all comes about through the operation of great natural laws, such as the survival of the fittest, etc. It has come about by the operation of laws which the white man himself has made for the white man's benefit. The Indian has never been given any power or opportunity to make laws of any kind, whether for himself or others.

The legal side of the question may be stated thus: The executive order establishing the Lummi Reservation (and all the tidewater reservations of this agency) stipulates low-water mark as the Indians' boundary line. Beyond that the Indians are in the jurisdiction of the State; yet it is beyond that low-water mark that he must go to secure his fish or his ducks, the natural foods upon which he lives and has always lived. It is beyond that low-water mark he must go to exercise his treaty-guaranteed privilege of "The right of taking fish at usual and accustomed grounds." The State issues fishing licenses and under the protection and permission thereof the white licentiate may lawfully approach the immediate littoral of Lummi Reservation and occupy in this manner the ancient communal fishery locations of the Lummi Indians *and to the exclusion of the Lummi Indians therefrom.* Where then is the Indian to fish — ashore — in his forest? Is he to exemplify the juvenile doggerel:

"Mother may I go out to swim?"
"Yes, my darling daughter!
Hang your clothes on a hickory limb —
But don't go near the water!"

When the treaty was made our Indians called to the attention of Governor Stevens and his party of white treaty makers that the Indians' interests lay in the water as much as if not more than the land. The Indian expected the treaty to take proper cognizance and care of those conditions. The Indian believed and he still believes that the treaty did so. Article V of the Treaty of Muckl-to-oh or Point Elliott, January 22, 1855 (12 Stat. 927), provides as follows:

The right of taking fish at usual and accustomed grounds and stations is further secured to said Indians in common with all citizens of the Territory, and of erecting temporary houses for the purpose of curing, together with the privilege of hunting and gathering roots and berries on open and unclaimed lands. *Provided, however,* that they shall not take shell-fish from any beds staked or cultivated by citizens.

The Indian claims that the above article in the said treaty secures to him that special privilege which was his right, his sustenance and therefore his life or the means of maintenance of it. In the Alaska Packers' Association case in the Federal Court of Judge C. H. Hanford of Seattle, Washington, it was held that the treaty guaranteed the Indian common rights but no special rights — that the Indian was guaranteed equal rights but not special rights, not exclusive rights; that the Indian in State territory was subject in all respects to all restrictions imposed upon white citizens at that point (in State territory). In the case of Winans, however, (*U.S.* v. *Winans*, 198 U.S. 371), there appears to have been a direct reversal of the said Hanford holding. Other cases bearing more or less on the issue in question are: *Seufert* v. *Olney*, 193 Fed. 200; *U.S.* v. *Taylor*, 3 Wash. Ter. 88; *Harkness* v. *Hyde*, 98 U.S. 237; In re Blackbird, 109 Fed. 139; and *U.S.* v. *Kagama*, 118 U.S. 375. The Winans case reverses Judge Hanford. The decisions in the Minans, Taylor, and the Seufert-Olney cases refer to the treaty and are strong decisions. In the Taylor case an injunction was granted restraining a property owner from maintaining a fence that cut off access to fishing grounds which were some fifty or sixty miles distant from the Reservation.

The first Act in the State of Washington relative to Indians fishing is found in the Session Laws of 1891, page 171; this has never been repealed and is now found in Rem. & Ball., Sec. 5207. It is as follows:

Section 5207. Nothing in this act shall be construed to prevent citizens of any state having a concurrent jurisdiction with this state over or upon any rivers or waters, from fishing upon such rivers or waters; provided that this Act shall not apply to Indians.

As has been said, this act has not been repealed and is now found in the later codes (Rem. & Ball., Sec 5207). Certainly there seems to be no fixed principle uniformly adverse to the Indians so far as these decisions are concerned. The most that can be said is that the question may be a moot one — certainly it is not one that has been definitely and finally settled.

During the latter half of the fiscal year 1914, there came into the Superior Court of the State of Washington in and for the county of Whatcome, at Bellingham, Washington, Judge Hardin presiding, a case of this nature bearing upon these phrases cited. In this case the State Commissioner of Fisheries had caused to be arrested two Lummi Indians (Patrick George and Dan Ross) who were not only fishing at the usual and customary fishing grounds of the Lummi Indians but at a point where the Nooksack river entered and was within the Lummi Indian Reservation. The said Indians were apprehended, arrested, and held for trial. Upon trial Judge Hardin exonerated, acquitted and released them, whereupon the Commissioner threatened to re-arrest the acquitted Indians. The decision in this case was forwarded to your Office under date of March 16, 1914. This case clearly shows the struggle which the Indian is compelled to make for his ancient right and ancient food. It also equally clearly shows the struggle which is being made upon the part of the State or its officers to take these things from the Indian, if possible, *even on the Indians' reservation.* Casimir Sam at Tulalip had a similar experience at duck shooting but was released by the court in spite of the testimony of the game warden (which was repudiated by the jury).

The contention has been made that the said cited Article V of the said treaty guarantees to the Indian the same privileges (including licensure) that it does to a citizen. The whites outnumber the Indians in this State more than ten to one. Most of the valuable fishery locations in this State are either adjacent to "Indian country" or else have been the usual, ancient and accustomed fishing grounds of the Indians from primitive times. The guarantee of equality, therefore is more apparent than real.

Several competent attorneys, furthermore, cite the Session Laws, Washington, 1909, page 143, and contend that inasmuch as the requirements for licensure are such qualifications of citizenship and residence as to make it an impossibility for a reservation Indian to lawfully obtain a lawful license, while citizens of the State may do so, the guarantee of equality is not maintained. If this contention is sound and can be maintained, then on still another ground is the Indian being discriminated against in the matter of his said treaty rights.

In the said Mattson fish trap case, Mr. Mattson had been licensed by the State to construct the said fish trap at the said designated point. This location is in navigable waters subject to the supervision and control of the commanding engineer officer of the U.S. Army for this District. Upon the requisite reference of this matter to him he considered solely the question of navigation (as is the custom and duty of his office) and approved the said application *subject to the approval of the Honorable Secretary of the Interior.* On the above presentation the Secretary of the Interior refused to approve the application and requested the Secretary of War to revoke the approval already given by a branch of his Department. This was done and the trap location ordered abandoned and vacated.

Pine Ridge Economy: Cultural and Historical Perspectives

RAYMOND J. DE MALLIE

INTRODUCTION

Pine Ridge reservation is one of the largest and among the poorest Indian reservations in the United States. As the home of the Oglala

ACKNOWLEDGEMENTS This report is based on published and archival materials, and on information gained during a five-week visit to Pine Ridge reservation in the summer of 1972. It would never have been written without the help of many individuals, both white and Indian.

I am indebted to Dr. Sam Stanley for inviting me to undertake this study and for providing funding from the EDA grant.

Mr. Stephen Feraca of the Bureau of Indian Affairs was generous with his advice, shared with me an account of his experiences on Pine Ridge, and allowed me to use his manuscript on Oglala tribal government. He has been very influential in shaping this study.

At Pine Ridge both present Tribal President Richard Wilson and former Tribal President Gerald One Feather graciously and patiently answered my questions. Joe Schneider, planning officer for the Oglala Sioux tribe, and David L. Varmette, Pine Ridge Agency program officer, were both very generous with their time and advice. They helped me obtain much of the statistical information contained in this report and provided important insights. In addition, the many members of the Oglala Sioux tribal government and of the Pine Ridge office of the Bureau of Indian Affairs whom I approached for information were uniformly courteous and helpful.

My debt to Bess Carlton Keller, who was my companion and coworker at Pine Ridge, is very great. She investigated economic and social patterns in the community of Kyle and was treated with great kindness and consideration by the townspeople. We found real helpfulness and sincere cooperation from all the Oglala we met on the reservation, making our visit a very meaningful and rewarding experience.

Albert Wahrhaftig, of Sonoma State College, was kind enough to lend me his notes on fieldwork done at Pine Ridge in 1965, which provided valuable insights.

S. Douglas Youngkin of the University of Wyoming did a thorough and competent job of extracting relevant historical information on Pine Ridge from government documents. His criticism and encouragement proved vital in writing up the final report.

Finally I must thank my colleagues who shared in this multitribal study of economic development. At our various meetings they both inspired and and instructed me, and this report reflects their influence.

Sioux — the people of Red Cloud and Crazy Horse — it is one of the best known of reservations and a frequent subject of reports appearing in newspapers and magazines and on television. The impression given of Pine Ridge is one of social degeneracy, terrible poverty, and general apathy. The federal government supports the people of Pine Ridge with both money and services, and still the people are poor. Why?

The popular answers are simple. The Indians will not work; they would rather live on welfare. They are not reliable. They are drunkards. They do not face up to the realities of the everyday world. Some claim such personality defects to be genetic; others claim them to be matters of habit. Some blame the inefficiency or corruption of the Bureau of Indian Affairs, while others blame the corruption of Indian leaders themselves.

But the problem of Pine Ridge is not simple. It is bound up with many factors that are inextricably intertwined. Unraveling the skein is not easy. To begin, we must identify the inhabitants of the reservation.

In the first place, the people of Pine Ridge are Oglala Sioux Indians. They have their own distinct culture, which differs from that of "white America" in basic ways. Their culture has continuity with the past, but it is not simply the heritage of the past; Sioux culture is *now*, the special outlook on the world that exists in the mind of every individual in the society. For many of the Oglala people, their culture is also bound up with Lakota, the native language of the Sioux — the first language, the language learned as a child, the language of thought and of the heart.

Second, the people of Pine Ridge have a history that is very real for them and that differentiates them from their white neighbors. This history begins with the Sioux as a proud and independent nation, the possessors of the Great Plains. With the buffalo and the horse the old-time Sioux were masters of the West. Then came the white man with his diseases, his weapons, his debilitating foods, his religion. Soon the buffalo were gone, and the Sioux found themselves stripped of lands, livelihood, and pride. Defeated by the whites, they were forced to confine themselves to small reservations. In return, the whites bound themselves by treaties to provide for the Indians forever, to give them food, medical care, and education. The treaty rights and the reservation lands are the special property of the Sioux.

Third, the people of Pine Ridge are poor. They have always been poor by white standards — ever since the reservation days began. Their poverty has become a cultural tradition, a part of the Indian way, accepted bitterly but without question.

In the fourth place, the people of Pine Ridge are under the direct domination of a particular arm of the United States government, the Bureau of Indian Affairs. To the Sioux, the BIA directly represents the president of the United States. It is the president who is responsible for the Indians' welfare, and the bureau is the white man's way of delegating that responsibility. The BIA has become an incredibly complicated organization over the years, more complicated than most Indians ever imagine. It has become so convoluted as to be ineffective, and it seems to lack overall direction and unity. Formerly the Sioux felt themselves to be entirely dependent on the bureau, particularly on its prime representative, the reservation superintendent. Today there is a growing tendency to bypass the Bureau when possible and to attempt to minimize its role on the reservation.

Finally, the people of Pine Ridge have their own government, the Oglala Sioux tribe. Unlike white Americans, Indians have a tribal loyalty and tribal identity. Tribal government, more immediate and more personal than the local government of most other Americans, is a political identity that is recognized by the United States government, and one that is uniquely available to Indians.

In these important ways, then, the people of Pine Ridge differentiate themselves from their white neighbors. They do not wish to become whites; they are proud of their status as Indians. But they are no longer willing to silently accept poverty, social degradation, and political domination. Their goal is to elevate Indian identity to a proud and positive image that is recognized by whites, to fit the Indian into white society as different but equal.

Few would argue against the proposition that the source of most of the ills of the Pine Ridge people is economic. Poverty is the keynote of reservation culture, its single overwhelmingly important characteristic. In order to understand the economy of Pine Ridge, it is necessary to have knowledge of the basic concepts of Sioux or Dakota culture and to be aware of the major events and trends in Sioux history; for the general principles that define Sioux attitudes toward economic concerns are deeply rooted in their culture and history.

CULTURAL BACKGROUND

The People of Pine Ridge: the Oglala Sioux

The Indians who were first settled on the Pine Ridge Agency belonged to the Oglala tribe, one of the seven tribes of the Teton (or Western) Sioux. All of the many Teton bands shared a common identity as Lakota "allies," but tribal identities were not so strong. Tribal identity was an intermediate category between national and band identity; it was more the recognition of a common origin and kinship than of membership in a meaningful group.

No chiefs had real authority at the tribal level, and bands and individuals passed constantly back and forth between tribal groups. At the tribal level there was not necessarily a sense of cooperation or any real commonality of purpose. Moreover, the Oglala were also split into two factions by a political murder in 1842, when Chief Bull Bear was killed by followers of a rival, Chief Smoke. After that date, the Bear people and the Smoke people became geographically separated, and the development of an Oglala tribal identity was blocked. In later years, dissension also resulted from the fact that, while some of the Oglalas chose to remain away from the agencies as long as possible in order to fight the whites, others, preferring the benefits of close contact with the agent and traders, had accepted the agency way of life from the beginning. These opposing groups had separate councils and leaders.

The Oglala who were appointed by the government to live at Pine Ridge Agency lacked a common organization, leadership, and sense of identity. For the first decade or so, many of the Bear people preferred to live with the Brules at Spotted Tail Agency. Later when the Great Sioux reservation was broken up into geographically separate reservations for each tribe, a group of Brule Tetons who were under the leadership of Chief Lip moved away from their assigned home on Rosebud reservation and insisted on being counted with the Oglalas of Pine Ridge. These diverse bands created problems, for the United States government insisted on dealing with the people of Pine Ridge as a single unit — the Oglala tribe. But the Sioux were very much divided. It was impossible for them to present a united front when dealing with the whites, at peace as in war.

After nearly one hundred years, the people of Pine Ridge are still faced with the problem of unity, with the task of developing a symbolic basis for unity as the foundation for effectively dealing with the white world.

Native Economy

The primary source of livelihood for the Sioux, ever since 1661 when the first report was given by whites, was buffalo hunting. Long before the introduction of horses, the Sioux were referred to by Europeans as the "nation of the beefe[buffalo]" (Radisson 1885: 20). The near-total utilization of the buffalo by the Sioux is well known; they used the flesh for food, the hides for clothing and shelter, and the bones for tools. The Sioux also hunted deer, elk, antelope, beaver, and a number of other animals. Antelope were sometimes hunted communally in drives, like buffalo (Denig 1961: 18). Chokecherries, wild plums, several kinds of berries, wild beans, and *tinpsila* (an edible root) were gathered and preserved to supplement the meat diet. But the plains west of the Missouri River were no paradise, and famines were frequent (Tabeau 1939: 73).

Supplementary food came to the Teton Sioux through trade with the sedentary horticultural tribes of the Missouri River, particularly the Arikara, who annually traded their corn and pumpkins for the Tetons' buffalo meat, hides, clothing, tipis, and bows. Frequently the trade was one-sided, with the Tetons demanding much food in exchange for their goods; frequently, too, they would simply steal part of the Arikara crops. The Sioux held horticultural tribes in disdain and referred to the corn-planting Arikara as "our women" (Tabeau 1939: 130). Every spring the Tetons also attended large trading gatherings with their eastern relatives, the Yanktons and the Santee, in the valley of the James River. Here they would trade their buffalo products for dried wild rice, corn, and items of European manufacture that first became available to the Santee and Yanktons along the Minnesota River in the mid-1600's.

The Teton Sioux owed their success in the high plains environment to horses, which they probably obtained in the early 1700's, although they were not plentiful until midcentury. A well-trained buffalo-hunting horse, swift and long winded, was a Sioux man's most valuable material possession. The approved way of obtaining horses was to steal them from enemy groups; although sometimes, early in the nineteenth century, various Sioux bands stole horses from one another (Tabeau 1939: 107). Horses were also obtained through trading and by the capture of wild stock. They very quickly became the medium of exchange and the primary unit of economic wealth.

White traders who pushed up the Missouri River in the early 1700's, eager to find gold and the wealth of beaver and other furs, found the Tetons equally eager for trade. European metal goods — especially knives, needles, pots, and guns, as well as mirrors, beads, trinkets, and some exotic foods — were all familar to the Sioux and were strongly coveted by them. Trade increased steadily with the Tetons, who tried to prevent white traders from ascending the Missouri and from dealing directly with the Arikara and other river tribes. By the early 1800's, there was considerable competition among the various trading companies. Whiskey was introduced as an inducement to trade and as a means of gaining a more favourable rate of trade. Feuds broke out among the Sioux, who were unable to deal with the effects of alcohol. Drunken fights became an integral part of trading with whites. The murder of the Oglala chief Bull Bear was blamed on the effects of whiskey.

By the time the Sioux first encountered the whites in large numbers, during the mid-nineteenth century, they had already completely integrated white manufactured goods into their economy. Knives and arrow points of flint had been largely — if not completely — replaced by iron, and large quantities of the white man's food had been added to the diet. The Sioux considered themselves to need, in an absolute sense, trade with whites. White traders had become a part of their environment, just as integral as their horticultural neighbors and their eastern relatives. In fact, with the increasing availability of white trade, exchange with the horticultural tribes and with the Yanktons and Santee was sharply diminished. The Tetons became more independent of other Indian groups, but at the same time became completly dependent on the whites for a vital link in their economy.

The economic system of the Teton was based on seasonal nomadism. In spring, in order to replenish their food supplies, the bands followed the buffalo herds. With the approach of summer — the season during which the buffalo gathered in large herds for mating — the Sioux bands also gathered together for an annual celebration of plenty. The Sun Dance was at once a prayer of thanksgiving and a plea for continued mercy from the powers, and one of the central symbols was that of the buffalo. Following the ceremony, communal hunts that provided much of the winter surplus were held.

Then the bands once again separated, heading for winter camps along the Missouri River or in the Black Hills. During the fall, the Tetons visited the white traders and exchanged their surplus buffalo robes, furs, meat, and grease for merchandise. Sometimes traders would spend the winter with a group, encouraging the trapping of fur. Winter camps were located in the shelter of trees, and the principal winter game animals were the deer, elk, and antelope of the river valleys. When the weather was very cold, the buffalo would also seek the protection of the valleys, where they became available to the Teton. The Tetons did not form large aggregations of people since forage and fuel were limited and hunting and warfare demanded speed of movement. The small group, the band, was most efficient in exploiting the economic potentials of the Sioux environment.

Social Order

The national identity of the Tetons as Lakota was very real and meaningful, but this identity was social rather than political. The Tetons had no national chiefs and no defined national council. There even seems to have been disagreement as to whether the two more easterly divisions of the Sioux — the Yankton and Santee — were really Lakota, although all three groups generally seem to have been conceded to constitute the legendary Seven Council Fires (*oceti sakowin*), the parent group of the Sioux.

Tribal organization for the Oglala, as for the other Teton tribes, was very weak. Groups larger than bands were formed only for the summer Sun Dance, for communal buffalo hunts, and during times of organized warfare. The tribe was composed of numerous bands, each of which was politically independent (Walker 1917: 73). Each band symbolized its autonomy by the establishment of a council fire, that is, a system of social control based on a council of adult men and elders that recognized the leadership of a chief. Each band was named, usually with a nickname. The primary group identity for any Teton individual was the name of his band. In 1879, seven such bands were commonly identified on the Pine Ridge Agency (Dorsey 1897: 220). One of these bands was sometimes referred to as *Oglala hca* (Real Oglala) and was considered to be the parent band of all the Oglala.

The essential unit of social order was the band, *tiyospaye*. The word, which means "a group of lodges," symbolizes a number of relatives who live together as a stable social group. The Oglala band was an extended family, which usually varied from ten to twenty lodges in size, each lodge housing a nuclear family consisting of parents and unmarried children. Typically, during the early and middle years of the nineteenth century, two or three of these *tiyospaye* would camp together, or very near one another, acknowledging the leadership of a single chief. Each *tiyospaye* had its own chief, but the chiefs of the two or three *tiyospaye* involved would defer to one of their number as the chief of the group. In such a situation it is likely that the chiefs were brothers or cousins. The group of two or three extended families would be considered by outsiders to be essentially a single band and would be referred to by the name of the *tiyospaye* of the leading chief. Largely because of divisive pressures brought about by wars with the United States and by the establishment of reservations, in 1884 the number of Oglala bands increased from the traditional seven to twenty-one (Dorsey 1897: 220–21). Individual chiefs pressed their own leadership, causing the bands of several *tiyospaye* to split up.

In the Lakota language, the term "*tiyospaye*" refers both to the individual extended families and to groups of two or three extended families. *Tiyospaye* is the cultural model or symbol of a social group which lives amicably according to the norms and values of the kinship system. (In a broad sense, the *tiyospaye* was a family.) The major sanctions for behavior in Teton culture were provided by the system of kinship or relationship. At broader levels of generality, the Sioux might refer to a tribe as a *tiyospaye*, as when they asserted that all the Lakota were a single tribe composed of seven *tiyospaye*. Sometimes this would refer to the seven tribes of the Tetons, but at other times the Teton tribes would be lumped together in order to also encompass the Yankton and Santee within the sacred number seven.

The meaning of kinship for the Sioux was very different than for white Americans, because kinship was used more extensively, including a greater variety of behavioral dictates. The structure of the kinship system was the "Iroquois" or "Dakota" type, the essential features of which are the classification of the father, the father's brothers, and the father's male cousins under the single term "father"; the mother, the mother's sisters and female cousins as "mother"; the father's sisters and female cousins and the mother's brothers and male cousins as "aunt" and "uncle." As indicated in Figures 1 and 2, every child was brought up with an abundance of people called father, mother, aunt, uncle, and, in parallel fashion, all the fathers, mothers, aunts, and uncles of these people were called grandfather and grandmother by the child. Thus the child who grew up in a band was surrounded with close relatives who gave bountiful attention and love to him. The individualizing effects of white American nuclear family life were foreign to the Sioux concept of kinship.

Membership within a band was not by birth but by choice; kinship was not so importantly a matter of descent as of behavior. If a person was called by kinship terms, he was morally obligated to respond in the appropriate ways, if he wished to interact. Thus, complete strangers could, and frequently did, move into the band and quickly become totally enmeshed in the system of kinship relations and obligations. Similarly, in-laws were not set apart but were amalgamated with the rest of a person's set of relatives. When it came time to marry, a man generally had to look outside his own band to find an eligible woman. After marriage there were no rules about where the new couple had to live, although they generally moved into the band of the husband or of the wife.

The important point is that in traditional Teton culture there was no distinction between the kinship system and the social system. They were both the same system, organized according to the same moral principles relating to the proper behavior between relatives. To focus on the kinship system is to see the social system from the point of view of a single individual; to focus on the social system is to see the kinship system from the point of view of the group.

All the structures of the Sioux system of social order were based on the kinship system and were modeled after the *tiyospaye*. The most important of these structures were the nation, *lakota*; the tribe, *oyate*; the band or extended family, *tiyospaye*; the family, as the constituent unit of the band; men's societies and women's societies; and the war party, which formed a temporary social group operating in terms of kinship norms.

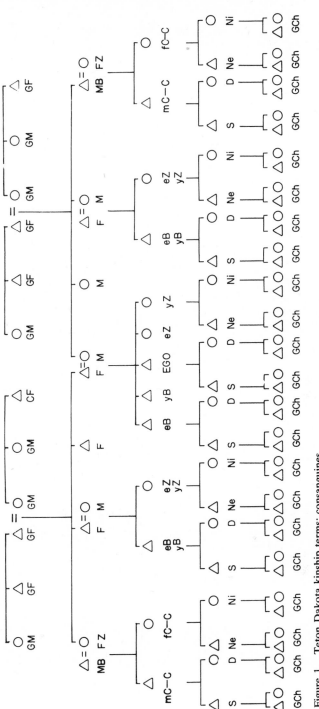

Figure 1. Teton Dakota kinship terms: consanguines

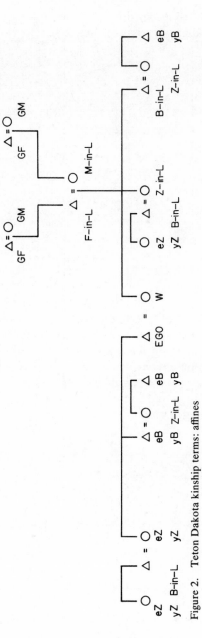

Figure 2. Teton Dakota kinship terms: affines

Political Order

The political order was not clearly differentiated from the social order. Political organization was necessary for the coordination of activities for the welfare of the group, but it was an outgrowth of the relationships in the *tiyospaye*. The central institution was the band council, an informal organization consisting of all the respected males of the band. The council appointed a chief — whose successor would likely be his son, although chieftainship was by no means hereditary. The chief had no real authority, only precedence in speaking at council meetings. His power lay in the number, prestige, and support of his relatives, and in the persuasiveness of his oratory. Official acts of the council were approved by acclamation, once a consensus or clear majority was recognized. Dissenters were free to leave and join some other band, or to form a new one.

The chief, as the leader of the council, embodied the wishes of the group. He was expected always to place the welfare of the group before his own welfare. The chief was called *itancan*. The word does not refer to a specific office but to the general role of leader.

The council — or the chief, with the approval of the council — appointed a number of officials called *akicita* [marshals]. It was their duty to do the bidding of the council and to enforce its proclamations. These men were most conspicious when keeping order at ceremonies, hunts, trading fairs, and during camp moves. The *akicita* were empowered to, and did, whip anyone who refused to comply with their orders. They might also destroy some of an offender's property — such as horses, dogs, or tipi — and in extreme cases they might kill him. In small camps the council might appoint all of the *akicita* directly, but it was more likely to appoint only one or two head *akicita* (*akicita itancan*) who would then chose their own assistants. Occasionally, all of the *akicita* might belong to the same men's society, but, among the Sioux, men's societies as units were not usually called upon to act as *akicita*. There was some tension between the younger *akicita* and the older men of the council, but this seems to have been settled over time by incorporating the leading *akicita* in the council.

The political order of a band, then, consisted of a council of older men presided over by a chief, and a number of marshals who carried out their wishes. The chief was considered to be a father to the band and was thereby brought into a close kin relationship with the entire band.

The Oglala also had a political organization at the tribal level. The most prestigious men of each band would meet together as a tribal council presided over by four appointed chiefs, the *wicasa yatapika* [men they praise]. The badge of office was a hair-fringed shirt, which was spoken of as being owned by the tribe. The *wicasa yatapika* were considered the supreme elder kinsmen of the tribe but had no actual authority. Organization on the tribal level seems to have functioned only on ceremonial occasions like the Sun Dance, large hunts, or large-scale organized warfare, such as war for revenge against another tribe or the several wars with the United States Army.

Political organization in the Red Cloud division of the Oglala (the Smoke people) was somewhat elaborated, especially during the late 1870's and 1880's. The entire council was organized to form a "chiefs' society" that appointed seven chiefs or *itancan*. However, they delegated their power to four younger men, the *wicasa yatapika*. Four *wakicun* were also appointed, who were responsible for the day-to-day organization and control of the camp; these men held office only for a year. (The office of chief was generally held for life.) In addition, there were the *akicita* or marshals (Wissler 1912: 36–41).

The chief, then, at whatever level, was the symbol of political order. As symbolic fathers, chiefs were enjoined to look after the welfare of the tribe as a whole, to look after the land, to ensure ample hunting territories, and, as a special duty, to look after the helpless, the poor, orphans, and widows (Neihardt 1930). A chief was expected to give his life for the people; this was the Teton conception of the leader, the maintainer of political order.

World View

To the Lakota, the basic characteristic of the universe was its unity, the ultimate "truth of the oneness of all things..." (Brown 1953: 95). Man is one with nature, and nature one with the supernatural. *Wakan tanka* symbolizes this oneness. *Wakan* indicates "anything that is hard to understand" (Walker 1917), anything mysterious, powerful, supernatural. *Tanka* means "great," or "big." *Wakan tanka* is thus the sum of what is mysterious, powerful, and sacred.

The circle was used as a symbol of *Wakan tanka*, because like *Wakan tanka* the circle has no end (Brown 1953: 92). The Lakota as a people were also symbolized by a circle, the "sacred hoop of the nation," depicted on the ground by the camp circle of tipis. As long as the circle was unbroken, the people would flourish (Neihardt 1932: 198). The unity of the circle is expressed in terms of "relationship," or kinship. This is a bond which has been established by *Wakan tanka* with the Lakota to create order in the world. The circle of relationships binds not only man with man, but man with the animals, plants, earth, and sky; "all are related and are one" (Brown 1953: 97).

Man was thus one small, integral part of the world and in no way superior to nature. Each individual man was considered to be the equal of all others, assuming compliance with the moral rules of the culture. Even children were to be treated with regard; they were not babied. "To even a small child, show him the regard of a man" (Bushotter n.d.). From early childhood children were encouraged to be independent.

There were two inequalities in Sioux society. The first was sexual. The distinction between male and female was sharply defined by the culture and was validated by strict standards for the division of labor. Men were primarily hunters and warriors (hunters were more essential, but warriors were more honored). Women took care of their lodges and the camp; gathered roots, berries, and fruits; and prepared the meat brought home by the men. The cultural distinction between sexes is set forth in this maxim: "That which is female is weak of heart, while that which is male must carry about a heart of stone" (Bushotter n.d.). Only the force of the council and the chief drew young men into the practical concerns of everyday life, by involving them in the *akicita*, by placing restrictions on war parties at the time of big hunts, and by charging them to remember the old and weak at home. In cultural terms, since fighting was the primary role of the man, the young men had to be restrained from throwing their lives away in attempts to perform impossible feats in battle with the enemy. Again, in cultural terms, the woman's primary role was to encourage and glorify her brothers, cousins, husband, and other male relatives in their manly pursuits. A woman would not marry a man until he had performed some brave deed against the enemy; she was taught from earliest childhood that she must honor and make life easy for her brothers, for their lives would be hard and dangerous.

The second inequality was that of supernatural power. Boys were instructed by shamans to fast and seek a vision. (Ordinarily this occurred after puberty, but some of the most powerful and important visions were experienced by very small boys.) The power of visions, in the supernatural support of various elements or creatures, was symbolized by the contents of the medicine bundle — animal skins, stones, dust, and other sacred items. Power was transferable, a man could sell or give it to other less fortunate men who did not experience visions.

Power was the means of accomplishing brave deeds and of acquiring prestige. Shamans (priests) and medicine men (healers) used their power for spiritual, philosophical, and curative purposes. Other men used it as a tool or weapon for solving the problems of life. Chiefs applied their power for the good of the people; the most prestigious chiefs were generally held to be shamans as well. As such they might be somewhat feared and revered, for power was held to be dangerous. A great vision indicating a course of action was a heavy burden for a chief who saw himself as the protector of his people. Women also experienced visions, but of lesser magnitude and importance, and were frequently granted curing powers.

In cultural theory, then, men were all equal and independent. Some had acquired power, but those who had acquired a great deal of power felt it as a burden to be used for the welfare of the people. Each person was a small part of the unity of society, as mankind was a part of the unity of the world. As a result of these beliefs individuals did not hoard material possessions. A chief was frequently among the poorest of people, because he was required to care for the needy. At communal hunts the chief would appoint young men to hunt for those who had no one else to hunt for them.

Other means for distributing material goods were also institutionalized. The giveaway has been considered the "very essence of Dakota communal life" (Deloria 1944: 73). Giveaways were for honoring someone on any ceremonial occasion. Thus, a man might honor a son who had killed his first small bird by giving away a horse, in the boy's name, to someone who needed it. To express his gratitude, the recipient would go the rounds of the entire camp, shouting out the name of the donor and the reason why the gift had been made.

There were also other forms of gift giving. A woman would honor her brother by giving gifts to his children. In all cases the gift giving was one-sided rather than reciprocal, but the exchange of material goods tended to even out eventually. After the death of a child, his father and mother might give away everything they owned, even their tipi. They would then be at the mercy of the society. The people of the camp would socially reintegrate the grieving parents by giving them a new tipi, new belongings, and everything necessary for a fresh start. Gift giving was the basis of the traditional Sioux economic system, which has been aptly called "giving to have" (Deloria 1944: 68).

Every aspect of Oglala life was regulated by and based on the moral system of kinship, which established reciprocal relationships between man and man, man and nature, and man and the supernatural. The controlling force of the universe, *Wakan tanka*, was entreated in the same way as other people were entreated: *wocekiye*. The word means to cry out, to pray, or to address somebody by a kinship term. To make oneself pitiful was at the center of the vision quest, the Sun Dance, and the giveaways following deaths. To make oneself pitiful and then to entreat the supernatural, nature, or man was intended to invoke common morality, to assert one's place in the universe and to demand that the universe recognize you by treating you according to the standards of rightness and goodness. This single moral system, embodied in the kinship system, was thus the overwhelming force of traditional Sioux culture, the basis of family relationship, the social order, the political order, the religious order. It was the strength and vitality of the traditional culture. Intellectually and emotionally it is the most important inheritance of the reservation Sioux. When all the outward signs of the old way of life were gone, the moral system of kinship remained as the primary source of identity for the Oglala as Indians.

HISTORICAL BACKGROUND

The Development of Pine Ridge Reservation (1896–1915)[1]

By the treaty of 1868, the various Dakota tribes made peace with the United States and agreed to a reservation in western Dakota Territory, which came to be known as the Great Sioux reservation. At the same time, the Teton were given hunting rights in the lands lying north and west of the reservation, in the Powder River country. The Dakota agreed not to molest wagon trains along the Platte River and to allow the building of a railroad along this route. In return, the United States government agreed to withdraw its troops from posts in the northwestern part of the reservation and to prevent white citizens from intruding on Sioux lands. Quantities of annuity goods were to be issued to each tribe for thirty years. Indian agents were to be stationed on the reservation, along with blacksmiths, teachers, and ministers. The Sioux were to be encouraged to settle around these agencies and to take up agricultural pursuits. The government intended to place these agencies along the Missouri River so that they could be easily supplied by steamboat.

The first agency for the Oglala people, the followers of Red Cloud, was established near Fort Laramie in 1869. In 1870 and 1872, Red Cloud and other Oglala chiefs journeyed to Washington, D.C., to talk to the president and to attempt to secure an agency in the western part of the reservation instead of the Missouri River country, which was hot, dry, and lacking in buffalo and other game.

With the discovery of gold in the Black Hills during the early 1870's, the fate of the Oglalas was sealed. The government recognized the impossibility of honoring its promise to keep whites out of the Sioux country, and a commission was sent in the fall of 1875 to secure the sale of the hills. It failed to convince the Sioux to sell at a price that the commission considered reasonable. To "protect" the United States

[1] Major sources for this section are Hyde (1937), Macgregor (1946), and the reports of the Indian agents at Red Cloud and Pine Ridge agencies printed in the *Annual reports of the Commissioner of Indian Affairs.*

citizens who were illegally trespassing on Sioux hunting lands, the Department of War ordered all Sioux to leave their hunting territories and return to the reservation by January 31, 1876, or be considered hostile. This led to the famous battles at the Rosebud and the Little Big Horn during the following June.

Congress sent another commission to the Sioux in the fall of 1876. The Indians were still opposed to the sale, but the commission nonetheless managed to return to Washington, D.C., with documents ceding the Hills, signed only by the Sioux chiefs. This violated the provision in the 1868 treaty which stipulated that any future land agreement would require the signatures of three-fourths of the adult male population of the Sioux. In return the Sioux were to receive annuity goods and farming utensils until such time as they would no longer need government support. Today the Oglala claim that they were betrayed at this council by their chiefs, whom they blame for the loss of the Black Hills.

In 1872, Red Cloud's agency had been moved northeast to a site on White River near the present Chadron, Nebraska. Camp Robinson (later Fort Robinson) was established two years later; here the surrender of Crazy Horse and his hostile Oglalas in the spring of 1877 marked the return of most of the Oglalas to Red Cloud's agency. Undefeated, but harrassed to exhaustion by army troops under command of General George Crook, the majority of the Oglalas had come together at the agency to await further developments. Immediately, there was friction between the returned hostiles and those Oglalas who had refused to fight. The army attempted to solve this problem by enlisting a considerable number of the returned hostiles, including Crazy Horse, as Indian scouts. But jealousies between agency chiefs and hostile chiefs were intense.

On September 5, 1877, Crazy Horse was murdered by the United States Army at Fort Robinson during an attempt to place him under arrest on suspicion of plotting to kill General Crook. Apparently older Oglala leaders who were afraid of Crazy Horse's intentions and influence helped to plan and carry out the arrest. Shortly afterward, the Red Cloud and Spotted Tail agencies were moved east to the Missouri River. Delegations of Sioux leaders again traveled to Washington, D.C., and won reluctant approval from the government to choose new locations for their agencies. Red Cloud wished to return to the White River Agency, but surveys indicated that the old agency site was outside the reservation and was actually in the state of Nebraska. The agency was therefore moved upriver some forty miles, near the mouth of White Clay Creek. The Oglalas were moved back west to the new agency in 1878; it was named "Pine Ridge" after a local landform, to minimize the prestige of the aging Red Cloud.

Red Cloud is said to have wanted to locate his new agency at this site because it was near the reservation boundary, allowing quick escape, and because the land was so dry and alkaline that it would have been absurd to insist that the Oglala attempt to plant crops. The remnants of the Northern Cheyenne, who fled from their reservation in Oklahoma, were temporarily located at Pine Ridge together with the Oglalas.

In 1879 a strong-willed and self-reliant man, Dr. Valentine T. McGillycuddy, was appointed agent at Pine Ridge. McGillycuddy's task was to "civilize" the Dakota and Cheyenne still living in scattered tipi villages in the vicinity of the agency. He attempted to break up the tribal system, which he felt was not compatible with civilization, by trying to discredit the chiefs and to destroy their power by fomenting jealousies among them and weakening their traditional prerogatives. It had long been the custom for chiefs to supervise the distribution of annuity goods and rations to their people through their *akicita*. Using the formula "every man his own chief," McGillycuddy attempted to force each man to act on his own initiative in the distribution of rations. When he arrived in 1879 there were eleven bands with as many chiefs; a year later the number had increased to thirty.

McGillycuddy organized a police force to carry out his own justice on the agency. He encouraged the adoption of white styles of dress and cooking, and log houses instead of tipis; he encouraged individual families to disperse along creeks, where arable land allowed the raising of crops; he encouraged stock raising; and he employed Indians in the hauling of freight. By 1881 he confidently reported that the influence of chiefs was rapidly dying out. In the following year he reported that the 1,500 cattle issued in 1880 had more than doubled by natural increase and that his system of distributing rations to individual heads of families was rapidly breaking up tribal groups.

In 1881 a "whiskey ranch" was established near the reservation boundary, just across the Nebraska line. This ranch, a source of annoyance for many years, developed eventually into the town of White Clay — still the major source of intoxicants for the people of Pine Ridge town.

McGillycuddy observed in 1883 that the Indian regard of stock raising was simple: horses are good to ride, cattle are good to eat. The economics of stock raising, he felt, would have to be slowly learned by the Sioux. He also felt that the most efficient method of teaching the Indians self-sufficiency would be to do away with the ration system, which merely encouraged dependency on the government. By this time the buffalo was virtually extinct on the northern plains; extensive hunting had made food scarce, and government rations as well as cattle were essential for survival.

Nonetheless, McGillycuddy reported that many young men were engaged in freighting and that, by utilizing their services during the year 1882–1883, he had saved the government some $50,000. Progress had been made in establishing traders on the reservation, as well; in 1883 there were ten traders — six whites, one half-breed, and three Indians. McGillycuddy's criticisms were not for the Sioux, over whom he had charge, but for the Bureau of Indian Affairs, which he felt reflected a "superfluity of bunkum" and was much in need of reform.

In his 1884 report, McGillycuddy noted that for the first time no Sun Dance had been held, and he attributed this to the good influences of the young progressives over the older traditionalists. In this year McGillycuddy decided to divide the reservation into districts, each under the supervision of a "boss farmer." The administrative system, apparently set up in the following year, used watersheds as boundaries; thus; each district had geographical unity. The system was planned to allow distribution of rations and other goods from decentralized areas, encouraging the Indians to scatter out more widely in the creek bottoms. Six day-schools were also established; the teachers were white, because no Indians were found qualified to teach. A boarding school was scheduled for opening in December.

In accordance with Indian Service directives, McGillycuddy attempted to set up a court of Indian offenses. He appointed three of the officers of the police force to act as judges, without payment, but they refused to serve. To function in such a capacity would surely have posed an onerous and thankless task. McGillycuddy also reported in 1884 that progressive Indians had, on their own initiative, organized a permanent board of councilmen. Delegates were chosen from each of the different villages, and Young-Man-Afraid-of-His-Horses was elected to serve as president.

McGillycuddy's last report, in 1885, is overall a discouraging document, suggesting that the Oglalas had little basis from which to become self-supporting. He noted that upon his arrival in 1879 not a single Indian family lived in a permanent house, while by 1885 two-thirds of the families, some 848, were living in log houses; he failed to add that the Oglalas no longer had access to large quantities of hides and were no longer being given canvas. Without material for tipis there was little choice but to build log houses.

For Red Cloud's immediate followers, McGillycuddy had no good words. He considered them obstacles to progress. They had killed and eaten their cattle instead of treating them as an economic resource to be developed. They continued to live in a village rather than to scatter out, and they spent their time feasting, dancing, and "mourning over the degeneracy of the young men" who were turning from traditional ways to working for a wage. The preferred work was not stock raising but freighting. Unfortunately, there was little future in freighting for McGillycuddy estimated that the work would be cut in half once the railroad was completed. He suggested that interest in stock raising was increasing, because the Sioux had sold 300 cattle during the year. The impression given by these reports is that the Sioux would prefer to work at tasks for which the payment was immediate, rather than wait for a slow return on their investment of labor.

Most of the Sioux, as McGillycuddy understood them, wanted only to sit around and wait for the return of the buffalo, the renewal of the power and authority of the chiefs, and the arrival of a new agent. They think themselves superior, he said, because they do not have to work, but must be fed by the white men.

There is undoubtedly some truth to this interpretation. Certainly the Sioux did feel that having taken their lands and the buffalo from them the white man owed the Indians all the necessities of life for "seven generations" — as specified at the Black Hills Council in 1876. Cultur- ally, for the Teton, this meant forever. The attitude was well expressed by Red Cloud in these words:

Father, the Great Spirit did not make us to work. He made us to hunt and fish. He gave us the great prairies and hills and covered them with buffalo, deer and antelope. He filled the rivers and streams with fish. The White man can work if he wants to, but the Great Spirit did not make us for work. The White man owes us a living for the lands he has taken from us (McGillycuddy1941: 103).

This attitude is firmly entrenched in Dakota culture. It is still expressed sometimes on the reservation particularly by old-timers who keep waiting for the government to pay the Sioux for the full worth of the Black Hills, at which time all the Indians will become rich.

In 1887 the new agent, H. D. Gallagher, reported that Red Cloud's band had finally been persuaded to leave the vicinity of the agency and locate some distance away, where they might attempt farming. He also noted, however, that drought had entirely ruined all crops during the year. This agent, like McGillycuddy, also felt himself to be the only source of justice for the agency; the court had not yet been established, and one of Gallagher's first official acts was to "dissolve" the council that had been established by the "progressives" several years before. Perhaps Gallagher was frightened by the size of the council — more than 100 men — or perhaps he simply felt that any organization among the Oglala was a threat to his authority. In any case, his refusal to recognize the Oglala political structure was one of a long series of overt actions designed to convince them that they could neither think nor act for themselves.

In 1889 Gallagher was still reporting the pernicious influences of the chiefs. In this year the commission to the Sioux visited the agency, attempting to gain the signatures of three-fourths of the adult males for sale of Sioux territories. Although the meeting was clearly in the best interest of the government, the agent complained that meeting with the commission had caused the Indians to neglect their crops.

The intent of this commission was to break up the Great Sioux Reservation and establish a number of smaller geographically separate reservations for each of the tribes. The remaining lands were to be opened for homesteading. Moreover, the commission required, under the Dawes Act, the allotment of lands in severalty to all adult Indians on the new reservations. It was felt that individual allotments would effectively break up the last vestiges of tribal organization and would also encourage individual agricultural activity on the part of each family, which would naturally be anxious to improve its permanent and privately owned lands and homes. By thus eliminating all nomadism and engaging the "barbarians" in the healthy pursuit of taming the earth, it was believed that the Indians could be raised, or rather could raise themselves to "civilization."

Soon after the Sioux commission left, the new religious movement, the Ghost Dance, claimed eager converts on the reservation. Many Indians abandoned their homes and farms in the firm belief that a new earth was coming. Cattle were killed and eaten to stave off hunger until the expected millennium arrived. The tragic massacre at Wounded Knee in December 1890 destroyed faith in the efficacy of the Ghost Dance, as well as the hope of a supernatural return to the good days of the past.

The agent in charge of Pine Ridge in 1891, Charles G. Penney, believed that, if the allotment system were put into effect on the reservation, it would lead to the extinction of the Sioux. Instead he felt that all lands should remain tribally owned in order to be most efficiently used for their only economical use, namely, stock raising.

As the years passed, Pine Ridge escaped the impending allotments of land, at least temporarily. Progress in stock raising was reported nearly every year. In 1901 agent John R. Brennan reported that beef was now being issued to the Sioux in a "civilized" manner. Previously, the animals had been turned loose to be run down and shot by the Indians; now, the cattle were butchered and meat was issued twice each month. Hides, instead of being given to the Indians, were sold, and the money was distributed to the Indians at the end of the year, averaging about $2 per person. Modernization was catching up with Pine Ridge. Telephone lines now connected each of the subagencies or district headquarters to each other and to the Pine Ridge headquarters, and Indians were no longer allowed to carry six-shooters.

A new program for employing Indians and paying them cash, in lieu of rations, began in 1902. Four hundred young men were put to work during the summer, building roads and tending stock. The 19,000 cattle of 1901 had increased to 31,000 in 1902, while horses had decreased from 17,000 to 12,000.

Brennan reported in 1903 that the Pine Ridge council, probably a continuation of the one once headed by Young-Man-Afraid-of-His-Horses, was controlled by the old chiefs, who remained hostile to innovations and to the involvement of Indians in physical labor. The year 1904 marked the establishment of an agency sawmill, and in 1905 the first allotments were made on the reservation. By 1911 the allotments had been nearly completed, and the unallotted portion in the east, organized as Bennett County, was opened for homesteading.

In general, the years since the Wounded Knee fiasco seemed to have been progressive in terms of physical well-being for the Oglala. Stock raising was definitely increasing, and more Indians seemed to be taking an active interest in it. At the same time, younger men were being hired by the agency whenever possible to work for cash, with the aim of reducing the attitude of total dependence on the government. By this time, hopes were high that the Sioux were well on their way towards successful cattle raising, with each family also growing vegetables and other crops on their allotments. After 1906 the agents' reports were no longer printed in the annual reports of the Commissioner of Indian Affairs, and printed sources of detailed information end. Nonetheless, it seems as though the first decade of the century was a progressive one, filled with promise for the Oglala.

The Period of Economic Crisis (1915–1934)

The period of crisis began in 1915. With war in Europe, cattle prices soared in the United States. Tempted by the high prices, the Oglalas had sold virtually all their cattle by 1916. Meanwhile, by 1917 the white owners of large cattle companies had leased nearly all of Pine Ridge reservation as cheap grazing land. The Oglalas entered a period of cash economy, and many of the luxuries of white civilization, particularly the automobile, became available for the first time. Oglalas lived off monies from selling cattle, lease payments, and the gradual sale of their extensive herds of horses (Macgregor 1946: 39).

During the winter of 1917–1918, the new superintendent of Pine Ridge quarreled with the traditional chiefs' council and ordered it officially dissolved (Grinnell 1967: 26). It was apparently at this time that the sons and grandsons of former chiefs organized themselves as the Treaty Council, also known as the Black Hills Treaty and Claims Council, or simply the Chiefs' Council. It is unclear whether the superintendent ordered such a group to form, or whether it was an entirely spontaneous action on the part of the Pine Ridge Sioux. In any case, the group held meetings, kept minutes, and was used by the superintendent as a forum for explaining BIA programs and policies (Feraca 1964: 24–25). But the explicit purpose of the council was to pursue treaty claims against the government. Specifically, the group attempted to obtain a large cash settlement for the loss of the Black Hills, as well as other lands. Thus, the intention of the group was to contribute to the growing cash economy of the reservation.

In 1921 came the postwar depression. The cattle market went under, and many cattlemen were driven out of business and had to default on their leases. At the same time, the Indians became eligible to sell their allotted lands, the period of government trust having ended. But only those Oglalas of half Indian blood or less were declared competent, so only these people could take advantage of land sales as a means of continuing their cash economy. By late 1922 the agricultural market had recovered, and there was much buying of Indian lands by both speculators and crop farmers. The government cooperated fully in the sale of Indian lands and advertised their availability, but the BIA took no steps to insure that fair prices were paid or that fair methods were used in securing the lands.

The white farmers who moved in to make their living on the reservation by growing flax, wheat, and other grains were the first successful dry farmers in the region. Citing their success as an example, the BIA began to encourage dry farming among the Oglalas and made loans for seed and equipment, entirely oblivious of the limited equipment available to the Indians as compared to the mechanized equipment of the whites. Government and farmers alike were also oblivious of the drought that began in 1924 (Macgregor 1946: 39–40).

A feeling of optimism and progress seems to have permeated the Pine Ridge reservation — at least among the administrators. In 1926 the superintendent attempted to reestablish an Oglala Tribal Council by scheduling an election; evidently he got no support whatsoever from the Indians, and the election fell through (Grinnell 1967: 26). Some of the younger, somewhat better educated and more acculturated Oglala were discontented with the Treaty Council, which they felt to be only a tool of the superintendent. They organized the Council of Twenty-One, composed of representatives from each of the seven reservation districts. This group wrote a constitution that was approved by the Secretary of the Interior in 1928. Subsequently an eighth district, LaCreek, was added and representation was increased to five per district. The new organization was immediately at odds with the Treaty Council, which termed itself The Council of one Hundred to symbolize its opposition and superiority (Feraca 1964: 31–32).

To assist the Indians in farming, the BIA established farm chapters at each of the day schools on the reservation. However, the Oglalas evinced little interest in farming, and, despite Indian officers, only the efforts of government officials kept the farm chapters alive (Mekeel 1936: 13). In the early 1920's, a five-year program was begun to develop the isolated community on Red Shirt Table. This was done in conjunction with the local farm chapter, and an attempt was made to see that each family would have milk cows, gardens, some farm production, and some livestock. However, the program was only successful for the first few years, and gradually the lands were leased to white livestock owners. Apparently these five-year programs were developed for other communities as well (Roberts 1943: 38).

With the financial crash of 1929, the short-lived prosperity of the entire region was ruined. The white grain farmers were entirely wiped out, and most of them moved away. The drought, with its hordes of grasshoppers and severe dust storms, ruined the Indian gardens and farms and killed the livestock. The Oglala economy was destroyed, and the Indians sold everything they could, even the dishes in their houses (Roberts 1943: 39).

The economic picture in 1930 was very grim. Some money came from land leased to white cattlemen needing additional grazing land because of the drought. Young people turning eighteen received their "Sioux benefit," as stipulated by treaty right. At this time the payment amounted to about $500 per person, but it could only be spent on equipment for making a start in life — wagons, furniture, livestock, clothing, etc., and could not be used for food. A few of the old-timers who had been Indian scouts for the army received modest pensions of $30–$50 per month. Some money came from cutting hay and selling it to the government or to traders and from hauling freight for the government. A few people received salaries — catechists, government farmers and their assistants, policemen — and a few received wages working for ranchers or traders. The most profitable enterprise was digging potatoes in Nebraska. Families traveled there to work together, earning wages and perhaps making some money hauling. When they left, they were allowed to fill up their wagons with potatoes for winter use. Nonetheless, Mekeel found that the average income per family (5.4 persons) in White Clay district in 1930 was $152.80. This income — supplemented with small government rations, chokecherries and other wild foods, and horsemeat — kept starvation just around the corner. There was no food surplus at all; traditional patterns of sharing leveled everyone to the same state of poverty (Mekeel 1936: 9–10).

In 1932 the Red Cross and the federal government supplied food and other necessities to the people of Pine Ridge, and in 1933, with the founding of the Civilian Conservation Corps, nearly all the able-bodied men were put on the government payroll (Macgregor 1946: 40). Programs of road building and the construction of dams, churches, schools, and public buildings gave Pine Ridge an aura of activity and development. Once again it seemed that progress was surely on the way.

The New Order (1935–Present)

The essential purpose of the Indian Reorganization Act (IRA) was to preserve traditional forms of Indian government by formalizing them with written constitutions and systems of elected officials. At Pine Ridge, however, self-government had long been dead. As on the other Sioux reservations, the Oglalas had placed their destiny directly in the hands of the "grandfather" — the president of the United States — and in his local representative, the "father" — the agent (later called reservation superintendent). The incorporation of the BIA official in charge of the reservation into the kinship system is very significant; it implied a relationship of trust and dependence between the people and their "father." In this way, a direct and personal relationship was established, which could be effectively manipulated by individuals. The traditional Sioux, the full bloods, were not interested in any intermediate body between themselves and the government; they would not trust any elected body. Only the treaty council, composed of respected leaders, had the people's trust to deal with the government and to fight for Indian rights.

After Benjamin Reifel, a prominent Sioux mixed blood (later a United States Congressman), and H. Scudder Mekeel, an anthropologist, traveled around the Pine Ridge reservation to explain to the people the provisions and intentions of the IRA, distrust and dissension followed. Superintendent Mcgregor reported in 1936 that the members of the Treaty Council had been informing the people that the acceptance of IRA meant that they would lose their lands and have to move elsewhere, that they would lose their treaty rights, that there would be no more rations, that they would not be allowed to belong to any church, and that the mixed bloods would control the reservation (see Feraca 1964: 34–35). In 1934 a vote was held to decide whether or not to accept the IRA: 1,169 voted in favor and 1,095 against (Feraca 1964: 37). Thus, the new way was accepted, but by a small margin. It is claimed that many full bloods did not vote, thinking that would be sufficient to negate the proposal. It seems certain that the majority of the Pine Ridge people did not want to change from the old way.

Mekeel drafted a constitution for Pine Ridge based on the IRA model provided by Felix Cohen. It was voted on in 1936 and accepted 1,348 to 1,041 (Feraca 1964: 37). The younger, more acculturated mixed bloods, represented by the Council of Twenty-One, were solidly behind the IRA. With the acceptance of the constitution, they had won out over the Treaty Council. The first president to be elected was a very acculturated mixed blood with no roots in any traditional community.

The constitution provided for eight voting districts, simply the old farm districts, with one councilman for each 300 persons, plus one if the remainder totalled over 150. It is difficult to understand how this provision entered the constitution, for Mekeel had been in favor of setting up voting districts according to the natural communities of the reservation, the remnants of the old *tiyospaye*. As a result, the voting districts had no unity or sense of common cause, and the dissension at this grass-roots level has plagued the Oglala ever since.

In addition to the councilmen, the constitution provides for the election of a president and vice-president. All enrolled tribal members over 21 are eligible to vote.

It is not necessary to summarize the constitution here, other than to state that it gives the council of the newly formed Oglala Sioux tribe the power to regulate lands and other property, to create tribal enterprises to charter subordinate organizations to carry on economic activities, and to set up a system of laws (including those regulating morality), police, and courts. It further provides for the establishment of district organizations, reproducing the tribal council at the level of each district.

It was the intention of the IRA that each organized tribe incorporate so that economic functions would be separated from governmental activities. However, the Treaty Council was able to sufficiently confuse the issue of incorporation with the tribal treaty claims and to denigrate the elected tribal officers, with the result that the charter of incorporation was defeated twice, in 1937 and 1938. The voting on this issue was heavier than on the acceptance of IRA and the acceptance of the constitution, suggesting that the Sioux were coming to grips with the mechanisms of elections. The Oglala Sioux tribe never did incorporate under the IRA, but in time all the economic privileges of the act were granted to them anyway.

Those who accepted the IRA and the new tribal organization were called the "New Dealers," and those who rejected it and supported the Treaty Council the "Old Dealers." The hostility between the two groups was intense, and each made fantastic accusations against the other. The Old Dealers denied the legality of the tribal council and refused to recognize it; when a delegation was sent to Washington each side had to be represented, or else each would send a separate delegation (Feraca 1964: 25–26).

About 1938 the government began to revive the cattle industry on

Pine Ridge, realizing, perhaps for the last time, that it was the only viable form of agriculture for the reservation. In 1942 the Civilian Conservation Corps ended, destroying virtually the only source of cash income for the reservation. Many of the Oglala joined the armed forces; 975 men and 35 women, or about 10 percent of the total Pine Ridge population, served in the armed forces during World War II (Thompson 1951: 78). A great many other Oglala moved off the reservation temporarily to work in war industries; many worked in the Army Ordinance Depot at Igloo, South Dakota, and some remained there until the closing of the depot in 1967. Those families remaining on the reservation during the war continued to receive rations, as well as cattle.

Stock raising increased slowly. In 1943 the Oglala owned 22,300 head of cattle. Horse herds were also built up; in 1942 there were 9,000 horses on the reservation. Economically, horses were needed for cattle herding (Macgregor 1946: 45).

Since the early 1930's, the economy of the reservation had definitely improved. In 1942 the mean family income was $457.90. Of this, 60 percent was earned, and 40 percent unearned income (Table 1).

Table 1.   Estimated breakdown of total family income (Macgregor 1946: 49–50)

	Percentage
Wages	43
Welfare (cash or commodities)	25
Agricultural (livestock)	16
Lease and tribal payments	14
Miscellaneous	2
Sources of income were estimated as follows:	
Government	52
Reservation resources	29
Wage work (nongovernmental)	19

Thus, the Oglala were earning a relatively small part of their income from the natural resources of the reservation. They raised livestock, cut some wild hay, and cultivated vegetable gardens. Little grain was grown; only 12 percent of Indian land at that time was judged suitable for the raising of grain. (This, of course, reflects the loss of good agricultural lands in Bennett County.) A little wage work was available on the reservation, and some money was derived from lease payments and craft work. Rations were still given to the needy; beginning in 1944 these were no longer provided in kind but in purchase orders to local merchants. In return, able-bodied heads of households were required to perform some work for the reservation. There was an increase on the availability of farm wage work off the reservation, particularly in the sugar-beet industry, which sent labor representatives from several adjacent states to hire entire families of Indians (who would be bused to and from their work) to help during the summer and fall.

However, the greater part of the income of the Oglala at this time was dependent, first, on the relief measures provided by the New Deal and, later, by work resulting from the war. When the many veterans and workers in army depots and other military industries returned to Pine Ridge after the war, they found virtually no work and were once again forced to depend on the resources of the land and the government.

PINE RIDGE RESERVATION TODAY

The Pine Ridge reservation includes a rectangular area in southwestern South Dakota, approximately 100 miles in length and 50 miles in width. The southern boundary of the reservation borders on the Nebraska line, while the western boundary is less than 50 miles from the Wyoming border. On the east, Pine Ridge adjoins Rosebud reservation, and on the north it abuts with Badlands National Monument. The area is fairly well watered by the tributaries of the Cheyenne, White, and Little White Rivers. Most of the land is rolling, grass-covered plains; these are dissected by water courses, along which cottonwood and other decidious trees are plentiful, and are broken by high, pine-covered ridges and buttes, many with eroded rock outcroppings. The northwestern portion of the reservation is high tableland and fantastic badlands formations. Altitude varies from 2,100 to 3,500 feet above sea level, being generally higher in the west and lower in the east. The western part of the reservation is basically cattle-grazing country, while the east is more suited to agricultural purposes (Maynard and Twiss 1969: 7–11).

Pine Ridge reservation is located in an area that, in terms of economy, is distinctly marginal. Cattle ranching and wheat growing are the major industries in the surrounding country. But Pine Ridge — because much of land is very poor and because it is located far from the railroad — presents a bleaker picture than the neighboring area of Nebraska. Much of Macgregor's classic description of the bleakness of Pine Ridge in the early 1940's is still appallingly accurate today (Macgregor 1946).

In order to develop a picture of Pine Ridge today, it is necessary to synthesize data collected during a ten-year period, from about 1962 to 1972. This unfortunately leads to some chronological confusion, as well as to some inaccurate comparisons, but it is the only way in which a comprehensive picture can be presented here.

Description and Statistics

POLITICAL DIVISIONS. For purposes of administration, Pine Ridge is divided into nine districts, representing the old farming districts plus the town of Pine Ridge, which has been recognized as a new political division because of its large population and divergent political interests. Map 1 shows the political boundaries as of 1969, and it is to these divisions that the statistics in the following pages refer. Map 2 indicates new, reappointed district boundaries that were apparently drawn up at the time of the admission of Pine Ridge as a separate district; this map was supplied by the Realty Division of the BIA at Pine Ridge, but nearly all politicians and administrators to whom I talked denied knowledge of these reapportionments. The maps do not account for the return of lands from the Aerial Gunnery Range to the tribe, a transfer now underway. It is likely that the old district boundaries will be followed northward to the reservation boundary, as they were before the range was confiscated by the government in 1942.

LAND AND RESOURCES. Within the reservation boundaries there are approximately 2,786,538 acres. The status of the land in 1968 was reported as shown in Table 2 (Maynard and Twiss 1969: 72).

Table 2.   Status of the land of Pine Ridge Indian Reservation.

Type of land	Acreage	Percent
Allotted land	1,089,076	39.1
Tribal land	371,845	13.3
United States Government	54,975	2.0
Other (deeded, state, county)	1,270,644	45.6
Total	2,786,540	100.0

Thus, at least 52.4 percent of the land is still owned by Indians. Indians also own at least 45,000 acres of fee land, in addition to an unknown amount of land purchased after being transferred to nontrust status. Maynard and Twiss (1969: 72) estimated that 55 to 56 percent of the reservation lands were owned by Indians. Of course, the amount of land actually owned by Indians is constantly changing. According to one report by Housing and Urban Development (HUD 1969 4: 25), an average of 30,000 acres per year are sold to non-Indians. Perhaps this land loss is decreasing, as the tribal council attempts to increase and consolidate its land holdings. In 1967 the tribal council was said to own 13 percent of the reservation (HUD 1969 4: 26). However, tribal funds are not adequate to purchase all reservation lands that come up for sale.

Much of the land area that has passed out of Indian ownership is in Bennett County, the ceded county in the southeastern section of the reservation that was opened to homesteading in 1911. Other non-Indian land is in the Aerial Gunnery Range, but much of this was returned to the tribe in 1968. The most recent figure concerning Indian-owned land obtained from the BIA at Pine Ridge (for calendar year 1971) was 1,749,420 acres (BIA 1971). Table 3 shows land use as classified by the BIA.

Table 3.   Land use on Pine Ridge as classified by BIA Report 50–1 for 1971

Types of land use	Acres
Open grazing	1,416,374
Timber	230,729
Dry farm	63,568
Irrigated farm	1,100
Wild lands (excluding timber)	32,683
Other nonagricultural uses	4,966
Total	1,749,420

Dry farming consists mostly of the raising of small grains for feed. Most of the irrigated farming, near the dam at Oglala, is a tribally owned enterprise.

In gross terms, 92 percent of Indian-owned land is native range, and 8 percent is used for the production of small grains. Indians operate approximately 48 percent of Indian-owned land, while 51 percent is leased to non-Indians (BIA 1972: 26).

Grazing land, then, is the primary natural resource of the reservation. In the southwestern portion of the reservation there are clay deposits suitable for ceramics that have been used by one potter in Pine Ridge town who has worked at her trade for more than twenty years. Despite a pilot study and much encouragement, however, there has never been any large-scale commercial ceramics industry on the reservation.

POPULATION.   Population statistics, like those for land, are easy to acquire but less easy to assess. The United States figures are not reliable, being consistently too low. This is because of the difficulty of reaching many of the remote areas of the reservation, as well as because of Oglala distrust of the census takers. During the last census,

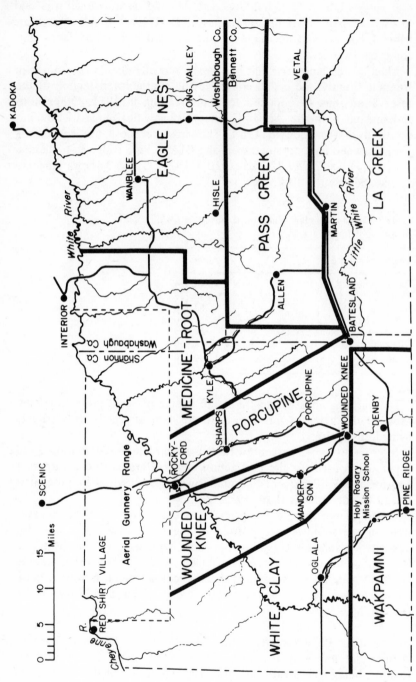

Map 1.   Pine Ridge political boundaries as of 1969

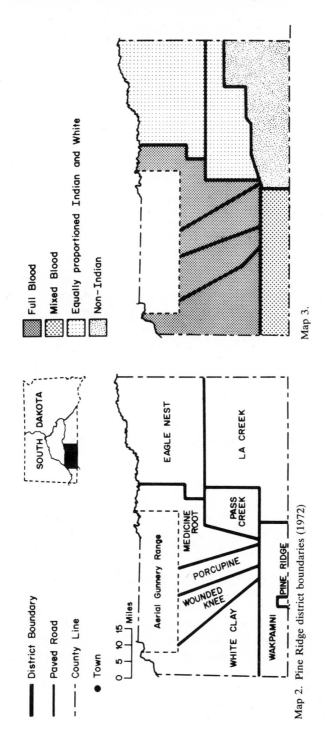

Map 3.

Full Blood

Mixed Blood

Equally proportioned Indian and White

Non-Indian

District Boundary

Paved Road

County Line

Town

SOUTH DAKOTA

Aerial Gunnery Range

EAGLE NEST

MEDICINE ROOT

PASS CREEK

LA CREEK

PORCUPINE

WOUNDED KNEE

WHITE CLAY

WAKPAMNI

PINE RIDGE

0 5 10 15

Miles

Map 2. Pine Ridge district boundaries (1972)

local people were hired to fill in the forms, but because of lack of supervision the 1970 census was again considered inadequate. Nonetheless, the census figures for recent years do not show a trend toward increasing population, and a disproportionate increase in the town population (Table 4).

Table 4. Population of Pine Ridge town (BIA 1972: 1)

Year	Pine Ridge town	Reservation
1940	750	11,329
1950	950	10,616
1960	1,256	10,095
1970	2,768	12,675

In 1967, however, members of the Mental Health Program at the Pine Ridge Hospital conducted a very thorough census, presenting questionnairs to about 96 percent of the population. Much of the information used in this report was supplied by this Baseline Data Survey, published in Maynard and Twiss (1969) and in the *Pine Ridge Research Bulletin* (1968–1970) and by the original data stored at the Community Mental Health Center at Pine Ridge. According to these 1967 data, the population of Pine Ridge reservation was approximately 13,500, as follows (Maynard and Twiss 1969: 17, 19): (1) Indians—10,000 with full bloods (2% non-Oglala) numbering 4,800 and mixed bloods (3% non-Oglala) accounting for 5,200; and (2) non-Indians—3,500.

The Baseline Data Survey placed the population of Pine Ridge town at 2,764 (Community Mental Health Center 1969).

Building on these figures, the population estimate for Pine Ridge reservation for 1972 is 14,800, and the estimate for Pine Ridge town is 3,500 (BIA 1972: 1).

DEMOGRAPHY.   According to the Baseline Data Survey, Indian residence on Pine Ridge reservation is as follows: villages, 50 percent; rural clusters, 15 percent; and isolated, 35 percent.

Of the non-Indians, 55 percent live in isolated homes and the remainder, presumably, live in towns (Maynard and Twiss 1969: 21).

Population density is computed at 3.1 persons per square mile, but, in fact, distribution throughout the reservation is very uneven. The town of Pine Ridge houses 20 percent of the total reservation population, while Wakpamni district as a whole includes 32 percent of the total population (36 percent of the Indian population). LaCreek is the next most populous district, accounting for 18 percent of the population. However, this district is predominantly white, with an Indian population of less than 4 percent. Pass Creek district is largely unpopulated, accounting for only 5.1 percent of the total population. The remaining population of about 44.9 percent is scattered fairly evenly throughout the other five districts. Table 5 gives the total population by district.

Table 5. Total Pine Ridge reservation population by district

District	Total population	Indians	Full bloods	Mixed bloods	Non-Indians
Eagle Nest	1,275	778	382	396	497
LaCreek	2,365	616	75	541	1,749
Medicine Creek	1,204	1,081	621	460	123
Pass Creek	667	512	243	269	155
Porcupine	1,085	965	621	344	120
Wakpamni	4,207	3,529	1,256	2,273	678
White Clay	1,081	1,040	710	330	41
Wounded knee	1,309	1,240	801	439	69
Total	13,193	9,761	4,709	5,052	3,432

Map 3 indicates the predominance of population within each district. more than one-third of the full bloods live in Wakpamni; the rest live mainly in White Clay, Porcupine, Medicine Root, and Wounded Knee. These four districts have the smallest proportions of non-Indians. Almost half of the mixed bloods live in Wakpamni; this is the only district in which they are in the majority. Nearly half the non-Indians live in LaCreek, where they are in the majority. The percentage of non-Indians is also high in Wakpamni and Eagle Nest (Maynard and Twiss 1969: 18–19, 21; Baseline Data Survey).

The respondents to the Baseline Data Survey identified 89 communities ranging in size from 5 to 2,764 inhabitants. Housing developments constructed since the survey may have altered these figures. Of these, 27 communities had a population of more than 100 (Maynard and Twiss 1969: 21; Baseline Data Survey). There are Indian communities in all reservation districts except LaCreek, which is predominantly white; most of the Indians in this district probably live in Martin and other towns.

The dispersion of the Oglala people throughout the reservation was the objective of the allotment system. The purpose, as we have seen, was to break up the bands as political forces and to make every man an independent farmer. Each band settled along a creek, the individual members choosing adjoining allotments. Here, between 1900 and 1920, the Indians built their first log houses. The fluid bands of old thus became fixed communities. The term for such a community was *tiyospaye*, the old word for band, or *wakpala*, meaning "creek." The unity of the community was expressed in the common identity of belonging to a certain named community, in allegiance to the band chief (for whom the government built substantial two-storey frame houses), and in the construction of a community dance hall, large structures in which community celebrations were held.

These first communities were kinship units, like the old bands. However, in time the kinship component of many communities was broken down by intermarriage, by expansion to find room for cattle herds and increasing population, and by the death of band chiefs and failure to appoint new ones. Many individuals moved away to new synthetic communities that arose around government installations. These factors were all part of the incipient change in the nature of Oglala social units.

When the reservation was established, districts had been set up according to watersheds. These were considered natural units, because movement from one to another was difficult at many times of the year without roads and bridges. In each district a commissary building was set up, with a "boss farmer" to supervise the district and to distribute rations. Around these distribution points, in time, Indians and whites alike began small businesses — stores, blacksmith shops, post offices, etc. Small towns grew up, such as Kyle, Allen, Wamblee, and Wounded Knee. During the depression men came to these communities to find work on WPA projects, building schools, churches, dams, and roads.

With the adoption of the constitution, the old system of leadership was formally discarded, and each district was forced to elect representatives. Often sons and grandsons of chiefs were elected, but frequently those who felt the pressure of community leadership considered it beneath their dignity to run for office. Mixed bloods began to gain the upper hand politically because of their facility in English and greater ease in dealing with the ever-growing complexity of BIA administration.

Today some small communities are still composed entirely of kinship groups, like the old *tiyospayes*. Larger communities, however, have generally lost the old patterns of social control based on kinship and are striving to replace them with a more "modern" and "white" system based on community pride and common Indian identity.

In each of the larger communities, housing developments have been built since 1961. These are low cost houses available to the poorest families: those who have sold their land and have no regular income. These most modern houses are therefore available to the socially disadvantaged, many of whom are looked down upon by the more conservative and provident people who have kept their lands and struggled through the years to make a livelihood from rasing cows and farming. Many of those moving into housing developments are mixed bloods, whom many full bloods disdain. This lack of cohesiveness weakens the community's ability to act as a unit in acquiring better services and facilities from the tribe and from the government.

INCOME. In 1967 the income received by the Oglala was $6,335,000. Only 23.5 percent was attributed to agricultural activities (HUD 1969: vol. 4, p. 21). Of the Indians on Pine Ridge, 67 percent of the households reported an annual income of under $3,000; this included 81 percent of the full blood families and 47 percent of the mixed blood families (Maynard and Twiss 1969: 60).

Forty-five percent of full bloods as opposed to 30 percent of the mixed bloods reported unearned income only (welfare, pensions, and land-lease checks). Twenty-two percent of all adults received welfare payments — 29 percent of the women (36 percent of full-blood women) and 12 percent of the men. Nineteen percent of all Indian women received Aid to Dependent Children payments — 25 percent of full blood women and 13 percent of mixed-blood women. About 50 percent of the Oglala receive land-lease checks. In addition, those families qualifying for it receive surplus commodity foods (Maynard and Twiss 1969: 67–68) (see Table 6).

Table 6. Sources of income for a sample Indian population in 1967 (Maynard and Twiss 1969: 67–68)

Type	Percent
Earned income only	24
Both earned and unearned	21
Unearned only	40
No income (mostly housewives)	14

Unearned income, particularly land-lease payments and welfare monies, composes a very large part of Oglala income.

EMPLOYMENT STATISTICS. The most reliable employment statistics are doubtless those of the Baseline Data Survey for 1967, which were reported in the *Pine Ridge Research Bulletin* (1967 1: 6) as shown in Table 7.

In a later publication of the Baseline Data Survey, the percentage of the labor force that was unemployed had risen to 36.6 percent. Among those employed, more than 25 percent were working part-time; of these, 73 percent were working on a temporaty basis. Thirteen percent of those employed full-time were working on a temporary basis (Maynard and Twiss 1969: 60). Strikingly, 46 percent of the full-blood men were unemployed, as compared to 31 percent of the mixed-blood

Table 7.   Pine Ridge labor force 1967

Labor force		Percentage
Employed full time		49.8
Employed part time		18.2
Unemployed		32.0
Males	33.1	
Mixed blood	27.8	
Full blood	38.3	
Females	29.6	

men. It is equally striking that only 66 percent of Oglalas over sixteen years of age were in the labor force, compared with the national average of 77 percent. Ten percent of the full-blood males and 3.7 percent of the mixed-blood males were unable to work because of disablement.

Among males, unemployment was greatest among those under 25 and over 55. There is a positive correlation between level of educational achievement and employment. There were no unemployed college graduates, although 22 percent of the high school graduates over 25 years of age were unemployed. However, this compares with 48 percent unemployment of males over 25 without high school diplomas. According to the Baseline Data Survey findings, education is the most important factor in employment on Pine Ridge (Maynard and Twiss 1969: 61).

The Baseline Data Survey reported the following statistics (see Table 8) from a sample population indicating which family members were working (Maynard and Twiss 1969: 64).

Table 8.   Workers on Pine Ridge reservation (sample population 1967)

	Percentage of Indian households	Percentage of non-Indian households
No one working	36	12
Household head only	30	62
Household head and wife	11	17
Only wife working	4	1

The Baseline Data Survey was taken just before the closing of the Wright-McGill fishhook factories on Pine Ridge, the largest employer next to the government. It was estimated that by late 1968, after the closing of these factories, the unemployment rate was about 40 percent (Maynard and Twiss 1969: 64).

The most recent published statistics concerning employment are for 1971 and are reproduced in Table 9 (BIA 1972: 5).

Table 9. Labor supply, Pine Ridge reservation

A. Employment (1971)	Male	Female	Total
Nonagricultural			
Manufacturing	120	115	235
Construction	90	1	91
Utilities	9	1	10
Trade, wholesale and retail	15	11	26
Finance, insurance, and real estate	3	2	5
Services	20	6	26
Government	170	180	350
All other nonagricultural	101	125	226
Total nonagricultural	528	441	969
Agricultural	306	140	446
Total employment	834	581	1,415
B. Current unemployment	1,292	323	1,615

C. Estimated number of housewives, seasonal and part-time workers who would shift from low-paying jobs that could be expected to work for industry:

	455	420	875

D. Estimated number of reservation high-school graduates in the next three years:

	130	120	250

E. Total potential labor supply (B, C, and D):

	1,877	863	2,740

Table 9 was prepared for the purpose of attracting industry to the reservation. It indicates that in 1971 more than 50 percent of the reservation labor supply was unemployed; it suggests an available labor force (including the estimated number of underemployed) in 1971 of 2,490 and projects an available labor force of 2,740 by 1974 (apparently taking no account of aging, deaths, accidents, or high school graduates leaving the reservation for further training, armed services, etc.).

A March 1972 BIA report gives the data for Pine Ridge as shown in Table 10.

Table 10. Employment statistics, Pine Ridge reservation

	Male	Female	Total
Resident Indian population, 16 and over	2,871	2,896	5,767
Population over 16 not in labor force	1,040	1,940	2,980
Potential labor force	1,831	956	2,787
Currently employed:	972	658	1,630
Permanent (more than 12 months)	519	488	1,007
Temporary (including seasonal)	453	170	623
Currently unemployed:	859	298	1,157
Those actively seeking work	230	105	335

According to these figures the unemployment rate is only 42 percent, and unemployment has declined to 1,157 in 1972 from 1,615 in 1971. These figures suggest that only about 25 percent of the unemployed are actively seeking work, which implies that a considerable number do not want to and will not work. This situation, although difficult to assess, seems to be a dominant opinion among BIA personnel, both white and Indian.

Although all these statistics point to an unemployment rate of about 40 to 50 percent, the president of the Oglala Sioux tribe told the writer in June 1972 that the unemployment rate on the reservation at that time was 85 percent. This statement, too, is difficult to assess, but it demonstrates a clear concern for employment. Lack of job opportunities, the need for employment, and speculation about the desire of the Oglala Sioux people to work are important themes in reservation politics.

The Oglala Sioux Tribe

The Oglala Sioux tribe represents the government of the people of Pine Ridge reservation. Tribal government is parliamentary; it assumes similar problems and a homogeneity of interest among the Oglala population. There is no separation of powers, all authority lying in the elected tribal council. Even the tribal court system is subordinate to the council.

Many of the problems of the reservation seem attributable to the tribal organization. It is, after all, an alien form of government that has been forced on the Oglala. The tribal organization has been made to accept administrative responsibility for the whole reservation, but it seems certain that the local people, the Oglala living in the various district communities, do not as a whole believe in a representative form of government. They do not identify with the tribe as a political group and would prefer to run their own affairs at the local level, under the direction of local leaders whose support comes from community faith in their abilities.

The Oglala Sioux tribe has reserved for itself a wide range of governmental functions. But because of the trustee relationship between the federal government and the Oglala Sioux, the government has practical responsibility for large sectors of reservation life. The Bureau of Indian Affairs has primary responsibility for the development of reservation resources, yet the bureau has not efficiently directed reservation development; instead, much of the responsibility for planning has been left to the tribe. The tribe, however, has not been able to gain the support of the people. Tribal programs are usually considered critically by the communities, acceptance is at best passive, and success has been minimal.

The problem is longstanding. The tribe attempts to get things done but meets opposition: first, from the people, who do not accept the legitimacy of tribal government — particularly as it touches their own lives — and, second, from the BIA, which will initiate projects for the Indians but is more reluctant to aid projects that have been begun and planned by Indians.

Gearing has called this type of problem "structural paralysis" (1970: 107). Because of the structure of the groups involved, nothing gets done; conflict is built into the system. Clearly, the key to development at Pine Ridge lies in understanding the structure of tribal organization and the interactions between the various structures involved in tribal government and planning.

THE TRIBAL COUNCIL.   Formal government of the Oglala Sioux tribe is the responsibility of the tribal council, an elected body composed of representatives from each of the nine reservation districts. Each district is allowed one councilman for each 300 residents, plus one more if the remainder of the population totals more than 150. All enrolled tribal members over the age of 21 who are reservation residents are allowed to vote. Elections are held every two years to fill all council positions, and at the same time a president and vice-president are elected by the reservation voters at large. Presidential and vice-presidential candidates run together as teams; the number of teams is reduced to two by the holding of a primary election.

The council selects a secretary, treasurer, and "fifth member," who may not be members of the council. Together with the president and vice-president, these five officials constitute the executive committee.

Regular council meetings are scheduled four times annually, and special meetings may be called by the president at any time. Only councilmen may vote at the meetings, although the president may vote to break a tie. When the council is not in session, governmental responsibility is in the hands of the executive committee, which meets weekly.

TRIBAL ASSETS.   In terms of wealth, the Oglala Sioux Tribe has little besides its landholdings. With all the monies accruing to the tribe through state tax returns, land sales, leases, and other means being allocated for operating expenses, there is never any surplus of funds, never any per capita distribution to tribal members. The annual budget, which in 1970 totaled more than $321,000 (*Oglala War Cry*, June 15, 1970), comes mainly from federal funds.

POWER OF THE COUNCIL. The power of the tribal council as an autonomous political body is severely limited by the Bureau of Indian Affairs. Any and all legislation passed by the council is subject to review by the bureau, and any tribal act may be vetoed by the secretary of the interior (Maynard and Twiss 1969: 137). Nonetheless, the tribe seems to be gaining somewhat in autonomy. About 1969 the tribal constitution was amended to remove the BIA superintendent from the executive committee. Shortly thereafter the council exercised its prerogative granted by the 1970 reorganization of the BIA to oust the superintendent from the reservation. This action seems to have been taken not because of any particular antipathy for the superintendent, nor from a feeling that he was incompetent, but rather as an exercise of political muscle, a symbolic gesture affirming new political self-sufficiency. The creation of a centralized planning office, directly responsible to the council, which incorporates officials previously responsible to the BIA, is another indication of the developing self-government on the reservation.

POLITICS ON PINE RIDGE. It may still be safe to say that the political process on Pine Ridge differs greatly from that of general American society. The people of Pine Ridge lack a real concept of "politician." Candidates for political office spend less time in making promises and outlining their platform than they do in maligning their opponents.

Today it appears that only a small minority of the Oglalas are interested in tribal politics (Maynard and Twiss 1969: 137). Normally, less than 30 percent of eligible voters take part in an election (HUD 1969 3: 22). Most Oglalas seem suspicious of tribal politicians, who are said to be dishonest and self-seeking. Furthermore, they are considered to be people who have sold out to the whites. Anyone engaging in politics on the reservation jeopardizes both social position and family relationships. Moreover, political careers are liable to be very uncertain. As a matter of course, the president and vice-president are never elected to two consecutive terms, and many of the councilmen are rotated as well. This hampers most development programs, which are just getting underway as one administration makes way for the next. To complicate the situation, each administration tries its best to discredit the preceding one and attempts to drop old projects and begin new ones. Maintaining continuity in development probably has been the most serious problem on Pine Ridge.

TRIBAL GOALS. In broad, general terms, there is little doubt that some consensus regarding tribal goals at Pine Ridge exists. The resolution of the tribal council in establishing an Oglala Sioux tribal planning office in 1968 states (HUD 1972: D):

The Oglala Sioux Tribe is fully committed to the development of a better way of life for the people of the Pine Ridge Indian Reservation — a better way of life which will be defined by the people themselves, speaking through the tribal and community organizations and as individuals.

In recent years, the emphasis has definitely been on community development and on the involvement of local people in the decision-making process.

A synthesis of tribal objectives prepared in 1971 listed three major areas. The tribe wished to develop its lands, to provide educational opportunities for the Oglalas, and to "preserve and revere the cultural heritage of its people" (OST 1971: 8). Other frequently heard desires are to provide job opportunities by encouraging light industry to come to the reservation, to increase the quantity and quality of goods and services available on the reservation, to further develop the cattle-raising industry, and to promote tourism.

DEVELOPMENT PLANNING. In order to overcome lack of coordination and continuity in planning, the Oglala Sioux tribe sought outside assistance. One of the periodic functions of the Bureau of Indian Affairs on any reservation is to prepare an Overall Economic Development Plan. Usually this is done by bureau personnel, but in 1967 the bureau contracted with a private corporation, Marshall Kaplan, Gans and Kahn, to develop a plan for the reservation. The two-year study was financed by a grant from the Department of Housing and Urban Development. Although based exclusively on Pine Ridge, presumably with the cooperation of the tribe, the final study was titled a "Model reservation program," and it was apparently designed to be generalized to other Indian reservations. Publication was in twelve rambling and repetitive volumes. While the study was in progress a change in tribal administration had occurred; when the final study was presented to the tribal council, it voted to condemn it to the waste-basket.

In 1969 the Economic Development Administration began a planning project on Pine Ridge, the stated purpose of which was to implement the HUD report (OST 1971: 2). This planning grant represents a contract between the Oglala Sioux tribe and the Economic Development Administration, the EDA planner being the administrator of the grant (EDA 1971: 3).

The first EDA planner apparently began work in 1970. His intention was to involve as many people as possible in the planning of economic development by holding frequent district meetings. However, when the grant was refunded for 1971, it was severely cut so that it was necessary to minimize popular involvement in the project (EDA 1971: 1).

The EDA planner spent the early part of 1971 reducing the HUD report to a modest document of some dozen typewritten pages outlining a basic planning framework. However, an attempt to get the tribal council to establish development priorities failed. As a result, legislation was drawn up to establish a tribal planning commission (EDA 1971: 1), which was established in August 1971 (BIA 1972: 18). Known as the "Crazy Horse Planning Commission," this body consists of one planner from each district, elected by popular vote. The term of office is four years, and terms are staggered to provide continuity (OST 1971). The tribal president, a nonvoting member of the commission, functions as its chairman (EDA 1971: 26). In order to maximize popular involvement, the legislation also calls for the election of one planner from each district community to work with the district planner. The commission meets regularly, and presumably the results will be reported to district and community planning meetings.

On April 27, 1972, the tribal council established an Oglala Sioux Planning Center, which gives the tribe more control over its own future than it has ever had before. Housed in a new building at the Pine Ridge airport, the center has consolidated all planning activity on the reservation. Under the control of a director, the center includes the EDA planner, the BIA programs officer, tribal planners, and officials employed by the Office of Economic Opportunity (OEO) and related government programs. The center is directly responsible to the tribal council through its director. Thus, the BIA planner is subordinate to the tribe, and the council has gained a greater degree of freedom from bureau domination. Presumably the center will promote continuity of planning from one administration to another. However, the center's director is appointed by the council, and it presently appears that the council is jealous of the planning center. Ideally, the council sees itself as the initiator of all reservation programs, but individual councilmen lack an understanding of professional planning problems and processes. There is likely to be resistance to programs developed by the planning center until the council feels that the center is taking its cues from them. This seems to be an area in which the persuasive powers of the tribal president will be needed to smooth over potential dissension in the council.

NONTRIBAL INSTITUTIONS.   Many nontribal institutions, particularly governmental ones, are an important part of reservation life, performing major functions in the areas of land management, education, and health services which would otherwise have to be handled by the tribe.

The major function of the BIA as it now operates on Pine Ridge seems to be to oversee the land assets of the reservation; it supervises all land sales, leases, stock raising, and agricultural projects. Although employment placement is also handled through the BIA, the net results are minimal. A longstanding job-traineeship program tends to train people in such skills as welding, truck driving, or electronics work—none of which is relevant to individuals who wish to remain on the reservation. The bureau also supervised the disbursement of funds to the tribe and plans public projects, such as road building, dam construction, irrigation projects, and public building projects.

Although the Catholic church runs a boarding school at the Holy Rosary Mission, the bureau runs most of the reservation schools, including the boarding school in the town of Pine Ridge. In the past these schools have been entirely independent of the communities in which they are located, but today at least token efforts are being made to involve the parents in school affairs. There is also much interest being shown in teaching the Lakota language as well as courses in Indian history and culture.

The Public Health Service Hospital provides health services for the entire reservation population. Nurses and nurses' aides serve each of the major district communities, and doctors hold regular clinics.

PLANNED ECONOMIC DEVELOPMENT

Throughout its history, Pine Ridge has experienced a number of attempts at planned economic development. They have centered on the involvement of Oglalas in construction and maintenance work generated by the Bureau of Indian Affairs, on agricultural development (both farming and stock raising), and, in more recent years, on manufacturing and tourism. In total, vast sums of money have been spent on these projects, but not one of them has generated real economic development. In the short or long run, many of these programs have been economically successful in terms of dollars, but none has provided the necessary driving force for meaningful, wide-range, long-term development.

That development is a goal, a felt need on the part of the Oglalas, is apparent. It has always been a stated goal of the BIA as well, but we may question whether, in the past, overly paternalistic bureau representatives at Pine Ridge have really desired it. In any case, both Indians and whites are in general agreement as to what development would mean: an economic program that would allow the Oglalas, as individuals and as a tribe, to be emotionally and economically independent of the United States government, while still maintaining their special identity and privileges as Oglala Sioux Indians. It would represent a logical continuation of Oglala history and would take advantage of the one real resource on the reservation: Sioux culture and its concomitant social patterns of cooperation, sharing, and reciprocity.

The three case studies that follow illustrate how past development programs have failed and, to some extent, why.

Red Shirt Table Development Association (1937–1944)[2]

In 1936 the BIA decided to initiate a development project in the community of Red Shirt Table at the extreme northwest corner of the reservation. A formal document was drawn up by the bureau after months of study in cooperation with local people, and the Red Shirt Table Development Association was formed in 1937 with eighteen families under the leadership of Moses Two Bulls, the local mixed-blood leader. The project was intended to develop three enterprises: livestock and poultry breeding and subsistence gardening. The bureau, having bought back land at Red Shirt Table that had been alienated by sale to whites, built facilities for the program, financed an irrigation project, loaned cattle and money, and provided the management. Originally set up as a five-year program, it was extended to eight years when it was apparent that the original loans could not be repaid as quickly as projected.

The association seemed a great success. After the first six years, the net worth of the enterprise was reported at $65,000. The cattle-raising program operated successfully, chickens and turkeys were being bred and sold, and about 130 acres were being irrigated. Potatoes and other root crops were being produced and stored in a community root cellar, and other surplus vegetables were being canned in a community canning kitchen. Winter feed for livestock was also being grown.

The project seems to have worked on an individual family basis, each family involving themselves as much or as little as they desired. Nine full-blood families, unwilling to join the formal association, formed an informal association of their own and presumably shared in the benefits of the project.

When government support ended, the association seems to have been financially solvent; the irrigation project was a success, and the poultry project, if not profitable, at least broke even. The number of cattle was reported to have risen to about one thousand. However, the individual members soon voted to break up the association and divide up the cattle. The raising of poultry and the irrigation project eventually died out, and the cattle herds dwindled, until the net results of the eight-year project were negligible.

Despite the appearance of success, the project failed to produce any

[2] This section is based on William O. Roberts (1943) and on an interview with Peter Two Bulls, one of the organizers of the association.

real development. The reasons for this are undoubtedly very complex. In the first place there is the problem of management. Superintendent Roberts reported that when the project began the Indians said to him, "You manage things; we do not agree among ourselves." When formal bureau management ceased, it seems that individual members lost faith in the association.

Two-thirds of the land being used for the project was owned by nonresident Indians, whose only interest in the project was to receive their regular land-lease payments. They preferred to lease their lands to white ranchers who could pay higher rates and were considered to be financially more reliable.

Moreover, World War II intervened. Many of the young men went off to fight, and large numbers of men and women who stayed behind were lured to war-time jobs off the reservation. This was particularly the case at Red Shirt Table. Although, from the perspective of Pine Ridge town, Red Shirt was the most isolated community on the reservation, it was at the same time the closest community to Rapid City, the largest white community in the area. In 1938 a bridge, which provided easy access to Rapid City, had been built across the Cheyenne River near Red Shirt Table.

After the war, some of the mixed-blood leaders of the association attempted to revive it, "for the sake of our children," but had no success. Interest and a spirit of cooperation were lacking. The community was losing population as residents were attracted off-reservation or closer to the conveniences and possible jobs available at Pine Ridge town. The area still has potential for a cattle-raising association, and the resident population, about 80 people, could surely be supported by this means. The problem today in the community, I was told, was lack of a popular leader. Until this is solved, nothing is likely to happen at Red Shirt Table, and the community may eventually fade away.

The Oglala Irrigation Project (1938–Present)[3]

The Oglala Irrigation project had its beginning in a CCC-PWA project. A storage dam was built on White Clay Creek near the present community of Oglala between 1938 and 1941. In addition to providing employment in the actual construction of the dam, it was originally planned as a rehabilitation project for some 200 families. It was proposed to give 5 to 10 acres of irrigated land to each family, and to organize livestock associations for the cooperative raising of cattle. This

---

[3] Most of the information for this section is taken from Missouri River Basin Investigations Project (Oglala Irrigation Project Cattle Enterprise 1969).

would have provided a diversified economic base for a substantial segment of the population.

However, during the construction of the dam, the bureau changed its plans, shifting emphasis from ranching to farming. Evidently the feeling was that 5 to 10 acre plots would be uneconomical, and the revised plan proposed to give about 40 acres to each of 50 families. Each family would have one acre for a kitchen garden, 38 acres for marketable crops, and would be provided with two milk cows and 100 chickens. In revised form, the project might have had some success, but selection of the 50 favored families would obviously have had divisive effects.

When the dam was completed both of the earlier plans, which had been the *raison d'être* for the dam construction, were dropped. Irrigated farming began there in 1942. Two hundred twenty-five acres were farmed under government financing and supervision. Farm machinery and operating expenses were provided by the BIA. The project employed twenty-five to thirty Indians who were paid in cash for their work, but housing for workers and their families at the site of the farm was not provided. The project was clearly an economic disaster.

In later years a share-crop program was initiated, and a few growers attempted to produce potatoes. Their success was uneven, and by 1947 only about 100 acres were being irrigated.

From 1948 to 1954 the area was leased out to ten or twelve Indian operators. By 1954, 859 acres were under irrigation. However, in the following year government supervision and assistance were withdrawn, and Indian operators lost interest. By 1960 most of the land was leased to cattle growers.

In 1963 the law and order branch of the Oglala Sioux tribe leased a small tract of the land for an honor farm. In that year, 55 acres were planted with alfalfa and 15 acres of row crops and vegetables were used as food for the jail personnel and for the prison labor.

By 1971 all of the irrigated area had been brought under the management of the Oglala Sioux Farm and Ranch Enterprise, which grew out of the honor farm. According to the mimeographed "Plan of operations," at least 90 percent of the employees of the enterprise must be members of the Oglala Sioux tribe, but the manager need not be. In 1972 the manager was an Oglala. The employees consisted of five or six men working under the Tribal Work Experience Program (TWEP, financed by the Department of Labor) who lived at the farm, and five trustees from the prison.

At the end of fiscal year 1971, the total number of acres under irrigation was 1,405, 100 acres of which were planted with row crops, 5 with garden crops, and 125 with small grains. The remaining 1,175 acres were used for hay and grazing land (BIA 1971).

The farm raises cattle — some 300 breeding head at the end of 1971 — as well as hogs. In 1971 the total value of livestock and equipment, including a bunkhouse and two houses, was put at $110,491. According to the farm plan, all profits "will be placed in an OST Reserve Fund for the express purpose of training and retraining potential heads of families for employment" (Oglala Sioux Farm and Ranch Enterprise 1971). As of 1972, as I understood it, all profits were still being funneled back into the farm in order to develop it to its maximum size.

Economically, then, the Oglala Farm and Ranch Enterprise seems successful. As a means of development, however, the dam project has been a dismal failure from the year of its construction. It has not only failed to involve any significant number of individuals, but also has relied entirely on heavy government subsidy for maintenance costs and on government management. Another dam is in the planning for the White River near Slim Buttes. The dam at Oglala should provide a good model of how a potentially effective development project can be rendered totally ineffective.

The Wright and McGill Fishhook Factories (1961–1967)[4]

By all accounts the Wright and McGill fishhook snelling plants on Pine Ridge constituted the most successful economic development project ever attempted on the reservation. Yet the "success" of this operation was deceptive and, in any case, had very little to do with the Oglalas themselves.

The BIA had long been looking for industrial work that could be located in isolated South Dakota, far from sources of raw materials and from major transportation routes. Fishhooks were particularly appropriate because of their light weight and subsequent easy transportation. The already manufactured fishhooks were trucked into Pine Ridge where the new factory would snell them, that is, tie on the various flies and lures.

In order to attract Wright and McGill to Pine Ridge, the Oglala Sioux tribe made available for company use a reconditioned tribal building as a base for operations, and the BIA provided on-the-job training funds to subsidize the workers. Initially the BIA decided that the tying of flies would be appropriate woman's work, arguing that woman were more dexterous with their hands than men, as witnessed by the quality of Sioux beadwork. It was foreseen, however, that such an action would contribute to the social degradation of Oglala men and

---

[4] The information for this section is taken from the Wright and McGill files, no. 1965-2276, Central Files, Bureau of Indian Affairs, Washington, D.C.

would aggravate the problems of idleness, drinking, and anomy. Instead, the BIA decided at least to start by encouraging men to do the work.

The immediate concern was to find an appropriate manager. This proved to be a major problem. The first plant opened at Pine Ridge town in March 1961 without benefit of a permanent manager, BIA employees temporarily overseeing the operation for the company. The need for an Indian manager was keenly felt. Although it is certain that qualified Indian managers could have been found on Pine Ridge, for one reason or another Wright and McGill hired Emil Redfish, a Brule Sioux from Rosebud reservation, to oversee their operations. The bringing in of this outsider to direct the Oglala workers was always a sore point.

From the beginning the factory proved successful. The company found the quality of the work higher than that of their other snelling plants (located in Mexico), and no doubt the Pine Ridge plant was economical. Redfish seems to have proven an efficient administrator. He insisted on punctuality among his workers, but was understanding of the peculiar problems of the reservation — problems of transportation, unfamiliarity with a time-clock, kinship obligations, drinking. Supervisors were appointed from among the best workers to encourage the others and to help with personal problems. Yet this placed the supervisors in an uncomfortable position of authority which many well-qualified workers refused to accept. To supervise one has to tread lightly on Dakota ideals of individual equality and autonomy and to risk being considered a bad relative and a white-man's Indian.

The majority of workers were men, although some women were also hired. Interestingly, it was found that men proved faster at the work than women. The weekly minimum salary was based on an average production of 96 dozen hooks during each eight-hour day. Some workers and engage them in conversation. As a result "No Visitors hooks per day. In 1965 the average take-home pay was reported at $104 to $150 per week.

During the early days of the operations, those Oglalas who had not been hired visited the plant and reportedly attempted to heckle the would aggravate the problems of idleness, drinking, and anomy. In-Are Allowed" signs were prominently posted and enforced.

By 1965 the fishhook operation was an accepted part of Pine Ridge life. Other factories had been opened in Wounded Knee and Kyle, and in 1966 a fourth was opened at Porcupine.

The number of workers needed in the factories fluctuated with the season, summer being the slack time. in February of 1965, 160 Indians were employed; at the end of June only 35 were working. The number climbed to 92 by the end of September and up to 200 by the beginning of December. This meant, of course, that workers had to be ready at all times to report when needed, but there was no certainty as to when they would be called to work. Announcements of who should work on any given day were very informal, operating by the "moccasin tele-graph" that is, relying on word of mouth. This proved to be an efficient way to ensure the right number of workers the next day. During 1965, the company was reported to be pumping $638,000 annually into the Pine Ridge economy, next to the government far and away the most important economic resource on the reservation.

During the period of the Wright and McGill operations, all problem workers were simply let go since there was a great demand to obtain jobs in the factories. There seems never to have been a labor shortage. Sometimes individuals who had been fired would be rehired at a later time. In 1966 it was reported that some 800 Oglalas had at one time or another been employed by Wright and McGill.

Working in the fishhook factories may have been viewed by some as a step in upward mobility. It was claimed that whenever any other job opened up on the reservation it was usually filled by someone from the fishhook factories, who had already proved their ability to work at steady labor.

By 1967, Wright and McGill considered the Pine Ridge venture a success and had closed down all its other snelling factories. An average of 90 workers per factory were employed, and at the high-point of company activities some 475 Indians were employed. Nonetheless, despite provision of facilities by the tribe and government wage subsidies, Wright and McGill were not making any profit on the fishhooks. Nor did they intend to. Their Eagle Claw fishhooks were a small link in the company's large interests in sporting goods, and they wished simply to keep their name in the fishhook business without losing money and still be able to compete with Asiatic imports. In other words while successful both from the point of view of the company and of the Sioux, nonetheless, the people of Pine Ridge were not involved in an economic enterprise that was truly self-sufficient and profitable.

Events of late 1967 forecasted disaster for the Pine Ridge reserva-tion. The first was a raise in the minimum wage which was to take place on February 1, 1968. The company's cost department reported that, with the increase, all the Pine Ridge operations would be running at a loss. The second was the loosening of trade restrictions with Asia. Eagle Claw fishhooks sold for 55¢ for a card of six; with the higher wages the price would be raised to 60¢. Japanese hooks of comparable quality could now be sold for 10¢ for a card of six. The company immediately announced that it would transfer all of its single-snelling operations to Mexico where labor was cheap, even if the quality were poorer. Only one Pine Ridge plant, employing about 100, would be retained to do double snelling. But even this proved unprofitable, and all of Wright and McGill's Pine Ridge operations ceased at the end of July 1967.

What were the results? The most extravagant claims had been made for the effects of the Wright-McGill factories. It was said that the drinking problem had been alleviated, that children attended school more regularly and did better work, and that the standard of living for the employees was raised with their ability to purchase more of the essential fixtures of an American life-style. Yet talking to the Oglala today, one gets the impression that this is greatly exaggerated. It seems that the income brought in by the factories was not enough to effect any substantial change in the economy. Probably the major effect was to replace monies and commodities previously received from the government welfare. With the closing of the factories, just as during slack hiring periods, it was necessary to return to government support. Yet there is no denying that the factories did have a social effect as well, although to attempt to measure it now seems impossible.

The Wright-McGill experience proved that the Oglala would work in factories if given the opportunity, and they would produce faithfully. But it also taught that there is little sense in involving the tribe in an economic venture that in the larger economic sense cannot prove profitable; it leads only to a precarious situation in which the future is forever uncertain and meaningful economic development is impossible.

THE ECONOMY OF PINE RIDGE

The economy of Pine Ridge Reservation has been characterized as a service economy. To a great extent it is outside the money economy common to most of the United States; based on the old treaties, the economic premise of the reservation economy is defined as dependence on the federal government for general welfare and main economic support. By accepting goods and services instead of cash, the Oglala find themselves in a rigid economic situation, where free choice is virtually nonexistent. Products and services are nonnegotiable; individuals are provided with surplus food, medical care, welfare monies, and educational facilities, but the individual has few choices to make. Thus, being brought up on the reservation is very poor preparation for facing the complexities of off-reservation life. It is this service economy that seems to be the basic reinforcing factor underlying the poverty of the Oglala and their general alienation from white society (HUD 1969: vol. 3, pp. 8–10, 13).

It has been estimated that during fiscal year 1966–1967, 91 percent of all funds expended or generated directly on Pine Ridge reservation originated in off-reservation public and private social service agencies; only 8.4 percent of such funds were directly attributable to the efforts of the Oglalas as individuals (HUD 1969: vol. 3, p. 14). The social service programs have annually expended some $14.4 million on Pine Ridge reservation. That this staggering amount of money has not produced any noticeable alleviation of poverty on the reservation suggests the ineffectiveness of a service economy in dealing with the real economic problems (HUD 1969: vol. 3, pp. 14, 18).

The economy of Pine Ridge may be subdivided into three major sectors and one potential sector. These are agriculture, manufacturing and commerce, government and services, and a potential trade sector based on tourism (EDA 1970: 18–19). A detailed examination of each sector fills in the overall picture of the contemporary economic situation at Pine Ridge.

Agriculture

The economy of the Oglala is still oriented primarily towards agriculture, particularly the raising of cattle. Nonetheless, the realty office of the BIA at Pine Ridge estimated that in 1971 only 270 families on the reservation made their living through agricultural pursuits.

Part of the problem is the pattern of land ownership. Over the years, because of the fractioning of allotments through inheritance, most Oglala have owned small, widely scattered parcels of land. The only profitable way to use these lands has been to lease them to cattle raisers through the BIA, which has established 346 range units that it leases on an annual basis. Lease payments must be divided among 39,635 ownership interests, which involves about 5,780 individuals (Lay 1970). Such a land-ownership pattern is entirely uneconomical, and the realty office of the BIA reported in 1972 that the tribe was negotiating a $4 million federal loan for the purchase of complex heirship units.

Of the 346 units, 142 are allocated for Indian lessors, at a minimal rate that is established at three-year intervals by the council. Only Indian ranchers owning fewer than 300 head of cattle are eligible for these range units; those owning more must compete against other Indians and white ranchers in bidding for range leases (Lay 1970). Long term leases are not available.

Because of the poor quality of much of the grazing land, it is calculated that one heifer needs 30 or more acres for sustained grazing. It is also estimated that a family needs at least 250 head to provide a minimum income (EDA 1970: 8). Even if every acre were utilized, less than half of the population of the reservation would be able to make their livelihood exclusively from the land (Lay 1970).

One answer to some of these problems would seem to be the formation of cattle cooperatives. One such land-use association was formed in the Slim Buttes area during the depression and was aided by CCC labor in fencing and other work. Each individual belonging to the association was required to provide a minimum of 54 acres for common use. The association apparently functioned with a good bit of success, but dissolved shortly after 1950. A similar association was formed at Red Shirt Table during the same period. Though quite successful, the co-op soon dissolved, and profits were divided among the members.

Today there is a cattle co-op in the Porcupine region, but it is quite small. During the summer of 1972, a group from the University of Colorado attempted to create interest in a cattle co-op in the community of Kyle but met with little success.

It would appear that there is only one workable basis for a cattle co-op: kinship relations. In particular, a group of brothers or cousins with in-married relatives are often able to cooperate well enough with one another. Nonrelatives, however, seem prone to quarrels and suspicion. Further, such cooperative groups apparently have a life-span of only one generation; interest in them does not seem to be passed on from one generation to the next. This may be related to Sioux attitudes which value an individual's right to organize his own affairs, on his own initiative, rather than fit into a prestructured situation that essentially denies his independence and autonomy.

Manufacturing and Commerce

Until 1966 the Wright and McGill Fishhook Factory, with branch plants in several communities, was a major reservation employer. This company was forced to terminate operations because of rising costs and increasing competition from Hong Kong. In order to overcome the disastrous effects of the shutdown, a group of individuals formed the Pine Ridge Reservation Development Corporation in 1966. Its major purpose was to make the reservation area eligible for financial help from the Small Business Administration.

The development company constructed a twenty acre industrial park around the old factory with the intention of encouraging light industry. A moccasin factory soon located in the old facilities. Moccasins proved popular and easy to sell, but because of management and financial problems the company was forced out of business in the spring of 1969. At that time the development company negotiated with Sun Bell

Corporation of Albuquerque, New Mexico, to take over the business. A white manager was brought in, and the business was renamed Pine Ridge Products (*Oglala War Cry*, June 15, 1970).

The factory has been a financial success and has expanded several times during the past few years. By September of 1970 the operation employed more than 80 Indians — 40 in the factory — and many others who lace moccasins as piecework in their homes. Thirty-eight different styles of moccasins were being produced at that time (*Oglala War Cry*, September 7, 1970). By the end of the year the factory was producing 1,500 pairs per day (*Oglala War Cry*, December 28, 1970). National sales have been consistently high, and in 1972 the company was investigating foreign sales as well. In April, 1971, the factory added a line of Indian dolls to its operation, considerably increasing the number of employees (*Oglala War Cry*, April 8, 1971).

Pine Ridge Products produces items that take off from traditional Indian themes but are not in the slighest degree reflective of Dakota culture. The moccasins are inspired by woodlands and Navajo styles, while the plastic dolls, with their buckskin and feather costumes, seem to be in many cases fairly objectionable representations of usual Indian stereotypes. They seem to be selling however, and during my brief stay I heard no complaints from the Oglalas regarding the nature of the materials produced by the factory.

Complaints were instead directed against the low wages. The factory, which has no competition for the labor market, pays the minimum wage to beginning workers, and salary increases are slow. These wages are very low to anyone who has worked previously on the well-funded OEO or other government projects. Similarly, workers who lace moccasins at home complain that the pay is low and that time is too short to get their allotted number finished. If they fail to have all allotted moccasins finished by the time the next delivery is made, they are no longer given work. So a woman doing such work may enlist the help of female relatives, and, when the wages are divided up, each individual's share is meager.

I was told that workers at the factory were allowed to vote on the hours they wished to work and choose a ten-hour work day four days a week. This innovative schedule was apparently followed for a considerable length of time, but normal work hours were reverted to as production increased. Most of the workers in the factory are Indian, but a few white women come from nearby Nebraska towns to work. The director of the factory is white, but the foremen are Indians, which has caused the usual problems of trying to get Indians to assume responsibility over others. Being in a position to order others about, clearly at odds with the kinship norms of the culture, places the foremen in an uncomfortable position. I was told that some good workers who would be promoted to foremen with higher pay have refused because they do not want to be placed in an awkward position of authority.

The development of Pine Ridge Products has been successful, but its success must be understood in proper perspective. Its financial solvency depends on a wage supplement program that is federally subsidized and on the fact that the capital burden has been borne by the development company that operates the industrial park. Officers in the company have a direct interest in the operation (EDA 1970: 19–20).

To date, no other responsible manufacturing tenants have been found for the industrial park. Other buildings on the grounds house a drive-in restaurant, the surplus commodities warehouse, and a tribal museum with an arts and crafts co-op in the basement.

In commerce, Pine Ridge has had less success. The Oglala Sioux tribe negotiated for the building of the Sioux Nation Shopping Center, which houses a large grocery store and a variety store. The tribe leases these facilities to a private, white-owned company, however, and makes only a small profit from this rental. The shopping center, like all of the other stores and trading posts on the reservation, charges very high prices. This has been attributed not merely to isolation, but more importantly to lack of competition (EDA 1970: 19).

Individuals attempting to start businesses on the reservation have not generally met with great success. There are a few old and established businesses — notably the pottery shop and a grocery store in Pine Ridge town — but others have been forced to close. One Oglala opened a grocery store in a district town but found that demands for credit from relatives were too much of a burden. To maintain his status as a good relative he had the choice of either going bankrupt, through indefinite extension of bad credit, or closing. He chose the latter option and now rents the building to Head Start. His livelihood is largely gained through cattle raising.

Another man obtained a loan from the Small Business Administration (SBA) to open a garage in Pine Ridge. Because there are no other garages on the reservation for repairing automobiles, he felt certain of a good business. However, he was unable to convince SBA to give him a reasonably large loan, and as a result his operation is so small that he can work on only one car at a time and does not have the room to hire a much needed assistant. Past businesses on the reservation have proven to be such bad investments that it is difficult for anyone to get financial backing.

This lack of success in business is always blamed partly on the lack of understanding of money. People say that the Oglala do not know how to use money or how to save it. A step toward improving the attitude toward money was made by the establishment at Pine Ridge in

January 1970 of a branch bank, which was managed by a representative from the parent bank. Set up in a trailer house, the new bank soon became a focal point of community pride. (Despite the insecure quarters, during the bank's existence it did not experience any robbery attempt.)

About 900 accounts (both checking and savings) were opened, but the amount of money involved was so meager that it was impossible for the bank to show a profit. It became largely a check-cashing facility. Unfortunately, the bank did not take advantage of the situation to encourage people to save by advertising campaigns and gimmicks, which would probably have worked well. Instead, the bank depended entirely on individual initiative for support. Those people who had long established accounts in Nebraska banks left them where they were rather than transferring funds. The new bank was not open on Saturdays, which proved a real inconvenience. Finally, the bank arrived at the position where it did not have enough cash on hand to cash paychecks; the parent bank soon decided not to continue support of the Pine Ridge branch in the red, and it was closed at the end of 1971.

The fate of the bank is unfortunate. If it had been able to hold out for the first years while losing money but gaining clientele, it probably could in time have shown a good profit as well as substantially benefited the reservation. In particular, the bank could have developed a number of local businesses by using the services of SBA. By judiciously choosing a few local people to support in business, it might have made a substantial start in promoting local commerce.

A bank may yet be possible in Pine Ridge, but to be successful the tribe, as well as the bureau, if at all possible, would have to use its services. Only in such a way could enough capital be kept on hand for loans and constructive purposes. In 1972 it was rumored on the reservation that the tribe was in the process of negotiating a large loan to establish a bank of its own. Whether such a project will be accomplished is as yet uncertain. However, its future seems precarious.

Government and Services

It has already been noted that the government and services sector of the economy is by far the largest. Approximately 40 percent of Pine Ridge households are employed in this sector (EDA 1970: 21). Yet these services are undeniably inadequate. A certain number of jobs and limited services are provided, but they do not seem to repay the great amount of money put into them.

The transportation system is an outstanding example. The BIA has only two major reasons for building roads: to provide school bus routes and access to off-reservation services. Clearly a more efficient transportation system is needed to stimulate a reservation development. A public bus system would allow centralization of services on the reservation at Pine Ridge and would encourage reservation business, which would greatly profit the economy.

In other areas — education and health care being two notorious examples — quality is quite poor despite a large outlay of funds and effort. The answer seems to lie in giving the Oglala people control over the planning and carrying out of services. What is true of federal government programs is also true of the many other agencies that operate social programs on the reservation. State government, tribal programs, and private social welfare agencies are all aimed at providing services without real initiative from the Oglala themselves.

Tourism

The fourth economic sector, revenues generated by developing tourism, remains as yet only a potential. Located between two popular tourist areas, the Badlands and the Black Hills, Pine Ridge undoubtedly does have some potential for tourism, although it is located off the interstate highway route that connects these two major tourist attractions. Tourism has long been considered a potential source of income for the reservation, but little has ever been done about it. The curious tourist who drives out of his way to see the reservation sees little beyond poverty and poor roads.

The Oglala Sioux tribe took a significant step in developing tourism by assuming the lease of the concession at Cedar Pass, the information center for Badlands National Monument. During the summer of 1972, the tribe hired a manager — the same man who used to run the Pine Ridge bank—and staffed the restaurants, sales shop, and camp ground. Most of the staff are Oglalas. The shop was stocked with beadwork and other craft items purchased from the Taopi Cikala co-op in Kyle — an arts and crafts shop that has been successful during its short existence but which has suffered from lack of publicity because it is far from the usual tourist routes. The tribal lease on the concession still has one more year to run, after which it may or may not be renewed.

In coordination with this venture to win the tourist trade, the Oglala Sioux tribe was granted $50,000 by EDA to conduct a feasibility study for the proposed Oglala Sioux Cultural Park. This park would incorporate parts of the land returned by the Aerial Gunnery Range with the Badlands National Monument. The Oglalas could use the park as a forum for interpreting Sioux culture to visitors and also capitalize on the tourist trade; the EDA planning program at Pine Ridge is considering the construction of a luxury motel, with an adjoining campground and cultural and historical attractions. A tipi village and a reconstruction of Fort Phil Kearney have been suggested. Presumably the Sun Dance would also attract more visitors if accommodations were available.

It is difficult to assess the potential of these ventures. Many feel that the tourist potential of the reservation is quite low, while others point to the fact that the Badlands are the top tourist attraction in the state. The Badlands areas inside the reservation are truly more spectacular than those areas now in the national park, but the problem lies in the possibility of developing these to the point of attracting tourists in their campers and air-conditioned cars. Clearly, a very expensive road-building project would be required. And, unless the Oglala evince a real desire to attract and satisfy tourists, such projects are doomed to failure. Oglala feelings towards tourists seem ambivalent. Most Indians seem to be more or less neutral when asked, but one hears complaints about tourists who drive past gawking, cameras clicking. Rosebud reservation has been developing its tourist facilities during recent years and has evidently had some success. The greatest enthusiasm has come from foreign, particularly European visitors, who evince much interest in Indians, and who are willing to spend considerable sums on quality beadwork and other craft items.

Pine Ridge has also developed a program catering to sportsmen. An area of land near Allen has been fenced in as the Oglala Sioux game range and is stocked with buffalo, elk, and other game. During the fall of 1972 the tribe organized a program to provide guides to white hunters for the hunting of buffalo and elk. Fees ranged from $1,000 for a packaged hunt for a bull buffalo or elk, down to $100 for a license to shoot a cow elk. This program is being run by the Oglala Sioux rangers, a group of tribal employees whose jobs center around range management. Some of the rangers were employed at the Badlands National Monument during the summer of 1972. The financial success of the fall hunts is not known, but certainly it can never provide any considerable income. With no services or goods available on the reservation, hunters, like tourists, will not generate much income for the area.

THEMES IN PINE RIDGE ECONOMY

A number of themes emerged during the course of this study that directly relate to economic concerns on Pine Ridge; they are outlined in the following discussion. To be appreciated, they must be considered within their total historical and cultural context as parts of the larger picture of Pine Ridge reservation.

Dependency

Dependence on the government of the United States for economic support is probably the most obvious theme. This dependence has a long history, traceable to earliest reservation days. At that time the Sioux felt that they had, albeit against their will, traded the old way of life for reservation life. They doubtless firmly believed that the government would support them indefinitely. This was not gratuitous support, but the Indians' just due for loss of lands and source of subsistence.

Through the years, this dependent attitude has remained the major orientation of conservative reservation Indians. Some, like the council of traditional leaders, put their efforts into attempting to get the government to pay for the Black Hills. In theory, this would provide enough money to make the Oglala rich, and their dependence on whites would then cease. In the meantime, all there was to do was to wait and keep pressing the claims case.

Dependence on the federal government has resulted in the establishment of a service-oriented economy on Pine Ridge. The Oglala are not recipients of negotiable money but rather of essential goods and services selected for them by the government. These include health care, house building, commodity foods, educational facilities, and so forth. Such a service economy tends to maintain the status quo; development does not occur.

Lack of Tribal Unity

The tribal structure of the reservation as an imposed system of representative democracy does not fit the cultural ideals of the Oglala. During the reservation period the first tribal council, established by Indians on their own initiative and modelled on an elective system, was "dissolved" by the reservation agent who refused to recognize its legitimacy. Later attempts to elect a tribal government were dominated by the mixed-blood element of the reservation and were systematically opposed by full bloods. Even today the IRA tribal constitution and tribal council are the subject of much harsh criticism. The term "the tribe" is used conversationally to mean "the tribal council" — which is understood to be a body of politicians each out for his own welfare.

The Oglala Sioux tribe lacks popular support. It would seem that recent trends to decentralize and delegate much of the responsibility to lower-level district and community organizations are the only way to increase the effectiveness of self-government on the reservation. At the tribal level conflicts are too intense and too many: mixed bloods against full bloods, townspeople against rural people, Pine Ridge town against the districts, BIA supporters against independents.

Measures initiated at a tribal level are distrusted at the community level. Local people cannot seem to muster enthusiasm for projects imposed on them from above. This reflects a general cultural emphasis on the role of the individual and his importance in shaping his own life. Small groups of people, nearly always relatives, want to join together and work in common to improve their economic situation. However, money is never readily available at the local level, whereas the formal tribal government can easily obtain large grants and loans. When the tribe receives such grants, it does not want to parcel them out to the districts.

In the long run, development projects tend to be tribal enterprises. No matter how successful, these soon lose the support of the people. The Sioux Nation Shopping Center and the Oglala Irrigation Project Cattle Enterprise are both good examples. Both projects were initiated by the tribe, with government funds, as attempts to improve local economy. Both have ended up without popular support. The shopping center has been leased to a white-owned corporation, and the only economic benefit accruing to the Oglala people is in the form of the wages earned by the few Oglala who work there. The irrigation project began as an attempt to provide irrigated farm lands as well as grazing lands to a number of families near Oglala, South Dakota. However, the project developed into a tribal enterprise and the profits are simply shuttled back into the farm or into tribal operational expenses, without any direct benefit to the people.

Management

Management has always been a particularly acute problem. There are few Indians anywhere trained to handle the major projects that need to be managed — shopping center, factory, planning center, bank, irrigation project, and so forth. The general pattern seems to be to try an Indian manager for a while and, when he fails to make a quick success of the operation, simply to hire a white manager from outside at a higher salary.

The problems of management are both educational and cultural. Certainly more Oglala need advanced training in order to learn how to function in managerial capacities within organizations modeled on those of white culture, whether a bureaucracy, a factory, a bank, a ranch, or a store. In such situations the Oglala manager will have to come to grips with the Dakota cultural system which dictates that every man is completely independent and equal and that no one has the right to tell anybody else what to do. To fill such a position, the Oglala manager is in a difficult situation, because he has to mediate between two opposing cultural systems. It is little wonder that such managerial positions are usually filled by whites or by mixed bloods who operate comfortably within white culture. In either case, to make a success of the operation with more traditionally oriented Oglalas, the manager must manage by suggestion, example, or praise, and be constantly attuned to conflicts of values.

On the other hand, still lacking at Pine Ridge are organizations based on traditional models and traditional types of leadership — leadership founded on personal loyalty of the followers, based on kinship, or charisma, or, simply, ability. These are the types of organization that might prove most successful and that would probably be very effective at the local level. But they are also gambles from the point of view of funding, and so far, despite the stakes, funding agencies have not been willing to take the risk.

Leadership

Part of the problem lies in the nature of leadership. Throughout the last century the Oglala have had impressed upon them the fact that they are incapable of running their own affairs. From the beginning of the reservation period, agents, later superintendents, have done everything in their power to suppress native leadership, which was seen as reactionary and dangerous. As long as the simple model of leading the Indians from their former way of life to "civilization" — understood as a Christian, agrarian society composed of economically independent families — remained the paradigm in which the BIA operated, any possibility of native leadership or group organization was seen as a threat to "progress." The educational system of the reservation reinforced the belief that Indians were too incompetent to think for themselves. The emphasis on mechanical and manual skills, and the system of rote learning of irrelevant knowledge, as well as the enforced competition of the school environment, likely discouraged many a potentially interested student. Provided with the basic necessities of life, Indian children were simply taught to play along with the system.

The earlier off-reservation boarding schools utilized harsh means to break their pupils of their native language and culture. Many of these students, now older generation, learned to speak English quite well, but the psychological cost was disastrous. They were taught that the greatest success lay in rejecting the reservation and attempting to achieve a pattern of life in harmony with white culture. It demanded no less than total cultural surrender.

The later on-reservation schools have been somewhat less harsh, but many of their students have not even obtained a fundamental speaking knowledge of English. At the same time, many are also inadequate in their native tongue. A greater condemnation of an educational system cannot be imagined.

The Oglala leader of today is one who has succeeded against all odds. He is a person who must combine traditional values of leadership — such as generosity, noncompetitiveness, and the ability to mediate harmoniously among all his followers — with the expectations of representativeness, efficiency, and effectiveness demanded by the white world. This is not a new dilemma: it is as old as the earliest contact between the United States and the Oglala, as old as the act of presentation of peace medals by Lewis and Clark to duly authorized "chiefs." Political factionalism, so characteristic of the nineteenth-century Oglala undoubtedly has its roots in patterns of "chieftainship" imposed by white traders, government officials, and military men. At least during the nineteenth century the patterns of leadership enjoyed an unbroken continuity with the past; each generation could look to its parents and grandparents for models of effective leadership. With the gap in effective leadership from the late nineteenth century to the present, today's Oglala leaders have no such immediate models. They are much more their own men, consciously and individually forging models of how to lead out of the values of traditional Sioux culture, reservation Sioux culture, and white culture, as they understand it.

With a heritage of factionalism, of lack of effective leadership to deal with the white world, and with the individual inventiveness demanded of the Sioux leader, it is little wonder that political quarrels are fierce, personal, and incessant on Pine Ridge today.

Multiple Planning Agencies

Formerly the various planning agencies on Pine Ridge, particularly the tribe, the BIA, EDA, OEO, and Department of Labor and Commerce programs, operated independently without any coordination. Duplication of effort was frequent. Today the planning center exists to coordinate these activities, and probably it will do much good. The extent of the remediable confusion may be suggested by noting that when I returned during the summer of 1972 to Pine Ridge, with a copy of an EDA planning document written a year before, it was treated as a resource, and it was borrowed by a center member in order to be xeroxed. Some members of the center seemed familiar with the document (OST 1971), but apparently the only copies had been forwarded to Washington or were otherwise lost.

Lack of Continuity

Lack of continuity in development programs is another frequently cited complaint. This may partly be blamed on the electoral system which replaces some 80 percent of tribal officials every two years, a procedure which is certainly not conducive to continuity. Moreover, given the nature of political behavior on the reservation, each administration seems to try its best to destroy any gains made by the previous administration.

However, it seems clear that merely making the term of office longer would not help the situation appreciably. The problem is a much deeper one, whose roots are in the general cultural conceptions of government on the reservation. Again the solution seems to be to seek continuity at a lower level: the district and community levels. This is the function of the new planning center. It is primarily conceived of as a coordinating center for the district planning commissions.

Lack of Profit Incentive

Finally, there seems little doubt that the economic system of Pine Ridge reservation is vastly different from that of general American culture. For the Sioux, economic profit is not a general cultural concept; expediency is more highly regarded. At an individual level, a $50 saddle bought one day may be sold the next for $10 if money is in demand, whether for some "serious" purpose or just to have a good time. The economic system of the reservation is not oriented toward profit.

Moreover, because of the reality of extended kinship ties, an individual finds that any money which he accumulates is not his own. The moral system of kin relationship demands that an individual share with his relatives or be branded as a sell-out to the white man's way. There is little doubt that this is one contributing factor to the greater relative economic poverty of full-blood households as contrasted with mixed bloods, who have adopted white American economic values.

Largely because the Oglala have never fully participated in the cash economy of the Middle West, they lack the skills and concepts necessary to function in such an economic system. Money takes on the aspect of a commodity to be bartered, rather than an asset of fixed value to be accumulated for protection against future need. The concept of an economic surplus is foreign to the Oglala today. Old values, particularly kinship values, remain paramount; money, however, has not found a place in the hierarchy of values.

PROSPECT

Poverty, as we have said, appears to be the keynote of reservation life for the people of Pine Ridge. The HUD study reported a median family income of $1,910 for Indian families on Pine Ridge in fiscal year 1966–1967. For the same year, it estimated that the total cost of social services provided to Indians on Pine Ridge was $8,080 per household (HUD 1969 1: 1). Despite this, the people are poor.

It is easy to conclude that poverty has become a way of life for the Oglala and that Pine Ridge should be approached as any other "culture of poverty." After all, poor people everywhere are forced to make out on less than enough, and everywhere they have developed similar strategies for dealing with those who have more than enough. Such an approach isolates poverty, defined simply as lack of money and lack of economic opportunities, and takes it as the cause of complex social and cultural situations.

However, a real understanding of the economic problems of Pine Ridge reservation is vastly different from that of general American domain of reservation life. This is precisely the weakness of prepackaged economic development programs whose goal is to stamp out poverty by applying the only known antedote: money. In traditional Oglala society, as in any tribal or folk society, all aspects of everyday life have some economic component. A defining feature of this type of society is the lack of institutional specialization. Western culture has taught us to differentiate economic, political, religious, and social activities as independent categories. Western white culture is based on a belief that man lives in an environment that is both impersonal and hostile. This view of the world is antithetical to Sioux thought, which does not isolate everyday activities into categories based on function. All relationships are face-to-face, on a personal level, and are multifunctional. For every individual, the entire universe is approached as an intensely personal presence.

The contrast between American Indian apperceptions of reality and those of contemporary white American culture could hardly be more striking. This is very clearly seen by comparing conceptions of bureaucracy. The impersonalized bureaucracies that impinge on every aspect of our daily lives merely reflect our understanding of an impersonal universe operating according to invariant physical laws. In contrast, the traditional Indian tries to approach bureaucracy on a personal level, as he would approach any other aspect of his universe.

For example, we see in the Bureau of Indian Affairs at Pine Ridge a complex structure whose function is to administer BIA programs on the reservation. Its effectiveness depends on its efficiency, and we demand that every individual who fills a role in the bureau structure should do so faithfully and thoroughly, within the confines of the job assigned to him. The traditionally oriented Oglala sees the same bureaucracy as the mediating link between himself and the president of the United States and attempts to deal with it as such. The BIA bureaucracy, however, does not consist of people who take a diffuse interest in every individual Oglala, but is rather a passive, impersonal structure composed of individuals with narrowly prescribed roles. Simply finding the right office, the right role bearer, to answer a question or file a claim can be a major task. For the Sioux, the bureau is the epitome of the white man's world.

White Americans know instinctively, as part of their culture, that bureaucracies are man-made and that, at least in theory, they can be controlled and shaped by individuals. Real people must, necessarily, fill the roles, and two role bearers in the system can and will interact with one another simultaneously at formal and personal levels. In the most tightly-run office, there is always someone who will treat a confused and unsure outsider with a degree of humanity not specified in his job description. Bureaucracy is an important part of American cultural history, an integral part of our heritage of literacy. We have learned to adapt to it as a useful mechanism for organizing nearly every aspect of life.

To the Sioux, however, bureaucracy is a relatively new phenomenon. The people of Pine Ridge have not chosen a bureaucratic organization on their own, but have had it forced upon them. They are still learning how to deal with it. Those Oglala who have joined the bureaucracy have done so with a deadly seriousness.

Nowhere is this clearer than in the reservation system of law and order, the tribal police force, and the tribal courts. These are the oldest bureaucratic organizations on the reservation in which Oglalas have filled all the major roles. The Oglala policeman or judge, generally speaking, compares with his average American counterpart as a model of conservatism. A boy may be imprisoned for a month for illegal drinking (in the name of morality), yet unscrupulous bootleggers (a traditional institution on the reservation) go unnoticed. The Pine Ridge police are prototypes of what the young in contemporay America call "pigs"; at Pine Ridge, during the siege of Wounded Knee in 1973, they were called (tribal president) "Wilson's goon squad." But they were only doing their duty, upholding the law and order of the reservation to the degree that outside intervention, on the part of United States federal marshals would allow.

Pine Ridge bureaucracy is highly institutionalized, rigid, and generally ineffective. White America has given the Oglala the rulebooks, but it has not passed along the associated cultural heritage. There is little doubt that, while most of the Sioux do not like bureaucratic organizations, some do play along with the system for their own good and for the good of their people or even try to effect changes. Others reject the system and refuse to cooperate; their contribution is to stall for time, waiting for the system to change, or simply to disappear. The bureaucratic system itself, as it exists on Pine Ridge today, is probably the primary cause of structural paralysis on the reservation.

In the past, the effectiveness of Indian bureaucracy was a moot point, since the BIA ran all the affairs of the reservation anyway. The obvious lack of unity and common goal orientation on the part of the Oglala merely fostered an ever-more paternalistic attitude on the part of the bureau. The BIA mouthed sentiments of Indian self-determination, but at the same time effectively prevented it. Today, at last, self-determination seems to have become a real policy of the bureau. The bureau is seen as receding into more of an advisory role, allowing the Oglala to administer their own affairs. What is manifestly clear is that the Oglala, despite their long apprenticeship under the BIA, have not learned the skills necessary to run their reservation in a rational way.

This failure may be interpreted as a failure of the system, not as a failure of the Oglala. If the Oglala cannot, or will not, adapt to the usual bureaucratic systems of white America, we must ask the obvious question: why should they have to? Why not develop alternate forms that may be more applicable to the situation at Pine Ridge?

It may be thought that the Sioux have no alternate forms for developing out of their traditional culture. This is greatly to underestimate the inventiveness of preliterate peoples. The Oglala political system in traditional times was a complicated and sophisticated form of social organization that proved resilient enough to allow the Teton tribes to survive as cultural and political entities during a very long period of tremendously disorganizing and disheartening wars with the United States. A reconsideration of the traditional jural forms (see subsection on "Political Order" in the section on "Cultural Background") can prove inspiring. Figure 3 restates the traditional form and provides, I think, a possible model for a redevelopment of tribal or local governmental or other organizational forms on the Sioux reservations.

This is not necessarily to suggest that the present tribal government should be abolished or that the Bureau of Indian affairs should be

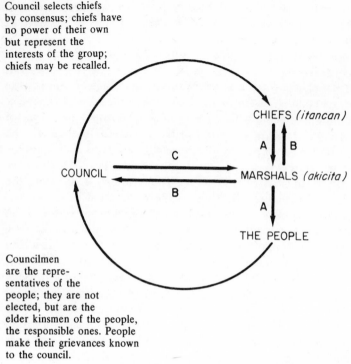

Council selects chiefs
by consensus; chiefs have
no power of their own
but represent the
interests of the group;
chiefs may be recalled.

CHIEFS *(itancan)*

A | B

C

COUNCIL

MARSHALS *(akicita)*

B

A

THE PEOPLE

Councilmen
are the repre-
sentatives of the
people; they are not
elected, but are the
elder kinsmen of the people,
the responsible ones. People
make their grievances known
to the council.

A. Authority expressed in terms of
kinship; chiefs are fathers, marshals
are elder brothers to the people.

B. Councilmen and chiefs are under the
jurisdiction of the marshals, just
as are all of the people, once the
marshals have received clear directives
from the Council, either through the
chiefs or directly.

C. Council approves selection of marshals
by the chiefs, may punish them for
misconduct, and may remove them at will.

Figure 3.   Model of traditional Oglala jural organization

reorganized on Pine Ridge. In one form or another, these bureaucratic structures are probably necessary to effectively coordinate Pine Ridge with the federal government. Even if, in the course of their history, the Oglala have not been a tribe *per se*, this identity has been largely accepted by them today, and it is probable that they can effectively build on a "tribal" basis. It provides the necessary corporate identity to deal with the outside world.

Internally, decentralization appears to be the most likely avenue of success. There is no reason why the Oglala cannot develop lower-level structures after their own models, innovating as they progress. The Crazy Horse Planning Commission has the potential to aid in this development. We have seen that lower-level projects involving smaller groups of people, all of whom are directly and actively represented, probably form the real development potential for the reservation. A strong point is the persistence of the kinship system to provide an organization for traditionally oriented communities — precisely those which are least likely to successfully use white bureaucratic models. This suggests that the society itself is the basic resource of the reservation. The idea is not new (Thompson 1951: 92), but, practically, it has never before been taken seriously. An exception, perhaps, was the development project at Red Shirt Table during the 1930's, an experiment that for its time was relatively successful. Its downfall, as we saw, was an historical accident—the intervention of World War II — and in the fact that the BIA has assumed all the managerial roles.

This approach to Pine Ridge development overcomes the traditional problems of lack of tribal unity and clearly stated tribal goals. Allowing each community, or self-detained group of any kind, the freedom to develop along lines of its own selection, with active support in the form of capital or whatever from the central tribal government, would not insure a uniform economic progress on every part of the reservation. But it would insure individual dignity, the right of the individual to work for the benefit of his family as he saw fit, and, of course, the right of every individual and group to take gambles and make mistakes. Funding such programs might seem to be expensive, but in the long run would probably be cheaper than the present system. What is more important is that it appears as a real remedy for the most deadly social problem on the reservation: apathy.

Economic development on Pine Ridge may be conceived of as a process that would upgrade both the social and material quality of reservation life without sacrificing Indian identity. It must be approached not as a break with the past, but rather, a development out of it. It is clear that economic development must be approached as a much broader program of social development. It is equally clear that no outsiders, whether white or Indians, are in a position to dictate or even to suggest to the people of Pine Ridge the lines along which their society should develop. To do so is both a moral wrong and a tactical error.

Instead, the many government agencies now providing social services to Pine Ridge need to concentrate more specifically on large-scale projects, capital development programs that may have no short-run economic return to individuals or to the tribe as corporate group.

Economic development cannot be thought of as a process of feeding money, and equivalent services, into the Pine Ridge economy until the common level of each family rises to some minimum standard. We already know that this will not work.

What can be done is to provide the Oglala with real opportunities for development by supplying them with capital, as needed, and with special privileges, as clearly spelled out in treaty agreements. At the same time, professional expertise, if and when needed, must be made available in an advisory capacity. Monetary grants must be provided in such a way that they may be subdivided and parceled out to smaller groups for local development projects. Attention must be paid to all aspects of the reservation that directly affect the economy, even if they have no immediately measurable economic returns — things like road improvement, street paving, lighting systems, transportation systems, communication systems, and educational and social facilities.

Development goals must not be aimed only at the survival of the Oglala in the modern world, rather the Oglala must be accorded the respect and integrity necessary to allow them to develop in their own terms. White America defines development in terms of progress — change. The Oglala do not share this conception of development. For them change is seen as bad, the usual white-man's plot underlying every seemingly well-intentioned plan, an attempt to change them from Indians to white men. For the Oglala, development instead means continuity, developing slowly, perhaps, but harmoniously. They have made their choice. From this point of view the structural paralysis that we have suggested for the reservation has been beneficial; it has served as a mechanism to stall what has frequently been seen as the inevitable final result, the destruction of the Oglala as a culture, the stripping of a people of their identity. The time is long overdue to stop playing games with the people of Pine Ridge and to work with them on their own terms. We must trust that their resilience as a people has outlasted our ill-conceived campaign to neutralize them in the melting pot, which, no matter how culturally real it may have been for the American dream, has always in reality been a myth.

EPILOGUE: WOUNDED KNEE 1973[5]

On February 27, 1973, a group of American Indians under the leadership of members of the American Indian Movement (AIM) entered the community of Wounded Knee on the Pine Ridge reservation and declared it "liberated." Carrying guns (which they did not use

[5] Information for this discussion is taken from new stories reprinted in *Akwesasne Notes* (1973).

except to shoot out the street lighting) the "invaders" took over the Catholic church, the trading post and store, and the houses of various whites and Indians living nearby. These people (eleven in number) became *de facto* "hostages" until it became clear, some days later, that most of them did not intend to leave, and, in any case, would not be detained from doing so. The "militants" retained control of Wounded Knee for seventy days, until May 8.

The selection of Wounded Knee for staging a protest was a careful and excellent choice. For Indians, particularly the Sioux, Wounded Knee has always been a symbol of defeat by the whites and of white brutality. It was here in 1890, not so very long ago, that two to three hundred Sioux men, women, and children were killed by the United States Army in a military action that can only be labeled a "massacre." For whites, Wounded Knee had always suggested the last battle of the Indian wars. Recently, however, the popularity of Dee Brown's *Bury my heart at Wounded Knee* (1970) transformed Wounded Knee into an equally powerful symbol for whites, connoting not only the unjust treatment of the American Indians by whites, but also the brutality of war and the participation of the United States Army in acts of unquestionable immorality. The parallel with the massacre at My Lai and the general similarity of the Indian wars to the undeclared war in Vietnam undoubtedly were important factors in the overnight popularity of the book. The time was ripe for the conscious use of Wounded Knee as a symbol that would speak equally effectively to both Indians and whites.

During the siege of Wounded Knee, while two to four hundred Indians held the village against an encircling force of a like number of United States federal agents, marshals, and BIA Indian police, the news media played a large part in shaping events. Perhaps without them the federal forces would simply have swept through the village, crushing the militants and ending the affair at the very beginning. But the adverse publicity would have been untenable. Again, the similarities to the war in Vietnam were too striking.

On the whole, the press and other news media had already taken the side of AIM before the struggle began. Following up on the Trail of Broken Treaties, the seizure of the BIA headquarters in Washington in 1972, as well as more recent publicity concerning the plight of American Indians as a discriminated minority in American life, American public opinion was ready to believe that Indian complaints were genuine. Moreover, they needed a scapegoat, and the BIA as a government agency was simply too impersonal to function in that capacity. Taking up the cry of the liberators of Wounded Knee, the press turned on Richard Wilson, mixed-blood president of the Oglala Sioux tribe, as a suitable scapegoat on whom to blame the problems of the reservation. He became, in the press, a symbol of the BIA. As a result, the "legitimate" tribal government was never given a fair hearing by the news media. In the media, it was supported only by the radical right. It is safe to say that the entire media record of the siege of Wounded Knee is one-sided, incomplete, and unreliable. In particular, news coverage emphasized the national significance of AIM's participation in this militant action and failed to consider the event fully from the point of view of the Pine Ridge people as a whole. To attempt to do this here would be to return to the historical and cultural perspectives we have already outlined for Pine Ridge economy. From now on, to approach any aspect of Pine Ridge, we shall have to consider the effects of the Wounded Knee take-over of 1973.

Two aspects of the events leading up to the take-over of Wounded Knee must be distinguished: first, the recent activities of AIM; second, the growing political problems on Pine Ridge reservation. The link between these two was Russell Means, the national coordinator of AIM and a resident of Pine Ridge.

There had been a growing national concern for the situation of American Indians. Part of this was caused by the activities of AIM; they focused attention on incidents of discrimination and harassment. On January 14, 1973, a Chicano-Indio unity conference held in Scotts Bluff, Nebraska, was disrupted by the local police's arrest of Means and other AIM members. In the press, it appeared as a clear case of harassment. Early on the morning of January 21, in a completely unrelated incident, an Oglala named Wesley Bad Heart Bull was killed by a local white in the crossroads town of Buffalo Gap, South Dakota, near the Pine Ridge reservation. Indian witnesses claimed cold blooded murder; the defendant claimed self-defence. Anti-Indian sentiment being an old part of the general white culture of western South Dakota, the possibility of a fair trial seemed remote. When the court charged the defendant with second-degree manslaughter (later, in May, the defendant was found not guilty) instead of murder, AIM stepped in. AIM declared February 6 a day of mourning for Wesley Bad Heart Bull and called for a peaceful demonstration in Custer, South Dakota, the county seat. Custer also is charged with symbolic value for Indians, who are sensitive to the irony of naming a town in the Black Hills (an area believed sacred by the Sioux) after the archetype of Indian fighters. Some two hundred demonstrators came to Custer and assembled at the courthouse, where they wished to make their grievances regarding the killing known. They were met by armed police, and a confrontation occurred that saw brutality, many arrests, and an attempt to burn down the courthouse. Western South Dakota armed itself as if expecting another Indian war, and spontaneous riots by Indians followed in Rapid City on February 9. The racial situation was tense; both sides were waiting for the slighest event to trigger violence.

During this same period, the Pine Ridge reservation was experiencing political problems. The current tribal president, Richard Wilson, was out of favor with a significant number of powerful reservation politicians. Wilson represents the younger, white-oriented mixed-blood population of the reservation who feel that the Sioux have been trying for too long to pretend that they are still living in the last century. He represents the entire mixed-blood segment of the population that has developed over the course of more than a century of intermarriage, and he represents as well a commitment to the present system of tribal government as organized under the IRA during the early 1930's.

Opposed to Wilson is an interesting coalition of other interests. Most vocal are the old-timers, the treaty council members who still oppose the IRA constitution, claim that it was never fairly adopted by the tribe and that the elected government is therefore illegal. Joined with them, generally speaking, are all the full bloods, those more traditionally oriented people who feel that Wilson's strategies do not reflect their interests. Lending more support to this side are a large number of young people on the reservation, both full and mixed blood, who are consciously trying to strengthen their bonds with traditional Sioux culture, and who feel that Wilson is a sell-out to the whites. All of these people are united by their suspicions that Wilson was unfairly elected and that his administration is rife with graft and nepotism. They are particularly resentful, too, of the large number of extra police who have been deputized by Wilson to prepare for possible trouble because of AIM threats to invade Pine Ridge. Finally, many of these people are sympathetic to AIM, though few are actually members.

The dissatisfied people of Pine Ridge began preparations to impeach Wilson. They planned to present the impeachment motion to the tribal council at its meeting on February 16, but at the last moment Wilson, using bad weather as his excuse, postponed the meeting by a week. By this time, over 80 federal agents had already arrived at Pine Ridge, and Wilson was deputizing a large police force. The reasons for these actions were not clear. A week later, on February 21, over 500 people met at Pine Ridge to consider impeachment. However, during the ensuing council meeting, Wilson waived the usual twenty-day waiting period that would have given both sides time to prepare their cases and demanded an immediate hearing. Five of the councilmen walked out in protest, and the council gave a 14–0 vote of confidence to president Wilson.

Previously, AIM representative Clyde Bellecourt had offered AIM support if the Oglala could not rid themselves of the "tyrannical" Wilson government. Now the newly organized reservation civil rights organization, together with the old treaty council and the land-owners association, invited AIM to come to Pine Ridge to aid them in their efforts. AIM responded wholeheartedly, and the result was the take-over of Wounded Knee.

The exact identification of the militants at Wounded Knee was always problematical. Wilson claimed they were all Communist-inspired agitators, outsiders, some Indians, others Chicanos, whites (some Russians), and blacks. He claimed that fewer than one hundred Oglalas supported AIM. The United States officials favored his view. From the very first, however, AIM claimed the three hundred to four hundred invaders to be mostly Oglalas and made it very clear that the take-over was not AIM's idea, but had been planned by the Oglalas themselves.

It is difficult to determine why the situation at Wounded Knee remained stalemated for so long. The militant demands as reported by newspapers on the first day of the take-over revolved around an investigation of the relations between the Oglala Sioux tribe and the BIA and Department of Interior, the right of the Oglalas to elect tribal officials who truly represent their interests, and a Senate investigation of Indian treaties. None of these demands were unreasonable, and all could have been sensibly and quickly agreed on. But using the excuse that human lives (those of the hostages) were endangered by a fanati-cal radical group, the government ringed the village with federal men and brought in the accoutrements of war. It was as if the government intended to reenact the massacre at Wounded Knee all over again and, having gotten into position, hesitated. The situation remained static, with the government men firing on the village as though it were a Communist bunker in Vietnam, while the Wounded Knee militants replied with what little fire power they could muster. Then, on March 26, a stray bullet struck a federal marshal causing serious injury. He was paralyzed from the waist down. No identification of the bullet was ever offered to determine whether it had come from the Wounded Knee defenders, or whether it had come, as the militants claimed, from a federal gun fired either by another federal agent or by a member of the Indian police, Wilson's "goons."

On April 5, after thirty-eight days, an agreement was signed by both the AIM leaders and representatives of the federal government. It essentially capitulated to the earlier demands, narrowing the treaty investigation to include only treaties with the Sioux, promising an audit of the Oglala Sioux tribe and an investigation of local civil rights cases. It was promised that Means and other AIM leaders would meet immediately with White House officials to negotiate the details of the evacuation of the village. Once in Washington, however, the White

House refused to meet with AIM leaders, perhaps partly because of the burgeoning problems of Watergate.

Meanwhile, tragedy struck at Wounded Knee. On April 17, a man who called himself Frank Clearwater and who claimed to be an Apache Indian was wounded by federal fire as he lay sleeping inside the church. He died on April 25. Two days later an Oglala named Lawrence Lamont was also killed at Wounded Knee by federal fire. It seems that it was only at this point, after real bloodshed, that the traditional Oglala leaders, the treaty council men, stepped in to take an active part in the negotiations. Up until then they had allowed the younger people to act as go-betweens in the negotiations; probably they felt themselves very much removed from the young militants whom they had invited to come to their reservation. An agreement was reached soon after, and the occupation of Wounded Knee came to an end on May 8. The terms were those of the April 5 agreement. In essence, the reservation returned to the status quo. Wilson remained in power, and, for the present nothing had changed.

But there were losses. In terms of money, the trading post and the churches of Wounded Knee were total losses. The BIA estimated $240,000 in damages to private homes in the area, and the federal government estimated a spending of five to seven million dollars during the Wounded Knee affair. (What if that money had been channeled into useful projects for the reservation population at large?) On the human side, the population of Wounded Knee, which had been exiled, had to move back and reclaim their homes, making a new start. Two were dead, several injured. The press had turned sour on the whole affair, discouraged by the secrecy and ineffectiveness of the long negotiations, angry at the waste of taxpayer's money, and attracted east by the complexities of Watergate. It remains to be seen whether the results will be worth the cost. But the fact of Wounded Knee cannot now be denied, and perhaps the government will be more careful in its Indian dealings in the future. It cannot afford any more bad publicity of this magnitude.

As of September, 1973, the situation at Pine Ridge remains little changed. The traditionally oriented Oglala still feel that their government is in the hands of half breeds who have sold out to the whites. They are unsatisfied with the form of government and feel excluded from running their own affairs. They feel that the tribal council has taken on powers never allotted to it by the people, and they are angry. The situation is not new, only aggravated by recent events. On the other hand, the mixed bloods feel that the reservation has been invaded by Communist infiltrators who prey on the "backwards" tendencies of the uneducated full bloods. They feel themselves to be in the right, leading the reservation progressively forward. They are relatively unconcerned with traditional culture. Their attitude was succinctly characterized by Wilson: "Culture is fine, but it don't feed you. You have to be in tune with the times" (*Akwesasne Notes* 1973: v (3), 33).

The tribal election of 1974 is fast approaching, and Russell Means has announced his intention to run for the office of president. If successful, he declares that he will abolish the office and help in constructing a new form of government for the reservation, one more in line with traditional methods of government. Wilson, on the other hand, promises to keep Means' name off the ballot. The outcome is uncertain, but it seems clear that the people of Pine Ridge have learned that in the long run it is probably wiser to solve their problems on their own, without calling outside forces, be they governmental or any other. The people of Pine Ridge need to use their indentity as the Oglala Sioux tribe to work in common for the good of all segments of the reservation; divided, they lose every advantage they have in dealing with the government as a tribe. The solution to the dilemma seems to lie in its leadership. Above all, the Oglalas need tactful leaders who, like the chiefs of old, can balance the interests of each factional group and still forge coherent strategies for dealing with the problems of modern life.

REFERENCES

Akwesasne Notes
  1973   *Akwesasne Notes* 5(2, 3). Rooseveltown, N.Y.
BIA (BUREAU OF INDIAN AFFAIRS)
  1971   *Land use inventory and production record.* Bureau of Indian Affairs, Division of Economic Development, Report 50–1. Pine Ridge, South Dakota.
  1972   *Industrial Facts/Pine Ridge, South Dakota.* Columbus, Nebraska: Nebraska Public Power District. (From data supplied by the BIA).
BROWN, DEE
  1970   *Bury my heart at Wounded Knee: an Indian history of the American West.* New York: Holt, Rinehart and Winston.
BROWN, JOSEPH E.
  1953   *The sacred pipe: Black Elk's account of the seven rites of the Oglala Sioux.* Norman, Oklahoma: University of Oklahoma Press.
BUSHOTTER, GEORGE
  n.d.   *Manuscript Autobiography.* National Anthropological Archives, Smithsonian Institution, Washington, D.C.
COMMISSIONER OF INDIAN AFFAIRS
  1872– *Annual reports of the Commissioner of Indian Affairs.* Washington,
  1906   D.C.: U.S. Government Printing Office.

COMMUNITY MENTAL HEALTH CENTER
1967 *Baseline Data Survey.* (A collection of questionnaires administered to the population of Pine Ridge during the late 1960's, as well as the tabular analyses of these data.)

DELORIA, ELLA
1944 *Speaking of Indians.* New York: Friendship Press.

DEMALLIE, RAYMOND
1971 "Teton Dakota kinship and social organization." Unpublished Ph.D. dissertation, University of Chicago.

DENIG, EDWIN T.
1961 *Five Indian tribes of the Upper Missouri.* Edited by John C. Ewers. Norman, Oklahoma: University of Oklahoma Press.

DORSEY, J. OWEN
1897 Siouan sociology: a posthumous paper. *Bureau of American Ethnology Annual Report* 15: 205–244. Washington, D.C.: U.S. Government Printing Office.

EDA (ECONOMIC DEVELOPMENT ADMINISTRATION)
1970 *1970 annual report of project 06–05–15003–02.* Washington, D.C.: Economic Development Administration. (In *Economic Development Administration* 1971: 17–24.)
1971 *Semi-Annual progress report, Oglala Sioux tribe, EDA planning grant 06–05–1500s–02.* Washington, D.C.: Economic Development Administration.

FERACA, STEPHEN E.
1964 "The history and development of Oglala Sioux tribal government." Manuscript loaned by author.

GEARING, FREDERICK O.
1970 *The face of the fox.* Chicago: Aldine.

GRINNELL, IRA H.
1967 *The tribal government of the Oglala Sioux of Pine Ridge, South Dakota.* Vermillion: Governmental Research Bureau, University of South Dakota.

HUD (HOUSING AND URBAN DEVELOPMENT)
1969 *Oglala Sioux model reservation program,* twelve volumes. San Francisco: Marshall Kaplan, Gans, and Kahn. (Report to HUD.)
1972 *Final report, Urban Planning Grant Project No. South Dakota P-49.* Planning Center, Pine Ridge, South Dakota: Department of Housing and Urban Development.

HYDE, GEORGE E.
1937 *Red Cloud's folk: a history of the Oglala Sioux Indians.* Norman, Oklahoma: University of Oklahoma Press.

LAY, BRICE
1970 "Views on the Pine Ridge reservation." *Oglala War Cry* 1:16, December 28, 1970.

MACGREGOR, GORDON
1946 *Warriors without weapons: a study of the society and personality development of the Pine Ridge Sioux.* Chicago: University of Chicago Press.

MAYNARD, EILEEN, GAYLE TWISS
1969 *That these people may live: conditions among the Oglala Sioux of the Pine Ridge reservation.* Pine Ridge, South Dakota: Community Mental Health Program.

McGILLYCUDDY, JULIA
1941   *McGillycuddy: agent.* Stanford: Stanford University Press.
MEKEEL, H. SCUDDER
1936   *The economy of a modern Teton Dakota community.* Yale University Publications In Anthropology, Number 6. New Haven: Yale University Press.
NEIHARDT, JOHN G.
1930   Interview with Black Elk. Manuscript collections, University of Missouri, Columbia.
1932   *Black Elk speaks: being the life story of a holy man of the Oglala Sioux.* New York: William Morrow.
OGLALA IRRIGATION PROJECT CATTLE ENTERPRISE
1968   *The social and economic effects of reservation industrial employment on Indian employees and their families.* Oglala Irrigation Project Cattle Enterprises, Missouri River Basin investigations Project, Report 189. Pine Ridge reservation, South Dakota.
1969   (Report No. 179). Oglala Irrigation Project Cattle Enterprise, Pine Ridge Reservation, South Dakota.
OGLALA SIOUX FARM AND RANCH ENTERPRISE
1971   "Plan of operations." Mimeograph. BIA, Oglala Sioux, Farm and Ranch Enterprise, Pine Ridge, South Sakota.
OST (OGLALA SIOUX TRIBE)
1971   "Extraction and modification of a project schedule from the basic 701 study recommendations." Unpublished manuscript. Washington, D.C.: EDA. (See also HUD 1969.)
Oglala War Cry
1970–   Articles in *Oglala War Cry.*
1973
Pine Ridge Research Bulletin
1968–   Public Health Service, Community Mental Health Program, Pine
1970   Ridge, South Dakota.
RADISSON, PETER ESPRIT
1885   *Voyages of Peter Esprit Redisson.* Edited by Gideon D. Scull. Boston: Prince Society.
ROBERTS, WILLIAM O.
1943   Successful agriculture within the reservation framework. *Applied Anthropology* 2: 37–44.
TABEAU, PIERRE-ANTOINE
1939   *Tabeau's narrative of Loisel's expedition to the Upper Missouri.* Edited by Annie H. Abel. Norman, Oklahoma: University of Oklahoma Press.
THOMPSON, LAURA
1951   *Personality and government: findings and recommendations of the Indian administration research.* Mexico City: Ediciones del Institute Indigenista Interamericano.
WALKER, JAMES R.
1917   The Sun Dance and other ceremonies of the Oglala division of the Teton Dakota. *Anthropological Papers of the American Museum of Natural History* 16(2).
WISSLER, CLARK
1912   Societies and ceremonial associations of the Oglala division of the Teton Dakota. *Anthropological Papers of the American Museum of Natural History* 11(1).

Passamaquoddy Economic Development in Cultural and Historical Perspective

SUSAN McCULLOCH STEVENS

CULTURAL AND HISTORICAL SETTING

The Passamaquoddy are an eastern woodlands people whose culture type was intermediate between sub-Arctic peoples to the north and agriculturalists to the south. Closely related are the Malecites of New Brunswick, the Micmacs of Nova Scotia, and the Penobscot Indians of central Maine. Archaeological evidence indicates the Passamaquoddy have inhabited their present region for at least 3,000 years and perhaps longer. Thus, unlike many Indians in America today, the Passamaquoddy live where their forebears lived, and they have a strong sense of belonging to the land.

Much of the material used in this study was gathered over a period of nearly three years while living on Indian Township Passamaquoddy reservation; therefore I would like to acknowledge my debt to innumerable Passamaquoddy, particularly those of Indian Township, for the many questions answered and the help and patience extended. Special mention must be made, though, of Mrs. Lena Brooks and Mr. George Stevens, Sr., who told me much about the old days; and of John Stevens, former tribal chief, and present state commissioner of Indian affairs, who helped me assess and understand the complex developments since the 1950's, answered hundreds of questions in formal and informal interviews, and without whose help the suggestions for future economic development programs on the Maine reservations would be far less authoritative.

Thanks are due Mr. Gregory Buesing for his information on the Wabanaki Confederacy, the Great Council Fire, and the role of the Passamaquoddy in the Revolutionary War, as well as the Seal Nose conspiracy of the early 1900's. Mr. Thomas Tureen, tribal attorney, was my primary source for materials concerning the history, progress and prospects of the Passamaquoddy land case.

Special thanks to Mr. Glenn Starbird for his additions and corrections concerning Passamaquoddy political history.

I am grateful also for access to written materials in the Maine Department of Indian Affairs, the Maine State Library in Augusta, and Bangor Public Library.

Reports of the early 1600's indicate that the Passamaquoddy were a seminomadic fishing and hunting people, who traveled within defined hunting territories in winter, converged as a unit at the spring salmon run, and lived together in a summer village (usually at Passamaquoddy Bay, part of the larger Bay of Fundy). At the summer village, agriculture was limited because of the soil characteristics and the short growing season; fish and seaweed were used as fertilizer, and beans, corn, squash, native tobacco, and other plants were grown. The summer mainstay was seafood, which was abundant, and wild fruits and vegetables. Whales, seals, and porpoises were hunted from canoes — porpoise is still a rare sort of Passamaquoddy soul food. Fish weirs reminiscent of those that appear in pictures painted in Virginia during the 1600's are still in evidence at Pleasant Point Reservation on the coast.

In the old days birch bark was the most commonly used material for everything from housing to household utensils to canoes; this region was the southernmost area of the birch-bark culture. The birch canoe made travel relatively convenient on the waterways that abound in the area, so that the rivers and lakes were akin to highways. The tribes of the area, therefore, have long been associated with particular rivers and lake chains; the St. Croix River, which serves as part of the boundary between Maine and Canada, is still associated with the Passamaquoddy, as was the St. John in earlier times.

Several types of houses were used in this transitional zone, including dome-shaped wigwams, longhouses, and conical tipis. Wigwams are still occasionally made, by hunters as overnight shelters and by children as playhouses.

Exogamous clans seem to have been prominent in early times. Today these have diminished to lineages whose members recall the former clan names but who do not practice a formal clan system.

The Passamaquoddy, who speak an Algonkian language known as Passamaquoddy-Malecite, are the only Indians left in New England who still daily use their native tongue. They are readily understood by the Malecites, less so by the Micmacs. The language is thought to be derived from a Proto-Algonkian structure with origins presumably in the Lake Ontario region and is relatively unchanged from that ancient form. English is also spoken by most people, although some old people are barely conversant in English.

The Passamaquoddy at one time belonged to the Wabanaki, or Abnaki Confederacy, and are thus referred to in some works as "Abnaki." Other names have been tacked on at various times by the French, the English, and by other Indians, and place names have also been confounded with tribal names. (Some Passamaquoddy pseudonyms are Etchimins, Openangoes, Schoodics, Unchagogs.) The Wabanaki Confederacy consisted of Algonkian-speaking tribes of New Brunswick, Nova Scotia, Maine, part of New Hampshire, and perhaps part of Quebec Province. The tribes were separate entities that united for common defense and were intimately involved in each other's political affairs. The confederacy was at war with the League of the Iroquois for many years, but eventually the two combined forces in a little-known coalition called the Great Council Fire. This organization, which by 1749 had expanded to include all the tribes east of the Great Lakes and Ohio, lasted until 1880. Incredibly, the Iroquois usually fought for the English and the Wabanakis for the French, yet the two groups remained at peace with one another. Later the same situation prevailed when the Iroquois again fought with the English, and the Wabanakis sided with the American Revolutionists. (Just how this peace was maintained from opposite sides of the fence would make an interesting study.) The Passamaquoddy finally withdrew from the Great Council Fire in the early 1800's, feeling, according to one old Passamaquoddy storyteller, that the Iroquois had gotten "too bossy." Other Wabanakis withdrew at different times, and the old confederacy seems to have simply withered away.

Today, Passamaquoddy social ties are most close with each other on the two Passamaquoddy reservations, with the Penobscots in the same state, with the Malecites, and, to a lesser extent, with the Micmacs (see Map 1).

The Passamaquoddy reservations are located fifty miles apart. Pleasant Point or Sebayick is a one-hundred-acre tract between Eastport and Perry on the coast, overlooking magnificent Passamaquoddy Bay (see Map 2). Indian Township or Medakmegook is a 23,000-acre township located inland on the Schoodic Lakes chain, which empties into the St. Croix River (see Map 3). This reservation, which consists of forests, lakes, and rivers in a quite pristine state, belongs to the whole tribe. On it are two Indian settlements, seven miles apart, known as the Strip and Peter Dana Point. This township is between Topsfield and Princeton but does not appear on most maps. Both reservations are on the Canadian border, and both are in Washington County, the nation's most easterly county.

POPULATION CHARACTERISTICS.   It has always been difficult to determine Passamaquoddy population figures, because of their migratory tendency. Many young people work in New England cities during the winter and return home in the spring, and others go to harvests in August and in the fall months. Decades may pass before a person returns home for good. But in all, there are probably about 1,300

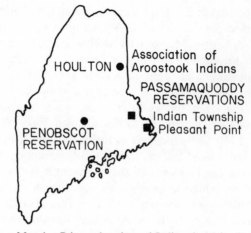

Map 1.   Primary locations of Indians in Maine in 1974

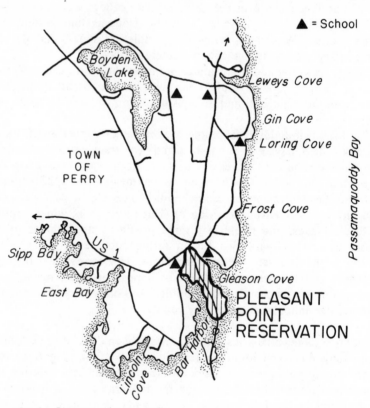

Map 2.   Pleasant point reservation

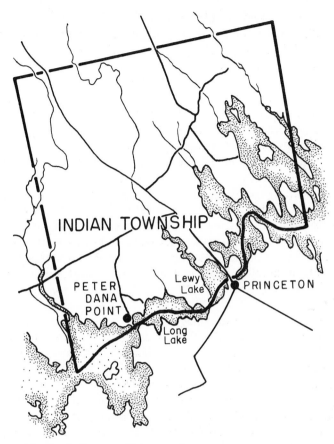

Map 3.   Indian township reservation

Passamaquoddies, both on and off the reservation. As good jobs and housing increase on the reservation, on-reservation Passamaquoddy population is slowly increasing.

At the present time the average population at Indian Township is around 300, and that at Pleasant Point around 400. The actual labor force is much smaller, however. A large percent of the total consists of children, or mothers with dependent children. Some of the population are elderly (not a large number, for it is an achievement to live to an old age in this poverty-stricken, low-health-care area). Alcoholism, a severe problem, received attention for the first time in 1972. Perhaps some of the best potential workers are working — somewhere else. But all indications are that large numbers of Passamaquoddy will return when economic development on the reservations takes hold.

PHYSICAL SETTING.   Pleasant Point reservation, the second most easterly point in the United States, faces Passamaquoddy Bay, a large bay that has some of the highest tides in the world. Ocean products are still important at this reservation, although their harvesting is no longer a big part of the economy. The reservation is curiously treeless and has been so for many years; presumably, existing trees were long ago used for firewood. Although the overall setting is magnificent, the reservation itself looks rather barren. Route 1, a main approach to the Maritime Provinces and the main coastal route in the state, borders the reservation. Because of this, Pleasant Point is potentially a good tourist stop, but it is so far undeveloped as such.

Very different in scenery and character is Indian Township, fifty miles inland. This is a heavily wooded area of spruce, fir, and tamarack, with second growth beech, birch, and maple. There are streams of enviable purity, several large fresh water lakes, and a shoreline estimated at about a hundred miles, which is almost entirely undeveloped. Because of its natural beauty, the reservation would be an ideal area for fishing, hunting, camping, and winter sports. It is completely undeveloped along these lines, except for a small but successful camping area.

RELATIONSHIP TO STATE AND FEDERAL GOVERNMENT.   The Passamaquoddy have never been under the Bureau of Indian Affairs, although currently they are lobbying to be so designated. They are not eligible in their present status for any of the services of the BIA, although occasionally a student has attended a BIA school.

When Maine was a province of Massachusetts, the Passamaquoddy were under this jurisdiction. At the separation of the two states in 1820, Maine agreed to assume the treaty obligations to the Indians formerly held by Massachusetts. The tribe had already been reduced to a little more than its present holdings. Maine has not been a good protector, but has nibbled away steadily at reservation lands, and has even assumed a fictional ownership of them. Essentially, these are the bases of an upcoming lawsuit and the source of most conflicts between the Indians and the state.

Maine has never been certain what to do about its Indians, who were supposed to "vanish" but never did. They have been under the state's governor and council, and the departments of forestry, wildlife, and health and welfare. Finally, because of Indian pressure, a State Department of Indian Affairs was formed in the 1960's to deal with the Passamaquoddy tribe and Penobscots, who are also on a state reservation. Although this was the first such state department in the country, Maine has been negligent about most other things pertaining to Indians. For example, Maine Indian people were among the last in the nation to receive the vote in national elections (1953); they received the vote in state elections that same year. In 1967 the reservations were apportioned into representative class districts, and Maine Indians could then vote for a district state representative.

Passamaquoddy pay all state taxes except individual property tax. Because some disrupted reservations lots presently in the hands of white "owners" are taxed, one could say a property tax, of sorts, is actually levied also. Indians pay federal income taxes. They can be drafted, yet, because of uncertain ownership of the land, cannot receive Veterans Administration or bank loans while residing on the reservation. This has hindered home improvements and the development of small businesses. Maine enforces all state laws on the reservations, must approve any changes in the operation of tribal government, and sends a state representative to conduct the biennial secret ballot elections on the reservations. (It does not, however, interfere with selection of candidates.) Finally, since at least 1823, there has been a tribal representative to the Maine legislature from both the Passamaquoddy and Penobscot tribes. The practice may go back as far as the Revolution. Until around 1941 they were seated and could speak on the house floor. Today they are neither able to be seated, nor speak, nor vote, but are there mainly to inform the tribes of legislative action pertaining to Indians.

In recent years the Passamaquoddy's ties with the federal government have been increasing, through War on Poverty programs of various sorts, through "Indian Desks," but most often simply as poor people (most Washington "Indian Desks" are set up to deal with federal Indians only). These programs represent a major historical change in Passamaquoddy culture and government relations.

Social Institutions Through Time

KINSHIP ALLIANCE.   The kinship system of the Passamaquoddy in early historic times seem to have been a matrilineal clanship — possibly with male subchiefs on each riverine district, and a head chief from a ruling clan over all. But, in any consideration of early kinship forms, one has to take into account the enormous devastation of disease; for wave upon wave of new European diseases swept the Eastern tribes, destroying existing social systems. Some of the fragmentary aspects of later Indian communities resulted most certainly from this unceasing loss of personnel. Indeed, it is only in the last three generations that there has been anything like a population increase, and that very small. The very early accounts give the impression of large populations with elaborate well-regulated clan systems. Each little tributary of any major river in the northeast had at least one village with a subchief — and there are innumerable rivers and tributaries in New England. The most recent studies of aboriginal American populations are turning up much larger population statistics than were ever suspected before, and this geographical area seems to substantiate the new larger estimates.

At any rate, by the 1600's several epidemics are known to have swept through the Eastern tribes. The beginning of the fur trade coincided with the first drastic declines in population; it was probably at this time that family hunting territories became more firmly established, with small groups fanning out over a large area to hunt and trap in the winter. These groups were probably no longer true clans, which by the usual definition are coalitions of related family lineages descended from a real or mythical common ancestor. Although these family hunting groups seem to have continued the use of clan names and symbols, by the 1600's they were far reduced from being true clans.

Today many people still remember their former clan names, but these have no real significance except as joking material or as glimpses into an unfathomed past history. Even so, kinship alliance is of prime importance. Today the kinship system is made up of lineages; that is, nuclear families or extended families related through one line of remembered ancestors. In most cases, Passamaquoddy lineages today seem to be patrilineal, but there are some examples, too, of strong lineage groups associated through a female line. Perhaps a merging of systems is at work here. People tend to be fiercely loyal to their lineage and will defend another member of it without hesitation. Lineages often vote as a block in an election, and there is competition and jealousy between groups. Factionalism falls along lineage lines as well, so that any program which ignores these social facts, as most do, is headed for trouble. At each Passamaquoddy reservation there are several strong lineages, and several lesser ones which usually side with one or another of the more powerful or influential groups. These smaller groups are wooed in various ways, especially at election time, for they, like independents in a two-party system, can determine the outcome of a political encounter.

Lineage members do not usually marry one another; those who do are said to be "just like dogs." Linguists and anthropologists have sometimes concluded that cross-cousin marriage was preferred in this area, because the language includes a special terminology for that relationship, and another for parallel cousins. Other evidence may refute such a conclusion, for even third cousin marriage is considered disgusting today and no distinction is made between the two types of cousin. Those who accept the cross-cousin marriage theory have proposed that the church has successfully eliminated the custom, but tribal practice today far exceeds the church's strictest dictates on cousin marriage. Restrictions include anyone of the known lineage. This restriction, incidentally, is not easily accomplished in a small population, and it drastically limits the choice of a marriage partner.

SEX ROLES. In former times the man provided the food, while the woman performed the rest of the work. Economic hardship and Aid to Dependent Children have undermined the man's role, which in many cases is one of bravado more than of economic usefulness. Women have a peculiar position in the culture, for, while they are the backbone of the community, often influencing the political attitudes of their family, and may also be the family's main breadwinner, yet they are frequently treated rather badly by their husbands, some of whom think it manly to be unfaithful, and, in public if not in private, "look down on" women. It is difficult to assess how much of this behavior is based on custom and how much reflects the beleaguered Passamaquoddy male's attempt to prove his manhood in a world that offers neither traditional nor modern outlets. Males who succeed economically display far less of the Passamaquoddy machismo syndrome than do the others, which may indicate that improved economic conditions on the reservation would lead to more stable family relationships.

AGE. To an outsider, the lack of social distinction between age groups is striking. Children are treated as small adults and are rather self-sufficient at an early age. Sexual encounters occur across a much wider span of ages than is normally true in a white community, and the ideal is not necessarily a situation in which the woman is younger than the man.

The respect traditionally accorded the elderly by Indians seems to be dying fast, particularly among teenagers and their younger siblings. This conceivably might have something to do with absorbing America's youth-culture attitudes over television; in any case, there are not many old people to respect, as few live to a ripe old age.

In the political realm, very few people under 25 are involved in tribal politics except at voting time, and they neither attend nor show much interest in tribal council meetings. Political interest seems to increase when one marries, however. Once again, it is not easy to assign this present pattern to former custom, although it may be custom. Until recent years, very few council meetings were held (as there was little to decide), but today there are meetings at least once a week. The sophistication of council members in dealing with various programs, proposals, and miscellaneous red-tape has increased vastly over the last fifteen years. Perhaps younger people simply feel intimidated by the complexity of some of these meetings. Or perhaps older tribal members feel they are too young to participate. In any case, they are conspicuously absent from important tribal decision-making situations and tend to finally become involved when they are already raising families.

SOCIAL CLASS.   There are no distinct social classes on the reservation. Indeed, it is a community of equals, and the social pressure to equalize everyone is intense. Some individuals may have more prestige than others, and one lineage may have more prestigious individuals than another; but prestige has its price, for trying to better oneself is resented and opposed in every possible way. As one old Passamaquoddy man said, "Indians are funny people; they hate to see another Indian get ahead." The idea seems to fit well into the concept of "limited good"; that is, "more for you is less for me." In former times, this homily was probably actually true; but today the idea is a major stumbling block in economic development programs, for, unless the whole standard of living of the tribe can be uplifted at once, there will be bitter resentment and outright attempts to thwart those who succeed over others.

The person with great prestige, particularly a leader, is one who does a lot for the community without thereby necessarily gaining something for himself. He must be exemplary in every way, unstinting in his day-to-day efforts for the tribe, and, above all, unselfish with his money, his car, and his time. He must help not only his lineage and its affiliates, but opposing lineages (who will not vote for him later in any case). If he does all this, and "gets ahead" as well, he will be the object of gossip and the search for his flaws will be unrelenting. If he works off the reservation, he will not be as popular as he would be if he worked on the reservation for the tribe. (OEO programs have made this latter a real possibility for the first time in centuries.)

TRIBAL GOVERNMENT.   There appears to be no solid evidence for the mode of tribal government at the time of white contact, but there is reason to think that it has not altered very much except for the fact that population decrease has perhaps made fewer chiefs.

During the period that is known, particularly the early reservation period of about 150 years ago, the Passamaquoddy had one chief, lieutenant-chief, and twelve counselors, one of whom was called (by whites, at least) "captain." The captain presided over the council. The council and the lieutenant-chief were appointed by the chief, who in turn was elected by the tribe — but elected from only one lineage, the Neptune family.

Maine, following Massachusetts' example, allowed one tribal representative to the legislature from both the Penobscot and the Passamaquoddy tribes. They could speak, and be seated on the floor of the legislature (but today cannot). They serve mainly as lobbyists and as sources of information for the tribe. The position was and is elective by the whole tribe.

In the middle 1800's, the so-called "War of the Flags" occurred at Pleasant Point reservation, then the seat of tribal government. The events leading up to this "war" are very complex and related to similar events which occurred among the Penobscots. Briefly, however, life-chief John Francis Neptune was progressive and for education, and the faction that did not go along with these ideas elected to follow the more conservative lieutenant-governor, Newell Neptune. When either group set up a liberty pole, symbolic of chiefship, the other would soon chop it down! The skirmishing went on for some time, until finally lieutenant-governor Newell Neptune and his followers split off, moving eventually to Indian Township reservation. The state then intervened and convinced the tribe to have a chief and lieutenant-chief of equal rank at each reservation, to divide the council in two (six at each place), and to select the legislative representatives, alternately, every two years from each reservation. The warring factions made a solemn treaty of peace with one another, agreeing to the arrangement, and vowing eternal brotherhood henceforth.

Today, each reservation elects a chief (more often called a governor) and a lieutenant-governor every two years. The appointment is no longer for life but for a two-year term, and it is no longer from one particular lineage, for anyone can be nominated. Until 1959 the chiefs still appointed their own councils, but the tribe requested the legislature to make the council elective as well. Thus, all official posts today are elective. The elections are held in September, and eligibility to vote is the same as that for other citizens of the state. In addition, voters must be on the census, which is taken annually just before election time. Off-reservation members usually do not vote, but this situation was recently challenged. Now if the tribal member returns to the reservation on election day, he may vote.

A council meeting may be called only by the chief, although he can appoint someone else, usually the lieutenant-governor, to conduct a meeting in his absence. Meetings are called as needed, rather than by a schedule, and are usually held at night. The council is considered representative of the tribe, and it votes on issues in the tribe's behalf. The chief may vote to break a tie, otherwise, he has no vote. The chief is definitely the servant of the people, and his power lies in his ability to interpret, to explain, and to point out the right path in a given situation to the council, who then may or may not do as he suggests. On matters that concern the tribe as a whole, joint council meetings with members of both reservation councils take place. They are held alternately at each reservation, and the host chief presides over the meeting. There has been a profound increase in joint tribal council meetings in the last decade, and relations between the two communities have improved greatly as a result.

Meetings of the council are usually open to tribal members or to invited outsiders. Although an agenda is usually followed, at the close of the meeting anyone may bring up an issue not on the agenda. Meetings were formerly conducted in the Passamaquoddy language and occasionally still are, but the influx of outsiders who are concerned with various programs has resulted in a much more frequent use of English at the meetings.

The tribal council also serves the reservation in other capacities, such as appointing constables, replacing an officer, and so forth. It is also the Community Action Program board of directors and the Overall Economic Development Committee on each reservation.

FACTIONS AND CONFLICT RESOLUTION. Factionalism is a real problem, and usually issues are secondary to basic conflicts among certain lineage groups, each of which usually has members on the tribal council. However, these factional differences seem to be better controlled than formerly and do not slow down tribal political processes as much as they used to. Perhaps this is because many of the issues the council now deals with are about new programs that are beneficial to everyone.

But when problems do arise, how are they solved? If the grievance concerns an individual (usually a leader or director of some program), a council member or ordinary citizen will air his complaint at a council meeting. If he has misunderstood something, perhaps his complaint will be explained away. If not, he does not say, "I think so-and-so should change his tactics"; instead, he usually stops speaking after making his complaint. The offender knows what he is supposed to do, and he is given a chance to improve; if he doesn't, the next time he might be warned in a roundabout way. If his misbehavior persists, the warnings get stronger. But rarely is anyone displaced from his position, unless actual funding of a program is seriously endangered by his actions. Even then he is given every possible chance to mend his ways. It is a terrible ordeal for all concerned when at last someone has to be removed from his post. Confrontation is not part of the Passamaquoddy life-style!

If the issue is broad and nonpersonal, most people trust the tribal leader, if he is capable. The leader goes to individuals separately, particularly to family heads and council members, and tries to explain the issues. If he does this, people will "think about it." This is a good sign, because if they don't "think about it," the answer is probably "no." (White outsiders who attempt to rush important decisions through the council often get a quick "yes," which is really a "no" without confrontation!) If there is no strong leader when an important tribal decision is pending, the people might postpone meetings and a decision until the incompetent man is voted out — which could take two years.

With the new programs, however, the council has learned to take two or three meetings, instead of four or five months, to make a decision. They have stopped delaying decisions, particularly policy decisions, and have learned to work together increasingly well. The two reservations are in greater harmony, and the increased meetings and public interest have acted as a sort of tribal group therapy, providing an outlet for complaints besides malicious gossip. There is now a more open atmosphere.

RELIGION AND THE SUPERNATURAL WORLD. Little is known of the "old religion," for the Indians in Maine have been Catholics for more than 300 years. Yet some of the old beliefs persist side by side with Christian ones and, more often than not, go unnoticed by the clergy.

The religious activities today are primarily those of the Catholic church, although there is a new, as yet unassessable, influence of the Bahá'í faith, which teaches brotherhood, world government, equality of the sexes, and the future importance of Indians in world and spiritual affairs. (This faith so far has only six or seven adherents, but among them are some of the more notable and intelligent members of the tribe. It will be interesting to see how this develops in the future.)

The Catholic patron saint of most Maine and Maritime Indians is St. Anne, whose special province it is to intercede in cases of illness. This selection may have been made because the tribes of the area were suffering greatly from European diseases at the time of the early conversions. Certainly conversion was speeded up by the fact that Indian doctors were inexplicably unable to help the people against smallpox, while Europeans, who were Christian, did not suffer as much in the epidemics. Today there is a Mission of St. Anne on each Passamaquoddy reservation, with a resident priest and teaching nuns. Baptisms, weddings, and funerals generally are held at a person's home reservation. Wakes take place in the home of a near relative and last for three days and nights, during which time someone is always in attendance to keep the soul company before it leaves the body through the mouth.

Passamaquoddy do not really believe in purgatory, but, on the other hand, never contradict the priest about this. They believe (with some justification) that hell is here on earth and that a person is repaid here, in his heart or by misfortune, for his transgressions against others. Hell is also not being admitted to heaven; but it is not the fire-and-brimstone place the church has taught about. Professional mourners are often called in to sing at the wake and at the burial service, and the old Indian dirges have an eerie, ineffably sad tone one never forgets. The mourners are paid with either food or nonalcoholic drink.

Other aspects of an older religion appear here and there; for example, many of the traditional dances are essentially religious in nature. In one, a pipe is offered to the four sacred directions; in another (the Green Corn Dance), the dance is actually a prayer for earthly fertility. Certain supernaturally endowed individuals still can dream or predict future events rather accurately; others can "will" events — particularly an injury or death — but this is considered an abuse of power. Some have a power to heal, which is simply bestowed upon them unbidden at birth.

These special powers are usually manifest in childhood, so that, even if they are not mentioned or used, people know who possesses them. Good leaders are thought to have special powers (and indeed they need them). The approach of death or danger to oneself or someone close is often signaled by the cry of Sqwowtemos [Swamp Woman] or other stereotyped signal, or in more individualistic ways. (Outsiders soon learn not to scoff at this ability, for the premonitions are usually correct.) Purposeful dreaming aimed at solving problems is another typically Passamaquoddy approach to life. One man told his successful son, "If you ever stop being able to dream, you won't amount to anything." Students of psychocybernetics (programming one's own computer to solve problems) might well look into this purposeful dreaming. It seems to work.

Finally, there are many nonhuman beings on the reservations, beings seen only by Indians or those with some Indian blood. There are at least two kinds of "little people," one from the shores and one from the forests, as well as an ill-tempered giant who prowls occasionally at night and has been seen as recently as two summers ago. These same beings, mentioned by Lescarbot in his 1606 account (Lescarbot 1907), affect social behavior mostly in the religious realm. One group of little people acts in conjunction with the Catholic church, even though the church probably doesn't know they exist. Thus, someone tried to steal the sacred wine, but the little people chased him out; when a dance was held during Lent, little people appeared, showed their disapproval, and the dance broke up. They do not seem to enter into day-to-day affairs, political events, or the new programs, but it is difficult to predict their future activities. Sadly, the most helpful little people, who taught the first Passamaquoddy all the good and useful things by which to live, sailed away about ten years ago in their stone canoes, saying someone more powerful was around; they would return with their goodness only when people again believed in them and needed them.

EDUCATION. The formal education of the Passamaquoddy began in the early French missions, but education was not the missionaries' main intent, and instruction was spotty; even after the fall of Quebec, however, missions were still the primary source of formal education for the Indians. After the education debates of the early 1800's, the few Protestants who attempted to teach on the reservation were replaced with Catholic priests and teachers. This situation has continued until fairly recently.

Formerly the schools were open only three months a year, for when the weather turned cold the teaching nuns departed to heated school-rooms elsewhere. (People who are today in their forties and fifties had this sort of education.) Given these circumstances and the distance to high school, very few Indians attended secondary schools at all until recently. About twenty-five years ago, heating facilities were put in convents and schools, and instruction lasted through the winter. Even so, instruction started later than at other schools, to allow children to accompany their parents on the fall potato harvest in Aroostook County.

The greatest advances in Maine Indian education have come about since 1965, when responsibility for Indian schools was turned over to the State Department of Education, and a specialist in Indian Education was hired. The school year was standardized to agree with that of other state-run schools, and the teaching nuns were required to be certified by the state. Because there were not always enough certified nuns, young lay teachers were sometimes hired, representing a radical change in school policy. (To many, this move was a good thing; but some of the more conservative element see it as a threat to Maine Indian' rights to have religious teachers.)

Adult education programs were introduced, and adult members of the community were incorporated into the grammar schools as teachers' aides and craft teachers. At about the same time, the legisla-ture passed an act creating Indian school boards on each reservation — at first appointed, but now elected. The school boards are a radical departure from past procedure and potentially weaken ties to the church, for now the people have the power not to renew contracts of teachers they don't like — including nuns. The church supported the creation of the boards, but one wonders if some of the eventualities of this new arrangement were foreseen. Indians themselves have not yet realized the power the boards give them, and to some extent are still accepting edicts handed down from "authorities." This, too, will change with time and experience, for, in this realm as in so many others on the reservations today, the chance to run their own lives is such a new thing that the people scarcely know where to begin.

Three years ago, after an extensive hassle with the state government, a new school was built on each reservation, replacing the dilapidated buildings that had served the communities for years. The planning, construction, and equipping was fraught with setbacks and contracting chicanery, but eventually good end products emerged, virtual monuments to perseverance!

In 1972 a first try at bilingual education was made at Indian Township, and it included the teaching of Passamaquoddy history in the schools. The great handicap here is that so little of the history is recorded in one place and therefore basic research must be done. Also, the Passamaquoddy language is not written and is still the object of linguistic research. But the new program is a start, and it aims at making students more facile in both English and Passamaquoddy: a worthy task where many people lack skills in both languages.

A Headstart program seems to be working well, and a hot lunch program is another innovation of great importance. Many adults who dropped out of high school (the dropout rate has been approximately 99.5 percent) have recently earned high school equivalency diplomas. Many young people are being sent to boarding high schools throughout the state, where they seem to fare better than in the local high schools, where prejudice is intense.

Upward Bound programs have lured a few Passamaquoddy to college, and this trend is increasing. Many colleagues throughout the state are now offering special financial aid and tutoring to Indian students, and in the summer of 1972 a conference of Indians and white educators dealt with problems specific to Indian students attempting to attend college.

In every way, it seems, the climate has improved on the Passamaquoddy educational scene. Proof is still to be demonstrated in the next few years, when grammar school children of today reach the point of decision on whether to drop out or stay in school. At present, there is still much to be done to appeal to students in the Indian community, but things can only get better than they were in the past.

Several years back, all of these innovations were threatened when the schools were declared segregated and ordered closed, and federal funds were given to the nearby white town to build a larger integrated school. The Passamaquoddy, incensed at this, wondered why the integrated school couldn't be on the reservation, which is actually most central to the attending towns; they pointed out that their schools were already open to anyone who wanted to attend. The Civil Rights Commission was sent to the scene by the state governor, and what it saw was a racially integrated group of blue-eyed blond children, side by side with dark-eyed black-haired children. Despite the genetics of the situation, however, the fair children are just as Indian in culture, language, and deed as the others and are fully accepted as Indian by both Indian and white communities. But the schools were not closed, and it is undoubtedly in the best interests of the children that it turned out this way.

TREATY RIGHTS AND WELFARE. Since 1794, the Indian agent has been a Passamaquoddy fact of life; indeed, for many he was the most important fact. The agent dispensed grocery orders, occasional clothing orders, house repair money, and sometimes medical funds to the impoverished Indians of the state. The agent often became a powerful figure among the people, a demigod with the power to grant or retract critical favors from his needy charges. But he also came to be seen as a natural resource — part of the natural order of things.

Likewise welfare, introduced in the thirties, came to be thought of as a natural resource. Nothing but desperation was required to get welfare — and nothing was required in return but a suitable gratitude, for there was no work one could do to pay it off if one wanted to. Aid to Dependent Children (ADC) came later, but immediately it fell into the same category as the agent and welfare, and in addition it worked to loosen family ties; the presence of a man in the house is enough to get one's Mother's Aid allowance cut off, and under these conditions a nonproductive husband is not welcome in the maternal home. Thus, ADC may have done more harm than good in the long run.

Now that there are other sources of income on the reservations, primarily through federal programs, the agent no longer has his grip on the people, and ADC doesn't break up as many homes. But nearly three hundred years of being given handouts, even though they were necessary, has resulted in many Passamaquoddy seeing the new federal programs as merely another fortuitous kind of natural resource. As Commissioner Stevens says, "They've been hand fed for centuries, but it's not been an easy life for them — it's been a hell of a life, a demoralizing life."

The self-help philosophy behind the federal programs is understood in Washington and by a few Passamaquoddy leaders, but is not understood by the majority of the Indian people. Even a good Passamaquoddy leader or director may not be able to get the people to work effectively in his program, if they see that people in another program are getting paid for doing nothing. The cultural tabu on criticism and direct confrontation inhibits a program director from "giving people hell" if they don't perform, and bossiness is not appreciated and does not get results. Therefore, people unfortunately often try to get into the program that requires the least of them: the director who most pleases the people and least worries about Washington is the most popular. If a director should insist that a person work or not be paid, the person can quit and go to the agent for a grocery order, claiming that he's been laid off. Conscientious Passamaquoddy workers are soon demoralized by being turned into errand boys for people who don't work, and soon give in to the nonwork ethic themselves.

Confounding all this is the fact that federal programs are frequently defunded, altered, or have their guidelines changed, so that there is little sense of continuity, from the people's point of view. Inevitably the programs are seen as temporary natural resources too — plums ripe to be picked while the season lasts.

In sum, then the Indian agent became a social institution, and welfare and ADC followed suit when they were introduced — even though all these programs were necessary because of the extreme poverty of the area. Now it appears that some of the federally funded programs are in danger of going the same way simply out of habit, and because the grass-roots people have lived hand-to-mouth for so long it is nearly impossible to think of any day but the present one.

The leaders, and increasingly the people who have served on the tribal councils, understand the government's ideals of self-sufficiency and home-based economic development at which the programs are aimed. But in order to be reelected, leaders and council members must in some measure also conform to the ideals of the community — ideals that include not telling another what to do, nonconfrontation, and unselfishly helping others. ("Unselfishly helping others" often means ignoring program guidelines as to who is eligible for hiring.)

It is clear that federal programs must be more closely geared to both the present values of the community and the past situation of the people to be really effective, and in addition the programs must include methods for reeducating the grass-roots element. A partial solution might be to show a series of entertaining teaching films periodically throughout the funded year of any program, films that reiterate the *point* of the program, the proper role of the director and the workers, and how the program has worked successfully in Indian communities elsewhere. The Passamaquoddy people previously have known few life alternatives, and it is not possible for them to choose an intelligent path towards self-help unless they are made aware, in a most basic way, that these programs *do* actually offer the choice of self-determination. Books and brochures certainly are not the answer, as many people are functionally illiterate, while the rest have little interest in the printed word. In a place where entertainment is almost nil, however, people *would* attend films, particularly if they concerned other Indians, in whom they are keenly interested.

Overall Organization of the Community

Of the institutions mentioned previously by far the most important in the community are kinship, tribal government, and the new federal programs. The importance of education is increasing, and it may become another stressed institution in a generation or so, particularly if the present trend towards Indian involvement in the creation and administration of program continues.

Although the role of the Catholic church was very important in the past, it seems to have lost some of its importance in recent years. Yet, the personalities of church workers on the reservations have a great deal to do with church attendance and attitude, and recently some young, nonpatronizing, and imaginative church people have come onto the two reserves. If this more liberal trend continues, it may bring about a resurgence of church involvement.

IN/OUT MIGRATION AND SEASONAL PATTERNS.   At the present time more than half the tribe lives off the reservations. Sometimes this is by choice, but more often it is because of the poor economic and living conditions on reservations. When housing and jobs improve, many of these people will return; indeed, many have returned already in the wake of improvements or promised improvements.

It is sometimes difficult for non-Indians to understand that most Passamaquoddy would rather make the reservation livable and reside there than "make it" in the outside world and live off the reservation. For on the reservation there is a sense of continuity, community, and belonging that many alienated Americans might well envy. There is also the fundamental difference between Indians and other groups in America that they were here first. The bright dreams of the immigrants and their descendants were not Indian dreams, and the mainstream holds no charms for most of them. Their basic values and orientations are not European, either, and do not mesh easily with those of most Americans.

There is also an almost abstract sense of loss: of land, of culture, and of self-sufficiency. This submerged sadness and anger expresses itself most strongly in the determination to hold onto whatever is left, particularly the land base that makes any cultural continuity for Indians possible. This continuity is real, not illusory, for the land the Passamaquoddy inhabit was inhabited by their ancestors thousands of years ago, even though its area is now much less extensive. Here they can be themselves, speak their own language, and see the graves of their ancestors. Though reservations are rife with every sort of problem, they are also home in the deepest possible sense. In spite of these home ties, the Passamaquoddy migratory behavior of old is still apparent. Until recently, entire families would pick up to go blueberry raking, potato picking, or on jaunts to visit relatives in Canada. Young men, particularly, still go to the larger cities in southern New England to work for a winter, a year or two, or even several decades, but most ultimately return. The increase of opportunity on the reservations, however, has sharply reduced the number of people who go as migratory workers to the seasonal harvest. Part of the motivation in the past was to have a good time and see other Indians, but now there are more cars available and people can simply drive to Canada to see their friends and relatives — and they do. There is still a good deal of traveling about, but, as more jobs open up on the reservation, the traveling is less and less for economic gain, and more and more for sociability.

INDIAN IDENTITY.   The question of social identity is currently undergoing changes in the direction of a stronger Indian identity and a greater pride in the Passamaquoddy background. This has resulted from the awakening of America to Indians, the considerable successes of the Passamaquoddy since the 1960's, and the emphasis currently being given to Indian culture in the schools and throughout the Maine reservations in general.

Not long ago, if a Passamaquoddy could pass for white in the cities, he might well do so. Today he more usually says, "I'm an Indian and proud of it." Those who "cop out" on their identity are looked down on by other Passamaquoddy and are not very welcome on the reservation. And those who play at being Indian, but in reality are ashamed of their people, are derisively called "radishes" or "apples" — red on the outside, white on the inside!

Relationships to the Outside World

The worst prejudice most Passamaquoddies face emanates from nearby towns. For example, two barbershops in Princeton, outside of Indian Township, chose to close down rather than serve Indians. In Perry, close to the Pleasant Point reservation, anti-Indian sentiment is not as vehement, but the commercial town of Eastport makes up for this lack.

Indians must trade in Princeton and Eastport, for the reservations have no real stores. The Indian agent does not deal out money, but calls a store with an order, which makes more trouble for the merchant, who grumbles even though he is getting business. The other white people of the area (usually poor themselves) see Indians getting something for nothing, which increases local resentment. The grocery and clothing orders, even though they are meager and irregular, give the impression that Indians don't have to work to live.

The local belief that Indians don't have to work but receive everything from the Indian agent makes it difficult to find a job in neighboring white communities. The attitude of white employers often seems to be, "What do you want a job for, when you guys don't have to work, but can just lay around the lake and drink beer?"

The developments of the past fifteen years have made local townsmen more resentful than ever, although they have often failed to apply for federal programs available to them as well. Several years ago the Passamaquoddy at Indian Township invited Princeton to submit a joint water treatment proposal to EDA, but the town refused. Later, when faced with a deadline and a state fine if they failed to clean up pollution in Lewey's Lake (which borders both Princeton and one of the settlements of Indian Township), Princeton asked to be included in the Passamaquoddy's project, which had been in planning stages for several years. It was then too late, and Princeton must now have a separate project. Some people in nearby towns are friendly to Indians, of course, and lately there have been many more marriages between Indians and whites from contiguous communities; but in general, relations between the groups are uneasy and sometimes even hostile. The Indian rule of thumb is that the farther away you get from the reservation, the better you'll be received.

WASHINGTON COUNTY. Washington County, where both Passamaquoddy reservations are located, is the poorest county in the New England States; it has more emigrants than immigrants and has been going downhill ever since the wooden ship-building industry of the district declined more than a century ago. Some relief was afforded by the sardine and other fishing enterprises, but for various reasons fishing in the area is no longer what it was. The educational level of most county residents is quite low, and the few college graduates usually go elsewhere, as there is little employment for them in the county. The general downward trend shows in attitudes and in a generalized apathy that is not too different from that encountered on the reservations.

The Indian communities are intimately tied up with the region's history, but otherwise they have little to do with the county. Until two years ago the communities were a delegate agency of the Washington County Community Action Agency, but they managed to separate themselves and become independently funded after making a stand to the OEO. The reasons for separation were that ordinary regulations did not apply on the reservation and were causing more harm than good and that the reservations could not seem to get on well with the Washington County Agency or the county commissioners. The separation seems to have benefited reservation communities. At present, the Passamaquoddy have no particular ties to the county, but they share its economic, educational, and social deprivation.

THE STATE OF MAINE.   The relationship of the Passamaquoddy to the state of Maine and its historical genesis has been detailed elsewhere. At the present time the state deals with on-reservation Indians through its Department of Indian Affairs, which is headed by a former Passamaquoddy chief. Funds for the department are granted biannually by the state legislature, which has consistently granted less than is needed to operate the program. This is in part due to the poor economic status of the state.

Since Maine Indians are not eligible for Indian Public Health Act Funds received by federal Indians, much of the budget of Indian Affairs in Maine goes towards health care. (Most such care is on an emergency rather than a preventive basis, and health is a major problem on the reservations as it is in Washington County in general.) Much of the rest of the budget goes for grocery orders, for occasional clothing orders; for children, for house repair — and, of course, staff salaries. In all, the expenditure per capita does not exceed around $300, and the largest part of this goes towards medical costs. Actual assistance for food and clothing is really very small; certainly, it is not enough to live on.

Most state laws are in force on the reservation, and any local variances have to be approved by state resolutions or acts. The state is trustee of the reservation land, but in the past has assumed an ownership attitude. A gratifying change in the official attitude of Maine has occurred recently, however, particularly through Governor Curtis, who has proven to be a friend of the Passamaquoddy people. He has openly favored the Passamaquoddy winning their land suit against the state, urging the legislature that it amicably right the old wrongs. His comments set off a chain reaction in which sentiments favorable to the Passamaquoddy were also voiced by Senators Smith and Muskie, soon followed by Congressmen Kyros and Hathaway. This official political stance of both parties marks a decided break with the past.

THE FEDERAL GOVERNMENT.   Until the new federal programs came on the reservations, the federal government had almost no contact with this tribe, except for the occasional child who was sent to a government Indian boarding school. (The total number has probably not exceeded ten.) This lack of concern of the federal government is in direct contradiction to the promises made the tribe on the eve of the Revolution and shortly after the Revolution, in which the new American government promised to always regard the tribe "as brothers and children, under the fatherly care of the United States, with every right and privilege ... " (Kidder 1867: 311). Further, it also conflicts with the Constitution, which states that only the federal government can make treaties with or manipulate lands of Indians residing within its borders. On this basis the Passamaquoddy sought federal recognition in 1972, for their treaty dates from 1794, which was *after* this Constitutional restriction was made. Part of the purpose of seeking recognition from the government is to gain various services, particularly those related to education and health, that federal Indians receive; it is also to be in a position to coerce the Department of the Interior and the Justice Department to sue the state of Maine in the behalf of the Passamaquoddy tribe in the land claims case, under the Indian Land Claims Act. Although the ability to sue under this act ended in 1972, the Passamaquoddy claimed that they were never notified when the act went into effect, partly as a result of their not being federal Indians, and that they were thus denied due process.

When these applications were made, the Bureau of Indian Affairs replied that having investigated the matter, they deemed that the Passamaquoddy were entitled to federal recognition. The Departments of Justice and the Interior failed even to respond, even though repeatedly requested to do so. While they dallied, the time limitation of the Claims Act drew ever nearer. At this point, the tribe brought suit against the two departments, charging that their case was being jeopardized by inaction. A federal court judge in Maine heard the case and ordered the two departments to state whether or not they would take the case, and, if not, why not. The departments stated they would *not* take the case, citing an 1800's Maine ruling that the Passamaquoddy tribe no longer existed! At least sixty Passamaquoddy were in the courtroom at the time, so the judge could only smile and rule that the two departments of the government must make suit in the Passamaquoddy behalf, appointing the tribal lawyers as monitors to assure that the case would be fairly handled. This ruling set a precedent in that a federal judge ordered federal departments to make suit in behalf of a third party; it also set precedent in that the tribe has been dealt with fairly in a matter concerning land.

One might ask why these two federal departments apparently wanted to see this case lost? Undoubtedly it is because the Passamaquoddy case may well set an expensive precedent for other neglected Eastern tribes. A close examination of actual (not BIA) population figures shows there are about as many off-reservation or nonreservation Indians as there are federal Indians, many of them Eastern tribal remnants. If these groups come to realize that they have ungranted rights and that their treaties are worth something, a very expensive can of worms is thereby opened. The federal stalling in this case was unmistakable, and the reasons seem equally clear.

CANADIAN MARITIMES. Relationships of the Passamaquoddy with the Maritime Indians of Canada (Micmacs and Malecites) used to be more political than they are at present, for they were all part of the Wabanaki Confederacy; later they joined with the Iroquois Confederacy to form the Great Council Fire. The Council Fire broke up in the 1800's, but even after that leaders from all the tribes ratified the election of leaders of single tribes. This eventually turned into a nicety rather than a necessity, and finally the practice was dropped altogether.

Today the relationships between the Maine and Maritime Indians are primarily social, and there is considerable intermarriage, particularly between the Passamaquoddy and the Malecites of the Fredericton and Tobique reserves in New Brunswick. The Malecites have, on occasion, been cooperative in joining Passamaquoddy confrontations with the state and the Georgia-Pacific Lumber Company, indicating that the old mutual help of the confederacy is not entirely dead. The Malecites are watching the development of the Passamaquoddy land suit with great interest, as some Malecite bands who assisted the Americans in the Revolution are also named in the treaties. There is also a rumor that the Malecites have been inspired to launch their own land suit in Canada in the near future. In the past three years there has been an increase of intertribal action between the Maine tribes and the Micmacs and Malicites in conjunction with TRIBE Incorporated (Teaching and Research In Bicultural Education) an international Indian high school for Maine and Maritime Indians that is presently struggling to stay afloat.

PAN-INDIAN INFLUENCES. Pan-Indianism has had negligible impact on the Passamaquoddy so far, primarily because they have not been federal and, therefore, have not had extensive contact with other tribes. Through new federal programs, some of the leaders have traveled widely and have been influenced by visiting other reservations, but this influence has been more in terms of economic progress that could be made at home rather than of dreams of national Indian unity. Maine Indians have found that, as members of national Indian organizations, they are of almost no interest to their federalized brothers, whose main concern is for problems of BIA Indians. This fact has diminished potential Passamaquoddy interest in Pan-Indian movements, and even when the Passamaquoddy do become federalized the memory of these slights will probably work against their being active in national movements for some time to come.

Among the Penobscots of Maine, renewed contacts with the St. Regis Mohawks have produced some "Unity Conventions," and shows by the "White Roots of Peace" have been well received. But many Penobscots are not involved, and few Passamaquoddy have taken part in this new movement. However, a movement to organize the Indians of the Atlantic seaboard into a unified action group was championed by some Passamaquoddy leaders and their supporters — particularly lawyers — who located funds for a preliminary visit to southern Indians and for setting up a conference of Eastern Indian leaders late in 1972. A powerful ally in this venture was the Native American Rights Fund. Prime goals of the conference were to clarify to Eastern Indians their rights and their eligibility for federal programs, and to form a unified voice. The conferees adopted the name, Coalition of Eastern Native Americans (CENA). It is likely that the resulting contacts will be more meaningful to the Passamaquoddy, who share a history similar to other Eastern Indians, than will future contacts with federal Western tribes.

TENTACLES OF ACADEMIA. Finally, there are contacts with academic America. The Passamaquoddy were overlooked for centuries, no less by academicians (except for a few folklore studies) than by politicians. Today they are getting their full share of attention. Linguists at the Massachusetts Institute of Technology, Harvard, and Wesleyan are working (not always in concert) on the Passamaquoddy language. Several students and an anthropology professor at Wesleyan are working on Passamaquoddy history, as is this writer. Many students from New England colleges have appeared in the last few years to make documentary films and write term papers on Passamaquoddy; the present writer, married into the tribe, came as the first full-time anthropological fieldworker in 1969.

It seems inevitable that interest in the Passamaquoddy will grow as the tribe continues to become better known and as Eastern Indians are put back on the maps of texbooks that have usually placed them under brief chapters entitled "The fate of the Eastern Indians" and dismissed them as dead and gone!

Capsule History of the Passamaquoddy

Maine Indians were in contact with Europeans long before the Pilgrims ever heard of Plymouth. The French, English, and Basque were actively engaged in fishing in northeastern waters by the mid-1500's, and a French schoolteacher, André Thevet, was Maine's first tourist in 1556. Thevet's accounts have been proven to be partly fictional, so it is tempting but unsafe to use his material in any historical reconstruction. The earliest accurate account of the Passamaquoddy is from Marc Lescarbot, a chronicler of Champlain, who published his *The history of New France* in 1606. Lescarbot accompanied Champlain on his second trip to the Americas and spent some time with Sieur de Mont in the

Passamaquoddy Bay region. Here he describes the Etchimins (the French term for the Malecites and Passamaquoddy) as full of fidelity, courage, generosity, and humanity . . . and said that the term "savage" hardly applied.

The French camped on St. Croix Island for the winter, having as frequent visitors the Etchimins and some Micmacs, with their great chief Membertou. The French and Indians got on well that winter, as they seem to have all through colonial history. In sharp contrast with the British, who would not eat at the same table with Indians and who enacted miscegenation laws, the French freely married into the northern tribes. French missionaries were active from earliest times among Indians of this area, and, within a Protestant enclave, Maine Indians are still primarily Catholic. At the time of Lescarbot, the Etchimins seem to have already been active in the fur trade, going seasonally to Port Royal in Nova Scotia to the main trading post of the area. Here they traded beaver, otter, and moose skins, as well as fresh meat, for guns, powder, shot, knives, kettles, flour, and such luxuries as scarves, jewelry, and sack.

Lescarbot in describing the main Etchimin village, said, "The town was a large enclosure upon a rising ground enclosed with trees, great and small, fastened one to another, and within the enclosure [were] many enclosures, large and small, one of which was as big as a market hall; that wherein they held their feasts, it was somewhat smaller," (Lescarbot 1907 [1606]).

Lescarbot noted that Indians of the area did not torture their enemies as some other groups did, that they were inordinately fond of children, that they engaged frequently in dancing and singing, and that "they have no law but that one must not offend another. So they have few quarrels; and if any such thing happens the Sagamore calls a halt, and does justice to him that is offended, giving some blows with a stick to the wrongdoer, or condemning him to make some presents to the other" (Lescarbot 1907 [1606]). Lescarbot described hunting, fishing, and agricultural techniques, as well as many other customs.

THE MISSIONARIES. The first record of missionary activity among Maine Indians is also from Lescarbot's account, where it is noted that Father Nicolas Aubry was sent along in de Mont's crew to Christianize the natives in the area as part of the obligation of his charter from the king. Apparently there were some Protestant Huguenots on this voyage who also had some luck at conversion. They did not demand that the Indian leaders give up their plurality of wives, and this made their religion more popular with some. Nevertheless, most of the French who came to Acadia, or New France (roughly, Maine and the Maritimes) were Catholic, and it was this religion which prevailed.

Throughout the first half of the 1600's the Jesuits and Recollet fathers operated several missions throughout Maine. These missions were constantly being obliterated by the English, who were also trying to claim the area, and they were moved or rebuilt innumerable times. Missionaries were also employed at the St. John and Port Royal trading posts, to which Maine Indians brought their furs, but these too were demolished by the British. Later the Capuchins were assigned to the southern part of New France (the Passamaquoddy region), and the Jesuits to the north. Unfortunately the Capuchin records are poor, and little can be learned of their activity in the area. Soon four Jesuit missions were established on the St. Lawrence, and Maine Indians are known to have frequented them. At these St. Lawrence missions Indians could find food, shelter, and protection from the Iroquois, as well as religion.

The record of Catholic missionaries in the area is generally admirable (and sometimes heroic), and they were not as determined to make Indians into Europeans to save their souls as were the Protestant missionaries in Southern New England. The priests were believed by the Indians to have supernatural powers, and it was said that when they had their black robes on, "they could see anywhere." Perhaps this was because their own supernatural men wore robes when practicing their arts.

After the fall of Quebec in 1759 and the consequent defeat of France in the region, the Indians of Acadia were left without their French allies or their priests. In 1764 a Passamaquoddy delegation went to the Massachusetts Bay Colony to protest land abuses and to request resident priests. The governor refused them a "popish priest," but offered them an Episcopalian minister instead, which the Indians refused. Several other requests were made by them to no avail.

Later, when Maine Indians served in the Revolution, they requested resident priests as part of their compensation. A French navy chaplain was all the Boston authorities could turn up, and he stayed only one summer. Finally, the disgusted Indians sent a delegation to Bishop Carroll in Baltimore, at that time the head of the Catholic church in the United States. He presented the chiefs with silver medals and applied to the Sulpician Order in France for a priest. The bishop had no funds to pay a clergyman for the Indians, and so an appeal was again made to the Massachusetts court to live up to its treaty obligations (still in existence) to support priests on the reservations. Finally, Massachusetts provided two hundred dollars a year for a priest who would serve alternately with the Penobscots and the Passamaquoddy. Later, a church and a priest were supplied to each reservation.

THE FUR TRADE. Fishing and the fur trade were the principal early industries in both Acadia and colonial New England. The Indians were involved in both, but the fur trade wrought greater changes in their economic and social life than any other development induced by Europeans.

In some ways Indians gained in the bargain, for they had the skills and knowledge to out-hunt and out-trap Europeans, while, for their part, Europeans relied heavily on the fur trade returns to support their expeditions and colonies. Fur and coin were interchangeable, and there was strong competition between fur traders and between the French and English. In competitive situations, the Indian temporarily came out on top. As early as 1610 Lescarbot wrote about the high cost of beaver, saying, "Eight years ago for two biscuits or two knives, one had a beaver, while today one must give fifteen or twenty," (Lescarbot 1907).

There can be no doubt that the economy flowered among the Indians of the Northeast in the 1600's but the ultimate price of the florescence was high. The Indians had tied themselves to the white man and to his guns, powder, and shot, so that ultimately Indians *had* to deal with Europeans to survive. They also were forced to take sides again and again in European wars for empire. And when the fur trade was effectively over, when the Indians had been reduced by war and epidemics, when Indians lands had been trimmed down to slivers of their former size — what was there for the Indians then? The answer is too well known to dwell on. Suffice to say that they had lost a precious thing: autonomy. They are struggling even today to gain back a few crumbs of control over destiny that they lost back when the first Indian traded a beaver skin for two biscuits.

The changes in the Indians' social structure and hunting economy produced by the fur trade have been well documented by anthropologists and historians, with some academic disagreements about details. Most agree, however, on a few essentials: that family hunting and trapping areas became more firmly defined and extended; that subsistence hunting gave way to hunting for market and trade; that economic automony gave way to dependence on the truck houses; and that economic arrangements changed from cooperation and sharing between members to competition between members for the European goods that had come to mean survival.

Maine was the frontier of both the English and the French, and consequently the source of ceaseless skirmishes until the fall of Quebec. For the most part, the Passamaquoddy dealt with the French, and because the French viewed Indians as basically human (something most English did not) there was intermarriage. The effect this had on the social structure is hard to assess, yet surely it must have had some; there are cases of Frenchmen becoming local chiefs.

THE FRENCH AND ENGLISH WARS.   In the colonial period there were several wars, which are usually called the French and Indian Wars by American historians. They could more properly be called the French and English Wars, however, for they were extensions of European conflicts, with Indians fighting on both sides. It is important to realize that those who gained least and suffered most in these conflicts were the Indians. Maine Indians almost always fought with the French, but, even so, they realized the great cost, for at one point they specifically asked to remain neutral. The French granted the request, but the English did not, declaring that, if the Indians would not take up arms against the French and the St. John Maliseats (their close relatives), they would be declared enemies. Naturally, they again joined the French forces. But with each successive war and its accompanying hardships and casualties Indian numbers were reduced. For the Indians, virtually every war was followed by devastating epidemics, for they were in a weakened condition and biologically were unused to European diseases. Not only that, their former native diet was infinitely more healthy than the European food they had adopted. In the end, it hardly mattered which side they backed, for in backing either one their population loss was so great that they would never again have the strength to maintain their own power.

The French had the upper hand in wars for some time, but in the late 1750's the British took the offensive at a time when the French were least able to reinforce their troops in Canada. In 1759 the fateful Battle of Quebec was decided in favor of the British. This turning point placed the Indian allies of the French in a most unenviable position. In the Treaty of Paris, signed in 1763, France relinquished almost every parcel of land it held in the New World — including the homeland of the Passamaquoddy.

THE POST-WAR PERIOD. The Passamaquoddy and their close relations on the St. John were the first tribes to sue for peace with the English, probably because they had been active on the side of the French and realistically feared reprisals. According to the excellent account, *The history of the state of Maine*, (Williamson 1832), Michael Neptune and Bellamy Glaube represented the tribes to Governor Lawrence of Halifax in February of 1760. They promised, among other things, to "Traffic only at the truck houses," as well as to have the treaty ratified by their principal men by a certain date, and to leave three hostages with the English until that time. Peace was also established between the Penobscots and the English.

English settlers emerged from their blockhouses and garrisons to begin life anew. As for the Indians, they were forced to declare their former rebellion against the English king and made to forfeit almost all their land — a convenient arrangement for the English. The English now controlled the fur trade in Maine, albeit both the Indians and the fur-bearing animals were on the decline. All trade with the Indians was regulated at two trading posts or truck houses, Fort Pownall and Fort Halifax, establishments that were carefully regulated and guarded. All commodities the Indians needed or were allowed to have were sold there. The Indians were desperately poor by that time and were no longer able to survive without guns and other necessities. They were perpetually in debt to the truck house, so much so that many people sold themselves into slavery or were forced to make their children liable for their debts. Parents sometimes even sold their children. (This among a people noted earlier for an inordinate love of children.) The legacy of poverty among Maine Indians today certainly gained a foothold in this period of their association with the white man.

In spite of their humiliating condition, Maine Indians were still feared by the English; when General Gage requested troops of Massachusetts to make war on the Indians south of the Great Lakes, the state refused on the basis of danger to the scattered settlements in Maine from the Indians remaining.

THE REVOLUTIONARY WAR.   In the years following the end of the French and English Wars in America, England imposed increasingly heavy taxations on its exports to America. Maine, in particular, had few manufactures and was heavily burdened by these taxes. By the late 1700's the atmosphere was again tense in the colonies.

In March 1775 British Captain Mowett "dismanteled" Fort Pownall on the Penobscot in violation of a British treaty with Maine Indians, upsetting the trade at a critical time of year. This and other indignities propelled the Penobscots and Passamaquoddies, by now the only tribes left in Maine, to side with the Americans against the British in the Revolution. Their fellows in the Maritimes, who had not enjoyed British rule either, soon joined the Maine Indians in an alliance that effectively prevented a successful British attack from the Canadian side.

The Americans entered into treaties of "peace and friendship" with the Maine and Maritime Indians, offering supplies and various guarantees, both during and after the war, in exchange for their help. Headquarters of the Eastern Division was set up on the coast at Machias, and an Indian regiment was headed by Colonel John Allen of Nova Scotia. Machias became the center of activity of Revolutionary Maine and a prime British target. But when four armed British vessels were sent against Machias, burning mills and buildings as they came, "Every man in the place able to bear arms was upon the shores; and when the barges were ascending the river, there were present between

40 and 50 Indian fighters, who raised and kept up a hideous yell; which being echoed by the white people in the same Indian tone, so reverberated through the forests, as to induce the supposition that they were full of wild savages" (Williamson 1832: vol.2, p. 462). Frances Joseph Neptune, a Passamaquoddy shaman who eventually became a famous chief, killed the British commander with one shot, at an incredible distance. The British, in a state of shock and consternation, withdrew. Machias was not visited again during the war. (The Americans said, of Neptune's shot, "Incredible"; the Indians said, "He had powers.")

The Americans' failure to set up and supply truck houses in Maine, as promised at the outset of the war, and the news that General Washington had decided against further attempts to send an expedition to Nova Scotia, where their Wabanaki allies resided, caused some Passamaquoddy to press for neutrality rather than further involvement in the war. But the same year France was induced to join the American cause, and the affection and affiliation with the nation brought in most of the stragglers and neutrals of the Wabanaki.

Passamaquoddy Bay, the principal home of the Passamaquoddy, was on the border, in a most disputed position. Privateers of both sides continually seized each other's goods. Some supplies were reaching the British from Nova Scotia through the bay, and at this realization Colonel Allen sought Passamaquoddy aid in stopping the traffic. The Passamaquoddy were most familiar with the treacherous bay and were good seamen. They were charged to go aboard any vessels, examine their papers, and force any ship that appeared to be connected with the British to go to Machias. They were also to turn over any Tories sending intelligence to St. John to Ambroise Bear, a Malecite chief, and assist him in bringing suspects to Machias. The Passamaquoddy performed well in this role, and Allen complimented them for "behaving with the greatest politeness and humanity to the prisoners." The real focus of the war, however, had shifted to the southern colonies, and Cornwallis' surrender in Virginia in 1781 was the decisive event. When the Treaty of Paris of 1783 was signed, the British grudgingly gave in to the demand that America be accorded full independence as a nation. Now was the time of reward for the Passamaquoddy and their Indian allies, the time when the promises made by Allen, as a representative of the government, would be met. Or would they?

Despite the repeating urgings of Allen and the Indians, virtually nothing had been done by the United States ten years after the Treaty of Paris. The Indians were destitute — in large part because of the war — and were beginning to make threats of retreating to Canada and joining the British, who had not completely given up the thought of regaining some territory. Allen went so far as to have the Indians take his two young sons hostage one winter, as proof of his sincere intentions to make the government honor the obligations he had made in its behalf. He appealed in an eloquent letter to the Massachusetts legislature, pointing out that the Indians still had letters from Massachusetts and General Washington promising that the widows and children of Indian veterans would be cared for, that the Indians should be guaranteed free exercise of religion and be supplied with a priest and a suitable residence for him, that they were to have exclusive rights of the beaver hunt, and that the wanton destruction of game by white hunters was to be curtailed. In addition, ammunition was to be provided for fowling in times of emergency, fair trade was to be established and regulated, and an agent was to reside near them to assist in business dealings and to redress wrongs. Finally, the Indians were to be viewed as "brothers and children under the protection and fatherly care of the United States" and to enjoy every right and privilege. (The Passamaquoddy are still attempting to gain such federal recognition.)

Somehow, during the course of the war, the St. John and Passamaquoddy were induced to resign most of their lands to the United States in return for a formal confirmation that certain of their ancient lands were inviolably theirs. In his letter, Allen reminded the Massachusetts legislature that it was at their urging that the Federal Eastern Indian Outpost was dissolved and ties between the federal government and the Indians in Maine were severed. (Massachusetts claimed this as the right of an original colony, but, having accomplished this, did nothing further.) Finally, in 1794 a treaty was made between Massachusetts and the Passamaquoddy which further reduced Indian land and was as notable for imposing restrictions as it was for fulfilling promises. The land reserved for Indians was somehow seen to be a benevolent gift of the state, rather than a miserly scrap of what was really their own territory. Later, the ultimate corruption was the leasing of much of this land for "999 years" to whites, without Indian consent.

Now, the Passamaquoddy have succeeded in having the Maine federal court judge order the reluctant Department of Justice and Department of the Interior to sue Maine and Massachusetts on their behalf for alienated reservation lands guaranteed in the 1794 treaty. It has been a long hard fight to reach this stage; "run around" is still the name of the game.

THE 1800's.   In 1820, Maine separated from Massachusetts and became a state. In the compact of separation between the two bodies, Maine agreed to continue the concern and care of Indians within Maine borders that had been exercised by Massachusetts. Massachusetts secured a release from its treaties with the Penobscots, but failed to do so with the more remote Passamaquoddy. It therefore set aside $35,000 for a trust fund to be established for the support of Maine Indians. Two large townships, the present Mattawamkeag and Woodville were set aside, and their timber, hay, and other produce were also to be used for Indian support. The trust fund still exists, although the interest continues to be placed in the general fund of the state. The fund was unavailable to Indians until recently, although occasionally it was used in their behalf or on behalf of others (without Indian consent); the townships were sold to the state for $50,000 by the Penobscots in 1833, by some inducement or other, and never used as intended by Massachusetts. A dreary recital of abuses of Passamaquoddy and Penobscot welfare trails through the 1800's, giving a good picture of the condition of Indians in the state, and the attitude of white inhabitants toward them. The culminating blow of that century occurred when, in a case concerning Passamaquoddy hunting rights, the state declared the tribe to be nonexistent. (With characteristic doggedness, however, the Passamaquoddy failed to become extinct.)

During this century, the Indians at Pleasant Point subsisted chiefly from fishing and sealing. Seal oil, much in demand, was sold in nearby Eastport. At Indian Township, farming was the mainstay, supplemented with hunting, fishing, basket-making, and guiding. Later in the century, Indians worked in logging and lumbering. Side occupations were fur trading and the making of snowshoes, axe handles, canoe paddles, and canoes. There was much shipbuilding in Washington County at this time, but there is no evidence that Indians engaged in this industry.

The Civil War brought out the strange rumor that confederate agents were at work among the Passamaquoddy. In a letter to a Calais newspaper, Chief John Francis denied that his people planned to rise and massacre the whites of the region. Passamaquoddy who wanted to join the Union Army were at first refused, but later this ruling was changed, and several served well in the cause of the Union. John Francis himself joined the Union Navy.

Education became a debated issue. Some Passamaquoddies wanted it for their children, but wanted it in French, taught by the Catholic clergy. Some thought it more realistic that their children now learn English, but feared Protestant proselytizing. Some thought it of no earthly use and wanted none of it. Protestant and Catholic clergy and missionaries vied for the chance to educate the Indians, while the state hung onto the purse strings. In the end the English language and Catholic priests won. The church has had a major hand in education on the Maine reservations ever since; only very recently have lay teachers been included in the reservation schools. During the 1800's, the dwindling fur trade was still carried on at the trading post in Robbinston on the coast by a few hardy souls, but the growing thing for Indians was making baskets for the tourist trade that was beginning to blossom in Maine. Passamaquoddy men of this era were still to be seen in fur hats, moccasins, and silver brooches and armbands; not really as they were in 1600, but not like the white men around them, either. Women wore tall beaver hats with silver bands, silver buttons and brooches, elaborately beaded leggings, and red and blue trade-cloth skirts; they were colorfully set apart from their white sisters of the time.

The 1800's brought many changes: English to American control; the Civil War; the emergence of Maine as a state; the entrance of Indians into the white economy other than in the fur trade; the jelling of methods of "dealing with Indians" (as, for example, the mythical extinction of the tribe); the introduction of education on the reservations, amidst power plays of Protestants and Catholics; and the changes in tribal structure, which resulted, in the last analysis, from pressures exerted from outside. It was an eventful hundred years for the Passamaquoddy.

1900's TO 1950's.   Little changed in the Passamaquoddy relationship to the state of Maine until the 1920's. In the twenties there was little work available on or near the reservations, and many men had been lost or disabled in World War I, creating further hardship. The tribe's representative to the legislature, disabled veteran George Stevens, Sr., appealed to the legislature for welfare relief for Indian communities. His appeal had effect, and assistance was given to the reservations, although no jobs were made available.

The problem of dealing with Indians was removed from the governor and council, where it had been dealt with from 1820 to 1927. Then the Forestry Department took over until 1933. Next Health and Welfare had its turn until 1965, when at last the Indians got their own State Department of Indian Affairs.

In the 1940's, a chunk of the larger Passamaquoddy reservation was taken by federal eminent domain for a German prisoner-of-war camp. (Internment was apparently not too grueling for the prisoners; dates between Indian girls and Germans were not uncommon.) After the war, the land was returned — to the state, not the Indians — and was sold off in lots to white buyers. Today it is an island of white homeowners within the reservation, and one of the parcels of land the Passamaquoddy are claiming in their lawsuit.

As for the economy in the first half of the twentieth century, the small amount of work available to Indians at Indian Township consisted of dangerous river drives where the logs were herded to the mills, and woods work, with seasonal potato picking in Aroostook County and blueberry raking within Washington County. At Pleasant Point, there was hard, low-paid work for women and children in the sardine factories that once dotted the region's coast. In the early part of the century there was still some sealing, but soon a bounty was put on seals, because fishermen found the seals troublesome. The Passamaquoddy, who could not so easily make a profit at fishing as they could at sealing, were the main losers in this shift in the economy. For a time they engaged in a "seal-nose conspiracy," counterfeiting many seal noses from one sealskin and turning them in to the game warden for the bounty. This was a successful means of subsistence for a while, but eventually three of the conspirators were jailed. (The game warden demanded the seal tail for proof of a kill, and the remaining counterfeiters resorted to making two "tails" out of each flipper, for a total of only nine "tails" per seal — but it was a living!)

The 1920's to the 1940's were economically very hard times in the region, for the Indians in particular, but during World War II there was work in the shipyards in Portland and in the fish factories on the coast. The isolated Indian Township people were taken by bus to the fish factories in Eastport, more than fifty miles away. Many Passamaquoddies joined the armed services. After World War II, the arrival of more cars on the reservation increased opportunities for work off the reserve, and the economy in general picked up. All things being relative, however, this still only meant things were better, not good, for Washington County has been an economically depressed area for many decades.

During the first fifty years of the twentieth century there were few changes in education or tribal government. Children still attended school only in the summer when the nuns came, and women were still not on the tribal council. There were changes, to be sure, during this period, but for the most part there were few signs that a burst of activity would begin in the 1950's.

THE 1950's TO THE PRESENT. The period from about 1955 to the present day has been one of profound change for the Passamaquoddy in almost every sphere, from educational and religious to economic and political. There are no signs of a slowdown in the recording of Passamaquoddy culture and its relationship to the world outside. The change seems to have resulted from a fortuitous combination of personalities, from changes in national policy regarding poor people, and from the realization on both the state and national levels that the American Indians have been treated unjustly.

First, the personalities. At Pleasant Point reservation, George Francis — who had been away from the reservation for over forty years — was elected chief. Francis, one of the few who had been educated at Carlisle Indian School, had later secured a good job in the auto industry in Detroit, where he lived and worked until his retirement. After his wife died and his children had married, he returned home to Pleasant Point, where he was accepted as naturally as though he had never been away. An intelligent man with experience on the outside, he had seen enough in other places to know that Passamaquoddies were worse off than they should be. After being elected chief, Francis exposed the situation of Maine Indians to the press, simultaneously working on the state level to increase revenues for Indians. Until this time, most people outside of Washington County were not aware that there were still Indians in Maine, so forgotten were they.

At about the same time, a young chief, John Stevens, was elected at Indian Township. Stevens had grown up in the poorest reservation in Maine under worse than usual circumstances, because his father, a former Indian representative, had been mistakenly imprisoned during most of Stevens' young life. His early experiences of going cold and hungry made Stevens react strongly to seeing young Koreans in that same condition. This new objective view of the effects of poverty made him resolve to change reservation conditions if he returned home alive. He did return and was elected chief at the age of twenty-one on the basis of promising to change things for the better. His early efforts were aimed at removing a despotic and dishonest Indian agent assigned to the Passamaquoddy.

Since the separation of the tribe into two main parts in the 1800's, there had been little cooperation or political exchange between the two Passamaquoddy reservations, but the young and the old chief were brought together because of George Francis' cultivation of the news media and, as one of them said, "publicity forced us to cooperate." The two men became good friends and began having joint council meetings whenever mutual problems and issues arose. Stevens said, "We learned we couldn't afford to be separate, but must unite. Today the reservation may have political squabbles among themselves, but when they go after something, they are united" (Stevens, personal communication).

In the 1960's Stevens read about the Office of Economic Opportunity, and he wrote asking if the Passamaquoddy, as "poor people," qualified for some of its programs. The response was that Maine wasn't set up to receive programs, but when it was the Passamaquoddy would be considered. This was not too long in coming, and the Passamaquoddies were made a delegate agency (later, an autonomous agency) of the Washington County Community Action Project. The tribe set up an OEO board and, in the process of groping through guidelines and regulations, learned not only of other programs available to them but also of OEO Legal Services. There was an awakening to a new set of possibilities having nothing to do with the state of Maine, which in the past had been singularly unresponsive to Indian needs.

Having gained a measure of control over their own destiny for the first time in 200 years with a CAP program, the Passamaquoddy had confidence to go on to other things. Their leaders began elbowing their way in to different committees that involved their welfare, including the Bureau of Human Relations Services of the Catholic church, which eventually formed a division of Indian Services.

Some of the first concentrated efforts of Indians were to introduce legislation and to lobby on behalf of Indians. Much latent hostility was stirred up in the legislature when Indians began speaking on their own behalf, so that while public awareness of Maine Indians increased, so did political resistance. Indian governors learned that without public support to pressure officials they would get nowhere, so they began speaking throughout the state, to the League of Women Voters and the Maine Teachers Association, to college and university students and professors, and to anyone else who would listen. More press coverage resulted; ultimately, sufficient pressure was put on the legislature so that it passed (on its fifth presentation) a bill forming a state Department of Indian Affairs, as well as other Indian bills.

Suddenly, the Indians of Maine had become visible. The United Council of Churches, in a survey of sanitary and health conditions, reported that there was no electricity, water, or sewage on the reservations, that more than half of the few available wells were contaminated, that houses were inadequate, that Maine Indians could not vote in state or national elections.

The Civil Rights Commission took notice, and soon a bill was passed giving Indians the right to vote in national elections in 1953. Maine was the last state in the Union to ratify the federal ruling of 1924 on Indians; even then the bill was introduced twice before passing. Only Utah was as lax.

In 1957 a bill was passed to take money from the Passamaquoddy Trust Fund and build homes under the aegis of the Department of Health and Welfare. Although many Passamaquoddy approved, they were not really consulted, and they were unable to get Health and Welfare to include Indians on the building planning board. Cracker-box houses were hastily built of substandard materials on concrete slabs, crammed into a tiny area in a way incompatible with Indian living preferences. They were too small for the typically large families and were firetraps as well; several deaths have occurred when people couldn't escape from the buildings.

The houses on Indian Township were built first. When the residents saw what they were like and how their trust fund money was being used, they appealed to the Civil Rights Commission. The commission sent Andrea Bear, a Canadian Indian who was a student at Colby College, to investigate. Her report was damning, but little action was taken — except that the houses built at Pleasant Point reservation the following year were made slightly larger and placed farther apart, although in many ways they were structurally inferior to those at Indian Township. Indians still had no say in the construction or placement of the houses, although they could choose the color of the kitchen floor. The state proudly claims to have "given" the Passamaquoddy this housing, implying somehow that it was at the taxpayer's expense rather than from the Indian trust fund — which despite years of state abuse miraculously still had something left in it.

Miss Bear also reported to the commission that Indians could not get haircuts in the nearby town of Princeton, and the barbershops were then ordered to accept Indian clients or close down. They chose to close down. Still, even that was progress of a sort, for it showed Indians that they had some control — however nebulous — over things.

In the late 1950's, the celebrated Passamaquoddy land case began — in a poker game. Years before, the state had illegally "leased" several parcels of Indian Township for 999 years to white men. One of the leasers put up, as stakes in a poker game, a piece of land that adjoined property leased for a motel. The motel owner "won" the lot that night, and the next day he began setting up stakes around it — including in "his" area the yard of an Indian home. The Indians held an angry meeting, deciding to stand guard and also to appeal to the state attorney general; he ruled that it would be up to the tribe to bring suit against the motel keeper. The tribe had no lawyer and no money to hire one, so it decided to provoke arrest in order to force the motel keeper to bring the suit to court. They stood guard on the land, threatening to cut down all the trees on the motel grounds if the road was begun on the disputed lot. The state police unsuccessfully tried to dissuade the Indians; finally, when only women were on guard, the police made their arrests and carted five Passamaquoddy off to jail. This news made the papers and prompted someone to tell Stevens of a new attorney in Eastport who might take their case.

The lawyer, for whom private funding was arranged, forced the presiding judge to disqualify himself on the grounds he had drawn up the deeds for the white leasers, and a second judge was appointed. He in turn dismissed the case for lack of evidence against the Passamaquoddy. Still, they needed to get the case into court, so the Passamaquoddy confiscated a gravel truck belonging to the motel keeper, who tried to shoot them. At this impasse, the tribal lawyer and the attorney general got the motel keeper to desist, and the zone was considered neutral until the question of Passamaquoddy land could be settled in court. Thus, further selling of Indian property was barred, and the land case began in earnest in 1959. Through various fits and starts it has finally reached a promising stage in 1972, is presently being handled by the Native American Rights Fund of Denver, and Hogan and Hartson of Washington, and may be finally settled by 1975. As for the motel keeper, he has had the foresight to sell "his" motel property.

As a direct result of this case, the formerly vague feelings of being "had" by the state have been crystallized into cold historical facts, and Passamaquoddies today know their rights and their history as never before. This new knowledge has brought changes in the schools and in relationships with the state, and a new determination not to be "had" again.

In 1968, land ownership was again threatened, and again the tribe rose to the occasion. Georgia Pacific Lumber Company, the main employer in the area, began cutting operations on Indian Township — apparently with the consent of the state but not with the consent of the Indians. The council appealed to the company to stop, with no results. Then it appealed to the cutting crews, augmenting the appeal with beer and picnic lunches; although the crews were sympathetic, the next day they were back on the job. Then the Passamaquoddy, joined by some Penobscots and Malecites, resorted to an imaginative tactic. They dressed, from oldest to youngest, in Indian regalia replete with paint and feathers, and, making the negative TV image work in their favor, staged an "attack" on the cutting crews, many of whom still had hangovers from the previous days' "picnic." The crews fled in such haste they left behind thousands of dollars worth of woods equipment, which was confiscated by the Passamaquoddy, who then were in a real position to bargain with the huge company. Company officials came to the reservation for a parley, appealing to Chief Stevens, as a company employee and a reasonable man, to talk sense to his tribe. He spoke to his fellow Indians briefly in Passamaquoddy, saying, in effect, "Give 'em hell!" They did, and Georgia Pacific withdrew. Negotiations were now open for a new land-management policy, the hiring of Indian cutting crews, and an Indian forest ranger. The tribe had accomplished another major victory, and its impact on tribal self-respect and pride is immeasurable.

In 1969, the state cut off aid for the summer — including medical supplies to the elderly and milk for children. When no appeals from the tribe were successful, the Passamaquoddy blockaded the road running through Indian Township. The road is virtually the only route through a vast wooded area to the paper mill, the market town of Calais, and the Canadian border. The turnout for the blockage was large, the plan organized, and the self-assurance high. During the land case the Passamaquoddy had learned that the road was built on land taken, but never recompensed, from the reservation, and that it had been built with monies from the Indian fund. By all rights, the road through the reservation was theirs, so they charged toll: $1 for cars and $2 for trucks. State officials were on their way immediately, and miraculously the funds were located to continue the needed assistance programs. Although several Passamaquoddy were jailed, all were soon released.

Again, after generations of apathy, the tribe had rallied to an occasion and emerged the victor. Confrontation is not a traditional Passamaquoddy approach to problems, yet they have learned during the past fifteen years that they have strength, backing from many sources, and power over their destiny. They are not about to accept injustice silently, ever again.

By 1965, the Indians of Maine had suffrage in state and national elections, electricity, some new homes, a land case in the works, the attention of conscientious white groups in the state, a church aware of Indian problems, a sympathetic press, some Title I education funds, several federal programs, and a new land-management policy.

Many more changes occurred during the final half of this decade: the state Department of Indian Affairs had been created, and soon Indians had a voice in choosing the commissioner and his deputy; federal water and sewage treatment facilities were being installed; an anonymous donor gave funds for travel expenses to the tribal governors and councils; an Indian education specialist was hired, and Indian education was placed in the Department of Education for the first time; women became active in tribal politics; and a school bond issue was passed for new schools on both reservations, and more federal programs were introduced, among them Headstart, Operation Mainstream, HUD (planning for new housing), and Indian Legal Services. Reservation conditions were and still are pretty poor; but they have come a long way from the standstill of the centuries preceding 1950.

In the early 1970's, the former chief George Francis died at Pleasant Point. The same year, his friend John Stevens left Indian Township in his seventeenth year as chief to become the Commissioner of Indian Affairs. His aim still, as always, is to get Indians in control of their own lives. He is presently working to introduce legislation that would give tribal councils control over the Department of Indian Affairs, so that, even if he is not succeeded by another Indian, control will still be in Indian hands. The trend towards self-determination is finally beginning to show results.

In the spring of 1973, the following programs were operating at the Passamaquoddy reservations: CAP, Headstart, Mainstream, HUD and EDA, Neighborhood Youth Corps, homemaker classes under HEW and the Catholic church, Office of Education, basic education courses, Opportunity Industrialization Centers under the Department of Labor, alcoholism program under state Department of Indian Affairs, home economics assistance from University of Maine Extension Service, scholarships and intern apprenticeships from the archdiocese of Portland, and, at Indian Township, a new program in bilingual education run by a Passamaquoddy. Each reservation also has a fledgling Basket Co-op in early stages of development.

The University of Maine recently opened its doors to Indian students, offering free tuition, room, and board — within a few months Indian enrollment had increased beyond anyone's estimates. Nearly every college and university in the state is trying to create Indian Studies programs, and the University of Maine is attempting to establish a talent development program for state Indians. Bowdoin College is working on a year-round recreation program for young people on the reserves in conjunction with the Newman Apostolate of that college, while Unity College is planning a program to help Indian adults obtain college degrees in a special part-time program. Indian speakers and Indian craftsmen are in great demand. There has been a renaissance of Indian crafts, songs, and dances; and newspaper articles about Maine Indians — once a rarity — are now commonplace.

Maine Indians are now on the map and in the news, and are beginning to believe in themselves. Although many programs are not producing sensational results, and the poverty cycle has not yet been broken, the seeds of a better life and of community autonomy have been planted and have taken root — and things will never be the same again.

FACTORS AFFECTING ECONOMIC DEVELOPMENT

Tribal Wealth

Most of the usable natural resources of the tribe are located on Indian Township, the larger by far of the two reservations. The township consists of approximately 23,000 acres, including around 16,000 acres of usable timberland, 100 miles of undeveloped freshwater shoreline on pure lakes and streams, and 7,000 acres relegated to bogs, heaths, open lands, and "alienated" (disputed) lots.

The timberlands produce mostly softwoods, such as spruce, hemlock, cedar, pine, fir, and tamarack. Some hardwoods are also found there; brown ash is sought in particular for basket making. The area is part of the watershed of the west branch of the St. Croix River, which is near the northeast part of the reservation. There are many fine lakes, including Lewey's Lake and Big Lake on the reservation, all with excellent fishing. Nearby West Grand Lake is famous for fishing, with many tourist homes and lodges. There seems to be no reason why Indian Township could not attract a similar development, for reservation lakes abound in trout, togue, bass, and land-locked salmon.

Hunting on the township is as good as any other place in Maine, a state famed for good hunting. There is an abundance of deer, bear, small game, and fowl, and a good-sized moose herd (although hunting moose is legal only for Indians). The potential for a sportsmen's tourist development is great, and plainly it is the avenue of income most likely to succeed — yet it is the one that has failed to receive funding to date.

At Pleasant Point reservation, some fifty miles to the east, a small but beautiful shoreline borders Passamaquoddy Bay. Beyond the shore lies the barren, hilly reservation of 100 acres. Some salt-water fishing and lobstering is done off the shores, and salt-water-oriented recreation seems to be the best bet for development at this reservation, with perhaps a marina and tourist comples to take advantage of the trade that comes through the reservation on Coastal Route 1.

The semiprecious minerals found along a coastal mineral belt are a secondary natural resource. Although the area is a haven for rock hunters, this resource is undeveloped. The Passamaquoddy have shown considerable potential for handicrafts, however, and might conceivably utilize this resource (with the proper backing, material, and training) to produce an Eastern Indian jewelry craft—but this is speculation only.

UTILIZATION AND MANAGEMENT OF NATURAL RESOURCES. By far the greatest user of the natural resources of the reservations is the tribe, which sees the lands as communally owned, although held in a sort of bondage by the state until the case is settled.

At Pleasant Point, tribal members do some porpoise shooting, operate two fish weirs, and swim, fish, and catch lobster as individuals. At Indian Township the lakes and woods are used freely by tribal members for hunting, trapping, and fishing, as well as for swimming, camping, and boating. Indians from both reservations collect balsam tips for the wreath-making business that flourishes in the county for a few weeks in winter, producing high-quality Christmas wreaths for sale throughout Maine and Massachusetts.

Besides procuring personal food, hunters may sell hides and pelts. Many Passamaquoddy act as seasonal licensed guides, both on and off the reservation. A new law requires that nontribal members who use the reservation for hunting must obtain a special license from the tribal council for $25, and that the hunters must hire an Indian guide as well. The hunting is very good, and the Passamaquoddy know their land intimately, so actually the arrangement is a good deal for the hunter.

A small picnic site on Indian Township, maintained by the reservation and the University of Maine, is well run by a tribal member. Despite a lack of advertising, there are usually more people wishing to camp than there are campsites — another indication that a tourist development would work here.

Finally, the natural resources are utilized by Indians in procuring the basic ingredients for home remedies that augment the spotty health care of the county; indeed, these natural remedies often work as well or better than those supplied by local doctors.

On Indian Township, timber is a planned resource and the main source of revenue for the Passamaquoddy Trust Fund. Until very recently there were virtually *no* Indians on the Indian Township Land Management Committee, which was made up of representatives from Georgia Pacific Lumber Company, the Maine Forestry Service, the University of Maine Forestry Department, and the Department of Health and Welfare. (Occasionally the reservation priest was invited to the committee meetings as a concession to the tribe.) After the confrontation with the Georgia Pacific Company in 1968, a new land-management committee was formed, made up of both the tribal governors and councils, and one member each from the Department of Indian Affairs, the Department of Forest Services, Georgia Pacific Lumber Company, and the University of Maine. This makes fifteen Indians to three whites, a real change in the balance of power. The Passamaquoddy Trust Fund is replenished yearly by revenue from lumber cut by Indians and bought either by Georgia Pacific for the nearby paper mill or by the state for firewood.

POTENTIAL DEVELOPMENT OF NATURAL RESOURCES. The Passamaquoddy, like most Indians, want to protect and keep their natural resources, but they also see the possibilities of developing these resources in a way that will not exhaust the environment. Economic concerns are clearly not paramount; a recent attempt to locate an oil refinery and oil storage depot on the two reservations was turned down unanimously by both councils, despite offers of large sums, jobs for everyone, and miscellaneous benefits.

The tribe *would* like to develop a recreation area, however. A recent bulletin of the Center for Community Economic Development noted that "the growth of recreation and tourism and the shifting pattern of development to less congested and polluted areas will in the next decade offer a tremendous opportunity for revitalizing rural America. But the rural poor who should stand to gain from these trends are being pushed out of the picture" (Faux 1972). The same bulletin mentions that, although outsiders are investing in real estate in Maine for the expected land and recreation boom, the official state stance is to attract industry, and "the attention of most regional offices of federal agencies [in Maine] is riveted to the mobility strategy and industrial development." Perhaps this official state attitude is why Passamaquoddy proposals to EDA for the funding of tourist complexes on both reservations have been turned down. But it is hard for people familiar with the reservation settings, including this writer, to understand how anything else would take precedence over so obvious a source of workable economic development as tourist facilities.

A good rundown of the recreation (and other) potential of the area is given by Tannenbaum in "Passamaquoddy Indian economic development" (Tannenbaum 1972). Besides mentioning the obvious advantages of marinas, picnic sites, craft outlets, motels, and cottages for the reservation, the author notes that a sawmill and equipment for producing cedar shingles and fences would have a good chance of success on Indian Township.

In 1969 the Clarkson Corporation did a traffic study on both reservations and found that Pleasant Point has almost a captive audience for a museum-restaurant-marina complex, while the traffic flow was lower at Indian Township. The roads to Indian Township are poor, discouraging all but the dauntless, but it would seem that pressure could be put on the state by the assisting federal agencies to rectify this.

Year-round recreation in Maine is a growing business, and it is at least as possible on Indian Township as anyplace else in the state. Here cross-country skiing, snowshoeing (on Indian-made snowshoes), and snowmobiling could be routed through numerous woods roads and still be kept clear of the Indian living settlements; ice fishing, iceboating, and skating are other winter possibilities. The summer recreation potential is even more obvious, with possibilities being limited only by money and imagination. Tourist development would correspond well with Passamaquoddy preferences for varying kinds of employment and seasonal cycles of activity, and with Passamaquoddy ideals of land use. From every angle, tourism is the best economic bet — yet it fails to be funded. Why?

CAPITAL RESOURCES. Capital resources of the tribe are currently fairly small, in terms of funds that are truly available, with no strings attached, for use as the tribe sees fit. The Passamaquoddy Trust Fund totals around $109,000.

The trust fund originated at the 1820 separation of Maine and Massachusetts. Massachusetts gave $35,000 for the establishment of the fund, stating in the compact of separation that the hay and timber proceeds of two large townships were also to be placed in the trust fund for the tribe. (These two townships were sold soon after the separation compact.)

Today, the proceeds of timber sales on Indian Township are the only source of replenishment of the trust fund. Still, much time has elapsed since 1820. One might well ask, "Where is all the accrued interest that should be in the trust fund?" Incredible as it may seem, no one ever has been made accountable for uses of the fund, and Indians have never received reports about expenditures until the past five years. Certainly they were never asked to approve uses of the fund. Research done both independently and in conjunction with the land case has shown that many towns have had access to the fund, including Biddeford, Wiscassett, Portland, Bangor, Oldtown, Houlton, and Eastport. Eastport, for example, borrowed from the fund to build toll bridges and then declared bankruptcy; it never repaid the large sums borrowed, even though it continued to collect tolls until the bridges were torn down. The road built through Indian Township, a state highway, was paid for by money from the trust fund, as were the bridges at either end of the township — although the Indians were not recompensed for land taken to build this road.

Abuses of the fund have been almost unremitting since Maine's inception as a state. To quote Indian Commissioner Stevens, "It was the slush fund for every politician around, and any campaign promises were paid for out of the Indian Fund. And then they say, 'Oh! Those poor Indians! No *wonder* we're poor — they've been stealing us blind for years!'"(Stevens, personal communication).

Until the new land-management policy was established after the Georgia Pacific showdown, the trust fund was controlled by the state governor and council, and Indians had no way of knowing how much money was annually received nor how much was taken out. Indians could not request use of the fund, and, indeed, very little of it seems to have been spent in their behalf. Now that the Land Management Committee consists of fifteen Indians and three whites, this picture has changed rather dramatically. The fund is now under the control of the Department of Indian Affairs, and each Passamaquoddy tribal council may request up to 40 percent of the fund if it sees fit, while 20 percent must remain to earn interest. Since this new ruling, however, the Passamaquoddy have left the fund almost entirely untouched.

The land case, of course, has a tremendous potential for increasing the trust fund. If the Passamaquoddy win their case, the state's failure to meet conditions of the compact of separation from Massachusetts will cause it to be held accountable for the abuses of the trust fund. If the tribe should win back what was taken from the fund, plus interest and damages, a very large sum would gather in the coffers. There might also be repayment of state taxes collected from illegally sold or leased Indian lands, taxes that even today are paid into the state's general fund.

Thus, although current capital resources of the Passamaquoddy are slim, their potential resources are substantial if they win their land case, and it appears that they do have a good chance of winning, even though the Departments of Justice and the Interior are resisting the case with every legal ploy possible. In effect, the Passamaquoddy, by asking the government to sue in their behalf, are asking it to admit its implicit blame in the case. This, in turn, would make it easy for Maine, if it loses, to turn to the federal government for aid in paying reparations. The federal government, in effect, is being asked to sue itself.

Tribal leaders and the lawyers involved in the case plan to convince the tribe of the importance of carefully managing any monies taken in. They hope to see the money invested with only the interest used, a sum that should still exceed the present budget of the state Department of Indian Affairs. Pending the outcome of the case, however, these funds are only a potential capital resource.

The budget of the Department of Indian Affairs is allocated approximately $300,000 a year for the Passamaquoddy people. Much of this is used for medical aid and staff salaries and cannot really be viewed as a capital resource; the legislature assigns budget categories, and the tribe has no control over these expenditures. The same is true of the federal programs on the reservations, for the budgets are relatively inflexible and must be spent as designated in the grant applications.

The tribe continually faces the problem of receiving funds that make *part* of a plan operative but supply no working capital. This has been the fate of the OEO-funded Basket Co-op, for example. Currently the co-op has a machine for pounding ash for basket splints, but there are no funds for getting the machine installed and running, so splints are still pounded by hand. The tribal council would probably not sanction the Basket Co-op using trust fund money for this, an unproved enterprise, and so the expensive machine sits unused.

Occurrences of a similar kind are not unusual in the implementation of federal programs. An MDTA program to train basket makers, for example, prohibited selling of the finished products — even though there was a market for baskets and even though the Passamaquoddy had bought the raw materials for production. Many of the finished baskets were taken apart, rewoven, and then sold. Most of them were given away, however — at a time when the Basket Co-op was in dire need of operating capital. This is clearly a silly way of doing things, and the Passamaquoddy can hardly be expected to show respect for program guidelines that are frequently foolish in application.

After the new basket makers had been trained, the co-op had accrued no working capital to hire them — partly because of the outlay in labor and raw materials for the training program, for which MDTA did not pay the promised sum after the program was completed (claiming that too few workers had been trained). Thus the bank loan that the co-op had taken out to pay the trainees had to be repaid with the co-op's only other revenue: money from making Christmas wreaths. This, too, was a disaster, for the winter was warm, the wreaths shed their needles, and sales were low; a church organization that had placed a large order failed to come up with the expected purchasers. The co-op was barely able to pay off the bank loan. The Passamaquoddy Basket Co-op now has managers paid by the CAP program, a building rented by the CAP program, equipment (some donated by the Universtiy of Maine), substantial orders from the army and other organizations, and personnel who already know the business or who have been trained on MDTA. Yet there is little activity, because of lack of operating capital to get the ash pounders operating and to pay labor until filled orders can take care of the payroll. In 1972 a capable co-op manager quit his job in frustation, and one can hardly blame him.

As another example, HUD installed the greater part of the water and sewage treatment systems on the reservations in the last two years, but did not provide hookups to homes. Thousands of dollars worth of equipment sat idle for more than a year, until the state was needled into assisting with the hookups; then the reservations were dug up all over again, at great nuisance and expense.

Federal programs frequently operate on the premise that the state will also do its part, but Maine is poor and is itself in need of economic development. The legislature's approach to poverty is to dole out welfare or Indian agent monies, which is rather like putting a band-aid on a bleeding artery. The federal government is wasting its time with reservation programs, until it takes a *total approach* to the total problems and ceases its fragmented attempts at economic development, which produces in Indians — and other low-income groups — a sense of failure, confusion, and a fear of trying again.

OTHER TRIBAL RESOURCES. The Passamaquoddy have a resource — as yet unrealized by themselves, the state, or the federal government — in their rich, if largely unwritten, history, for there is considerable potential for an historical tourist attraction. What does this potential consist of?

1. The Passamaquoddy were among the first Indians of New England to meet with Europeans (long before the settlement of Plymouth), and Champlain's St. Croix Island, a national historic monument is nearby.

2. They were among the first Christian converts in North America, and church history is extensive for the area.

3. They were important during the Revolution, primarily as a bulwark against the British in Canada.

4. The tribe was part of the Wabanaki Confederacy and later of the Great Council Fire of the Iroquois League, a formidable third force in the French-English struggle for empire.

5. The Passamaquoddy were essential in resolving the international boundary dispute between Maine and Canada.

6. They invented the canvas-covered canoe, which dominated the market for 75 years.

7. Franklin Roosevelt frequented Pleasant Point reservation, across the bay from the family summer home at Campobello (today an international historic site containing many Passamaquoddy baskets, rustic furniture, birch canoes, and other handiwork).

8. The Passamaquoddy are unique among Northeastern Indians in the retention of their language, and many of their customs, crafts, and authentic tribal dances are well known to most tribal members.

Recent historical studies are turning up more information on this really interesting tribe, and it does seem that an entrepreneurial mind could make a paying attraction out of this wealth of historic material. A side benefit would be a boost to the morale and pride of the tribe, which, after years of depletion, could well use such a lift.

The tribe also has itself as resource; first, in the potentially increased population that should result from better housing, jobs, schools, and medical care, which appear to be coming in; and second, in the sense that the Passamaquoddy harbor a potential for outstanding craftwork, evidenced not only by the expert basketwork and woodworking, but also in the new crafts that recently have been introduced, with considerable show of talent among both young and old. Economic development plans that direct this tendency towards skill in handiwork and craftsmanship could do quite well, provided such plans are approached in total perspective, not piecemeal, as they were with the ill-starred Basket Co-op.

Tribal Income: Its Sources and Uses

HUNTING AND FISHING. Fish and game are more than the products of sport to the Passamaquoddy: they are important in the sustenance of life. Indian Township reservation has both hunting and freshwater fishing, while Pleasant Point has saltwater products, and many families have members who pursue these natural resources at least some of the time. Commonly, those who hunt and fish distribute some of their catch to friends and relatives throughout the tribe, so that there is a wide distribution of these goods on and between the two reservations. Because fish and game are usually outright gifts, they can be considered edible income.

SEASONAL WORK. Quick income from short bursts of hard work is available through blueberry raking, potato harvesting, and wreath making. Guiding sportsmen also provides seasonal work for a few. The emphasis on seasonal labor has dropped dramatically during the last few years, apparently because of the increase of reservation jobs (low-paid but full-time), and also because of the increased availability of transportation, which enables Passamaquoddy to visit their Indian friends in Canada any time, rather than only at harvest times. Presently, only a small fraction of Passamaquoddy income is from seasonal labor, a definite break with practices of even five years ago. Wreath making on the reservation in the early winter season is the main seasonal work survivor, probably because the incentive for this work has always been economic and not social — it is the main way Passamaquoddy prepare for the Christmas gift-giving season. About $12,000 was made in 1971 by the tribe as a whole, but people of all ages worked at making wreaths around the clock, seven days a week for two months; for the actual effort involved, the profit is not great. Although the wreaths sell in Boston and other cities for from $3.50 to $6.00 each, the Passamaquoddy make about 15 cents a wreath and supply the materials as well.

LOCAL EMPLOYMENT. An average of 15 percent of the people at Pleasant Point work off-reservation locally, while only about 3 or 4 percent do so at Indian Township. These figures increase somewhat in the winter. Approximately 25 percent of the population on both reservations is currently employed in federally sponsored on-reservation programs such as CAP and Operation Mainstream; yet if these funds should be eliminated, 75 percent of the tribe would be effectively out of work, for relative prosperity of a few gives income to the 50 percent of the tribe who are self-employed, who provide various services and handcrafted articles. Some tribal members who have a little ready cash buy Passamaquoddy crafts for resale elsewhere.

The unemployment rate is around 10 percent at Pleasant Point, and around 22 percent at Indian Township, if those who are self-employed at least some of the time are considered as employed. If full-time employment is used as the criterion, employment figures are much higher.

DISTANT EMPLOYMENT. Approximately 35 percent of tribe works in various New England cities for the winter, and this figure includes large numbers of young men. At winter's end they leave their jobs and return to the reservation for the spring and summer social season, where they live off their winter earnings and occasional odd jobs. But as more jobs open up on the reservation, the winter exodus decreases, so that a viable economic system could well change the whole employment pattern.

ANONYMOUS DONOR FUNDS.   For the past four years, an anonymous donor has contributed a stipend to each of the tribal officers and councilmen to help with expenses, such as travel costs and babysitting fees. This was a great boon to the continuation of joint council meetings, which involve a round trip drive of more than 100 miles for one reservation's governing body or the other's. The fund amounts to $6,000 a year, divided among 16 people. This is probably the last year these funds will be available, however. If so, the governors and their councils will revert to the status of unpaid public servants whose jobs increase in complexity each year. The Department of Indian Affairs intends to include tribal officer stipends in the next budget proposal to the legislature, which at present pays only the tribal governors, at $300 per year.

CATHOLIC BUREAU OF INDIAN SERVICES.   The Archdiocese of Portland Division of Human Services has an Indian Services Bureau that is currently funded at $36,000 a year for the three state reservations and for the Association of Aroostook Indians in Houlton. This money is divided four ways, at about $9,000 per location, and is used primarily for secondary school and college scholarships. In the past a visiting nurse was funded by the Indian Services Bureau, as were recreation programs and homemaker classes. The amount and use of these funds changes yearly.

THE STATE DEPARTMENT OF INDIAN AFFAIRS.   The Maine State Department of Indian Affairs, funded biannually by the state legislature, covers only those Indians who reside on the three Maine reservations. The funding changes from budget to budget but agent's reports indicate that from the 1800's onward underappropriation has been the most consistent aspect of Maine Indian Affairs. The total current budget for Indian affairs is about $408,553 for the year, of which approximately $237,934 goes to the two Passamaquoddy reservations. Eighteen percent of the budget goes for staff salaries (commissioner, bookkeeper, secretaries, two agents, and three chaplains). Of monies allocated to the Passamaquoddy, as much as 34 percent is used for medical care, because Maine Indians are ineligible for federal Indian health services. Twenty-four percent goes for grocery orders, mostly to old people and families receiving Aid to Dependent Children. The Department of Indian Affairs also assists with clothing orders (usually for school children), with small household needs on an emergency basis, and with fire truck and ambulance service.

BUREAU OF PUBLIC IMPROVEMENT FUNDS. The Bureau of Public Improvements contributes approximately $20,000 a year to Indian Affairs for home repairs and improvements on the three reservations. This is a small amount when one considers that reservation Indians are unable to secure veterans' or bank loans for home improvement and that this is a climate inherently destructive to wooden houses.

AID TO DEPENDENT CHILDREN. The State Department of Health and Welfare administers federal Aid to Dependent Children in the reservation communities, but does not supplement this aid, as do many other states. Indian Affairs supplements ADC payments when there is no other income, but the department does not have enough funds to adequately support these families. Thirty-seven families receive ADC on the two reservations combined. The payments are $95 a month for a mother and one child, $40 addition for a second child, and so on, in decreasing amounts per child. People on this program also are eligible for Medicaid, which is a help to them and to the already beleaguered Indian Affairs budget.

SOCIAL SECURITY. Thirteen elderly Passamaquoddy receive Social Security Old Age Assistance, and sixteen receive State Old Age Assistance, which is granted to those whose total income is not over a certain base amount. People who receive this assistance also have Medicaid.

Eight Passamaquoddy receive Social Security disability payments, but are not eligible for further assistance from the state.

Seven Passamaquoddy receive either veteran's pensions or Veterans Administration disability payments at present.

Two persons from Pleasant Point receive Aid to the Blind.

Because labels on the surplus commodities foods say "Not to be sold . . . ," this food is ubiquitously called "Noddabee" on the reservations. Most families are eligible to receive "Noddabee" and take advantage of the monthly distributions.

FEDERAL PROGRAMS. No overall figure is available for the amounts granted to the Passamaquoddy reservations in the various federal programs. The figure fluctuates radically from year to year, as programs are augmented, discontinued, or completed. The Department of Indian Affairs plans to delineate these figures in the future.

PATTERNS OF INCOME ACQUISITION AND USE. In 1965, the average annual Passamaquoddy family income was estimated at $430 per capita. Indian agent's orders, welfare, and fruits of the chase somewhat augmented the incredibly low standard of living, but did nothing toward teaching anyone how to handle a family budget. Today reservation employment has risen, with a concomitant rise in the cash income of almost every family. The newness of this situation cannot be overstressed: people now have actual cash income to manage. That they do not always manage it very adroitly should come as no surprise.

The largest part of the family income today goes for groceries, which reflects not only high food costs but the deprivations of the past. Careful shopping and elimination of "junk foods" is practiced by very few when a paycheck is in hand, and no consumer courses have been taught on the reservations to date.

Because of economic conditions, Indians in Maine were as a group poorly dressed until recently. When they became news worthy, boxes and even truckloads of used clothing poured in, usually to be distributed by the church. They are still arriving. But the people who three years ago eagerly sought out usable items from these donations ignore them today — to the puzzlement of the donors who have heard that Indians are poor. They are poor, but not as poor as they were: after groceries, they spend their new money on clothes for themselves and their children. This is very important, especially to the young people, who until recently were shabbily dressed compared with white children in the neighboring towns and high school. (An attitude survey showed as one of the reasons why local white children were glad they weren't Indian was that whites had nicer clothes.)

Another result of improved income is the number of telephones installed on the reservations. Three years ago there was only a public pay phone at each settlement and in each CAP office. Today there are about twenty phones in various homes. Home improvements have been made by some families, but any extra income is more likely to be spent on bigger and better television sets, tape players, and other luxuries. Unfortunately, many of these items are bought on time from local price gougers, at exorbitant interest rates.

In general, one could say that the spending of the new income is done from the belly outwards, with the last consideration being the exterior of one's home; the effects of the new relative prosperity cannot be observed on a casual drive through the reservation.

The idea of savings and investments for an individual family is completely foreign. With or without consumer education, it is doubtful that this aspect of financial management will ever take hold. On the tribal level, investment of profits from an enterprise such as the Basket Co-op would be very hard to accomplish until everyone on the reservation is well-off. It can be predicted that, if the Basket Co-op or other enterprise should make profits above payroll and overhead, the surplus would not be invested but everyone would receive a pay increase. The only conceivable way around this disinclination to invest would be to write into laws and grant awards the requirement that certain percentages of profits would be seeded back into the enterprise. Even this move would have to be carefully explained and jointly approved by the tribe. Passamaquoddy life has had a "here and now" immediacy that will be eradicated only by many years of prosperity — and "economic development" means something rather different on the reservation than it does in Washington, D.C.

Products, Services, and Markets

PRODUCTS. Most of the manufactured products of the Passamaquoddy reservations are made at home in cottage industries.

Pleasant Point, on the coast, specialized in scale baskets for commercial use in the nearby fisheries. These baskets are used in collecting fish scales for the manufacture of pearlescence, an iridescent substance used in nail polish, buttons, and fake pearls. The men at Pleasant Point usually make these heavy-duty baskets, which withstand repeated soaking and abuse. The market varies according to the catch and the fishermen's search for basket substitutes that might cost them less than eight dollars. Usually, however, they return to the superior Passamaquoddy baskets, Many laundry and pack baskets are also made on this reservation, again mostly by men, who generally work on the heavy utilitarian items. Women at Pleasant Point make the more colorful fancy baskets, which incorporate saltwater sweet grass in the design. The "fancy" items include sewing baskets, jewelry baskets, tissue holders, wastebaskets, pincushions, and even toy cradles. One Pleasant Point woman has had a contract with the state for many years to make pie baskets, which are filled with Maine products and presented to miscellaneous dignitaries who visit the state.

Leather, shell, and bead pendants are also made at Pleasant Point, as are birch-bark toys and wastebaskets, carved war clubs, and other knickknacks. All are made at home by individuals or by families.

Marine products are gathered at Pleasant Point, and one man has a Small Business Administration loan for a lobstering operation. Although he is the only Indian lobstering at present, there has been talk of pressing for exclusive fishing rights off the coast of the reservation, and if this is accomplished more might take up lobstering. Another family has two fish weirs and does a fairly good business.

Pleasant Point people also make Christmas wreaths in season, as do their counterparts at Indian Township, but they have the added problem of having to make a 100-mile round trip to obtain raw materials. Nevertheless, one man at this reservation has been a prime distributor of the wreaths for years.

Other products produced here, such as firewood holders and medicinal herbs, play a minor role in the economy.

At Indian Township, manufactured products are similar to those of Pleasant Point, but there are more extensive products because of the more varied land and forest base.

In the basket industry there are more women than one finds at Pleasant Point. Perhaps this is because more of the Indian Township men are involved in cutting ash for raw basket materials. In any case, because fewer men make baskets, fewer heavy utility items are produced, although the Basket Co-op is producing some laundry baskets for the army. The women make fancy baskets similar to those at Pleasant Point. Although Indian Township has fewer market outlets the demand is invariably greater than supply.

Beadwork and leatherwork are produced with increasing skill and frequency at Indian Township, and a resurgence of competent carving is taking place among some of the men and older boys. Two men in particular are deft at making lightweight canoe paddles and rustic furniture of ash. They also make snowshoes, albeit rarely. Many novelty carved toys are made here, and finger weaving was recently reintroduced, resulting in proliferation of belts and headbands, which are worn locally and sold in craft fairs around the state.

During hunting season, "sports" (white city hunters) often come to the reservation and pay up to $150 for a deer or $100 for a bear, in order to return victorious to suburbia. This trophy game can be considered another reservation product.

Although the fur trade is assumed to have ended in the 1700's, it persists in attenuated form. Nearly every family on Indian Township reservation relies on the fur trade for some small augmenting of income in the winter. A buyer from the neighboring town comes every week to purchase what has accumulated since his last visit. He pays $1 for a deer hide, $2 for a muskrat pelt, $50 for beaver, and $75 to $80 for mink. The obvious profit that someone is making on deer hides causes one to speculate on the profits that are being made (not by Indians) on beaver and mink. The Passamaquoddy have found it impossible to eliminate the middleman; fur companies will not deal directly with the reservations.

SERVICES.   The Passamaquoddy provide outsiders with some services, such as chair rushing and caning, making wood holders and rustic furniture on order, and performing miscellaneous odd jobs and carpentry. But by far the greatest number of services are provided within the tribe on an exchange basis; cash transactions for services between tribal members are rare.

Tribal members provide one another with many kinds of services, including woodcutting, cooking, barbering, carpentry, making axe handles and canoe paddles, providing transportation, supplying baskets and beadwork products, and doing occasional gardening. In the exchange of these services, the general rule requires return of equal value or equal time. Professional mourners who sing old Indian songs at funerals provide another kind of service, usually paid for in food.

Medicine is a special area of service. The sick person appeals to one knowledgeable in herbal lore for a diagnosis and a cure. One must "give up something" for the medicine to work, and this may vary according to the ability of the sick person to pay. A pack of cigarettes might suffice, or a small cash payment, or some other tangible thing; but even if one is a friend or a close relative of the curer, something must be offered for the medicine. Otherwise, a cure cannot be effected.

On the day-to-day level, there is a complex borrowing system. For example, a person who runs short of bread or sugar may borrow from a friend or a neighbor, but to actively repay this loan in kind would be to degrade the lender. Therefore, care is taken to avoid obviously repaying him, lest it be implied that he is ungenerous. Eventually, the original lender will run short of something of equal value and will borrow from the original borrower. A gauzy network of mutual obligations is thus built up, often crossing traditional faction lines. This borrowing system, then, also serves as a social cement.

There is also an underground system of services that involves alcoholics, bootleggers, the Indian agent, and the reservation man-on-the-street. It works this way: the alcoholic cadges an order for clothing, groceries, or house repair money from the Indian agent (who by necessity must be torn about whether or not to assist this obviously needy person). The alcoholic makes his purchases, perhaps keeps some, but usually sells all he acquired at very low rates. His goods are bought by the reservation man-on-the-street, who can ill afford to turn down a real bargain. The alcoholic then takes his small profit and goes to a bootlegger on the reservation, who will sell him cheap wine or beer at inflated prices. The alcoholic, of course, is the loser, but he doesn't see it that way. Everyone has "beaten the system" — a favorite pastime of any red-blooded Passamaquoddy — so there is a psychological as well as an economic gain all round.

The fact that there is profit, challenge, reward, and structure explains why attempts to rid the reservations of bootleggers have always failed. Alcoholism is a serious problem, about which most people are increasingly concerned; but leaders who attempt to remove the bootleggers are subtly resisted, because too many people directly benefit from their presence. (On the other hand, leaders are also condemned if they don't try to eliminate the bootleggers.) Clearly, substitute elements should be inserted into the system, to replace alcohol and the bootlegger — but no one yet has figured out what these substitutes might be.

MARKETS. Most of the handicrafts produced on the reservations, except for the commercial utility baskets, are sold to other reservation members, who either use them, give them as gifts, or resell them to gift shops. A few things are sold to tourists through the Basket Co-ops on each reservation, and near Pleasant Point many items are bought up by local white merchants who run Indian trading posts. Some Passamaquoddy items also find their way to stores on the Penobscot reserve. Lately several Maine crafts groups are carrying Passamaquoddy handicrafts and would probably take more if they could get them, and increasingly, articles are sold at summer New England craft fairs. Each reservation has a summer festival or "pow-wow" where items are also sold, but there are never enough to meet the demand.

The commercial baskets (scale, pack, and laundry) are bought, respectively, by local fishermen, L. L. Bean Camper Supply in Freeport, Maine, and by the United States Army. The potential market for Passamaquoddy baskets is far greater than the amount produced. If production were increased, many other markets would be possible. Museums, for example, usually have poor collections from the Northeast, and most would welcome representative quality samples of splint-and-sweet-grass basketry. (The Bureau of Indian Affairs outlet carries some Passamaquoddy items now.) Various Indian shops around the country would also carry Northeastern baskets if they could get them, and several outlets in New England that deal only in baskets have indicated they would take orders. Visitors from Denmark were certain the baskets would sell in Scandinavian countries, where there is great interest in American Indians and a fondness for handcrafted items. The Passamaquoddy could also have their own outlets at tourist complexes, if they ever get them. Not least, they could expand their repertoire of toys and Christmas ornaments and do very well with these, as there is a steady demand for the few items that are produced.

Christmas wreaths presently are sold cheaply, but with better contacts the tribe could probably make a profit. Some wreaths are sold to a Passamaquoddy who delivers them to Connecticut, but many others are bought by non-Passamaquoddy middlemen and taken to Boston, where they sell for much more than when they are purchased from Indians. Decorated wreaths fetch still more, and if it could be arranged to bring several Passamaquoddy to the city for a week or so of concentrated work, they could themselves do the decorating and reap the profits.

The fur trade is another area where Indians might conceivably increase profits by dealing directly. In addition, if they were trained to tan deer hides as they did in the past, they could afford to manufacture all manner of deerskin items and sell them at a handsome profit. As it is, many more people would engage in leatherwork if they could afford the leathers; the present arrangement (selling an untanned deerskin for $1, but paying $20 or $25 for a tanned one from the leather company) makes leatherwork prohibitive for most.

The seafood industry at Pleasant Point could probably be augmented. It was suggested recently that the Pleasant Point Passamaquoddy might also engage in the preparation of biological ocean specimens for educational purposes. So far nothing has come of this suggestion, and nothing will, unless the proper equipment and training are made available.

There is a greater market for Indian hunting and fishing guides than there are guides. Because guides in Maine are required to have a license, perhaps this market could be better filled by giving courses in guiding for young Passamaquoddy men. Certainly there is good money in guiding, and Indian Township is surrounded by some of the best hunting and fishing territory in the Northeast. Here, then, is one more undeveloped market that could be tapped by the tribe.

Another potential market is the production and processing of fiddlehead ferns, which grow along brooks and rivers in the area and are harvested by hand when they are still coiled in fiddlehead form. They are laborious to clean but make a delicious gourmet vegetable: bright green, slightly crunchy, and tasting like delicate asparagus. They are processed in nearby New Brunswick and sold frozen in standard sized boxes for about 98 cents a box. Gourmet restaurants in New York are the main buyers, in addition to local enthusiasts who can't wait until spring. The Passamaquoddy and Penobscot enthusiastically gather fiddleheads every spring for home consumption, for fiddleheads are a native Indian dish. A program to farm, freeze, and promote these delicacies would probably produce a good market.

PROBLEMS. The problems the Passamaquoddy have with products, services, and markets all return to a single factor: demand is greater than supply. This may be caused by lack of business and marketing experience, by the need for immediate cash (which causes people to sell to whomever buys first rather than to those who would pay a fair price), by inability to get raw materials when they are needed (particularly in basketry), by lack of personnel (related to lack of jobs), by lack of operating capital to get started, and by the existence of factions that interfere with the smooth operation of the programs that could help in these matters. However, the talent and the possibilities are all there. It only remains for the Passamaquoddy people and those who would help them to become sensitized to how the Passamaquoddy economy can best be developed. This, in turn, requires an honest appraisal of the problems. What is Passamaquoddy culture really like? And how can one swim with the cultural stream instead of against it, in the implementation of economic development programs?

Psychosocial Factors Affecting Work Patterns and Economic Development

The work habits of the Passamaquoddy are geared to periods of intense activity, followed by relaxation and enjoyment of the fruits of their labor. This pattern is probably a remnant of precolonial times when the rigors of winter demanded serious attention to hunting, while the abundant summer allowed a season of relative relaxation and socializing; the pattern was reinforced in later periods up to the recent past, when employment other than seasonal work was difficult or impossible to secure. The sporadic Passamaquoddy work pattern and seasonal-cycle approach to labor is diametrically opposed to the Puritan work ethic of this country, and particularly of the Maine towns surrounding the reservation.

Despite the criticism of neighboring whites about Indian work habits, production in any Passamaquoddy endeavor goes up in direct relation to the flexibility of the work schedule. A case in point was a wreath-making project at the Indian Township Basket Co-op two years ago. On the initial "sensible" schedule of work hours — from 8 to 5 — production was very low and only a trickle of wreaths were produced, despite good wages, good working conditions, and supplied materials. (Previously, wreath making had always been done at home.) When the hour restrictions were dropped and the building remained open from 7 A.M. to midnight, production soared — even though many people worked in the formerly shunned 8-to-5 time slot. Choice and freedom are everything!

The disinclination to be regimented is stronger in some Passamaquoddy than in others, and a few tribesmen are notable in both the Indian and white communities for their fine work records in local mills. People in the white community see these workers as "good Indians," but other Passamaquoddy admire them for being good providers (i.e. they have stable incomes) more than for being steady workers.

Passamaquoddy work patterns also differ from those of whites in that they are oriented toward the present rather than the future. A Passamaquoddy generally works for today to live for today; if anything is put away for the future, it is for a real, soon-to-be-realized future, not a theoretical one. With many people this attitude affects job training incentive. One is what one is, yet everything is subject to change — one may be something else tomorrow. Thus, why train for something one may never become?

In actuality, however, many people have had training of some sort and have successfully used it. Almost always the accepted training had the immediate reward of on-the-job training pay. More people might be encouraged to seek training if all job training programs offered pay with training, had the same pay scale, and were in accord with local wages, and if trainees were actively assisted with placement or were helped in starting their own enterprises on the reservation.

Finally, the planning required for the tribe to set up a program, seek funding, and organize its operation takes a tremendous amount of psychological energy, both because of inexperience in this realm and because such planning goes against the preexisting natural order of Passamaquoddy life. The tribe has, in seeking help in the approved manner, made a major concession to the methods of an alien culture. Isn't it then asking too much that it also be required to meet guidelines and restrictions from that alien culture that cause factionalism and discontent in its own? The benefits presently cost too high a price, and the results are far less than they might be if the Passamaquoddy expended less energy in serving two masters.

SOCIAL OBLIGATIONS. Social obligations vary from family to family. In general, however, people rally behind a family leader who looks out for his own when he can. Brothers and sisters also have close ties and help each other where possible. And finally, tribal leaders and program directors are expected to distribute goods, jobs, and funds as widely as possible throughout the tribe.

Into this realm of social obligations come the program guidelines, which usually provide a limited number of job slots and rules forbidding nepotism. Much better would be programs in which the tribal council assigned job-slot quotas to families — perhaps according to the number of potential workers available in the family. A job slot then could be filled by more than one family member on an alternating basis to be determined by each family. The family head would still be in a position to help out particularly needy family members, and leaders would not be forced to walk the tightrope that is presently strung between the reservation and the federal government.

The personal world view still obtains among the Passamaquoddy. Nepotism is a means of survival, evil only because it is at the center of a cultural conflict.

THE IDEA OF LIMITED GOOD. A useful concept was developed by George Foster at the University of California (Berkeley), which he called "the idea of limited good." The essence of the idea is that "more for you means less for me" — the cultural idea, in other words, that all good things are limited. Foster's use of the term was in the context of peasant villages in Latin America versus outsiders. Among the Passamaquoddy the idea exists on an individual, or, more especially, on a family basis. Such an idea mitigates against the development of improved methods and profit-increasing techniques, because in this context getting ahead becomes an aggressive act against one's neighbors. The idea of limited good prevails among the Passamaquoddy as a whole, leading to an intensive pressure to level everyone to the same relative economic condition. It is a major obstacle to economic development. For this reason, it was previously stated that unless the standard of living of the entire tribe can be raised at once, there will be bitter resentment and attempts to thwart the person who succeeds over others.

The idea of limited good is intimately connected to the factionalism between lineage groups, and it also explains why the even distribution of goods, jobs, throughout the reservation community is the only assurance that one man's — or one family's — gain is not another's loss. Poverty and want intensified the idea of limited good, and this nonproductive cultural element contributes to the problem. More than anything else, it perpetuates the cycle of poverty.

Federal programs have further exacerbated the idea, guaranteeing at least partial defeat of their aims at the outset. The limited job slots of a program, for example, are perfect monuments to the limited good idea. If a program director is from a major faction, he is practically certain to aid his own group over others, making factional divisions even more bitter. If he is from a minor faction, a third party, he is in a position to play both sides against each other, promising jobs to this one and that one. By community standards, the only way to be fair is either to give everyone a job at once, and prematurely exhaust program funds, or to rotate community members through positions, firing and hiring by a system only another Passamaquoddy can comprehend. The suggestion is here reiterated, then, that at least some of these problems could be alleviated if the council could assign jobs to families as a *whole*; this would at least distribute the "good" to every group, and the decisions would be interfamilial rather than between lineage factions.

Finally, the constant shuffling of federal programs (available one year and not the next; funded one time and defunded the next) further fulfills the basic tenet: that good is limited and all grace is transitory.

The only answer — except for an ideal and consistently generous federal government — is the development of a viable Passamaquoddy economic development program that would exist through time and beyond the winds of political change. Such a program would involve the whole community and would be run by the community — ideally, by using tribal practices constructively instead of considering them a detriment, as is presently the case. Eventually, as business acumen developed and income for everyone improved, the idea of limited good might recede to a manageable size and be put away on the cultural shelf. The Passamaquoddy might then recognize that there could be "more for us all."

ANTIWORK INCENTIVES.   What reasons can be given to explain why some Passamaquoddies, as the white local townsmen would have it, "don't want to work?"

Because work in itself is not a virtue to a Passamaquoddy, other things will have an equal or greater priority in his mind. Some of these other priorities may also make good economic sense. For example, to the man who doesn't come to work but goes fishing, fishing is not only enjoyable — it also brings food to his table and probably to someone else's as well. If he sells some fish, this also brings him monetary profit. In any case, the fish may not always be available and may have to be caught in season. Should he wait, merely because of a job that goes on indefinitely and that will still be there after the fish have gone? Usually, the answer is "no." Flexible work hours would work well in such a situation. But prior to federal programs the only steady jobs Passamaquoddy had were in the white community, so they have used its standards as a norm in setting up their own hours of work. Perhaps work hours could be rethought by the Passamaquoddy in their own terms, in *all* programs, as they were in the Passamaquoddy-run wreath enterprise. This would eliminate at least one existing antiwork incentive.

Many Passamaquoddy value freedom over regimentation or being tied down, even if this choice means poverty. Only jobs that are changing in content, location, and hours would appeal to them. People with this type of occupational claustrophobia would perhaps adapt best to the varied jobs provided by a home-based tourist development, which would allow considerable variety in hours and work.

Another antiwork incentive is the poor self-image that has been generated by 300 years of poverty, paternalism, and discrimination. A generally prevailing attitude is that, "oh, an Indian couldn't do this (or that) anyway." This ineffective image is slowly dissolving, as more and more Passamaquoddy find they can indeed "do it." Programs that are feasible, and that don't run counter to community practice, make for more confident managers and directors. The more culturally manageable programs there are, then, the better it will be for the Passamaquoddy's self-image as a capable people.

An area that surely touches on production and the area of antiwork incentives is health. There is widespread incidence of debilitating health problems such as tooth infections, anemia, diabetes, respiratory ailments, ulcers, alcoholism, and sight and hearing disorders. Economic development will inevitably have to consider the physical person, if it is to overcome the major obstacle of unattended health problems, which invariably affect the performance of the whole community.

The teenage dropout is yet another work-incentive problem. Federal programs invariable require workers and trainees to be 18 years old, except for the Neighborhood Youth Corps, which requires that the employee be enrolled in school. In a community with a dropout rate of 90 to 95 percent, this means that many able-bodied young people between 15 and 18 have virtually nothing to do. What the young people *do* do, then, is drink with their friends and finish developing a sense of social impotence, which their brush with schools in the white world has already implanted. They also learn to beg grocery orders from the Indian agent and to steal the things that they cannot earn money to buy; many of them set out on the downhill road into alcoholism. Yet all around them are trainee jobs of various kinds: concentrated employment programs they cannot enter, vocational training requiring them to be 18, and jobs in the world outside that demand a high school diploma. Economically and psychologically, they are a burden to themselves and to the community. After bumming around for several years, is it any wonder that many of these young people, on turning 18, no longer have any interest in taking advantage of the programs and jobs offered? Here, then, is one of the most misguided aspects of federal programs. The age rule in federal programs does *not* work to keep young people in school; it merely makes their almost inevitable dropping out more debilitating than it needs to be and kills off whatever ambitions and work incentives they once might have had.

Other antiwork incentives occur at the management level. Directors or managers are constantly caught between program guidelines and community practice. Frequently they are subjected to having to administer a program in which a major element has not been funded, so that ultimately nothing works — in what might be called the "fanbelt effect." (With a defunct fanbelt, nothing in a car works right, and it soon won't run; just as, without working capital, the Basket Co-op won't run.) Managers thus become frustrated, quit, and often move off the reservation where their talents can better be put to use.

Another antiwork incentive is the lack of community cohesion, which has several sources, among them the rivalry created by many of the federal programs. The Mainstream program produced some community improvements, but not nearly as many as it might have. Part of the trouble can be traced to the factionalism that Mainstream itself engendered because of hiring policies and limited positions, in what everyone knew was a "make-work" program, anyway.

As one watches the panorama of programs, classes, and other recent innovations on the reservations, few are seen that do not create some kind of disruption. But the few that have really worked show that there is, under all, a latent but strong sense of community. This sense of community, which is waiting to be nurtured and developed, could be the most important factor of Passamaquoddy economic development. The potential is obvious in certain joint efforts of community-wide concern, planning, and execution that were the binding forces of Passamaquoddy life in recent years. (Significantly, none were related to federal programs, except in the sense that federal programs provided a sense of importance and control over their destinies.) The unifying activities were the strike against Georgia-Pacific, the road blockage against the state, the initiation of the land case, and the summer dance pageants.

The most successful program from outside has probably been Bermuda North, an annual craft program instituted by the Newman Apostolate of Bowdoin College. Community cooperation and morale is extremely high during Bermuda North every year. Somehow (and one suspects it was through sensitivity to the Passamaquoddy and their culture), the Bowdoin group has done what almost no other has: they have brought in a program from outside that really works on the reservation. Their successful operation has been based on the following points:

1. Including the total community — all lineages, both sexes, all ages.

2. Fostering the sense of community cooperation and sharing. Sit-down dinners in the parish hall have augmented the sense of community involvement.

3. Bolstering Passamaquoddy self-image by stressing Indian heritage and Passamaquoddy ability to produce superior craft products.

4. Providing variety in instruction and choice of crafts.

5. Providing adequate instructions.

6. Taking a total program approach by leaving no gaps — enough supplies, alternative offerings, and so forth.

7. Providing a sense of continuity — by leaving supplies behind (craft items, guitars, leather, cloth, a treadle sewing machine for every home) and by reliably returning each year.

8. Sending representatives who are flexible, sensitive, and well trained.

9. Consulting with the tribal council at every phase of planning and activity enrolling its assistance in administrating the program.

With donated materials, a minimum of funding, and a maximum of sensitivity to the realities of the Passamaquoddy community, Bowdoin's Bermuda North has done more, and done it better, than many heavily funded programs. Through its success, we may glimpse possibilities as yet unrealized for the Passamaquoddy community.

PROWORK INCENTIVES. One kind of work incentive is created by competition between lineage groups: for example, if one family is doing particularly well at woods operations, members of another lineage may set out to exceed them. If the first family discontinues the work, however, the second may also, because competition is now removed. Therefore, lineage competition can be both constructive or destructive in any given economic endeavor, depending on how the force is channeled. It would be advantageous, for example, to have competing woods crews composed of single lineages, but utterly disadvantageous to have two or more crews, each composed of several lineages. The latter could expectably result in competition within the crew, rather than the cooperation necessary (see Figures 1 and 2).

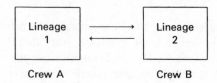

Figure 1.   Constructive competition

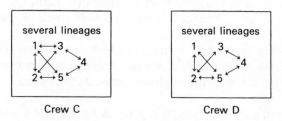

Figure 2.   Destructive competition

In the implementation of federal programs on the Passamaquoddy reservations, and elsewhere in Indian communities, lineage rivalry has not been acknowledged or used constructively. Even Indians have not generally tried to approach the matter openly, perhaps through fear of loss of funding, or of revealing inner conflicts to outsiders. Nevertheless, if the matter were dealt with squarely, both economic development and community relations might be improved. In the Passamaquoddy Basket Co-op, for example, an ideal arrangement would be for the community-owned co-op to receive funds and give out minigrants of equal value to lineages for the year's craft supplies. The co-op could then buy back finished products throughout the year, for resale whenever the best market was available. In this way family rivalry could be channeled into producing the most or the best crafts, or creating new lines of craft items. This system would also serve as an incentive for families to specialize and perfect those crafts in which they have especial interest.

Another work incentive is the hope of income coupled with independence. Trades that require independence or self-management are considered more desirable than those that require working under someone. Hunting, trapping, or guiding are traditional pursuits which have the qualities sought in a job by many Passamaquoddy. The freedom *not* to work at all is in itself a work incentive, in the sense that an occupation that occasionally allows this option is more desired than one that does not. Noting this, it would seem that training groups of Passamaquoddy to be ship's welders (who must leave the reservation and work under someone else in rigid time patterns) is less practical than training for jobs that can be performed on or near the reservation, with a measure of independence. Such jobs might include occupations that are scarce in the county — auto mechanics, electricians, carpenters, and plumbers; or trades connected with maintaining a sports-tourist complex — boat and snowmobile repair, laundromat operation, garage management, campground maintenance, guides, and craft entrepreneurs.

Passamaquoddy women work as productively and as steadily as the men, if not more so, and are increasingly interested in employment. Federal programs should give attention to training by providing child-care facilities on the reservation. Passamaquoddy women, who are strong in both character and muscle, could perform a wide variety of jobs if they were trained. (Often, in fact, the woman gives work incentive to her husband, urging him to provide the family a decent living standard, or to get ahead. Indeed, a man who is not pressured by his women is less likely to be found at his job than one who is.) Many Passamaquoddy women already have the incentive to work — but they have little chance for training that can be used on the reservation, and scant hope of obtaining a child-care center in the near future. The problem is not so much one of motivation as it is of the tendency to see women as a kind of cultural wallpaper, rather than as viable human resources.

Another work incentive is common among Passamaquoddy young men, who — like other young men — would like to have cash to enjoy themselves and to impress their peers. Much of this motivation, as previously noted, disappears during the years of under-eighteen ineligibility — often for good. Personal or family crises provide some of the most common incentives to work, but it is difficult to see how this type of incentive could fit into an economic development plan.

Finally, some Passamaquoddy are highly self-motivated to get ahead and to make a decent living, and they work reasonably well in white work situations. These Passamaquoddy are a group apart; they are often viewed by others as inordinately greedy, for they infringe — or seem to — on the "limited good." As a result, they sometimes move off the reservation. On or off the reservation, however, these people maintain friendships with each other that transcend traditional kin boundaries. Often in their backgrounds is an uncommonly difficult childhood, considerable intelligence, and more than ordinary outside contact and travel. This atypical group is viewed by other community members with a mixture of respect and resentment; members of the group are often either in leadership positions or are working toward them.

PERSONAL GOALS. Until very recently, it was impossible for most Passamaquoddy to exercise a choice in either economic or educational realms, and the fact that some choice *is* now possible has not really registered. As a result, personal goals — as they would be conceived in a white community — are ill-defined at best. Most people have some vague hope of having a good life economically, perhaps a house, and the respect of others; but a lack of experience in planning or even thinking about personal goals prevents them from either formulating or working toward goals of any but the most day-to-day kind. This may account, in part, for the low interest in formal education.

Many of the goals a Passamaquoddy might form are possible only if he or she leaves the reservation. This necessitates a sacrifice of both security and identity — a high price, indeed. As a result, few Passamaquoddy dream of a career, except in times of crisis, when they might say, "Why didn't I become this, or that?" In good times, though, they will not be career-minded, and may even pass up training in the career they have coveted during crisis periods. Most Passamaquoddy have little or no idea about saving or sacrificing to achieve a personal goal; history, culture, and fatalism have seen to that. Furthermore there is little likelihood of a change in the foreseeable future. Therefore, programs that attempt to stress career planning, pensions, etc. will fare less well than those which hold forth immediate personal rewards, freedom, and variety.

TRIBAL GOALS. Although the Passamaquoddy have been devoid of voice and of choice for several hundred years, yet an unspoken tribal goal has persisted: the goal simply to endure. Many predictions have come and gone about the supposedly vanishing Passamaquoddy people and culture, but objective evidence tells another story. They are still here, and their numbers are growing. They are not as they once were, true. But who is? The Passamaquoddy no longer daily wear feathers, any more than whites still wear pilgrim buckles; yet each culture has retained its essential core, even though it has borrowed extensively from the other. As the minority group — religiously, historically, and racially — the Passamaquoddy have been, and are still, subject to unrelenting pressures to become assimilated (or, in Anglo-language, "like us"). Instead, they have sifted the outside elements through their cultural screen, retaining what they could profitably use while tossing out the rest. Today the goal of cultural persistence, stronger than ever, is expressed in a keen interest in tribal lore, dances, songs, history, crafts, and language. Today it is no longer enough simply to endure: now one must endure with dignity and pride.

The federal programs that first sparked some hope of self-determination also gave a measure of self-respect, despite the fact that by outside objective standards many of the programs "failed." Actually, they never failed at all; they were only badly judged, and for the wrong things. Today adults in their late twenties and early thirties are the ones promoting Passamaquoddy language, culture, and history; they are the people who are both old enough to remember growing up ashamed to be Indian and young enough to remember when the shame was transformed into pride. That pride, once fragile, is fragile no more. It has grown strong, feeding on new knowledge and self-respect.

The primary tribal goal today is independence, particularly from the state. The land case represents a move in that direction and is not simply a legal exercise. In a cosmic sense, it is both a symbol of all that was lost and all that might be gained. White observers who think the main Passamaquoddy motive is a cash settlement have woefully misunderstood. What does matter, to the exclusion of nearly everything else, is the land itself and all it represents — historically and spiritually. Winning the case would have economic usefulness, true, but the real victory would be moral. It would prove that the Passamaquoddy have been wronged and that they have held on, asserted themselves, and ultimately prevailed: in short, that they are a people to be reckoned with.

The tools necessary for dealing with independence have not had a chance to develop over the years of forced dependence on the state. Therefore, the most difficult lesson — that every freedom bears a responsibility — is slowly being learned today. Some people, of course, want the benefits of self-determination without the work it inherently entails; but natural leaders are constantly emerging who are proving increasingly adept at their tasks, despite an almost total lack of experience. Self-doubts about capabilities are diminishing, too, as individuals learn that they are indeed capable persons.

The Passamaquoddy pitch for federal recognition is tied to the land suit, and to them it does not seem antithetical to the dream of independence, for they plan to insist on considerable autonomy.

Should they win the case, they will be in a position where they will *not* need the BIA economically and may choose to be terminated. Or, if they lose the case but win recognition, they will be better off under the lumbering BIA than under the bumbling state.

Loss of the land case, however, would have chaotic effects on Passamaquoddy morale, for in their hearts they have always known the land is theirs. To be officially told it is not would be a devastating psychological blow whose effects would be hard to predict.

RED AND WHITE GOALS IN OPPOSITION. Irving Hallowell has said that people with different culture patterns live in different orders of reality. Perhaps this is why programs designed for red men by white men — even those with the best of intentions — don't work. Indeed, even the conclusion that a program "didn't work" is culturally determined; it may, as far as the program recipients are concerned, have worked very well.

The Passamaquoddy of Indian Township would not agree, for example, that the apparently chaotic Operation Mainstream program "didn't work." Even though guidelines were largely ignored, threats rumbled periodically from the granting agency, and the director ultimately lost his job, many people in a largely jobless area had sporadic income for several years, everyone's house got painted, some costumes and baskets were made, and, best of all, people had some rare spending money for relatively little effort. The program failed? Never!

By the standards of the program planners, however, Operation Mainstream on the Passamaquoddy reserves was a disaster arrived at through an unremitting series of crises. People were fired and hired (seemingly at random), budgets were consistently overspent, nepotism was rampant, nearly every guideline was ignored, steady work habits were not established as had been hoped, and visible community improvement was slight. After all these trials the Passamaquoddy were not one iota closer to the "mainstream of American life," and, worst of all, they didn't even seem to care. The program, viewed from the intended goals of the creators, was an unmitigated flop.

It is apparent, in Mainstream and other examples, that not only were the goals different between the two cultures at the outset, but the results were inevitably judged differently. While the federal planners might say, "Here was a program. Did it produce the desired results?" A Passamaquoddy might say, "Here was a program. What did it do for us while it lasted?"

Certain sentiments and hopes for the downtrodden are implicit in most federal programs, but these fine sentiments are also culturally tinged. It is as if the planners were saying, "We really want you to succeed; but there are certain ways you must go about succeeding, and, furthermore, we will define what success is."

Some of the sentiments implicit in programs guidelines are: (1) effective management must be developed; (2) a good man should be assisted to get ahead; (3) steady work habits are essential to success; (4) career interests should be encouraged and developed; (5) planning for the future is a good and necessary thing; (6) surplus capital from tribal enterprises should be invested to produce even further tribal profits; (7) all people — including minorities — of a development area should work together in the common cause; and (8) people should be self-sufficient and able to stand on their own two feet.

Passamaquoddy assumptions, taken in a parallel fashion are quite different: managers and management by definition are distasteful necessities, which are required only as long as the job at hand exists. Trying to get ahead is in bad taste. Steady work is a bore — variety and choice are more important. People change and fortunes change, so why plan a career? Planning for the future usually proves futile, because one never knows what will happen. Surplus capital produced by the tribe should result in higher wages all around. Indians are Indians and really don't have a common cause with other groups. It is good to live near friends and relatives who will tide you over the bad times.

Both points of view make sense when couched in their own cultural contexts, but out of context they may appear perverse. This is why the white goals embedded in most federal programs, even though applied in blind good faith, must inevitably be seen as cultural perversions by the Passamaquoddy. It is the reason guidelines are ignored. It is the reason programs "don't work." It is one reason aspirin sales have increased.

The solution to this dilemma is laughably simple, and has been suggested more than once by Indian people in general, and Vine Deloria in particular: Free the funds and give them to the tribes; then let each tribe do its own thing, in its own way — for its own reasons.

Management

Almost all of the Passamaquoddy enterprises requiring management are government funded. Office of Economic Opportunity funds are managed by the Community Action Program (CAP) director on each reservation. The CAP director does not have to be the tribal chief, although this arrangement has already become almost custom. The tribal council won status as CAP boards of directors in a pitched battle with OEO. The CAP director's job is one of the most important on the reservation and one of the best paid. The directorship generally strengthens the role of chief, while the chiefship gives support to CAP projects. If the chief does not support some CAP aims (as perhaps spelled out in a previous political period on the reservation), he is also in a position as CAP director to hold up projects.

Some Department of Labor funds are managed by the Operation Mainstream director, who is generally faced with problems originating in limited funds, job slots, and the creation of jobs. Mainstream seems to operate in fits and starts, sometimes accomplishing really useful tasks on the reservation, sometimes foundered by problems.

Other Department of Labor funds are managed through the Opportunity Industrialization Center program (OIC), which contracts with different agencies to guarantee jobs and adequate training or retraining. Ideally, the needs of the community are assessed, and funds for training are supplied accordingly. OIC is presently preparing some Passamaquoddy for jobs in the forthcoming housing development project sponsored by the Housing and Urban Development Administration (HUD).

Each reservation has a Passamaquoddy Housing Authority, which manages the funds of HUD and deals with housing development, water and sewage treatment, and community planning.

The Neighborhood Youth Corps (NYC) on each reservation is sponsored federally by the Department of Health, Education and Welfare and, locally, by the Maine State Department of Education. NYC, which provides some Passamaquoddy youth with after-school, vacation, and summer jobs, is directed by a Passamaquoddy adult on each reservation.

The Passamaquoddy Basket Co-op has a branch on each reservation and requires managers in both places. The manager's salary is paid by the local CAP agency, as are a few of the co-op's operating expenses. The co-op's board of directors, however, are chosen by the workers and not by the CAP board. The American Freedom From Hunger Foundation formerly funded some operations of the Basket Co-ops, but do so no longer; Operation Mainstream labor is being used presently, but this is not a permanent arrangement. The lack of funding sources and the diversity of those available make management of the co-ops a tricky job.

The newly formed Passamaquoddy school boards perform a very complex type of management and do it very well, considering the total lack of previous experience in this realm. School board members must sort out laws and regulations (some of which conflict) relative to Indians, Mainers in "unorganized territory," the state education department, and guidelines of federally sponsored programs such as Headstart, the hot-lunch program, and the bi-lingual education program. The regulations and customs of the Catholic church must also be considered. School board members, all new to their work, have walked headlong into a net made of threads running from the state and federal governments, the reservation itself, the Department of Education, and the Catholic church.

The management job *par excellence*, of course, goes to the chief and his council, who must coordinate, as far as possible, all the preceding activities and many more besides.

SELECTION OF MANAGEMENT.   Chiefs and councils, the ultimate reservation managers, are elected by the tribe at large every two years, in secret ballot vote. The turnout of eligible tribal voters is generally very high, and tribal political races are often close; generally, the councils are quite representative of the community at large. Chiefs may stay in office for years, or turnover may be frequent.

The Housing Authority on each reservation is appointed by the local chief and approved by the council; the Authority then chooses its chairman. The tribal council appoints the Operation Mainstream director and NYC directors. The council originally appointed the tribal school board, which now is elected at large for staggered terms.

The manager of the Basket Co-op is presently chosen by the CAP board of directors (which is also the tribal council). This arrangement pertains only as long as the co-op receives CAP funds; should the co-op become self-sustaining, and therefore able to pay the manager, CAP will have no further powers of appointment. Instead, he will be appointed by the board of directors of the co-op, who are chosen in turn by the workers.

OIC directors are chosen by the community at large in a general meeting called for the purpose. The positions last only as long as the OIC training programs are in effect on the reservations.

DECISION MAKING.   Decision making is a peculiarly difficult business for Passamaquoddy management personnel, for several reasons. First, there is so little previous tribal experience in management, in the modern sense, that no one knows exactly where the managerial boundaries are. Neither the manager nor the managed know what is expected in this new relationship — managers and directors, by definition, are un-Passamaquoddy institutions. It's the old story retold: no Passamaquoddy tells another what to do.

Decisions are reached by roundabout methods expertly calculated to offend no one. Even the supreme manager, the chief, does not "manage" as such, except in the most subtle ways. Instead, he influences the council to direct him to do what he already thinks best. (Without council approval, he will not long remain chief.) Federal program guidelines and bylaws direct the managers and directors to make decisions, yet managerial inexperience combined with a community-wide dislike of being bossed results in managers turning to others in council and leadership positions for advice and reaffirmation of ideas. They seek justification at many levels for most of their actions, for they don't feel free to act on their own. They are both unsure of their abilities and that the community gives them authority the federal proclamations say they have. The federal program mandates "to manage" are outside mandates to "tell others what to do" — something one can*not* do in a Passamaquoddy community. Clearly community ideals and management, per se, are in conflict.

Management, then, is basically an intrusion (however necessary) from outside. Furthermore, it is not in accord with the only kind of management situation the tribe is accustomed to — the council and chief. Although it may seem to the uninformed observer that a manager and a board of directors are much like a chief and his council, actually there is a basic philosophical difference between the two.

The manager in a program or a company operates at the top of a pyramid, with a considerable amount of direct power vested in his position. The Passamaquoddy chief, however, sits at the bottom of a reversed pyramid, with no particular power vested in his role except what the council grants him. The council, in its turn, receives its power from the people (see Figure 3).

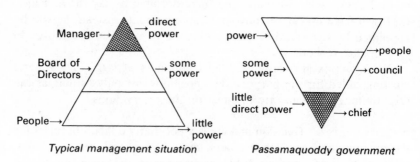

Figure 3.   Power and Passamaquoddy government

It is no wonder the Passamaquoddy manager, then, doubts that he has real authority. Everything in his culture tells him that he does not. Generally, he is pulled in two directions until paralyzed into inaction, or he makes his decision for or against the "Passamaquoddy way." If he supports Passamaquoddy culture, he is happily received by his community but is in trouble with the district directors of his program. If he follows the official guidelines, he finds that no one on the reservation will work for him. Perhaps the manager could turn to his board of directors for direction and support, as a chief turns to his council. But no — the board will not come to his aid; they too sense, however unclearly, the basic philosophical difference in the two systems. Management by white standards simply does not culturally "fit" into Passamaquoddy life. The people will not allow excess amounts of power to be invested in one individual.

Dealing with this problem will take considerable thought — preferably by Indians, for this management problem is not unique to the Passamaquoddy. The mimicking of white management methods has not worked so far, and it is not likely to work in the future. Certainly, whatever the "Indian way" of management may turn out to be, it has to be more comfortable and effective than present methods. If an Indian brand of management is ever discovered, it should be given full reign, no matter how it looks to another culture.

Source of Expertise

LAW. The most important source of expertise available to the Passamaquoddy is the Indian Legal Services Unit of Pine Tree Legal Assistance, Incorporated, a nonprofit OEO legal service. This organization has been consistent in its willingness and capability to help the tribe secure a variety of federal programs, has assisted in the land case, and has counseled in private matters. The Indian Legal Services Unit provides advice and representation to the Passamaquoddy CAP's, the Basket Co-ops, the Housing Authorities, and a women's club. It negotiated with the Native American Rights Fund to assist in the land case and was instrumental in helping establish the Eastern Seaboard Coalition of Indians, which was originally spearheaded by the Passamaquoddy. The legal service also has been reliably supportive in dealings with town, county, state, and federal governments. The Passamaquoddy have benefited greatly from this organization, which has upheld their rights, explained their legal status, used Indians in their offices, and, in general, operated efficiently behind the scenes.

Until the Indian Legal Services Unit was established, the law was more often an enemy than a friend to the Passamaquoddy people and was frequently used as an instrument to obtain Indian land or to save the state money; now, the Passamaquoddy are suing the state and federal governments. The Indian Legal Services Unit represents federal War on Poverty programs at their best — a "best" that probably exceeds the government's original plans.

CONSTRUCTION, SANITATION, PLANNING. In 1969 the tribe hired a civil engineer to oversee the construction of new schools on each reservation. Later he was hired by the housing authorities to assist in planning and managing the installation of water and sewage treatment plants. Today he is the housing coordinator for both reservations, in the hire of the two Passamaquoddy Housing Authorities. In 1971 an architect was also hired by the housing authorities; he works primarily on community centers.

EDUCATION.   Shortly after the Maine Department of Indian Affairs was established, Indian education was placed under the state Department of Education and an "Indian education specialist" was hired to work with the three Maine Indian reservation schools and the Department of Education. The specialist, who formerly worked with Eskimo education projects, today works closely with the Passamaquoddy director of the bilingual, bicultural program at Indian Township. Several linguists and anthropologists are consultants to this program, providing assistance in putting the language in written form and in compiling Passamaquoddy history. Several Passamaquoddy also provide the bilingual program with expertise in dance, song, crafts, and other lore.

GOVERNMENT.   Expertise in government has been made available on the state level to the Passamaquoddy Commissioner of Indian Affairs by Governor Curtis and his staff, and by a handful of interested legislators. On the federal level, senators and representatives from both parties have been quite responsive to Maine Indian needs and have helped Maine Indian delegations manoeuvre in Washington. It is safe to say that Maine Indians never before have had such a sympathetic government at the higher state levels; from the legislature on down, Indians still often encounter difficulties.

BUSINESS AND MANAGEMENT.   Most federal program agencies provide consultants of some sort in administering their programs, but the advice provided is often too theoretical or too general, the language too technical, and the knowledge of Indian culture too vague for these experts to effectively impart their "expertise" to the people. All too often agency consultants come and talk learnedly while the Indians nod pleasantly; but out of earshot the Passamaquoddy ask each other, "What the hell did he say?"

Professional consulting firms have been hired for several Passamaquoddy projects or grant preparations, but they mostly leave the Passamaquoddy with the feeling that much of their money has been spent for little in the way of results — a feeling based on fact. Trusted friends are now more often the Passamaquoddy consultants — paid or otherwise.

The expertise expounded in business and management situations seldom has anything whatever to do with the realities of Passamaquoddy life, and no social scientist is ever employed in these projects. The training or advice should be geared, but usually is not, to the exact task at hand, because Passamaquoddy are not generalizers. The language itself is very detailing and particularizing. Passamaquoddy minds ask questions like "How *exactly* do we operate the Basket Co-op?" rather than "How are cooperatives usually run?"

Federal or private advisers and consultants need to be far better attuned to the culture they are dealing with. Studies such as this one, detailing Passamaquoddy lifeways, history, and present tribal systems, should have been done in the beginning, not at the end, of federal programs. The mistakes have all been made by this time, and many of the programs are labeled failures, yet it is debatable where the "failure" lies. We suggest that the real failure lies in the failure of program planners and administrators to recognize cultural differences, and in the planning, implementation, and evaluation of the federal programs.

Bushels of dollars have been spent for every conceivable kind of consultant but one, the person with an understanding of the Passamaquoddy culture: the one person who has the kind of information necessary to make the programs work.

The Implementation of Federal Social Programs

FAILURES. Some of the federal programs were failures by Passamaquoddy standards, and some were failures by white standards. The examples that follow were failures by everyone's standards.

The first Passamaquoddy Community Action Program (CAP) was created several years ago as a delegate agency of the Washington County Agency, even though the Passamaquoddy administratively have had few ties with the county. The Passamaquoddy irreverance for "white tape" and the county CAP director's strong adherence to procedural regulations rapidly led to disharmony. This was augumented by the fact that Indians weren't yet sure what they wanted to do, but they *did* know they wanted to do it themselves. Under the larger agency, this was seldom possible. The county commissioners often presented a conservative stumbling block to both the Indians and the outsider agency director. In short, the whole thing was not a successful arrangement.

The Passamaquoddy lobbied for their own independent agency, and the second year they got it. They now had to have their own board of directors separate from the governmental body of the community, that is, the tribal council. (This rule was a federal guideline.) A board was created and the Passamaquoddy set off with high hopes for their new program.

Before long, however, the CAP board and the tribal council began to wrangle. The council felt that CAP was preempting some of its rights and responsibilities. They were also jealous that CAP was able to promote programs because it was funded, while the legitimate governing body was penniless. It was a period of drastic change when many decisions affecting the community had to be made. But who should make them, CAP or the council? On one reservation, CAP and council were at loggerheads most of the time; at the other, much of the time. The facts were that traditional rights were in the council, and money rights in the CAP board. With these groups opposed, community paralysis resulted. CAP was still not working on reservations that desperately needed community action.

In the midst of this dilemma, a few Indian people began to grasp the nature of the illness and thereby came to recommend the cure. Once realized, it was obvious that the board of directors of CAP and the tribal council should be one body on each reservation. The body then would have both the money and the power; it could not fight itself, and the unproductive arguments about who should handle what would vaporize. That this arrangement would be the answer was self-evident; that is, to the Passamaquoddy.

The "keepers of guidelines," however, said it couldn't be done. It was against the rules. It was an unorthodox and unreasonable demand for the Passamaquoddy to make. It was, in short, "not possible." "Has to be," said the Passamaquoddy. Here began a long series of negotiations with the OEO area representatives. They begged and pleaded and said the Passamaquoddy were making it impossible to give them all that lovely money. "If you don't do it our way, no funds," they said. A joint tribal council meeting was held, with the OEO officials attending. They were certain the Passamaquoddy would see the light and vote sensibly, but the joint council proceeded to reject the next year's CAP grant by a unanimous vote. They had voted down a $100,000 grant. In so doing they had shown a sense of self-preservation and that they couldn't be bought off. For once, they had insisted on doing something their way or not at all.

The sequel to the story is that OEO was dunned with angry letters from more imaginative segments of the public and was forced to reexamine its position. For the first time it occurred to them that perhaps it was not the Passamaquoddy who were intransigent but OEO itself. They found a way to have the tribal council and the CAP board be one and the same; and the Passamaquoddy got their grant on their own terms. A year later an OEO evaluator gave the Passamaquoddy one of the highest ratings of any CAP in the country. OEO collectively gulped and began trying the method out in other Indian communities, usually with success. What had once been anathema had now become *de rigueur*.

The CAP program episode represents a failure turned into a success. The success resulted from fitting the program to the culture instead of fitting the culture to the program. Most program failures, however, have not had such a fortunate outcome.

A good example of a total flop is a recent Army Special Forces paramedical training project. In 1972 this organization sent a medic to each of the three Maine reservations; their purported mission was to set up a reservation clinic with army surplus materials, provide first aid while they were there, and, most important, train paramedical people who could replace them when they left. They were also to make a survey of health problems on the reservations. The well-intended program, however, was fraught with problems from beginning to end, doomed inevitably to failure because it was built on false premises.

First of all, there was no room on any of the reservations to set up a clinic or even an office. (There are no community centers, houses are already overcrowded, and none are vacant.) The medics found they were lucky to have any cramped space to work in at all. Certainly there was none to put a clinic in, so the supplies were cancelled.

The people did look forward to having a medic, however, for they thought he could do what a doctor did, without the travel and expense usually involved. Indeed, the medics had performed surgery on the field in Vietnam; but, back in the United States and the American Medical Association, they were not allowed to stitch up a cut or administer a shot of penicillin. Most of the simple services they *were* allowed to provide were already available in the community through the native medical practitioners. The medics had some business, because they were always available and always free during their three-month stay. But they offered little in the way of new services.

The paramedical people the medics planned to train in their stead did not come forward. Certain people in the community could already take care of many of the things the medics wanted to help them with. In some instances, as with poison ivy, for example, the local remedies were more effective than were those of the medics. The medics, however, could have profitably taught two things to the local native practitioners: facts about nutrition and the rudiments of how infectious diseases are spread and controlled. They never got the chance. Their strict rule from higher up was not to train any native practitioners, on the grounds that they would practice native medicine along with what the medics taught them, and thus bring wrath to the medical profession and shame to the Green Berets! It was pointed out by this observer that, the American Medical Association and Green Berets notwithstanding, the Passamaquoddy would continue to seek and receive treatment from native practitioners long after the three-month enterprise was over. It was pointed out that the sane thing to do was train the Passamaquoddy who were already talented in medicine and who were the people already sought out for medical aid. This rather obvious advice fell on ears that were unwilling or unable to hear. The local practitioners in some cases came forward to be trained and were turned away. Other Passamaquoddy who tentatively ventured forth withdrew. No one, in the end, was trained, The medics have gone, and the native doctors are still curing infections, burns, bites, rashes, pains, and, in some cases (though they would deny it), have helped kidney disease, gangrene, cataracts, and other serious ailments. They are good doctors; but because the Green Berets came and said (like so many others), "We are here to help you — our way," —Passamaquoddies are no wiser today about healthy nutrition and the germ theory of disease than they ever were.

The Green Beret's medic episode shows very clearly how futile it is to fight the culture and how disastrous it is not to have the facts first. Goodwill is just not enough.

The Passamaquoddy, it is true, are not without flaws themselves. They make mistakes: they succumb to unproductive infighting; they are not always clear about the essential relationship between freedom, which they covet, and responsibility. Even so, most failures of reservation programs cannot be placed at their doorstep, but usually can be traced to the blithe ethnocentricity of well-meaning federal program planners, who cannot shake the belief that all Americans shoot for the same goals, reach them by the same means, and assess results by the same standards. Social scientists who might somewhat alleviate this disorder are rarely called into planning these programs; particularly absent are anthropologists, who are, at least, more knowledgeable about American Indians than most other white people. (Ideally, of course, Indian anthropologists should be consulted, but they are in short supply.) It is even more apparent that what is needed, generally, is flexibility, not guidelines created for administrative comfort in a distant city.

Despite the lack of Indian and social-scientist input into federal Indian projects, it should have needed no special expertise to realize that if you don't provide operating capital for a potential business enterprise (the Basket Co-op), you are probably dooming it to failure. And what logic lay behind preventing the MDTA basket-maker trainees from selling the completed baskets if they were of acceptable quality? We have to ask what purpose was fulfilled by having the workers weave and unweave baskers when the co-op needed capital? If these are the strange and mysterious ways of the white man, the Passamaquoddy are wise to remain Indian!

How, too, is an Indian (or anyone) supposed to grasp the logic behind installing a sewer and a water supply system that is attached to no house? After enduring bulldozers and steam shovels tearing up the reservations, two years later the Passamaquoddy were still burning tires to unfreeze community wells.

The Economic Development Administration (EDA) had an economic development plan prepared by an EDA consultant, and many Passamaquoddy were interviewed for their ideas, which were included in the plan. The plan was basically sound and well researched, but it was rejected. No one is quite sure why.

These are but a few of the federal bombs that have hurtled through the reservations these last few years. A common element of pigheadedness runs through them all. We say the Indians will not bend; it is *we* who will not bend.

Reality, Indian style, is what the federal planners must work with in the Indian communities. Is this really so difficult? With money saved from program disasters, it would be possible to hire competent Indian or anthropological researchers to predict likely snags and unforeseen disasters-in-waiting of a program. This should not be a luxury at all, but a necessity. The one reason it may never happen is that, if all the separate realities of the Indian communities were faced, it would be impossible to make universally applicable program guidelines. But of course it always has been impossible.

SUCCESS.   A few years ago on the reservations, schools were not happy places for the Passamaquoddy. There were no Indian school boards, no Indian teachers, no Indian history of Maine, and no teaching in the native language. The schools were run entirely by outsiders, mostly nuns, who were not even required to be certified by the state. The quality of teachers, thus, ran the gamut from excellent and enlightened to substandard and prejudiced. The problems faced by a child in a bilingual situation were never acknowledged, let alone dealt with. The schools were generally shunned by parents, who in some cases were made unwelcome there. Children all too often put in their school time as one puts in time at a penitentiary.

With Catholic church awakening to the Indians' new demands that they be included in planning and running their own affairs, little by little some Indian elements began to be included in the curriculum, usually in the arts and crafts realm. One nun taught Indian dancing, using a drum she made herself. Not knowing that the songs give directions to the dancers, she cried out, "left, right, left," while the children plodded glumly through their lackluster paces.

In 1968, the state Department of Education took over Indian education for the first time. Some Indian teaching assistants were hired and, eventually, an Indian education specialist. Through the efforts of many a legislative act, the first Indian school boards were created on each reservation, and two new schools were built at last.

Around this same time a Passamaquoddy man, Wayne Newell, went to Harvard for a Master of Education degree in Indian education. He was from Pleasant Point reservation, but after graduation he settled with his family at Indian Township, where — with a grant from the Department of Health, Education and Welfare, the good wishes of the state Indian Education specialist, and a tentative go-ahead from the tribal council — Newell began a bilingual, bicultural education program in the Dana Point (Indian Township) Grammar School. His underlying belief was that personal pride and dignity is a prerequisite to learning, as well as a motivational force that could carry Passamaquoddy children through the many crises encountered in getting education. The pride and dignity was to come through cultural awareness and pride in Passamaquoddy history and arts and through a real skill in both the native language and English.

Today, the Dana Point School is a happy place. (Newell's aim: "To make this the happiest place on the reservation.") The children work hard, learn a lot, and still keep smiling. Regimentation is minimized, use of Indian personnel is maximized, and the whole community is involved in capturing the language in writing (with the help of linguists at the Massachusetts Institute of Technology). The program includes courses that teach Passamaquoddy and other Indian history, the development of the land case, and the basis for the present status of Maine Indians. Indian adults in various careers and positions, including people in political offices of the tribe, talk to classes about their jobs and what they do. Displays and posters stressing Passamaquoddy life and language abound in the school, and twice-a-week gym consists of Indian dance classes, taught by a Passamaquoddy woman proficient in the art. Language games have also been created in both Passamaquoddy and English, and a small bilingual newspaper (*The Wahanaki Times*) is issued every week or two. Three books for beginners in Passamaquoddy writing have been developed, and a dictionary is planned. The school library, which is always open, is being filled with books of all sorts, with an emphasis on Indian subjects. (The library, such as it was, used to be closed most of the time, no books could be taken home, and one had to be "good" to have reading privileges.) It is used now by both adults and children. Adult classes are in progress to teach the new writing system, and every house has a sign describing in Passamaquoddy terms who lives there. The nonnative staff is learning the writing systems, too. Everyone, in short, is learning and contributing to the enterprise, and the school truly belongs to the community for the first time. It is a most heartening development to have witnessed.

To imply that every Passamaquoddy approves of this revolution in education would not be true, for many doubt that the children are "learning anything." They know from sad experience that learning should be painful and school miserable, and these children are enjoying themselves! It is a safe bet, though, that Newell's thesis is right: The program does engender self-respect and pride, which will carry at least some children through the vicissitudes of education in white schools later on. Those who don't break the dropout barrier at least will understand their place in the universe better. They will know their history, their language, their traditions, and their rights. They can only be better off than they would have been without this new program.

By almost any standards the program is a resounding success; and the key to its success is that it is Indian planned, staffed, and run (even though various nonnative staff members and consultants are freely used). Twenty years from now, in retrospect, the new school program may turn out to be one of the most important innovations of this entire dynamic period.

Another tribal success already detailed was the Community Action Program (CAP) after it was run the "Indian way." Yet another success is the Indian unit of Pine Tree Legal Assistance. This organization is not Indian run, but it is genuinely dedicated to Indian causes, has hired Indian staff on a fairly regular basis, and deals with issues important to the people it serves. Lack of funding results in having to deal mainly in class-action suits rather than with individual cases, which occasionally leads to misunderstandings; but on the whole Pine Tree Legal is in touch with the tribe and therefore with the "Indian reality" promoted in this paper.

Other successes were some training programs that taught skills useful on the reservation in ongoing projects. Some basic education programs have also been successful, and many people have earned their high school equivalency certificates. Finally, Bermuda North's craft program stands out in the crowd as a winner.

All of these successes have the following in common: extensive Indian input and constant contact with the community, adapting to the culture rather than vice versa, and goals in accord with those of the people.

The most prominent success of all is the hardest one to see, an unplanned-for by-product of all the government programs that have rolled in, out, or over the reservations in the last ten years: the development of Indian leadership. Programs that ostensibly "failed" nevertheless provided travel money, conferences, and decent incomes for enough people to help a few break out of the rut of isolation and gain knowledge and confidence in themselves. Perhaps one of the most important lessons some Passamaquoddy learned is that white people don't always know what they're doing, and that Indians sometimes do! Another revelation is that some people out there really do want to help. True, they want to do it their way, usually, but at least somebody cares. The message has begun to come through: "We are a worthwhile people."

People who a few years back were afraid to address any group off the reservation today lecture all over New England and chat freely with congressmen in Washington. They know the ropes politically, and what they don't know they know how to find out. In addition, after many years of relative isolation they have become acquainted with Indians of other areas of the country and have become increasingly aware of their losses in not being federally recognized.

Leadership, a sense of worth, and access to knowledge — these are the greatest gifts provided (inadvertently) by the federal programs. Through these gifts Maine Indians have gained their own department on the state level, have rallied concerned citizen's groups to their side, have started a historic suit for land rights, have created the Coalition of Eastern Native Americans, have increased interreservation cooperation and good will, have improved education, sanitation, and economic conditions, and have begun to regain control of their lives again, after nearly 300 years of being under the "big thumb." "Knowledge is power." For the Passamaquoddies, with their new knowledge, there will be no turning back on the long, long road to better days.

Other Indians in the state and throughout New England are reacting to the developments on three Maine reservations by seeking funds, recognition, and a chance at a decent life, even though many are landless and powerless at present. The pebble is in the water and the ripples are widening out.

ANALYSIS.   For an outsider, analyzing another culture is like putting a jigsaw puzzle together with no picture on the box to go by. Are you making geraniums or windmills? Scattered on the table top, the pieces are incomprehensible. The corner and edge pieces are the crucial ones to place in beginning to grasp the puzzle's makeup. So, with understanding another culture, one must place the cultural values of the people in their proper places, for they represent the corners and perimeters of the culture, showing the limits and boundaries of cultural behavior as well as much about the arrangement of the other pieces in the center.

For these reasons much of this paper has been devoted to explicating the cultural values of the Passamaquoddy, values which for them represent "the way things are." Certain of these values persist through time historically, as well as in many contemporary situations, for values in any man's world are all-pervasive, whether he recognizes them or not. If an outsider attempting to promote a program among a different people fails to perceive (or worse yet, to believe) the other culture's value system, he will probably both disrupt the culture and waste his efforts. Cultures, besides being like puzzles, are like living creatures whose immunoreactions throw off incompatible intruding organisms. They are out of kilter for awhile (sick, if you will), until the offending element is thrown off. Then they return to normal. Such has been the fate of many a federal program that tried to operate in ignorance of, or in opposition to, Passamaquoddy values. The Passamaquoddy themselves have often contributed to this sequence while trying to cooperate with a program that someone wants to give them, which they want to have. But, whenever they make too many concessions to doing things someone else's way, they find disaster in the wings. For too long, they have been brainwashed to believe that the white man knows best. He doesn't — at least not about the Passamaquoddy reality.

An admonition therefore follows for both program planners and the Passamaquoddy: understand the Passamaquoddy world, its history, continuity, vicissitudes, and most of all its values. Work with the values. Use them, don't fight them. Be creative and dare to do what may look silly to people in the next town or at the next desk.

A brief review of some of these values is appropriate:

1. Good is limited; if one man gains, another must lose.

2. One person does not tell another what to do.

3. Work is not a virtue in and of itself.

4. Families or lineages have strong social obligations to other members of the group.

5. Freedom of action and movement is more important than steady work, if a choice must be made.

6. Independence and self-management are ideals, even when working side-by-side with another person.

7. One is specific in speech and meaning. Generalizations are meaningless.

8. There is pride in being Indian.

9. An excess of power in one individual is not to be tolerated.

10. One will say "yes" when one means "no" in order to avoid a rude confrontation.

11. Intertribal difficulties will not be made known to outsiders.

12. One's fate, to a greater extent, is preordained.

13. Economic development is desirable, but not at the expense of everything else.

Preferences and custom are very close to being values and must be as well understood as values are. Here are some preferences and customs:

1. Seasonal cycles of activity are customary — winter is the hard work time, summer the take-it-easy time. Cycles of extremely hard work followed by total relaxation are a commonplace way of life.

2. There is "Indian time" and "White time." Indians check their watches when meeting a white man but may not when meeting one another. Punctuality in itself is no special virtue. Working from 8 to 5 has no meaning to anyone but the mill timekeeper.

3. In living close to the land one uses the season's bounties as they appear. Other things, like jobs, can wait.

Much can be learned by the nature of recent basic changes in the Passamaquoddy community, for, as we have pointed out, incompatible elements are ultimately rejected. Here are some significant changes of recent years:

1. The reduction of migratory workers shows that economic patterns *can* change if jobs are made available.

2. The development of viable leadership through exposure to new experiences, information, and travel shows that the capability for self-determination is undeniably present in the Passamaquoddy people.

3. The newly gained legal and historical knowledge that the tribe has is now part of the culture. It cannot be taken away, and because knowledge is power the people are not likely to become subservient again.

4. The general direction of change is toward a reaffirmation of two things: a decent life, and the right to be Indian.

5. Prosperity's fruits are used from the belly out, for personal satisfactions. In a place where everyone intimately knows everyone else, paint on the house will impress no one but nonresidents.

6. Women are emerging as important tribal decision makers on a more than behind-the-scenes basis, and are increasingly active in tribal politics.

7. The Passamaquoddy are willing to make some concessions to the white man's way and have amply proved this in working through the alien red (white) tape's program applications and sometimes really ridiculous guidelines.

8. Indians in general, and the Passamaquoddy with them, are now demanding cultural concessions from white agencies who want to help. "Help us our way, for our reasons," is the message.

We have noted various built-in problems in federal programs on the Passamaquoddy reserves. Some of these problems are the Passamaquoddy's own, some are those of the federal agencies, and some belong to both:

1. The agent, welfare, and ADC have all been a part of Passamaquoddy life and are used like natural resources that must be harvested while available. Federal programs (which disappear and reappear and change their shape in the night) are often seen in this light, rather than as long-range aids to self-determination.

2. Developing management is a problem to be thoughtfully worked out, for a Passamaquoddy can't tell another what to do, no matter *what* the job description says!

3. There are lineage factions whose competition must be channeled constructively to avoid tugs-of-war that could ruin a program.

4. Women's capabilities must be used to a fuller extent. This means training and day-care arrangements.

5. Teenagers are in a never-never land of dropping out and are ineligible for everything going; they are a great disruption on the reservation through no fault of their own.

6. Supply never meets demand in the Passamaquoddy market. Although poor, they cannot produce enough goods to meet the market demand.

7. Finally, there are great differences in values among the nonnative program planners, as well as differences in judgment over what "failed" and what "succeeded."

SUGGESTIONS. This final section will be devoted to specific suggestions that could bring improvements to the Passamaquoddy economic development scene. Many have been mentioned in other parts of the paper in context and are extracted and summarized here; others are new entries.

Present economic pursuits that could be augmented Many people could augment their incomes during hunting and fishing season as guides, because the recreation potential of Maine is increasing, and nearly every "down-country sport" would prefer an Indian guide to anyone else. Demand is already greater than supply, so that training courses to license more Indian guides is an obvious need.

The fur-trade practices, casually accepted at present by nearly everyone, should be re-examined. Why, for instance, isn't a reservation person able to serve as the go-between with the fur companies? What prices are being granted for pelts in other places? Certainly, a dollar is not adequate recompense for a deer hide!

At Pleasant Point, exclusive Indian fishing and lobstering rights should be secured off the coast of the reservation, and any other similar rights that were stated in the treaties should also be re-established. In this way, several more people could probably make a living as lobstermen and fishermen.

Christmas wreaths are made throughout Washington County and on the reservations, and are sold for very low prices — sometimes as low as 25 cents each. The large wreaths are made of balsam "tips" wired onto a form. When decorated, they sell on city streets in other states for between five and ten dollars. Perhaps decorations could be purchased wholesale and applied by tribal members, and the tribe could establish direct outlets in the cities.

A few Christmas novelties are already made (of the ash material used in baskets), and these items could be produced as a specialty. Some people already make poinsettias, crosses, and birds, and by borrowing some ideas from the Scandinavian Christmas ornaments of straw, the Passamaquoddy could quite easily develop distinctive ornaments of ash and sweetgrass, which should have high saleability in gift shops and wreath markets.

In the basket industry, operating capital is a must. More efficient ways of securing and replanting brown ash need to be established, and more effective ways of getting the pounded strips to the weavers must be developed, both for those who work at home and those that work in the co-ops. Basket dyes should be improved, for they sometimes fade.

Beaded or carved jewelry, knick-knacks, and toys are made, but there are never enough to meet the demand. Encouragement of this cottage industry is in order, and it ought to be at least minimally organized, perhaps with an outlet through the co-ops. Some people who are old or semi-invalid could work at these crafts at home, if they had supplies.

Finally, better roads and maps would greatly facilitate tourists going to the reservations to buy these goods. The reservations are almost impossible to find, if one doesn't know where to look for them.

Possible new economic pursuits If the social and health needs of the tribe are not met (and United States Indian Health Services so far will not help this tribe), economic development schemes will have minimal returns. Reservation clinics are necessary but unfunded, and mental health services are almost totally lacking. Alcohol treatment facilities are in the planning stages, but funds are shaky at present. Funding agencies should, therefore, automatically relegate a small part of every program budget toward helping existing reservation health facilities or creating new ones.

Day-care centers for working mothers need to be encouraged, for in these small communities one can't afford to waste talent, male or female, and many of the tribe's potential leaders, craftsmen, and creative thinkers are women. They need to be freed, at least part of the day, to use their talents in tribal enterprises.

Guaranteed federal loans for business projects operated by Maine Indians would be a great boon, but these Indians are not presently eligible for loans available to Federal Indians. It is most difficult for the tribe to borrow funds for operating capital, because they have no collateral.

The historical resources of the tribe could be developed for the benefit of the tribe's morale, the edification of the state's other residents, and the stimulation of tourist trade. If similar projects could be developed in other Indian communities on the Eastern Seaboard, perhaps a coordinated "Eastern Indian Historical Trail" could be developed from Maine to Florida. Many members of the Coalition of Eastern Native Americans are dreaming, too, of developing their own historical resources.

At Pleasant Point, a small marina could be developed. Passama-quoddy Bay is fairly treacherous; therefore, Indian guides who know the bay well could be part of this complex. A possible small industry for the collection of specimens for biological research (suggested in Tannenbaum's EDA report) is another income potential. A Penobscot who has seen the Lummi aquaculture project on the northwest coast wondered if a similar effort might not work at Pleasant Point. A feasibility study of this possibility may be in order.

At Indian Township, there is an ample deer herd and a strong interest and talent in leather work. It would be eminently worthwhile to establish tanning facilities on at least a small scale for leather preparation. It is certainly one of the most obvious improvements that could be made for the least outlay.

Northeastern Indians have distinctive floral designs; Maine Indians, besides these, have a unique "double curve motif" type of design that could profitably be used in eastern Indian silver jewelry craft. Given the talent exhibited by the Passamaquoddy in other crafts, and the boom-ing market in Indian jewelry and arts, with good training and promo-tion, Northwestern Indian jewelry would seem a very good bet. Local Maine semi-precious stones might be incorporated in this work as well.

Indian Township has potential wealth in its ample supplies of cedar and other woods, and a portable lumber mill would be a boon to the tribe. Perhaps direct sale arrangements could be made with various island communities off the New England coast, where houses are often sided with cedar shakes and shingles. Cedar fencing could also be produced at Indian Township quite easily.

Fiddle-head fern cultivation is another distinct possibility on Indian Township; it has been mastered in New Brunswick, so that the techniques are already developed and presumably could be copied here.

Most important in the realm of new economic pursuits, and one that would incorporate almost all of the foregoing suggestions, is the development of a good-sized tourism complex. A multistory motel with museum, stores, marina, deep-sea fishing trips, boat rentals, restaurant, and gift shop could be created at Pleasant Point, even though the land base is small. Perhaps a small ferry could operate from this complex to Deer, Moose, and Grand Manan Island, as well as to nearby Campobello.

At Indian Township, the possibilities for a tourist complex are even greater because of the large land base, brooks, rivers, and lakes. Here, where fish and game abound and the lakes are pure, it would be feasible to have a year-round tourist haven, with camping, swimming, boating, canoeing, snowmobiling, hunting, fishing, ice-fishing, snow-shoeing, cross country skiing, nature walks, cook-outs, and other sporting pursuits. Supportive facilities could include a small boat marina, gift shop, laundromat, museum, craft demonstrations, grocery and tackle store, restaurant, motel, cabins, boat rentals, camping and canoeing outfitting, drive-in movie theatre, tennis courts, and garage, as well as sales and rental outlets for snowmobiles, boats, skis, small engines, trail bikes, and so on. Jobs would be made available to everyone in such a comprehensive program, and a successful tourist complex would generate new jobs constantly through the necessity for new units, the demand for craft, and the need for babysitting, guides, and other services. Besides benefiting from the growing tourist industry of northern New England, the tribe could also benefit from the recreation provided to itself in this tribal-wide enterprise (as well as from the income). Such a complex would be self-generating, and ideally would put the tribe beyond the winds of political change, which presently keep them swinging from program to uncoordinated program.

The tribe has attempted to have such a project funded before (from EDA), with negative results. Some have suggested they seek help from the BIA, which currently is developing similar programs on reservations across the country. But the BIA and Maine Indians, as we have shown, have no official ties, and no help is forthcoming from that quarter.

Avoiding problems in the presentation of federal programs   The first necessary step is avoiding problems is for federal agencies to eliminate nonsense guidelines. A typical example is the guideline requiring job trainees to be 18 before receiving training. It would be much better to allow training to anybody over 14, and to attach a rider requiring all those under 18 to work also on a high school equivalency certificate.

Another important goal of federal programs should be to take a total approach, and to finish jobs once undertaken (for example, the water and sewerage project, and the Basket Co-op). Continuity of programs is obviously a must.

In planning reservation programs, federal agencies should first know the tribe well. This could be accomplished by having and using studies such as this one, by using native specialists wherever possible, by using anthropologists familiar with the area, and in general by learning the cultural values, history, and present status of the community to be helped. True, it is a lot of work, but it would be well worthwhile. Federal agencies also need to examine their own inevitable ethnocentricity in regards to goals and methods. They need to keep it clearly in mind that, although intransigence may appear to be the dominant feature of the culture they are attempting to assist, intransigence may also be *their own* most dominant feature in the eyes of the program's recipients. Finally, consultants who come to give technical assistance need to know more than "facts": They need to know the people.

We have emphasized throughout that when the Passamaquoddy culture bends too far to fit itself to some program, disaster or rejection of the program inevitably follows.

Programs, then, must be fitted to the culture, and not the reverse. How can this be done? Hours, and even work days, should be flexible. Minigrants should be made to individual families or lineages, which would then sell their crafts to the tribally owned Co-op. There must be, as far as humanly possible, an even distribution of good jobs. (This would be most easily accomplished in a tourist development program.) There must be training for the kind of jobs where one can be one's own boss. Advice and training should be geared to the exact task at hand. (How do you fill out THIS particular form? What does a "quarterly report" mean? How do you set a fair price, for a basket?) Lineage competition should be used constructively, by having different families work on different projects and programs. The tribe, and tribal government, should be consulted at every phase of planning and execution of any program. Get Indian input all the way. Training must be adequate. Don't assume anything about a people's past experience in a job. They may have no acquaintance with an item at all. Use total approach programs (such as the tourist complex) that give the community-at-large common goals and similar opportunities.

The presentation of programs could certainly use some upgrading, too. People often are unclear about programs, how or who supplies them, how long they will last, or what they are supposed to accomplish. Personal roles in the programs, not to mention job duties, are often just as obscure. Films, therefore, need to be developed to accompany every program, explaining in three dimensions what EXACTLY is supposed to go on and who is supposed to do it. Federal agencies need to coordinate their efforts at higher levels, so that similar programs from different agencies don't leave everyone standing around wondering what the program difference is, and who should do what?

Some general suggestions: Provide a total program, which will involve the whole tribe. Run the tribe, or at least each reservation, as a corporate body with the elected chief and council as the overall board of directors. Funnel in all separate program monies into one fund, which is earmarked for the total tribal project. Let Indians, perhaps with consultant assistance, set the properties on the use of the Composite Fund. Build reseeding money into all programs (so much profit requires so much to be reinvested in the enterprises). Get the tribe itself to figure out how to increase production and how to make management work. Get good health care, nutrition, and personal money management programs underway. Work on the development of a sense of community and on Indian pride.

Finally, let the words of a Passamaquoddy woman who spoke at the 1972 Maine Indian Civil Rights Hearings be engraved in bronze and placed on every "Indian Desk" in the land:

We are sick to death of people telling us what's good for us and cramming it down our throats. We would like to have the opportunity to decide our own destiny.

REFERENCES

"Act relating to the separation of Maine from Massachusetts, June 19, 1819."
  1819   Sec. 1, Art. 5, "Indians of Maine." Doc. Hist., Maine Hist. Soc., Coll., Sec. 2, Vol. VIII, Portland (1902).
ASSOCIATED PRESS
  1968   "Logging, Indian dispute quiets; work is resumed." *Portland Press Herald*, July 6, 1968.
  1969   "Quoddy toll gate on route 1 gets tribal go-ahead." *Maine Sunday Telegram*, July 4, 1969.
Bangor Daily News
  1969   "Indians say if talks, they may not block." *Bangor Daily News*, July 5, 1969.
BAXTER, JAMES P.
  1908–   "Documentary history of Maine." Maine Hist., Soc. Coll., Sec.
  1916   2. (Vols. XII, XIII, XXIII, and XXIV, pertain to Maine Indians.) Portland, Portland, Maine.
BEAL, CLAYTON
  1969a   "Indians vow road blocks, seek milk, medical funds." *Bangor Daily News*, June 7, 1969.
  1969b   "Demonstration by Quoddy Indians wins concession from State bureau." *Bangor Daily News*, July 8, 1969.
BECK, HORACE P.
  1966   *Gluskap the liar and other Indian tales.* Freeport, Maine: The Bond Wheelwright Company.
BELMORE, BRUCE W.
  1945   *Early Princeton, Maine.* Portland, Maine: Southworth-Anthoensen Press.
BROWN, W. W.
  1892   'Chief Making' among the Passamaquoddy Indians. *Journal of American Folklore* 5: 57–59.

Brunswick Times-Record
  1968 "Indians to plan next step on disputed timber cutting." *Brunswick Times-Record*, July 2, 1968.
  1968 "Indian picnic halts timber cutting." *Brunswick Times-Record*, July 5, 1968.
BUESING, GREGORY P.
  1970 "Notes on Wabanaki history." Middleton, Connecticut: Wesleyan University. Unpublished honors thesis, Department of Anthropology.
Calais Advertiser
  1969 "Indians collect their scalps — and milk and medicine." *Calais Advertiser*, July 10, 1969.
"Cession of lands to the State of Maine for support of the Indians, by commissioners under the Act of Separation, Dec. 28, 1822."
  1822 Doc. Hist., Maine Hist. Soc., Coll., Sec. 2, Vol. VIII, Portland (1902).
Committee on Labor and Public Welfare, U.S. Senate
  1969 "The education of American Indians. Field investigation and research reports." (see pp. 245–251 for Maine.) Prepared for the subcommittee on the Ind. Ed. Vol. II. Washington: U.S. Government Printing Office.
CLARKSON CORPORATION
  1969 "Analysis of transient motor vehicles near lands owned by the Passamaquoddy Indians and analysis of marine traffic on Passamaquoddy Bay near lands owned by Passamaquoddy Indians, Washington County Maine." Fairfield, Maine: Clarkson Corporation.
DAVIS, HAROLD A.
  1950 *An international community on the Saint Croix.* Orono: University of Maine Press.
DAVIS, REVEREND JOHN P.
  1971 "Project, Bermuda North II." Mimeograph. Brunswick, Maine, Bowdoin College Newman Apostolate.
DESJARDINS, RT. REV. PHILLIP E.
  1952 "Indian missions in Maine in chronological order." Portland: Archdiocese of Portland.
DOYLE, LL., G. BUESING
  1970 "A five year developmental program for the Indians of Maine, submitted to the National Conference of Catholic Bishops' Campaign for Human Development." Bangor, Maine: Division of Indian Services, Diocese of Portland.
DUNNACK, H. E.
  1920 "The Maine book." Augusta, Maine. Copyright held by H. E. Dunnack (no publisher).
ECKSTORM, F. H.
  1932 "The handicrafts of the modern Indians of Maine." Bar Harbor, Maine: Abbe Museum. Bulletin 3.
  1939 *A reference list of manuscripts relating to the history of Maine, Part II.* Orono: University of Maine Press.
  1945 *Old John Neptune and other Maine Indian shamans.* Portland, Maine: Southworth-Anthoensen Press.
ECONOMIC DEVELOPMENT ADMINISTRATION
  1971 Federal and state Indian reservations; and EDA handbook." Publ. by U.S. Dept. of Commerce.

ELWELL, E. L.
  1968   "An overall economic development plan; Promote Recreation and
         Industry Down East, Inc. (PRIDE). (Hancock, Knox, Penobscot,
         Piscatiquis, Waldo, and Washington Counties.) Submitted to
         Economic Development Administration; U.S. Commerce Dept. Con-
         gress, Washington, D.C.
FAUX, G.
  1972   Rural poverty and land ownership in Maine. *Community Economics*
         May (occasional bulletin). Cambridge, Massachusetts: Center for
         Community Economic Development.
FITZPATRICK, D. W.
  1968   "Quoddies to gain control of disputed timber lands." *Brunswick
         Times-Record*, July 9, 1968.
FONTAINE, D. F.
  1971   "Evaluating Pine Tree Legal Assistance, Inc." (see esp. "Report on
         activities of the Indian Legal Services Unit of Calais, Maine".)
         Prepared for Auerbach Corp. (no publ. info.)
FORD, DANIEL
  1971   "The natives are restless. Maine's desperate Indians are creating a
         new kind of school to save their kids." *Boston Sunday Globe*, January
         10, 1971.
GERETY, BISHOP PETER L.
  1971   "A coordinated plan for human and social development." Portland,
         Maine: Archdiocese of Portland.
GUSTAFSON, ROBERT
  1971   Passamaquoddy Indians weave their way to economic success. *Op-
         portunity Magazine*, June. United States Office of Economic Oppor-
         tunity.
HACKET, B. MC., JR.
  1971   "Meni-Countri Products, Inc. economic development trip to the
         Passamaquoddy Indian reservations at Dana Point and Pleasant
         Point." (Cost-analyses of basket and wreath making.) Waltham,
         Mass; Meni-Countri Products, Incorporated.
HASBROUCK, SARAH S.
  1968   "The Catholic Indian Missions in Maine: 1611–1820." Mimeograph.
         Augusta: Department of Indian Affairs.
INTER-CULTURAL STUDIES GROUP OF CONCORD ACADEMY
  1973   *Indian leadership in New England, 1973.* Inter-cultural Studies
         Group, Lexington, Massachusetts.
ISAACSON, DORIS, *editor*
  1970   *Maine: a guide 'Down East'* (second edition). Rockland, Maine:
         Courier-Gazette, Incorporated.
JOSEPH, A. M., JR.
  1971   *Red Power: the American Indians' fight for freedom.* New York:
         American Heritage Press.
KALISS, ANTHONY
  1969   "A report on Passamaquoddy tribal lands on Indian Township,
         Nemcass (Governors) Point and Pine Island." Mimeograph.
  1972   "Maine Indians today; Penobscots, Micmacs, Maliseets, Passama-
         quoddies; a study of current programs and services." Bangor, Maine:
         Division of Indian Services Bureau of Human Relations, Archdio-
         cese, Portland.

KIDDER, FREDERIC
  1867 *Military operations in eastern Maine and Nova Scotia during the Revolution.* Albany, New York.
KILBY, W. H.
  1888 *Eastport and Passamaquoddy.* (see Chapter 18, "The Passamaquoddy tribe of Indians.") Eastport, Maine.
KIP, REV. WM. I.,
  1847 *The early Jesuit missions in North America.* Compiled and translated from the letters of the French Jesuits, with notes. Part I. New York: Wiley and Putnam.
LANGLEY, WILLIAM
  1971 "Maine Indians: net gain in five years — zero." *Maine Times,* July 2, 1971. (Interview with Passamaquoddy tribal governor, John Stevens.)
LEACH, D. E.
  1966 *The northern colonial frontier, 1607–1763.* New York: Holt, Rinehart and Winston.
LESCARBOT, MARC
  1907 *The history of New France* (1606). English translation, notes, and appendices by William Grant, three volumes. Toronto: Champlain Society.
LEVINE, JO ANN
  1967a "Rising expectations stir Indians in Maine." Boston: *Christian Science Monitor,* May 29, 1967.
  1967b "Maine Indians find a voice." Boston: *Christian Science Monitor,* May 31, 1967.
  1967c "'Outsiders' awaken Maine Indians." Boston: *Christian Science Monitor,* June 1, 1967.
LIPSKY, J., J. BAKER
  1971 "The Passamaquoddy: gentle red militance." *The Phoenix* (Boston), December 29, 1971. (Note: This is an outstandingly informative article on values, relationship to Maine, and developments of the late 1960's among the Passamaquoddy.)
LORD, R. H., SEXTON, J. E., HARRINGTON, E. T.
  1944 *History of the Archdiocese of Boston* (three volumes; see volume two "The missions of Maine, New Hampshire, and Vermont.") New York: Sheed and Ward.
MAINE COUNCIL OF CHURCHES
  1951 "Our Maine Indians." Mimeograph. Maine Council of Churches.
MAINE DEPARTMENT OF EDUCATION
  1969 "Indian education in Maine." Mimeograph. Department of Education, Augusta, Maine.
MAINE DEPARTMENT OF INDIAN AFFAIRS
  1968 "The Department of Indian Affairs." Mimeograph. Department of Indian Affairs, Augusta, Maine.
  1971a "Maine Indians: a brief summary." Mimeograph. Department of Indian Affairs, Augusta, Maine.
  1971b "State of Maine: a compilation of laws pertaining to Indians." Revised mimeograph. Department of Indian Affairs, Augusta, Maine.
MORRISON, A. H.
  1968 "Ramblings in Wabanakia and Wabanakiana." (Bibliography of Maine Indian sources.) Buffalo: Department of Anthropology, State University of New York.

MORRISON, K.
1968 "Legal action hinted on Indian land case." *Brunswick Times-Record*, June 27, 1968.
1970 "Maine Indians fight back." *Maine Times*, April 3, 1970.
NEWELL, WAYNE
1973 "Report on bilingual-bicultural education program at Indian Township, Maine." Indian Township, Maine, Dana Point School.
New York Times
1968 "Maine woods pact heartens Indians. Passamaquoddy get right to cut trees for concern." *New York Times*, July 21, 1968.
1972 "Judge backs Indians in Maine land suit." *New York Times*, June 24, 1972.
NICHOLAS, BARRY
1970 "Report on the Indian Education Workshop held at T.R.I.B.E., Incorporated, Learning Center, Bar Harbor, Maine, August 3–22." Mimeograph.
NICOLAR, JOSEPH (Penobscot Indian)
1893 *The life and traditions of the red man.* Bangor: C. H. Glass.
NUTT, GEORGE W.
1860 "Annual report of the agent to the Penobscot and Passamaquoddy tribes of Maine to the Honorable Governor and Council of Maine." Published by State of Maine.
O'TOOLE, F. J., TUREEN, T. N.
1971 State power and the Passamaquoddy Tribe: a gross national hypocrisy? *Maine Law Review* 23(1). University of Maine School of Law.
PASSAMAQUODDY INDIAN TRIBE OF MAINE
1969 "Overall economic development program for Passamaquoddy Indian Tribe of Maine." Submitted to the Economic Development Administration of the United States Department of Commerce. Washington, D.C.
PEASE, DUSTIN
1968 "Reconnaisance report for Passamaquoddy reservation comprehensive planning proposal." Manuscript from Maine Washington County Regional Action Agency.
PECORARO, JOSEPH
1970 "The effect of a series of special lessons on Indian history and culture upon the attitudes of Indian and non-Indian students." Department of Education, Augusta, Maine.
PORTER, C. H.
1886 "Annual report of the agent to the Passamaquoddy Tribe of Indians to the Honorable Governor and Council of Maine." Published by State of Maine.
Portland Press Herald
1971 "Stevens sworn in to Indian Post." *Portland Press Herald*, August 7, 1971.
PRATSON, FREDERICK J.
1970 *Land of the four directions.* New York: Viking Press.
PRINCE, J. D.
1897 The Passamaquoddy wampum records. *American Philosophy Society Proceedings* 26.
PROCTOR, R. W.
1942 "Proctor report on Maine Indians; prepared for the Maine Legislative Research Committee." Xeroxed typescript, Augusta State Lib-

rary, Maine. (Note: A most important source for history and relation to state into 1940's)

QUINLAN, E.
1972 "Unity College studies Indian culture — color it proud." *Morning Sentinel,* August 2, 1972. Waterville, Maine.

RAINEY, FROELICH G.
1956 A compilation of data contributing to the ethnography of Connecticut and Southern New England Indians. (1936). *Bulletin of the Archaeology Society of Connecticut.* Third reprint.

RAY, ROGER B.
1972 *The Indians of Maine: a bibliographical guide.* Portland: Maine Historical Society.

ROBERTS, ELEANOR
1969 "Channel 56 shows plight of Maine Indians." (Article describing the documentary film on Passamaquoddys, "So we will stand and fight.") *Boston Herald Traveler,* July 10, 1969.

SCHERMER, ANDREA
1967 "The Passamaquoddys — Maine's stepchildren." *Boston Sunday Globe,* November 19, 1967.

SOCKABASIN, A. J., STONE, J. G.
1971 "Off-Reservation Indian survey: Maine." Department of Indian Affairs, Augusta, Maine.

SOULE, W. H., *ed.*
1970 "Prehistoric peoples of Maine." Augusta: Maine State Museum.

SPECK, F. G.
1915 The Eastern Algonkian Wabanaki Confederacy. *American Anthropologist,* n.s. 17: 492–508.

1940 *Penobscot man.* Philadelphia: University of Pennsylvania Press.

SPINDLER, G. D., SPINDLER, L. S.
1957 "American Indian personality types and their socio-cultural roots." in American Indians and American Life, Annals Amer. Acad. Pol. & Soc. Sci., Philadelphia.

STARBIRD, GLENN, JR.
1971 "Brief history of Indian legislative representatives in the Maine Legislature." Mimeograph. Department of Indian Affairs, Augusta, Maine.

STEVENS, J., FRANCES, E., HINCKLEY E.
1969 "A proposal for the use of the job corps training center facility at Acadia National Park: Abenaki Indian High School." *Ellsworth American,* December 18, 1969 Ellsworth, Maine.

STEVENS, SUSAN M.
1972 "A brief history of the Passamaquoddy Indians." Mimeograph. Department of Indian Affairs, Augusta, Maine.

STEVENS, S., BUESING G., BUESING J.
n.d. "Once we were brothers; historical sketches of Maine and Maritime Indians." Unpublished manuscript.

TANNENBAUM, A.
1972 "Passamaquoddy Indian economic development; a report under EDA contract 0-35417 (January). Washington, D.C.: Continental-Allied.

TAYLOR, T. W.
1972 *The states and their Indian citizens.* United States Department of the Interior. Washington, D.C.: Government Printing Office.

TEETER, KARL V.
  1967   Preliminary report on Malecite-Passamaquoddy. *Contributions to Anthropology: Linguistics I.* Ottawa: National Museum of Canada, Bulletin 214.
TUREEN, T. N.
  1971   "Remembering eastern Indians," in *Inequality in education.* Symposium on Indian education, Center for Law and Education, Harvard University 10. Cambridge.
UNITED PRESS INTERNATIONAL
  1969   "Maine Indians sit, demand wampum." *Boston Herald Traveler,* July 8, 1969.
UNITED STATES DEPARTMENT OF THE INTERIOR
  1967   "Indians of the Eastern Seaboard." Bureau of Indian Affairs. Washington, D.C.: Government Printing Office.
VETROMILE, REV. EUGENE
  1866   *The Abenakis and their history.* New York: James B. Kirken.
Vista Magazine
  1969   "In the state of reservation." (Passamaquoddy Indians.)
WEINBERG, PAUL
  1973   "The Indians of Maine in the first half of the nineteenth century." Unpublished term paper prepared for Bowdoin College, Brunswick. (Prepared by Department of Indian Affairs, Augusta, Maine.)
WIESENTHOL, M.
  1969   "Quoddies tell their side on TV tonight." *Maine Sunday Telegram,* July 13, 1969.
WILLIAMSON, W. D.
  1832   *The history of the state of Maine; from its first discovery,* A.D. *1602, to the separation,* A.D. *1820, inclusive,* volumes one and two. Hallowell, Maine: Glazier, Masters.
WILLIAMSON, W. H.
  1967   "Maine's Indians: once they owned the entire State." (Series of 5 articles on : Struggle for tribal identity; dispute with Indian agent; beginnings of the land case; Vistas workers experiences; and budgetary problems with the state.) *Maine Sunday Telegram,* February 22, 1967.
WOOD, ETHEL
  1921–   The Maine Indians, and their relations with the white settlers.
  1922   *Sprague's Journal of Maine History,* volumes nine and ten.
WOOD, WILLIAM
  1898   "New England's prospect." (1634). Boston: E. M. Boynton.
WRIGHT, PIERCE, BARNES, WYMAN
  1966   "Report on proposed improvements at state Indian reservations." Prepared for the Department of Indian Affairs, Topsham, Maine.

Making Do with the Dark Meat: A Report on the Cherokee Indians in Oklahoma

ALBERT L. WAHRHAFTIG

INTRODUCTION

The general consul of the Cherokee nation is recognized as a Cherokee by United States law. This is because his name appears on the "Too-Late Roll," a supplementary listing of infants attached to the final roll of Cherokee citizens, which was closed for all time in 1907. In all other respects, however, the general consul is the image of a rural white Southern politician — a florid, portly, verbose lawyer who can be, when the occasion demands it, courtly. One day not long ago, he sat behind the expanse of desk in his office in Fort Gibson, Oklahoma, suspiciously interrogating a young white man who, with his wife, had come to do research for a dissertation on the history of contemporary "full bloods" in the Cherokee nation. On one side of the lawyer sat his elderly legal secretary and on the other side sat his chauffeur/general

Data for this report have been gathered since 1963. While an associate of the Carnegie Corporation Cross-Cultural Education Project of the University of Chicago (directed by Sol Tax and Robert K. Thomas from 1963 to 1966), I made demographic and socioeconomic surveys of tribal Cherokee settlements, collected data in depth at two settlements, and closely observed political and ceremonial events among the most traditional Cherokee; these observations were extended during the summer of 1967. I returned to the Cherokee nation in January 1972 to collect additional information specifically for this report, joined by Janet Jordan, who contributed cultural anthropological data; Bonnie Chism, who interviewed several tribal officials and observed the Cherokee community representatives' meeting; Donald Paquin, who prepared an analysis of the Cherokee housing program; Richard Hughes, who constructed a chronology of recent events as reported in the *Cherokee Nation News*; and Robert Buchanan, who journeyed to Tahlequah as a consultant.

From the first days of my fieldwork, Robert K. Thomas has unfailingly given of himself as a friend, teacher, and colleague. I am expressing my appreciation to the many Cherokees who have been friends and generous informants by preserving their anonymity.

assistant. The lawyer calls these men "full bloods," and, indeed, both are dark skinned and of unmistakably Indian physiognomy. At noon the lawyer sent the assistant to bring in a lunch, and he soon returned with a bucket of fried chicken. Tucking a napkin under his chin, the lawyer turned to the young white couple and said, with expansive gallantry, "Now you-all take the white meat you want. These boys can make do with the dark."

This vignette stands as a metaphor for life in the Cherokee nation today and as an abstract of this report. The Cherokee Indians are a people who live on leftovers. Moreover, even the leftovers are dealt to them by a locally powerful group of people who are white in culture, loyalty, life-style, and appearance — yet are legally Cherokee. Therefore, although this report is concerned with the economic situation of Cherokee Indians in Oklahoma, it must commence, as all discussions of the modern Cherokee must, with the question of who is and who is not a Cherokee.

As described in the body of this report, there is a relatively small group of people in eastern Oklahoma who pursue, in modern form, traditional Cherokee ways of life; most of them can speak the Cherokee language. People living outside their way of life call them "full bloods." There is a larger population in eastern Oklahoma (and elsewhere) whose members also identify themselves as Cherokees; many of these people are legally Cherokee, although some are not. There also is at present a legal entity known as the Cherokee nation of Oklahoma, or, as it is called locally, "the tribe." Although these groups of people — each Cherokee by different criteria — overlap, they do not correspond. Eastern Oklahoma is an ethnically and culturally complex region. Within it, the group that lives a Cherokee way of life is not the same as the group whose members call themselves Cherokees, nor does either population coincide with the legal membership of the Cherokee nation. Indeed, as this report demonstrates, as often as not these categories of people are adversaries.

To understand events among the contemporary Cherokee, the situation must be considered from three points of view: (1) that of an outside observer — preferably trained to recognize cultural, social, and cognitive boundary lines — who can conceptualize a complex social system containing distinctive populations, all acting in terms of their own unique perceptions of themselves and of other populations in their environment; (2) that of "Indians," that is, the culturally conservative Cherokees who are here called "tribal Cherokees"; and (3) that of the personnel, both technically Cherokee and white, who administer Cherokee affairs. In addition, one must become habituated to the fact that the different populations involved disagree irreconcilably on the issue of who is and who is not a Cherokee. In fact, a conclusion to be drawn from the final section of this report is that *in this regional social system, those who control regional systems of cultural definition thereby control the allocation of political and economic power.*

In earlier descriptions of the Cherokee (Wahrhaftig 1966a, 1968), I commenced with an explanation of the various populations that are called "Cherokees" before proceding to other subjects, but this approach is tedious for the reader and does not communicate effectively. In this report, the issue of cultural definition has been deferred for another approach. In the first three sections words such as "Cherokee" and "white" have been used exactly as the tribal Cherokee use them, drawing the reader into one gestalt so that he will be able to perceive the Cherokee situation as tribal Cherokees themselves perceive it. To the extent that this approach has been successful, the reader will have internalized one set of cultural definitions when he arrives at the section entitled "The Cherokee establishment," and this will provide a holistic background for the formal discussion of the various criteria for determining Cherokee membership that are presented in that section.

In organizing this report, I have attempted (1) to describe the Cherokee situation both from the viewpoint of an analytic observer and also as it is seen and experienced by Cherokee participants and (2) to keep description of the Cherokees in context, so that they are understood as participants grappling with existence in a complex and rapidly changing social system. The first two sections of the report establish the context. First of all, the Cherokees are at the bottom of the heap in a regional economy; they are the poorest and most isolated population and are excluded from present currents of economic development. This aspect of the situation is described in the first section. Cherokees are poor because their assets have been stolen through processes described in the next section, which is followed by a section dealing with the ways in which tribal Cherokees keep their settlements together and survive. It includes a description of the internal economy in traditional, culturally conservative Cherokee communities, an economy that is efficient and flexible, within the limits of the scanty resources upon which it operates. Description of that economy is related to a more inclusive description of traditional Cherokee life in order to identify processes through which the Cherokee ceremonial and ritual ideas are the core of the adaptive process — a proposition that I think may well be true of many other American Indian peoples. These ideas provide an orientation that causes Cherokees to remain attentive to changes in their environment; hence, the ideas define a sort of feedback mechanism, which causes Cherokees to reconsider and refashion their way of life whenever they perceive that their adaptation is breaking down. The social system in which Cherokees are enmeshed is dealt with as a whole in the final section, which documents the emergence of a regional center of power — the "Cherokee establishment" — created by entrepreneurs who have made an asset of their legal designation as Cherokees and who have devised techniques for exploiting Cherokee poverty in itself as a resource. In closing this section, the effect of these economic endeavors on tribal Cherokee settlements and the response to it are described.

THE CHEROKEE SCENE

Of all the tribes of American Indians, none has so distinguished a reputation for accomplishment as the Cherokees. Once corn-gardening villagers in the mountains of America's Southeast, the Cherokee evolved an autonomous and self-sufficient republic. While continuing to be an Indian nation, they not only learned from but often surpassed their white neighbors. To their basic subsistence pattern of hunting, foraging, and gardening, they added plantation agriculture, animal domestication, crafts, and trade, which extended the dimensions of their native prosperity. Cherokees of the eighteenth and nineteenth centuries created for themselves a written form of their own language, a written constitution and code of laws, a bicameral legislature, a national supreme court, a national police force, a national book press, and a newspaper with international circulation. When Cherokees became interested in Christian thought, they were able to read an edition of the Scriptures that a Cherokee had translated directly from the original Greek into his own language. In the middle of the nineteenth century, when the Cherokees decided to add to their national school system seminaries (the equivalent of modern colleges), they selected a faculty from the finest academies of the eastern United States. After the Civil War, Cherokees were near universal literacy in their own language, and their degree of literacy in English exceeded that of whites in states bordering the Cherokee nation. Both in the "old country" before the forced removal that followed the 1835 Treaty of New Echota and in the Cherokee nation in the West thereafter, the most affluent Cherokees built handsomely furnished mansions that set the standard for frontier elegance. These houses embody a principle that Cherokees applied generally: when they built, they built first class. Having developed this advanced way of life, the Cherokees thought of themselves as civilized. Admiring intellectuals in the United States and throughout Europe concurred, calling the Cherokees a "civilized tribe."

Less celebration has been made of the fact that no tribe of Indians has had more taken away from them than the Cherokees. No tribe now lives in greater poverty, nor suffers greater indignity. The Cherokees, who were only a century ago an internationally renowned people, now scramble for simple survival as a community, for mere subsistence as individuals. They now live in a rural part of the United States that is poor even without taking into consideration its Indians. In this impoverished environment, the Cherokees are the poorest among the poor, a minority population enclaved and exploited within its own homeland in the Ozark hills of eastern Oklahoma.

Reliable statistical information about Cherokees is scant. From 1907, when Oklahoma became a state, until about 1960, the Cherokee-country "Establishment" systematically maintained the fiction that the Cherokees had "progressed" to the extent of complete assimilation into the general population (Wahrhaftig and Thomas 1968). The Cherokees as a tribe and as a nation were spoken of glowingly, in the past tense. They were one's distinguished ancestry. Scholars were deflected toward studying tribal history, or toward lamenting a priori a dying culture. As historian Angie Debo points out:

The agency [as the Bureau of Indian Affairs was called in earlier days] maintained contact only with those [Indians] still owning restricted land .... A whole generation born too late to receive allotments was growing up in illiteracy and squalor with no land and no tribal relations. Even their names were unknown to the Indian service (Debo 1970: 281).

In the 1960's, the myth of Cherokee assimilation was dispelled, partly through the dissemination of the first comprehensive studies of traditional Cherokee communities in modern times, made between 1963 and 1966 by the Carnegie Corporation Cross-Cultural Education Project of the University of Chicago. These studies coincided with the inception of the Office of Economic Opportunity, which made program funds available for distribution wherever it could be proved that needy Indians existed.

But the establishment in eastern Oklahoma continued its hostility to research, for, while it was expedient to document the presence of impoverished Indians, the outrageous poverty of the Cherokees itself was an indictment of past leadership. There has been no effort to update the demographic, social, and economic data gathered in 1963–1964 nor, as the present head of the Cherokee tribe's community development program said with a shudder, is there any probability that there will be.

The Cherokees are miserably poor. In the four Cherokee settlements surveyed in 1963, median per capita income ranged from $450 to $650 a year (Wahrhaftig 1970: 45). In the counties where these Cherokee settlements are located, a substantial number of white families fall below the poverty index accepted at that time, an annual income of $3,000 per family. Adair County (in which the largest and most concentrated population of Cherokees resides) was featured in a *Newsweek* article on the War on Poverty as one of the hundred poorest in the nation. Yet in eastern Oklahoma, where there are large populations of Cherokees, there is not one county in which Cherokee income is even half the income of whites. The per capita income of Cherokees as compared with the per capita income of whites in 1963 was 43 percent in Adair County, 47 percent in Cherokee, 42 percent in Delaware, and 41 percent in Sequoyah (Wahrhaftig 1970: 47).

Among Cherokees the degree of poverty, deprivation, and cultural isolation is uniform from county to county and from settlement to settlement. In 1963, I selected for study four Cherokee settlements, in four different counties of eastern Oklahoma, that represented extremes in the existing range of geographic isolation, cohesiveness, and traditionality. When the results were tabulated, the data varied surprisingly little from one settlement to the next. Marked differences in native culture and social structure had no effect on the level of material well-being (Wahrhaftig 1970: 1–7).

Cherokee income, such as it is, comes from the stingiest and most precarious sources. Principal among these are short-term, seasonal menial labor and welfare, the latter administered by capricious and vindictive local officials (Wax 1971: 103–105). In the settlements I surveyed, from 42 percent to 66 percent of the heads of households were not in the labor force at all; many were prematurely disabled by the combination of a life of heavy physical labor and employers who provide no workmen's compensation. From 22 percent to 46 percent of the employed men were working seasonally, for short terms, or at odd jobs. Further, the amount of unemployment among Cherokees was obscured by their desperation.

To avoid falling into the hands of welfare officials, whom they fear, Cherokees will accept jobs from which they can profit but little. For example, men were traveling at their own expense from Adair County to Lincoln, Arkansas, each night in hope that a chicken processing plant there would need them as "chicken grabbers." Two or three times a week they would be hired to work all night at $1.00 per hour. Elsewhere, Cherokees worked at farms, commercial nurseries, and canneries, sometimes for as little as 85 cents per hour and often for lower wages than whites were paid for comparable jobs. Hardly a third of Cherokee households are able to support themselves by their own earnings, and more than half of all Cherokee households are dependent in whole or in part on welfare. As telling as these figures from a survey of households are, it is more realistic to talk about whole Cherokee communities as the relevant economic unit. In this case, the source of total income for Cherokee communities in 1963 was as follows: wages, 57 percent; welfare, 29 percent; social security and pensions, 12 percent; other, 2 percent (Wahrhaftig 1970: 45–52).

Not long ago the Cherokees were a nation of subsistence farmers, plantation owners, ranchers, and tradesmen. Today Cherokee self-sufficiency is entirely destroyed. The Cherokees are at the mercy of currents in the larger economy of the Ozarks.

The Cherokees are a social and cultural isolate within the larger society that has invaded their homeland. The most dramatic index of this estrangement is that, although in 1963 a total of 10,450 Cherokee-speakers were participating in Cherokee society — and there is every reason to believe that the population of Cherokee-speakers has grown since then — not one full-time, well trained Cherokee–English interpreter could be found anywhere, employed or unemployed. Nor is there one today. Whites maintain the fiction that Cherokees merely pretend they don't understand English whenever it serves their interests to "act dumb," and Cherokees long ago gave up any hope for recognition of the reality of a bilingual society that interpretation implies. For generations, whites have been saying that the present generation of Cherokee-speakers will be the last, for the young are speaking English. They do not realize that the Cherokee community, closed and isolated itself, is withdrawing from whites. It is not at all uncommon for Cherokees to forget much of their English, as, in middle age, they become increasingly immersed in the affairs of their own community. Hence, the bilinguality of the young is deceptive. In the four Cherokee communities sampled, I found that 14, 24, 40, and 42 percent of the heads of households were unable to speak any but the most rudimentary English (Wahrhaftig 1970: 12).

At the end of the 1880's, it became clear that the United States would not tolerate an autonomous Cherokee nation. Cherokees had educated themselves, both in the narrow sense of "schooling" and in the broader sense of mastering the English language and the mechanics of Anglo-American legal proceedings, in an effort to fend off white men and to survive as a nation. Those efforts proved fruitless. As a Cherokee elder warned an Indian ecumenical conference in Canada last year: "We had Christian preachers, and we had educated men, but that didn't do us no good when the white man come after our land." In a family of Cherokee, the older brothers — now men in their nineties — speak fluent English; their father drove them to school with a whip, they say, for he was convinced of the necessity of education. The younger brothers, born after 1890 when it was clear that Americans would dissolve the Cherokee nation no matter what Cherokees did, cannot speak English. Cherokee alienation from American institutions became complete in that decade. A tribe internationally known for its school system and the educational attainments of its citizenry was plunged into a state of unscholarliness (Thomas and Wahrhaftig 1971).

At present the Cherokees are an uneducated and an illiterate people. In 1963, Cherokees had completed a median of 5.5 years of school, one of the lowest levels of attainment in the United States. Forty percent of the population was functionally illiterate, and only 39 percent of the population had completed the eighth grade or beyond (Wahrhaftig 1970: 28–30). What must be understood is that these figures do not indicate ignorance. They are an index of the thoroughness with which Cherokees have rejected the role demanded of them in American society.

The result of sixty years of disinvolvement from American society is a crippling lack of sophistication, which renders Cherokees evermore easily victimized. That Cherokees are victimized outright is a matter for discussion later. It is worth mentioning here that the more severe cases of theft, brutality, and negligence occur in an everyday atmosphere of fear, contempt, and barely veiled discrimination. In Tahlequah, the former capital of the Cherokee nation, Indian children are bussed out to rural schools on the peripheries of the city by covert agreement, while the children of suburban white professionals are bussed in to town. When "the law" (as they call the sheriff) walks into the Tomahawk Bar in Stilwell, Indian drinkers fall silent, hunch their shoulders, stare down into their beer, and silently wait for the hand of authority to drag them away. An informant in Cherokee County said: "One time several Indians came to the construction job looking for work. The boss told them to start next morning. Next morning they drove up in time for work, but they were shy, so they stayed in their cars. After a while the boss asked me, 'What happened to those guys I told to come to work today?' I told him they were waiting around in their cars, but the boss said he didn't have time to go around to each car and get those guys. So they gave up on waiting and left."

The Cherokees are not, as much of the foregoing discussion has implied, simply a population category, a mass of individuals bearing certain characteristics. For as far back as history and archaeology can trace them, the Cherokee were a people who lived in many cohesive, small, fluidly linked settlements. This is still true today. At present, sixty-nine identifiable, named Cherokee settlements are distributed throughout six counties of northeastern Oklahoma (Map 1). The core of the Cherokee population resides permanently in these settlements. In addition, there are Cherokees who work in other locations and come home to participate in the definitive social events of Cherokee community life on weekends or during vacations. There are also individuals who were raised in these settlements, were socialized and enculturated as Cherokees, but have divorced themselves from participation in Cherokee community life. Some of these people live in northeastern Oklahoma but not among Cherokees; others have moved away. In 1963, I attempted to estimate the Cherokee population in each of these categories. The estimates were conservative; the actual population in each category was probably no lower than estimated and might well be from 10 to 20 percent higher (see Table 1).

Table 1. Residence and social participation

Population participating in Cherokee life	
Residing in Cherokee settlements	9,500
Participating in Cherokee life, regardless of place of residence	11,500
Population reared as Cherokees	
Reared in Cherokee settlements and residing in northeastern Oklahoma	10,500
Reared in Cherokee settlements but not necessarily still residing in northeastern Oklahoma	16,500

In 1902, an estimated 8,000 Cherokees lived in these Cherokee settlements. Since the destruction of the Cherokee nation — despite continuing statements that the Cherokees are "dying out" — the core Cherokee population has grown slightly, and the number of people participating in Cherokee community life has grown rapidly. In 1963, I predicted that the Cherokees were on the threshold of a population explosion, and my impression after visiting Cherokee settlements in 1972 is that this rapid population growth is now underway. Meanwhile, growth of the base Cherokee population has been so rapid (and pressures for assimilation so great and the carrying capacity of the Cherokee environment so limited) that as of 1963 a minimum of 4,500 Cherokees have "spun off" into the general society and, intentionally or not, are detached from the life of the Cherokee community. It is the presence of these individuals — living in the "white world" and therefore socially visible, while Cherokee settlements remain isolated and inconspicuous — that fuels the local establishment's certainty that the Cherokees have nearly all assimilated.

Cherokee life takes place in small, named communities of relatives. Cherokee settlements are the same old social units which were the basic units of Cherokee social structure in the "old country." When the Cherokees were forced to remove to Indian territory, entire towns resettled together under the dirction of their own officials, in environments that their own scouts selected as being similar to the places they had been forced to leave.

Some Oklahoma Cherokee settlements bear the names of noted towns in the "old country" (Echota, for example), and "old country" dialects exist unscrambled in Oklahoma today. There are areas in which Cherokee communities have been destroyed, in most cases, through the creation of artificial lakes. Balancing the destruction of old

KEY

⬤ less than 20 households

⊜ 20 to 30 households

◍ more than 30 households

1. Grove
2. Honey Creek
3. Drowning Creek
4. Jay
5. Brush Creek
6. Ribbon
7. Spavinaw
8. Eucha
9. Piney
10. Wycliffe Creek
    New Jordan
11. Kenwood
12. Bull Hollow
13. Cloud Creek
14. Salina
15. Locust Grove
16. Little Rock
    Snake Creek
17. Rose
18. Leach
19. Twin Oaks
20. Bittle Kansas
21. Ballou
22. Oaks
23. Rocky Ford
24. Chewey
25. Johnson Prairie
26. Moodys
27. Fourteen Mile
    Creek
28. Hulbert
29. Spring Creek
30. Tablequash
31. Red Oak
32. Elm Tree
33. Briggs
34. Christie
35. Old Green
36. Peavine
37. New Greenleaf
38. Park Hill
39. Welling
40. Barren
41. Wauhillau
42. Sugar Mountain
43. Echota
44. Mulberry Hollow
45. Fairfield
46. Stilwell
47. Barber
48. Lyons Switch
49. Cherry Tree
50. Honey Hill
51. Salem
52. Qualls
53. Burnt Cabin
53. Cookson
54. Bunch
55. Greasy Creek
56. Bell
57. Oak Ridge
58. South Greasy
59. Rock Fence
60. Nicut
61. Vian Creek
62. Marble City
63. Bellefont
64. Braggs
65. Sourjohn
66. Notchietown
67. Blackgum
    Mountain
68. Vian
69. Sycamore
70. McKey
71. Prices Chaple
72. Warner
73. Oak Grove
74. Muldrow

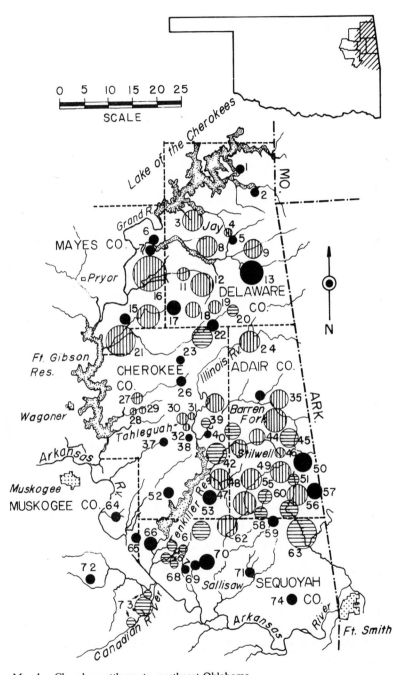

Map 1. Cherokee settlements, northeast Oklahoma

Cherokee settlements is the emergence of new, cohesive Cherokee communities, often within or on the outskirts of small towns. Of seventy-two identifiable Cherokee settlements in eastern Oklahoma, forty-eight are old and stable, fourteen are disintegrating, and ten are emerging. The basic framework of Cherokee settlement is intact and adaptive. A core of old settlements provides continuity while forced-out populations coalesce into new settlements located in more hospitable environments (Wahrhaftig 1968: 515–517). The Cherokees have maintained their population and have preserved the core of settlements from which their nation was built, although they have been reduced from an independent nation to an ethnic minority submerged within a culturally complex region.

Demographic changes within eastern Oklahoma are forcing the Cherokees into an increasingly disadvantaged position. They are concentrated in "hollows" through which flow creeks that lead to the Verdigris, Grand, and Arkansas river valleys, which do not coincide with Oklahoma township and county boundaries. Although Cherokees predominate in some geographic areas, they are a minority within existing administrative units.

From the Depression until the 1960's, poor white farmers fled eastern Oklahoma, while Cherokees left in lesser numbers. As a result, eastern Oklahoma populations dwindled, but the proportion of Cherokees relative to whites increased. From 1960 to 1970 the overall loss of population was arrested, but at the same time the numbers of Cherokees appear to have sharply increased, and the ratio of Cherokees to whites continued to increase (see Table 2) (Wahrhaftig 1968: 514–515; Jordan 1972a, 1972b).

Table 2.   Cherokee population relative to white population

County	Percentage Cherokee 1940	Percentage Cherokee 1960	Percentage Cherokee 1970
Adair	19	23	27
Cherokee	10	13	20
Delaware	10	14	20
Sequoyah	5	6	9
Mayes	—	—	11

However, numbers do not tell the whole story. Generally, as rural white subsistence farmers have departed, their small farms have been consolidated into large ranches, often owned by Texans. New lakes built as part of the Army Corps of Engineers Arkansas River Flood Control Project have attracted vacationers, retired city folk, weekenders from nearby cities — and increasing numbers of small-town businessmen to service them. Population growth in eastern Oklahoma has been in small towns and in urban areas. This means that Cherokees have been stranded. Rural whites, with whom Cherokees used to have neighborly relations, have been replaced by city folk. Cherokees now appear to have fewer personal relationships with whites than they did a generation ago, and a widening gulf in wealth and sophistication is separating them from whites.

Cherokee settlements, having survived in rocky crannies that did not tempt whites in an agrarian age, may yet be doomed to disintegration, as Oklahoman profiteers exploit their environment. Eastern Oklahomans have taken to calling this area "Green Country." This appellation — backed by the Phillips Petroleum Company, which detailed an employee to "serve virtually full time" as executive vice-president of Green Country, Incorporated—represents an adroit bit of identity managing. It evokes a new future for the region, as a paradise of woods, lakes, bass, legions of free-spending tourists and vacationers, second homes for Tulsans and Dallasites — the playground of Texas and Kansas. This image submerges the old realities: Indians, lawlessness, failed farms, poverty, cultural and economic backwash. The new image, and the national advertising that is merchandising it, has the timeless ring of God-created wilderness, revealing that Oklahomans are apparently oblivious to their impact on the environment. In less than a century it has been transformed, certainly to the disadvantage of the Cherokees and, perhaps, to that of everyone else. Cherokees say that, when they first came to the area, the Ozark forests had trees so big and so widely spaced that through them you could see a man on horseback a quarter-mile away. As whites gained control, forests were logged and bottom lands were planted to cotton. Hillsides were leased to cattlemen or in tiny tracts to thousands of tenants, to be subsistence farmed into exhaustion (McWilliams 1942: 189–190). Cherokees were enjoined from the annual burnings that had cleared underbrush from the woods. Game was hunted out of existence. And finally came the army engineers, with an orgy of dam building that has yet to reach its climax. In the 1940's, Cherokee settlements along Greenleaf and Drawning creeks were covered by Lake Greenleaf and by the Lake of the Cherokees. In the 1950's, a large Cherokee community at Yonkers was covered by the Fort Gibson Reservoir, Lake Tenkiller covered a Cherokee settlement at Linder Bend and another along the Illinois River bottom, and Lake Eucha covered a Cherokee community at Eucha. Dozens of additional lakes, which will inundate the areas most thickly populated by Cherokees, are on the Corps of Engineers drawing boards. The price the Cherokees have paid for Green Country is scrub-choked, tick-infested, second-growth forests; fishing lakes that have drowned former Indian settlements; and a displaced Cherokee population which is either on welfare or in California.

Where Cherokee settlements are intact, Cherokees survive, poor and frustrated, but not yet demoralized nor alcoholic. Unfortunately, the future survival of Cherokee settlements is not under Cherokee control.

HOW THE CHEROKEES GOT THAT WAY

To understand how the Cherokees came to be as poor as they are and, more importantly, to understand the premises guiding Cherokee conduct today, it is necessary to confront what the Cherokees regard as the blunt facts of their existence. First, they know that wealth was stolen from them. Second, they know that the most eminent institutions of Oklahoma society were the instruments of this theft: Angie Debo (1970: 277) flatly concluded that "the entire legal system of eastern Oklahoma was warped to strip [Indians] of their property." Third, they consider some of the most respected members of Oklahoma society (including many who are by genealogical and legalistic definitions "Cherokee") to be brazen criminals who gained their wealth and standing through profiteering from Cherokee affairs.

The theft of Cherokee assets reached its zenith in the twentieth century. Most of it occurred within the lifetime of the fathers of the men most influential in Cherokee settlements today. Cherokees are convinced that thievery continues, by the very processes that operated successfully in the past; therefore, they consider that lessons essential to their survival are to be found by reviewing history. Local whites try to prevent Cherokees from "dwelling on past history," for it is only by forgetting (or ignoring) the past that Oklahoma white people can justify the present. But for Cherokees to obligingly ignore their history would be suicidal.

In 1828, Cherokees who had voluntarily removed to lands in Arkansas were persuaded to vacate them in exchange for seven million acres of land in the Verdigris, Grand, and Arkansas river valleys. In 1835, Andrew Jackson forced the Cherokees still remaining in their Arkansas homeland to sign the Treaty of New Echota, which dictated their removal to lands already in possession of western Cherokees. Under terms of that same treaty, Cherokees purchased from the United States the "neutral lands," an additional 800,000 acres in Kansas, and also were assured of a "perpetual outlet west, and a free and unmolested use of all the country west of ... said seven million acres." During Jackson's administration each of the "Five Civilized Tribes" (Cherokees, Creeks, Choctaws, Chicasaws, and Seminoles) was similarly forced to abandon its homeland and relocate in Indian territory. These Indian nations owned all of what is now the state of Oklahoma except the panhandle (see Map 2). They had already lost the western

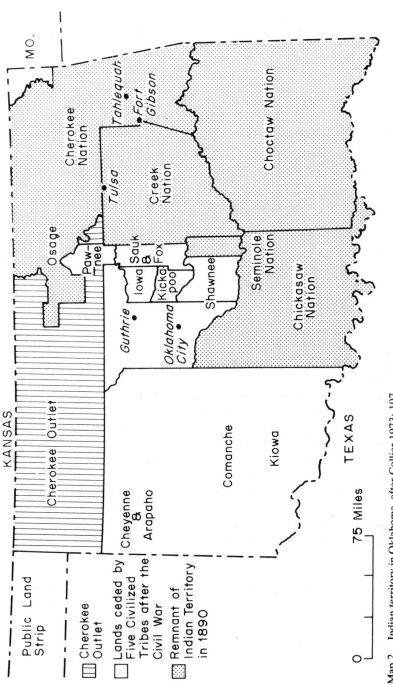

Map 2. Indian territory in Oklahoma, after Collier 1973: 107

portion by 1898, but they retained the east — 19,500,000 acres of lands rich in timber, coal, oil, minerals, and pasture. "No other exploiters of Indian property in the history of the United States had ever been offered so rich a prize" (Debo 1970: 276).

It took white men scarcely fifty years to strip the Five Civilized Tribes of their remaining resources. Of the 19,500,000 acres held in 1891, there remained in 1956 only 316,902 acres of restricted land, and this was the most barren and isolated acreage. Before 1891, the Cherokee Outlet, Cherokee Strip, and neutral lands were totally lost to the tribe. Of the seven million acres still retained by the Cherokee nation in 1891, less than 146,598 acres of restricted land remain[1] (United States Department of the Interior, 1971). The "orgy of exploitation" has been described by Angie Debo (1940) in *And still the waters run*, a comprehensively documented account of the fate of the Five Civilized Tribes between 1898 and the 1930's. Her investigation of the means by which Indian assets were stolen confirms that the contemporary Cherokees' distrust of lawyers, judges, bankers, written documents, officials of the state of Oklahoma, and the Bureau of Indian Affairs is based on solid historical precedent.

The existence of an autonomous Cherokee nation was an impediment to white speculators, for there was no private ownership of land, no possibility of acquiring land from individuals, and both law and national sentiment forbade either sales or cessions of Cherokee national lands. But whites jumped the border after the Civil War and illegally settled in such quantity that Cherokees were outnumbered in their own nation. Whites, whether poor intruding settlers or influential businessmen, favored dissolution of the Cherokee government and the creation of a new state from territories held by the Indian nations.

Around 1880, the highest offices in the Cherokee nation were taken over by the least traditional of Cherokees. These men resisted incorporation of the Indian nations into a new American state, but when it became apparent that statehood was inevitable, they seized the opportunity to cut themselves slices of the pie. At that point, the interests of prominent Cherokee politicians were merged with the interests of others who scrambled for wealth.

In this period dealers in Indian land were called, and called themselves, "grafters." The term implied no dishonor, for they viewed themselves as bringing progress, which all races would ultimately share, to an area that Indians had failed to develop. Grafters bankrol-

---

[1]   This figure combines acreage under jurisdiction of the Tahlequah Agency of the BIA, which serves only Cherokees, and the Miami Agency, which serves Cherokees, eastern Shawnee, Senaca-Cayuga, and Quapaws. These two agencies also administer 21,987 acres of tribal land and 19,808 acres of government land, utilized primarily by Cherokees.

led newspapers all over the Indian territory as well as on the borders of Kansas, Missouri, Arkansas, and Texas, to present the view that Indians were victims of their own dishonest and inefficient governments, that only by emancipating them from tribal despots could these victimized populations progress, and that each Indian would personally benefit from equality of individual opportunity in the society of a new state. Congressmen also propagandized this vision of reality and blasted all who cast doubt upon it. In the new state of Oklahoma, grafters became the backbone of the establishment.

In the 1880's, and 1890's, eastern Oklahoma commerce was built on speculation in Indian land, timber, coal, and railroad rights of way. (A decade later, oil boomed to the top of the list.) The Cherokee nation, dissolved when Oklahoma became a state, no longer controlled these resources; they remained in possession of the individuals among whom tribal lands had been allotted. Because many of these Cherokees did not speak English and were innocent of business procedure, they were restricted from selling their allotments. Title to their land was held in trust by the United States government, and the Bureau of Indian Affairs supervised their interests.

The grafters were consistently able to arrange for the appointment of cohorts to key BIA positions, and they had little trouble in disposing of the few Indian agents who attempted to make decisions contrary to the grafters' interests. Grafters were among Oklahoma's first congressmen and they could also count on cooperation from judges in Oklahoma courts, many of whom they had put into office. Some judges built their own political machines, by handing out guardianships over minor and "incompetent" Indians and by approving lavish attorney's fees for even the most straightforward cases; others were perhaps honest, but they shared the grafters' exploitative view of land, money, Indians, and progress.

When reformers attempted to direct attention to the swindles being perpetrated through the BIA and the courts, their allegations were refuted by a torrent of editorials and congressional oratory. To Cherokees, all lawyers, courts, politicians, Indian agents, the press, and even powerful individuals of Cherokee origin seemed to be solidly interlinked against them. An older Cherokee summed it all up with chilling understatement: "[The lawyers and the descendants of those opportunistic Cherokee politicians], they'll be joined with the rich people. When they do that, it be pretty hard to get along with."

For seventy years or more, Cherokee have lived amid ingeniously contrived schemes for divesting them of their property. Their survival as a people demands that somehow they both eat and hang on to their remaining possessions. The acreage that Cherokees have already lost represented land, timber, and oil that might have provided them with a living — and a handsome one. That loss can be endured and even interpreted by Cherokees as a punishment from which they will one day emerge, chastened but pure and strong of will.

Present and future land losses are of a different order. The lands that are left are the sites of Cherokee homes and settlements, the pared-down territory to which the social fabric of Cherokee community is fastened. Cherokee survival skills, based on the support of an intact settlement, are of little use to the isolated individual. When Cherokees lose these lands, they are losing their physical place in the social order of the settlement into which they were born. These settlements are efficient social units, welded by time and geared to an effective sharing of resources and income that levels out the risks of survival, even on reduced and uncertain resources. However, Cherokee settlements are knit by continual person-to-person interaction, which is disrupted by the intrusion of whites or other strangers. In order to keep their settlements together under present conditions, and their person-to-person system of interaction closed, Cherokees must own the land to which their settlement is attached (Wahrhaftig 1966; 1970: 52–58).

Given this context, what adaptive survival techniques can a people develop in an environment of smiling swindlers? Cherokees have schooled themselves to sign nothing, to expect the worst from even the most seemingly friendly and innocent dealings with whites, and to anticipate that any promise of a project that will lead to future economic reward is the prelude to fraud.

In the contemporary Cherokee parable of "The pretty colored snake," a hunter returning home encountered a little snake. "It was a beautifully colored snake with all pretty colors all over it, and it looked friendly, too" (Spade and Walker 1966: 788–789). He fed it, and so did others as time went on. The snake grew bigger and hungrier until it was consuming a whole deer for a meal. One night the Cherokees were dancing around the fire,

...when the snake came and started going around too ... That snake was so big and long that he stretched all around the people and the people were penned up. The snake was covered all over with all pretty colors and he seemed friendly; but he looked hungry too, and the people began to be afraid. They told some boys to get their bows. They all shot together and they hit the snake all right. That snake was hurt. He thrashed his tail all around and killed a lot of the people. They say that snake was just like the white man (Spade and Walker 1966).

It cannot be too strongly emphasized that the Cherokee experience teaches them that courts, the law, and the legally established authority are still the primary instruments of their distress. In 1956 and 1966, I was the English-language secretary for the Five County Northeast

Oklahoma Cherokees (later called the Original Cherokee Community Organization). Devoted originally to establishing the Cherokees' right under treaty to hunt and fish without restriction, the organization became a forum at which the Cherokee-speaking population met to define their current problems. At meeting after meeting in Cherokee communities people told what was happening to them, in an effort to define the pattern of their exploitation (Buchanan 1972; Wahrhaftig i.p.). By their own accounts, Cherokees are presently losing land and other assets through illegal removal of restrictions and consequent sale, through the machinations of court-appointed guardians, through disadvantageous leases, through illegal sale forced by welfare agencies, and through partition and adverse possession. Land losses are presently estimated to be 5,000 acres per year (Collier 1970).

At each meeting, there were families seeking to regain land recently lost through the fraudulent removal of tax exemption. In 1898, in preparation for statehood, the United States government began to survey Cherokee lands, which the tribe had owned communally, and to make allotments to Cherokee citizens. Those of one-half or more Cherokee blood were protected from grafters by restrictions on the sale of their allotments.[2] The Bureau of Indian Affairs now supervises the administration of these restrictions. Because alloted lands are held in trust by the United States government, they are tax exempt.

Cherokees insist that when modern grafters desire a tract of alloted land, they conspire with the county assessor's staff to place the tract on the county tax rolls. The Cherokee allottee is almost certain to remain ignorant of this "mistake"; consequently, he neither pays tax nor is he informed of the need to set matters straight. When taxes have gone unpaid for three years, the county auctions the land to recover unpaid taxes and the grafter buys it.

An exceptionally short statute of limitations — five years — applies to this category of transaction in Oklahoma. Eight years after the grafter has set his plan into motion, the land is irredeemably his. Characteristically, Cherokee allottees remain unaware of the transaction until the new owners arrive, backed by the sheriff, to dispossess them. This may not happen until after the statute of limitations has run out. The success of this basic scheme and its many variants depends on the interaction of five factors, in addition to the presence of greedy and unscrupulous land speculators. There must be county employees who are willing to illegally transfer land to county tax rolls; BIA officials

---

[2] The first United States census of the Indian territory, made in 1890, classed inhabitants according to physical appearance without regard to citizenship. The census categories do not correspond exactly to cultural categories of Indian and white, but they are a useful approximation. In 1890, the population of the Cherokee nation was 56,035 persons of whom 29,166 were white, 5,127 were Negro, and 22,015 were Indian. Indians were 39 percent of the population (Debo 1940: 13),

who consistently lack vigilance; a gap in language, culture, communications, and sophistication that prevents Cherokees from grappling with the complexities of the white man's ideas about land tenure; state laws such as the short statute of limitations, which promote fraud; and finally, a general suppression and intimidation of Cherokees, which fosters their conviction that resistance to even patently illegal transactions is sure to prove futile.

Historically, the removal of restrictions on the sale of Cherokee lands (on categories of land or on individual holdings, by act of Congress or by neighborhood bribery) has provided the grafter's greatest windfalls.[3] To date no adequate defense has been developed. But then, no one has tried very hard. Neither the present Cherokee government, nor the Bureau of Indian Affairs, nor the Cherokees themselves have devised some simple system for monitoring county tax rolls and sending "land loss alerts" to threatened allottees. The newspaper printed by the tribal government faithfully lists the names of Indians admitted to local hospitals, but never the names of Indians whose homes are in jeopardy!

Cherokees also bitterly insist that property rightfully theirs is administered for the benefit of white men, through leases which operate to the disadvantage of existing Cherokee settlements. Populous settlements at Kenwood and Bull Hollow, for instance, are in the middle of a large area known as the Kenwood Indian reserve. Inside the Kenwood reserve there are Cherokee allotments, lands owned in fee simple by whites, and an extensive area — most of it in 40- and 80-acre tracts — that is locally called "Indian land" or "government land." Most of the acreage in this last category is submarginal agricultural land, which the United States government bought up during the Depression in order to take it off the market. Although the question of title is confused, in recent years these lands have been administered by the Cherokee government with consent of the BIA, following established bureau precedents. They are leased, sometimes complete with a "government house" and a well, to cattle raisers — many of whom are technically Cherokees, although they are culturally and socially white and live apart from local Indian settlements.

Cherokees in Kenwood and Bull Hollow are firm in their conviction

---

[3]   The grafters ... found ways of having restrictions removed from land they controlled. An allottee could apply to the agency and establish his competence to manage his land, but many applications were made without the knowledge of the Indian by dealers who held sales contracts or merchants who had extended extravagant credit. Another method was to have the restrictions removed by special acts of Congress by slipping the Indians' names into the Indian Appropriation Bill. A study of the individual victims named in this act in 1906 shows shocking spoliation in every instance. Some of them had given powers of attorney to a merchant to whom they owed money; then as soon as the bill was enacted, he gave deeds to a fellow conspirator. In another case a guardian sold his ward's valuable oil land without the knowledge of the child's father.

that any poor and homeless Cherokees ought to be permitted to settle freely on these "Indian lands." In allocating land, the first priority they recognize is that every Cherokee has a right to a home. Instead, they see it leased to people whom they regard as white men, who don't really need it, anyway. Indignation over the administration of these lands is ceaseless. Discussion of the subject sometimes ends with halfhearted inflammatory muttering about "getting together and cutting the throats of all them cattles." Fires do seem frequent in the area, and it is indicative of Cherokee sentiment that such fires are not attributed to accident. When the "government house" of a Cherokee family that was under threat of eviction burned, Cherokee opinion had it that "that's one house they won't put white people in, to let their cows wander around on the roads at night. If Cherokees can't have it, nobody's going to get it."

Historically, enforcement of unconscionable leases has been a long-standing practice. It is an old swindle, an example of which was provided by Robert L. Owen, an opportunistic Cherokee politician who entered the United States Senate at statehood. "An extensive dealer in the rich valley land of Cherokee and Creek allottees . . . [one] of his leases dated December 18, 1901, would run for ninety-nine years and the entire rental was discounted as follows: $10 had been paid November 29, $30 was paid when the lease was made, and $320 would be paid upon execution of a deed" (Debo 1970: 277–78).

Another means of grabbing Indian assets has been to secure a court appointment as legal guardian of an Indian who has been adjudged incompetent. In a recent instance widely discussed among Cherokees, a county judge was said to have appointed his own secretary as guardian of a Cherokee man who, although elderly, was spry and sound of mind. Hearing of this, the Cherokee's brother and sister petitioned the court to appoint them as guardians of their own brother. The petition was denied, but, even before that, the court-appointed guardian had sold the Cherokee's land in order to pay for his burial expenses — although he was alive and in sound health.

Angie Debo writes that,

> . . . a neglected field of exploitation was opened up by the discovery that Indian adults also needed guardians. It had always been recognized that mentally defective Indians like other defective adults could be placed under guardianship, but it was not until about 1913 that it began to be apparent that all Indians and freedmen who owned oil property were mentally defective . . . . Even those Indians whose wealth came from restricted allotments and who were therefore adequately protected by the Government were declared incompetent, and a horde of guardians and attorneys were richly compensated for services consisting mainly of cashing royalty checks from the Agency. Young allottees approaching their majority began to hide or to seek refuge in distant states to avoid being brought into court and declared incompetent (Debo 1940: 305–306).

Cherokee dependence on welfare, inevitable in the poor and jobless region they inhabit, leaves them vulnerable to still further losses. Oklahoma welfare regulations contain exemptions relating to allotted land. Among other rights, a Cherokee may retain his last forty acres of allotted land and still receive Old Age Assistance. According to Cherokees, it is a common practice for welfare officials to deny knowledge of these exemptions and to force elderly Cherokees to sell their allotments. Following such a sale, they can insist that the Cherokees exhaust the proceeds on their own subsistence before they are considered eligible for further assistance.

Ever since "the state come in" (as they put it), Cherokees have lived fearfully and in expectation of being plundered. Their adaptation to being preyed upon can be witnessed in the layout of their homesites and in the etiquette for approaching them. From inside a house in any Cherokee settlement, the main road may clearly be seen; when strangers approach, those within the house become wary and silent. Women move into the rear rooms or peep nervously through the curtains. There is always one person who is depended upon to handle newcomers. The one who approaches is expected to get out of his car to unfasten a gate at the roadside, to proceed up the drive, but to stop short of the house and wait inside his car — honking the horn impatiently if necessary — until a member of the household emerges to invite him to "step down." The entire visit may be transacted with the visitor remaining in his car while his "host" leans against the car door. To walk up and knock on the door is an unacceptable intrusion. This etiquette creates a no-man's-land in which the household's specialist in English-speaking and "foreign relations" can negotiate, while less sophisticated members are sheltered. To be invited into the house is a gesture of considerable trust and acceptance; thereafter, the visitor may feel free to enter the house as though it were his own, without knocking. The Cherokee cannot afford to trust just anyone.

Cherokee material resources — the bottom lands, the minerals, the timber — have almost entirely passed into the hands of whites. Cherokee monetary resources — even their award from the Indian Claims Court, which was distributed early in the 1960's — have also circulated into the hands of white shopkeepers. The Cherokees are, as they put it, "pretty far down." Still, economic growth in eastern Oklahoma is based on exploitation of a final Cherokee resource — the Cherokee themselves. The establishment has only begun to exploit Cherokee labor, and it has barely commenced to grasp the possibility for capitalizing on the Cherokee as a presence.

As for the exploitation of Cherokee labor, overall economic development programs and economic base reports for eastern Oklahoma have in recent years been uniformly pessimistic about prospects for future agricultural and industrial development in the counties that were formerly part of the Cherokee nation. Studies cite high transportation costs, distant markets, unsophisticated local government, and insufficient development of the social, cultural, and educational facilities that are necessary to attract and satisfy corporate executives and their families. Studies also emphasize the presence of cheap labor — primarily Indian — in an area with low prevailing wages, no state minimum wage laws, no right-to-work law, and few unions. Cherokee County, for example, pointedly noted that "many of these Indians subsist on minimum standards of living" (Oklahoma State Employment Service Research and Planning Division 1962: 31.) Although ethnic groups are becoming increasingly sensitive to patronizing and cant, W. W. Keeler, principal chief of the Cherokees, still advertises that patience and manual dexterity make his people suitable for employment in monotonous manual tasks.

A more recent trend has been to bank on the presence of Cherokees to draw tourists into the Ozark Hills. Adair County claims that "the cultural activities of the Cherokees and their assimilation in the population of Adair County [sic] offer some excellent opportunities to create new attractions within the County that can enhance its economic development" (Adair County Development Committee 1962: ii).

Essentially, such plans involve hiring Cherokees to "play Indian" in enterprises developed by local entrepreneurs (with as much state and federal investment as they can promote), for the benefit of the business community. The most ambitious of these schemes is a complex consisting of a reconstructed ancient Cherokee village, an amphitheater in which to present a pageant based on Cherokee history, a Cherokee museum, and a Cherokee archive, all to be located outside Tahlequah (the former Cherokee capital) in a neighborhood where high officials of the Cherokee nation once lived. It is always claimed on behalf of these projects that both their construction and their operation would create jobs for Indians who would otherwise be on welfare. "In addition to kindling pride in heritage [which the local establishment gratuitously assumes is lacking in Cherokees] the project is planned to be of substantial economic benefit through employment, both direct and indirect" (Cherokee National Historical Society n.d.). Initial estimates for the costs of the construction of the Indian village were $150,000 and for the amphitheater $300,000, in funds largely solicited from the EDA and other federal agencies. These projects gall Cherokees. Cherokees have contested the authenticity of the Indian village and protested the commercialization of their sacred dances within it. Employment return has been small: 50 to 75 jobs during the six months of the year when employment is least hard to find. Most of the jobs are for "villagers" who must wear wigs and imitation buckskins, and speak

Cherokee at all times on the job, while whooping, weaving baskets, and dancing. In the first (and only) such demonstration in Cherokee history, Cherokees picketed the inauguration of the village. Many of them refer to it as "the monkey house."

Of the pageant presenting Cherokee history after the Trail of Tears, an emeritus professor of Cherokee history wrote: "A stranger would never suspect it was a Cherokee performance, were it not for the fact that one or another of the actors yell out from time to time that 'the Cherokees are the greatest people on earth'" (Ballenger n.d.) A Cherokee reviewer said, "The drama concentrates mainly on the split within the Cherokee Nation and what a grand and glorious thing it was for the Cherokee when the Indian Territory became the state of Oklahoma .... The only point the drama makes is that tidy white minds with their neatly arranged myths about the Cherokees should not be disturbed" (Racoon [1969: 11] quoted in Fites n.d.)

Benefits to the Cherokees consisted of employment as construction laborers and in the nonspeaking, nondancing, walk-on parts of the performance. Of 85 persons that the drama employed during the summer months of 1971, only 47 were of Cherokee descent. Very few of these were culturally Indian. Compared to this small return to Cherokees in employment generated by investment of their own funds, the president of the Tahlequah Chamber of Commerce calculated that in 1971 the total impact of Tsa La Gi (as the village is called) on the Tahlequah area amounted to $10,660,420.47. The force that provided increased annual revenues of nearly $11 million to Oklahoma businessmen by ostensibly providing summer jobs for indigent Cherokees was the Cherokee National Historical Society, an organization composed of members of the chamber of commerce, bankers, realtors, and Cherokee politicians. In this combination, an observer with a sense of the continuity of complex social systems might see the grafters of old times in modern dress. The Cherokees do.

HOW CHEROKEE SETTLEMENTS SURVIVE

The Cherokee way of life is to live in a small, autonomous settlement. As far back into the past as Cherokees can be traced, this has been the case, and it is true today. The number, size, and total population of Cherokee settlements in Oklahoma now correspond closely to the number, size, and population of Cherokee settlements observed during the 1700's in the Cherokees' native environment, the mountains of the southeastern United States (Wahrhaftig 1968). Each Cherokee settlement is a social unit, knit by kinship and small enough for face-to-face interaction. Through a classificatory system of defining relatedness (in which the matrilineal clan was once important), large numbers of Cherokees interact with one another as close relatives (Gearing 1961; Gilbert 1934). Each Cherokee settlement is also a ceremonial unit, with its own central meeting place for ritual and its own curers, preachers, and holy men. Until the 1930's, each Cherokee settlement was a subsistence unit, producing and consuming what it needed from lands available to all Cherokees.

The Cherokees who live in these settlements are one single, unique people. Their name for themselves may be translated as "the principal people." They conceive of themselves as a "nationality" (an English word they often use) bound by shared tradition and shared concern for one another, and not as a people legislated by citizenship of geopolitical boundaries. They conceive of the world as a system of many interdependent populations, each of which must live in a proper way in order that all may survive — and all of them, including the Cherokees, must survive in order for the world to stay together. Modern traditional Cherokee teachings say:

For God said, if the Cherokees be destroyed and become extinct,
Then that will be the destruction of the whole world.
This is the word of the forefathers of our own land (Keetoowah Society 1972).

Cherokee settlements are related through ties of kinship, intermarriage, and participation in a common ceremonial cycle. These ties are the pathways for interaction through which Cherokees residing in different settlements share their experiences, make up their differences, and synthesize new interpretations of their culture. This last task is the special function of old men, the opinion definers in individual settlements, who continually travel to consult with one another. So, while each Cherokee settlement is an autonomous social unit, all the Cherokees residing in each of the settlements participate in a shared culture and a shared definition of themselves as one people.

Perhaps every anthropologist has had, at some point in his studies, an insight that brings into focus what he has learned of the people he is observing. Mine came on the eve of the trial of a Cherokee named John Chewie before a tribunal of federal judges in Tulsa, Oklahoma, on charges of hunting deer out of season and without a license. Having just completed a socioeconomic study of households in four Cherokee settlements, I had been asked to testify as an expert witness to the poverty of Cherokees and to the importance of fish and game in their diet. At that time, I pictured Cherokees as subsistence farmers with a strong sense of solidarity who had become imprisoned as wage earners in the rural backwash of the society we had imposed on them.

John Chewie and I sat on a bluff over the Illinois River through a moonlit night and reviewed his life as a hunter. He was then in his early thirties, an ex-marine with enough training to hold industrial jobs in Tulsa, when he was in the mood for city living. Usually, he preferred to stay with his elderly father in the Cherokee settlement at Bull Hollow. We counted the number of deer John had killed during the last full season, guessed their dressed weight, multiplied, and came up with a rough estimate of the quantity of meat he had provided "for the pot." The amount was one ton! I was astounded, and I think John was too, for he was used to thinking of his deer kill by kill, and I to thinking of mine by the meal.

Not realizing the quantities involved, I had never before thought to ask about how the kill was distributed. John told me which cuts he brought to his father (who took pieces to his friends when he wasn't feeling too lame) and which went to his brothers and his sister (each of whom received joints large enough to share with their neighbors, for John's siblings have not managed to live next to each other). And the meat that was left? By this time most everybody knew a kill had been made. John habitually deposited the rest of the carcass at a cross-roads store. Anybody who needed meat knew it would be there and could feel free to come and get what he could use. The deer was totally consumed as fresh meat.

I knew well enough that the Cherokee diet is a bland monotony of beans, potato, biscuit, salt pork, and pan gravy if it is not supplemented with game, fish, nuts, and wild greens — but I had never before realized the larger picture. Taken in context, John Chewie could be understood as a specialist, a hunter who with one or two fellows kept an entire settlement supplied with fresh meat — while, meantime, other members of the settlement followed other economic pursuits. Here is a pattern of hunting and distribution of game that could have been found in any of the "classic" hunting-gathering societies that abound in anthropological literature.

This revelation, coming after two years of fieldwork, brought many previous observation into focus. I recalled the group of men and boys who went rabbit hunting together in the snow around the settlement at Cherry Tree, and I remembered the pride of a Cherokee father telling me how much his sons fished and how none of them could be intimidated into buying fishing licenses. ("We're Cherokees, ain't it?" they told him.) And a Cherokee doctor and his apprentice who often sat silently together for hours, not lost in thought but turned outward, joined in the observation of the hills and trees and sky. I realized that it was almost entirely within the context of the hunt, and the stockpiling of knowledge of nature that goes into hunting, that young Cherokee men model after their elders, learn from them who they together are, and develop their strongest affective bonds. I began to think that the relations of hunter-to-hunter and of hunters-to-environment were the models on which the structure of modern Cherokee settlements is based. And it occurred to me that a society that retains within its present subsistence adaptations the possibility of falling back on previous adaptation has developed a sort of "fail-safe" mechanism.

The presence of John as a hunter for his settlement of wage laborers involved more than just the retention of the social relations (especially the distribution of meat through a network of kinspeople) characteristic of hunting societies. John has a hunter's culturally derived mentality. When we were talking about what he did with the meat, John told me:

I just hunt to feed people now. I learned better. It didn't used to be that way, though. I used to hunt deer for money. I was a good shot, shit, couldn't miss! I could get a deer anytime, me and my buddies, and sell it to a white man for 15 maybe 20 dollars. And get drunk, whoowie!

Dad kept telling me it wouldn't do. He said God put those deer here to feed the Cherokees. He didn't put them here to sell to no white men for drinking money. I didn't pay him no mind.

We were hunting one morning and a buck rose up no farther than from here to there and stood dead still. There wasn't no way to miss. I shot, and then again and again. Couldn't hit him. Same thing another time. That deer was close enough to throw a rock at. I fired and couldn't hit him no way.

I told Dad, and he said I might as well put my gun up, cause I done lost my power. That come of killing deer to sell to white men. I knew it wasn't no use to hunt. I laid off it for years.

A time come when Dad said he thought I might be straightened out. He said he could try and purify me. After that, I took my gun down again and went hunting. Got a deer that day, sure enough. I'm a sure shot right now, but I only kill what people need to eat....

I used to see a little white deer sometimes when I was hunting. It wasn't a fawn. It was full-grown, but very small and perfectly white. I used to try to kill it, but I never could.

I told Dad. He said that deer was part of the Little People's herd. He said it wasn't no use for me to shoot at it. That wasn't a deer meant for people. It was the Little People's food, and they wouldn't let anybody kill it. I sure couldn't (personal communication).

The Cherokees are not a hunting-gathering band. John is a modern Cherokee, a Marine veteran, a beer drinker, a resident in a sedentary settlement, whose brothers commute to work at a steel plant in Tulsa. He is a skeptic who sometimes doesn't pay much attention to what the old people try to tell him. Still, it is in the context of his experience as a hunter that his self-esteem is tested, his understanding of the inner working of the world is derived, and his relationship to his father, brothers, sisters, and other kin is stabilized.

Cherokees perhaps no longer make their living from the surrounding natural environment, but they depend on it to define their life and power. They would not know what to do if they could not cue to it. Cherokee doctors say that when you are sick, if you have faith, you have but to walk in the woods watching closely, and the plant that will cure you will make itself known. Unlike whites, Cherokees rarely build storm cellars, for if you live right, storms will spare you. They feel confident when they see eagles flying in a propitious direction and apprehensive when they hear owls nearby at night. Psychologically, at least, their adaptation involves paying attention to their environment in order to better live in it, rather than try to control and manipulate it.

For the sake of argument, we might accept the proposition that there are two general paths that human societies have followed in their efforts to survive on earth. I do not want to caricature the path of white Americans. Suffice it to say that it involves a willingness to transform our life to conform to our latest adaptation, and to expect that the consequences of this will inevitably reshape the totality of our society. Phrases like "the machine age" and the "automated society" are comfortable, in our syntax. We tend to identify the adaptation as a whole by its characteristic means of production, too. This makes it difficult for us to imagine societies that survive, without stagnation, by continual accretion to, and refinement of, their *earliest* adaptation. It is also difficult for us to find a vocabulary for adaptations in which means of subsistence are incidental to a customary and desired quality of relationships among people and other members of the environment. Yet this is exactly the adaptation that Cherokees appear to have made. There is a sufficiently large, yet satisfyingly intimate size of community, coordinated by flexible relationships among people that occurs in modern societies of hunter-gatherers with "magical" frequency (Lee and DeVore 1968: 245–248; Sahlins 1972). Cherokees seem to have retained that small social system and the complex of ideas that symbolize its ideal relation to its environment as the basis of their continued social and cultural development.

The blueprint for Cherokee settlements developed over an enormous length of time in the forests of the eastern United States. In a synthesis of the archaeology of that area, Joseph Caldwell concludes that hunting bands, entering the forests around 8000 B.C., spent 6,500 years working out techniques for living efficiently in the forest environment. The next 3,000 years saw men elaborating and refining their primary adaption into the forest. During the final few centuries before Europeans came, new ideas and activities from the native civilization of Mesoamerica were received, reinterpreted, and incorporated within the forest-based way of life (Caldwell 1958: 1962 [1971]).

Studies of modern hunting-gathering peoples suggest that the hunters who entered the eastern forests 10,000 years ago already had a life based on cooperation and sharing within loosely structured bands of kinsmen (Lee and DeVore 1968). From birth, modern hunting peoples must be programmed to ceaselessly scan their surroundings, noting them in minute detail, storing away information, and learning to relate their observations to the ongoing task of feeding and ensuring the safety of their relatives (Laughlin 1968). Given time, the members of a hunting band can know an extensive environment in intimate detail. Through such experience, hunters in the eastern United States broadened their utilization of the forest. They learned the habits and habitats of more varieties of game and devised new methods of hunting — a "forest hunting pattern" evidenced by the appearance of new forms of projectile points in environments where they were not previously found. They accumulated an encyclopedic knowledge of plants and increased the number of those they knew how to prepare for eating. They noted the places and seasons in which many plant and game species increased and were available, so that they could substitute for random wandering a regular cycle of moving seasonally from one abundant foodstuff to the next. Caldwell (1962 [1971]: 362) calls this adaptive trend, "represented by changes in hunting methods, emergence of economic cycles and food specializations, and achieving a kind of balanced reliance on almost all sources of natural foods" the establishment of "primary forest efficiency." He believes that "the establishment of forest efficiency in eastern North America was primary in the sense of providing an economic foundation, a sine qua non for later developments. It was also primary in representing an economic system from which later peoples never really departed" (Caldwell 1958: vii.).

The forest adaptation that had developed by 2000 B.C. was sufficient to support sedentary communities. For the next 3,000 years, men continued to live in small settlements widely distributed in the forest, a pattern of settlement appropriate to an economy based heavily on hunting and gathering. "The hunting-gathering pattern was developed to a peak of efficiency and jelled, so to speak, in the very heart of eastern cultures" (Caldwell 1958: 72). People in these small settlements learned how to cultivate food plants, including maize, but gardening was of only incidental importance. There was no "agricultural revolution"; rather, gardening as another use of the woods' fertility was fitted in among earlier techniques.

Perhaps, Caldwell suggests, diversified hunting and gathering was more efficient. Modern studies of hunter-gatherers who understand and yet eschew agriculture indicate that they consider it an unnecessarily risky way of life. On the base of small forest-adapted settlements, the development of other aspects of life was impressive. Men devoted their energies, it seems, to expanding, ritualizing, and commemorating their relations to one another and to the supernatural. They became "mound builders" and constructed enormous ceremonial centers. The mounds and tombs and burials in these were furnished with beautiful objects worked from materials traded in from all over the East. People in settlements distributed over large regions seem to have related to one another through trade in ritual objects and the sharing of sacred concepts. The ceremonial centers are the works of "advanced cultures" with priesthoods, the capacity to amass labor, engineering competence, material riches, widespread trade, and aesthetic sensibility — so much so, that for generations Americans could not be convinced that Indians had been the "mound builders" — yet it was accompanied by no major transformation of settlement or subsistence. The East was "economically on a plateau, continuing and developing an exploitative pattern which had been formulated during Archaic times" (Caldwell 1958: ix).

In a final development trend, which lasted from about A.D. 1000 until the arrival of Europeans, ideas and activities from the farming civilizations of Mesoamerica were brought to the eastern United States. The people in the eastern United States did not become Mesoamerican farmers: they simply added new technical and spiritual facets to a way of life that was stable in its basic orientation. They began to garden, especially maize, more intensively — although Europeans saw whole "towns" with cultivated fields in the Southeast empty when the hunt was on. They organized in relatively more compact "towns" that incorporated their own central ceremonial plazas. In association with these appeared "cults," as evidenced by a succession of distinctive ceremonial structures and similarly decorated ritual objects. All of these factors were incorporated into the life of kinsmen who lived by a diversified exploitation of the forest. "Thus, the Mesoamerican features of the Gulf Tradition, the Mississippian radiation, and the Southern Cult all appear in what are essentially indigenous formations and so thoroughly re-interpreted that archeologists have sometimes been unwilling to consider them Mesoamerican at all" (Caldwell 1958: xi).

Cherokee ceremonial institutions reveal a great deal about the manner in which Cherokees have integrated new experience. Before the Removal, the high point in the Cherokee ceremonial cycle was a series of agricultural ceremonies celebrating the planting and harvest times, which climaxed with the Green Corn Ceremony. Yet, when examined, these ceremonies did not have much to do with crops and harvests. Fire, tobacco, the tongues and hide of white deer, and the boughs and barks of several trees — all products of the woods — are the most important offerings made in them, and the ceremonies principally had to do with reconciling people to one another while strengthening their health and fertility. The dances performed at a nominally agricultural Green Corn Ceremony were animal dances.

When James Howard (1968: 14) recently showed Cherokee ritual specialists decorated objects excavated from Mississippian, and even Adena and Hopewell, sites, they unhesitatingly gave consistent interpretations of the motifs. He concluded that, while other tribes originally from the Southeast may have preserved more of the outward form of ancient Southeastern ceremonialism, the Cherokees have preserved more of the underlying symbolism. And now, in Oklahoma, a system in which forty-two Cherokee Indian Baptist churches of individual Cherokee settlements convene annually on their own central campground, at roughly the time of year when the Green Corn ceremony was held, preserves old meaning in a new form. The Baptist faith, as practiced by Cherokees, does not emphasize individual salvation and redemption nearly so much as it does prayerful healing and "love" — caring for one another within the church-settlement-community. The ideas that express and stabilize people's relationships in Cherokee settlements belong to one of the oldest unbroken ceremonial traditions in the New World (Howard 1968: 88).

There is a powerful ritual metaphor that still defines their adaptation and allows Cherokees to consider its meaning in a sacred-intellectual context. This is the White Path (a motif that Cherokees share with other Iroquoian peoples). The teachings of the Keetoowah Society, one of the principal congregations of non-Christian Cherokees, are codified in the form of seven beaded belts of wampum. When these are interpreted, the theme of traveling the White Path is central in the explanation, and three of the seven belts specifically symbolize this concept (Thomas 1953: 121–124). The White Path reminds Cherokees that a way of life has been set out for them. A way of life that is specifically theirs exists. The White Path defines that which is important about that way of life — not specific customs or ways of doing things, but a condition of human relationships. This is what Christian Cherokees mean when they say "love" and what Keetoowah people mean when they say "peace":

This is more of what Keetoowah is teaching:
The way of peace (Keetoowah Society 1972).

Europeans and white Americans called the Cherokees "civilized" because of their tangible accomplishments. They developed literacy, a constitutional government, formal education, and so forth. Cherokees see themselves as being civilized *before* these developments took place. Their concept of "civilized" is the antithesis of "wild." It is an idea related to "tame" or "domesticated," in that it is a condition of life that involves two requisites: *sedentariness*, or being permanently located in a home environment, and *responsiveness*, or the capacity to enter into relationships based on reciprocity (such as the relationship between kinsmen, or the relationship between men who sacredly strengthen all life in the universe, and the plant and animal populations that support them). The civilized life is harmonious and ordered. The White Path is a way of peace. It is living that keeps to autonomy, tranquility, consensus, and avoidance of crowding others. The White Path involves the continuity of a certain emotively felt quality of life.

Also in this metaphor there is the implication that it is possible to not follow the White Path, perhaps even without knowing it. As in the case of John Chewie, who discovered that he could no longer kill deer, this alerts Cherokees to always watch for signs that they are straying and to take corrective action. This disposition to observation and action enables Cherokees to regulate their lives.

We *plan* a way of life. Cherokees do not; they *regulate* theirs. Always, there is the implication that the way of life for them exists, though they may stray from it and be forced to rediscover it over and over again. This is what the Cherokees' history of the Cherokees is made of. As the Keetoowahs speak of their origins:

When we lived by the waters of the ocean in the east,
We had our first laws to live by,
The Four Mothers,
Laws that protected us.
So long as we kept together and honored them,
Then the Lord kept all evil from us.

Right in that place,
Our own people fought among themselves.
That fighting left them open to worse things.
The Laws of the Four Mothers were broken up.
So their killings grew into a way so awful that
The trails ran with blood.
They brought this on themselves.

The older people gathered to think,
Knowing this could not go on,
That they had to find their way back to peacefulness ... (Keetoowah Society 1972).

So the Cherokees monitor their own way of life, and, when they sense that things have gone wrong, their response is to rely on knowledge — to gather new information and learn from it how things must be set straight.

When white men took over the Cherokee nation, and their surveyors began measuring the land while registration parties forcibly enrolled Cherokees in preparation for Oklahoma statehood, Cherokees knew they had strayed from the path. They "took a wrong turn and now we find ourselves in a deep, dark hollow" (Thomas 1953). Their reaction was to "gain knowledge (Thomas 1961). They retrieved their old wampum belts that were being kept as heirlooms, their interpretation forgotten, and sent them with an emissary to their fellow tribes, asking elders there to speak their meaning. From this effort to "get back what they had lost" came the modern Keetoowah Society and its offshoots, organizations that boosted Cherokee morale and furnished the base for experiments in communal economic innovation from 1898 until the 1930's (Littlefield 1971). The wampum are all the more precious for embodying this gained knowledge.

Their sense of being one people with an ordained share of the world's riches has enabled Cherokees to create complex superstructures in order to coordinate actions in their settlements. This happens especially when Cherokees conclude that their existence as a people is threatened, and with men learned in sacred knowledge as spokesmen. Fred Gearing (1962) coined an appropriate term when, in *Priests and warriors*, he described how Cherokees of the eighteenth century followed this path towards the development of a "voluntary state" (which in turn was the basis for the creation of the Cherokee nation). He points out (1961: 132) that in many village-organized societies in the archaeologically known past of both the Old World and the New, and consistently in the case of the Cherokees, "the move toward statehood starts only in the presence of commonly perceived duress," and "the first unification is under the priesthood."

We are dealing with the joining together of coequal villages, an action which would seem to require a large measure of cohesive public sentiment. Under such priestly leaders...a cohesive public sentiment had the best possible chance to form .... Given the need to coordinate the actions of more than one village, that priestly leadership was especially equipped to sense minute jealousies and to nurture trust (Gearing 1961: 132).

Throughout Cherokee history, encroaching white populations got away with taking what they wanted, but, when their activities intruded into the life of Cherokee settlements and disrupted life within them, Cherokee unification was sparked. This was the case when the Cherokees first formed their "voluntary state," and again, when resistance to statehood united settlements all over the Cherokee nation into the Keetoowah Society, which was led by a reconstructed native priesthood. I witnessed the same process in the 1960's, when the local establishment's first steps toward consolidation of their control over Cherokee affairs provoked spokesmen from Cherokee settlements in five counties to pull themselves together into the short-lived Five County Cherokee Organization.

The first chairman of this modern revival of "voluntary statehood" was chief of the Keetoowah Society and the second chairman was chief of the Seven Clans Society (Wahrhaftig i.p.; Buchanan 1972). It is within the framework of such organization that Cherokees look forward to the solution of their economic difficulties. Among Cherokees, however, political and economic and ritual organization on a scale that transcends the individual settlement seems to arise only when necessary and to atrophy, or meet "grass-roots resistance," whenever it outlives its usefulness or develops in a direction incompatible with the basic adaptation of Cherokee settlements.

Some years ago, I attempted to describe how Cherokees actually *do* survive in their settlements — to isolate the principal mechanism of their cultural adaptation. I wrote then that:

All people [in the Cherokee social world] share the job of existing in the physical and social world. The surrounding physical world provides the wherewithal for this way of life. It can be combed over, learned about, and nurtured to produce the elements for food, shelter, medicine, defense, recreation and whatever else man needs. Life depends on profound knowledge of the world, on exploration of each new way that men can find to sustain themselves within the world. The basis of [Cherokee] tribal life, for this reason, has never settled into a single technology such as intensive farming or commercial fishing. It depends, rather, on a closer and constantly adaptive relation to the surrounding environment. Southeastern tribesmen lived aboriginally and continue to live now by hunting, fishing, gardening, gathering, domesticating animals, and by continuing to respond to new economic conditions. The purpose of continual economic and technological adaptation has continued to be the prosperity of the whole body of people. Since Indians live as members of large groups of people involved in a mutual enterprise, successful maintenance of life is also dependent on profound knowledge of the people with whom one co-exists. Discord among people means economic and social disaster. An Indian community depends on the experiences of all its members, experiences of the resources of nature and of the ways of men, for its survival (Wahrhaftig 1966: 62).

It follows from this summary that, if Cherokees are blocked off from gaining new knowledge or are prevented from using new knowledge in their own way, the basis of their adaptation is destroyed and settlements will disintegrate into disoriented and unsupported individuals. This is why the autonomy of Cherokee settlements is so crucially important.

There are presently sixty-nine Cherokee settlements in eastern Oklahoma, but a modern Cherokee settlement is not much to see. It will be in rugged terrain bypassed by major highways. Small houses, hidden under shade trees, stand along the sides of unpaved roads that are strewn with tire-tearing flints. Some homes are gleaming "Indian project houses" built in recent years, their fresh paint already reddened with dust and mud. Most are spartan wood-frame houses, weatherbeaten and homely. A few, beneath a veneer of imitation brick siding, are log cabins. All are surrounded by a clutter of cars, some running and some cannibalized, and other potentially useful debris — the Cherokee bank account. There is little land under cultivation, and less in the way of kitchen gardens than one might expect to see. Almost no one has the beautiful peach and plum trees that travelers saw in old Cherokee towns and that give rise to a Cherokee surname: Peacheater. Unless people are "doubling up" on small pieces of land, the houses are relatively distant from one another, for the Cherokee ideal, which today is seldom possible to realize, is to have neighbors just close enough that their chimneys can be seen.

A place of worship occupies the center of the settlement. In most, this is a member church of the Cherokee Indian Baptist Association. The churches are built where baptisms can be held in clear waters running from east to west (for "going to the water" is an ancient Cherokee rite of purification expressed through the church). The complex of buildings — which usually includes Sunday school meeting rooms, a kitchen, a dining hall, and facilities for "dinner on the ground" — serve as an all-purpose meeting place, a community hall, a place for older men to consult one another under shade trees, a base for sending "love offerings" of groceries and labor to the poor and the sick, and a women's house, where, under the umbrella of the Women's Missionary Union, the Cherokee matriarchy can assemble. As the church (or, in non-Christian settlements, the "stomp ground" with its outdoor facilities for prayer, sacred dances, ceremonial ball games, and feasting) is the only institution in a Cherokee settlement that remains under Cherokee control, a host of political, educational, and economic functions have been grafted on to it.

When Andrew Jackson marched the Cherokees out of Georgia, they removed by "companies." Whole settlements traveled together, coordinated by their local "captains." Scouts preceded them and selected, in the West, sites in the kind of environment they had adapted to in the "old country." They looked for abundant game, sweet drinking water, a site where water flows to the West, and fertile garden spots, probably placing their priorities in just that order. Entire "towns" from the East resettled intact. The major dialects of Cherokee spoken in the "old country" are still discrete in Oklahoma. Probably most Oklahoma Cherokee settlements are hundreds of years old.

Still, it is possible to drive through the resulting settlement today without having become aware of its presence. Cherokees live lightly upon their environment. An anthropologist driving through a

Cherokee settlement once remarked that the houses looked like flies perched on a sugar cube, as though you would never know they had been there if they flew off.[4] A Cherokee's home is not his palace. It is the base of operations for a life lived outdoors as much as possible. Although Cherokee material culture has grown to resemble that of local poor whites, the Cherokee settlement pattern is not oriented toward agriculture.[5]

There are usually twenty to fifty households containing a population of 100 to 250 people in each Cherokee settlement. Households average five persons each. About 60 percent of the households containing children house a "nuclear family" of father, mother, children, and no others. But the distribution of Cherokees into small households belies a more extensive structure. The individual household is not the basic social or economic unit in Cherokee life (Wahrhaftig 1970: 65–66).

Over time, a Cherokee settlement tends to be maintained as a single group of kinsmen. Having been together so long, the problem is usually not that people are related, but that they are related so extensively. The customary practice at present is that Cherokees do not marry anyone known to be a relative. Given this broad proscription, it is not long before all the kin groups within a settlement are integrated. Thereafter, the members of that settlement may have to find mates in neighboring settlements, which tends to extend the

---

[4]   I would like to be able to say that where Cherokees live, the material transformation of the environment is minimal, but this is unfortunately not the case. The timber has been logged, and brushy second growth replaces woods thinned and cleaned by the Cherokee custom of annual burning. Most of these transformations, I think, result from activities forced on Cherokees by whites. During the Depression, for example, many men were able to feed their families only by "tie hacking," that is, cutting timber into railroad ties. During that same period, a geographer remarked that "In many Indian districts, even though the population may consist largely of restricted Indians and most of the land may be owned by them, more Indian land is used by white men than by Indians. This is particularly true of pastureland and of the better cropland. Some Indians have returned to poorer land because they have leased their land to whites. The Indians have not wasted the land resources to the extent that the whites have, but often the waste has been on Indian-owned land" (Hewes 1942: 280).

[5]   Whites in the Cherokee nation make less intensive agricultural use of the land than do whites in similar environments in Arkansas. This phenomenon was studied by Hewes in the 1930's (Hewes 1942, 1943) and was reobserved by Robert K. Thomas and myself in 1964. As compared to Arkansas farmers, Oklahoma whites build less substantial houses and outbuildings, are less likely to plant orchards, plant smaller and less diverse "kitchen gardens," plant flower beds and other adornments less frequently, and construct less varied improvements on their lands. Hewes reported on the basis of data from the 1930 census that; "In both value of farm buildings and of dwellings per farm the best of the Cherokee counties was poorer than the poorest of the four border counties, although it had more valuable farm land than two of the four border counties" (Hewes 1943: 140). Hewes attributed some of the difference to the high proportion of tenants in Oklahoma as compared to Arkansas. He also believed that Oklahoma whites "preserve more of the pioneering traits" than those who stayed behind in Arkansas.

framework of relationships.[6] Any Cherokee family moving to a different Cherokee settlement is soon incorporated through marriage. The next generation are consanguineal kinpersons.

The backbone of a modern Cherokee settlement is a generation of men who are like brothers to one another.[7] A man usually brings his wife to his parents' home and soon thereafter builds a house of his own nearby. This separates a married woman from the companions of her childhood. The infant males who crawl together (watched over by elder sisters) become boys who hunt, fish, and tussle together, and later adolescents who chase girls together. In young adulthood they work alongside one another, and at maturity they preside together over the affairs of the settlement (influenced greatly by the diversity of strong opinions represented by the women they have married). The men of a Cherokee settlement tend to be born already related to one another. Those who live conveniently nearby come to know one another individually and profoundly through a lifetime of hunting, fishing, fighting, drinking, womanizing, sobering up, repenting and settling down — all in the same shared environment. Under these circumstances, the distinctions we make between brothers, first cousins, distant cousins, and so forth are inapplicable. Male kin of the same generation who interact together are "brothers." The structure of a Cherokee settlement is organized around a very few (and often overlapping) clusters of "brothers."

In general, all the relationships of people within a Cherokee settlement are like the relationship between "brothers"; with the exception of women recently married in, they are relationships between people who have lived together for a long time in the same environment in a small and intimate community, and they are relations extended from the primary kin relationships. In a Cherokee settlement, one is surrounded by grandfathers, grandmothers, fathers, mothers, uncles, aunts, wives (or husbands), brothers, sisters, sons, daughters, nieces,

---

[6] Centuries ago, Cherokees reckoned descent matrilineally and encouraged marriage with certain relatives, namely women of the clans of either of a man's grandfathers. At present, Cherokees reckon descent bilaterally and theoretically there is no limit on the degree of relatedness within which marriage is incestuous. There has been enough internal migration within the Cherokee nation in the last century to alleviate the problem, but Cherokees ought to be grateful to Detroit, for the automobile, which has increased the "courting range" of the young, has helped get this generation off the hook.
[7] The relationship between classificatory brothers can be extremely close. The relationship between "real" (biological) brothers is sometimes almost pathologically close. Although they frequently live in adjoining households and work together, in this relationship they have less freedom to express anger or hostility than in any other. The combination of deep affect and repression is sometimes explosive. Fratricides seem to be unusually frequent, and there are cases in which, after one brother killed another in the heat of anger, the remorseful murderer then committed suicide.

nephews, and grandchildren. That is, all persons in a Cherokee settlement quite naturally and unconsciously relate to each other through behaviors that derive from these primary, "close" relationships. Fundamentally, the Cherokee social system operates by perfecting a few fundamental models for behavior.

One attribute of this system of social relations within a Cherokee settlement is that the settlement can field a very flexible yet well articulated work force. This can currently be seen most clearly in the Cherokee tradition of community labor, for in this context Cherokee arrangements are unaffected by our cultural practice of hiring an individual wage earner. Cherokee settlements ("towns" as they were then called) once produced their food together. Bartram, who visited the Cherokees in the 1770's, observed that:

An Indian town is generally so situated, as to be convenient for procuring game, secure from sudden invasion, having a large district of excellent arable land adjoining, or in its vicinity. . . . This is their common plantation, and the whole town plant is one vast field together; but yet the part or share of every individual family or habitation is separated from the next adjoining, by a narrow strip, or verge of grass, or any other natural or artificial boundary.

In the spring, the ground being already prepared on one and the same day, early in the morning, the whole town is summoned, by the sound of a conch shell, from the mouth of the overseer, to meet at the public square, whither the people repair with their hoes and axes; and from thence proceed to their plantation, where they begin to plant, not every one in his own little district, assigned and laid out, but the whole community united begins on one certain part of the field, where they plant on until finished; and when their rising crops are ready for dressing and cleansing they proceed after the same order, and so on day after day, until the crop is laid by for ripening (Bartram [1791: 400–401] quoted in Fogelson and Kutsche 1961: 95–96).

A Moravian missionary who journeyed through the old Cherokee towns in 1783–1784 added to this description that: "They dare not go from their Work till in the Evening, but the Women must bring them their Victuals into the Field" (Williams [1928:261] quoted in Fogelson and Kutsche 1961: 96). Men organized into a community work group, which was complemented by a community work group organized among women. In that period, "this same communal organization of men who tilled the fields also rapidly erected both private and public buildings in the town, and the men of one town or neighborhood frequently helped those of the next" (Fogelson and Kutsche 1961: 96).

During the next two centuries, the structure of the Cherokee "town" altered considerably, as did the organization of the community work group. Among the Cherokees of North Carolina, the end product was an intricately organized settlement work group, the *gadoogie*, headed by a chief and an assistant chief who decided what work should be done and where, supported by a secretary and treasurer, and filled out by a number of specialists (e.g. gravedigger, carpenter, head cook) who coordinate their respective male or female work crews (Fogelson and Kutsche 1961: 98–110). The Oklahoma Cherokees followed a slightly different path. There, the tradition of settlement work parties as a primary means of crop production persisted, although no one knows for how long, or how intensively. Hewes (1942: 274) mentions "town work" as characteristic of the Cherokee "pioneer economy" in Oklahoma. Thereafter, the *gadoogie* became an occasion, as opposed to an organization. Oklahoma Cherokees use the word to mean a work party called together to accomplish some specific task, usually with the expectation that the work will be accompanied by a feast collectively prepared by the workers' women. Now, the *gadoogie* remains in the background of Cherokee settlement life, as a form of disaster relief to be called upon when the primary economy fails. This is possible because the population of a settlement is so related that they can "fall together" when called out.

Voluntary work groups bring baskets of food to the poor and the shut-in, and cut their firewood, clean their houses, wash their clothes, and cook their meals. Groups appear to sing and pray over invalids. When a home or a church is destroyed by fire it will be repaired by a voluntary work group. Even quite unusual tasks may be performed *ad hoc* by such work groups. John Chewie, accused in 1966 of shooting a deer out of season and without a proper license, pleaded innocent. When the ACLU agreed to enter the case, Cherokees began to hope that it would be the definitive test of the legality of their right to hunt and fish throughout eastern Oklahoma. In the settlements of Kenwood and Bull Hollow, Cherokees were deeply interested in the case, but worried, too, for they knew John was fond of drinking and they feared that county authorities would find a way to get him drunk enough to accept a bribe and drop the case. To handle the situation, they called together the young men and detailed them to search for John, find him, and act as his bodyguard.

More often than not, the work group of a settlement is organized within the framework of its Indian church. North of Stilwell in Adair County, Cherokee members of a Methodist church have trained together as ambulance attendants. They schedule themselves so that some trained member of the congregation is on call twenty-four hours a day, by telephone or by short wave radios that they have distributed in remote parts of their settlement, to tend patients and rush them to a hospital. As a final illustration of the propensity of this tradition to appear in new context, in the winter of 1972, the Original Cherokee Community Organization, which had become the organization uniting Cherokees who opposed the incumbent tribal government, was attempting to build its following by traveling from its offices in the town

of Tahlequah to Cherokee settlements where members of the organization cut wood, repaired bridges, cooked meals, and extended their
relationships through the ease with which voluntary work groups may
be entered. They mended their political fence literally.

Not long ago Cherokee settlements were economically self-sufficient.
The Cherokees brought to the West a knowledge of farming, as well as
hunting, fishing, and plant collecting. Nearly a century ago one of them
testified:

Nearly all of us have our own houses. We raise our own corn and wheat; we
have hogs, cattle, and plenty of chickens and live comfortably. We may be
poor, but we are independent. You can go anywhere and find enough to eat.
They are therefore satisfied and happy. Some live in valleys that are very
narrow, but they are rich. They have farms of four or five to twenty acres. The
people don't care to go elsewhere (Report of the Committee on Indian Affairs
[1886] quoted in Hewes 1942: 275).

Although this account fails to mention the diversity of subsistence
enterprises, it reflects the enormous importance Cherokees attach to
their autonomy, to determining their own adaptation. That was when,
as Cherokee memories go, the quality of life was as it was supposed to
be. Older Cherokees look back to the times when they lived this way
and insist that then people lived longer, were healthier, and got along
with each other better. It was the Cherokee Golden Age. An elderly
man told me:

It wasn't as neighborly [that is, crowded] as it is now. People used to live five
and ten miles apart. They farmed with an ox, and they used to have hogs up to
six years old. They were not in need of food. They raised a *lot* of corn. They
had no use for money. No use for grocery store. Even today people look for
hidden treasures because back then, the farmers had no use for money and just
hid it away.
   Then they changed to using horses and visited a little more. Not too long
after it, began to use machinery. People began to close up. Some quit farming.
They started working. Now one man can farm with a little gas! . . .
   In those days all people were Keetoowah. There were no churches.
Churches started from people visiting in groups at night. Believing in "do unto
others." Before then people worked together. Loved one another. Had lots of
gadoogie. Helped one another. They built rail fences and did farm work. They
didn't use herb medicine [against one another to conjure]. They doctored
among themselves. They ate lots of wild game. No guns. They used bow and
arrows to hunt deer, turkey, wild hogs, and they made hominy and kenutchie
from hickory nuts, and corn bread and beanbread from corn.
   My dad said years ago people didn't marry until they were in their seventies
[i.e. in those days seventy was early adulthood and people lived much longer]
(personal communication).

Cherokee subsistence farming settlements were boxed in by farms
leased to white men. Overpopulation, overfarming, and overexploita-

tion of the woods destroyed the environment and the last possibilities for Cherokee economic self-sufficiency. The process of encapsulation and destruction of economic self-sufficiency has not yet run its course. Even before statehood, Cherokee settlements were islands of Indian farming. Land hawks, as they were called, collaborated with Indian agents to lease large sections of Indian lands and, in turn, to sublease them to settlers. At hearings held in 1915, one witness told of a firm of speculators that controlled 30,000 acres of land in the Indian territory and leased it to more than 1,500 tenants, and this was not an exceptional example (McWilliams 1942: 189). Time only made matters worse:

As oil, mining, and lumbering activities began to decline, workers from these industries crowded into the already overpopulated areas in search of subsistence farms. The number of farms increased in precisely the poorest, therefore the cheapest, farming areas in the state. As farming units got smaller and smaller, soil erosion, already far advanced, began to claim the land (McWilliams 1942: 191).

The Cherokees were boxed in by these manipulations. The Depression, together with severe droughts in 1935 and 1936, completed the destruction of their self-sufficiency. Observers saw Indian farmers near starvation (Hall 1934). A geographer who gathered data during those times reported that:

The Cherokee economy is not well suited to present conditions. Generally, the Indian farmer is able to supply his own food but does not have sufficient cash income to buy clothing and other necessities. The average family cash income for the year 1934 in the northern part of the region was estimated by Indian Service workers at $95. A considerable part of the cash income is derived from the sale of wood, particularly of railroad ties, in the cutting of which the Indians have acquired the reputation of being skilled workmen. Generally, the culture of the restricted Indians is that of the pioneer period, but much impoverished and no longer adequate (Hewes 1942: 281).

Toward the end of the 1930's, there seems to have been less wood for ties, and there was less employment for farmhands. The cash that Cherokees needed to supplement their subsistence farming became harder to acquire. The failing subsistence farms of the 1930's were replaced by cattle ranching. In Adair and Delaware counties, submarginal agricultural land was bought by the United States government and turned over to the Bureau of Indian Affairs to administer.

The BIA leased to cattle raisers. Subsistence farmers from Cherokee settlements were poor risks, compared with the culturally white but technically Indian entrepreneurs who were awarded leases. Speculation in cattle land began. In the late 1960's, local opinion in Adair and Delaware counties was that Texas investors were consolidating large tracts for cattle. Census figures compiled in 1964 do show recent decreases in small holdings, and increases in the number of landholdings of more than 220 acres, including a rather large jump in the number of holdings of 500 to 1,000 acres (Jordan 1972a).

Meanwhile, construction of a large number of lakes as part of the Army Engineers' Arkansas River Flood Control Project transformed eastern Oklahoma into a potential recreation area and brought into being a whole new set of possibilities for speculation in land. Together with the white population's new uses for land came new restrictions on Indian usage. Prohibitions on burning the woods were enforced, increasing the tick and chigger population, and decreasing the ease of hunting. Where once Cherokees allowed their hogs to fatten by roaming the woods, "hog-fencing laws" made that enterprise untenable. County officials began to enforce state hunting and fishing regulations with tenacity.

Cherokees were increasingly blocked from their generalized utilization of the woods and streams, deprived of sufficient cash supplement to capitalize even a subsistence farm, and confined to the tiny island of their allotments. Cherokee self-sufficiency had seriously declined by the time World War II arrived.

Historically, Cherokees have suffered two traumatic events, of different orders, with distinct effects on their way of life. The first occurred in 1907, when the Cherokee nation lost its political autonomy and its citizens were incorporated into the state of Oklahoma. The more recent occurred between 1920 and 1940, when the economic self-sufficiency of Cherokee settlements was undermined. Cherokees no longer found it possible to devise an autonomous adaptation to their environment, and life in Cherokee settlements was severely jolted.

Cherokees who were teenagers in the 1920's describe a life that was strained and violent. Cherokees say that young men then were "mean." (We would say "homicidal.") A number of the people who are now white-haired, "beloved men" in Cherokee settlements, models of peacefulness and sobriety, had explosive tempers and were vicious fighters when they were young. It has been said of the honored and elderly retired chief of a modern Cherokee ceremonial society that when he was a young man he used to show up on the ceremonial grounds so drunk that participants in the ritual had to tie him to the sacred ball game pole for his safety and theirs. The permanent effect of this turbulence, at least as Cherokees explain it, is the abandonment of a host of seemingly useful and pleasurable activities.

An outward harmony in personal relationships is enforced among Cherokees (Hudson 1970; Thomas n.d.a, n.d.b, n.d.c). A Cherokee is expected to unhesitatingly give of himself to others and to suppress any outward show of emotion, especially anger. It is characteristic of

Cherokees that this almost saintly behavior is demanded as a normal and continual state. Neither children nor adults are rewarded for attaining it, but deviation is punished. People will "get mad." This means that they will, while maintaining an outward facade of serene cooperation, retaliate through sorcery or through treachery. Or they will repress their anger until some final slight explosively releases it, for in the Cherokee way of life there are no approved ways to discharge tension (Holzinger 1961). When times are tense and interaction among Cherokees is strained, the Cherokee response is to "pull in" — to avoid places and events where they might be uncertain of the response of others to them. The decades between 1920 and 1940 were a time of general "pulling in," which adversely affected life in Cherokee settlements.

I think that as Cherokee economic self-sufficiency slipped away, relationships within Cherokee settlements broke down. To defend the integrity and cohesiveness of their settlements, Cherokees abandoned valued events. There were too many brawls. Drunkenness was followed by homicide, which was followed by recriminations and vengeance extracted through vicious gossip and then through conjuring and evil medicine. This in turn led to more deeply ingrained hard feelings, latent and ready to precipitate another brawl. When Cherokees identified an event as one likely to precipitate this cycle, public opinion unified against it, and they "let it go," whatever its other values to them. Hard feelings were too high and too dangerous a price to pay.

For instance, many Cherokees were talented fiddlers and guitar players, and in some settlements there used to be weekly music parties and square dances. The fighting at these got out of control, and public music making, dancing, and partying have not been condoned in Cherokee settlements ever since. Cherokees used to enjoy gambling, and horse races and poker parties used to provide them with some excitement. But there were quarrels over bets, and killings, and Cherokees gave up public gambling. There used to be a very old tradition of team sports, in which the men of one settlement challenged men of another. There was "men's ball" (an aboriginal game in eastern North America, from which lacrosse is derived), a "marble game" (which bears some resemblance to Italian *bocce ball* and English bowling on the green), and cornstalk shooting, in which teams of archers shoot at distant bales of cornstalks and score by counting the number of stalks their arrows have pierced.

In each of these sports, teams were assisted by sorcerers, whose task was to strengthen the home team and to disarm the opposition. One of the reasons for abandoning these sports was that the sorcerers were thought to be doing unnecessary harm to their opponents. Worse, they were suspected of using their position on the teams as a cover for sorcery in which they duelled to the death with their personal rivals. It was all right for arrows on a direct path to the target to magically break in two in midair. It was not all right for an archer to draw his bow and at that moment have his shooting arm "cripple up" — not just for the duration of the match, but for life. Furthermore, as there was no limit to the amount or the kind of body contact allowed in the men's ball game, which was played with sturdy wooden rackets, men expressed their hard feelings by braining one another. The game was abandoned because there were too many injuries. People began to feel uneasy about crowds and even to fear that an enemy might have set "doctored" food out for them at a church supper or feast. Perhaps for these reasons, the custom of regularly building houses by *gadoogie* disappeared. All of these events were sociable, recreational, lively, stimulating, and colorful. None was replaced by a substitute.[8] Without them, life in a Cherokee settlement is drab, oppressive, and monotonous. In the aftermath of losing economic autonomy, Cherokees did hold their settlements together, but the pleasure and joy in life went out of them.

A host of useful productive activities were either curtailed or abandoned in Cherokee settlements at this time. Cherokees no longer plant as large or as varied kitchen gardens, preserve produce by drying and canning, raise and butcher hogs, smoke meat, brew beer, distill whiskey, squeeze sorghum, mill flour, log for construction lumber or firewood, or make furniture nearly as much as once they did (Mildred Dickeman, personal communication). To the loss of land, the restricted use of the woods, and the increasing and unpredictable amounts of time demanded by wage labor — reasons sometimes given for passing of these practices — we might add also demoralization.

Today Cherokees are the laboring caste of eastern Oklahoma. They haul rocks and carry hod on construction jobs. They frame buildings. They ditch roads and chop brush for the "high lines" of utility companies. They harvest beans, peas, and strawberries. They bale hay. They glean huckleberries from the woods and sell them to grocers. They pump gas and wait table. They plant and pack seedlings in commercial nurseries. They grab chickens in the yards of packing plants. They sort fruit in canneries. A few now are factory laborers in tribally subsidized industries.

Cherokees do work that is heavy, dangerous, and dirty for em-

---

[8] Cherokee settlements do field softball teams, which compete with teams from other Cherokee settlements. Sometimes heavy bets are made on these games, but as "ballgame medicine" has not been incorporated into Cherokee softball, this sport is not fully a substitute for men's ball — which was a substitute for ritualized warfare.

ployers who often provide no workmen's compensation and no social security. They work at jobs that are seasonal, and jobs where there is work only during fair weather. They work for employers who lay them off a week before they would qualify for unemployment insurance and then hire a new crew. They work for incredibly low wages. In 1972 there are Cherokee women who clean, cook, and baby-sit for $2.00 to $4.00 per day. They are trapped by the expectation that they ought to be grateful for any menial work. Last winter, we conversed in the sitting room of an energetic young Cherokee couple, pressed to the walls by a king-sized quilt stretched on a quilting frame in the center of the small room. The wife had been working on the quilt for days, and the husband was tired of the sight of it. She explained that the patterned quilt top, batting, backing, and even the thread had been thrust upon her by a white lady from Tulsa who expected to pay $2.50 for its completion. Her husband listened silently as she counted up how many evenings she had spent on the quilting and then said indignantly, "It's just not right. You ought to be getting at least fifty cents an hour out of this"!

Poor whites do this kind of work too, of course, but Cherokees are restricted to such jobs by strong local prejudices. They are subjected to all of the conflicting stereotypes one hears about Indians. On the one hand, Cherokees are said to be heavy drinkers, unreliable, prone to unexplained absenteeism, and a little violent. At the same time, they are also thought to be docile, methodical, patient, careful to do a good job, but slower than Mexicans. So long as Cherokees "live like Indians" they are victims of an intense and covert discrimination, no matter how educated and capable they may be. I know, for example, a well-educated, attractive, and distinctively Cherokee looking lady who had lived in a midwestern metropolis for many years. After she and her family moved back to a rural Cherokee settlement, she repeatedly looked for work in Stilwell, the principal town in Adair County. She admired the life-style of small-town whites, and they were the models for her dress, grooming, and gestures. Nevertheless, the best job she ever found was waiting table in a cafe, and even there she was made to feel uncomfortable. Several years later, her husband became a prominent official of the Cherokee tribal government, in which capacity he was functionally a member of the local establishment. After that, his wife quickly was offered a satisfying job in the town's most prestigious dress shop.

If Cherokees are employed as skilled laborers in eastern Oklahoma, it is usually because they are temporary trainees in projects supported by the Bureau of Indian Affairs and allied agencies. The welders, mechanics, and heavy-equipment operators thus trained seldom find appropriate employment after the project ends. One afternoon a young Cherokee was asking an older man about the school for heavy-equipment operators situated in the Cherokee settlement at Bull Hollow. "When you're done, do you get a job?" he asked. "Yeah, lots of jobs," was the answer, "in Arkansas, picking grapes."

In 1963, there were no Cherokees with white collar jobs living in Cherokee settlements. The only ones that I know of in 1972 work for their tribal government. Yet Cherokees are desperate for jobs. When Murray Wax (1971: 11) interviewed Cherokee parents about the value of sending children to school, he found that: "The principal value of an education is seen as economic: if a person were able to finish school he would get a job — a better job, a job secured more easily, an easy job, indeed *any* job."

In any Cherokee settlement, kinsmen perpetually pass tips about jobs to one another. Information circulates about who is hiring whom, where, and for what. People drive to one another's houses at night with the news. Sometimes things work out. Too often, the information is inaccurate, or out of date, or others got there first. There is, in addition, a simple and paralyzing fear of whites and a conviction that there is no point in trying for a job. "I just wouldn't know how to act right." From their settlements, Cherokees will travel considerable distances to take advantage of the relatively higher wages and lesser prejudices in areas outside the Cherokee nation. At five in the morning, cars full of Cherokees leave Bull Hollow in Delaware County, bound for jobs as forgers and welders in Tulsa. The workers seldom return before eight at night. Similarly, Cherokees drive from Marble City, Oklahoma, to work at a chair factory in Fort Smith, Arkansas, and from Hulbert to work in Muskogee. They are away from home for twelve to fifteen hours in order to earn eight hours' pay, traveling the initial miles away from their settlements over roads that shred tires and shake cars to pieces.

Even the jobs created by the Cherokees' own government tend to extend this pattern. Workers commute from their settlements to factories located (with one exception, still in the planning stage) in county seats, where most of the employment is for laborers soldering together electronic components.

Observers of the Cherokees in modern times have been amazed that Cherokees can survive on as little as they do. In the 1960's, I lived with Cherokee families and participated in the life of Cherokee settlements while conducting a survey. I knew quite well that people were poor, but I was more impressed with the orderliness and functionality of Cherokee households than with their brute poverty. I could scarcely believe the results, when the survey questionnaires were tabulated and then carefully checked. They were dead accurate. The Cherokees are *that* poor (see first section). A Bureau of Indian Affairs employee who surveyed Cherokee settlements in the 1950's raised the crucial question. He said that "conditions such as those here reported have prompted the question "How can they manage to live on so little income?" ... These questions have been put frequently by the writer to those who live alongside [the Cherokees]. The answer invariably has been, "I don't know" or "that's something I've never been able to figure out" (Cullum 1958: 15).

Cherokees get by on so little, I am convinced, because at least the system of primary relationships among kin in their settlements is still intact. Formally organized institutions for organizing collective work, for political decision making, for self-defense, and for social control no longer exist, but there remains a network of person-to-person relationships within a Cherokee settlement that is a pathway for an efficient distribution of resources and labor through sharing. So long as these person-to-person relationships do not break down, the Cherokees are not so poor as they might be.

In the old Cherokee nation, lands were communally owned; today Cherokee settlements still function as though this were the case, even though the United States government has since allotted Cherokee lands to individual Cherokees, and relatives sometimes quarrel bitterly over inheritance. Even so, no Cherokee will deny another a place to live. The facilities in Cherokee settlements are stretched to house the needy, even though overcrowding may result. As a result, the array of people living on any given tract of restricted land is likely to be bewildering.

The principle of allocation, however, is clear. Parents reserve home-sites on their allotments for their children and thereafter "lend" unoccupied portions of their land to any Cherokee who requests it. Figure 1 shows the households on two typical tracts of restricted land in a Cherokee settlement in Adair County in 1965. On the larger tract are the households of the elderly heir to the tract and of two married sons and one married daughter, and sites that have been chosen by the remaining sons and daughters, who were then living either in Chicago or Dallas. On the neighboring tract of land are located households of the widow of the original allottee and her present husband, the daughter of the allottee by an earlier marriage and her husband, the son of the widow of the allottee by a former marriage and his wife, and the allottee's widow's son's stepdaughter with her husband. In addition, a site has been reserved for the children of the widow of the allottee by her present marriage. Returning in 1972, I found more people living on the first tract. A new house had been built for the son who lived at "C," and in his old house lived the brother of the wife of the heir of the original allottee, together with his sons. The daughter of

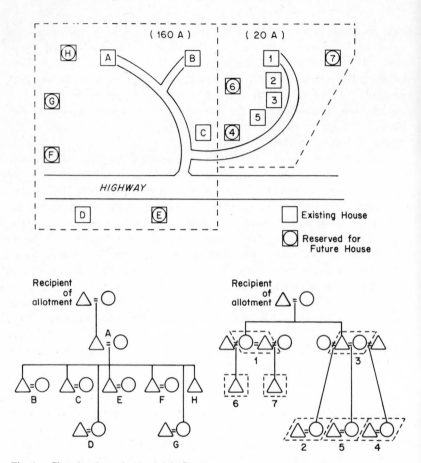

Fig. 1.   Cherokee households, Adair County

this man had been given a site next to "E" and lived in a new house
built there. Daughter "G" had moved out of her parents' house and
into a new house on a site she had chosen.

When there is freedom to do so, Cherokees work communally. All
summer long, people band together to pick strawberries, peas, beans,
tomatoes, and huckleberries. Whole families, including very young
children, may work together, or groups of women together with their
female children may work while men are employed elsewhere. Although Cherokees resent having to scrape by at stoop labor, they at
least make this an occasion for sociability. Cherokee migratory labor
follows the same pattern, with gangs of young men, usually "brothers,"
traveling to Colorado for the broom corn harvest and following the
crops from there. Each worker, even those who are children, keeps his
own wages and spends them as he pleases.

In the more common circumstance where communal labor is not possible, the Cherokee adaptation to wage labor is nevertheless based on intricate chains of reciprocal services that may include the whole of a settlement. Figure 2 shows three typical households in Cherokee settlement in Delaware County. An elderly man lives with his wife in Household I; his son with his wife, children, and aunt live in Household II; and another son lives in Household III with his wife and child. House III is a trailer placed behind House I. A shortcut footpath through the woods connects House II with the others. The women in Houses I and II cook together in the big house, where both households eat together.

On a typical working day, the young man and his wife in the trailer are ready to leave for work at dawn. They leave their daughter in charge of her grandmother in House I and drive west. The wife is dropped off at her job in the city of Pryor, and the husband continues on to work in Tulsa. It is late in the evening before they return to their home. Meanwhile, the other son also leaves his home at dawn. He

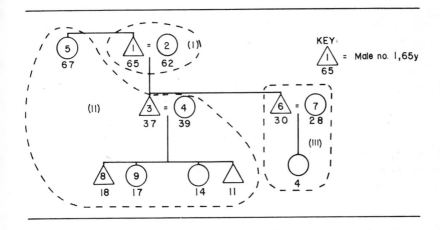

Source of Income

Household	Individual	Income
I	1	Welfare/Old age
	2	None
II	3	Road construction crew
	4	Cannery worker, seasonal
	5	None
III	6	Steel plant labor (Tulsa)
	7	Office work (Pryor)

Fig. 2.   Characteristic Cherokee economic unit, Delaware County, 1963

picks up his wife's brother (not on the diagram) and other young men, and together they drive to work on a road crew. His elderly aunt stays home, minding his children. The old man gets up later. He comes to fetch his daughter-in-law from House II and, picking up women from other houses along the way (not on the diagram), he takes them to work at a cannery. He waits there while the women work, then drives them home in the evening. This particular extensive pattern of cooperative relationships is interesting in that it is fairly recent. The young couple in the trailer lived in Tulsa and had moved back to the settlement just a few months before my observations were made. They found that they could live better by commuting to their distant jobs from this settlement. It took but a short time to incorporate them into the neighborhood pattern of cooperation and wage earning. This example makes it clear that in the less disrupted Cherokee settlements, each person plays a role in facilitating production. As chauffeurs, chaperones, and baby-sitters, older people play roles that free more young people to earn wages. In turn, older people are supported and looked after by the younger. The boundaries of Cherokee households are fluid. When expedient, they may merge, as when two nuclear families cook and eat together, or individual persons may shift from one household to another, if that proves more satisfying and convenient.

While these pervasive cooperative arrangements enable Cherokees to earn and survive on their meager wages, the adaptation is difficult and is continually jeopardized. The priority whites place on dependability and punctuality on the job conflicts with the priority Cherokees place on dependability and punctuality in responding to the needs of their companions. As whites are ignorant of the kind of Cherokee relationships just described, and as these are also "taken for granted" by Cherokees and therefore exist below the threshold of conscious awareness, Cherokees would find it difficult to explain themselves to their white employers even if these employers would listen.

Cherokees always seem to be in some bind. Last winter we visited Cherokee friends on an icy February day. As the husband stoked his wood stove — for he has never had the time or money to insulate his house and therefore cannot hope to afford the amount of propane gas that would be necessary to heat it — he worried aloud. While he is working, framing houses for a contractor, he doesn't have time to cut wood. He counts on buying it cheap from a relative who is a wood-cutter. But now this relative had the flu, and there was no cheap wood to be had. He stayed home to cut a supply of wood for his own family and for his sick relative, but was concerned that the boss would be angry at his absence and kick him off the construction crew.

When relationships are disrupted in a Cherokee settlement, the results are demonstrably costly, both to Cherokees and to the public. The realigned settlement may be both more culturally isolated and less self-sufficient. The Cherokee settlement around the town of Hulbert provides an example. It is among the least isolated of Cherokee settlements, situated on a major east-west highway linking Tahlequah (the former Cherokee capital and now a regional trade center) with Tulsa, and linked by paved roads with the cities of Muskogee and Wagoner. So the Cherokees around Hulbert are more exposed to the acculturative influences of town and city life than is usually the case. Nor is the terrain as rugged as that surrounding most Cherokee settlements. Cherokees around Hulbert live interspersed with neighboring white farmers and ranchers. The settlement patterns of Cherokees and whites interpenetrate.

I expected to find an acculturated Cherokee settlement at Hulbert and even wondered if it would really be necessary to use an interpreter. It was. In tabulating the results, I found that as many Cherokee heads of households around Hulbert were unable to speak English as in the most isolated Cherokee settlement, and twice as many heads of households were unable to speak English as in the remaining two more isolated Cherokee communities (Table 3).

Table 3.   Percent of heads of households unable to speak English*

Settlement	Percent
Hulbert	40
Cherry Tree	14
Marble City	24
Bull Hollow	42

*   Where both husband and wife were present in the household, both were counted as househeads.

Clearly, Cherokees here were not acculturated; moreover, their inability to speak English evidenced an enormous amount of social isolation from English-speaking whites in spite of the lack of geographic isolation from whites. Absence of geographic isolation and exposure to town life have not led to an acculturated settlement around Hulbert.

In general, the Cherokees around Hulbert were not only poor, but were also more fearful and "closed" than Cherokees in more isolated communities. Young Cherokee workers were also migrating from this area to live near jobs they had found in Wagoner, Tahlequah, Muskogee, and more distant cities. With a shortage of young adults to support and care for them, older Cherokees were moving off their restricted lands and into town. This process was encouraged by social workers and welcomed by landlords in the economically stagnant town of Hulbert who were eager for welfare-supported tenants. Many Cherokees were forced to sell their lands in the process of moving. Around Hulbert, there were more landless Cherokees renting homes than in any other Cherokee settlement (Table 4). Because Cherokee wage earners have migrated away from Hulbert, there were more households with no source of support but welfare (Table 5).

Table 4.   Status of Cherokee residential sites

Settlement	Allotted	Purchased and restricted	Being purchased through welfare	Rented	Tribal lands (former "government land")
Hulbert	46%	6%	3%	40%	0%
Cherry Tree	66	16	0	11	11
Marble City	48	24	12	13	0
Bull Hollow	61	33	0	0	5

Ironically, the overall income of Cherokees around Hulbert is no less than in Cherokee settlements supported principally by wage earning. (Table 5). However, Cherokees at Hulbert have higher expenses (as for rent) and could count less on help from kinfolk. In the Cherokee settlement most exposed to white life-styles, the standard of living was a little lower and the amount of welfare assistance required for even that level of living was far greater.

Table 5.   Source of total income of settlement — 1963–1964

Settlement and Median per capita income	Wages	Welfare	Social Security Pensions	Miscellaneous
Hulbert ($500)	39%	42%	18%	0%
Cherry Tree ($500)	64	19	11	5
Marble City ($650)	60	29	10	1
Bull Hollow ($450)	64	25	8	1

The conditions to which Cherokees around Hulbert have been exposed lead not to acculturation of the Cherokee settlement but to *fragmentation*, at least in the sense that individuals are drawn out of the diminishing body of the settlement. Cherokee life is communal, and Cherokees prefer to learn and work in kin groups, but involvement in American institutions demands participation in which the isolated individual is the principal actor. Demands that Cherokees perform as individuals start with their first days of school, before they even understand the English language (Dickeman 1971). These demands continue into their other relationships to our society — as students, employees, billpayers, or welfare recipients.

Furthermore, eastern Oklahoma whites, especially schoolteachers and the more paternalistic of employers, are cultural evangelists in their interactions with Cherokees. They conceive of each Indian as individually free to make a choice between his own backward ways and "progress," between Satan and the angels, accordingly, and they heavily reward a Cherokee who "forgets" his language and his tribal "superstitions." Some individuals respond to these pressures by becoming zealous converts to white values, some by militant repudiation, some by withdrawal, and some by oblivious imperception. The results of the process are tangible in Hulbert. Although it is commonplace for workers in other Cherokee settlements to commute even greater distances to their jobs, Cherokees from Hulbert are more willing to abandon life in the settlement and live near their jobs in towns and cities.

Because the experiences that decrease commitment to the Cherokee settlement are so individual, the effects on individuals cut across kinship ties. In a given group of brothers, there may be some who find satisfaction in their attachment to the hills and to the Cherokee-speaking relatives, while others are uncomfortable there and deeply ashamed of their Cherokee upbringing, asking only the opportunity to leave it far behind. Thus, individual persons may repudiate their places in a Cherokee settlement and move away from it, but as a Cherokee settlement is an extensive system of related people, the system of relationships simply closes up again. The settlement remains socially cohesive, but its economic and cultural characteristics are altered.

Paradoxically, the effect of the process just described seems to be a settlement that is, in the narrow sense of the word, more "traditional." Originally, there were three Cherokee settlements near Hulbert, each clustered around a Cherokee Baptist church on one of the westward flowing creeks north of the town. The churches at Fourteen Mile Creek, Keehner, and New Hope are still functioning ceremonial centers for settlements that are being reduced by fragmentation and dispersion. At the same time, Cherokees who have moved from the settlements to the town of Hulbert have formed new relationships to one another and have established a new settlement whose social center is a Cherokee Methodist church in town.

As young workers migrate from Hulbert, they fall back on the acceptable Cherokee practice of "lending" or "giving" children to older relatives to raise. It is hard for a working couple to raise children in the city, and it makes sense to "give" them to grandparents, which is the common pattern, but in the absence of their parents, which is not.

The generation that participates most directly in American society, through employment and recreational activities, is absent from the household during the years in which their children are being socialized. Children are raised by adults who are at the stage in the normal progression through a normal Cherokee life when they are most withdrawn from surrounding whites and most concerned with traditional Cherokee community affairs. Hence, the isolation of Cherokees in Hulbert.

The result, at Hulbert, is a settlement with an enthusiastic sense of identity, yet one crippled by naïveté and innocence of white ways. The Cherokees around Hulbert have been among the most active in attempting to devise their own communal institutions and economic base. Early in the 1960's, they somehow persuaded the United States Public Health Services to establish in their settlement the only local clinic serviced by the main Indian hospital in the region. (The clinic has since been removed.) In 1965, members of the settlement independently made a survey of their own economic needs, in hope of receiving funds through the proposed community action program of the Office of Economic Opportunity. At about that time, they had also been enthusiastic over a proposal to establish a cottage industry for the manufacture of canvas golf bags. Unfortunately, the proposal emanated from a utopian-minded white preacher and his retired brother, neither of whom had the resources to back production. Undaunted, Cherokees around Hulbert are now the backbone of a feeder-pig marketing cooperative sponsored by Oklahomans for Indian Opportunity (see next section).

There is evidence suggesting that acculturative pressures finally pare Cherokee settlements down to a stable core of "diehards." The process extracts those Cherokees whose ties to settlement life can be weakened, leaving behind a population whose commitment is strong. The interest that Cherokees showed in 1965 in clarifying their treaty rights to hunt and fish without restriction was kindled by Cherokees at Park Hill, a settlement nearly in the shadow of the city of Tahlequah that is now reduced to a very few households. It was there that Cherokee men first proposed that a group of Cherokee hunters should simply gang together to hunt through the woods and see if any state or county authorities would try and stop them. This plan awakened interest in the issue of Cherokee hunting rights among other Cherokees, who decided that they should first seek a lawyer who could examine the treaties and advise them of their rights. When this consensus was reached, Cherokees from Park Hill dropped out of the movement. They were certain that American justice would produce nothing and were not about to waste their time. Rather, they were willing to wait until the results of their fellow Cherokees' actions could teach them, too, to trust nothing but their own actions.

While Cherokees have been able to utilize the strengths of their shared settlement life in order to survive in the white man's eastern Oklahoma, this has nothing to do with the life Cherokees want for themselves. Cherokees want autonomy, independence, and economic self-sufficiency. They have tried consistently to reattain these goals for the last 160 years, and they are still trying. Cherokee attempts to regain self-sufficiency have followed one of two avenues; migration or development of a self-sufficient community within the state of Oklahoma.

Cherokees expect the United States government to defend Cherokee territorial integrity and sovereignty. They believe that their earliest treaties commemorate an agreement for perpetual reciprocity between the Cherokees and the United States government. Cherokees gave up land and later offered military assistance. In return, the United States government obligated itself to "take care of the Indians." If it becomes apparent that the United States is not going to honor its commitments, then Cherokees are prepared to move entirely outside American jurisdiction. If they cannot find land not controlled by some other nation, then they will look for a nation that can be trusted to honor its guarantees.

Each time life in Cherokee settlements has been dislocated by white political and economic expansion, Cherokees have envisioned migration as a solution. There have been four waves of actual or seriously contemplated migration. The first, which brought a fourth of the tribe to the territory between the Arkansas and White rivers before 1812, coincided with the expansion of white colonization on the Cherokee frontier and consequent intensification of border raids and reprisals. By 1822, entire Cherokee settlements had moved to Texas, where there were "climatic conditions auguring favorable to the pursuits of agriculture, stock-raising and hunting." Cherokees were under the impression that they had a "perfected right" to occupy lands granted by the monarch of Spain (Starr 1921: 187).

The aftermath of the Cherokees' forced removal to Indian territory produced a second wave of migrations in the 1840's. Some bands of Cherokees did in fact colonize in Mexico, while others asked the United States to provide them a home upon relinquishment of their lands in the Cherokee nation (Littlefield 1971: 409–10).

The traumatic events that preceded incorporation of Cherokees into the state of Oklahoma precipitated a third series of plans for migration. A delegation of Cherokees opened negotiations in 1895 with President Diaz for a tract of land in the Mexican state of Sinaloa. The

Cherokees may have been supported by prospective emigrants from the others of the Five Civilized Tribes, for they claimed nearly 100,000 Indians of several tribes and nations would be glad to settle in Sinaloa, bringing with them some $150 million in capital (Littlefield 1971: 411). This was only the first of several plans for emigration which involved lands in Tamaulipas in 1898: a reported migration of 5,000 Cherokees, Creeks, and Delawares to Guadalajara in 1899; new plans for migrations to unspecified locations in Mexico in 1901: and an effort by a body of Indians from all five of the Civilized Tribes to colonize a 9,000-acre tract they bought north of Tampico. John Henry Dick, who bought a large tract of land during this migration, told the Oklahoma newspapers, " ... should the restrictions be removed from our lands, we can move to Old Mexico and buy ten times as much land with the money derived from the sale of our small holdings here and be a free people" (Littlefield 1971: 414–19).

Predictably, renewed interest in migration to Mexico accompanied the loss of economic self-sufficiency in the 1930's. The plan was organized by officers of the Four Mothers Society, an organization that arose during the resistance to statehood, which has ceremonial grounds and priesthoods among each of the Five Tribes. In 1932 a party of Cherokees and Creeks made a reconnaissance of prospective sites for colonization in northern Mexico, and early in the 1940's a delegation traveled to Mexico City in hope that the Mexican government might still recognize cessions made to Cherokees by President Diaz, and before that by the Spanish Crown.

The other direction that Cherokees take in their attempts to live according to their own wishes involves bolstering their present settlements. Not a day goes by without a scheme for some form of collective production being debated in a Cherokee settlement somewhere in the Cherokee nation. There is perennial talk about consolidating land, either by getting people to combine adjacent allotments or by selling restricted lands and using the proceeds to buy large tracts for communal use. On this land base, the Cherokees involved then propose some additional means of earning an income.

A project that still provokes heated discussion among older Cherokees was conceived around 1915, when a man named C. P. Cornelius became advisor to the Keetoowah Society, then at the height of its strength among Cherokees. Redbird Smith, founding chief of the Keetoowahs, had met Cornelius during a visit to Washington, D.C., and hired him to come to Oklahoma and help the Cherokees. Smith told Cornelius, "I want my people to be self-reliant, and some day I want the strong to build up a surplus that will make it possible for the weak to receive an education and never want for anything" (Littlefield 1971: 424).

Cornelius was a broadly educated man, a lawyer, and a member of Wisconsin's Oneida tribe. "He had everything in his favor to be received favorably by the Cherokees. He was an Indian, an educated man, and he came from the sacred direction, east" (Thomas 1953: 182). Cornelius advised Keetoowah Society members who were scattered all over the Cherokee nation, to congregate in the area of the head fire (ceremonial ground) in the Illinois district:

... Late in November, 1921 over one hundred [members] did prepare to move. The members of thirty-five families belonging to the Brush Creek Fire and Yellow Locust Fire of the Keetoowah Society made ready to leave their homes near Jay in Delaware County. They were all going to live in the same locality in the Wild Horse Mountains in the extreme southeastern corner of Cherokee County, some seventy-five miles away. There Cherokees boxed up their household goods, sold their corn, hogs, and cattle for whatever price they could get, and attempted to rent or lease the homes they left behind. If the latter were not possible, they planned to leave their farms untended and unoccupied. A farewell dance was held, and the group departed November 27, 1921, to be followed by fifteen families from Saline Creek in Mayes County on January 8, 1922.

It was the intention of these people to establish a colony in which they would have their own schools, revive their old customs and practice their own religion without interference. To assist them in their project the Keetoowah Society notified the colonists that there were funds to meet their expenses in moving. Houses had already been built to receive them. Once the colonists were there, however, they were expected to work for the common good since one purpose of the project was to revive the old tribal custom of holding lands in common (Littlefield 1971: 423).

An anthropologist whose informants included two of Redbird Smith's sons described the way in which the Keetoowah hoped to support themselves:

After Redbird Smith's death, C. P. Cornelius continued with his plans. The restrictions were removed on several ... allotments and they were mortgaged. With this money, a bank was set up in Gore, Oklahoma, with C. P. Cornelius as president. A herd of black Angus cattle was purchased in Wisconsin and driven to Oklahoma. These cattle were placed on different tracts of [Cherokee] land, each smaller herd with cowboys appointed to look after it, and with a general foreman to supervise the whole project...

Sometime in the early 1920's the bank at Gore failed, the cattle herd was taken by creditors, and the [Cherokees] who had mortgaged their allotments lost their land. George Smith [Redbird's son] said,

"We bought the cattle when times were good, and then prices went down. We had a bad winter that year with deep snow all over the ground. C. P. Cornelius tried to get more restrictions removed so he could mortgage that land and get some more money to tide us over. But the government found out what the Keetoowahs were trying to do (set up a reservation) and they wouldn't remove any more restrictions from full-blood land."

This failure of the bank probably happened in the post World War I depression in the early 1920's when many sound businesses and banks failed. Many [Cherokees] today feel that C. P. Cornelius cheated them out of their land. But George Smith says, "C. P. was awful smart: you couldn't get ahead of him. The white people was scared of him all the time, watching what he was doing with the Keetoowahs. He was a good man, but the white people were against him, and we had some bad luck" (Thomas 1961).

The story of C. P. Cornelius and the Keetoowahs is typical of a great many Cherokee endeavors between the 1890's and the present time. No one has studied the subject, and it is therefore impossible to even guess how often Cherokees have attempted similar reconstruction of their communities. The spark is far from dead, and similar plans are still being made. For example, members of the Seven Clans Society, whose ceremonial ground is at the Cherokee settlement of Chewy in Adair County, have been working on a plan that includes consolidating what little land they have left in order to set up a communal farm, buying a microbus and setting up a daily "run" through the hills to transport people to the Indian hospital and to their errands in town, establishing a community hall work center and laundromat, founding a co-op store to break the hold that white proprietors of country stores have on their Indian creditors, and forming a credit union. They intend to employ young Indians, give them business experience, and plow the profits into other community development programs.

There can be no doubt that Cherokees do have aspirations toward developing a more secure and self-sufficient economic base for their settlements. In every Cherokee settlement, there are people who have a clear idea of what they would do to make life better for everybody in the settlement — if they just had some capital and some freedom to use it. But Cherokees also doubt that they will be allowed to develop in this way. They are aware that any success on their part will threaten white economic and political control over the region. As the Keetoowah say,

This is about Indians.
Today they are held down.
They are a poor and sorrowful people.
They can't get out of it (Keetoowah Society 1972).

Any talk about what Cherokees might be able to do is soon permeated with a deep and bleak pessimism. Cherokees do not imagine that the destiny of their settlements is theirs to control. Worse, there have been many experiments like the two described, and many failures, and these occur in the context of a society that regards Cherokees as stupid and incompetent. To the things that Cherokees do not believe whites will let them do are added the things that Cherokees themselves have begun to believe they are not "smart" enough to do.

The Cherokee conception of the future is very different than that of white Americans. We consider the future to be unknown and unknowable, and wonder what it will bring. Cherokees know. They are a people who live under prophecy. Their priests have seen into the future and told them what is going to happen. The prophecies are common knowledge among Cherokees, and, although many Cherokees are reluctant to admit (to whites, at least) that they "believe them," it is hard, too, to disbelieve them. The prophecies explain what it is that is happening to the Cherokees right now.

The prophecies date back to the trauma of Oklahoma statehood. In those difficult times, Cherokees realized that they were "going downhill," and the people were deeply worried. Deciding to "do like in the old days," they picked seven men to ask God for direction. The seven men met and, taking fire from the ceremonial ground, went to sit out on a little bluff, where they prayed and fasted around a small fire throughout the night. They received their answer in the form of a long, symbolic dream or vision, the content and interpretation of which is esoteric knowledge known to older Cherokees. The gist of the message was contained in a sort of anecdote, which is familiar to, and readily understandable by, the mass of Cherokees. Toward dawn, one of the old men got thirsty and went to the drinking bucket for a dipperful of water. By the light of the fire, the others could see him pick up the bucket and discover that it was empty; they could see where the water had leaked out. Everyone laughed, and they did without water the rest of the night. Then at daybreak, when they were packing up their things to go home, they looked at the bucket again. It was full of water.

What this meant, they said, was that Cherokees would be like the water. They would dwindle down to nothing, just like water leaking out of that bucket. Everything they had would be taken from them. They would be offered pretty things, things they would think that they wanted, to tempt them away. Pretty soon there wouldn't be any Cherokee left, except the very few who could stand to lose everything and not be tempted. Then, when everything seems lost, the Cherokees will be made whole again. Just as the water miraculously reappeared in the bucket, the Cherokee nation will be restored: the few Cherokees who have stood fast will form its nucleus.

In February 1973, in preparation for this report, I asked a Cherokee who knows the prophecies well to describe what would happen when, as was foreseen, things begin to get better for Cherokees. He said that the prophecies do not say exactly what will happen. If Cherokees who have stayed with their settlements and resisted the seductions of the white man's way of life can sit down together to try and find what they can do for themselves, a plan will be revealed to them. The rebirth of the Cherokees can start with just a handful of men. They have to deliberate among themselves and determine something that suits *them*: "See, if I sit down, think it over, something that works for go a long way . . . Three four, five [of us] sit down . . . . Not going to ask *nobody*! Not going to ask Indian bureau, or old people. Not going to ask nobody. Just going to set down thinking."

The enterprise they decided on will start on a small scale and build slowly. It will take a long time before its results are to be seen: "When they find out something good for them, when they start it, they gone to start three generations. Fourth generation they might change this. That's how long it goin' to start. Bigger. And get bigger and bigger. Now that's what I been telling. Oscar, I told him. Been telling these other people. We got to sit down, think of something. That's what prophecy says. We'll find something good for *us*. We kin start it. They goin' to start it and get bigger and bigger. That's what prophecy says."

And accompanying this economic revival, there will be a new spokesman and a new doctrine — and a new place to meet, to interpret the changes that will keep people socially and emotionally healthy: "All it says, someday . . . one of these fire place [ceremonial grounds] it's going to be called chief. Be one called chief. Anyway, it's going to be called chief all time [Not just a chief in the narrowly political sense of the word]. If they listen to him, they find good medicine for the Indian . . . . They say he's goin' to appear some time 'bout this time, [the one] they gone to call chief. It's goin' to be poor man. Not goin' to be rich. Not goin' to be educated. Just really ordinary Cherokee. But he'll be called chief. He's the one goin' to start it."

The promised restoration of the Cherokees involves both an economic base for Cherokee settlements and a doctrine, a new ceremonial structure that will unify the Cherokee people. It will find its roots in subsistence activities satisfying to the ordinary Cherokee, at one pole, and in teachings drawing on the accumulated knowledge of the Cherokee priesthood, at the other. The Cherokees will rise in a sacredly defined social movement.

White America plans. A nation living under prophecy watches. The question for them is, has our rise started? And by what sign can we know? This is why prophecy is wedded to social movement. For once it is accepted that an authentic sign heralding the turning point has been seen, there can be no doubting the definition of the situation. It means that everything that is tried will have to come out all right. Despair turns to glee, and anguish to energy. In February, things were bad. People were poor, as always; but, worse than that, new tribal programs were intruding on life in the settlements. Cherokees regard their tribal government as an arm of the white establishment, as people pretending to be Indian in order to get their hands on Cherokee money. The rapid development of tribal programs was being met with rapidly developing resentment. People felt pushed around — especially by the tribal housing program, which forcefully merchandized to them houses they were not sure of wanting. And roads the size of highways were suddenly being pushed through the remote hills of Adair County. To poverty now was added final penetration of the protective isolation of Cherokee settlements. It was a worrisome scene. Yet the older Cherokees — men of an age to influence consensus in Cherokee settlements — were gleeful. Looking around them in light of the prophecies, they chortled hopefully, "We're down about as far as we can go!"

THE CHEROKEE ESTABLISHMENT

In 1965, a previously unnoticed natural resource was discovered in eastern Oklahoma. The development of this resource has furnished the base for a major and prestigious industry and, in this economically depressed area, promises to be the single force that will create new jobs, attract new investment, and collect substantial federal subsidies. Its directors are the Cherokee Establishment, and the future of eastern Oklahoma is increasingly in their hands.

The Cherokee Establishment emerged over a period of some fifteen years. Like any establishment, it is an alliance of powerful persons and agencies that are united by a shared conception of the proper state of society, as well as by the mutual political and economic advantages to be gained (or preserved) through continued association. The Cherokee Establishment unites a core of Americans, who are recognized as Cherokees by United States law, with their white and their culturally Cherokee allies.

Eastern Oklahoma's newest industry is headquartered in a complex of buildings just outside the southern limits of Tahlequah, Oklahoma — buildings whose plate-glass windows and rich wood interiors overshadow even the banks in the center of the Cherokees' former capital. In these buildings things are run in an obviously business-like way. Make no mistake, this complex is a showplace — the executive facilities of a modern corporation. Within it, the corporation life-style has been imported to rural Oklahoma, right down to the last detail of a parking lot subdivided according to status and a franchised restaurant for the expense account entertainment of bankers, oilmen, chamber of commerce directors, and visiting high school classes. The buildings belong to the Cherokee nation of Oklahoma, or, as its employees and its supporters usually call it, "the tribe." The complex houses both white-collar employees of "the tribe" and also the entire Tahlequah Agency Office of the United States Bureau of Indian Affairs.

The newly discovered resource that is being developed is the poor Cherokee Indian. From the Cherokee Establishment's point of view, "the tribe" and its present operations are a great American success story. The Cherokees are Indians helping Indians, those who have "made it" showing those who have not how to pull themselves up by their bootstraps. Here are people who have had the discipline to refrain from licking their wounds and nursing a grudge against the United States, who instead work toward their own prosperity. Although there may still be a lot of work left to do, and a large population of poor and disadvantaged Cherokees to upgrade, there is also leadership and an inspiring example of success in the person of W. W. Keeler, principal chief of the Cherokee nation. Born poor and an Indian on an Oklahoma ranch, Mr. Keeler worked himself up to become president of Phillips Petroleum Corporation — and an Indian chief, too. He has been honored by business and civic organizations all over the United States for his personal success and for his devotion to the needs of his people. Five successive presidents have sought his advice on national policy toward American Indians.

When President Johnson declared a war on poverty and it became clear that federally financed programs would be piped into economically stagnant areas through the Office of Economic Opportunity, eastern Oklahomans began to move. When Appalachia became eligible for special support through recognition of its prevasive poverty, Oklahomans realized that "Ozarkia" could equally be brought to the attention of the Congress. Oklahomans began to grasp that having poor Indians in your county could be worth even more than having oil under your land. They came to understand that more money and power is now to be gained from helping Indians than from swindling them. The recent history of eastern Oklahoma appears to revolve around that homely observation.

In order to maintain its credibility and power as the principal helper of Cherokees, the Cherokee Establishment must control the definition of who is and who is not a Cherokee. They must appear to be Indians, for, if not, they might appear to be grafters. To keep up appearances, the Cherokee Establishment manipulates legislation and plays upon public opinion,[9] and is assisted in doing both by the deep and consis-

[9]   A key member of the Cherokee Establishment once claimed that he and his associates "got rid of" local newspaper and television reporters who were critical of activities and policies of the Cherokee nation. While I have been unable to verify this information, reporting of Cherokee Nation activities by the *Muskogee Phoenix*, the *Tulsa Tribune*, and the *Tulsa Daily World* has been noticeably more positive in tone since 1968.

tent myths through which Oklahomans justify the sanctity of Oklahoma social structure.

In the view of Oklahomans, the destruction of the Indian nations is metamorphosed into a tragic necessity that freed Indian individuals from tribal backwardness and permitted their rise according to personal merit in a new commonwealth. The classic expression of this unconscious conviction is to be found in a review by a widely respected native Oklahoma historian, herself the granddaughter of a Choctaw principal chief, of Angie Debo's *Rise and fall of the Choctaw Republic*, in which the reviewer insisted that the title of the book is "a misnomer in itself."

The Choctaw Republic rose but *it did not fall.* From its inception over a century ago, it was planned as a training ground for the Choctaw people, in preparation for a time when they of their own volition would become citizens of their protector Republic, the United States. When at the end of almost three quarters of a century they cast a majority vote in favor of such a step by adopting the Atoka Agreement, they as a nation had attained a position where their leaders were counted among the leaders in the new State of Oklahoma organized soon afterward. Thus, the Choctaw Nation as a republic did not fall: it attained its objective (Wright 1935: 108–120).

How Cherokees are defined affects, then, not only how people in Oklahoma think about Indians, but also how they think about themselves and their own society. The Cherokee Establishment can count on public sentiment, on the desire of Oklahomans to believe that all is right in the world. For so long as W. W. Keeler and his colleagues are defined as "Cherokees," then it follows that the people who live in Cherokee settlements are a neglected population that is making great strides forward under the administration of "successful business and professional leaders of unquestioned ability and integrity." However, if W. W. Keeler is not a Cherokee, then what is an executive of an Oklahoma oil company doing in command of Cherokee affairs? Then, there exists the possibility that the people who live in Cherokee settlements have been made the victims of an outrageous colonial situation — that they have been handed over to the captains of the very industry that reduced them to poverty.

There is no possibility of understanding the state of contemporary Cherokee affairs without first understanding the evolution of the issues involved in the question of who is a Cherokee.

By 1827, the Cherokees already had an elective bicameral legislature presided over by John Ross, their first principal chief. The majority of Cherokees, known as the "Ross party," called upon Ross to resist American pressure to remove them from their homelands. A minority, which later became known as the "Treaty party," sympathized with the signers of the Treaty of New Echota, which in 1835 committed the Cherokees to move west to Indian territory. When the Cherokee nation was reestablished in Indian territory, antagonism between the two parties continued in the form of a series of political murders. Political differences were accompanied by an increasing difference in life-style. Although there were plantation owners and slaveholders in the Ross party, most of that group preferred life based in the traditional Cherokee settlement; and, although there were members of the Treaty party who lived primarily by the hunt, more of them farmed, herded cattle, and engaged in commerce. In the Cherokee nation, the Civil War was also a devastating war between the two bodies of Cherokees. Afterward, their bitterness was so intense that they separated completely. Under Cherokee law until 1907 and under United States law since then the descendants of both factions are equally and legally Cherokee, although for a century they have lived as two separate and antagonistic communities.

After the Civil War, the Cherokees who had been members of the Ross party stayed to the east of the Grand River. They remained a Cherokee-speaking community and continued a life based on the Cherokee settlement, marrying almost entirely among themselves. By the 1880's, they were spoken of as "the full-blood faction" of the Cherokee nation. The culturally Cherokee population of today comes from the "full-blood faction" settlements.

Meanwhile, the people who had formed the Treaty party moved west of the Grand River. They were familiastic more than settlement-minded and became increasingly oriented toward ranching and commerce. Their part of the Cherokee nation was filling up with whites, and members of the Treaty party intermarried extensively with these whites and became part of a Cherokee-white English-speaking community. By the 1880's they were known as the "mixed-blood faction" of the Cherokee nation, which gave rise to the socially and culturally assimilated Americans who are "proud of their Cherokee ancestry."

In preparation for Oklahoma statehood, all citizens of the Cherokee nation were listed on a final roll, which was closed in 1907 and has never since been reopened for addition. Because the roll was a list of the persons who were to receive allotments of Cherokee land, speculators made every attempt to cram it with extra names. A few of the certifiably fraudulent entries have been removed from the roll by court order. A great many of the persons listed are entered as being 1/16, 1/32, 1/64, 1/128, and even 1/256 Cherokee! In all, the roll includes 41,824 names: 8,703 full-blood Indians: 27,916 mixed-blood Indians: 286 whites: and 4,919 freedmen (Negro ex-slaves and their descendants). Under United States federal law this document determines who is legally Cherokee.

It is quite obvious that the *cultural* and the *legal* definitions of

"Cherokee" are in conflict. In this report, "Cherokee" has been used much in the way that the people I call Cherokee define themselves. These Cherokees (in their/my terms) see themselves as an entire *community* of people who *participate* in a specific ancient yet continually evolving way of life that is *permanent* (although not unchanging). Their focus — which is on participation, on the whole body of people who share in their way of life at any given time — tends to be fuzzy about marginal individuals. Because participation in a Cherokee settlement is at the heart of Cherokee self-definition, it is a matter of where an individual's life is rooted. The Cherokee conception allows for the fact that many individuals are lost from the Cherokee way of life; they are "ashamed" of being Cherokee and have "joined up" with whites. But whether this makes such individuals Cherokee or white seems to be a question that Cherokees themselves have understandably avoided for two generations — for what could possibly give any one Cherokee the right to imply to another Cherokee that the latter's grandchildren are not Cherokee?

Oklahomans of course, would heatedly object that this definition is too restrictive. It includes only the full bloods, they would say. When Oklahoma whites wish to specify the people here called "Cherokee," they say "Indians" — meaning "people who live like Indians." They unconsciously use "Cherokee" to refer to a "better class of people."

"Cherokee," as Oklahomans habitually use the word — and as the Cherokee Establishment insists that it be used — has nothing to do with social participation or even with race (although it does mean that the person specified has "some Indian blood"). "Cherokee," as the Cherokee Establishment uses the word, means an individual who is legally entitled to a share of Cherokee assets. The Cherokee nation, from this point of view, was significant as a political entity. When it came to an end, some of its [Cherokee] citizens were just like white men, while a few were still [Cherokee] Indians, but what is significant is that all had the same *legal right*, as *individuals*, to a share of the tribal property. These rights are conceived of as inheritable, and the 1907 final roll was drawn up to facilitate the distribution of individual allotments to Cherokee citizens. A Cherokee is still anyone whose name is on the roll of citizens and anyone descended from a person named on that roll.

Oklahomans are deeply committed to believing that Cherokee culture is temporary and inevitably must vanish. It does not seem inconsistent to them that individuals isolated for generations from the life in Cherokee settlements should be equally as Cherokee as monolingual Cherokees living in those settlements. Indeed, from their point of view, the fact that they have been assimilated into American life is precisely what qualifies such men for leadership over Cherokees. It is, after all, knowledge of white ways, not Indian ways, that counts in the world today.

The Cherokees who live "like Indians" in Cherokee settlements are overwhelmingly outnumbered by the people who have a legal claim to the Cherokee estate. The population of "tribal Cherokees" (a term that will here be used to designate residents of Cherokee settlements) has probably grown to at least 10,000. There is no way to count the number of "legal Cherokees" (that is, the tribal Cherokees together with the greater number of "white" men of Cherokee descent).

The Cherokee claims award was distributed to 44,000 people who by 1962 submitted applications proving that they or a lineal ancestor had been named on the 1907 roll of Cherokees. In 1962 there were more than 9,000 tribal Cherokees (Wahrhaftig 1968). Some refused to apply for claims, maintaining that an individual payment of $260 could never compensate for the loss of a perpetual homeland. Others were ineligible, either because they (or their ancestors) had escaped the enrollment parties, or because they were children of two living enrolled Cherokees. Thus, there can be at most no more than 8,500 tribal Cherokees on the 1962 per capita distribution list. The other 36,500 persons are "whites" and "blacks" of Cherokee descent. The tribal Cherokee are outnumbered by more than four to one.

The Cherokee Establishment protects its power both by legitimizing its own leadership as being Cherokee and by discrediting the opinions of the Cherokee-speaking population that lives in Cherokee settlements, which are as numerous and as populous as in aboriginal times. So long as it remains possible to present the entire legally Cherokee population as being the true constituency of the Cherokee tribe, then the opinions of tribal Cherokees can be passed off as the views of a small (and backward) minority.

The Cherokee Establishment has seen to it that all legal Cherokees can register to vote in Cherokee elections. The result is that culturally white voters living east of the Grand River, in counties with no tribal population at all, as well as culturally white voters living outside of Oklahoma are in the overwhelming majority. Absentee voters provided 41 percent of the total in 1971 (Jordan 1972b). Yet this portion of the electorate selects the "Cherokee leaders" who, in terms of their own cultural standards, they think will best help Indians.

The Cherokee nation's complex outside Tahlequah houses a confusing array of activities. It provides offices for employees of the Cherokee nation and for the Tahlequah Agency of the Bureau of Indian Affairs. It is a center for the coordination of the Cherokee National Housing Authority, Cherokee Nation Industries, the Cherokee Neighborhood Youth Corps, the Cherokee Skills Center, and many other projects dealing with job training and education.

Closely tied to this complex is the Cherokee National Historical Society, which claims that it annually brings more than $10.6 million dollars into eastern Oklahoma by running a replica of an ancient Cherokee village and a "historical" pageant. Northeastern State College works in close alliance with Cherokee nation administrators through their mutual involvement in various bilingual education projects, which reach into local school systems in the neighboring counties. The activities of the Cherokee nation and the Cherokee Establishment that radiates from this center are a pastiche. They just grew, and grew fast — ostensibly to benefit Cherokees in their rural settlements, but more realistically to claim federal grants and funds.

No organizational chart relating these activities, projects, and programs to one another exists. They sprang up so fast that their structure has never been systematized. Yet beneath the apparent diversity there is one consistent principle of organization. Power is, and always has been, centralized in the hands of a culturally white elite. The Cherokee Establishment is an empire that has evolved through four distinguishable phases.

From 1907 until 1948, the Department of the Interior held that under United States law the Cherokee nation could no longer exist as a legal or political entity. For the sole purpose of having someone to sign deeds disposing of Cherokee national property, it was customary for the president of the United States to appoint a principal chief of the Cherokees. Some of these "chiefs" were appointed for a twenty-four hour term. The BIA managed the affairs of individual Cherokees whose lands were restricted from sale and held in trust by the United States government. Cherokees living traditionally in rural settlements were otherwise ignored, and eastern Oklahoma society was presided over by a local elite that proudly traced its roots back to distinguished ancestors among the culturally white branch of the Cherokees.

The first phase in the development of the Cherokee Establishment was precipitated by passage of the Indian Claims Act of 1946, which invited Indian suits against the United States government. Bartley Milam was then the token, federally appointed chief. In 1948, the BIA and Chief Milam called for a meeting in Tahlequah to select attorneys to prosecute a tribal claims case. They hoped to win monetary settlements for Cherokee lands fraudulently disposed of by the United States government. At this "convention," Milam appointed an executive committee, which in turn selected the tribal attorneys. When decisions were presented to the few dozen people present for a voice vote of ratification, the handful of tribal Cherokees who had attended withdrew from the convention. Milam died shortly thereafter, and W. W. Keeler, originally appointed by Milam to represent Texas Cherokees on the executive committee, became principal chief. Keeler,

appointed chief by the Secretary of the Interior on the recommendation of the local BIA agent, and a committee selected by Keeler or by
his predecessor have directed Cherokee affairs since 1948. Members of
the executive committee have been culturally white individuals, locally
regarded as being from "old families" of the region's elite.

A woman who was a member of the Cherokee executive committee
from 1953 until her resignation in 1966 painted a vivid portrait of
its procedures in testimony she presented to a Senate Special Subcommittee:

Comparatively few of the Cherokee people, of course, came to Tahelquah and
participated in the election of this Executive Committee. The election, however, gave it a semblance of popular approval. This committee has been
continued to the present time [1968], though no election by the people has
ever been held since 1941. New members of this committee have been
appointed by the chief from time to time as needed. After the appointment
they usually go through the form of an election of the new appointees by the
committee itself. Thus it has come to be purely a self perpetuating body, in
reality appointed by the chief. At first these members were supposed to live in
the district they represented, but this required site has long since been ignored.
They are now selected from anywhere. The present committee has four
lawyers on it.

This committee is altogether a confirming body. It never acts against the will
of the chief. It always confirms his suggestions. It in no way sponsors the will of
the Cherokee people, whom it nominally is supposed to represent ... It is not
recognized in any way by the Federal Government.

In other words, the chief, appointed by the Department of the Interior, is
the sole ruling agency of the Cherokee tribe. The Cherokee people haven't a
word to say about any of their affairs. The chief is as absolute in authority as a
ruler could ever be ... " (Special Subcommittee on Indian Education 1968:
559).

Between 1948 and 1962, the Cherokee chief and his executive
committee performed three functions. They prosecuted Cherokee
claims against the United States government, perpetuated the myth of
Cherokee assimilation, and worked energetically to deflect any
"separatist" activities among Indians, and dispensed charity to "needy
full bloods." They did little more until 1962, when the Cherokee tribe
acquired $2,000,000 and additional projects could be considered.
Anticipating awards in the tens of millions of dollars, the chief and
executive committee contracted four attorneys, who agreed to prosecute Cherokee claims in return for 10 percent of any settlement. The
chief and executive committee found a way to perpetuate the myth of
Cherokee assimilation in dramatic form, creating a "Cherokee National Holiday," which is still held in Tahlequah each fall. The holiday
is a memorial to the death of the Cherokee nation, an occasion upon

which members of the establishment's elite present flowery eulogies to the past accomplishments of the Cherokees.

In addition to this manipulation of social symbols, executive committee members have extended their ties to Indian politicians in other tribes. Together with their counterparts among the Creeks, Choctaws, Chicasaws, and Seminoles, they formed a Five Civilized Tribes Intertribal Council and, more importantly, they had a hand in the policies of the National Congress of American Indians from the time that organization was founded. Wherever they suspected that Indians might demand more tribal autonomy, or accuse the Department of Interior of mismanaging tribal resources, or cast doubt on the inevitability of Indian assimilation into the American melting pot, delegates of the Cherokee executive committee went.

In 1961, Professor Sol Tax of the University of Chicago coordinated a massive conference at which it was hoped that Indians from all over the country might author a "Declaration of Indian Purpose," advising the new administration of their wishes. At a meeting of the Five Civilized Tribes Intertribal Council, Cherokee delegates advised that the meeting was a Communist-backed effort to stir up discontent among Indians. One of those present recalled:

The chief had been on a trip, with several other oil men, to Russia some time before this. When he returned the executive committee was given a rather bizarre account of the trip, bugged rooms, things they already knew about the chief. Indians here in the United States are being kept in leg-irons [the Russians said]. The chief [said he] asked where they got their information and was told from the University of Chicago.

When this meeting at Chicago was announced, the chief, tribal lawyers, and others, began plans to send representatives to see what went on there. In the executive meeting that spring some of the main discussion was this Chicago meeting. It was decided that two of the tribal lawyers would go, which they did. The resolutions passed by the Chicago conference were rather ineffective, so far as our information goes. The lawyers returned quite jubilant and recounted what they had done blow by blow (Special Subcommittee 1968: 556).

The Cherokee executive committee created the Cherokee Foundation, Incorporated, in 1952, to "improve the welfare, culture, health and morale of the Cherokees." The foundation was "administered by successful business and professional leaders of unquestioned ability and integrity" (*Cherokee Nation News*, September 23, 1969). It was something of a "charity drive," supported by tax-deductible contributions solicited from local businessmen. The foundation presented baskets of food and clothing to Cherokee families at Christmas time and once "bought a special type mattress for $635 for a young Cherokee,

25 years of age, who is a paraplegic" (Special Subcommittee 1968: 973). Until 1962, the direction of Cherokee affairs was a civic duty performed by prominent and socially responsible members of eastern Oklahoma's older elite families.

The Cherokee Establishment entered a second stage of development in 1962, when the tribe came into possession of about two million dollars in funds left over after per capita distribution of an award from the Indian claims court. The chief used this money to finance a number of projects proposed to him by business interests in eastern Oklahoma, local officials of the BIA, and advisors at the Phillips Petroleum Company — with the sanction of the socially prominent citizens of Cherokee descent who sat on the executive committee.

Cherokee money was used to underwrite projects that enriched the general economy of eastern Oklahoma, under the justification that these projects generated needed jobs for destitute Cherokees. But the man who was the first business manager of the Cherokee nation said, "The Cherokee tribe is controlled essentially by non-Indians. They don't do anything that will harm non-Indians. Fact, they go even further. They don't do anything that will not *benefit* non-Indians. Of all the programs that the Cherokee tribe has, none were started with the prime objective of helping Indians (Wahrhaftig 1972). When new programs were announced by the Office of Economic Opportunity, the Cherokee Establishment moved to incorporate and control them. The result was a hodgepodge of projects and programs, opportunistically embarked upon with neither the knowledge nor the consent of the Cherokees residing in Cherokee settlements.

The court of claims awarded the Cherokees nearly $15 million as an additional payment for the Cherokee Outlet. After the per capita distribution of this award in October 1964, a residue of about two million dollars remained in the tribal fund. Chief Keeler and a small number of his associates "wanted a fund left in the treasury to use in the promotion of future projects of their own choosing" (Special Subcommittee 1968: 560), and this was arranged.

The group's most controversial proposal was the financing of the early activities of the Cherokee National Historical Society, which was incorporated in April 1963. The society was backed by leading politicians, bankers, chamber of commerce officials, BIA employees, and distinguished citizens of Cherokee descent. Its principal project has been an unabashed imitation of tourist attractions already developed on the Cherokee reservation in North Carolina. There was a great deal of publicity about the employment that would be generated by this attraction, but the benefits in the form of wages for Cherokees are minor compared with the benefits to the overall economy of eastern Oklahoma. The president of Tahlequah Chamber of Commerce called the project "the most exciting quality tourist attraction in the area — a magnet, it draws tourism to other parts of Tahlequah." The project was seen as a major economic "break" for the area. Although the Cherokee National Historical Society has financed this project by raising hundreds of thousands of dollars in grants — principally from EDA — the seed money was provided from Cherokee tribal funds. The business manager of the Cherokee nation from 1967 to 1969 said, "The tribe loans money to the Cherokee Historical Society at prime interest rate with no security. The initial loan of $100,000 was finally repaid — with money from EDA. But every time the historical society goes broke, the tribe loans them money again" (Wahrhaftig 1972).

Tribal Cherokees have no part in deciding how Cherokee residual funds are to be invested, and even the tribal executive committee seems not to have been informed of planning. A former member of the executive committee testified:

Everyone knows the value of a surprise move, and none better than the chief, as he is a past master in handling people and situations. At a committee meeting in 1965 that was called to discuss housing there was present at least seventy-five people — visitors, Cherokees, and Bureau officials. Housing was discussed, but quite unexpectedly the chief asked the Executive Committee to allow a hundred thousand dollars from the Cherokee residual fund for the Cherokee cultural project. It seems quite evident now that the chief must have had an understanding as to who he intended to appoint as manager of this project. The writer was the only abstaining vote. If there is any question or objection to what the chief has done, the chief assures the objector that the Executive Committee passed the measure. In this way the responsibility is shifted and the objector is silenced (Special Subcommittee on Indian Education 1968: 557).

A clique or "inner circle" within the growing Cherokee Establishment appears to have been making the major decisions.

A former tribal official says bitterly, "Keeler's idea was for the tribe to have a desk in Harrington's [the BIA Superintendent] office in Muskogee.... He never could imagine the Cherokee tribe as anything but a legal fiction for the BIA to work through." Keeler, as a principal executive of Phillips Petroleum, drew on Phillips Petroleum's Director of Special Cooperative Projects to devise means of attracting new industries into the Cherokee area. Maximum advantage was taken of wage subsidies available through the BIA on-the-job training programs and sites furnished free of charge by the Cherokee tribe. For a subsidiary of Phillips Petroleum that by 1966 was employing 29 workers, 20 of them [legally] Indian, in the manufacture of plastic pipe, the tribe even acquired 25 houses "near the industrial area where Indians are currently employed and where many jobs will be created for them" (Special Subcommittee on Indian Education 1968: 975).

However, it does seem that the Cherokee tribe invested large amounts of money to create a very few jobs. The tribe's first general manager says that the Cherokees "sunk over $150,000 in Glassmaster," a company that manufactures pleasure boats in Grove, Oklahoma. "Not only does this plant not employ many Cherokees," he said, "they haven't paid anything back. They were only obliged to sign a five-year lease, and they don't have to begin repaying capital until after five years." Glassmaster employed 11 [legal] Cherokees in 1968 and 14 in 1970.

During this second period, the elite who were directing Cherokee affairs became very secretive about their activities — and they still are. A former member of the tribal executive committee says, "Minutes don't mean a thing. Whenever they want to talk about something important or the least bit controversial, Keeler says 'Now this is off the record.'" When I asked the former general manager of the Cherokee nation where I could get some reliable figures about tribal operations, he laughed a little hysterically and said, "There aren't any. A budget is passed. Then when the tribe runs out of money on a project, they just vote more. When that runs out, they vote more. They never amend the budget. They don't even have profit and loss sheets on such operations as the restaurant [that the tribe invested in]. In that operation, tribal funds were channeled through BIA which has its own way to disguise losses on accounting sheets. It used to take eight weeks for us to requisition the tribe's own funds from the BIA" (Wahrhaftig 1972).

One reason for secretiveness, perhaps, is that some costly blunders may have been made. The Cherokees built a plant in Tahlequah for McCall Manufacturing Company of Greenville, South Carolina, expecting that employment would reach 125 by 1969, but McCall never materialized and the tribe was stuck with the facilities. There has been gossip around Tahlequah that the Cherokee Foundation had guaranteed the loan by a Bartlesville Bank of $250,000 to McCall and that the funds have disappeared into South Carolina. Some unexplained factor also upset highly publicized plans for Bates Manufacturing Company to move into a new plant in Pryor, Oklahoma, which was furnished by the Cherokees.

The rationale for the kind of development favored by the Cherokee Establishment has always been that it would lead to the "economic upgrading" of individual "Indian people" [tribal Cherokees] into the overall social and economic system of Oklahoma. The "stated goals" (a phrase used with monotonous insistence) were concerned with "trying to educate the [white] people to understand the Indian, while ... the Indian must learn to pat himself on the back and not be afraid to set his goals big." As if to refute these premises, around 1965 the presence of tribal Cherokees with aspirations of their own, living in traditionally organized settlements, became undisguisable. First, there were a number of efforts by tribal Cherokees to protest the executive committee's use of Cherokee funds. They argued that tribal Cherokees had no voice in decisions that were made about the disposition of Cherokee money; that they wanted the funds used for directly charitable purposes, such as helping the poor, sick, and homeless in their own settlements; that when they were employed on tribal projects they were really being forced to work for their own money; and that the Cherokee National Historical Society's village and pageant misrepresented Cherokee culture and made a commercialized travesty of Cherokee sacred rites (Fites n.d.).

Some of the arguments of tribal Cherokees were sympathetically reported by Tulsa newspapers. Then the Carnegie Corporation Cross-Cultural Education Project of the University of Chicago published the results of the first modern research on Cherokee demography and the socioeconomic conditions of the tribal Cherokee population. These research reports, distributed in a bilingual Cherokee/English edition written for relatively unschooled Cherokee readers (Wahrhaftig 1966b), were also summarized in local newspapers. The reports forced whites and Indians to lay to rest the myth of Cherokee assimilation and prosperity.

Later, when officials of the recently created Community Action Program of the Office of Economic Opportunity invited proposals from eastern Oklahoma, white politicians quickly tried to define the entire northeastern Oklahoma region as one "community," but CAP personnel were initially sympathetic to a more sociologically realistic definition of a "community" (Wahrhaftig 1966b). They responded to individual Cherokee settlements as potentially viable communities, and they held unprecedented meetings in which the proceedings were fully interpreted into Cherokee. Although the usual tribal Cherokee response to meetings is to send an observant young man to listen and report back to residents of his settlement, some five hundred settlement residents attended an all-day meeting with CAP spokesmen held in southern Adair County. The crowd was enthusiastic and Cherokee settlements quickly responded to the OEO with proposals of their own (Wahrhaftig 1965).

Next, as an experiment in "action anthropology" designed to study conditions under which literacy and bilingualism can be promoted, the Carnegie Project subsidized tribal Cherokees, who produced a Cherokee-language newspaper and Cherokee-language radio programs, as well as other Cherokee-language and bilingual textbooks, informative guides, and readers (Walker 1965: Spade and Walker 1966; United States Public Health Service n.d.). Tribal Cherokees began to sense that it was not impossible for Cherokees to do things as

Cherokees in a Cherokee way. In this context of hope that Cherokee settlements might at last be on the move, tribal Cherokees again turned to the eternal first item on their agenda, their right to hunt and to fish, and the Five County Northeastern Oklahoma Cherokee Organization quickly emerged.

The initial response by the Cherokee Establishment was to attribute these events in Cherokee settlements to the activities of Communist agents and "outside agitators" who were preaching hatred of white people to Cherokee "full bloods." Their next response consisted of attempts either to compete with or to absorb the projects initiated in Cherokee settlements. The Cherokee tribe began publishing its own newspaper (in English). The tribe and the BIA each hired Cherokee-speaking community workers — for the first time. A Cherokee Public Relations Association was organized to explain what the executive committee was doing with Cherokee funds. The proposals made to the CAP by tribal Cherokees were sidetracked in the political quagmire of the OEO regional office in Austin, Texas, and the official most responsible for encouraging them was kicked upstairs; thus the OEO was taught to never again relate to Cherokees in any way other than through the chief and executive committee. Other branches of OEO awarded contracts to the Cherokee government, for a Cherokee Neighborhood Youth Corps and other programs. Through this process, "the tribe" was saddled with a great number of unrelated programs. Some of these they may have wished to administer, but others they had to take on simply to prevent other institutions — or still worse, the tribal Cherokees — from running them.

Another response pursued by the Cherokee Establishment was to work intensively on a program that would impress both tribal Cherokees and the public that "the tribe" did have the interests of Cherokee settlements at heart. In June 1965, a Cherokee Housing Authority Board of Commissioners was established and five Cherokees were later appointed to serve a (powerless) advisory committee. The board promptly submitted the first of a continuing series of proposals for low-rent and mutual-help housing to be supplied to Cherokee settlements under the auspices of the HAA. Although most housing in Cherokee Settlements is dilapidated by the United States Census standards, no one troubled to ask the Cherokees who lived in such houses how high new housing stood on their list of priorities.

By 1967, Cherokee affairs were in a state of confusion. A bewildering assortment of programs were in operation, many of them run by hastily created subsidiary organizations. Areas of jurisdiction and interrelationships were unclear, and there was no overall plan for development. The only coherent factor was that all the programs were run by like-minded men, personally appointed by the Cherokee chief with ratification by his appointed executive committee, and were firmly interlocked by overlapping boards of directors. BIA personnel, Cherokee tribal directors, OEO administrators, welfare department supervisors, bankers, business organizations, elected politicians, school and college administrators, and, to some extent, the local press — all were becoming increasingly dependent on programs generated by the Cherokees' two million dollars. And all looked forward to future claims settlements, which are expected to result in awards of between fifteen and fifty million dollars.

In addition, businessmen and bureaucrats were beginning to take advantage of a new aspect of Cherokee exploitability. In the usual situation, a colonial power may extract native resources and use them for its own purposes, or a colonial system may harness native labor for its own use. The system in which Cherokees are enmeshed adds a new dimension to these relationships. The very *presence* of Cherokees is negotiable. In the case of nonhuman resources, the pattern is well established. If a firm can prove a reasonable possibility that there is oil under land it controls, it can raise money. If its drilling operations are large enough, they will generate a host of new businesses — suppliers of drilling tools, derrick builders, cafes to feed workers, stores to supply them. All of these businesses are economically and often politically dependent on the firm that initiated exploitation. If the firm fails to strike oil, the new businesses that it has generated, which now depend on it, will clamor that it be granted additional funds for continued drilling.

The War on Poverty converted Cherokees into an asset similar to oil. When the Office of Economic Opportunity, the Economic Development Administration, or the Office of Education become convinced that a poor and "culturally deprived" target population exists, they will grant funds for the development of this population. The resulting programs may be of considerable benefit to the "target population." The resulting investment may benefit local "Cherokee-helping" businesses even more.

By pointing to the existence of a large population of non-English-speaking Cherokees in Cherokee settlements, the Cherokee government has recruited money for a number of bilingual education programs, which have added employment and have also added to the power and prestige of Northeastern State College and the county school systems. Ironically, the "Cherokee-helping" business has been founded and managed by the architects of the social system that impoverished Cherokees and keeps them poor. Unlike timber and oil resources, the supply of poor Cherokees is not likely to be exhausted. The possibilities for continuing development of the Cherokee-development industry are unlimited.

In June and July 1967, the small body of people who govern Cherokee affairs began to consolidate a position. The tribe acquired a general manager, adopted a plan of operation, and opened its first tribal office, in Tahlequah — steps that inaugurated a third stage in the development of the Cherokee Establishment. Between 1967 and the fall of 1971, in addition to further institutionalizing itself, the Cherokee tribe greatly expanded its commitment to build new houses in Cherokee settlements, altered its methods of importing industrial employment into the Cherokee area, and tried to make it appear that tribal Cherokees had a voice in decisions made for them by the tribal government. Although new personnel were appointed, decision-making power remained concentrated among the chief and his appointed executive committee.

The newly hired general manager apparently tried to differentiate "the tribe" from the BIA. (As he tells it, the chief and executive committee were reluctant to approve particulars of his plan.) The finances and personnel of the Cherokee nation and the BIA were thoroughly intertwined in 1967. When, after nineteen years, the Cherokee nation finally opened an office where Cherokees could walk in and speak with representatives of the people who decided their tribal affairs, two of the five employees staffing it were BIA people who were paid with Cherokee tribal funds. The tribe's first general manager claims that,

The tribal office building was my idea. I thought the tribe had to have identity . . . . Keeler never could imagine the Cherokee tribe as anything but a legal fiction for the BIA to work through. When I wanted to rent a place in Tahlequah for a tribal office, the Chief really dragged his feet. Then, later, they thought about building a building to lease to the BIA. Keeler wanted simply to put a couple of extra rooms in that one to house tribal affairs. I refused to build that one. Eventually they built the BIA a building with no provisions for the tribe's office at all. Keeler turned down proposals for an office building for the tribe twice. He finally approved the idea the third time I submitted a set of plans (Jordon 1972b: 128).

At the time the general manager was hired, the Cherokee tribe had already started construction of a restaurant and an arts and crafts salesroom near its industrial site on the outskirts of Tahlequah. The general manager says, "This was a plan from the BIA. They said it would give Cherokees pride in their culture! The project was financed with tribal money, but the workers were being paid by the BIA with federal checks. The first thing I did was get some checks printed."

With an office near Cherokee settlements as a base of operations, the Cherokee nation staff began to push their housing programs *within Cherokee settlements.* Previously, Cherokees had been summoned to meetings held in county seats, where they were informed of programs devised for their benefit; they were expected to come to BIA offices to submit their application. Now "the tribe" began to convene meetings in church houses at rural Cherokee settlements. If Cherokees responded through their usual tactic of passive resistance, sending a few young men to listen closely and later tell older men what they heard, the Cherokee nation staff spoke its piece (although usually without even *ad hoc* interpretation, and no "official" translation into Cherokee of the terms of a housing project has ever been attempted). Then the staff waited for word to get around and convened another meeting. They were persistent salesmen.

Housing program proposals were altered continuously, in a sequence that cannot be detailed here. Different projects were requested at different times, each with different building designs, different terms, and different contract regulations — until there were eighteen programs in all. This situation was thoroughly confusing, especially when Cherokees who did not understand that there was not one housing program but many attempted to compare notes. Meanwhile, the Cherokee Establishment was expanded by corporations attracted to Oklahoma by the prospect of housing contracts, the most active being the New York-based International Basic Economy Corporation (IBEC).

The Phillips Petroleum Company is keenly aware of the public relations benefits that accrue both to specific corporations and to the free enterprise system in general, when business helps American Indians (Phillips Petroleum Co. n.d.). The company's Special Cooperative Projects engineered "the tribe's" programs for developing jobs for Indians. The earlier programs involved creating a package of subsidies, such as those available through the Bureau of Indian Affairs On-the-Job Training Program, which might tempt employers to locate in the Cherokee area. The first taker was a Phillips subsidiary company. Soon, Special Projects changed its tactics; instead of trying to attract companies, it used available subsidies to attract contracts that the Cherokee nation could set up a factory to fulfill. Cherokee Nation Industries, Incorporated (CNI) was established in March 1969 to produce electronic components under a training grant from the Great Western Electric Company of Oklahoma City. As new contracts are brought in, CNI has expanded its facilities in Tahlequah and Stilwell. Although creation of CNI made it appear that Cherokees were shaping their own development, in reality Cherokee employment became increasingly contingent on the good will of Phillips Petroleum, with no assurances that its future resources or knowledge of past contracts would be available to future Cherokee chiefs and administrations.

The Cherokee Establishment was embarrassed when television networks featured poor tribal Cherokees in documentary films on poverty, particularly when it was revealed that the affairs of these thousands of Cherokees were managed by a federally appointed chief and a committee of prominent citizens who qualified as Cherokee only through a legal technicality. Hearings on the Study of the Education of Indian Children, presided over by Senator Robert Kennedy in a Cherokee settlement in 1968, produced testimony highly critical of the tribe's "leadership" (Special Subcommittee on Indian Education 1968). Something had to be done about the obvious lack of articulation between the Cherokee Establishment and Cherokee settlements.

In addition to underwriting television specials of its own, the Cherokee Establishment responded to criticism by setting up a system of "democratically elected community representatives" to link Cherokee settlements to the tribal government, and by working — through the Department of the Interior and the Oklahoma Congressional delegation — toward the drafting of laws authorizing a Cherokee election (on terms it could accept).

A Cherokee-speaking community worker was assigned to organize the tribal Cherokee settlements. (In the vocabulary of the Cherokee Establishment, this employee was called a "Cherokee tribal field specialist" until 1971 and a "community development officer" thereafter; the tribal Cherokees were called "field traditional Cherokees" [Special Subcommittee on Indian Education 1968: 984].) At meetings that were usually held in Cherokee Indian Baptist church houses, residents of Cherokee settlements were encouraged to elect community representatives and assistants, who were then invited to meet as a body at the tribal offices. Although publicity statements about the community representatives emphasized their role as advisors to Cherokees' administrators, their main function was to serve as a pipeline through which tribal programs could be "explained" to residents of Cherokee settlements.

The community representatives had difficulty in understanding that they were intended to be powerless. After discussing the fact that their wishes and work were not being heeded by the tribe's directorate, they voted to draft their own bylaws and to define and clarify their own existence. In 1970 they were granted voting privileges within the Cherokee executive committee, whose meetings they are now allowed to attend. (Simultaneously, the tribal chief suggested that he might appoint vice-chiefs in each community, thereby moving to contain this brief rebellion by creating higher ranking community representatives under his personal control.)

Concurrent with the development of a system of community representatives, the Cherokee Establishment, together with its counterparts in other civilized tribes, set about obtaining legislation authorizing an election, on terms that would least upset the existing distribution of power. Five features in the resulting legislation were critical. First, at least some of the Five Tribes Chiefs would not consent to legislation that committed them to holding election. An Oklahoma congressman introduced a bill in 1969 authorizing each tribe to *select* its principal officer. The bill was revised to state that the principal chief be *popularly selected* (after the Department of the Interior had suggested that such officials should be popularly *elected*). Second, existing claims payment rolls were established as the official basis for voting lists, ensuring that the electorate would consist of legal Cherokees, not just tribal Cherokees. Third, the "officially recognized tribal spokesman and/or governing entity" was charged with writing the election rules and regulations, which were then to be subject to the approval of the secretary of the interior. Fourth, it was specifically stated that "Nothing in this Act shall prevent any such incumbent . . . as being selected as the principal chief." Fifth, the legislation bound tribes only to "popularly select" a principal chief, without stipulating the means of organizing, staffing, or operating the tribal government (Jordan 1972b).

In an election held on August 14, 1971, W. W. Keeler was popularly selected principal chief of the Cherokee nation by an overwhelming 7,495 votes out of 10,086 cast. Two features of the election were notable. Tribal Cherokees passively resisted the election by not registering to vote; and a remarkable amount of money and energy was spent by non-Indian businessmen on behalf of "their" candidate. In February 1971, businesses and organizations in eastern Oklahoma received letters stating, "First, let me say that I am not writing this letter in my official capacity as secretary-manager of the Tahlequah Chamber of Commerce. I am writing it as [personal name]." The letter continued, "it seems imperative to me that we, as residents of Northeastern Oklahoma Cherokee Country, both Indian and non-Indian alike, need to insist that Bill Keeler continue on as leader of the Cherokee Tribe . . . ."

In similar style, the *Tahlequah Times* reported on May 6 that "Members of Citizens Concerned for Cherokee Leadership met with Keeler last Wednesday (April 28) and presented him with a petition urging him to run for re-election" (*Tahlequah Times* 1971). An officer of one of the largest banks in northeastern Oklahoma (himself a legal Cherokee) sent out personal letters in support of Keeler to customers who had heavy obligations to the bank (Jordan 1972b). And at the end of June, Green Country, Incorporated (the promotional group whose executive vice-president is supplied by Phillips Petroleum) staged a television ceremony at which Keeler, who was presented an award, was described as "a person who can talk business with one of the biggest oil executives in Australia one minute: meet with the President of the

United States the next minute: and eat and mingle with a fullblood Cherokee at Bull Hollow" (*Cherokee Nation News,* June 29, 1971). Keeler's victory was a victory for the Cherokee Establishment.

In these five years the Cherokee Establishment has come a long way from the legal fiction which once hid behind the BIA and had so little sense of its own autonomy that it didn't even have checks with its own name to its present position as *the* establishment of eastern Oklahoma.

With Keeler's election to a four-year term as principal chief, the development of the Cherokee Establishment has entered its fourth and latest stage. Now "the tribe" is *the* power in eastern Oklahoma. An official of the tribe said, "Before his election, the Chief was kind of cautious in his programs. He felt like he lacked a mandate. But now he feels like he is 'the choice of the people'. He has bold ideas, and pretty soon the tribe will be dealing with fifty to one hundred million dollars." The bold ideas have yet to be announced, nor is there yet any indication that there exists a coherent economic plan for the future, but there are already indications of the direction in which the Cherokee Establishment is moving. There will be a greater appearance of democracy, a greater concentration of power, and heavier pressure towards assimilation.

In October 1971, Keeler began to restructure the Cherokee tribal government. The executive committee was finally dissolved. Keeler announced that he would appoint a cabinet of Cherokees familiar with tribal programs to act in its stead, but this was to be provisional, for he intended the Cherokee tribe to be governed under new bylaws and a newly revised constitution. The new constitution will define the manner in which Cherokees will be represented by their tribal government, and, when it is ratified, presumably the old pattern of concentrating power by direct appointment of tribal officials will appear to be ended. In reality, continuity of power will be ensured, because all twenty-four members of the new Cherokee Constitutional Revision Committee, announced in February 1972, were appointed directly by the present chief. No timetable for writing the new constitution has been announced.

Cherokee officials and BIA personnel formerly indulged in rituals of mutual congratulation, but the tribe is now cool toward the bureau, especially at levels above that of the local area superintendent. When students demonstrated against conditions at Chilocco Indian Boarding school, Keeler accused the BIA of "not only permitting outside militants to come to Chilocco, but apparently . . . encouraging them." In a long article reprinted in the Cherokee tribal newspaper, Keeler declared that "the majority of Oklahoma Indians, and most of the older Indians in other areas, do not buy militant programs. On the other hand, it appears the Bureau of Indian Affairs goes out of its way to back up militant groups" (*Cherokee Nation News*, January 25, 1972). Several Oklahoma informants believed that the falling out between the Cherokee nation and BIA occurred when "young Turks" (as they were often called in bureau newsletters) appointed to high BIA positions called for the compulsory rotation of area superintendents, a reform that would have jeopardized one of the key relationships underlying the Cherokee Establishment. Whatever the reasons, the Cherokee nation is now proposing to administer services formerly entrusted to the BIA. The tribe is especially interested in taking over the Sequoyah Indian School, a BIA boarding school outside Tahlequah that serves children from the Five Tribes.

In the year since the election of the Cherokee principal chief, the Cherokee Establishment seems to have intensified its efforts to establish a definition of the Cherokee that, racist in the extreme, glorifies assimilation. Public honors are heaped on individuals with traces of Cherokee blood who have distinguished themselves in American life, no matter how distant their connection with existing Indian settlements. In 1972, a recently deceased admiral, who "remains the highest ranking person of American Indian descent in United States military history," was named to the Cherokee Hall of Fame. By request of Chief Keeler the tribal newspaper is now publishing articles "covering persons of Cherokee Indian blood who have achieved in the various fields of entertainment, industry, the professions, the arts, etc." A two-part profile featured Anita Bryant — singer, beauty contestant, author, and outstanding example of love, faith and trust in Christ and her religion" — whose father is French and whose mother is "Dutch, Scotch, Irish, English and of Cherokee descent." These are the models of success revered today by the Cherokee establishment.

What kind of society shall Cherokees live in? The Cherokee Establishment has never prepared an explicit statement of its philosophy nor described its vision for the future. No overall economic or cultural plan exists, nor any criteria for evaluating the effectiveness of development. The Cherokee Establishment acts extemporaneously, convinced that any development is *de facto* good for tribal Cherokees so long as it does not violate the unwritten laws governing the relationship of tribal Cherokees to America. This set of laws, embodied in monuments, symbols, the content of interaction, and pervasive social expectations, defines a relationship in which tribal Cherokees are expected to utilize "opportunities" offered by the tribe as a means of advancing themselves toward "first class citizenship."

The first such law is that what is done is done. Cherokees are expected to accept unprotestingly their station in society and to repeat this acceptance to themselves as a catechism. On the eve of a visit from the Commissioner of Indian Affairs, the community representatives worried about the possibility of a demonstration, although they did not wish to say so except by indirection. A tribal Cherokee who is also a strong supporter of the present tribal government orated before the group. He told the story of a man who buried his tomahawk, but the winds blew and the lands eroded. In time the handle of the tomahawk cropped up, and he had to bury it deeper, again and again. The orator said that the mission of the Cherokees is to bury the past deeper and to work for now.

Next, and perhaps most crucial, Cherokees are expected to internalize American ideas about the importance of one's individual status. They are to work their way up the ladder according to the rules that govern American social and economic behavior, and to accept, as Americans have, the consequent disruption of settlement and family.

Cherokees are also expected to agree that, with hard work, they can overcome their "racial inferiority." The point is seldom presented this nakedly, but it is clearly to be seen in the compulsion of the Cherokee Establishment to reassure the public, as though there were reason to doubt, that "The fact that Indians have excellent, inherent manual dexterity, eye-hand coordination, and an appreciation for fine detail equips them to become outstanding employees in a wide variety of occupations" (Phillips Petroleum Company n.d.). This point is over and over repeated to Cherokees.

Finally, Cherokees must subscribe to a monumentalization of their lives. Just as the Cherokee village and pageant reinterpret Cherokee history, making it appear that Cherokees improved on their savage situation by embracing the Amercian ideals of education and toil, a Cherokee who is lucky enough to find work at Cherokee Nation Industries, thus bringing a paycheck home to his or her family, must also expect that his efforts will be on public display as living testimony to the progress that minorities can make under the American system of free enterprise.

While the Cherokee Establishment has been expanded considerably in size, power, and status, it has delivered to tribal Cherokee settlements principally houses and a few jobs. New houses are conspicuous everywhere. There is no doubting that the greatest part of the housing programed by the Cherokee Tribal Housing Authority is actually inhabited by tribal Cherokees. The complexity of the terms under which the houses have been acquired is staggering. By June 1972, 28 separate housing projects had been approved — each with its own set of terms involving from 10 to 150 housing units, for a total of 1,646. At this time 309 units were completed and occupied, 198 were partially completed, 588 were under construction — and the paperwork preceding construction was in process for an additional 551 units (*Cherokee Nation News* June 27, 1972).

The Cherokees who are acquiring houses (1,407 of them) through the twenty-one tribally sponsored mutual-help projects commit themselves to a twenty-year-long relationship with a federal-tribal bureaucracy. Although the Cherokee Nation Housing Authority (CNHA) never phrases the matter this way, tribal Cherokees realistically perceive the program in terms of their potential obligations within a new relationship. To acquire a house, an eligible Cherokee must provide an acre of land. The CNHA states that "How the participants acquire the acre is of no consequence to us, as long as it is clear of any encumbrances and is transferable to the Housing Authority." In practice, if the participant owns restricted land, he applies to the BIA to have restrictions removed from an acre, then deeds his land to the Housing Authority until such time as the house is paid for. On approval of these arrangements, the participant and the CNHA enter into a contract. The participant and/or any adult member(s) of his household make a "down payment" by working for 500 hours fabricating house panels in the factories of builders contracted by the CNHA. The labor is evaluated at $2.50 per hour, and the value of the down payment is calculated at $1,250. The down payment fulfilled, builders contracted by the CNHA then erect a prefabricated house on the participant's acre. For twenty years, the participant makes monthly payments that in no case are to exceed 20 percent of his monthly income, however little that may be, plus insurance and administrative fees. The rest of the cost of the house is provided by a subsidy supplied to the CNHA by the Indian Housing Authority of the Department of Housing and Urban Development. At the end of twenty years, the participant receives title to the house and land.

Through the CHNA mutual help program, a Cherokee can acquire a home that he would otherwise be entirely unable to purchase, but the principal beneficiaries of the program are the predominantly white contractors, suppliers, and subcontractors with whom CNHA does business. The 28 housing projects so far approved represent an expenditure of $27,768,401 pumped into an impoverished economy. The Cherokee's first general manager estimated that contractors are making a profit of $1,000 per house. Housing the Cherokees is big business.

A Cherokee friend recently greeted me by saying, "There's nothing new around here but the election and the houses." The houses are a divisive issue and a focus for Cherokee anxiety. Cherokees are certainly attracted by the prospect of better and cheaper homes, but their introduction to the program scared them. To begin with, it involved signing papers written in English — an act that for centuries has been the prelude to disaster. Cherokees said they had difficulty understanding the complex English in which the staff explained the program, and there was no careful "authorized" translation of the terms of the program into Cherokee. Cherokees sensed that they were being given the hard sell, and they worried about it. People wanted to know what would happen if they couldn't keep up payments. What would happen if a man paid on his house for fifteen years and then died? Most of all, they worried that a person could lose not just his equity, but his land — and his children's land. The suspicion that in accepting a house, a man might be jeopardizing the land of his children and his children's children, was agonizing.

Seven years later, this agony has been neither recognized nor responded to. The same questions are asked, and go unanswered, today. People who do not have new houses are uncertain and anxious about the contracts, as are many people who now occupy new homes. The ambivalence is overwhelming.

Some residents of Cherokee settlements ask about taxes. They realize that until the house is "paid out," neither house nor land is taxable. By then, twenty years hence, land values will have greatly appreciated. At that point they will be handed their titles and become taxpayers. How will they earn money for taxes? Or can their lands be rerestricted? Other Cherokees insist that when they receive title to their house and one acre, they will be "living on their own land." This will mean, they say, that by definition they will not be living on the remainder of their holding of restricted land. To not live on restricted land, they say, causes the land automatically to be unrestricted, alienable, and taxable. In view of the amount of Cherokee land that has been lost by fraudulently adding it to county tax rolls and then selling it for nonpayment of taxes, these questions are crucial.

In addition to the overall tendency of the Cherokee Establishment to decide for tribal Cherokees what is good for them, there are two reasons why after seven years the deepest concerns of the tribal Cherokees are still unanswered by the CNHA. The first is that the CNHA is directed by legal Cherokees who are openly contemptuous of tribal Cherokees. The second is that CNHA is big business. Its personnel have been so busy promoting and selling houses that are self-evidently good for clients that they have not taken the time to deal with what seem to them distant and irrelevant questions. A very light-skinned and urbane Cherokee university graduate, who recently conducted interviews with Cherokee tribal officials, found that they related to her as being a fellow member of the legal Cherokee elite. Her interview with one prominent official of the CNHA was interrupted by a telephone call; concluding a lengthy conversation, he shook his head in exasperation, slammed down the phone, and said in a tone of voice that assumed the interviewer's empathy, "Damned little full-blood. Sometimes you just can't get a thing through to her."

When the interviewer asked for an explanation of the circumstances under which a CNHA house would be taxable once the owner received title, the official first maintained that the "tribe," not the CNHA, was at fault for the failure to explain these matters. He then said that before an Indian could lose his land, he would have to "go through the BIA" and "the BIA would not let that happen."

"You see," he said, "the Indians use the tribe as a mother hen. It's one of their characteristics. So whenever they get in trouble, they run to the tribe. This is probably what would happen if they got in trouble with taxes, and the tribe would work it out with the BIA." Nor was this official alone in his views. His assistant, too, in a separate interview, explained that the CNHA and the tribal government "were like a mother to the Indians," taking care of everything for them from building them a house to finding them a job.

If "the tribe" is a mother, she is a most negligent one. It would appear that "the tribe," the CNHA and the BIA are more than happy to assist a Cherokee in removing restrictions on his land, as necessary for participation in a CNHA program — but none of these agencies accepts the responsibility for preserving the restrictions on that Cherokee's remaining land, or for rerestricting his one acre after he has received title from CNHA. The Tahlequah Agency of the BIA states that,

The present procedure that we use for people who live on restricted land who want to participate in the mutual-help housing program is to issue a removal of restrictions on the one acre . . . .
This question came up quite a bit when this program was new whether or not they could put this acre back in trust status after the Housing Authority deeded it back to them, but we can find no authority under which this can be done. At the present time we are telling people that when the restrictions are removed in order for them to participate in the mutual-help program that the land will remain unrestricted. This would also apply to homestead allotments (Wahrhaftig 1972).

When interviewed, a prominent official of the CNHA said that all of a Cherokee's land must be removed from restriction in order to do anything with part of it. In order to deed one acre to the CNHA, all of the land must be unrestricted. He repeated the grafter's classic allegation, that most of the Cherokees who do have their land in trust are glad to get it away from the BIA anyway, because then they can do what they want with it. In response to a written request for clarification of this issue, the same official explained that "if a person has a number of acres from which restrictions were removed in order to secure the acre for the house site, the property, other than the one acre house site is taxable. There is a way for them to place the unrestricted land in trust to the Cherokee tribe, thereby making the land nontaxable once more. Many Indian people do not understand this procedure and consequently must pay taxes or lose the property at tax sales."

In the case of the CNHA's contractors, the abdication of this responsibility is total. When an official of IBEC was asked at a "kick-off meeting" for a mutual-help housing project whether a Cherokee owner would have to pay property tax after receiving title to his house, he answered disparagingly, "That's twenty years from now." Reminded by the interviewer that twenty years is not such a long period of time, he said, "I won't hang myself from my thumbs over it."

A graduate of the management department of a university who has had considerable experience in residential contracting analyzed the CNHA's Mutual-Help and Occupancy Agreement and reported that "the Cherokee when entering into a contract with the Housing Authority does so only on a great deal of faith, for there are few avenues of recourse if difficulty arises." A point-by-point analysis of the contract convinced him that "the contract is designed not to help and protect the Cherokee, but to help and protect the Housing Authority." In addition to objectionable features in various of the specific articles of agreement, he finds,

... the lack of any statement which verifies that the house will be paid for in twenty years if the terms and conditions of the contract are met. Despite the personal assurances of [CNHA administrators] there is no clause which guarantees the ownership of the house and property after twenty years. The participant does sign a lease in which he agrees to lease his land and house from the Authority for twenty years, but nowhere in that lease or in the contract is there a guarantee or even hint of ownership in twenty years" (Paquin n.d.).

The houses, imposed from the top down as they have been, are a divisive force in Cherokee settlements. The Cherokees of modern times have evaded the factionalism that plagues so many Indian reservation communities. When faced with a matter that threatens to polarize them into one group that favors white ways and another group that rejects them, Cherokees simply withdraw from the whole issue. There has been no possibility of withdrawing from and avoiding the issue of houses. This program, unlike all others, has been brought right into the center of Cherokee settlements and "sold" persistently, over several years, from the pulpit of neighborhood churches. The three choices — accept, reject, or evade — that Cherokees have preserved for so long have been narrowed in this case to a fatal two — accept a house or reject it. On the basis of their acceptance or rejection of a house (and the twenty years of supervision by federal and tribal authorities, who can legally impose their standards of cleanliness and home maintenance on Cherokee clients) Cherokees are beginning to brand one another.

Further, there is a marked division of labor by sex within the Cherokee settlement. Women manage affairs within the household. Men determine the relation of the household to the world without. The issue of new housing invades a "gray area" between these jurisdictions, creating a new pressure on Cherokee male-female relations. Women apparently consider the acquisition of the new houses to be one of the workaday matters over which normally they have exclusive jurisdiction. Every Cherokee woman who talked with us about the new housing used the words "my house," never once "our house." Frequently, as a woman spoke glowingly of the house she would have, the man turned away and gazed silently at the corner. We found households — without knowing how common they might be — where the man was the breadwinner and the woman was the house earner. One family daily cared for two sets of grandchildren, whose fathers were earning wages while their mothers worked out their 500 hours at the housing factory.

Although women want the new houses and move to acquire them, the men, in their traditional role as bearers of the responsibility for looking beyond the affairs of the household, worried about taxes, and land, and the historical consequences of signing semiunderstood documents. An older man, asked what he thought about the situation, replied, "Most of the men know what's this house and what's happen after you take this house, but the women don't. All they think about is pretty house, big house. They don't think about what will happen after years."

This man's wife is fully convinced that he has already signed up for her house. She showed us where it is going to be. When his wife couldn't hear the conversation, he continued, "I think about this house [his present one], all I need is put a big room in front, and bathroom, and [running] water. That's all I need. I won't be owing nobody much. If I do owe, I'll be able to get out [of debt], come out some time."

Even after seven years, tribal Cherokees perceive the houses as a white man's program for Indians. One family, asked where they had applied for their house, they said they went to "that brick building next to Sequoyah school" (the palatial Cherokee nation's office). When asked to whom they made payments, a spokesman said, with a sort of a chuckle, "some rich man." When asked who that might be, he replied, "Rockefeller." Because Cherokees see the housing projects as something pressed on them by whites, it follows that the necessity to accept or reject a house — with no possibility of simply withdrawing and avoiding the decision — forces Cherokees to declare themselves unequivocally as white-following or white-rejecting. Divisiveness that has long been successfully avoided is now beginning to surface in Cherokee settlements. People who are convinced that they are doing the right thing by accepting a house write off their Cherokee critics as "crossed-up people." Those who eschew a house, fearing loss of land and the connection to white authority, feel that they are resisting the temptations spoken of in Cherokee prophecy, and that those who accept houses are the Cherokees who are going to be "lost" — seduced away from the tribal fold. One man explained that the prophecies say that legal Cherokees ("they're Cherokee who won't be no Cherokee, but they'll say 'I'm Cherokee'") will collaborate with "the rich people," "And they're gone to grab the land. They're gone to stop this everything what belongs to the Indian, to Cherokees . . . They're going to take *everything* . . . ."

And [the prophecies] just talk about this building, too, this new house. They didn't say "new house." They said they gone to give something good that the Cherokees think is good. They gone to see a pretty. They gone to believe that's what they want. That's what the Cherokees gone to say, [the prophecies] said. They gone to say "We got everything what we need. We got what we want." That's what [the prophecies] say the Cherokees gone to say. They gone to all agree, most of the Cherokees. Gone to agree to that. Go for it. But it's not going to do any good for the Cherokee. It's going to be belong to devil, this thing. That's what they said. [The informant laughed ironically.] Everybody's getting new house! ! !

When tribal Cherokees are asked what they need most, the answer is not "houses" but "more jobs." They are grindingly poor and jobs are a clear and unarguable necessity. Cherokees must scrabble for whatever is available in the way of employment. But their quiet desperation does not prevent them from being aware that their money is used to stimulate jobs for them without their knowledge or their control, that the jobs created are of the lowest order — often seasonal and degrading and brainlessly monotonous — and that such jobs exist because employers have been promised cheap and docile labor. As Cherokees see it, white people force Cherokees to work for Cherokee money, keeping the profits for themselves. The tribe's own Cherokee Nation Industries (CNI) is viewed no differently, for it perpetuates the low wages prevailing in the local economy and messianically imposes the white man's enthusiasm for property ownership, while disregarding traditional Cherokee work patterns.

It is impossible to say how many Cherokees receive jobs from the tribe's efforts to stimulate employment. G. E. Durham of Phillips Petroleum said, of the Phillips plastic plant at Pryor, "It's predominately Indian and God they've been real happy with them. They are real good employees." Sensitive to criticism that Indians are hired only in menial positions, he added, "Here's some good names for you: Tony Mouse and David Standingwater. They are supervisors at the plant"

(Personal communication). Yet, when asked how many of the plant's employees are Cherokee, Durham insisted that it is difficult to maintain statistics because of federal civil rights laws that forbid specifying race on job applications. Statistics may further obscure the situation, because legal Cherokees are included. Tribal Cherokees are tolerant, but they can reach the flash point when jobs that they regard as theirs are given to white men who are "technically" classified as Cherokees. These projects have been financed with Cherokee money — with the compensation extended for stolen Cherokee homeland. Hence, the bitterness of tribal Cherokees who see these jobs and moneys passing into the hands of whites is understandable. When the Cherokee tribal offices were being built, a contractor arrived with laborers recruited in the city of Muskogee, who had claimed to be Cherokees. Tribal Cherokees working on the job armed themselves with pick handles, refused to let the new workers get off their truck, and stayed away from work for a day to underscore their point. They said that, having already stolen the land and everything worth much, white men were now after the crumbs left for Cherokees.

The Cherokee Cultural Center was the first example of what tribal Cherokees are getting for their money. Through the efforts of the Cherokee tribe, the Cherokee National Historical Society, and the state of Oklahoma, nearly two million dollars were programed for development for the first phase of the center's operations. It is estimated that the amount of business drawn into eastern Oklahoma by the center will soon reach fifteen million dollars per year. In return for the investment tribal Cherokees receive work as laborers on the crews that built and maintain the complex, plus employment during the five months that the complex is open to tourists. No figures for the number of Cherokees employed by the village have been released; fifty would be a high guess. The drama hires 85 persons, 78 of whom are Oklahoma residents. Sixty-five percent of the cast and staff have "some Indian blood" and 47 percent were "of Cherokee descent," but it is widely known by local college students that when it comes to getting jobs at the drama, "everybody is a Cherokee."

Employment at the Cherokee Cultural Center re-creates and perpetuates the caste-structured society in which Cherokees are imprisoned. Dark-skinned, "Indian-looking," Cherokee-speaking people are hired as "villagers" for minimum wages. Younger, better educated, English-speaking, but Indian-looking people are hired at slightly higher wages as "guides," to direct tourists among the villagers. College students with legal claims to being Cherokee are hired at still higher wages as pageant actors, and the members of the old legally Cherokee elite fill managerial positions. Tribal Cherokees are in no position to decline employment at the center, but they bitterly resent working as a source of amusement for white tourists. They call the village "the monkey house." The director of the Cookson Hills Community Action Program reported that a Cherokee mother came to him to ask him to find her son a job "where he could learn something." She did not want him out in the village "playing Indian." A Cherokee listening to this conversation commented, "If they come from Sequoyah [the local BIA Indian boarding school] they're encouraged to be dumb, so they'll do fine working there at $1.60 an hour."

The basic economic pattern is repeated in other job-producing enterprises encouraged by the Cherokee tribe before the creation of CNI. Costs of establishing industry are high, returns to the general economy of the region are significant, and the benefits in terms of jobs for Cherokee are small.

For example, a South Carolina manufacturer negotiated with the tribe. A former Cherokee official reported that "his plant was run down, and he was faced with the cost of building a new one. Out here there are old buildings he could stick a factory into. He didn't need to put in any paved parking lot, or worry about unions, or fringe benefits, and he could get money at a full percent less interest. He said by coming out here, he could gain twenty years."

In a similar vein, the plant manager of Phillips Petroleum's factory at Pryor said,

We hire Indians here because of Mr. Keeler's interest in them, but also because it makes good economic sense. Your minority people, they aren't so transient. There are a lot of Indians living in this area with their families and all, and you know they aren't going to pick up and leave. I mean, if you train up a group of them, they aren't likely to go running off to a place like Chicago hunting a better-paying job with the skills you've given them. We hire a lot of Indians here because we have the kind of jobs they qualify for because of their lack of education. Now if we had a lot of jobs paying $4.00 or so an hour, you'd see our ration of Indians to white workers flop right on over" (Collier 1970: 40).

In the summer of 1970, there were 60 employees at the Phillips plant, 40 of whom were to some degree Indians. Three quarters of these were referred by the BIA, which for the first six to eighteen months of employment reimbursed Phillips for 50 percent of their salaries (Collier, personal communication). The Cherokee and Creek tribes jointly made a loan to Stephens Manufacturing Company which permitted it to expand its facilities for the production of school heating and ventilating systems. The Cherokees' $60,000 loan at the minimum prime rate of interest resulted in twelve jobs for Cherokees in 1969. The tribe's purchase of $150,000 worth of bonds for Glassmasters Plastics in Grove, Oklahoma, resulted in the employment of fourteen

Cherokees (eleven of whom initially were subsized by BIA on-the-job training programs), plus fifteen non-Indians.

With the creation of Cherokee Nation Industries, Incorporated in March 1969, the Cherokees formed an industry of their own. At present, CNI operates factories in Stilwell and Tahlequah, manufacturing electronic components for Western Electric and tailoring carpets for airliners. Seemingly independent, CNI actually represents a merger of the interests of the local establishment and of the Cherokee directorate. Its board of directors includes representatives of the region's largest banks, Phillips Petroleum, and the tribal government. The industry is dependent on contracts negotiated at higher levels of the corporate world by an executive of Phillips' Special Cooperative Projects division. CNI presently has no competitive product and no sales force and, in all probability, no means of surviving if Phillips Petroleum were to terminate its support.

When asked what makes CNI competitive when bidding on contracts, especially when Economic Baseline Reports for Adair County predicted conditions unfavorable to industrialization, the chairman of the CNI board of directors replied, "our performance record." Western Electric has found that work in the Cherokee nation is some 40 percent better in quality and in quantity than work performed in its own plants in Oklahoma City and elsewhere. Yet the Cherokees *had* no production record when their contract with Western Electric was negotiated.

Beneath an attractive-looking series of incentives, CNI perpetuates the region's usual employment practices. Workers are eligible for a 10¢ an hour incentive wage increase if they exceed production quotas, and there is an elaborate plan whereby stock is awarded to employees who complete a year's employment. Nevertheless, CNI policy is to "try to stay just a little above the prevailing wage." In the winter of 1972, workers at CNI's carpet-cutting plant were starting at $1.65 and receiving raises of five cents every 60 to 90 days, until they reached $2.15 an hour. Wages in the electronic assembly plant are comparable. There, a high proportion of employees are women and/or part-time workers; all workers must expect layoffs because of recessions in the electronics industry.

Although a Cherokee-run industry might take advantage of traditional Cherokee work habits, CNI disregards them entirely. An anti-nepotism rule forbids employment of more than one member of any family, thereby spreading job opportunities but also making it impossible for fathers, sons, and brothers or mothers, daughters, and sisters to work as teams. The regimentation imposed by a management that is dedicated to "instilling good work habits" conflicts with Cherokee expectations of noninterference and sensitive cuing as the basic form of interaction when working together.

A young woman, sitting with her husband, told about her work at CNI. She said, "I worked one year at CNI and quit. I only missed one-half day in one whole year." She didn't want to say why she had quit, but when pressed did so.

The woman: "They got a new boss that thought he was real big. He thought he knew my job better than me. He thought he knew what I should do. He tried to tell me what to do. I knew what to do..."
Her husband: "Quit."
The woman: "Yeah, quit" (Wahrhaftig 1972).

The Cherokee nation is the scene of a one-sided battle over the shape of the Cherokees' future. On one side is the Cherokee Establishment, backed by heavy political and financial commitments from federal bureaucracies. It moves toward centralizing power, toward expanding towns into cities filled with industries and blue collar Cherokee populations, toward emptying the forests of farmers and transforming them into profitable vacationlands. The establishment insists that funds for the aid of Cherokees be expanded in projects that are tangible and showy, that attract a "good press" and can stand as monuments to responsible leadership and minority advancement. Its emphasis is on further development of a unitary society, in which each person has equal opportunity to make something of himself, so long as he compliantly starts from his existing position in the local caste structure.

Working in opposition to this current are occasional groups and persons with a different vision of appropriate development for the region. They suspect that one of the strengths of the region may turn out to be its inability to support industry and concentrations of workers, and that this limitation may eventually stimulate small communities, whatever their ethnicity, to support themselves through diversity of economic specialities. A society that is decentralized and culturally plural is intolerable to the Cherokee Establishment, for it implies that Cherokee settlements are viable and that tribal Cherokees now, without further leadership and grooming, are competent to make decisions for themselves. Whenever proponents of the autonomy and viability of small communities emerge, the Cherokee Establishment moves to neutralize their effects by discrediting them, buying them off, or coopting them.

The Cherokee Establishment will not countenance development that recognizes the economic potential and cultural permanence of Cherokee settlements, even when that development is entirely under its control. The Cherokee nation's first general manager, Ralph Keen, was devoted to the philosophy of modest development of existing Cherokee settlements. He says,

This is a poor area and transportation costs are enormously high. It has been proven time and time again that it can't support industry. If you are going to develop it, you must capitalize on what it does have. There are two alternatives. Reliance on such agriculture as there is — chickens and cattle — or reliance on industry for which there is a permanent local demand — food processing. Setting up chicken houses is not hard at all, but you can tie up a lot of money and still only provide two or three jobs. A herd of cattle can easily tie up $100,000 and only provide a very few jobs. Still, development here is going to have to be in terms of small and scattered projects. You just can't provide hundreds of jobs in one place. The tribe wants big, showy projects, but it won't work. They aren't economically viable (Ralph Keen, personal communication).

Keen claims credit for developing the tribe's system of community representatives. He saw these representatives not just as a link between tribal planners and rural Cherokee settlement-dwellers, but as the nuclei of community action programs based in the settlements. When he was manager, he says, the tribal government offered up to $1,000 to any Cherokee settlement that wished to build or renovate a community building. Two accepted. The tribal government was always on the look-out for projects initiated by individual settlements and never turned one down. Keen says that he originally thought the development of adequate integration between Cherokee settlements and the existing tribal government would have to evolve in three steps. The first step was to encourage the settlements to elect representatives. He was certain, he says, that initially no settlement would elect either a militant or one of the older traditional opinion makers, but would choose "the safe person" who would go to meetings and report what he had heard. Keen went around from settlement to settlement pounding on doors. Settlements held meetings often with no more than fifteen people present, and always elected "the safe man." During the term of the first elected representatives, Keen hoped that people would realize that this could be a complex and important job, "one that demands alert and educated people." He suspected a different kind of person would be elected to represent settlements in subsequent annual elections.

Keen's proposals assumed the viability of Cherokee settlements, the legitimacy and the viability of the Cherokee government he had entered, and the eventual correlation of the interests of settlement Cherokees and that government. After a year and a half, however, the principal chief asked for Keen's resignation. Nothing remains of his plans for buttressing Cherokee settlements. There have never been new elections, and community representatives have become self-perpetuating, like the executive committee. The "safe men" who were chosen by ten or fifteen of their fellows carry on, filling vacancies by appointment of *ad hoc* arrangement. No longer does the tribe stimulate projects in individual settlements. Instead, discussions among community representatives are directed toward consideration of tribe-wide programs planned at the top of the Cherokee-BIA hierarchy.

While the Cherokee Establishment proceeded with its arrangements for industrial employment in town factories, another organization, Oklahomans for Indian Opportunity (OIO), attempted to stimulate self-sufficiency in existing Cherokee settlements. Instead of considering the activities of OIO as a useful complement to its activities, the Cherokee Establishment has dealt with it as a rival. In a request for funding, OIO stated the premises for its rural development program in Cherokee country:

> ... if Indian communities are to survive in the non-reservation atmosphere of Oklahoma, then Indian people must have the opportunity to gain control of the economic situations that most vitally affect their daily existence. That is, they must have the opportunity to work in a business owned by themselves or by other Indians: they must be able to buy the goods they need in stores owned by Indians if they so choose: they ought to be able to borrow from an institution controlled by other Indian people ... they ought to be able to live together, to preserve what they think is worth preserving, to discard what is not: they ought to be able to live in any way they please. But there must be an economic base for such freedom, and really one cannot talk about freedom to be different in our society unless one recognizes the need for the economic security of minority groups (Harvard Business School 1970a: 7).

OIO appears to have had modest success with programs developed along these premises. For example, the Lost City Cooperative Marketing Association supplies Cherokees in four counties with feeder pigs — young hogs that are fattened until they reach two months or 40 pounds: then the cooperative collects the hogs and ships them to grain-growing areas, where they can be sold for further fattening (Harvard Business School 1970b). As the Cherokee Establishment becomes an increasingly potent force in the local economy, it becomes less probable that these modest and rural-based projects can survive without its collaboration. One strongly suggests that the Cherokee Establishment is inclined to withhold support and to allow potentially beneficial projects sponsored by its rivals to fail.

The Miami Brick and Stone Corporation of Sequoyah County, a small business started by a former OIO field staff coordinator and a local landowner, received a direct loan from OIO and a loan of $53,000 guaranteed by the Small Business Association. There are Cherokee-speakers on Miami Brick's board of directors, and the plant provides employment for members of Cherokee settlements north of Marble City. Miami's management expanded the plant because the CNHA was about to begin constructing brick houses and it alleges that all four CNHA contractors (AZTEC, IBEC, Southern Construction, and Allen Construction) promised to buy Miami Brick providing the CNHA so directed. The company was confident of such a recommendation, because Section 3 of the Housing and Development Act requires that

... interagency cooperation with the Small Business Administration to award to locally owned and operated businesses contracts for work to be performed, including but not limited to planning, construction, and maintenance. The Indian housing authority should take the initiative in requiring preferential employment for Indians .... The area Director may also waive the competitive bidding and advertising requirements where such action is the only way of achieving the employment, training, and economic benefit objectives of the Indian housing authority. Such action might be necessary to actively support a fledgling Indian contractor (Indian Legal Information Development Services 1971: 21–22).

Although the management of Miami Brick insists that test results certify that its brick meets all applicable FHA and HUD standards and that these results were delivered to all contractors, CNHA refused to recommend the brick. Miami Brick was told to deal directly with the contractors, who then said that the brick did not meet FHA specifications. The company, denied the anticipated tribal market, fell heavily into debt. It then asked the Cherokee nation to buy a half interest in its operations, in the hope of preserving the jobs of local employees. As of February 1972, the managers of Miami Brick were pessimistic about future prospects. Although they said that Chief Keeler had formally directed the CNHA to work toward an agreement with their company, they also felt that local tribal officials have a long-standing hostility and suspicion toward OIO projects and would drag their feet until Miami's loans were no longer negotiable. They bitterly believed that CNHA's reluctance to do business with them was robbing Cherokees of jobs and profits that were delivered to white contractors.

On the rare occasions when they get a chance, Cherokees express their opinion of these recent developments. They clearly do not feel that the Cherokee tribal government is their government. They do feel that it ought to be. There is no doubt that they think that they ought to be running their own affairs in their own way. They are beginning to demand recognition.

A year ago, for example, federal investigators held hearings on the Adair County Community Action Program. Ordinarily only a few Cherokees come to silently observe such proceedings, which are reported back to consensus makers in their settlements. This time a crowd of three hundred Cherokees showed up at the Adair County courthouse. The proceedings which were, as usual, conducted in English, were soon interrupted when a spokesman for a Cherokee settlement in southern Adair County took the floor. In an action that was recklessly aggressive (particularly by Cherokee standards of behavior), he declared that he had been given to understand that the meeting had been called to listen to Cherokees, He is a Cherokee, he said, and Cherokees speak Cherokee. They also expect to listen to Cherokee. He finished his statement in Cherokee. County officials, having failed to provide an interpreter for the benefit of non-English-speaking Cherokees, had to scramble to find an interpreter for the benefit of the investigating officials. This, then, like Cherokee participation in a welfare rights organization founded that year, was an act in open defiance of the white power structure. From the perspective of the white civil rights movement, such acts might seem to be token or even symbolic. It must be remembered, however, that when Cherokees had their nation taken away from them, their reaction was covert consistently and underground. Open and public actions, to them, bespeak reckless fury.

Cherokees are beginning to talk back through the system of community representatives. Although community representatives were installed in order that "the tribe" might communicate its wishes to Cherokee settlements, members of some Cherokee settlements are pressuring their representatives to "go to Tahlequah and speak up." Cherokee settlements have occasionally sent along extra observers, to make sure that their representatives says what they want said.

As a body, community representatives have spoken out against a number of "giveaways" proposed by tribal officials. Because the city of Stilwell wants a new airport, tribal officials included one in plans for an industrial site to be developed near the Cherokee settlement at Cherry Tree. Community representatives argued that the tribal government had already given the city of Stilwell a whole lake from which it draws its water supply. They could see no reason to give Stilwell white people an airport, too. An airport is something for rich people. No Cherokee is going to be able to make use of it, many Cherokees will suffer the nuisance of it, and the land ought to be devoted to something Cherokees can use.

Bearing in mind that Cherokees habitually refrain from public displays of hostility, preferring instead to express disapproval and displeasure by silent withdrawal, the events that are taking place in recent meetings of Cherokee community representatives are startling. In their open criticism of the actions of tribal officials, Cherokees are now reacting with behaviors that are traditionally tolerated only among warriors in battle. At a meeting of community representatives called on February 3, for example, representatives of the Cherokee Establishment made an appearance to report on their travels to various meetings outside Oklahoma. After a longwinded description of a trip taken to discuss the reservation area program with the commissioner of Indian affairs, a special presidential assistant, and three Oklahoma congressional representatives, the community representatives pointedly interrupted to redirect the meeting to their own concerns. They began to discuss the Cherokee Constitutional Revision Committee, and were angered to discover that the committeee had been single-handedly appointed by the chief. A representative rose to say that the people who should have been on that committee are the ones who know the most about everyday Indian life; they should be mostly from the counties that have large concentrations of tribal Cherokees, but his county has almost no representation. He said he is tired of things like that. "Maybe we should secede from the Cherokee Nation and make up our own district. Then we could demand equal representation. I won't accept this constitution unless I have a part in it." After further discussion, another representative commented, "Sometimes we let our respect for Keeler's helping us stand in the way of what is good."

Following this discussion, another representative brought forward a newspaper article and demanded that it be read. The article said that the general consul of the Cherokee nation had appointed a committee of thirty-five Cherokees to protest the construction of a dam being built in Tennessee that will flood the site of Sequoyah's birth. The representative argued hotly that once again he had read in the paper about what Cherokees were doing, having no voice in the matter himself. He asked by what authority the Cherokees' lawyer could go around doing things like this without the Cherokee people having any opportunity to have their say.

The representatives then passed a motion demanding that all Cherokee business be presented to them before action is taken by boards appointed by the chief, the general consul, or other officials. They decided to send a letter to appropriate bodies and individuals, informing them of the decision.

Toward the end of the evening, a representative who had not said a word during the meeting asked for the floor. Speaking in Cherokee, he said that things had been deleted from the minutes of the last meeting, among them a discussion of discrimination against Cherokees in employment, and a discussion between contractors and the community representatives concerning CNHA housing. He insisted that these discussions be restored, and he demanded a report on how many Cherokees are actually being employed by contractors building CNHA housing.

The behavior of Cherokee community representatives demonstrates that Cherokees have not internalized their own powerlessness. They are a self-confident people who assume that if the white man were not "keeping them down" they would certainly be a well-educated and self-governing community. Recruited as window dressing, community representatives are reaching for the reins of government, believing it only natural that the authority of the Cherokee settlement has belatedly been recognized. Similarly, Murray Wax and his colleagues, who asked Cherokee parents how much schooling they would like their children to obtain, found that about half wanted the children to finish college. Wax (1971: 115) says, "For a people so impoverished, whose children experience such difficulties in the school system, this pattern of responses is phenomenal. At the present time, few of the children endure throughout the high school trials, and almost no one completes college. The hope for education is almost religious." It seems to me that tribal Cherokees believe that they, the so-called "full bloods," developed and ran the Cherokee nation in the past and that they can and will do so again. That is what power and education are for, as they see it.

At present Cherokees have neither power nor education nor much wealth. What they do have are strong, resilient, and intact communities, and a vivid sense of the kind of cultural and economic redevelopment they expect to attain. Cherokee settlements — socially cohesive, and rich in traditional motivations — are entities that could rapidly develop economically now as they did in the past. Yet Cherokee settlements cannot develop along these lines without jeopardizing the Cherokee Establishment's exploitation of Cherokee labor and the Cherokee presence. Until recently, the expansion of the Cherokee Establishment has been benign. Its further expansion will be against the grain of dogged resistance from Cherokee settlements, which are formulating independent views of development that do not include their own use as a natural resource. It looks as though the next chapter of Cherokee history will be grim.

REFERENCES

ADAIR COUNTY AREA DEVELOPMENT COMMITTEE
    1962   "*Overall economic development program.*" Prepared by Hudgins, Thompson, Ball and Associates, and Industrial Planning Associates. Offset print for private circulation.
BALLENGER, T. L.
    n.d.   "*Trails of tears*, a review." Unpublished manuscript.
BUCHANAN, ROBERT W.
    1972   "Patterns of organization and leadership among contemporary Oklahoma Cherokees." Unpublished Ph.D. Dissertation, University of Kansas.

CALDWELL, JOSEPH R.
1958 *Trend and tradition in the prehistory of the eastern United States.* American Anthropological Association, Memoir 88.
1962 "Eastern North America," in *Courses toward urban life.* Edited by Robert J. Braidwood and Gordon R. Willey, 288–308. Chicago: Aldine. (Reprinted 1971 in *Prehistoric agriculture.* Edited by Stuart Streuver. New York: American Museum Sourcebooks in Anthropology, The Natural History Press.

CHEROKEE NATIONAL HISTORICAL SOCIETY
n.d. Prospectus. Mimeograph. Tahlequah, Oklahoma City.

Cherokee Nation News
1969 Article in *Cherokee Nation News,* September 23.
1971 *Cherokee Nation News,* June 29. Official publication of the Cherokee Nation of Oklahoma. Weekly, Tahlequah, Oklahoma.
1972 Article in *Cherokee Nation News,* January 25.
1972 Article in *Cherokee Nation News,* June 27.

COLLIER, PETER
1970 *The theft of a nation: apologies to the Cherokees. Ramparts.* 9(3): 35–45.
1973 *When shall they rest? The Cherokees' long struggle with America.* New York: Holt, Rinehart and Winston.

CULLUM, ROBERT M.
1958 *The rural Cherokee household, study of 479 households within fourteen school districts situated in the old Cherokee nation.* United States Department of the Interior, Bureau of Indian Affairs, Muskogee Area Office. Muskogee, Oklahoma. Mimeographed.

DEBO, ANGIE
1940 *And still the waters run.* Princeton, New Jersey: Princeton University Press.
1970 *A history of the Indians of the United States.* Norman, Oklahoma: University of Oklahoma Press.

DICKEMAN, MILDRED
1971 "The integrity of the Cherokee student," in *The culture of poverty: a critique.* Edited by Eleanor B. Leacock. New York: Simon and Schuster.

FITES, GAIL
n.d. "The Cherokee cultural center at Tahlequah, Oklahoma, a dramatic tribal dispute." Term paper for Anthropology 231, Department of Anthropology, University of Kansas.

FOGELSON, RAYMOND D., PAUL KUTSCHE
1961 "Cherokee economic cooperatives: the Gadugie" in *Symposium on Cherokee and Iroquois culture.* Edited by William N. Fenton and John Gulick, 83–124. Smithsonian Institution Bureau of American Ethnology Bulletin 180. Washington. D.C.

GEARING, FRED O.
1961 "The rise of the Cherokee state as an instance in a class: The 'Mesopotamian' career to statehood," in *Symposium on Cherokee and Iroquois culture.* Edited by William N. Fenton and John Gulick, 125–134. Smithsonian Institution Bureau of American Ethnology Bulletin 180.
1962 *Priests and warriors: social structures for Cherokee politics in the 18th century.* American Anthropological Association Memoir 93. *American Anthropologist* 65(5): part 2.

GILBERT, WILLIAM HARLEN, Jr.
1934 *The eastern Cherokees.* Smithsonian Institution. Bureau of American Ethnology Bulletin 133.

GULICK, JOHN
1960 *Cherokees at the crossroads.* Institute for Research in Social Science. Chapel Hill: University of North Carolina.

HALL, TOM ALDIS
1934 "The socio-economic status of the Cherokee Indians." Unpublished M. A. thesis, University of Oklahoma.

HARVARD BUSINESS SCHOOL
1970a "Oklahomans for Indian opportunity (A): A program for rural economic development." Case Study 9–671–030/IM 1964. Harvard College. Mimeographed. Cambridge, Massachusetts.
1970b "Oklahomans For Indian opportunity (B): The lost city cooperative marketing association." Case Study 9–671–031/IM 1965. Harvard College. Mimeographed. Cambridge, Massachusetts.

HEWES, LESLIE
1942 The Oklahoma Ozarks as the land of the Cherokees. *The Geographical Review* 32: 269–281.
1943 Cultural fault line in the Cherokee country. *Economic Geography* 19: 136–142.

HOLZINGER, CHARLES H.
1961 "Some observations on the persistence of aborginal Cherokee personality traits," in *Symposium on Cherokee and Iroquois Culture.* Edited by William N. Fenton and John Gulick, 227–238. Smithsonian Institution Bureau of American Ethnology Bulletin 180.

HOWARD, JAMES
1968 *The Southeastern ceremonial complex and its interpretation.* Missouri Archaelogical Society Memoir 6. Oklahoma State University, Stillwater, Oklahoma.

HUDSON, CHARLES
1970 Cherokee concept of natural balance. *The Indian Historian* 3(4): 51–54.

INDIAN LEGAL INFORMATION DEVELOPMENT SERVICES
1971 Housing. *Legislative Review* 4(1): 19–23.

JORDAN, JANET
1972a "Demographic changes in a five county area of northeastern Oklahoma, 1960–1970." Unpublished manuscript.
1972b "Restoration of the right to elect tribal leadership: the Western Cherokee election for chief, August 14, 1971." Unpublished manuscript.

KEETOOWAH SOCIETY
1972 "Four talks about the Indians from the Keetoowah Society of the Cherokee Indians in Oklahoma, February 1972," Mimeographed.

LAUGHLIN, WILLIAM
1968 "Hunting: an integrating biobehavioral system and its evolutionary importance," in *Man the hunter.* Edited by Richard B. Lee and Irven DeVore, 304–320. Chicago: Aldine.

LEE RICHARD B, IRVEN DEVORE
1968 *Man the hunter.* Chicago: Aldire

LITTLEFIELD, DANIEL F., Jr.
1971   Utopian dreams of the Cherokee fullbloods: 1890–1930. *Journal of the West* 10(3): 404–427.

McWILLIAMS, CAREY
1942   *Ill fares the land: migrants and migratory labor in the United States.* New York: Barnes and Noble.

OKLAHOMA STATE EMPLOYMENT SERVICE RESEARCH AND PLANNING DIVISION
1962   Economic base report: Cherokee County mimeograph. Oklahoma City.

PAQUIN, DONALD
n.d.   "The Cherokee Mutual-Help Housing Project." Unpublished manuscript.

PHILLIPS PETROLEUM COMPANY
n.d.   "*Path of many ways.*" Phillips Petroleum Company, Bartlesville, Oklahoma.

SAHLINS, MARSHALL
1972   *Stone Age economics* Chicago: Aldine.

SPADE, REV. WATT, WILLARD WALKER
1966   *Cherokee stories.* Middletown, Connecticut: Wesleyan University, Laboratory of Anthropology.

SPECIAL COOPERATIVE PROJECTS, PHILLIPS PETROLEUM COMPANY
n.d.   "*The human potential.*" Draft for a proposed book. Phillips Petroleum Company, Bartlesville, Oklahoma.

SPECIAL SUBCOMMITTEE ON INDIAN EDUCATION
1968   *Hearings on the study of the education of Indian children, Part 2, February 19, 1968, Twin Oaks, Oklahoma.* Committee on Labor and Public Welfare, U.S. Senate, Ninetieth Congress, First and Second Sessions. Washington D.C: Government Printing Office.

STARR, EMMET
1921   *History of the Cherokee Indians and their legends and folk lore.* Oklahoma City, Oklahoma: The Warden Company. Republished 1967 by Jack Gregory and Rennard Strickland as *Starr's history of the Cherokee Indians*; Indian Heritage Edition. Fayetteville, Arkansas: Indian Heritage Association.

Tahlequah Times
1971   Article in the *Tahlequah Times*, May 6.

THOMAS, ROBERT K.
n.d.a   "Cherokee values and world view." Unpublished manuscript.
n.d.b   "The present 'problem' of the eastern Cherokee." Unpublished manuscript.
n.d.c   "Individual acculturation among Oklahoma Cherokees." Unpublished manuscript.
1953   "The origin and development of the Redbird Smith movement." Unpublished M.A. thesis, University of Arizona.
1961   "The Redbird Smith movement." in *Symposium on Cherokee and Iroquois culture.* Edited by William N. Fenton and John Gulick, 159–166. Smithsonian Institution Bureau of American Ethnology Bulletin 180.

THOMAS, ROBERT K., ALBERT L. WAHRHAFTIG
1971   "Indians, hillbillies and the 'education problem'" in *Anthropological perspectives on education.* Edited by Murray Wax, Stanley Diamond, and Fred O. Gearing. New York: Basic Books.

UNITED STATES DEPARTMENT OF THE INTERIOR
  1971   *Report of program activities, fiscal year 1971.* Department of the Interior. Bureau of Indian Affairs, Muskogee Area Office.
UNITED STATES PUBLIC HEALTH SERVICE
  n.d.   Public Health Service Indian Hospital. Social Service Department. Tahlequah, Oklahoma.
WAHRHAFTIG, ALBERT L.
  1965   An anti-poverty exploration project: a suggestion for non-reservation Indian communities. *Journal of American Indian Education* 5(1).
  1966a   Community and the caretakers. *New University Thought* 4(4).
  1966b   The Cherokee People Today Tahlequah Printing Company, Tahlequah, Oklahoma. Originally published in Cherokee.
  1968   The tribal Cherokee population of eastern Oklahoma. *Current Anthropology* 9(5): 510–518.
  1970   *Social and economic characteristics of the Cherokee population of eastern Oklahoma.* Anthropological Studies 5, American Anthropological Association.
  1972   Fieldnotes.
  1976   More than mere work. *Appalachian Review.*
  i.p.   "Institution building among Oklahoma's Cherokees, in *Four centuries of southern Indians.* Edited by Charles Hudson. University of Georgia Press.
WAHRHAFTIG, ALBERT L., ROBERT K. THOMAS
  1968   Renaissance and repression: the myth of Cherokee assimilation. *Trans-action* February 1968: 42–48.
WALKER, WILLARD
  1965   Cherokee Primer. Northeastern State College Press, Tahlequah, Oklahoma. Originally published in Cherokee.
WAX, MURRAY
  1971   *Indians and other Americans.* New York: Prentice-Hall.
WRIGHT, MURIAL
  1935   Review of the rise and fall of the Choctaw republic by Angie Debo. *Chronicles of Oklahoma* 13: 108–120.

Dressing for the Window: Papago Indians and Economic Development

HENRY F. MANUEL, JULIANN RAMON, and
BERNARD L. FONTANA

The trouble is that Indians who get into big tribal jobs or tribal politics don't even talk to you anymore. You go to Sells [the tribal capital] and see them driving around in tribal cars or government cars with their noses stuck up. But what's sad is that the white men are really running things. These Indian people think they're important, but they're really not. To the whites they're just dressing for the window.
(Papago Indian discussing tribal government in 1972)

INTRODUCTION

The saguaro cactus of southern Arizona is much more famous than are the humans whose ancestors inhabited this region in ancient times. Yet, like the saguaro, the unassuming and unpretentious citizens who today are known collectively to outsiders as the Papago Indians have also been influenced by the region's physical environment, and an understanding of their present situation requires familiarity with that environment as well as a knowledge of the past 250 years of their history.

The following report is the result of a study commissioned by the Economic Development Administration through a grant to the Center for the Study of Man, Smithsonian Institution, Washington, D.C. The concern of the EDA was with economic development on Indian reservations. To quote the introduction to the grant proposal: "Need has been expressed by EDA offices concerned with Indian reservation development projects for a research study to analyze components of different systems of production and distribution on the reservations. Traditional tribal organizations of production, distribution, and management of resources differ significantly from those of the white community. This study will consist of a comparative examination of the various organizational and value

The Sonoran desert, which includes the "Papago country" of south-western Arizona, is the lowest and hottest of the North American deserts. It is also the most varied. Its total area of more than 100,000 square miles comprises innumerable microclimates and scores of habitats — "a multitude of little worlds, fragmented and varied, all existing within the larger framework of 'a desert'" (Hastings and Turner 1965: 7, 8, 11).

---

systems currently being applied on Indian reservations. It is hoped that suggestions for maximizing economic returns within the framework of Indian values will be developed" (Stanley 1971: 2).

The Papago study was one of seven assigned by Dr. Sam Stanley of the Center for the Study of Man. Similar reports have been written concerning the Navajo (Shonto community), Pine Ridge, Morongo, Lummi, and Passamaquoddy reservations and the Cherokee communities of eastern Oklahoma.

The methodology of these reports, the present one included, has been influenced by a consideration of a statement made by Vine Deloria, Jr., in his book *Custer died for your sins*: "Tribes that can handle their reservation conflicts in traditional Indian fashion generally make more progress and have better programs than do tribes that continually make adaptations to the white value system" (1970: 28). We have attempted to discern whether or not this is so in the case of the Papagos, and, if so, to suggest reasons why.

The report which follows represents a joint effort among its three authors. Henry Manuel and Juliann Ramon are Papago Indian students at the University of Arizona, Tucson, majoring in government. Manuel was born and raised at the village of Ali Chuk (Menager's Dam) in the Gu Vo district of the Papago (Sells) reservation; Ramon was born and raised in the village of Bac on the San Xavier reservation. Both are fluent speakers of Papago, their native language. Both have been involved in tribal affairs in various official capacities.

Fontana is an ethnologist in the Arizona State Museum at the University of Arizona. Since 1956, he has lived immediately adjacent to the San Xavier reservation, and in 1962–64 he served as the Papago Tribe's sole expert witness in its claims case against the United States government in its attempt to receive compensation for lands and minerals wrongfully taken.

Manuel and Ramon gathered all of the contemporary field data for the case studies involving Kitt Peak National Observatory; Kitt Peak "Gateway"; Papago Explosives, Inc.; San Xavier Cooperative Association, Inc.; San Xavier Industrial Park, Gila Bend Tourist Center; and Gila Bend Fortress Village. Fontana alone is responsible for the case studies concerning ASARCO and Mission Mine; Papago Industries; and E. K. Landscapers. Manuel collected the information concerning the organizational charts for the Bureau of Indian Affairs' Papago Agency; the Sells Service Unit of the United States Public Health Service; and the Papago tribe.

Virtually all of the sections, "Primería Alta" and "The Papago Reservation," are the responsibility of Fontana. Fontana supplied most of the historical data throughout the report, drawing largely on an extensive newspaper file concerning Papago Indians he has been compiling since 1956. He is also responsible for the final written version of the text, having edited and drawn together the materials collected by Manuel and Ramon. All three of us discussed the text at length after reading the initial version, and this final product represents our joint thinking.

We wish to thank the many individuals who cooperated in the preparation of this report by freely supplying us with information. They include Papago people; tribal, Bureau of Indian Affairs, and Public Health Service officials and employees; and innumerable non-Papago citizens of Tucson and Gila Bend. We regret that their numbers are so great that it would be impractical to list all of them.

And, if our report has a dedication, it is to a better future for Papago people. They have earned it.

Although Europeans first explored the Papago scene in 1539, the religious and secular conquests of New Spain were not extended into the northern reaches of the Sonoran desert until late in the seventeenth century. Spain's clerical, military, and civil representatives found the region inhabited by several groups of Indians, whose dialects were mutually intelligible with the languages spoken by people the Europeans called "Pimas," who had already been encountered to the south. By extension, the northerners became "Pimas Altas" [Upper Pimas], and their vast domain was called Pimería Alta.

Pimería Alta

Although Pimería Alta lay almost wholly within the Sonoran desert, most of its native inhabitants lived in the lower valley of the Colorado River and on the uplands of Arizona (Map 1a). The few who lived beyond the desert — in the grassy steppe and the evergreen woodlands of oak, pine, and juniper — were dislodged permanently by Apaches in the eighteenth century.

Based on the availability of water, Pimería Alta may be subdivided into three major zones: the extremely arid west, where annual rainfall averages 5 inches or less; the seasonally more moist central areas, where it averages 5 to 10 inches; and an even more moist perimeter to the north, east, and south where rivers once flowed perennially and today's rainfall averages 10 to 15 inches a year. Local variability within each area is enormous, as in all arid regions, and averages conceal the fact that rainless years may be interspersed with brief storms that dump more water in one day than a locale has received during the previous decade (see Shreve and Wiggins 1964: 21, for rainfall map; Hastings and Turner 1965: 11, for detailed discussion).

Not surprisingly, the inhabitants of Pimería Alta seem to have adapted to the three general types of environment. Differences among them were noted by the Spaniards, who called the western Pimans of the arid desert "Sobas," the central Pimans (at least seven major groups) "Papagos," and the riverine Pimans "Sobaipuris," "Gilenos," "Piatos," and "Pimas."

The modern Arizona descendants of all these people are the "Papagos" of the Papago, Gila Bend, and San Xavier reservations, who are considered here (as well as the "Pimas" of the Gila River, Salt River, and Ak Chin reservations). All refer to themselves in their own language as *o'odham* [the people]. Papagos call themselves *tohono o'odham* [desert people], to distinguish themselves from the Pimas or *akimel o'odham* [river people].

EUROPEAN CONTACT.   Contacts between non-Indians and the inhabitants of Pimería Alta were sporadic and superficial during the interval
between the earliest explorations of Marcos de Niza in 1539 and
Francisco Vasquez de Coronado in 1540 and the arrival of Jesuit
missionaries in 1687. With the Jesuit missionization program, however,
the riverine Pimans and, to a lesser extent, the central Pimans were
introduced to cattle, horses, sheep, and goats; to wheat and to
European fruits and vegetables (Boulton 1948: vol. 2, pp. 265 ff.);
and to new architectural styles, a new religion, and new political systems.

Between 1687 and 1767, the Jesuits established more than a dozen
mission headquarters and mission *visitas* [outlying stations] in Pimería
Alta in early times were soldiers, missionaries, prospectors, and immigrants en route to California, rather than colonists. A few small Spanish
villages. After the Jesuits were expelled from New Spain in 1767, their
work was carried on in the same locations by Franciscans until the
1830's, when the secularization that resulted from Mexican independence brought an end to proselytizing efforts among the Indians.

In addition to these culturally isolated mission communities, a few
mining camps were established in Piman country early in the eighteenth century, although these were quickly abandoned as silver deposits were exhausted. The raids of Apache Indians and the periodic
rebellions of Pimans themselves brought Spanish and Indian troops —
primarily Opata Indians — into Pimería Alta, and presidios were built.
Among the earliest forts were those established in 1752 at Tubac,
adjacent to a Piman village on the Santa Cruz River in southern
Arizona, and in 1776 at Tucson, across the river from an Indian village
of the same name.

NON-INDIAN SETTLEMENT.   Most of the Europeans who came to Pimería
Alta in early times were soldiers, missionaries, prospectors, and immigrants en route to California, rather than colonists. A few small Spanish
ranches were established during the eighteenth century, and a few
Indian villages became non-Indian pueblos towards the end of this
century. After Mexican independence in 1821, however, large grants
of land were formally given to Mexican ranchers — some of whom had
been civilians in the presidios. The grants were located along the
eastern riverine boundaries of Piman country (Mattison 1946: map
following 326).

In 1854, as a result of the Gadsden Purchase, Pimería Alta was
divided. The southern part, and the Pimans who lived there, remained
under the jurisdiction of Sonora and Mexico; the north became part of
Arizona and the United States. In 1857 an Indian agent arrived in
Tucson to take charge of Papago affairs — "Papagos" by then being

considered as all the southern Arizona Pimans except the "Pimas" who lived near the Gila River.

Set aside for Papago Indians by executive order were San Xavier reservation in 1874, Gila Bend reservation in 1882, and Papago reservation in 1916. In 1919, the Bureau of Indian Affairs moved its principal offices from San Xavier to Sells, on the much larger Papago reservation, which became the administrative headquarters for the three combined reservations. (In this paper the combined reservation is referred to as the "Papago reservation," the smaller unit as the "Papago (Sells) reservation.")

The Roman Catholic church began to reassert its influence in 1873, when a parochial school was established at San Xavier — the first school of any kind for Papago children; in 1908, the Franciscans returned to the Papago missionary field throughout Arizona. Presbyterians began to proselytize among the Papagos later in the nineteenth century, building a school for Indians at Tucson.

The Papago Reservation

The Papago Indian reservation is today one of the largest Indian reservations in the United States, with a combined area approaching three million acres (resulting from executive orders dated July 1, 1874; December 12, 1882; January 14, 1916; and from acts of Congress dated February 21, 1931 and July 28, 1937).

The Papago (Sells) reservation includes 2,773,358 acres; San Xavier reservation, 71,095 acres; and Gila Bend reservation, 10,337 acres. The 1972 population estimated by the United States Public Health Service was Papago (Sells), 7,719; San Xavier, 702; Gila Bend, 151; plus 4,927 Papagos who live off the reservation — for a total of 13,499 Papago people.

Natural resources on the Papago (Sells) and San Xavier reservations include minerals (principally copper), grazing lands, and irrigable acreage. Modern irrigation on the reservation, however, like that elsewhere in southern Arizona, depends on pumping from deep wells. There are no longer any perennial streams. Stands of mesquite trees along the intermittent Santa Cruz River continue to supply Papago woodchoppers at San Xavier with small cash incomes, however.

The Gila Bend reservation, small as it is, has lands that are potentially irrigable and lands that are useful for the grazing of cattle on a small scale. But its chief "natural resource" may be the potential development of a prehistoric ruin within its boundaries as a tourist attraction.

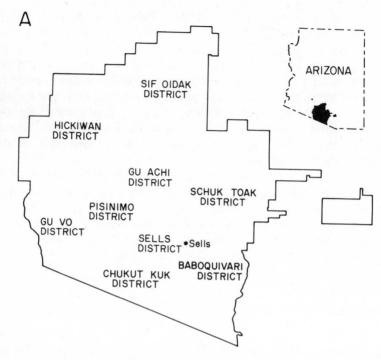

A

Map 1a and 1b. Papago Indian reservation and dialect areas

BOUNDARIES AND TRANSPORTATION. The southern boundary of the Papago (Sells) reservation is also the international boundary between the United States and Mexico (see Map 1). Most of the reservation lies within Arizona's Pima County, although it also extends into Maricopa and Pinal counties. State Highway 86, which is paved, bisects the reservation from east to west, linking it with Tucson and Ajo. A paved reservation road runs from Casa Grande through Chuichu and Santa. Rosa, connecting with Highway 86 at Covered Wells; much of the road from Sells south to San Miguel is also paved. Most of the reservation's roads, however — hundreds of miles of them — remain unpaved. Some are occasionally improved by grading and hole filling, and most of the time it is possible to travel by passenger car or pickup truck to any inhabited location. No railroads cross the reservation, but there are a few landing strips for small planes.

The San Xavier reservation, wholly in Pima County, shares part of its boundary with that of the city of Tucson. Interstate Highway 19, a four-lane freeway, runs north-south across the eastern section of San Xavier, and three paved county roads are also located within its boundaries. This reservation is literally across the street from Tucson International Airport, and the tracks of the Southern Pacific Railroad are nearby.

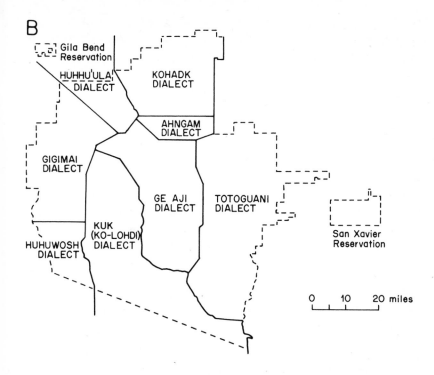

The Gila Bend reservation, in Maricopa County near the non-Indian town of Gila Bend, is on Interstate Highway 8, and the Southern Pacific's main east-west line through Arizona passes nearby. San Lucy Village, the only inhabited site on the reservation, is easily accessible by a good road from the town of Gila Bend.

PHYSICAL ENVIRONMENT. Physiographically, all three units of the Papago reservation lie within the desert region of the basin and range province (Wilson 1962: Figure 13), which is made up of a series of parallel mountain ranges and valleys. These alternating landforms trend generally from southeast to northwest, and altitudes increase generally from west to east. On the western boundary of the Papago (Sells) reservation, the Ajo Mountains rise to 4,770 feet above sea level; the crest of the eastern boundary is Baboquivari Peak, at 7,730 feet. Elevations of the intermontane valleys increase correspondingly, from La Quitun Valley, some 1,500 feet above sea level on the west, to the Baboquivari Plain, which is about 2,500 feet high.

The San Xavier reservation is in Santa Cruz Valley, which is bordered by the Tucson and Sierrita mountains on the west and the Rincon and Santa Rita mountains on the east. The Gila Bend reservation is in the lower valley of the Gila River, at the southeastern end of the Gila Bend Mountains.

The vegetation of all reservations is characteristic of the lower Colorado and Arizona upland zones of the Sonoran desert. Landscapes are dominated by giant saguaro cactus, barrel cactus, chollas and prickly pear, mesquite, palo verde, catclaw, white thorn, desert willow, ironwood, creosote bush, saltbushes, and white bursage.

The notion that Papago country is a barren and sandy waste is altogether false. Large sections of it have a luxuriant plant cover, on mountains as well as in valleys.

Subsistence in Pimería Alta

The ancestors of the Papagos appear to have had three different types of subsistence economy, according to whether they lived in western, central, or riverine areas. In all three regions, surpluses were either small or nonexistent.

In 1694, Jesuit priests Eusebio Francisco Kino and Marcos Antonio Kappus, with a military escort commanded by Ensign Juan Mateo Manje, traveled through the lands bordering the northeastern shores of the Gulf of California. Here they "came upon some squaws who were filling some *tinajas* [earthenware jars] with water from a small hole . . . . The Indians went about naked, covering their bodies only with small pieces of hare furs . . . . We gave them a supply of food since they were poor and hungry, living on roots, locusts and shell fish" (Manje 1954: 14, 17). Later in the same year, the explorers described Indians in the same vicinity as "poor people who lived by eating roots of wild sweet potatoes, honey, mesquite beans, and other fruits. They traveled about naked; only the women had their bodies half covered with hare furs" (1954: 30).

WESTERN PIMERÍA ALTA. Manje's account provides the first known written description of the western Piman-speaking Indians called "Sobas" by the Spaniards, who in later times came to be called "Sand Papagos." These people probably never numbered more than 500 men, women, and children. They wrested a livelihood from the arid west of Pimería Alta by hunting wild game, collecting plants and insects, and gathering shellfish and other foods from the Gulf of California. They traded shells, ceremonies, and salt, gathered from deposits at the head of the gulf, for the earthenware pottery and agricultural products of the Yuman-speaking Cocopas who lived on along the lower Colorado River and on its delta.

The western Pimans were true nomads who had no fixed village locations; "home," to them, was much of the lower valley of the Colorado River. They were divided into an undetermined number of bands of extended family members; under optimum conditions the size of band may have been as large as 80 or 90 people. One band, the so-called "Pinacateños," had its principal territories near natural rock water catchments in the Sierra del Pinacate, where in 1701 the Spaniards "counted 50 persons, poor and naked people, who sustain themselves by roots, locusts and lizards, which they call iguanas, and some fish" (Manje 1954: 160; Hayden 1967: 341).

The sparseness of vegetation and fauna made it necessary for these Indians to range throughout western Pimería Alta in a continual exploitation of the foods and water sources on which they depended. They moved from place to place in seasonal cycles — usually with some degree of regularity — but always within the limits of the huge area that is bounded by the lower Gila and Colorado rivers, Rio Concepción, and the Ajo Mountains.

The western nomads, unlike other inhabitants of Pimería Alta, have disappeared as cultural entities. Many of them died of yellow fever in the 1850's; others were killed by Mexican and Anglo-American intruders in their territory; the rest left their homeland to become assimilated among other Indians or in non-Indian towns and mining camps during the second half of the nineteenth century. A Pinacateño hermit, Juan Caravajales, survived in the mountains until the 1920's. It is also possible that Piman-speaking Indians who now live at Dome, Arizona, are descendants of the nomads of western Pimería Alta (Hayden 1967: 341 ff.; Vivian 1965: 125 ff.).

CENTRAL PIMERÍA ALTA. The Papago Indians described in historic literature and by ethnographers were members of the many extended-family groups whose aboriginal range was in the central part of the Arizona upland, where there were no perennial streams. These were "two-village" people, who maintained winter habitations in the mountain foothills near permanent springs of water, as well as summer habitations on the intermontane plains, where they farmed after the rains of late summer had moistened their fields. This seasonal migration pattern, from summer field to winter foothills and back, was once a way of life for more than 4,000 Piman-speaking Indians of the central region.

The central Papagos, unlike the western nomads, constructed permanent shelters. Their brush houses — dome-shaped structures of mesquite, covered with branches or grass — were arranged in village clusters, although the houses were often widely separated. Village members were related either by blood or by marriage.

When a village became too large for available resources, a group of its residents would found a new village in another location. As a result, throughout central Pimería Alta there were geographically separated winter villages whose related members usually farmed in the same valleys during the summer. In aboriginal times there were at least a dozen such groups of related villages, in which were spoken at least seven dialects of the Piman language: Huhhu'ula, Gigimai, Huhuwosh, Ko-lohdi, Ge Aji, Kohadk, and Totoguani (Map 1).

Each major or "parent" village had a recognized headman and a council of elders, but government was strictly by consent of the governed. No one had autocratic powers. Above all, there was no central or binding authority among members of all the village clusters — no "chief" of all the Papagos. Kinsmen attended to their own affairs and had little interest in what other Piman-speakers were doing.

Before the coming of white men to their country, the central Papagos lived mainly by hunting, gathering, and trading and probably raised about one-fifth of their total food supply on family farm plots that varied in size from one-quarter acre to two acres. The planting of crops of corn, beans, and cucurbits was man's work, and there was only a single planting period and a single harvest each year. This was "flash-flood" agriculture. As soon as rain brought water to fill the *charcos* [valley catchment basins] and to flood the plains at the mouths of arroyos, men and older boys went to the fields. Seeds were dropped into holes made with digging sticks, and dirt was then scraped over them with the feet.

During the rainy season, central Papagos attempted to control the distribution of water in the fields by judicious placement of low embankments, brush dikes, and short, shallow ditches. The idea was to keep the crops well watered until they began to set fruit. On higher mountain slopes, rocks were aligned to channel rainwater into strategically situated arroyos. The result was a kind of *arroyo grande* — a natural ditch, modified by man to carry large volumes of water to fields.

The harvest, which was woman's work, usually began in October or November. Crops were either eaten or stored, and families remained in the valleys until the food supply had been exhausted and there was no more water in the *charcos* [water hole].

RIVERINE PIMERÍA ALTA. The largest Indian villages were situated in the fertile valleys of the river systems that formed three-fourths of the perimeter of Pimería Alta. Villages were fixed fairly permanently in their locations, although residents might move from one side of a river to the other after a flood or the death of an important person. Sometimes people would sleep next to their fields for convenience, but the fields were seldom more than a mile from houses. In short, it was along the perennial streams that Piman life assumed its most sedentary form.

Crops were the same as those grown in central Pimería Alta, with the addition of cotton, which was raised in a few places. Planting and cultivation, which were based on the ditching and irrigation of fields (or "floodplain" farming, rather than the flash-flood farming practiced by the two-village people), required a fairly complex organization of manpower and division of labor. (Floodplain farming seems to have reached its highest development along the Middle Gila River, a region that has since become the Gila River Indian reservation, which is not considered here.)

The largest village in Pimería Alta at the opening of the historic period was the Sobaipuri settlement of Bac (now San Xavier del Bac), which had more than 800 inhabitants. Other villages along the San Pedro, Santa Cruz, Middle Gila, San Miguel, Magdalena, Concepción, and Altar rivers varied in size from 20 to 50 houses, with from 100 to 600 inhabitants. Their oval houses, made of mesquite and brush, were often covered with plaited mats.

The riverine Pimans were probably much like other Pimans in many aspects of their culture, and it is unlikely that they could be easily distinguished on the basis of items of material culture, religious beliefs and ceremonies, social organization, or musical and oral traditions. But greater supplies of food and larger, permanent villages suggest that political and economic organization within these settlements was more detailed. The riverine people had to supplement farming with hunting, gathering, and fishing to a lesser degree than did other Indians of Pimería Alta — and the natural resources that could be exploited along rivers were the richest in the desert. There was more leisure time and, consequently, a greater number of part-time specialists at certain trades and a greater production of goods. In addition, the main routes of travel through the Sonoran desert followed streams, and villages beside them were more likely to become centers of trade and commerce than were villages elsewhere. The greater wealth that accrued to riverine Pimans because of this combination of circumstances was reflected in more and better clothing (including that made of locally grown cotton) and in ornaments of turquoise and shell.

In Pimería Alta, the riverine people were decidedly the aristocrats. A Spanish missionary described their characters as "haughty and proud, a fact which can be recognized in the manner in which they talk — with little esteem — about those Indians of the west. These western Indians [Central Pimerians], either because of being less haughty or because of some other motive, consider them superior and look up to them with special respect" (Manje 1954: 242).

Indians whom the Spaniards called "Arenenos" are frequently grouped with the western nomads in historic and ethnographic accounts, although they should probably be considered as riverine Pimans who farmed part of the year along the Sonoyta River or near the few large springs in southwestern Arizona and northwestern Sonora that were capable of supporting agriculture. Their habitations may have been less permanently situated than those of other riverine people; thus agriculture supplemented, in only a small way, the food that they garnered by hunting, gathering, and collecting. Major Areneno settlements were at Quitobaquito, now in Arizona, and at Sonoita, where their descendants live today as Sonorans.

In summary, the Pimans of the arid lower valley of the Colorado were of necessity nomadic, because the lack of surface water made farming and fixed habitations impossible. The two-village Pimans practiced agriculture, within the limits of their technology and those presented by the lack of perennial streams in their domain. The riverine people were able not only to plant the biggest crops but also to plant the biggest and most permanent villages.

INTRODUCED CHANGES. The Spaniards, and ultimately other non-Indians of European extraction, introduced innumerable changes in Pimería Alta: cattle, horses, goats, and sheep were brought in; wheat became an important crop along the rivers; money supplanted salt and ceremonial songs as mediums of exchange. A different technology — based in the final analysis on coal and iron, neither of which is found in the Sonoran desert — made it possible to tap deep supplies of underground water, to build all-weather roads, and to make gasoline-powered transportation the mode of the day.

The ancient inhabitants of Pimería Alta controlled the resources of their local environments. Today their descendants, the Papago, obviously cannot control coal and iron and the foreign economy based on these resources, which have brought about a totally new economy.

The New Economy

In prehistoric times, the Indians subsisted almost entirely on products grown in or gathered from the local environment, but, in the first two-and-a-half centuries after the coming of Europeans, they became dependent on products and economic systems that are foreign to the soil of Pimería Alta. This is evident in the story of cattle raising, the most important Papago-controlled industry, as well as in the histories of wage labor, federal employment, welfare, and leasing — which have also become key elements in the attempts of modern Papagos to make their way in the world.

CATTLE RAISING.   Jesuit missionary Eusebio Kino introduced cattle to Pimería Alta. Between 1687 and his death in 1711, Kino worked tirelessly among some 30,000 Indians, establishing more than 25 mission headquarters and visiting stations, primarily in Indian villages on the riverine perimeters of his mission territory. In addition to cattle, mission ranches were stocked with horses, burros, mules, oxen, sheep, goats, pigs, and fowl.

Kino's Jesuit and Franciscan successors continued to be involved in animal husbandry, but, during the Franciscan period (1768 to about 1828), herds were gradually concentrated in a few of the larger missions along the rivers in eastern and southern Pimería Alta. By 1821, Tumacacori Mission, on the Santa Cruz River, had become a mixed Pima-Papago settlement, with 5,500 head of cattle, 2,500 sheep and goats, and 600 horses (Kessell 1969: 57). It is not known how many of these animals made their way into the central parts of the Papago country, but they probably effected very little change among the two-village people and none at all among the western nomads.

Land Grants. Toward the end of the Spanish period, and increasingly during the Mexican period, non-Indians applied for grants as a means of securing title to ranch lands. Papagos, of course, did not apply for ownership of land that they felt already belonged to them, even though they were regarded as citizens under Mexican law. By the 1830's, Mexican ranches where stock was raised were scattered throughout the river valleys and higher grasslands of Sonora, as far north as Tucson. Parts of central and western Pimería Alta were left to the Papagos, but the legal titles of lands belonging to most of the riverine Indians were preempted. Eighteen land grants, issued between 1821 and 1850, covered most of the Santa Cruz, Sonoita, Babocomari, San Pedro, and Arivaca river valleys and included more than 800,000 acres of land (about 1,250 square miles). The United States eventually confirmed title to about 100,000 acres.

Mexican cattlemen not only grazed their stock on lands issued under formal grants, but also used what were called "overplus" lands, to which they might eventually acquire title by payment of current market price. Thus, the aboriginal Papago Indian domain of eastern Pimería Alta was eventually taken over by freely wandering herds of cattle.

The immediate effects of Spanish and, subsequently, Mexican ranching on the lives of Papagos are difficult to assess, in the absence of documentation. It is clear that the southern and eastern riverine perimeters of Papago country were eventually filled with Mexican ranchers. It is probable that Papagos soon became dependent on these ranchers for employment during at least part of each year and that, when Papagos were not tending their own little fields, they were trading their labor to Mexican rancheros for food or money, rather than following the aboriginal pattern of hunting and gathering or that of trading with other Indians. With large Mexican ranches on their borders and in their midst, some of the Papagos probably became partly dependent on non-Indians.

Papago Ranching.   It is presently impossible to estimate how many Papagos had acquired cattle and had themselves become ranchers by the 1850's. Geographic logic suggests that the first to own cattle were those along the rivers and on the adjacent desert lands and that the two-village people were the last. (There are no data implying that western nomads ever became herders.)

Rolf Bauer, who has studied the implications of the Papago cattle industry (1971: 87), notes that some investigators believe that during most of the eighteenth and nineteenth centuries cattle were only a minor part of Papago subsistence and that, before the 1870's, the cattle that were beyond mission or presidio influence were semiwild. Bauer further states:

Southern Papagos, close to the Anglo and the Mexico ranchers, were acquiring animals through the abandonment of ranches due to Apache raids and drought, and as pay for their services with the soldiers. There are some strong indications that herds had become in one century more than a minor portion of Papago subsistence before the Indian Service began introducing changes to develop cattle ranching as a permanent Papago industry in the early twentieth century. Between 1711 and 1912, that is, between the time Father Kino's missions lapsed and the time the Indian Service made their first development effort, *there were two centuries during which time the Papago had the opportunity to adapt ranching practices to their subsistence economy.*

There is some indication that during the early portion of those 200 years those stock that bred outside the influence of missions were hunted like deer, or caught as 'Mustang' and 'tamed and used ... in the manner taught at the mission.' During those two centuries there seems to have been a merging of hunting and cattle practices, the latter adapted from or fitted to the former, ending with the shift from emphasis on hunting to emphasis on grazing, especially in the southern district of the present-day reservation (Bauer 1971: 87).

Bauer quotes evidence that Papago family hunters, who were always males, began to hunt and kill half-wild cattle, distributing the meat precisely as they had distributed venison. In time, hunting shifted to herding, but with males still in charge. Ruth Underhill described the situation on the Papago reservation during the 1930's:

Now cattle raising has taken the place of hunting, its arrangements are very similar. A village unit used the neighboring range as it had formerly used the hunting, but that range has no definite limits and no objection is raised if the cattle of other units are found there. A few families have accumulated enough cattle so that their ownership ranks as a business, managed on modern lines. Many, however, sell only two or three a year to local buyers and butcher about as many for the family as they formerly butchered deer. They distribute gifts of beef as they once distributed venison (Bauer 1971: 87).

The livestock introduced into Papago country by Spaniards and Mexicans was supplemented by a second wave of cattle, brought in during the 1870's and 1880's by Texans and other Anglo cattlemen. This increase in stock also served to increase the conflict between Indian and non-Indian cattlemen.

In 1871 the Arizona superintendent of Indian affairs stated that stock raising had become the Papago specialty. Five years later the agent at the Gila River Indian reservation noted that the Papagos had many more cattle and horses than the Pimas and that herds were increasing yearly. Livestock raising had become a most important factor of Papago livelihood, and many non-Indians agreed that Papago independence related directly to their ability to manage cattle. Papago settlements were said to be "wherever they could find springs, marshes, or low lands, that would furnish water for their stock" (Stout 1878: 5).

Soon, Indians began to lose out in competition with non-Indian cattlemen. In 1871, Henry Clay Hooker released about 4,000 head of cattle in the Baboquivari Valley, on Papago lands. An Indian agent, describing San Xavier five years later, said: "thousands of cattle belonging to Mexicans and others are grazing on the reserve, crowding the stock of Indians to an inconvenient distance from where they now belong" (Hudson 1876: 8 ff.). Later, a Tucson newspaper reported that "the country between Tucson and the belt of country in which these mines are located [Papago Mining District] is fast filling up with herds of stock and ranchmen" (*Arizona Daily Star* 1879). The increasing numbers of complaints filed against Papagos for stealing cattle, too, indicate that more and more cattle belonging to white men were being grazed in Papago country.

Conflict. For Papagos, the situation had become critical by 1887. The agent for the Pima and Papago Indians wrote in his report for that year that the Papagos:

... have been able heretofore to prosecute and carry on this industry by reason of springs and water and wells at the foot of mountains, where there is fair grazing land. When the spring or well at one point becomes dry, or the grass exhausted, they drive their stock to another point, and only use their homes in villages a small portion of the year.

This small privilege is fast being wrested from them, for the country is fast filling up with cattlemen (whites), and now at almost every spring or well some white man has a herd of cattle, and the inevitable result follows, the Indian is ordered to leave, and the 'superior race' usually enforces such order. The large scope of the country over which they are scattered, and the distance from this agency, renders it practically impossible for the agent to protect them against these wrongs, though I have traveled one hundred miles over a desert to secure an Indian the privilege of taking water from a well he had dug himself (Howard 1887: 6).

Two years later, another Pima and Papago agent argued that Papagos should be placed on reservations because they could:

...not hope to hold the vast cattle ranges belonging to the public domain against the influx of white population that is constantly flowing into this Western country; the Indian office may expect constant difficulties arising out of disputes between whites and Indians over the land which is now the support of the Indian, and which he will defend, in one way or another... (Johnson 1889: 120).

The "constant difficulties" became a crisis in 1895, when non-Indian cattlemen threatened to take armed action against the Papagos. They claimed that Indians had cost them more than $300,000 in damages, that Papago thievery had put some livestock operators out of business, and that they, not Indians, had legal compensable interest in grazing lands. They added that unless the federal government did something to stop Papago cattle stealing, they would take matters into their own hands. A spokesman said:

The cattleman of Pima County has...sunk wells 600 to 1,000 feet in depth and [is] pumping waters therefrom; he has built great reservoirs to impound the rainwaters, and will work out his own prosperity and will develop the country if left alone. He would ask no protection from the Government if the Indians were not its wards. He fears not the Indians but respects the long arm of the law.... The Papago Indians and kindred tribes should be removed to and kept confined on the reservation set apart for their use (Cameron 1896: 253).

Although there was no shooting war, the Papago cattle industry continued to be threatened. In this century, an Indian agent wrote that the Papagos were still in danger of "being driven out of their present possession and holdings, which most of them have held since time immemorial, by white cattlemen, either by threats or otherwise .... It will be the usual process of freezing out the red man from the public domain" (Berger 1903: 168).

A drought seriously depleted Papago herds in 1904, but by 1915 their stock had been replenished sufficiently to convince federal officials and members of the Indian Rights Association that steps should be taken to make the Papago role in the cattle industry secure.

An act of Congress on August 1, 1914, provided $5,000 for "development of a water supply for domestic and stock purposes and for irrigation for nomadic Papago Indians in Pima County, Arizona." The same act appropriated additional funds to be used, in part, for "improvement and sinking of wells, installation of pumping machinery, construction of tanks for domestic and stock water...." (United States Statutes at Large 1914). All this for Indians who as yet had no "legal" title to their lands.

The extraordinary size (more than 2,750,000 acres) of the Papago reservation, set aside by executive order in 1916, was based at least partly on the fact that each head of cattle needed about 140 acres for grazing. A subsequent reduction in size made the following year indicated the power of non-Indian cattlemen, who succeeded in having the heartland of the Papago country restored to public domain.

Most Papago families who acquired cattle apparently did so on a very small scale. Their initial model appears to have been the pattern still familiar among non-Indians throughout northwestern Mexico. In this culture, which has been labeled "Norteño," ranching is a single-family enterprise that may include the farming of small fields, the husbandry of chickens and pigs, the cutting and selling of mesquite and other fuel woods, the herding of goats and cattle (usually less than a dozen), and the owning of a few riding animals. Such ranchers are often expert cowboys, who also sell their *vaquero* skills to the owners of large ranches for whom cattle are an industry rather than a means of simple subsistence.

After larger scale Anglo-American and hacienda models were established in the 1870's, a very few Papago families acquired extensive herds of cattle, which they raised and marketed in the manner of non-Indians. It was estimated that more than 50 percent of all Papago families had livestock by 1959 — but two families had herds of more than a thousand cattle (even thousands), five families had between 500 and 999 head, nine families had 100 to 499, ten families had 50 to 99, twenty-nine families had 10 to 49, and four hundred families had 1 to 9 head (Metzler 1960: ch. 4, 5 ff.). Thus, fewer than 5 percent of the Papago people living on the three reservations owned about 80 percent of the cattle. As Metzler notes: "the figures distinguish roughly between the cattlemen and the families that just have cattle" (Metzler 1960: ch. 4, p. 6).

Obviously, the cattle industry on the Papago reservation actually exists in two quite different — although interlocking — forms. One of these may be considered as an extension of subsistence, and the other as a profit-and-surplus enterprise that is a "business" in the non-Indian sense of that term.

Subsistence Cattle Raising. This pattern has been described by a range management specialist employed by the Bureau of Indian Affairs:

... to a Papago a cow may represent a walking checkbook .... If a man needs a hundred dollars for his family, or a fiesta, a funeral, or a marriage, or for whatever purpose, he literally goes and cashes one cow or perhaps two or three cows, ... whatever his needs are. He doesn't keep money in the bank. His bank's walking out on that reservation, and therefore, as ... he needs cash, he goes out and sells. But the selling procedure is in itself unique, and in itself poses a problem for the Papagos because today they probably have a 5¢ spread in total income per pound that they get by the method of the traders buying individual stock, one to thirty, perhaps, at a time .... The trader cannot afford to go down ... with a bobtail truck and pick up livestock at this rate and pay the maximum market price for those cattle. But the Papago is the one that's hurting or suffering as the result of this system. Now they sell cattle over the scale. There are no public auctions where you can get the best bidding in, no competitive bidding to get the best price. But it's brought about the dual problem of the system of traders being on the reservation and making individual purchases and also the extended credit. Obviously these traders extend credit to these people, which many of them prefer. But at the same time the total income of the people is certainly reduced per ... hundredweight by this system (Whitfield 1970: 49 ff.).

An important aspect of the relationship between the small-scale cattle owner and the cattle buyer is that many Papagos have established long-term acquaintance with particular buyers, and dealings transcend purely commercial considerations. There are social overtones to the relationship, and a buyer is one to whom a Papago might be able to turn in time of need or crisis. Although the relationship is embodied in the notion of the willingness of the buyer to "extend credit," the credit is not strictly economic in nature.

In 1968, Papagos belonging to the Gu Achi Stockmen's Association described the pressures on small-scale cattle owners that make them decline the chance to sell their cattle at a few large sales and thereby derive greater profit. Bauer lists these in order of most general occurrence:

a.   Selling cattle for money, as when they [Papagos] return from cotton camps, or just before they go to Magdalena [for an October religious fiesta], or in hard times.
b.   Exchange of cattle with someone for beans, etc. That's been going on for a long time.
c.   For church feasts, saints' days, weddings, other fiestas. Catholic families have pictures of their saints. On the day of their saint, these people organize the fiesta and butcher cattle for the meals. But it's also a community fiesta, so some people will make donations of meat to help out (Bauer 1971: 89).

Bauer believes that "not only Papago social organization and economy, but Papago values have been in contradiction to Western-type economic development" (1971: 89 ff.). Metzler also notes similar conflict:

Anglo values emphasize individual initiative, responsibility, aggressiveness, and getting ahead. Papago ideals are cooperation, harmony, and doing your part.... This type of moral code created an individual who was highly subordinate and submissive .... Any desire to get ahead was outside his realm of thinking. This type of moral code created a society in which cooperation and sharing were the key values. Individual or family advancement was sinful, as it tended toward inequality and lack of unity.... This culture produced friendly, cooperative human beings, but had no goals in the way of material progress.... The white man, who simply assumes that the Papago can adopt his way of life, is ignoring the depth of the Papago system of life (Metzler 1960).

A reservation superintendant, John Artichoker, has summed up these contradictions between Papago and Western values with the comment, "Their priorities are backwards" (personal communication 1968).

Contrasted with the priorities of the small cattlemen and their "backwards" mores are those of the large-scale cattlemen, for whom stock raising is a commercial enterprise. A few of these Papago "cattle barons" live in ranch houses surrounded by all the auxiliary buildings and other appurtenances one would expect to find on a large ranch in Sonora or Texas. There are garages and sheds, private wells and water tanks, new automobiles and pickup trucks — and sometimes private chapels, as well as smaller homes for the adult children of the head of the family. One observer has written:

Some men, misers, have hundreds of cattle. They are criticized for receiving more help than they give at roundups by statistically inclined and less wealthy cowboys. They are not roundup bosses .... The cattle misers have stayed aloof from the present institutions [which enables one to become powerful by being generous]. They have a great deal of money on the hoof. Such men have existed since about 1900 .... They are said to be buried with lard cans full of their unspent silver dollars. We can regard them as outside the generosity system .... Lard buckets of silver dollars are proofs that their deceased owner didn't get anywhere in Papago society (Bahr 1964: 5).

One of the immediate effects of the adoption of cattle by the Papagos has been overgrazing of the range and consequent erosion. It has been estimated that by 1914 there were between 30,000 and 50,000 cattle and from 8,000 to 10,000 horses in Papago country. Further increases resulted in attempts by the Bureau of Indian Affairs to reduce the numbers of Papago stock; in 1930, each Papago family was theoretically limited to ownership of 100 cattle and 50 horses. By 1950, drought and an infectious disease, dourine, had reduced the 1930 totals — 27,000 cattle and 18,000 horses — to 13,000 cattle and 7,000 horses. Cattle had increased to 15,000 by 1960, and in 1967 there may have been as many as 18,000 cattle and 3,000 horses. (These numbers conflict, incidentally, with a 1944 BIA estimate that the maximum carrying capacity of the Papago range is 11,000 cattle and 1,000 horses [Bauer 1971: 89].)

In 1935 the Papago reservation was divided into eleven separate grazing districts, nine on the big reservation and one each on the San Xavier and Gila Bend reservations. Although previously there had been six ill-defined but commonly understood grazing areas on the Papago (Sells) reservation (Jones 1969: 202–235), the new boundaries and three new districts approximate Papago notions of areas belonging to related villages, which may have been consistent with traditional pre-cattle hunting-and-farming territories. There is also a crude correlation between Papago dialect areas and grazing districts, although Totoguani speakers were placed in the Schuk Toak and Baboquivari districts, Ge Aji speakers in the Gu Achi and Sells districts, Kuk (Ko-lohdi) speakers in the Chukut Kuk and Pisinimo districts, and Huhhu'ula speakers not on the Gila Bend reservation were included in the Hickiwan district with speakers of Gigimai.

Each livestock district is fenced, and, with rare exceptions, the enclosed cattle are run in common. Individual Papagos have their own brands, which can be passed to one's heirs. In the absence of a formal livestock association, coalitions of villages go together to handle a particular range, taking care of the roundup, branding, and preparation for sales. Every family with cattle on the range is expected to provide a cowboy to help in the roundup, and his presence also lessens the risk of a family's losing calves to someone else or of having mavericks turned over to the Papago tribal herd.

Each coalition of villages selects a cattle boss, and during roundup the cowboys meet each night with him to discuss the work of the day and to make plans for future work. The cattle boss is often a man who owns much stock but is not necessarily a "cattle baron"; in at least one recent instance, the cattle boss of a district was also the person in charge of Indian religious observances and Christian fiestas (Bahr 1964: 4 ff.; Jones 1969: 208–210; Whitfield 1970: 48–49).

Tribal Herd. In 1935 the Bureau of Indian Affairs brought in stock from New Mexico to be issued for slaughter, but the animals were so thin that they were turned out onto the reservation for fattening. The twelve cattle that survived became the nucleus of the Papago tribal herd, which has been used by the BIA as a kind of school for the demonstration of range management principles and modern ranching procedures to Papago cattlemen. The tribal herd also supplies the services of registered bulls to Papago livestock owners, on a rental program.

Initially, the Papago Agency of the BIA created a livestock board, which was assigned the task of overseeing operation of the tribal ranch. Although the Livestock Board was a part of Papago tribal operations, there is evidence suggesting that the tribal ranch was in fact run and controlled by the Land Operations division of the BIA's Papago Agency. In 1956 the BIA's Papago Agency turned the herd over to the Papago tribe; in 1962 the tribe requested additional technical support and supervision of the herd operation from the agency; in 1966 the tribe resumed full responsibility for the herd, and since then the herd and ranch have been handled by the Papago tribal herd manager.

The reasons for these shifts in responsibility have been analyzed by Bauer (1971: 91–93). He notes that the BIA made a successful economic enterprise of the ranch, but, when Papagos assumed control in 1956, no Papago cowboys had been trained specifically to take over jobs that previously had been done by BIA personnel. The Livestock Board "fell apart," and in 1962 the tribe, which could no longer afford to run the herd out of its own meager resources, called to the BIA for help. What looked like "help" in 1962 looked like "planning, supervision, and repossession" in 1966, so the tribe reduced the role of the BIA and hired its own tribal herd manager, a non-Indian, to oversee management of the ranch.

Beginning in 1935, the BIA tried to encourage Papagos to form district livestock associations as a means of coping with problems related to overgrazing, marketing, and other matters. Most Papagos viewed such encouragement as a BIA attempt to force Papagos into a stock-reduction program, which they had staunchly and bitterly resisted. However, district land codes and cattle associations were formed at San Xavier in 1953, Sif Oidak in 1954, Vaya Chin-Kaka-Ventana in 1957, Gu Achi in 1962, and Vamori in 1964. Of these, only the Gu Achi Stockmen's Association has been judged successful by both Papago cattlemen and BIA personnel.

The details of the successful enterprise, analyzed by Bauer (1971: 93–95, 98–101), will not be repeated here. His conclusions, however, have broad implications that extend far beyond the limits of the cattle industry's technicalities and into other programs. The following are Bauer's suggestions, which deserve to be more widely disseminated in the literature:

When members of a community or local group describe a program (project, organization, etc.) as their own, as opposed to belonging to an outside group or change agent, they will take responsibility for directing and maintaining it after the change agent has left.

In order for them to call a program their own, the members must participate in some combination of the following aspects of the program's development:
a.   *They have to come to accept the initiator (or change agent) of the development process* as a person who can be trusted, who has demonstrated concern for the well-being of the community and has respect for its members and their potential for developmental change. He must possess the knowledge, skills, and potential resources sufficient to help them solve their problems. Once the change agent has been accepted by the community, the following kinds of participation can be initiated.
b.   They have *to help identify the problems that they wish to resolve.*
c.   They must *participate in planning a program solution* to the problems they have helped to identify.
d.   They must *believe that there will be benefits for themselves to be derived from the program's success.*
e.   They must be allowed the time and opportunity needed to *adapt the planning, organization, project, and evaluation* to their own socio-cultural life.
f.   They must *recognize as their own the organization* responsible for carrying out the program, and then participate through it.
g.   They have to *(1) accept the major responsibility for organizing and carrying out the program solution,* and *(2) do the work themselves or select those who do.*
h.   They must (1) decide whether or not new *skills and technical knowledge are necessary to carry out the plans* and (2) *identify and obtain the resources* that can assist them.
i.   They have to *recognize the results of their efforts, success or failure, as their own* (Bauer 1971).

In 1955, total gross receipts from sale of Papago cattle were estimated at $634,000; in 1959, they were as high as $750,000; and in 1967, $846,000, or some 31 percent of the total Papago income from all sources. Because a very few families own most of the cattle, this means that great wealth is concentrated in the hands of a relatively small number of people. It is not surprising that many of these wealthy Papago cattlemen have been prominent in tribal politics, exerting considerable influence on tribal affairs.

There is no reservation-wide grazing ordinance; there are no reservation grazing fees. A flat 3 percent sales tax on all animals sold on the reservation accrues to the Papago tribe. Livestock associations, such as they are, collect small fees in their own areas for operational costs.

In 1969 a well-publicized drought caused the deaths of about 1,200 head of Papago cattle. To help alleviate the crisis, the BIA was able to expend some $200,000 for hay, other feed, and veterinary supplies. Some of the tribal and BIA employees were paid overtime wages for helping to haul water and feed during the emergency; others worked long extra hours at no extra pay. At least one of the families who raise cattle on a large scale refused all proffered federal or tribal help, electing to handle the drought situation in its own way; other families accepted whatever help they could get, regardless of their relative wealth or the size of their herds. Hard feelings resulted.

It was obvious that the small cattle owner was more seriously hurt as a result of the drought than was the owner of many head. The man who owns a thousand cattle and loses half is still fairly wealthy, but the man who owns five animals and loses two is left even more poor. On the Papago reservation, moreover, most federal or outside efforts aimed at improving the range and stock benefit to the wealthy more than they to the poor. As Metzler has commented: "the large livestock owners have been reaping profits for years from the activities of the Bureau in regard to water resources and range improvement" (1960: ch. 4, p. 17).

Little did Father Kino know, when he brought cattle from Mexico to nourish the Indian converts of Pimería Alta, that these domesticated Old World beasts would eventually nurture the development of an elite class of wealthy Papago cattlemen, cattlemen's associations, grazing districts and village-coalition cattle bosses; of a Papago livestock board, tribal herd and ranch; and of BIA supervision of various aspects of the cattle-raising industry. But the Jesuit legacy has remained, and the raising of livestock — with its attendant sociological, psychological, and political implications — continues to exert a powerful influence over the lives of the desert people of the Papago Indian reservation.

WAGE LABOR. Although it is impossible to pinpoint the exact time at which Papagos first began to exchange their labor for either goods or cash, it seems reasonably certain that at least as early as the eighteenth century — and perhaps historically — the western nomads and the central two-village people were trading labor to their Yuman and riverine Piman neighbors for food. There is also reason to suspect that during the 1700's, at least some Papagos were employed in mines and on ranches by Spaniards, and it is assumed that the Piman Indians who served as soldiers in the Spanish army received pay and rations for their efforts.

A silver strike was made in 1737 in Papago territory southwest of Guevavi, near the Santa Cruz River. In 1771 extensive deposits of placer gold were discovered near Cieneguilla, south of Caborca in Sonora, and by the 1830's innumerable small Mexican mines were scattered throughout Pimería Alta. Although mining had not been a native Papago pursuit, it is probable that a great many Papagos soon became familiar with the value that non-Indians placed on certain minerals and that they became involved in mining operations.

Between 1860 and 1890, Anglos, too, began to search for gold and silver in Papago country. Mines were opened at Fresnal, Cababi, Gunsight, and dozens of other locations in the heart of Papago lands. At least a few Papagos were hired as mine laborers, and many Papagos sold goods to the predominately non-Indian residents of boom mining camps. Women sold their earthenware pottery and men supplied fuel wood. A calendar-stick account of Papago history, kept at the village of Covered Wells, noted that in 1887 the Quijotoa mine shut down and there was no more work and that in 1900 the long closed Picacho mine reopened and the Indians secured much employment.

The Indian agent reported in 1876 that Papagos "find considerable employment among the settlers, providing valuable aid in their harvest fields, and adapting themselves to various kinds of labor" (Hudson 1876). Large numbers of Papagos were employed in off-reservation cotton farming in 1918, when World War I cut off the United States from supplies of Egyptian long-stable cotton, and a boll weevil infestation simultaneously hit the South. The invention of the pneumatic tire, which requires cotton thread, established Arizona as one of the cotton-growing centers of the world. Papagos supplied the labor force to cultivate and pick the crops, and the cotton industry eventually became the principal provider of Papago family income.

New Migration Pattern.   The labor of Papagos was as cheap as it was unskilled, and because nearby cotton fields surrounded the reservation a new kind of migratory cycle was established. From their winter villages, people moved in summer to the white man's cotton fields. A few of the more prosperous white farmers established permanent cotton camps, with diversified operations that employed Papago farm laborers throughout the year. Thus tied to wage labor, many Papagos were born and grew up with cotton camps rather than reservation villages as "home." The pattern persisted until the early 1960's, when mechanization of cotton farming greatly reduced the need for unskilled labor.

Metzler, quoting from a 1947 report, says that income from wage labor accounted for 27 percent of total Papago income in 1937, and for 56 percent ten years later (1960: ch. 6, p. 1). By 1967 wage labor had declined to 41 percent of Papago total income, reflecting a decline in cotton-camp labor and a concomitant increase in welfare allotments (Figure 1).

In 1960, Papagos' wage labor came chiefly from employment in agriculture; from employment in nearby cities such as Tucson, where men and women worked in construction, manufacturing, public agencies, hospitals, hotels and motels, tree and plant nurseries, stores, and private homes; from employment in distant cities, as a result of the BIA relocation program; and from on-reservation employment as "clerks, secretaries, nurses, nurses' aides, sanitarians, mechanics, machine operators, truck drivers, bus drivers, cooks, maintenance men, interpreters, teachers, and telephone operators" (Metzler 1960: ch. 6, p. 4). The 1972 list is much the same, except that the

Office of Economic Opportunity and other federal programs have increased the range and number of employment positions on the reservation since 1965, as opportunities for off-reservation agricultural employment have decreased.

Although we recognize the dangers of generalizations concerning modern Papago people — and although we cannot endorse his entire statement — the views of Papago wage labor expressed by Metzler in 1960 continue to be very applicable in 1972:

The change to working for wages in a money economy has been a financial boon to the Papagos. Earning a living by collecting food from the desert was hazardous. Crop and livestock production were helpful additions to their sustenance, but both had limited possibilities.

Yet the change has been most difficult and it is still too early to say that it constitutes a solid gain. First of all the Papagos strongly rebel against the regimentation of the industrial economy. They deeply prefer to be able to follow their own inclinations each morning rather than to have to report to the same place and task. To change from a life of unhurried living to one of never-ending routine work fails to evoke any enthusiasm. So they get "fed-up" with a steady job and take French leave. They prefer odd jobs to steady employment.

Equally important, the Papago has only a vague idea as to how to utilize the money he receives in his paycheck. Hands reach for it from all sides, and it may all go for alcohol, police court fines, and other empty purposes. His family may still lack food, clothing, and a decent place to stay, particularly if he also loses his job because he failed to report for work at the prescribed time and place. To get money and then be exploited for it can be much more destructive to the individual than to be ill-nourished on the desert.

Consequently, many Papagos say, "We were better off before the white man came in and began destroying us with his vices. Our people are gradually being destroyed by alcohol and we are helpless to do anything about it. We ought to close off the reservation and live in our own way."

The transition to a wage work economy means a change in their entire way of life. They have received very little practical guidance in making this change. The number of failures made during this process is so high as to warrant the misgivings of the Papago people. The number of changes in the direction of personal and social disintegration may be as great as the number in the direction of greater economic security.

Their change to a wage economy is practically inevitable and will continue .... The sooner a broad program is devised to meet the adjustment problems of these people, the less the social costs will be. The Papagos themselves must be active participants in the development of such a program (Metzler 1960: ch. 6, p. 2–3).

FEDERAL EMPLOYMENT. Since the beginning of official contact between the Papagos and the United States government, direct federal subsidies have assisted the Indians. Colonel John Walker, who became the first Papago agent when he arrived in Tucson in 1857, issued rations of flour and beef, as well as shovels, hoes, brass kettles, butcher knives,

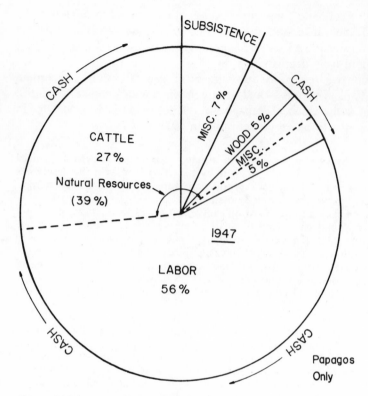

Source: U.S. Department of the Interior, 1949; *Papago Agency Newsletter,* November 21, 1967.

Figure 1.   Papago income sources

scissors, saddlers' awls, needles, square axes, helved axes, steel shovel-plow points, tin cups, and spools of cotton.

Although Papagos were hired by the Bureau of Indian Affairs at San Xavier for various kinds of jobs throughout the 1890's and early 1900's, it was only when the Papago (Sells) reservation was created and BIA headquarters was moved there in 1919 that the full impact of federal employment opportunities was felt among Papagos. Sells, which had been little more than a farm area in the nineteenth century, became one of the most heavily populated areas on the reservation — as it remains today. Many Papagos, especially the Protestant minority who had been educated at the Presbyterian boarding school in Tucson, were employed in government service.

During the Depression of the 1930's, the Civilian Conservation Corps–Indian Division (CCC-ID) established a branch on the Papago

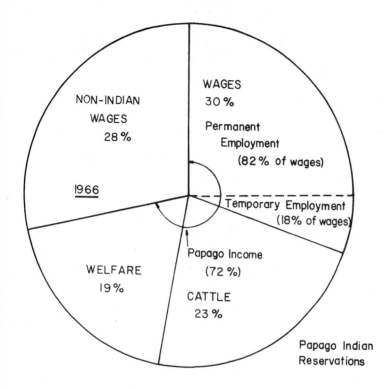

reservation, and large numbers of Papago people were set to work in groups, for the improvement of wells, cattle-watering places, trails, roads, and fences. Many Papagos who had made fairly satisfactory adjustments to off-reservation life apparently returned during the 1930's, simply because more work and more money were available on the reservation than off it.

During the last ten years, federal payrolls and federally derived income have increased on the Papago reservation. The Bureau of Indian Affairs and Public Health Service have been joined in hiring Papagos by the Office of Economic Opportunity and by the federally supported public school district — as well as by the Papago tribe, which administers federal grants, such as those received from OEO.

A former superintendent of the BIA's Papago Agency has reported that during 1966 a total of $3,745,780 was generated on the Papago reservation. Indians received $2,680,197 of this amount. (Presumably, the remaining million-plus dollars went to high-salaried non-Papagos working on the reservation.)

The BIA was the largest single employer of the reservation, with a payroll for Papagos and non-Papagos totalling $781,298. The United States Public Health Service–Division of Indian Health was second, with a combined payroll of $616,357. Papagos working for the federally subsidized Kitt Peak National Observatory on the reservation earned $121,636. When welfare payments are included in the total, it becomes apparent that about three-fourths of the income on the reservation in 1966 was federally derived (see Figure 1). The percentage is probably lower today because of income from mining leases, but the duration of these high bonus payments for exploration and development leases is unpredictable. Meanwhile, it is clear that the federal government has become the principle source of on-reservation Papago wage income.

WELFARE.   If the issuing of food and implements by Colonel Walker, the first Indian agent, can be called "welfare," then Papagos have been recipients of welfare for many, many years. Welfare in terms of cash payments to individuals is a twentieth-century phenomenon, yet it is not surprising that the Papagos have received monetary assistance. In 1968 it was established that the average Papago reservation family had an annual income of $2,377, or $554 per capita. The "average" Papago family had about one-fifth the annual income of the "average" family in the state of Arizona as a whole. William Kelly has written:

> There is little or no evidence that Papago Indians have taken undue advantage of welfare programs. On the contrary, there is much evidence that state and federal welfare payments make the difference between complete and painful poverty and a bearable standard of living for many reservation families. This last statement holds particularly true for the old people — close to 60 percent of all welfare payments go to individuals over 65 — who are especially vulnerable under modern conditions (Kelly 1963: 188).

Welfare payments to Papagos are made in the form of Old Age Assistance, Aid to Dependent Children, Aid to the Blind, child welfare, and general assistance. (The figures given do not take into account Social Security, retirement, or veteran's benefits.) In 1958 the estimated total of welfare payments made annually to Papago reservation residents was $354,252 and the total had risen to $473,796 by 1962 (Kelly 1963: 120). A former superintendent of the Papago Agency has estimated that the 1966 total had risen to $718,685, which probably reflects the loss of seasonal agricultural labor (primarily in cotton), as well as the increasing population, particularly of older people.

Padfield and van Willigen have reported that, in 1965, 35 percent of the reservation Papago families were receiving welfare assistance, as contrasted to 13 percent of the off-reservation Papago families (1969: 214). This report also indicated that the on-reservation population was older, less well educated, less committed to participation in the labor force, more disabled, and almost totally dependent economically. We suspect that this picture has been altered at least slightly by changes that have occurred on the reservation since 1965, most notably those brought about by OEO programs, income from mineral leases, and a rapidly growing tribal bureaucracy.

LEASING. The fifth major element in the "new economy" of the Papagos involves the leasing of their land and resources. It has not been possible to determine when the first leases of Papago lands were made, but the Senate's *Survey of conditions of the Indians in the United States* (United States Congress 1931) made it clear that legally there had been no leasing at all. Papagos were not in permanent possession of mineral rights until 1955, so legitimate leasing of mineral rights was previously impossible.

Some time after 1931, however — most probably during the 1950's — Papago farmlands at San Xavier were leased to non-Indians, who grew crops and later ran cattle into the fields after the harvest. But such leasing has always been on a fairly small scale. Not until 1955, when mining companies became interested in leasing copper resources, did this source of income become significant in Papago lives.

Mining Leases. The American Smelting and Refining Company (ASARCO) obtained an exclusive mineral exploration permit for 15,360 acres of the San Xavier reservation in 1957, a lease that granted the company the right to develop any ore bodies that might be discovered. ASARCO paid $1,066,007 to obtain this lease and has subsequently made additional rental payments, royalty payments, and a $2,100,000 settlement of a lawsuit brought against the company by Papagos.

In 1967 three other companies paid Papagos a total of $757,938 as bonuses for exclusive mineral prospecting permits on the San Xavier reservation; no commercial ore bodies have been located and no mines have been developed in the area involved. In 1969 Hecla Mining Company and El Paso Natural Gas Company paid the Papago tribe $3,700,000 in rentals and bonuses for development of a copper mine in the Sif Oidak district, in the northern part of the Papago (Sells) reservation. Additional leases of Papago lands for mineral exploration, such as a 1967 lease with Newmont Mining, Ltd., have also been negotiated — and there are prospects for others in the future. Of a total of $7 million that the Papagos have acquired through the leasing of mineral rights since 1957, some $6 million has been negotiated since 1967.

Land Ownership. The nature of Papago land ownership is one of many complex factors involved in leasing. The San Xavier reservation is alloted largely under the terms of the Dawes Severalty (or General

Allotment) Act of 1887. Some 41,622 acres of the 71,095-acre reservation were assigned in restricted or trust status to individual Papagos in 1890, and most of the mineral-bearing land is in these areas. Thus, the heirs of the original allottees divide the lease money in accordance with their proportionate shares in an allotment, and comparatively little of the payment goes to either the San Xavier district or the Papago tribe.

Leases on tribal land, however, are of financial benefit to both the tribe and the political district in which the land is located, with half of the money going to each political unit (as provided for in the Constitution and bylaws of the Papago Tribe, Arizona, approved January 6, 1937). This division has been contested by many of the Papagos living in districts with high lease incomes, who argue that the district should get all or most of the money and the tribe little or none.

In the "new economy," leasing has surpassed all other categories in gross income during recent years. Mineral resources are not unlimited, however, nor will the magnitude of annual royalties be as great as initial bonus payments. Moreover, these large sums of money tend to be inequitably distributed among Papagos, especially at San Xavier, where payment rests solely on chance — the heritage of allotted lands everywhere. The large sums of money have also attracted many non-Indian advisers and consultants, most of them extremely well-paid people who, intentionally or not, have preempted the Papagos' ability to make decisions in their own behalf. Money has also stimulated the growth of a tribal bureaucracy — which may or may not always act in the interest of the majority of Papago people.

The Ruling Elite

In every political structure there are centers of power and authority, and the Papago Indian reservation is no exception. The influence of at least six major organizational units is felt reservation-wide, or nearly so, and these units can be considered as the loci of power on the reservation.

This does not mean that the 80-plus individual villages that are scattered over some 2,700,000 acres of Papago land lack internal political structure; for some villages are highly organized along rather traditional lines, and they exercise a high degree of autonomy in the management of their internal affairs. Reservation-wide structures and programs are becoming increasingly influential at the local level, however, and, to the non-Indian outsider who approaches the Papago world, the key decision makers are those who represent one or more of the six major centers of power. It is not surprising that these power centers control the on-reservation Papago economy — for that economy is the source of their power.

THE PAPAGO INDIAN TRIBE.   The Papago Indian tribe was organized in 1937, with a constitution and by-laws in accordance with the Indian Reorganization Act of 1934. Following the lines of grazing districts that had been created in 1935 (which, in turn, to some extent had followed the aboriginal concepts of related-village boundary units), eleven political districts were created: one each for the San Xavier and Gila Bend reservations, and nine on the Papago (Sells) reservation (Baboquivari, Chukut Kuk, Gu Vo, Gu Achi, Hickiwan, Schuk Toak, Sells, Sif Oidak, and Pisinimo).

Each district has its own democratically elected chairman, council, and two elected representatives to the tribal council. The twenty-two tribal councilmen elect — either from among their own number or at large — a tribal chairman, vice-chairman, secretary, and treasurer. The tribal constitution requires that, at a minimum, the council meet on the first Saturday of each month. Elections are held annually.

Papago Democracy.   In theory — the traditional theory of Western democracy — Papago councilmen represent the interests of constituents in the districts from which they are elected. By Papago tradition, however, each person is regarded as having precisely the same rights as everyone else, and Papago people are, therefore, reluctant to speak for anyone other than themselves. In the old days, the governing of village or groups of related villages was strictly by consent of the governed; all interested parties were consulted before important decisions were made, and it was customary to forestall action until consent was virtually unanimous. Until very recently, almost all votes of the tribal council have been 22–0, a good indication of the survival of traditional Papago notions of democracy.

From the viewpoint of outsiders, the traditional machinery of Papago tribal democracy was cumbersome, slow and hopelessly inefficient. The council was likely to postpone action on any matter — large or small — until councilmen could return to their district villages and consult with local people, which delayed most decisions for at least a month and some for several months. In other instances, no decisions were made at all, either because concensus could not be achieved or because either the people or the councilmen were indifferent to the outcome.

The extent to which councilmen actually reported back to their constituents is lost to history, although it may be assumed to have varied widely from district to district. A fact that emerges clearly, however, is that Papagos do not share the Anglo tradition of representative government. Unlike white men, the Papagos have not believed that simply because one is elected to a representative position he is justified in making decisions that affect others without first consulting them. (Indeed, the first three decades of Papago tribal government under a constitution and bylaws were very similar to the "town-hall" government of the colonial United States.) To non-Papagos, a democracy so intensive is suitable for running the affairs of villages where individuals know one another personally, but it is not suitable for running the affairs of a nation — Papago or otherwise.

Imposed "Efficiency."   Very soon after the Offices of Economic Opportunity programs came to the reservation in 1965, with funds to be administered by the tribe, changes were made in the nature of Papago tribal government. In a tape-recorded interview, a former Papago tribal council member expressed his views on this subject very well:

You know, you have proposals that goes off to the people [from the tribal council to the villages]. Well, this would take years, or something like that. So he [the tribal attorney] didn't like that. So he decided, well, we'll put up committees. So now they propose some [thing] and they send it to the committee, and supposedly each committee is representing the people, saying 'okay.' So they leave out the people. They [outsiders dealing with the tribe] just work with the council and the committees, and most of the time the committee is the council themselves. They're particular who they have in those committees (Whitfield 1970).

The committee system — devised in attempts to bring efficiency, *as defined by non-Indians,* into Papago tribal government — has short-circuited direct and meaningful village involvement in tribal affairs. It brings Papago government more in line with non-Papago ideals of representative government, which are essentially much less representative than those of Papago tradition. Councilmen are encouraged to make immediate decisions on behalf of their constituents and are discouraged from consulting with villagers on many issues.

Moreover, because the entire elective system of government, as exemplified by the tribal constitution, is foreign to traditional Papago political systems, the turnout of voters is usually small, and Papagos have asserted that money bribes are sometimes offered in attempts to stimulate voters to go to the polls and vote on specific issues.

The tribal constitution and bylaws provide only for a tribal council, chairman, vice-chairman, secretary, and treasurer; the tribe operated with such a group from 1937 until 1965. The committee-and-board system, and the growth of tribal bureaucracy, occurred after the introduction of OEO funds in 1965 and have continued under President Nixon's program of "self-determination." Increasingly, BIA services are being contracted to the tribe and put under tribal control. The Tribal Work Experience Program, for example, has been funded by the BIA but is controlled by the tribe.

Figure 2 charts a somewhat idealized version of Papago tribal government (as of Summer 1972). By no means are all the services indicated on the chart paid for with tribal income from leases or from other reservation-generated sources. Major contributors of the funds that maintain the system are the Office of Economic Opportunity, the Economic Development Administration, the Department of Housing and Urban Development, the Bureau of Indian Affairs, and the Department of Health, Education and Welfare. The Tribal Utility Authority and the Tribal Mining Committee, however, are a direct outgrowth of leasing activities.

COMMUNITY ACTION PROGRAM. Although it is administered within the framework of tribal government, the Community Action Program (CAP) — formed (1965) and still largely funded by the Office of Economic Opportunity — has for part of its history been nearly autonomous within the tribal structure. Today, CAP is probably less autonomous than it has been in the past, but as a branch of tribal government that controls the expenditure of substantial federal grants, its potential remains for continuing to be a locus of power. It is probably no coincidence that the first director of CAP, Thomas Segundo, subsequently became tribal chairman. The director of this program has patronage to dispense, a large budget and many vehicles under his control, and his work takes him repeatedly into the villages to deal at the "grass-roots" level of Papago society.

Contemporary Papago critics of OEO activities on the reservation point out that the Community Action Program's facility for providing free transportation is, in itself, a means of power, in an area where great distances and poor roads make transportation a critical factor in everyday life. In former times only wealthy Papagos — most notably, the cattlemen — had pickup trucks or automobiles, and people in more remote areas depended on such transportation in getting from their villages to tribal headquarters at Sells, to the nearest trading post, or to Tucson, Phoenix, and Ajo. Thus, CAP's free transportation has eroded some of the influence and power formerly enjoyed by comparatively wealthy Papago individuals.

Subsidiary Services. The Community Action Program is also responsible for other reservation programs. Papago Legal Services provides advice, assistance, and counsel in court for those who could not otherwise afford legal help. The Community Development Program funds the employment of workers — all Papago Indians — in several

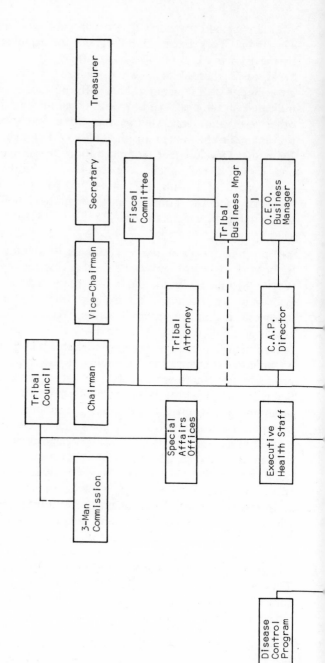

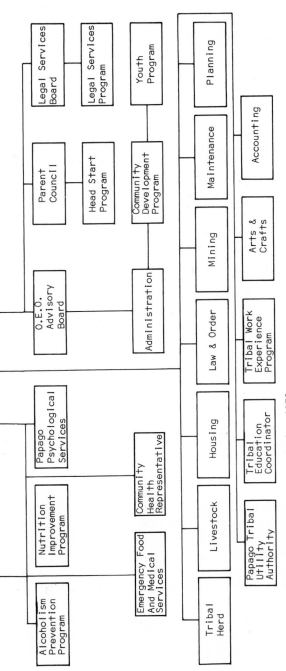

Figure 2. Paradigm of Papago tribal organization, 1972

reservation villages. CAP also operates a Neighborhood Youth Corps and a Headstart preschool program that is very popular among Papago parents. Funding for most CAP programs comes from OEO and the Department of Commerce, although money has also been contributed by the Department of Labor and the Department of Health, Education and Welfare.

THE BUREAU OF INDIAN AFFAIRS.   Whatever else the role of the Bureau of Indian Affairs on the Papago reservation may be, its ultimate function is as federal trustee for Papago lands. Lands within the Papago reservation, like Indian reservation lands elsewhere, are held in federal trust, which means that approval of the BIA or Department of the Interior is required before contracts between the tribe and potential leasers or purchasers of land can be made final. The same provision applies to contracts made with Indian owners of allotted lands in restricted status.

The BIA's role goes far beyond that of property management, however. Its wide-ranging activities also include land operations, education, and employment — as well as credit, housing, law enforcement and social services (Figure 3). It is presently being argued in a federal court that the BIA should also provide services for off-reservation Indians, in a case involving a Papago Indian living at nearby Ajo who requested general assistance from the BIA at Sells after his union went on strike against the local copper company and who was refused on the grounds that he did not live on Indian trust lands. Papago Legal Services sued the secretary of the interior on behalf of the Indian. (The decision presently stands in favor of the plaintiff, but the case has not yet been heard by the United States Supreme Court, and the decision could also be overturned on appeal.)

Official Approval.   The BIA also has the power to approve or disapprove contracts between the Papago tribe and other agencies and individuals: for example, traders on the reservation and tribal attorneys. Many actions of the tribal council cannot become effective without BIA approval. The phase, "with the approval of the secretary of the interior," who is represented by the BIA, is even inserted in the Papago Constitution.

Because of the very real authority it has acquired through various acts of Congress and because of its large payroll, the Papago Agency of the Bureau of Indian Affairs continues to be one of the most important centers of power on the reservation.

INDIAN OASIS PUBLIC SCHOOL DISTRICT.   Until the 1960's, all schools on the Papago reservation were administered either by the Bureau of

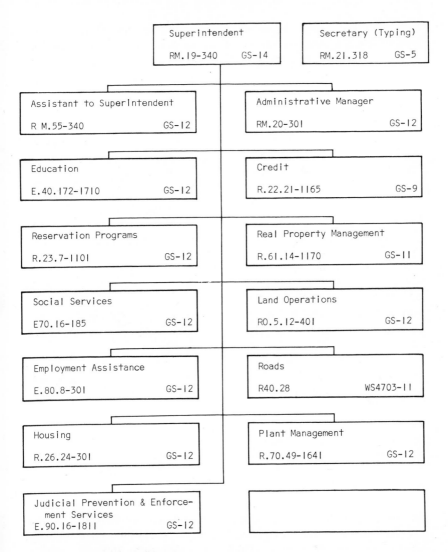

Figure 3. Office of the superintendent: organizational chart of the Papago Agency, Bureau of Indian Affairs, 1972

Indian Affairs or by the Roman Catholic church. Today, the church operates only two schools on the reservation, the elementary schools at San Xavier and Pisinimo. The BIA presently has schools at Santa Rosa, Santa Rosa Ranch, and Gu Vo (Kerwo), and it has plans to build a large boarding school at San Simon.

Public schools were established on the reservation in 1963, with the creation of Pima County Public School District No. 40 (Indian Oasis), which is administered by an all-Papago school board. The district is responsible for the operation of elementary schools at Sells and Topawa, and Baboquivari High School at Sells. The Papagos within the school district have taken a lively interest in the operation of their schools, as evidenced by the fact that two board members have been subjected to recall elections.

The public school district, with its operating and capital outlay budgets, its many employees, and its board, clearly represents another important locus of reservation power — although this influence is limited largely to the boundaries of the Indian Oasis School District, within the Papago (Sells) reservation.

UNITED STATES PUBLIC HEALTH SERVICE.   On the Papago reservation, the payroll of the Public Health Service is exceeded only by that of the Bureau of Indian Affairs. The Health Programs Systems Centers, located on the San Xavier reservation where it maintains a clinic, is also responsible for administration of the Sells Service Unit, which operates a hospital at Sells and a clinic at Santa Rosa. Although the administrative center at San Xavier employs many Papagos, it is not directly involved in health-care services. The center carries out health research among the Papago people, supplying supportive data to those who deliver health-related services.

Public Health Service programs are related to tribal programs that are funded through grants administered by the tribal council. The organizational structure responsible for various health services is charted in Figure 4. The three-man commission is intended to "serve as a watchdog (or stirring stick) on the program activities of the various programs. The 'Special Affairs Office' is a tribal provision for leadership in emergency situations, but is not always occupied by tribal personnel. It is designed to be filled by health program representatives who will serve as a team to meet some specific health problem, such as an epidemic or floods," according to an explanation issued in 1972 by the Papago Executive Health Staff, which is made up of the directors of the tribal health program (Papago Executive Health Staff 1972).

ROMAN CATHOLIC CHURCH.   About 90 percent of the Papago Indians are Roman Catholics, at least nominally, and many of them are devotedly so. In the history of the reservation, this church has exerted enormous influence over the lives of Papago people and reservation affairs. The first schools for Papagos were Catholic schools. A Franciscan friar was influential in having the Papago (Sells) reservation created and also partially responsible for the delineation of tribal district boundaries; and in recent years, Franciscans have been involved in the affairs of the Indian Oasis schools. Since 1971, a Franciscan priest has served as

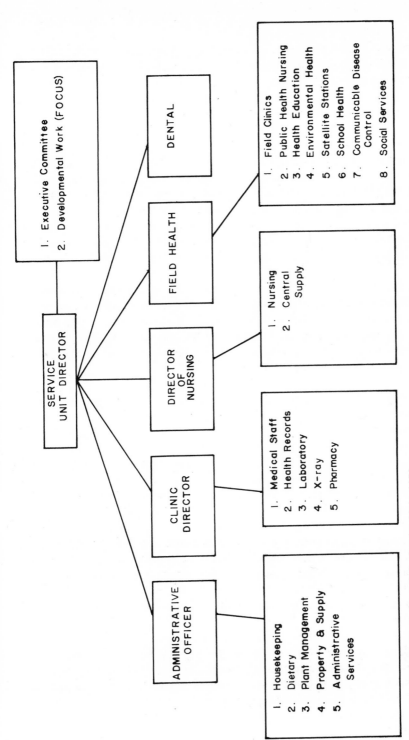

Figure 4. Organizational chart, Sells Service Unit, 1973

principal of Baboquivari (public) High School, and the only school on the San Xavier reservation is a parochial school operated by Franciscan nuns.

It is also obvious that the influence of the church in Papago affairs has gradually diminished over the years, and that, in 1972, for example, it is not nearly as powerful as it was in 1930. Today the church has fewer schools, fewer active missions, and fewer personnel. There are churches at Topawa, where Franciscans have a headquarters, and at Sells; at Pisinimo, a school and a church; at Covered Wells, a resident priest and three nuns are involved in religious education. The frequently photographed settlement at San Xavier del Bac includes four resident priests, a brother, and the Franciscan sisters who run the school. At Chuichu, there are two nuns whose sole concern is religious education.

Protestant Influence. Protestants are also active on the reservation. There are Presbyterian and Nazarene churches, and Mormon and Baptist missions. Of the Protestants, Presbyterians have historically been the most influential group in tribal affairs. A Presbyterian minister, as well as the Franciscan friar, was involved in the creation of the Papago (Sells) reservation.

POWER PLOYS. An outsider who approaches the reservation with a proposal concerning its lands or its Papago residents will almost certainly have to face one or more of these power structures, through its "ruling elite." People at the village level are increasingly insulated — and isolated — by these rather complex structures from direct contact with non-Papagos.

Tactically, which structure should be approached first? From time to time the answer changes, as power shifts. The Bureau of Indian Affairs once wielded sufficient "clout" to obtain tribal council approval for almost any projects that it backed. Since the advent of Office of Economic Opportunity funds, which go directly to the tribe, the locus of strength has shifted toward the tribe itself. Most proposals are now made first to the tribe rather than to the bureau, putting the tribal councilmen and non-Indian employees and advisers "in the driver's seat."

At the same time, case studies indicate that Papago people at the village level are increasingly being relegated to seats "in the back of the bus." Our investigations have led us to conclude that Papago tribal government is becoming more responsive to the needs of outsiders than it is to the needs of most Papago individuals and that the average Papago is becoming less able to make effective decisions in his own behalf.

CASE STUDIES

In attempting to understand the economic development of any group, it is helpful to examine individual instances in which changes aimed at general economic improvement have been proposed, either by those involved directly or by outsiders. Among the Papago, several dozen such changes have been suggested over the past twenty years, but an examination of the facts has brought us to the conclusion that most of the suggested changes fall into definite patterns, which can be exemplified by specific case studies.

ASARCO and Mission Mine

In March of 1957, after the Bureau of Indian Affairs had brought the record of allotment ownerships on the San Xavier reservation up to date, the BIA's Papago Agency (1957) issued a notice that it intended to advertise the leasing of exclusive mineral-prospecting permits on this reservation. On April 8, a four-page mimeographed announcement appeared: "Notice of competitive sale exclusive prospecting permit with option to lease restricted Indian lands for mining, San Xavier Indian reservation." This notice indicated that bids for the prospecting lease had to be submitted to the superintendent of the Papago Agency no later than 2 P.M., May 13, 1957; that three adjoining tracts of land, each containing 5,120 acres, would be opened for mineral exploration for a two-year period upon approval of the bid; and that the successful bidder would have an option to mine as many as 2,560 acres of land within each of the three tracts, provided he could obtain signatures of owners of at least 80 percent of the land involved.

Tract 1 includes sections 10, 11, 14, 15, 22, 23, 26, and 27 of Range 12 E., Township 16 S. Tract 2 includes sections 12, 13, 24, and 25 of the same range and township, and sections 7, 18, 19, and 30 of Range 13 E., Township 16 S. Tract 3 includes sections 8, 9, 16, 17, 20, 21, 28, and 29 of Range 13 E., Township 16 S.

Four mining companies submitted bids. American Smelting and Refining Company (ASARCO) was high bidder on all three tracts, offering a total of $1,066,007.04 for the 24 sections of land involved.

Representatives of the BIA and ASARCO worked together during the summer of 1957 to acquire the signatures necessary to cover 80 percent of the interest in the land in each of the three tracts, and early in September the required number was delivered to the Papago Agency superintendent by the mining company. Authorization for mineral exploration was issued through the BIA on September 13,

1957. ASARCO had paid Papago landowners approximately $70 per acre to obtain the exclusive right to prospect for minerals on 15,360 acres of land and to obtain an option for exclusive mining rights on a maximum of 7,680 acres.

ALLOTMENTS OF 1890. Prior to this juncture in the history of San Xavier, residents and nonresident allottees had paid scant attention to the allotments made in 1890. Despite sporadic attempts of BIA employees to persuade allottees to write wills so that their shares in the land would go to heirs of their choice, nearly all allottees died intestate. (They still do.) In terms of the Dawes Act of 1887, this means that the secretary of the interior determines the heirs in accordance with the state of Arizona's laws of succession — a system of inheritance that certainly is not native to Papago culture.

Until 1955, the BIA had been rather lax in probating the estates of deceased allottees. Papagos, neither knowing nor caring about this imposed and foreign system of land ownership, continued to build their houses in areas of their choice, close to relatives; they continued to farm small fields, to chop wood, and to graze their cattle as if the entire reservation were owned in common.

With the prospect of mineral income, however, all this began to change. People were informed if they were living on an allotment belonging to someone else, and they moved. Concern for private ownership of land was awakened — especially for land on the southern part of San Xavier reservation, where mineral explorations were to be made.

A great many heirs had accumulated by 1955. It was not unusual to find people who had a 5,040/1,108,800 share in a 20-acre allotment. Since that time, fractionations have become even more astronomical.

Few Papagos understood the state's laws of inheritance or the nature of their share in allotments. Many people living at San Xavier had no allotments at all. Other nonresidents, including a few non-Papago Indians who had become related to heirs through marriage, had a compensable interest in San Xavier land. And many allottees — perhaps most of them — had no more than a vague idea of where their allotments were located physically on reservation lands. (A confusion that still applied in 1972.)

Meanwhile, the people living at San Xavier, who had a sense of local autonomy, believed that district and tribal council permissions were needed before land on the reservation could be leased. In 1955 San Xavier residents were not aware that allottees, with the approval of the federal trustee — the BIA — could lease reservation lands without district or tribal approval. In the end, the district council approved the proposed lease, and the allottees — or those close enough to the reservation to care — felt free to sign lease agreements once such approval had been granted.

Instead of converting the mining-lease situation into a tool that could be used to make the Papago people aware of the intricacies of Arizona inheritance laws and of their own rights and responsibilities as landowners, BIA officials chose a much simpler solution: Papagos were told that if they signed the lease agreements, they would get money. On this level of understanding and sophistication, the signing of leases proceeded. No one knew how much money he would be getting, nor did anyone know precisely why he would be getting it.

PAYMENT DISTRIBUTION. When bonus payments were finally distributed, several Papagos who had worked hard all their lives, struggling to better their economic circumstances through their own initiative, received nothing. Others, including a few alcoholics, inherited large sums of money. Individual payments ranged from $26,000 to as little as $4. The amounts fell randomly among rich and poor, drunk and sober, respected and disliked, lazy and industrious.

Moreover, the BIA, as trustee, elected to show "big brotherly" concern over the allottees' use of their funds. If individuals who had been on welfare received sizeable shares of money, they were removed from welfare rolls and given biweekly or monthly checks in the same amount they had been receiving as welfare recipients. Only now the money they were getting was "their own." Others who were deemed to be "responsible" by BIA personnel were given their money in lump sums. The money of at least one individual, a chronic drunk, was turned over to a bank, which was appointed as trustee. Some Papagos were forced to apply for their funds as they needed them — and to justify the need by showing BIA personnel their bills, or by explaining that they had to buy school clothes for their children. In the initial stages of distribution, the reservation was visited weekly by the Papago Agency administrative assistant, who sat a table in the council house while Papagos queued up outside, waiting their turn to ask him for some part of their money.

There is no very useful way to generalize how the million dollars were eventually used — indeed, no one recorded how all of it was spent. Some of those who could afford it had domestic water wells drilled at their homes — they couldn't foresee that a few years later the Public Health Service would install a reservation water system free of charge. People bought groceries, new and secondhand pickup trucks and automobiles — even a tractor. Improvements were made on homes. And people bought wine, beer, and hard liquor; they wrecked or neglected their vehicles; they had a good time; they went broke. It is perhaps safe to say that the money seems not to have changed anyone's life-style. The drunks did not become more sober. The industrious were no less hard working than before, and the thrifty no less thrifty. And, tragically, in some instances the aged poor died without discovering that they had become rich.

EXERCISE OF OPTIONS.   ASARCO had completed its mineral explorations on the reservation by 1959, and the company chose to exercise its mining options within Tracts 1 and 2, where workable ore bodies had presumably been discovered, but not on Tract 3. Altogether, ASARCO leased for mining 560 acres of Tract 1 and 1,920 acres in Tract 2, for a total of 2,480 acres.

The leases for these two tracts, formally executed in August of 1959, provided for a royalty of 10 percent of the value of the ores or concentrates, as indicated by reduction returns after deducting freight charges to the point of sale; for an annual rental of $1 per acre per year and, after the first four years, a minimum royalty payment of $4 per acre per year — or a total of $5 an acre annually, whether there was mining or not; and for a one-time payment of $25 per acre once mining commenced.

Each mining lease was good for ten years and for as long thereafter as minerals were produced in paying quantities. Leases were subject to review and adjustment by the secretary of the interior at the end of each ten-year period. Finally, the leases provided that Indian labor was to be used in all positions for which they were qualified.

OVERBURDEN DUMP.   As early as 1959, ASARCO began separate negotiations to lease four sections of land within Tract 3, where no exploitable ore deposits had been found, for use as a dump for overburden from the adjacent off-reservation open pit. The company initially offered to lease the four sections needed for a dump at $1 per acre annually. The Papagos had no attorney in 1959, so the BIA was their sole protector against exploitation. A BIA land appraiser counted the cattle then being grazed on the four sections and evaluated their worth to the Papagos at about 75 cents per acre.

After some very stormy council meetings, at which typically no more than ten or fifteen people showed up, the annual rental offer rose to $6 per acre, and in April of 1959 both sides accepted these terms. The lease was to run for 25 years. In effect, ASARCO bought this land — for it is doubtful that any practical use will be found for the mountain of overburden — at a cost of $150 per acre, with payments to be spread out over 25 years. One of the writers of this report (Fontana) criticized the arrangement in 1959, predicting that within ten years the sale price of adjacent off-reservation land would be at least $1,000 per acre (a prediction that unfortunately proved to be correct).

ASARCO did not begin mining operations on its properties in Tracts 1 and 2 until September of 1966 — eleven months before the expiration of its first ten-year lease. By June 14, 1968, ASARCO had paid $1,129.89 in royalties for copper mined within Tract 1. On June 5, 1970, the Papago tribe canceled the leases, on the grounds that a small amount of unallotted tribal land was located within the leased area.

The mining company's attorney decreed the cancellation void, because the BIA and not the tribe had signed the original agreement. In mid-June, the Papago Indian tribe and individual allottees filed a lawsuit in U.S. District Court seeking more than $20 million from ASARCO, alleging violations of the two leases on Tracts 1 and 2.

Once again, most Papagos who owned shares in the land involved knew nothing of the details of the lawsuit nor of the complex reasons for filing it. They had been assured by the tribal attorney that ASARCO had violated an agreement and that the case against the company looked very promising. The district and tribal councils agreed, and one of the Papagos helped the attorney get signatures on a contract that enabled him to represent individuals in the case as well as the tribe.

Even though royalty payments made by ASARCO had been very small, dissatisfaction became widespread after the company stopped all payments. Then, in December of 1971, it was announced in the press that the suit had been settled out-of-court for $2,100,000. The settlement, which involved several adjustments in the original leases, still had to be approved in federal court — but it would not go to trial.

NEW COUNCIL. In January of the following year, a new district council was elected at San Xavier reservation. Most of the new councilmen were young people who had little or no understanding of the terms of the proposed settlement. They contacted individuals at the University of Arizona, none of whom had previously seen the proposed agreement, for an objective explanation of the terms. Additional persons in the Tucson community were contacted; the Papagos asked the federal judge for a delay to allow more time for their investigations; he agreed to the delay — and a horrendous squabble ensued.

In a meeting held at San Xavier, which was attended by a very large number of Papagos — allottees and otherwise — BIA officials and the tribal attorney explained the settlement. One of the attorneys helpfully translated $2,100,000 into the number of candy bars that could be bought with it.

Because most Papagos were already impatient about having waited so long to receive royalty payments and because many of them could feel $2,100,000 within their grasp, the district council decided to approve the settlement agreement. In typical Papago fashion, the council did not vote. Those present at the meeting, including those who had no immediate interest in the outcome, were asked to vote by a show of hands.

A few allottees, however, were still not satisfied that they understood the terms of the agreement. They were represented gratis by a Tucson law firm, and several meetings were held so that each point of the proposal could be carefully explained. Just before the agreement went into federal court for a hearing before the judge, the "hold-out" allottees agreed that all the terms of the proposed settlement were fair except two. They did not want to lease additional lands to ASARCO for the dumping of overburden, and they felt that the fees of the attorney representing Papagos were too high. ASARCO attorneys immediately replied that they would not pursue the attempt for additional land, because the company wanted to get on with its mining operations — which left the attorney's fees as the only point of dissension.

In the end, the attorney who represented the tribe and individual allottees received about $300,000 of the $2,100,000 settlement — some $100,000 less than he had originally asked for.

Once again, the level of Papago understanding of leasing proved to be negligible. As before, choices were presented to them in simplistic "either/or" alternatives. Refuse this offer, and you don't get any money; accept it, and you'll be paid. Neither the BIA nor anyone else has attempted the incredibly ardous task of trying to explain complex legal situations so that Papagos can understand them, of listing the many alternatives that are always possible, of encouraging people to make choices based on factual appraisal of their own best interests.

Kitt Peak National Observatory

Early in the 1950's, the National Science Foundation (NSF) began to search for an observatory site that would be remote from city lights and polluted air, in an area where a mild climate and clear nights would allow maximum astronomical research.

The Papago Tribe in 1956 gave permission to the NSF and the Association of Universities for Research in Astronomy (AURA) to test Kitt Peak, in the Shuk Toak district of the Papago (Sells) reservation, as a potential site. After two years of testing, the selection of this site for a national observatory was announced by the NSF. The contract by then had been approved by both the tribe and the NSF.

Kitt Peak National Observatory is today one of the more important centers of astronomy in the United States, but this did not come about without considerable persuasion on the part of Papagos and non-Papagos alike. The district within which the observatory is located is inhabited by many traditional and conservative Papagos, most of whom depend on cattle for their livelihood and who had little or no interest in leasing lands for an observatory or anything else. In addition, some Papagos regard Kitt Peak as a sacred mountain, which should not be desecrated even by a road — much less a building atop its crest. Villagers of Coyote Sits (Ban Tak), just beneath the peak, objected that approval of the lease would eventually bring white men to the area and that such men would have a bad influence on Papago children. Mark Manuel, then tribal chairman, countered this objection by saying: "You people shouldn't feel that way. You never can tell. Some of your kids might want to go into that line of work."

Some Papagos also objected (and still do) that the agreed leasing fee was too small. Papagos were authorized to lease 2,400 acres for the observatory, for an initial payment of not more than $25,000 plus an annual rental amounting to about $2,550—half of the total to go to Schuk Toak district and half to the Papago tribe.

For a time it appeared that the Papagos would not approve the lease. Then, at the suggestion of University of Arizona astronomer Edwin Carpenter, Papagos who objected to the proposal were brought to the observatory on the university campus and given a demonstration of what could be seen through telescopes. This reasonable approach to better understanding, combined with the prospect of employment opportunities, carried the day for NSF and AURA. Papagos have since been employed almost continually at Kitt Peak; the payroll to Papagos in 1966, for example, amounted to more than $100,000.

The Papago tribe in 1956 gave permission to the NSF and the by Papago people themselves, and in no way do the Papagos exercise any control or input concerning this activity on their reservation. But relationships between Kitt Peak personnel and Papagos have been excellent on both the personal and the institutional level.

Kitt Peak "Gateway"

Early in 1962, a group of Tucson businessmen foresaw that the opening of Kitt Peak National Observatory would probably increase the number of tourists visiting the area. These businessmen, who philanthropically wanted to help the Papagos by increasing employment and business opportunities, formed a nonprofit corporation and presented a proposal to the BIA superintendent for construction of a service station and auto repair and towing facility; a trailer camp and a motel; a Papago museum and a "model" Indian village (primarily for exhibition); and a small planetarium — all to be built at the intersection of Arizona State Highway 86, which links Tucson and Atjo, and the turnoff to Kitt Peak.

The planning of the corporation members, all of them non-Indian, called for a complete Papago takeover of the facility at the end of 25 years, with at least part of the profit being set aside for scholarships for Papagos.

After receiving enthusiastic endorsement of their plans from BIA officials, in August of 1962 the group approached officials of the tribe and of the Schuk Toak district in which the project was to be located. By mid-October the Schuk Toak people were actively considering the proposal, and the businessmen proceeded with their planning.

In July of the following year, Schuk Toak Papagos asked for more information. Ten months later — much to the surprise of the would-be philanthropists — the proposal was flatly rejected by the Indians.

What went wrong? One of the businessmen believes that the approach taken to the Papagos brought about the group's failure. Its members naïvely — and mistakenly — believed that BIA approval would automatically be followed by Indian approval, particularly since the project (as viewed by outsiders) would clearly benefit the Papagos.

A few Schuk Toak Papagos did approve of the idea. One elderly man indicated he believed that Papago people would benefit from the operation of such a business. Another elderly Papago, a respected leader, said the proposal was rejected because most people didn't really understand it. An anonymous shaman regarded the plan as being a further intrusion on the sanctity of Kitt Peak and its surroundings.

Still others, primarily cattle-raising residents of Coyote Sits, objected because they — like cattlemen everywhere — are generally opposed to any kind of intrusion on their range lands. They share a general abhorrence of tourists, hunters, and other aliens who might disturb their stock, cut or knock down fences, or damage water sources and grazing land.

In retrospect, the Papagos of Schuk Toak district today bear no ill feelings toward those who proposed the "Gateway" complex. They are neither any richer nor any poorer than they were, and the landscape of the area of proposed development also remains the same, without buildings, trailers, asphalte or concrete slabs, restrictive fences — or intrusive strangers.

The rejection of the proposal apparently resulted from varied motives, ranging from a simple lack of understanding to the outright hostility of the cattlemen and at least one medicine man. The negative feelings of people living in the district outweighed the acceptance of those who were in favor of the plan. Essentially, many Papagos apparently believe that if one proposal is approved, other changes are almost sure to follow.

Papago Tribal Utility Authority

Through Papago Council Resolution No. 8–70, the Papago Tribal Utility Authority (PTUA) was created on July 28, 1970, and was authorized to acquire, construct, operate, and maintain a utility system throughout the Papago reservation, "where such services are determined to be feasible and economic."

A flyer explaining the project announced that the PTUA was established "to create an enterprise of the Papago Tribe with the authority and responsibility for securing the objective of furnishing utility services of all types to all areas of the Papago reservation. These services will be geared to provide the maximum employment of Papago people and to further carry out the purpose and intent of promoting the betterment of the Papago Tribe" (Papago Tribal Utilitary Authority 1970).

A more immediate inspiration, however, was the fact that Hecla Mining Company and Newmont Exploration, Ltd., were going to need large amounts of electrical power for their mining operations on the northern end of the Papago (Sells) reservation — and that supplying such power would perhaps be a profitable venture for the tribe.

Until 1951, the reservation's scant power supply, which was generated at plants using gasoline or diesel oil, serviced no more than a few homes in smaller villages. A power plant at Sells, operated by the BIA, was taken over by Trico Electric Cooperative, Inc., in 1951, at the bureau's request. Trico bought the BIA generator for one dollar, discarded it and built a new facility, which by 1972 was serving more than 700 homes on the Papago (Sells) reservation and another fifty or so at San Xavier.

Around 1967, Trico's engineers alerted the company to the fact that the Sells circuits would be overloaded unless something were done to increase the capacity of the Kitt Peak Observatory line with a new transmission. Trico subsequently spent about $5,000 staking out new lines on the reservation and was making plans to extend an additional forty miles of lines to whatever areas or villages the tribe wished, when, in 1969, "someone" told the company that the tribe itself was planning to go into the utility business.

All attempts by Trico officials to discuss the matter with tribal officials met with failure, for the tribe never responded to Trico requests. Although Trico's operation on the reservation was losing money, officials of the cooperative continued to hope that it would someday run in the black. Not until after the PTUA was formed, in 1970, did Trico discover that it lacked a legal franchise to do business on the reservation. What the company had, in effect, was a certificate saying that it could serve the reservation "on request." A hearing was held before the Arizona Corporation Commission in October of 1971, and a month later the state attorney general ruled that Papago-owned utility lines could not be taxed and, in effect, that a state-issued certificate authorizing a utility company to do business is not binding on an Indian reservation. The commission, however, disagreed.

Negotiations have begun between Trico and PTUA for the purchase by the latter of Trico's lines and facilities on the reservation. PTUA hopes to borrow money for the sale price — rumored to be slightly more than one million dollars — from the Rural Electrification Administration. Included in the negotiations is a stipulation that Trico will continue to serve the reservation for about two years after the purchase is finalized.

In March of 1972, PTUA began selling retail electricity to its first customer, Hecla Mining. PTUA buys this electricity wholesale from Arizona Public Service, a private, profit-making corporation. Meanwhile, after Trico learned that it might not have a binding franchise to serve the reservation, the company, in an effort to protect its investments, raised its rates for extending lines and connecting homes. The nominal hook-up charge at San Xavier, for example, became a $500 fee. Thus, until PTUA can service the whole reservation, individual Papagos are paying the costs that indirectly support a tribal venture.

Most Papagos who are presently being served by Trico know almost nothing about what is going on — and others who do know are sceptical about the ability of PTUA to service remote areas of the reservation in the foreseeable future. They cannot see why the tribe should profit at the expense of individuals or of remote villages.

On the other hand, PTUA has some experienced people on its board and an experienced man, a non-Indian, as its manager. He argues that "the whole idea behind the PTUA is the implementation of President Nixon's program of self-determination for the Indians. The tribe will be controlling its own destiny. The PTUA should provide employment for the Papagos, and at the same time allow them to direct the development of the resources on the reservation." He has also stated that the company eventually plans to extend its service to include telephone, water, gas, and sewer lines.

Papagos serviced by Trico are voting members of this cooperative who read their own meters, pay their bills, and are eligible for election as company directors. Papagos will own PTUA collectively, but it is uncertain how strong a voice individual consumers will have in the operation. In any event, those involved most directly — present and prospective Papago customers for electric power — were never consulted. All negotiations were handled at the tribal level, and, as mentioned previously, some Papago consumers of electricity are still unaware of what is happening.

Papago Explosives, Incorporated

In November of 1971, it was announced that the Papago tribe and Phillips Petroleum Company were planning to operate an explosives mixing plant and storage facilities, to be built on tribal land south of Casa Grande. The BIA provided a $25,000 industrial development grant, the Papago tribe provided an additional $5,000, and Phillips purchased a $30,000 interest (to become a major stockholder in the new firm).

The idea for this project was brought to members of the Sif Oidak district by a sales representative of Phillips. When the proposal was first made to the district, tribal councilmen objected, saying that the project should be decided by the tribe rather than district. The Papago Mining Committee was commissioned to make a feasibility study, and some of its members visited Ft. Wingate, New Mexico, to examine an existing facility that is owned and operated by the Navajo tribe. (The petroleum company helped to underwrite costs of the trip.)

Ownership in Papago Explosives is presently shared by the tribe, which has a 70 percent interest, and Phillips Petroleum, which holds the remaining 30 percent. The idea of an explosives plant was very favorably received by the tribal council, after the mining committee reported on the Ft. Wingate facility. Navajos are managing and operating this entire operation by themselves, something that Papagos hope to be able to achieve with their plant.

Operation of Papago Explosives is delegated by the Papago tribe to a seven-member board of directors, three of whom are Papagos, the remaining four being non-Indians. Four members represent the tribe, and three are employees of Phillips. A Papago was the first manager of the plant, which was built in 1972, five miles south of Chuichu Village in the Schuk Toak district. It is conveniently located near the Hecla mine (its first customer), with easy access to highways and to the railroad at Casa Grande. Two sales were made during the first two months of operation. The plant employs six people, all Papagos, and it is estimated that eventually as many as twelve Papagos will be working for Papago Explosives.

So far as we have been able to determine, there have been no adverse criticisms of this project from Papago people, nor were there any serious objections to it at any time. Thus far, the venture appears to be successful from the points of view of all who are involved in it.

San Xavier Cooperative Association, Incorporated

Formed in June of 1971, the San Xavier Cooperative Association is the result of a need perceived by Papago people themselves — the farming of some 1,100 acres of land that had been lying idle for several years near Mission San Xavier del Bac. Some of these lands had been farmed by Papagos until the early 1950's; most of them were leased to non-Indians for farming during the next decade, and expired leases had not been renewed.

In 1970 a former chairman of the San Xavier district suggested that a Papago cooperative be formed for the purpose of putting the land back into production. A similar model already existed in Arizona on the Ak Chin (Maricopa) reservation, where a few years earlier Papagos and Pimas had begun a successful cooperative farming venture.

The 1,100 acres put together by the cooperative were owned by 189 allottees, and all allottees who are legally adults have become members. Some of these allotments were incredibly fractionated — one 19.5-acre unit belonged to 90 third-, fourth-, and fifth-generation heirs. In computing the share of each allottee, a common denominator of 8,870,400 was used. Were the group's land to be physically divided into separate parcels, one heir would have owned 0.04 acre. "If he were to die on his land," commented a BIA official, "they would have had to bury him standing up."

The cooperative initially received a $25,000 grant from the Indian Business Development Fund, which was used for repairing irrigation pumps, clearing land, and fixing and installing fences. In December of 1971, the Farmers' Home Administration extended the cooperative a $90,000 loan, to be paid back over nine years at $4\frac{1}{8}$ percent interest. Within a month, more than half of some 720 acres that had been committed to production had been planted, with grain sorghum and alfalfa as the chief crops. By August, plantings included 150 acres of corn as well as 125 acres of cotton, which was planted for the University of Arizona on an experimental basis at $20 per acre. The corn was harvested in late fall, and by midwinter cattle were being pastured on harvested lands. (The cattle do not belong to the Papagos.)

The hardworking president of the seven-member all-Papago board that runs the cooperative has been one of its most vigorous champions; the cooperative's attorney is a member of the law firm that represents the tribe as well as many Papago allottees.

A status report issued by board president Patrick J. Franks in mid-1972 included the following statement:

We are now starting to use the $90,000 which the Farmers Home Administration has given us as a *loan*. Some of the money will be used to pay for employment but we still need lots of *volunteer help* from you member people so that we can get something out of the Farm and make it a success. I am writing you this status report letter to inform you Farm Members on what we have been doing since June 19, 1971, when the Board was formed.

Any of you can see by looking over the Farm areas how much work has been accomplished out there in the fields so far and also how much work that still needs to be done to get the Farm going right. We still need more support from you Farm Members. In order to make the Farm a financial and economic success, we really do need lots of cooperation from all of you!

So you can see, we need your full cooperation for the development of your farm land. We just cannot let it lie there and let the City of Tucson take over the water rights! We don't want that to happen to us so make your voice heard by speaking up loud and doing your part for the San Xavier Farm Association and for the San Xavier Papago Indian Reservation (Franks 1972).

Franks's letter makes clear his interest in developing idle farmlands and his concern over water rights. (The water table of much of the eastern reservation is dropping because of off-reservation pumping.)

At times, members of the cooperative — who have first preference for employment — have had to work for more than seven consecutive days without breaks. The biggest difficulty, in addition to the fact that weeds grow unless something is done to stop them, has been that some of the Papago labor force occasionally disappear for days or even weeks at a time. Non-Indians hired to do the labor have left because the hourly wage is only $1.50. It is not likely that an increase in this pay scale would attract steady Papago employees. Some Papagos, among them many from San Xavier who are unemployed, have yet to adopt the notion of working regularly. It is also clear that the emotional feeling that "this is our farm" is not yet shared by most members of the cooperative. But nearly everyone who lives on the San Xavier reservation seems to be pleased that long-idle fields are again being farmed, and there are few skeptics to scoff at the idea of the farm's eventual success.

The farming venture has demonstrated visibly that fractionated allotments can be combined into a single association in which members receive benefits in proportion to their alloted shares in the land. Unlike the lands leased for mineral exploitation, which are comparatively out-of-sight and out-of-mind, the cooperative's fields surround the inhabited parts of the reservation and are seen daily by almost everyone. All roads to Tucson pass the farmed fields.

Whether the San Xavier Cooperative Association fails or succeeds, the fact that crops have been grown and harvested at all has been a measure of success, and Papago people working on the project have a degree of control over the outcome.

Papago Farms

In December of 1957, the Papago tribe and two Phoenix firms — Freesh Land Ventures, Inc., and the James Stewart Company — entered into a lease involving about 12,000 acres in the Chukut Kuk district, on the southern part of the Sells reservation. The leased acreage was to be developed under the name "Papago Farms." The Stewart Company was to construct and maintain at least eighteen wells on the farm during a 25-year period, and at the end of this time — in 1982 — the entire farm was to be turned over to the tribe. The tribe and district were each to receive half of an annual rental fee, the amount to be determined by the returns on each year's crops. Papago Farms is wholly non-Indian owned and controlled (the farm superintendent was a former mayor of Coolidge, Arizona, and other members included a Phoenix attorney and two Phoenix farmers). At the end of 1957, the company announced that within one year it planned to have at least six wells drilled and from 1,800 to 3,200 acres under cultivation. The attorney representing Stewart said, "Papago Indians will be given preference in employment at Papago Farms, and the venture should act as a strong deterrent to the Indians' leaving the reservation in such numbers as before. Within 25 years that we'll be working the land, they will receive the benefits of employment, water, roadways, and ultimately, gas and electric power. And when our lease expires, it's all theirs."

In June of 1958, the president of the company told the Tucson Chamber of Commerce that 2,900 acres had been cleared and planted, that the development was "strictly a business venture" to be "operated for a profit," and that the business would inevitably benefit Tucson.

On October 13, 1961, the superintendent of the Papago Agency of the BIA cancelled the Papago Farms lease. He gave the following explanation:

The premises of the lease were bustling with activity shortly after negotiations on the lease were completed. Buildings were erected, wells were drilled and equipped, and irrigation structures were installed. The first summer, during which a large melon crop was planted, the lessees were, among other things, victims of weather and marketing conditions [only a dirt road goes to the site]. A modification to the original 12,000-acre lease was requested and granted wherein the total acreage was lowered to an amount more nearly in line to the restrictions on pumping. The modification also decreased the rate of development requirements.

In 1959, the second year of the lease, the highlights of the activity on the lease were the harvest of a large silage crop and the sacking of some 3,000 50-lb. sacks of onions from a 17-acre field that had originally been planted for raising seed. The silage crop was placed in two pits, one of which remained untouched at the time of lease cancellation. Many of the onions which were sacked were not sold due to falling market conditions and were left to rot under a packing shed which was almost totally destroyed during a windstorm during the summer of 1960.

During the third year of the lease the only crop grown was a relatively small amount of grain sorghum. The fields were not properly cared for and much of the grain was harvested by the birds. The lessee would not be obligated, but for a minimum lease fee of $10,000 would be able to use the premises as he saw fit. The only activity during the fourth season of the lease saw the lessee placing the land in the grain sorghum reserve program of the ACP and collecting more from the program than the minimum annual lease payment of $10,000. The Papago people saw fit not to allow further modification to the lease and requested that the Superintendent cancel the same.

Due to mismanagement and neglect, the one thing that offered the Papago Tribe a certain amount of income from rent and wages for the people was fast getting away from them. For these reasons the Superintendent cancelled the lease (United States Department of the Interior 1961: 36, 39).

The report also points out that although 5.59 miles of concrete-lined ditches were constructed in 1955, 2.5 miles were never used and were allowed to deteriorate, and by 1961 the entire irrigation system had become unusable.

In May of 1963, the non-Indian owners of Papago Farms filed a $1 million suit in United States District Court, charging the superintendent with improperly canceling the lease. The tribe countered in October with a suit requesting $343,000 in damages, alleging that the firm had failed to fulfill the terms of the lease. The matter was settled out of court in 1965.

By April of 1967, the new superintendent of the Papago Agency was encouraging the tribe and the Chukut Kuk district to negotiate a new lease for operating Papago Farms, noting that during the previous six months the agency had been approached by at least six large agricultural enterprises, which had expressed interest in leasing the farm's area. He pointed out that the tribe and district would have to make the decision but that the Bureau of Indian Affairs was anxious to assist the tribe in any way possible in order that Papago Farms would be put to its best use. In recommending that a lease be negotiated, the superintendent cited the value of lease income to the tribe and district, noted the value of on-reservation job opportunities, and added that putting the land into maximum production would help meet the increasing demands for food in this country. Finally, he argued that the disadvantages to the Papago tribe in leasing Papago Farms are small compared to the advantages. Agricultural use of the type proposed will bring in

income on an unused reservation resource. One or two Papago cattlemen would have to make some adjustments on grazing cattle.

What the superintendent failed to take into account is that the
Chukut Kuk district, which has within it one of the wealthiest cattle-
raising families on the reservation, has no "unused" resources. All the
arable land is used for grazing.

On May 24, 1957, the Chukut Kuk District Council approved a
request for an experimental lease on a small part of Papago Farms,
with eight of the thirteen members voting in favor of the lease. When
the tribal council met in June, however, it was decided that not enough
notice had been given for the Chukut Kuk District Council meeting and
that the action of the eight councilmen had, therefore, been illegal.
This decision was made after two members of the wealthy cattle-
raising family had retained a Tucson attorney, who had notified the
tribal chairman and council that the family considered the district
action to be null and void.

Since 1967, various half-hearted attempts have been made to bring
Papago Farms back into production. A Franciscan priest who had
formerly been stationed at Pisinimo tried to encourage people in the
district to take over operation of the farm, and at least one district
cattleman has considered planting part of the area for pasturage, as an
individual enterprise. But the lands continue to lie idle save for what
nature chooses to grow on them, and Papagos have not received the
benefits of employment, water, roadways, and ultimately, gas and
electric power. It is clear that the concept of Papago Farms was not a
Papago concept and that the farm's development has little to do with
the aspirations of Papago people.

San Xavier Industrial Park

Early in 1967, according to the superintendent, John Artichoker, who
was then in charge of the BIA agency at Sells, the Papago Agency was
visited by a group of "industrialists" who were interested in locating on
Indian lands in Arizona. The superintendent continued:

Because of its proximity to transportation facilities, an area of the San Xavier
Reservation was tentatively selected for leasing to the group. Within a short
while, other lease proposals were received for San Xavier lands. A land title
investigation disclosed that approximately 400 acres of land in the northeastern
corner of the reservation were owned by ten individual Papago Indians. A
series of meetings were held with the landowners to discuss the proposals and
to ascertain their thinking on the matter. Out of the meetings grew the idea of
a partnership which would facilitate decision making by vesting authority in
three of the landowners to act on land proposals. The thought was also

generated that the partnership should also have an attorney to advise them independently of the Bureau of Indian Affairs. As a result, the landowners formed the Papago del Bac Partnership [May 7, 1967] and selected Barry DeRose of Globe, Arizona, as its attorney.

One of its first acts was to lease [on December 1, 1967] 110 acres of its holdings to Papago-Tucson (non-profit) Development Corporation for an industrial park site. The sixty-five year lease calls for a guaranteed minimum annual rental of $10 an acre which is increased to $70 an acre as the land is subleased to other companies. In addition, the lessee pays to the partnership 50 percent of its annual net income from the sub-leasing of land to others. The Papago-Tucson Development Corporation presently has pending before the Economic Development Administration (EDA) an application for a grant-loan of $180,000 for site preparation. A decision on the application is expected soon (*Papago Agency Newsletter* June 14, 1968).

The nonprofit Papago-Tucson Development Corporation was formed late in December of 1967; Edward Berge of Tucson, who is the tribal attorney, also serves as attorney for the corporation. A grant of $171,200 and a loan of $42,800 were awarded to the corporation by the Economic Development Association in April of 1969, with the loan to be repaid over a 40-year period at an annual interest rate of $4\frac{3}{4}$ percent. The work of putting in roads, sewers, landscaping, and other improvements was contracted to a Scottsdale firm, which entered a low bid of $145,456; this work was completed in October of 1970. Eleven months earlier, the BIA had placed a full-time employee at San Xavier to assist in promotion of the industrial park. A real estate firm was chosen to handle listings on the unleased land belonging to the Papago del Bac partnership.

In November of 1970, it was announced that seven firms were considering locating at San Xavier Industrial Park. A month later the Tucson Realty and Trust Company was appointed exclusive agent for leasing and management of the park under a five-year contract.

The following January, Samsonite Corporation announced plans to open a die-cutting plant at the park; for reasons never made public, negotiations fell through and in March this company leased for its plant a building owned by the Tucson Airport Authority. The park had no further potential customers until late in 1972, when it was announced that a company which assembles mobile homes intended to move into the park. At the end of 1972, however, nothing but weeds occupied the 40-acre site that had been prepared out of the 110 acres leased in 1967 by the Papago-Tucson Development Corporation.

All officers of the development corporation are Papago Indians. Their principal adviser is their legal counsel, and they are also advised by the industrial development man assigned by the BIA to San Xavier (whose office is in Tucson). If any of the allottee owners of the land has received rental payments after the first of the park's operation, the allottees who were queried were unaware of it. So far as we were able to learn, the EDA had not received any payments on its $42,800 loan. The Papagos on the board of the corporation have no assets of their own, and it is clear that the corporation will have no assets unless leasers are found for the industrial park.

A rumor, which we were unable to confirm with documentary data, says that the San Xavier District Council has assumed part of the burden of financial responsibility for the industrial park. This may be true, but the nature of the relationship between the council and the Papago-Tucson Development Corporation remains unclear.

But it is clear that from the very outset, the San Xavier Industrial Park was conceived, promoted, and operated by non-Indians. Although the board members of the corporation are all Papagos, there is no evidence that they have any meaningful voice in planning. Indeed, few — if any — of the members seem to know very much about the events in the history of the park, and they have little knowledge of financial commitments.

The idea of the park originated with the superintendent of the Papago Agency, who, with his administrative assistant, bypassed the district council entirely and went directly to the allottees, selecting their attorney and getting them to form an informal "partnership" that is registered neither with the state of Arizona nor with Pima County.

The attorney prepared lease arrangements for the allottees, most of whom have never lived at San Xavier reservation. When contacted in the fall of 1972, the attorney — who had almost forgotten about the industrial park and the "partnership" — was not sure whether or not he still represented the clients.

The district and all but about a dozen Papagos living at San Xavier have never had anything to do with the park — unless, of course, the district has secretly assumed some of the park's financial obligations. Papagos living at San Xavier can hope to receive, at most, only lease payments — and it is not presently known whether the district or the corporation would get this money.

Prospects for Indian employment at the industrial park are not very bright; presently, it has no employees. It is also highly questionable that San Xavier has a labor force sufficient to fill even a half-dozen jobs requiring steady work hours. Most of the able-bodied people at San Xavier who want to work are already employed or can find employment without much difficulty. The San Xavier farm cooperative, which can use all the part- and full-time employees it can get, is unable to find them. Thus, to argue that the San Xavier Industrial Park is for the benefit of Papagos is to be cynical in the extreme. The need for the enterprise was defined by an outsider to the community, its development proceeded largely because funds to make it possible were available, and — in our opinion — it has gone nowhere because it has nothing to do with Papagos, except on paper and ceremonially.

Papago Industries

The story of Papago Industries is similar to that of San Xavier Industrial Park. In June of 1967 the Papago Agency Superintendent, John Artichoker, made the following announcements:

> What appears to be an outstanding possibility for creating jobs on the reservation has developed during the past week. There has been received a definite proposal from a company which wishes to locate an electronic component assembly plant in Sells. It is anticipated that the assembly plant will employ 50 to 60 people within the first 12 months of operation, increasing to an employment total of approximately 150 people within two years.
> The Sells assembly plant is expected to begin operations on July 17, 1967 and applicants for jobs are being actively sought. Anyone interested in applying for work should contact the Agency Branch of Employment Assistance in order that testing and job interviews may be arranged. The jobs will involve light work suitable for women. Work tasks would include winding small transformers, soldering, testing and inspecting (*Papago Agency Newsletter*, June 1967).

The superintendent, who apparently had bypassed the tribal council and the Sells District Council completely in arranging for the plant to locate in a BIA-owned building on the reservation, in January of 1968 reported that during the previous year eleven Papago people had been employed at Papago Industries in Sells and that he anticipated the number would increase to forty during 1968. The venture collapsed, however, and the Papago Tribal Council formally asked the commissioner of Indian affairs to remove the superintendent, charging that he was implementing programs on his own initiative and was not working within the structure of Papago government. We were unable to gather details, in either written or oral form, of the Papago Industries project, which died rather quietly. The local off-reservation press took no notice of its passing, and today few Papagos have any recollection of it.

Gila Bend Fortress Village

In June of 1963, it was announced that plans were being made to excavate some fairly spectacular prehistoric ruins that are situated atop a mesa on the Gila Bend Indian reservation. The mayor of Gila Bend, the non-Indian town nearby, said he was enthusiastically behind plans to make the site a tourist center. The Gila Bend District Council had given approval of the idea, agreeing that it would be profitable to exploit the site as a tourist attraction and that excavation and stabilization would prevent further deterioration of the ruins. The "fortress," which is about 700 years old, is made up of stone breastworks and the remains of more than two dozen living units.

In January of 1964, the Arizona State Museum received $13,700 from the National Science Foundation for archaeological work on the site; Indian labor from a Papago village — the only settlement on the Gila Bend reservation — was employed to excavate and partially restore the ruin, under the direction of museum archaeologists.

In June of the following year, Chambers and Campbell, Inc., of Albuquerque issued a feasibility report, "Tourism potential of the Fortress Village, Gila Bend Indian reservation, Arizona," which had been paid for by the BIA. The firm reported that development of the site as a tourist attraction "can at best be considered marginal in an economic sense," pointing out that the costs of developing the site and an all-weather road into it would be very high and that at most only 40 to 55 persons per day might be expected to detour from the interstate highway to visit the ruins (Chambers and Campbell, Inc., 1965).

In spite of the somewhat negative position of the feasibility study, interest in the potential of the site has persisted, especially in the non-Indian community of Gila Bend. A new freeway will bypass this town, but the community's businessmen believe that tourists who could be lured to visit the ruin would pause to buy food, gasoline, meals, and lodging at Gila Bend. Moreover, some BIA officials feel that the 1965 feasibility study is outdated, because it does not take into account increased American interest in camping and sightseeing since that time.

During the first five months of 1968, meetings were held that included Papago and Gila Bend district councilmen, Papago tribal employees, BIA officials from both the Papago reservation and the Phoenix Area Office, and citizens from the town of Gila Bend. People from the University of Arizona and from various state agencies, such as the Arizona State Parks Board, also attended some of these meetings. However, only three Gila Bend Papagos were present for any of the meetings: the chairman and vice-chairman of the Gila Bend District Council, and the Papago tribal vice-chairman (whose home is in the Gila Bend village).

In June of 1969, the ruin was officially added to the National Register of Historic Places as Fortaleza Archaeological Site. By April of 1972, the BIA was still working toward opening the site as a tourist attraction, one that might include campsites and trails and that might employ a few Gila Bend Papagos as guides and manitenance workers.

Fairly recently, an organization called the Papago Bend Commission was formed by Papagos from the Gila Bend reservation and non-Indians from the town of Gila Bend. At a meeting on June 27, 1972, attended by one of us (Ramon), the Papago Bend Commission met with a representative of the National Park Service to discuss Fortaleza. No Papagos from the Gila Bend reservation attended. The group wanted the National Park Service man to explain the steps necessary to transfer Fortaleza from Indian ownership to federal ownership, through having it declared a national monument (as was done with the prehistoric ruin of Snaketown on the Gila River Indian reservation in 1972).

It is not clear to what extent Papagos living on the Gila Bend reservation understand the various proposals that are being made, ostensibly in their behalf, for Fortaleza. Nothing has happened to the ruins since they were excavated in 1964, and, at the moment, it appears that it may be many years — if ever — before anything further happens to them.

The idea of developing the site for its tourism potential is one that was initiated and has been largely promoted from outside the Gila Bend Papago community. The very small representation of Gila Bend Papagos at meetings — almost all of which have been held off the reservation in the town of Gila Bend — is probably a measure of the lack of interest that Papagos have in the project. Certainly, interest is much greater among the non-Indians of the town of Gila Bend.

The Fortaleza project, in any case, has now been overshadowed by another proposal, which also involves the Gila Bend Papagos.

Gila Bend Tourist Center

At the June 1972 meeting held at Gila Bend, a second tourist-oriented project was discussed by members of the Papago Bend Commission, after a realtor had announced that she wanted to donate 160 acres of land to Gila Bend Papagos as a site for an industrial-tourist complex. The land is located about nine miles from Fortaleza, on the opposite (south) side of the planned freeway from both the reservation and the town of Gila Bend. The realtor owns considerable property adjacent to the 160 acres, and an interchange leaving the freeway at this point would lead to the proposed complex — as well as to her adjoining land. (It was mentioned at the meeting that the tribe would have more weight in being able to get an interchange than would a private developer.)

Official announcement of these plans, which apparently originated as early as 1965, was made to the press early in October of 1972. By then the Federal Bureau of Roads had already agreed to build an interchange at the desired location, and the nonprofit Indian Development District of Arizona (IDDA) had become involved and was promoting the plans on behalf of Gila Bend Papagos.

The official announcement said that the Papago tribe would undertake construction of a $1.4 million commercial complex, to include a 70-room motel, a restaurant, and 82-pad mobile-home park, a 136-space travel-trailer park, a 34-acre man-made lake, and — in time — an Indian craft center, a Western town, a rodeo ground, and an industrial park. No dates for construction were mentioned, and we have not learned where the $1.4 million is to come from.

Non-Indian citizens of the town of Gila Bend immediately protested the proposal, arguing that it would mean the death of their community. They had wanted the Indians to develop a tourist attraction on the reservation that would bring people into Gila Bend, not to build a competing project on a site far removed from the town. The mayor and townspeople began to circulate petitions opposing the move, and newspaper accounts made it appear that the non-Indians of Gila Bend and the Indians of the reservation were in conflict.

Our investigation leads us to conclude that the 160-acre development would involve very few Papago people. The project was not promulgated by Papagos, and most of the people living on the Gila Bend reservation are only dimly aware of the plans that are being made. The enterprise is being promoted by Papago tribal officials — largely through their non-Indian advisers and employees; by IDDA, which has to show results to justify its existence; and by real-estate developers in Gila Bend and elsewhere throughout the state. In short, the real conflict is among non-Indians, not between Indians and whites.

On the other hand, the few people in the Gila Bend village who do know about the proposed complex seem to be more favorably disposed toward the development of this site than toward the development of Fortaleza. The prehistoric ruin and its environs have some religious significance to Papago people, and, given the choice, they would probably rather have tourists nine miles away than in their back yard. Moreover, the leader of the village with whom Ramon spoke, could see no reason for not accepting a 160-acre gift.

Optimistic planners have predicted that when the complex is completed it will employ about fifty Papagos — although there may not be fifty employable Papagos looking for jobs. Certainly, there are not that many available workers — steady or otherwise — living on the Gila Bend reservation; its total 1972 population is reported at 151.

E. K. Landscapers

E. K. Landscapers, which is owned and operated by Edward N. Kisto, has been in business on the Papago reservation since July 1, 1967; the company specializes in the construction of fences and gates of ocotillo and saguaro ribs, in building the rustic shade shelters called "ramadas," and in other landscaping projects that give a desert, "Papago look."

Edward Kisto *is* the firm; he hires workers — all fellow Papagos — as they are needed. The company's first contract was for work on the Papago Agency grounds at Sells. Since then a great deal of work has been done for urban home owners and commercial firms in Tucson.

Kisto was born near Fresnal Canyon on the Papago (Sells) reservation. Orphaned at the age of twelve, he attended the Indian boarding school in Phoenix, served in the army during World War II, and later spent several years in the urban jungles of Los Angeles. The suicide of a brother shocked him into joining Alcoholics Anonymous and returning to the reservation, where he leased forty acres in the Baboquivari district from the tribe, bought cattle with savings, and borrowed money to buy a home and drill a well.

Kisto went into the landscaping business in 1967, to supplement his farm income. He and another Papago, using bicycle chains and other spare parts, devised a machine that would make fences of the long, slender branches of the ocotillo — which will sprout leaves after being cut and placed in the ground, making a dense fence. Kisto advertises by taking a booth at the Pima County Fair; newspaper publicity has also helped to popularize his work.

In an interview with reporter John Winters of the *Tucson Daily Citizen*, Kisto said:

"I like it here" [at the ranch], he said simply. When I was in Los Angeles, I used to be alone. It was very lonely out there. Here I never feel alone.

"I would like to keep up traditions, like my father and mother. They used to milk cows, make cheese and tortillas. I'd like to keep everything Indian.

"Yes, I live in a modern house, but I like to keep things Indian."

His big dream, he said, is to convert part of the ranch into a recreation area. On a pickup tour of it, he pointed out the riding and hiking paths he has cleared, and the areas he intends to set aside for camping.

"I would like to put trailers here, have horse-back riding, even go up on the peak (Baboquivari) for rides," he said. "I'd like to get me a wagon, bring 'em up on the hills.

"Maybe," he grinned, "you can never tell, we could have a swimming pool out there.

"I am a proud man," he beamed (May 19, 1972).

E. K. Landscapers — although Edward Kisto obviously doesn't think of it as an industry — is an eminently successful business enterprise. The conception, planning, and execution of the company's efforts have been Kisto's own. He has found a way to live in a modern house and to enjoy all the conveniences of suburbia, while living in a remote area of the Papago Indian reservation.

REFERENCES

Arizona Daily Star
1879   Article in *Arizona Daily Star,* February 9, page 3. Tucson, Arizona.
BAHR, DONALD M.
1964   Untitled and unpublished manuscript concerning Papago resources. Nine chapters, each numbered separately. Copy on file in the Arizona State Museum Library, University of Arizona, Tucson.
BAUER, ROLF W.
1971   "The Papago cattle economy. Implications for economic and community development in arid lands," In *food, fiber and arid lands.* Edited by William G. McGinnies, Bram J. Goldman, and Patricia Paylore, 79–102. Tucson: University of Arizona Press.
BERGER, JOHN M.
1903   "Report of the farmer in charge of the San Xavier reservation," in *Annual reports of the Department of the Interior for the fiscal year ended June 30, 1902,* part 1 (report of the commissioner of Indian affairs), 167–169. Washington, D.C.: Government Printing Office.
BOLTON, HERBERT E., *translator and editor*
1948   *Kino's Historical Memoir of Pimería Alta,* two volumes in one. Berkeley and Los Angeles: University of California Press.
BUREAU OF INDIAN AFFAIRS
1957   "Notice of competitive sale exclusive prospecting permit with option to lease restricted Indian lands for mining, San Xavier reservation." Mimeographed report of April 8 by the Papago Agency, Bureau of Indian Affairs.
CAMERON, COLIN
1896   Letter to B. J. Franklin, governor of the territory of Arizona, written August 10, 1896, from Rancho San Rafael de la Zanja, Pima County, Arizona, in *Report of the governor of Arizona to the secretary of the interior* (annual report of the secretary of the interior for the fiscal year ended June 30, 1896, volume three, 207 ff.), 252–253. Washington, D.C.: Government Printing Office.
CASTETTER, EDWARD F., WILLIS H. BELL
1942   "Pima and Papago Indian Agriculture," In *Inter-Americana studies,* volume one. Albuquerque: University of New Mexico Press.
CHAMBERS AND CAMPBELL, INC.
1965   "Tourism potential of the Fortress Village, Gila Bend Indian reservation." Report to the Bureau of Indian Affairs, June.
DELORIA, VINE
1970   *Custer died for your sins: an Indian manifesto.* New York: Macmillan.
FONTANA, BERNARD L.
i.p.   "Man in arid lands: the Piman Indians of the Sonoran desert," in *Desert biology,* volume two. New York: Academic Press.

FRANKS, PATRICK J.
1972 "Status report on San Xavier Cooperative Association." Unpublished manuscript on file at Arizona State Museum Library, Tucson.

HASTINGS, JAMES R., RAYMOND M. TURNER
1965 *The changing mile.* Tucson: University of Arizona Press.

HAYDEN, JULIAN D.
1967 A summary prehistory and history of the Sierra Pinacate, Sonora. *American Antiquity* 32(3): 335–344. Salt Lake City: Society for American Archaeology.

HOWARD, ELMER A.
1887 "Report of the agent for the Pima, Maricopa, and Papago Indians to the commissioner of Indian affairs," In *Annual report of the commissioner of Indian affairs to the secretary of the interior for the year 1887,* 4–7. Washington, D.C.: Government Printing Office.

HUDSON, CHARLES
1876 "Report of the agent for the Pima, Maricopa, and Papago Indians to the commissioner of Indian Affairs," In *Annual report of the commissioner of Indian affairs to the secretary of the interior for the year 1876,* 6–9. Washington, D.C.: Government Printing Office.

JOHNSON, CLAUDE M.
1889 "Report of Pima Agency," in *Fifty-eight-annual report of the commissioner of Indian affairs to the secretary of the interior, 1889,* 119–121. Washington, D.C.: Government Printing Office.

JONES, RICHARD D.
1969 "An analysis of Papago communities, 1900–1920." Unpublished Ph.D. dissertation, University of Arizona, Tucson.

KELLY, WILLIAM H.
1963 *The Papago Indians of Arizona: a population and economic study.* Tucson: Bureau of Ethnic Research, Department of Anthropology, University of Arizona.
1967 "Social and cultural considerations in the development of manpower programs for Indians." Text of a talk delivered at the National Conference on Manpower Programs for Indians, Kansas City, Missouri, February 16, 1967. Unpublished; 9 pages. Copy on file in the Arizona State Museum Library of the University of Arizona.

KESSELL, JOHN L.
1969 Father Ramon and the big debt, Tumacácori, 1821–1823. *New Mexico Historical Review* 44(1): 53–72, January. Albuquerque: University of New Mexico Press.

MANJE, JUAN M.
1954 *Unknown Arizona and Sonora, 1693-1721.* Translated by Harry J. Karns. Tucson: Arizona Silhouettes.

MATTISON, RAY H.
1946 Early Spanish and Mexican settlements in Arizona. *New Mexico Historical Review* 21(4): 273–329. Albuquerque: University of New Mexico Press.

METZLER, WILLIAM H.
1960 Untitled series of manuscript chapters concerning the economic potential of the Papago Indians. Eight chapters each numbered separately. Dittoed. Copy on file in the Arizona State Museum Library, University of Arizona, Tucson.

PADFIELD, HARLAND, JOHN VAN WILLIGEN
  1969   Work and income patterns in a transitional population: the Papago of
         Arizona. *Human Organization* 28(3): 208–216. Lexington: Society
         for Applied Anthropology.
Papago Agency Newsletter
  1967   Article in *Papago Agency Newsletter*, June, volume one, number 23.
  1967   Article in *Papago Agency Newsletter*, November 21, volume one,
         number 44.
  1968   Article in *Papago Agency Newsletter*, June 14, volume two, number
         24.
PAPAGO EXECUTIVE HEALTH STAFF
  1972   "Explanatory statement on organization." Unpublished manuscript
         on file at Arizona State Museum Library, Tucson.
PAPAGO TRIBAL UTILITARY AUTHORITY
  1970   "Explanatory flyer on establishment of PTUA. Unpublished manus-
         cript on file at Arizona State Museum Library, Tucson. (Statement of
         John R. Raley quote 1972 in Tucson Daily Citizen, p. 17, March 25,
         1972.)
SAXTON, DEAN, LUCILLE SAXTON
  1969   *Papago and Pima to English, English to Papago and Pima dictionary.*
         Tucson: University of Arizona Press.
SHREVE, FORREST, IRA L. WIGGINS
  1964   *Vegetation and flora of the Sonoran desert,* two volumes. Stanford:
         Stanford University Press.
SPICER, EDWARD H.
  1962   *Cycles of conquest.* Tucson: University of Arizona Press.
STANLEY, SAM
  1971   "Economic development of Indian reservations." Proposal submitted
         to the Office of Economic Research, Economic Development Ad-
         ministration. United States Department of Commerce Grant number
         OER-400-G-71-18.
STOUT, J. H.
  1878   "Report of the agent for the Pima, Maricopa, and Papago Indians to
         the commissioner of Indian affairs," in *Annual report of the com-
         missioner of Indian affairs to the secretary of the interior for the year
         1878,* 2–6. Washington, D.C.: Government Printing Office.
Tucson Daily Citizen
  1972   Interview with John Winters in the *Tucson Daily Citizen*, May 19.
         Tucson, Arizona.
UNITED STATES CONGRESS
  1931   "Survey of conditions of the Indians of the United States, part 17."
         Hearings before a subcommittee of the Committee of Indian Affairs.
         U.S. Senate 71st Congress, 3rd Session. U.S. Government Printing
         Office.
UNITED STATES DEPARTMENT OF THE INTERIOR
  1949   Data from *The Papago development program* (May). Washington,
         D.C: U.S. Department of the Interior.
  1961   "Narrative highlights of the branch of land operations of the Papago
         Agency, Phoenix Area Office, Bureau of Indian Affairs." By William
         Karty and others. Mimeograph.
United States Statutes at Large
  1914   Act of Congress. Public Law 160, 63rd Congress, 2nd Session,
         volume 38, p. 587. August 1.

VIVIAN, RICHARD G.
1965   An archaeological survey of the lower Gila River, Arizona. *The Kiva* 30(4): 95–146. Tucson: Arizona Archaeological and Historical Society.

WHITFIELD, CHARLES
1970   Transcript of a tape-recorded seminar conducted at the University of Arizona on February 16, 1970, in *Papago seminar, 1970*, 26–68. Copy on file in the Arizona State Museum Library, University of Arizona, Tucson.

WILSON, ELDRED D.
1962   A resumé of the geology of Arizona. *Bulletin of the Arizona Bureau of Mines* 171. Tucson: University of Arizona Press.

Conclusion

SAM STANLEY

COMPARATIVE ANALYSIS

Ever since its foundation, the United States government has treated the Indians of North America as if they constituted one undifferentiated whole. This policy has been embodied in the constitutional provision that the government has the power to make treaties with and regulate trade among the Indian nations. What started as an individual negotiating authority to come to equitable terms with each and every Indian tribe has become a means for turning each tribe into a bureaucratic facsimile of every other tribe. Countrary to this pervasive view of Indians, the accounts of tribal life and history in this volume testify to each Indian group's uniqueness. The recognition of this uniqueness is at the heart of the whole Indian "problem" and certainly that of their economic development.

In the following section a brief comparative analysis of the seven tribes will be presented. The reader will see what they all share in common; what some share with others; and what makes each singular. One should also bear in mind that the processes which have shaped the fates of these tribes are broadly similar for all North American Indian tribes.

The analysis has tried to focus upon the specific socioeconomic circumstances of each group studied. There are many commonalities. All have been conquered militarily or forced by other means to give up their sovereignty to the United States; have maintained their identity and asserted their uniqueness throughout historical time; have been forced to cope with strange and startling changes in their traditional relationships to their environments; have been compelled to establish very foreign systems of political organization in order to survive. The same holds in different degrees for adaptation from a religious, social, and economic perspective. All have suffered a severe loss of land with little or no understanding of how it happened or why; have had to deal with faceless bureaucracies that have dipped deeply into their daily lives; have had to recognize daily that they have had little or no control over their own future; had an adequate fully functioning and satisfactory economic system prior to Western contact, have had to look across the "translation line" and try to understand what proposal is being put to them; have had to face an arrogant demand from a very powerful force to "get in line and start acting as if their values were the same as those of non-Indians"; and all have been told to give up their children to be educated in the powerful Western way.

There are doubtless many other commonalities shared by Indian tribes throughout the United States, but these are the most obvious. They testify to a series of shared experiences and relationships which Indians have had vis-à-vis the expansion of the United States government. The single most common relationship is that of negotiated treaties, though not all tribes have this sort of formal connection with the federal government. Whether or not an Indian community has a treaty can be a very crucial factor in economic development.

Setting aside, for the moment, the commonalities of the seven studies, it is instructive to see what some share and others do not and in what way they effect economic development. The reader has seen that the outstanding "success" to date has been achieved by the Lummi Indians of Washington state. This coastal group has characteristics in common with two of the other tribes in our study: The Passamaquoddy and the Morongo. All are small in total population and land base. Each, of course, speaks a completely unrelated language — on the order of difference between Bantu, German, and Chinese! They have some other important things in common. Morongo and Lummi have related to the BIA, but never in a close supervisory manner. Passamaquoddy has had to deal with, until recently, a state apparatus which pretty much ignored them. Hence, all three of these groups appear to have had minimum help or interference from legal representations of the larger society. At the same time, each of these groups has remained small enough to maintain community control over its leadership. As social groups they have always relied on face-to-face interaction in order to function, and they have maintained this mode into the present. Each has a sense of what the community can do and wants to do as well as what it will reject. The Lummi refused programs that would have turned them into farmers, into wage earners, city people, and cottage industry craftsmen. Yet as soon as aquaculture was proposed they embraced it as a meaningful activity consistent with their own view of themselves. In a word, it was an undertaking which spoke to the heart of the community. Similarly, the Passamaquoddy, though desperately poor, refused to participate in an Office of Economic Opportunity program unless they could do it in their own way. They rejected $100,000 until the OEO came to its senses and agreed to let them do it as they saw best. No one should be surprised at the high rating which their program received the following year. These are examples of Indians being permitted to develop in their own way, on their own reasonable terms, at their own pace, with results satisfactory to all. The Morongo are another example of this. After months of painstaking effort by their planning committee, they turned down an Economic Development Administration offer to finance their efforts. True, they could have used the money, yet the community did not feel comfortable with it. This is not to say that they are against improving their own standard of living, but rather that they cannot do anything which will violate their own sense of themselves. The smaller tribes are a special case in that they still maintain traditional Indian values, especially those associated with face-to-face relationships. They are little communities with integrity that reach far back into the past. When everything else is forgotten, they will still remember how to behave to one another.

The other four tribes differ from those already discussed on several counts. First, they are much larger in population and in tribal and individually allotted land. Second, they all relate to the federal government by means of treaty or executive order. Third, they are all amalgamations of smaller, in many cases, disparate units, sharing only a language in common. Fourth, they are all governed by a system which is foreign and does not respond readily to their notions about how people should relate politically one to another.

At Pine Ridge there is a clear division between the "breeds" and the "full bloods." In this case the former have traditionally controlled the tribal government, as established under the Indian Reorganization Act after 1936. Full bloods were aware of this situation but have always regarded it as a way of dealing with whites. In effect they gave power to the "breeds" to deal with the United States government, because the breeds understood the English language better and would keep the "Feds, et. al." off their backs. The meaning of Wounded Knee 1973 is to be sought in precisely these terms. The tribal leadership of Richard Wilson was not successfully keeping the whites at bay—in fact, its leadership became a threat to the full bloods; hence, in desperation, they called for the American Indian Movement. Dr. DeMallie has pointed out that the bureaucracy, most tellingly represented by the BIA, has been one of the single most pervasive institutions which have hindered development on Pine Ridge. The formal relationships which characterize the Federal bureaucracy are foreign to American Indian experience. Indians have little or no experience in relating to such faceless and impersonal, albeit powerful, organizations. Where Indians from disparate backgrounds have been put together and declared a "tribe" as in the case of Pine Ridge, there is clearly trouble ahead. If one adds the authority of a BIA and loss of any real autonomy by Indians, then we can begin to understand why Pine Ridge Sioux have had such a difficult time getting on their feet. In a sense, bureaucracy is a disease that is difficult to transmit to Indians, but when they catch it they are often rendered more bureaucratic than their donors. As Dr. DeMallie points out, most non-Indians have had considerable experience with bureaucracies and know how to look for the "give" in them — after all, they created them.

The distinction between full bloods and other legal members of the tribe is very marked with the Oklahoma Cherokee. Again, the full bloods are effectively cut off from the actual administration of any tribal affairs. In one sense this is in the nature of the case — communication between people who speak different languages is almost impossible. The situation becomes insidious when one realizes that the full bloods have no interpreters and that the officers of the tribe can, therefore, speak freely without fear of contradiction from them. It is a serious problem and vitally effects the economic development of the Oklahoma Cherokee full bloods.

Professor Wahrhaftig's analysis focuses on the exploitation of the full bloods as part and parcel of the power system of eastern Oklahoma. In his view the full bloods are not only a cheap source of labor but their "tribalness" is also an asset which attracts both tourists *and* federal dollars for programs which will "relieve" their dire financial position. These dollars turn up in the pockets of establishment whites and "legal" but not tribal Cherokee.

From the full blood point of view, the Cherokee "government" is another white man's institution for doing something to them. If something (like housing) comes from them, then it is seen as some kind of white payment to the Cherokee for a part of what has previously been taken from them. In a word, their present government is "illegal" when set in the context of their own ideas about Cherokee political institutions. They know that the laws of the Cherokee people predate those of the whites. Only adherence to those laws will enable them to continue as a people. Obviously white man's laws are different and to follow them is not to be Cherokee — this in essence is their position *vis-à-vis* legal Cherokee who are not full bloods.

The Papago people also have a problem with their tribal council, although it is not nearly as acute as the Cherokee and Sioux cases. Fontana, Manuel, and Ramon make it clear in their paper that it is more in the communication between tribal council and people that a problem arises. Even more specifically, there has been the problem of communication between the former tribal lawyer and the council and between the BIA superintendent and the council. The council, which is a representative body, finds itself pressured into making decisions on questions which it would like to understand better. If they feel uneasy, imagine how the people living in the areas which councilmen represent must feel about the projects which mysteriously arise from time to time. As Manuel et. al. point out, most of the people simply do not understand what is happening. The Papago "track record" bears this out — 11 failures out of 12 cases. Once again a foreign form of government has been imposed upon a group of people who have never before functioned as a cohesive political unit. They are not only told to act together; they are admonished to be competent, representative, and to deal quickly with the complexities of the modern, powerful, white industrial world. Perhaps too much is expected too soon.

The one successful Papago case of economic development is instructive. A sophisticated tribal member returned to the reservation after several years in Los Angeles. He leased land, bought cattle, drilled a well, and built a home. In 1967 he went into the landscaping business. With the aid of an ingenious machine, constructed from spare parts, he makes fences by splitting and planting the long slender branches of acotillo. After planting, the fence sprouts leaves and becomes quite dense. This Papago entrepreneur, Edward Kisto, now has jobs throughout the Tucson area and always hires fellow Papago to carry out the work.

Though Kisto would not conceptualize his work as economic development, it certainly would fit the definition. The lesson of his enterprise is clear: he brought an idea to the resources of his environment; the result has been a near monopoly on processing a natural resource and employment opportunities for Papagos. There is a continuity to this kind of development which deserves to be replicated for all Indians.

The Navajo tribe is the largest in population and landholding. It possesses mineral resources, and since World War II it has been moving toward industrialization. The pace has not been rapid, and, aside from the sawmill, industrial development has been mostly directed by whites. Dr. Ruffing makes two important points about the Navajo. She argues that development programs which do not take account of the interdependence of Navajo social structure and economy entail heavy social and economic costs. There are human costs as well, since programs which are inconsistent with Navajo values and identity will not only take a heavy toll, but will surely fail. For this reason she urges that more consideration be given to strengthening and updating the traditional economic base — specifically, stock raising and farming—through support of residence groups and organization of livestock cooperatives. The second point which she makes concerns the whole complex of development and exploitation of mineral resources on the reservation. She points out, following Aberle, that Navajos are deriving little income by collecting lease payments for mineral extraction. As a result they have been unable to accumulate sufficient capital for future development from this income. One can infer from her analysis that the Navajo would derive more benefit from their resources by managing them as the Middle Eastern countries are now doing with their oil. At a minimum, it might be far more beneficial to the tribe if they were the "board of directors" and hired the experts, i.e. the oil companies, to provide their talents when needed. This would put the tribe in the driver's seat and permit a quantum jump in economic development. A patient give and take dialogue between tribal leaders and the people conducted at the Chapter house meeting level could speed the process. Dr. Ruffing's most telling point is that up until now there have seemed to be no alternatives to doing things the way they have been done.

The recent announcement (the *Washington Post* 1974) by the Northern Cheyenne tribe that they were requesting the Department of the Interior to cancel their mineral leases so that they could assume full responsibility for mineral exploitation, processing, and marketing may well represent the future for tribes with these kinds of assets. Indians are beginning to realize that people with skills are for hire and will work for them depending upon the challenge and the pay. None of us would be surprised if the Navajo "nationalized" their resources and took full responsibility for developing them.

The Navajo are a key group in any discussion of the Indian future. They are presently looking closely at a ten-year program of economic development. Other tribes will watch them closely. It remains to be seen if they can achieve their goals, and not at the price of sacrificing their Navajo way.

RECOMMENDATIONS

From its conception, it was planned that this volume would be of service to at least three different groups: American Indians, federal agencies, and social scientists and others interested in Indians and economic development.

We hesitate to say very much to American Indians. The facts documented in the seven reports have long been known to most of them. They have been trying to direct attention to them since early on. They need not be told that United States policy was deliberately aimed at crushing the institutions which held Indian communities together, i.e. religious, educational, political. Nor do they have to be urged to take control of their own destinies — they have made it clear that this is what they want to do. Our only real conclusion for them is that their most economically productive path is to continue to assert their right to be themselves and to develop economically only on terms that are compatible with their community integrity.

There are a number of conclusions of particular interest to federal agencies and other developers based on the experience of our study:

1. Indian tribes need time to study, think, and talk over the implications of any given economic development program.

2. For any given program suggestion there should be alternatives to select from.

3. Development takes money, regardless of the cultural differences. Tribes appreciate the fact the EDA and other agencies are a source of development funds which did not exist until recently, giving them new alternative resources in addition to the conventional BIA assistance.

4. It seems clear that the Lummi case is a success on a number of grounds. It has pulled the community together after years of factional division. It has had a multiplying effect in terms of jobs generated, trucks purchased, education advanced, and it has attracted back skilled members of the tribe. It has raised the status of the Lummi within the surrounding white community. Finally, the project should result in a considerably increased income for the tribe as a result of sales of the seafood which they have harvested.

The lessons seem obvious:

a. A project which captures the imagination of the whole community is a good candidate for success — note that this is not sufficient as witness some of the cases from the Cherokee and Morongo.

b. A multiplier effect, i.e. one that produces other modes of livelihood, seems to be an important desideratum of any successful development plan — Lummi is the outstanding example.

c. An increase in income and skill levels within the community is desired by the Indians if community integrity is not to be violated.

d. Perhaps the most important single factor is the sense on the part of the community that they are negotiating their own future.

5. The study suggests some important clues about investment:

a. Innovative enterprises where Indians might have a natural advantage have the best chance of success.

b. One example is to give them a public utility type of monopoly in exploiting some resource on their own land. None of our studies provides us with an example of this, but what if the Fort Berthold Reservation Dam project had actually been operated by the Indians? Rather than receive money for their land, they could have been given jobs and authority to regulate any public services which stemmed from the construction of Garrison Dam. Why couldn't Navajo exploitation be done by the Navajo?

c. In those cases where mineral wealth is present on Indian land, improved living conditions for the Indians can be achieved through greater Indian involvement in the exploitation of that wealth. One reason for Indian reticence about exploitation of their resources is their feeling that they are losing control of the management. They are "out of it," either for conservationist feelings or because they have no sense of participating in the ultimate wealth which may accrue from it. They also feel at the mercy of the people who have the technical know how to develop their mineral resources — a good example is the Navajo-Hopi Black Mesa strip mining. There is no inherent conflict with traditional Indian systems in exploitation of mineral resources by Indian management.

d. Careful attention ought to be paid to the possibility of awarding exclusive franchises to American Indian tribes to perform certain services. This is the case with airlines and some defense contracts. Why not for Indians?

e. In any funding proposal for American Indians, particular concern should be given to the degree of originality and innovativeness, because this is the only realistic way in which Indians will be able to get enough elbow room to develop. It appears very unlikely that Indians are going to succeed if they try to compete directly with whites in what are primarily white enterprises. The real clue is again in the Lummi project, which is both innovative and based on some fundamental Lummi skill and knowledge.

f. Economic development efforts are successful when, among other things, they are based on the Indians' intimate knowledge of their own environment. This was the case with the Lummi and helps account for their success.

6. When Indians have considerable latitude in choosing experts to assist them in developing economically, chances of success increase. A crucial role was played by Dr. Heath in proposing the aquaculture project to the Lummi. He was able to project a vision of what could be done with an apparently useless tideland, and the picture was immediately grasped by the Lummi.

7. Economic development is closely related to other forms of development and depends on existing institutions. Most of the time this is presupposed, but not recognized. In Western Europe and Japan the spectacular growth after World War II was possible because institutions already existed to foster it. The institutions of American Indian tribes can also facilitate economic development, but they need to be heavily supported. Though their World War II was over a hundred

years ago, their key institutions have been under assault almost up to the present day. The Passamaquoddy governor and his council saw a separate OEO organization as a threat to them as the representative governing institution. The tribe would not accept an OEO grant until it came to the governing body. This is an example of support for an institution which had legitimacy with the people and some continuity with their past. The important point is that there are native institutions which *must* be supported before there can be economic development. A good example is the Creek Indians of eastern Oklahoma. They are a divided people similar to the Cherokee in this respect, yet they have some 18 sacred ball grounds presently on white-owned territory. Each year they perform their ceremonies on those grounds, yet it is always at the sufferance of the white-farmer-rancher-owner. They (the Creeks) are acutely aware of the precariousness of the situation and spend an inordinate amount of time worrying about the future of their sacred grounds. Why not buy these grounds for the traditional Creek and see what happens? There is good reason to suppose that, if they really felt secure about their sacred places, they would be much more disposed to think of a future in which they might even control their own destiny positively.

On the whole it would make good sense to support American Indian indigenous religious beliefs as fully as possible. There is precedent for this in the recognition of Taos Pueblo's right to their sacred mountain. Any official act which strengthens the fundamental religious posture of a tribe will almost certainly enable them to pull together more closely as a people.

8. Though it is important to work with tribal governments as closely as possible, it ought to be recognized that some are closer to the people than others. This raises problems and dilemmas which are difficult to solve or resolve. There is no clearcut solution, but provision should be made for acting constructively. In the case of the Cherokee, there are viable full blood organizations which might undertake specific development projects for the people they represent. The Cherokee Seven Clans Society is one such organization. With the Navajo it might be appropriate to support the local extended kin group in matters pertaining to sheep or cattle production, while it would be equally suitable to fund the tribe to carry out the marketing function in wool, hides, and meat.

9. Something should be done about the problem which might be labeled the "good intentions" gambit. This problem starts with Congress, which votes appropriations for a particular program in the sum of millions of dollars. A bureau of the federal government is charged with the task of administering the program and the dollars. Unbelieving Indians are usually unprepared for the sudden appearance of the

money, and it takes them time to develop coherent programs. In the meantime, government agencies must work against a July 1 deadline to get all of the appropriated money committed to specific projects. They find themselves pressuring the tribes to come with any kind of proposal so that the money will be spent. The tribes feel a lot of pressure to respond and in the end often support programs they have little faith in just so they won't "lose" the money. Naturally, the outcome is almost always failure. To the Indians it is a choice of "take it or leave it and never mind if you don't understand." Later the Indians are marked once more as failures because the program did not go as expected. For this problem it is clear that there must be some way to carry over development funds from year to year so that: (1) government agencies will not be under intense pressure to literally force programs on Indians and (2) Indians will not be under such pressure to accept programs which they do not understand. Nowhere is the folly of forcing programs on Indians so evident as in the Papago cases.

10. Urging Indians to get "off the dime" and start behaving like white men has negative results. This is precisely what they cannot and do not want to do. They want to be Indians, and only when whites accept this fact will they (Indians) begin to feel free to pursue the kind of development which they desire. Indians know what whites expect of them, because they are close observers of their conquerors, so when they do not cooperate wholeheartedly in a developer's scheme it is because to do so will violate their internal Indian charters for correct behavior.

11. The diversity of Indian tribes cannot be ignored. This means that a single formula for development will not work. There are no across the board solutions. Each Indian tribe must be considered separately and uniquely, and, as we have already noted, it is often necessary to recognize natural economic units within tribes. Though it is difficult to deal with scores of special cases, this is what must be done. In other words, while it is sound bureaucratically to deal with masses, it is disastrous when applied to economic development for American Indians.

The conclusions of this report would not be complete without some attention to the myths and assumptions which have characterized Indian-white relationships since contact. One assumption is that Indians must discard all of their ancient wisdom, their notions about how to relate to their fellow tribesmen, and their feelings about nature and its enjoyment. It is difficult for non-Indians to accept the Indian view of time, man, and nature. Yet this is precisely where there is the least amount of understanding and the greatest preponderance of myth.

The classic assumption is that Indians were savages prior to European discovery. This is nonsense — all prehistorical and early historical evidence marks them as a people who knew how to live with nature. There was an evenness and balance in their life that caught the attention of every careful European explorer. Indeed, the life they lived contained all of the benefits of what can be called the "good life" in the twentieth century. In his book *Stone Age economics,* Marshall Sahlins describes how tribal peoples managed their own affairs while maintaining ample leisure time for satisfying human relationships. The important point is that they managed their own affairs competently and satisfactorily. Now they are faced with the problem of getting back on the track, but not at the price of changing their fundamental values.

A recent evaluation of Indian economic development done for EDA illustrates the complexity of understanding the problem (Boise Cascade Center for Community Development 1973). In discussing cultural values (p. 13), the authors point out that traditional entrepreneurial or managerial values seem lacking in Indian traditions. They have no entrepreneurial or managerial class, and they are not habituated to contemporary money-making patterns. Furthermore, ". . . the creation of economic values and self-sustaining entities does not come easily to Indians." None of these allegations are new or surprising. They have been made by everyone who has taken time to observe the contrast between Indian and non-Indian values. What is disappointing is the recommendation for doing something about the situation. The authors conclude that, "thinking in monetary terms, comparing costs and benefits, and engaging in producing and selling are activities which must be transplanted to the reservation for economic development projects to be viable" (p. 13). Once again it is the Indian who gives up his cherished values and identity. Once more there is a refusal to accord any dignity to the Indian way — always it is up to him to change and no alternative is explored. Like a record ever replayed, there is recognition of Indian values, and the solution is always to ask him to change them. When will non-Indians accept the validity of the Indian position and let them develop in their own way?

Another myth which must be put to rest or at least seriously challenged is that an Indian tribe must adopt the traditional laissez-faire, entrepreneurial attitude in order to develop economically. The weakness of this approach is that it will not admit any alternative means for increasing production, but a glance at the world literature on economic growth suggests that there are viable alternatives. In particular, Indians might profit by looking at the experiments in labor managed economics described and theorized about by Jaroslav Vanek in his *Labor managed market economics.* The economy which he analyzes is one in which decisions about the production, pricing, and distribution of goods are made within a community composed of labor and management. In this system labor has a more active role than management, but the dialogue between them generates a common community of interest in the productive processes. The economic system which he presents is different from both capitalism and centrally planned socialism. It is a system which might be closer to the Indian value of community than any other offered to date.

The recent publication of *Small is beautiful* (Schumacher 1973) suggests another way of looking at economic development which might be useful for American Indians. Schumacher emphasizes the importance of doing something productive, i.e. having a job rather than drawing welfare. He suggests that a labor intensive economy though less efficient than a capital intensive one may still be more desirable from a psychological and sociological perspective. He also advocates local processing of regional resources. There is something for American Indians in his book.

APPENDIX: OUTLINE OF MATERIAL NEEDED FOR EACH TRIBE OR RESERVATION IN THE STUDY

For each tribe or reservation being studied, descriptions of the organization of economic activities are required in terms of the following areas:

HUMAN RESOURCES. Social organization or customs that affect labor force participation, scheduling of work hours, desire on the part of the individual for personal growth and for material growth (better housing, more modern possessions, higher incomes, etc.).

CAPITAL RESOURCES. Who owns the factors of production (land, machinery, buildings, livestock, etc.)? What is the relative importance of community-held property versus individual ownership?

MANAGEMENT. How are the managers selected? Are they Indian or non-Indian? Who makes the management decisions — an individual or a group?

NATURAL RESOURCES. What is the attitude toward natural resources? Are they regarded as primarily to be conserved, or to be exploited for profit? Are there tribal policies for managing resources?

MARKETS. (Relative emphasis on competition versus cooperatives.) How are the goods produced by the tribe or by its individual members used? Are they sold to outsiders, within the tribe, or are they divided among tribal members? How are prices determined?

PROFITS. Is the profit incentive present? If so, how important a factor is it in economic activities? Are other incentives important? If so, what are they?

INCOME DISTRIBUTION. How is the total tribal income (money and other) divided? What effect does this have on the material well-being of individuals and on the quality of life in the community?

METHODS OF DEALING WITH CRISES. What systems are followed in dealing with droughts, floods, and other natural or man-caused disasters?

ECONOMIC, POLITICAL, AND SOCIAL INSTITUTIONS.

TRIBAL WEALTH. What constitutes the wealth of the tribe, in terms of natural resources or intangibles?

VALUES AND GOALS OF THE RESERVATION WITH REGARD TO ECONOMIC DEVELOPMENT. How are conflicts in values and goals between individuals and tribes resolved? What goals, other than economic, does the tribe have? How are these goals pursued, reconciled?

This descriptive material will be used for analytical purposes in comparing the systems operating in the different tribes.

REFERENCES

Boise Cascade Center for Community Development
  1972 Indian economic development: an evaluation of EDA's selected Indian reservation program, Volume one. Boise, Idaho.
MORTON, ROGERS B.
  1973 Speech on economic development at Menlo Park, California. Office of Communications, U.S. Department of Interior, Washington, D.C.
SAHLINS, MARSHALL
  1972 *Stone Age economics*. Chicago, Illinois: Aldine-Atherton.
SCHUMACHER, E. F.
  1973 *Small is beautiful: economics as if peoples mattered*. New York: Harper and Row.
SPICER, EDWARD H.
  1952 *Human problems in technological change*. New York: Russell Sage Foundation.
TAX, SOL, SAM STANLEY
  1969 "Indian identity and economic development." 75–96 Joint Economic Committee, Congress of the United States, Washington, D.C.: U.S. Government Printing Office.
U.S. Congress Joint Economic Committee
  1969 *Toward economic development for native American communities*, Volume one and two. Washington, D.C.: Government Printing Office.
VANEK, JAROSLAV
  1970 *The general theory of labor managed market economies*. Ithaca, New York: Cornell University Press.
Washington Post
  1974 "Cheyennes set plan to process coal." *Washington Post*. March 3.

Biographical Notes

LOWELL JOHN BEAN (1931–) is Professor of Anthropology and Curator of the Museum of Anthropology at California State University, Hayward. He received his Ph.D from the University of California, Los Angeles in 1970. He has been closely associated with the Indians of the Morongo reservation and assisted them in the establishment of the Malki Museum and its publications program. He is interested in cultural ecology, California Indians, North American Indians, ethnohistory, and ethnobotany. He has published numerous articles and books on California Indians including *Mukat's people* (University of California Press).

VINE DELORIA, JR. (1933–) was born in Martin, South Dakota and is a member of the Standing Rock Sioux Tribe. He has degrees in Science, Theology, and Law from Iowa State University (1958), the Lutheran School of Theology, Chicago (1963), and the University of Colorado (1970), respectively. He is the former executive secretary of the National American Indian Congress and was a founder of the Institute for the Development of Indian Law. Deloria has authored numerous books on Indian affairs, religion, and science, knowledge, and philosophy.

RAYMOND J. DEMALLIE (1946–) is Assistant Professor of Anthropology at Indiana University. He received his B.A. (1969), M.A. (1970) and Ph.D (1971) from the University of Chicago. He has taught at the University of Wyoming and was a post-doctoral fellow at the Smithsonian Institution. He has carried out extensive field research with Sioux Indians. North American Indians, ethnohistory, kinship, and contemporary Indian affairs are his major interests. He has most recently written a long article on Dakota kinship and an Introduction on Dakota tribes for the forthcoming *Handbook of North American Indians*.

BERNARD L. FONTANA (1931–) is a field representative for the University of Arizona. He has been an ethnologist at Arizona State Museum and Lecturer in Anthropology for the University of Arizona. He has a B.A. from the University of California, Berkeley and a Ph.D. from the University of Arizona (1960). He has resided next to the San Xavier Indian reservation since 1954. He has written numerous articles on the Papago and was once employed by the tribe in their claims case.

HENRY F. MANUEL was born in Ali Chuk on the Papago Indian Reservation in southern Arizona. After service in the U.S. Navy, he received his B.A. from the University of Arizona and is now a graduate student in a special counseling program at that institution. He has been employed by the tribe in legal services.

JULIANN RAMON was born and raised on the San Xavier Papago Indian Reservation in southern Arizona. She studied political science at the University of Arizona.

LORRAINE TURNER RUFFING (1943–) is presently writing a comparative study of American Indian and Third World development problems. She received her Ph.D. in Economics from Columbia University in 1973. Her main area of interest is the economic development of indigenous peoples. Her dissertation examined how a traditional Navajo community could increase income per capita without incurring major social disruption. In 1975–1976 she organized a study of obstacles to reservation and resource development for the American Indian Policy Review Commission. She has also spent five years in Venezuela and Chile studying worker participation in firm management. Her publications include "Navajo economic development subject to cultural constraint", "Shonto revisited: measures of social and economic change in a Navajo community", *Las experiencias autogestionerias chilenas*, and *Report on reservation and resource development and protection.*

SAM STANLEY (1923–) is a Research Anthropologist at the Smithsonian Institution. He received his B.A. in Philosophy (1951) and M.A. in Anthropology (1954) from the University of Washington and his Ph.D. in Anthropology (1958) from the University of Chicago. He has taught at the University of Illinois, the University of California, Riverside, and California State University, Los Angeles. His fieldwork has been with North American Indians and in Indonesia. Since 1966 he has organized and coordinated research programs in the human sciences at the Smithsonian Institution.

SUSAN McCULLOCH STEVENS (1934–) is a doctoral candidate at the University of California, Berkeley. She has a B.A. from the University of Connecticut (1957) and an M.A. from the University of Massachusetts (1965). She is married to John Stevens, long-time governor of the Passamaquoddy tribe and former Commissioner of Indian Affairs for the State of Maine. Ms. Stevens has done research in biochemistry, medicine, and ethnohistory. Recently she conducted extensive research on New England Indians and on alcohol use and abuse.

ALBERT L. WAHRHAFTIG (1935–) is Associate Professor of Anthropology at California State College, Sonoma. He received his B.A. from Stanford University and his M.A. (1960) and Ph.D (1975) from the University of Chicago. He has done extensive field research on the Cherokee Indians of eastern Oklahoma. He has also carried out fieldwork in Mexico. His research interests include anthropological theory and method, applied anthropology, and psychological anthropology.

Index of Names

Index of Subjects